C++ Plus
Data Structures

The Jones and Bartlett Series in Computer Science

C++ *Plus*
Data Structures

Nell Dale

University of Texas, Austin

JONES AND BARTLETT PUBLISHERS

Sudbury, Massachusetts

BOSTON   TORONTO   LONDON   SINGAPORE

World Headquarters
Jones and Bartlett Publishers
40 Tall Pine Drive
Sudbury, MA 01776
978-443-5000
info@jbpub.com
www.jbpub.com

Jones and Bartlett Publishers Canada
2100 Bloor Street West
Suite 6-272
Toronto, ON M6S 5A5
CANADA

Jones and Bartlett Publishers International
Barb House, Barb Mews
London W6 7PA
UK

Library of Congress Cataloging-in-Publication Data

Dale, Nell B.
    C++ plus data structures / Nell Dale.
       p.   cm.
    Includes index.
    ISBN 0–7637–0621–3
    1. C++ (Computer program language)   2. Data structures (Computer science)   I. Title.
    QA76.73.C153D334   1998
    005.7′3—dc21   98–12284
                                                      CIP

Chief Executive Officer: Clayton Jones
Chief Operating Officer: Don Jones, Jr.
Publisher: Tom Walker
Senior Managing Editor: Judith H. Hauck
Marketing Director: Rich Pirozzi
Production Manager: Anne Spencer
Manufacturing Director: Jane Bromback
Development Editor: Karen Jolie
Production Editor: Joan M. Flaherty
Assistant Production Editor: Rebecca Marks
Designer: George H. McLean
Typesetting: Tradespools Ltd.
Cover Design: Anne Spencer
Printing and Binding: Banta Company

Printed in the United States of America
02 01 00 99   10 9 8 7 6 5 4 3

PREFACE

Historically, a course on data structures has been a mainstay of most computer science departments. However, over the last 13 years the focus of this course has broadened considerably. The topic of data structures now has been subsumed under the broader topic of *abstract data types (ADTs)*—the study of classes of objects whose logical behavior is defined by a set of values and a set of operations.

The term *abstract data type* describes a comprehensive collection of data values and operations; the term *data structures* refers to the study of data and how to represent data objects within a program; that is, the implementation of structured relationships. The shift in emphasis is representative of the move towards more abstraction in computer science education. We now are interested in the study of the abstract properties of classes of data objects in addition to how the objects might be represented in a program. Johannes J. Martin puts it very succinctly: ". . . depending on the point of view, a data object is characterized by its type (for the user) or by its structure (for the implementer)."[1]

Three Levels of Abstraction

The focus of this book is on abstract data types as viewed from three different perspectives: their specification, their application, and their implementation. The specification describes the logical or abstract level. This level is concerned with *what* the operations do. The application level, sometimes called the user level, is concerned with how the data type might be used to solve a problem. This level is concerned with *why* the operations do what they do. The implementation level is where the operations are actually coded. This level is concerned with the *how* questions.

Within this focus, we stress computer science theory and software engineering principles, including modularization, data encapsulation, information hiding, data abstraction, functional decomposition, object-oriented decomposition, the analysis of algorithms, and life-cycle software verification methods. We feel strongly that these principles should be introduced to computer science students early in their education so that they learn to practice good software techniques from the beginning.

---

1.   Johannes J. Martin, *Data Types and Data Structures*, Prentice-Hall International Series in Computer Science, C. A. R. Hoare, Series Editor, Prentice-Hall International, (UK), LTD, 1986, p. 1.

An understanding of theoretical concepts helps students put the new ideas they encounter into place, and practical advice allows them to apply what they have learned. To teach these concepts to students who may not have completed many college-level mathematics courses, we consistently use intuitive explanations, even for topics that have a basis in mathematics, like the analysis of algorithms. In all cases, our highest goal has been to make our explanations as readable and as easily understandable as possible.

Prerequisite Assumptions

In this book, we assume that the students are familiar with the following C++ constructs:

- Built-in simple data types
- Stream I/O as provided in `<iostream.h>`
- Stream I/O as provided in `<fstream.h>`
- Control structures `while`, `do-while`, `for`, `if`, and `switch`
- User-defined functions with value and reference parameters
- Built-in array types

We have included sidebars within the text to refresh the student's memory concerning some of the details of these topics. If the students do not know these C++ concepts, an intensive introduction to them is available in *Essentials of C++ as a Second Language, A Laboratory Course*, also published by Jones and Bartlett.

Content and Organization

Chapter 1 outlines the basic goals of high-quality software and the basic principles of software engineering for designing and implementing programs to meet these goals. Abstraction, functional decomposition, and object-oriented design are discussed. This chapter also addresses what we see as a critical need in software education: the ability to design and implement correct programs and to verify that they are actually correct. Topics covered include the concept of "life-cycle" verification; designing for correctness using preconditions and postconditions; the use of deskchecking and design/code walk-throughs and inspections to identify errors before testing; debugging techniques, data coverage (black box), and code coverage (clear or white box) approaches; test plans, unit testing, and structured integration testing using stubs and drivers. As we develop ADTs in subsequent chapters, we discuss the construction of an appropriate test plan for each.

Chapter 2 presents data abstraction and encapsulation, the software engineering concepts that relate to the design of the data structures used in programs. Three perspectives of data are discussed: abstraction, implementation, and application. These perspectives are illustrated using a real-world example (a library), and then are applied to built-in data structures that C++ supports: structs and arrays. The C++ class type is presented as the way to represent the abstract data types we examine in subsequent chapters. The principles of object-oriented programming—encapsulation, inheritance, and polymorphism—are introduced here and covered in stages in the next four chapters. The case study at the end of this chapter reinforces the ideas of data abstraction and encapsulation in designing and implementing a user-defined data type for generalized string input and output.

We would like to think that the material in Chapters 1 and 2 may be a review for most students. However, the concepts in these two chapters are so crucial to the future of any and all students that we feel that we cannot rely on their having seen the material before.

Chapter 3   introduces the most fundamental abstract data type of them all: the list. The chapter begins with a general discussion of operations on abstract data types and then presents the framework with which all of the other data types are examined: a presentation and discussion of the specification, a brief application using the operations, and the design and coding of the operations. Both the unsorted and the sorted lists are presented with an array-based implementation. Overloading the relational operators is presented as a way to make the implementations more generic. The binary search is introduced as a way to improve the performance of the search operation in the sorted list. Because there is more than one way to solve a problem, we discuss how competing solutions can be compared through the analysis of algorithms, using Big-O notation. This notation is then used to compare the operations in the unsorted list and the sorted list. The C++ class constructor and class destructor are covered. The case study takes a simple real estate data base, demonstrates the object-oriented design process, and concludes with the actual coding of a problem in which the sorted list is the principal data object.

Chapter 4   introduces the stack and the queue data types. Each data type is first considered from its abstract perspective, and the idea of recording the logical abstraction in an ADT specification is stressed. Then the set of operations is implemented in C++ using an array-based implementation. The concept of dynamic allocation is introduced, along with the syntax for using C++ pointer variables, and then used to demonstrate how arrays can be dynamically allocated to give the user more flexibility. Templates are introduced as a way of implementing generic classes. A case study using stacks (postfix expression evaluator) and one using queues (simulation) are presented.

Chapter 5   reimplements the ADTs from Chapters 3 and 4 as linked structures. The technique used to link the elements in dynamically allocated storage is described in detail and illustrated with figures. The array-based implementations and the linked implementations are then compared using Big-O notation.

Chapter 6   is a collection of advanced concepts and techniques. Circular linked lists and doubly linked lists are discussed. The insertion, deletion, and list traversal algorithms are developed and implemented for each variation. An alternative representation of a linked structure, using static allocation (an array of structs), is designed. Inheritance, class copy constructors, assignment overloading, and dynamic binding are covered in detail. The case study uses doubly linked lists to implement large integers.

Chapter 7   discusses recursion, giving the student an intuitive understanding of the concept, and then shows how recursion can be used to solve programming problems. Guidelines for writing recursive functions are illustrated with many examples. After demonstrating that a by-hand simulation of a recursive routine can be very tedious, a simple three-question technique is introduced for verifying the correctness of recursive functions. Because many students are wary of recursion, the introduction to this material is deliberately intuitive and nonmathematical. A more detailed discussion of how recursion works leads to an understanding of how recursion can be replaced with iteration and stacks. The case study develops and implements the quick sort algorithm.

Chapter 8   introduces binary search trees as a way to arrange data, giving the flexibility of a linked structure with $O(\log_2 N)$ insertion and deletion time. In order to build on the previous chapter and exploit the inherent recursive nature of binary trees, the algorithms first are presented recursively. After all the operations have been implemented recursively, we code the insertion and deletion operations iteratively to show the flexibility of binary search trees. The case study discusses the process of building an index for a manuscript and implements the first phase.

Chapter 9   presents a collection of other branching structures: binary expression trees, heaps, priority queues (implemented with both lists and heaps), and graphs. The graph algorithms make use of stacks, queues, and priority queues, thus both reinforcing earlier material and demonstrating how general these structures are.

Chapter 10   presents a number of sorting and searching algorithms and asks the question: which are better? The sorting algorithms that are illustrated, implemented, and compared include straight selection sort, two versions of bubble sort, quick sort, heap sort, and merge sort. The sorting algorithms are compared using Big-O notation. The discussion of algorithm analysis continues in the context of searching. Previously presented searching algorithms are reviewed and new ones are described. Hashing techniques are discussed in some detail. Finally, radix sort is presented and analyzed.

Additional Features

Chapter Goals A set of goals presented at the beginning of each chapter helps the students assess what they have learned. These goals are tested in the exercises at the end of each chapter.

Chapter Exercises Most chapters have more than 35 exercises. They vary in levels of difficulty, including short programming problems, the analysis of algorithms, and problems to test the student's understanding of concepts. Approximately one-third of the exercises are answered in the back of the book. The answer key for the remaining exercises is in the *Instructor's Guide.*

Case Studies There are seven case studies. Each includes a problem description, an analysis of the problem input and required output, and a discussion of the appropriate data types to use. Several of the case studies are completely coded and tested. Others are left at various stages in their development, requiring the student to complete and test the final version.

Program Disk The specification and implementation of each class representing an ADT is available on a program disk that can be downloaded, free of charge, from the Jones and Bartlett Student Diskette page on the World Wide Web (www.jbpub.com/disks). The source code for the completed case studies and the partial source code for the others is also available.

Programming Assignments A collection of recommended programming assignments for each chapter is included at the end of the book. The assignments represent a range of difficulty levels and were carefully chosen to illustrate the techniques described in the text. A large selection of additional programming assignments is also available in the *Instructor's Guide.*

Instructor's Guide An instructor's guide is available that includes the following sections for each chapter:

- Goals
- Outline
- Teaching Notes: suggestions for how to teach the material covered in the chapter
- Workouts: suggestions for in-class activities, discussion questions, and short exercises

- Quickie Quiz Questions: additional short-answer questions that can be used in class to test student comprehension
- Exercise Key: answers to those questions that are not in the back of the book
- Programs: suitable programs in ready-to-copy format

Transparency Masters   A set of overhead transparencies is available in hard copy or in PowerPoint.

Acknowledgments

We would like to thank the following people who took the time to review this manuscript: Donald Bagert, Texas Tech University; Susan Gauch, University of Kansas; Pamela Lawhead, University of Mississippi; Pat Nettnin, Finger Lakes Community College; Bobbie Othmer, Westminster College of Salt Lake City; Suzanne Pawlan-Levy, Allan Hancock College; Carol Roberts, University of Maine; and Robert Strader, Stephen F. Austin State University.

A special thanks to John McCormick, University of Northern Iowa, and Mark Headington, University of Wisconsin—LaCrosse. John graciously allowed us to use some of his analogies from *Ada Plus Data Structures*, and Mark's ideas, suggestions, and sharp eyes were invaluable. Thanks also to David Teague, Western Carolina University, who not only reviewed the manuscript in minute detail the first time, but agreed to review the final-draft changes under pressure at the last minute.

Thanks also to the students at Uppsala University in Sweden who used the final draft of the manuscript in a course in the fall of 1997. Because non-English readers see what is written, not what they expect to see, their comments were invaluable in cleaning up ambiguous wording.

Thanks to my husband Al, our children and grandchildren too numerous to name, and our dogs Maggie, who keeps my feet warm, and Bear, whose role in life is to protect me from delivery people—especially from those bringing packages from the publisher.

A virtual bouquet of roses to the people at Jones and Bartlett who have worked on this book: Dave Geggis, our editor, friend, and confidant; Karen Jolie, our development editor with whom we have had the pleasure to work before; Joan Flaherty, the packager; Barbara Pendergast who did the copy editing chores; Anne Spencer, whose "can-do" attitude got this book out months ahead of the original schedule; and last, but certainly not least, the people at Tradespools, the compositor in England who implemented Anne's "can-do." Thanks to each and every one of you!

About the Cover

The recurrent cover image features a unique aspect of the 40-room Centre Family Dwelling, a 164-year-old building in Kentucky's Shaker Village of Pleasant Hill. Built to accommodate 100 celibate inhabitants, Centre Family Dwelling boasts two entranceways, dual stairways, and a wide common passageway on each floor that separates brothers' and sisters' apartments.

Completed in 1834, the massive building's exterior is hand-hewn Kentucky River limestone quarried from the nearby Kentucky Palisades. In the hallways, the floors are quarter-sawed white oak. Oak and ash run throughout the remainder of the building. The original woodwork paint still clings to the walls of the kitchen and the main hallways.

Centre Family Dwelling's high ceilings and vast windows are exceptional features for architecture of the time. These unusual characteristics reflect a concern for proper ventilation and lighting, embracing small, high interior windows and transoms to permit light into intimate spaces.

Essentials of C++: A Lab Course Through Arrays Program Disk

Jones and Bartlett Publishers offers free to students and instructors a program disk with the complete programs found in *Essentials of C++: A Lab Course Through Arrays*. The program disk is available through the Jones and Bartlett World Wide Web site on the Internet. *

Download Instructions

1. Connect to the Jones and Bartlett student diskette home page (www.jbpub.com/disks/).

2. Choose *Essentials of C++: A Lab Course Through Arrays*.

3. Follow the instructions for downloading and saving the *Essentials of C++: A Lab Course Through Arrays* data disk.

4. If you need assistance downloading a Jones and Bartlett student diskette, please send email to help@jbpub.com.

*Downloading the *Essentials of C++: A Lab Course Through Arrays* program disk via the Jones and Bartlett home page requires access to the Internet and a World Wide Web browser such as Netscape Navigator or Microsoft Internet Explorer. Instructors at schools without Internet access may call 800-832-0034 and request a copy of the program disk. Jones and Bartlett grants adopters of *Essentials of C++: A Lab Course Through Arrays* the right to duplicate copies of the program disk or to store the files on any stand-alone computer or network.

CONTENTS

10 *Sorting and Searching Algorithms*   *585*

Programming Assignments   707

Glossary   747

Index   765

CHAPTER

1

Software Engineering Principles

GOALS

- To be able to describe the general activities in the software life cycle
- To be able to describe the goals for "quality" software
- To be able to explain the following terms: software requirements, software specifications, algorithm, information hiding, abstraction
- To be able to understand the fundamental ideas of top-down design and object-oriented design
- To be able to identify several sources of program errors
- To be able to describe strategies to prevent various categories of software errors
- To be able to specify the preconditions and postconditions of a program segment or function
- To be able to show how deskchecking, code walk-throughs, and design and code inspections can improve software quality and reduce software effort
- To be able to state several testing goals and to indicate when each would be appropriate
- To be able to describe several integration-testing strategies and to indicate when each would be appropriate
- To be able to explain how program verification techniques can be applied throughout the software development process

At this point in your computing career, you have completed at least one semester of computer science course work. You can take a problem of medium complexity, write an algorithm to solve the problem, code the algorithm in C++, and demonstrate the correctness of your solution. At least, that's what the syllabus for your introductory class said you should be able to do when you complete the course. Now that you are starting your second (or third?) semester, it is time to stop and review those principles that, if adhered to, guarantee that you indeed can do what your previous syllabus claimed.

In this chapter, we review the software design process and the verification of software correctness. In Chapter 2, we review data design and implementation.

Software Design Process

When we consider computer programming, we immediately think of writing a program for a computer to execute—the generation of code in some computer language. As a beginning student of computer science, you wrote programs that solved relatively simple problems. Much of your effort at the start went into learning the syntax of a programming language such as C++: the language's reserved words, its data types, its constructs for selection (`if-else` and `switch`) and looping (`while`, `do while`, and `for`), and its input/output mechanisms (`cin` and `cout`).

You may have learned a programming methodology that took you from the problem description that your instructor handed out all the way through to the delivery of a good software solution. There are many design techniques, coding standards, and testing methods that programmers have created to help develop high-quality software. But why bother with all that methodology? Why not just sit down at a computer and write programs? Aren't we wasting a lot of time and effort on techniques, when we could just write our programs directly in C++, Ada, C, Pascal, or Smalltalk?

If the degree of our programming sophistication never had to rise above the level of trivial programs (like summing a list of prices or averaging grades), we might get away with such a code-first technique (or, rather, *lack* of technique). Some new programmers work this way, hacking away at the code until the program works more or less correctly.

As your programs grow larger and more complex, however, you must pay attention to other software issues in addition to coding. If you become a software professional, someday you may work as part of a team that develops a system containing tens of thousands, or even millions, of lines of code. The activities involved in such a software project's whole "life cycle" clearly go beyond just sitting down at a computer and writing programs. These activities include

- *Problem analysis* Understanding the nature of the problem to be solved
- *Requirements definition* Specifying exactly what the program must do
- *High-* and *low-level design* Recording how the program meets the requirements, from the "big picture" overview to the detailed design
- *Implementation of the design* Coding a program in a computer language
- *Testing and verification* Detecting and fixing errors and demonstrating the correctness of the program
- *Delivery* Turning over the tested program to the customer or user (or instructor!)
- *Operation* Actually using the program
- *Maintenance* Making changes to fix operational errors and to add or modify functions of the program

Software development is not simply a matter of going through these steps sequentially. Many activities take place concurrently. We may be coding one part of the solution while we're designing another part, or defining requirements for a new version of a program while we're still testing the current version. Often a number of people work on different parts of the same program simultaneously. Keeping track of all these activities is not an easy task.

We use the term **software engineering** to refer to a disciplined approach to the development of computer programs through *all* of these software life-cycle activities. What makes our jobs as programmers or software engineers challenging is the tendency of software to grow in size and complexity and to change at every stage of its development. Part of the discipline in the software engineering approach is the use of tools to manage this size and complexity. Usually a programmer has several toolboxes, each containing tools that help to build and shape a software product.

Software Engineering   A disciplined approach to the design, production, and maintenance of computer programs that are developed on time and within cost estimates, using tools that help to manage the size and complexity of the resulting software products

---

Hardware   One toolbox contains the hardware itself: the computers and their peripheral devices (such as monitors, terminals, storage devices, and printers), on which and for which we develop software.

Software   A second toolbox contains various software tools: operating systems to control the computer's resources, text editors to help us enter programs, compilers to translate high-level languages like C++ into something the computer can execute, interactive debugging programs, test-data generators, and so on. You've used some of these tools already.

Ideaware   A third toolbox is filled with the shared body of knowledge that programmers have collected over time. This box contains the algorithms that we use to solve common programming problems, as well as data structures for modeling the information processed by our programs. Recall that an **algorithm** is a step-by-step description of the solution to a problem. How we choose between two algorithms that do the same task often depends on the requirements of a particular application. If no relevant requirements exist, the choice may be based on the programmer's own style.

Algorithm   A logical sequence of discrete steps that describes a complete solution to a given problem computable in a finite amount of time

---

Ideaware contains programming methodologies such as top-down and object-oriented design and software concepts, including information hiding, data encapsulation, and abstraction. It also contains some tools for measuring, evaluating, and proving the correctness of our programs. We devote most this book to exploring the contents of this third toolbox.

Some might argue that using these tools takes the creativity out of programming, but we don't believe that to be true. Artists and composers are creative, yet their innovations are grounded in the basic principles of their crafts. Similarly, the most creative programmers build high-quality software through the disciplined use of basic programming tools.

Goals of Quality Software

Quality software is much more than a program that somehow accomplishes the task at hand. A good program achieves the following goals:

1. It works.
2. It can be read and understood.
3. It can be modified without excruciating time and effort.
4. It is completed on time and within budget.

It's not easy to meet these goals, but they are all important.

Goal 1: Quality Software Works   The program must do the task it was designed to perform, and it must do it correctly and completely. Thus the first step in the development process is to determine exactly what the program is required to do. To write a program that works you first need to have a definition of the program's **requirements**. For students, the requirements often are included in the instructor's problem description: "Write a program that calculates . . . ." For programmers on a government contract, the requirements document may be hundreds of pages long.

Requirements   A statement of what is to be provided by a computer system or software product

---

We develop programs that meet the user's requirements using **software specifications**. The specifications indicate the format of the input and the expected output, details about processing, performance measures (how fast? how big? how accurate?), what to do in case of errors, and so on. The specifications tell exactly *what* the program does, but not *how* it is done. Sometimes your instructor provides detailed specifications; other times you have to write them yourself, based on the requirements definition, conversations with your instructor, or guesswork. (We discuss this issue in more detail later in this chapter.)

Software Specification   A detailed description of the function, inputs, processing, outputs, and special requirements of a software product. It provides the information needed to design and implement the program.

How do you know when the program is right? A program has to be *complete* (it should "do everything") and *correct* (it should "do it right") to meet its requirements. In addition, it should be *usable*. For instance, if the program needs to receive data from a person sitting at a terminal, it must indicate when it expects input. The program's outputs should be readable and understandable to users. Indeed, creating a good user interface is an important subject in software engineering today.

Finally, Goal 1 means that the program should be as *efficient as it needs to be*. We would never deliberately write programs that waste time or space in memory, but not all programs demand great efficiency. When they do, however, we must meet these demands or else the programs do not satisfy the requirements. A space-launch control program, for instance, must execute in "real time"; that is, the software must process commands, perform calculations, and display results in coordination with the activities it is supposed to control. Closer to home, if a desktop-publishing program cannot update the screen as rapidly as the user can type, the program is not as efficient as it needs to be. In such a case, if the software isn't efficient enough, it doesn't meet its requirements, and thus, according to our definition, it doesn't work correctly.

Goal 2: Quality Software Can Be Read and Understood   The first goal says that the computer must execute the program as expected; this second goal is more concerned with our ability to read the program.

You might wonder why anyone would want to read a computer program. Chances are you have already read a number of them in programming textbooks. Reading a well-written program can teach you techniques that help you write good programs. In fact, it's hard to imagine how anyone could become a good programmer *without* reading good programs.

Think of the last time you had to debug one of your programs. You probably spent a lot of time reading it. A well-designed, clearly written, well-documented program is certainly easier for human readers to understand. The number of pages of documentation required for "real-world" programs usually exceeds the number of pages of C++ code. Almost every organization has its own policy for documentation. We're sure that your instructor does.

Although the computer is the ultimate reader of the program, it is likely that a program that cannot be understood by its human authors contains errors.

Goal 3: Quality Software Can Be Modified   When does software need to be modified? Changes occur in every phase of its existence.

Software gets changed in the design phase. When your instructor or employer gives you a programming assignment, you begin to think of how to solve the problem. The next time you meet, however, you may be notified of a small change in the program description.

Software gets changed in the coding phase. You make changes in your program as a result of compilation errors. Sometimes you suddenly see a better solution to a part of the problem after the program has been coded, so you make changes.

Software gets changed in the testing phase. If the program crashes or yields wrong results, you must make corrections.

In an academic environment, the life of the software typically ends when a corrected program is turned in to be graded. When software is being developed for use, however, most of the changes that are made take place during the "maintenance" phase. Someone may discover an error that wasn't uncovered in testing, someone else may want to include additional functions, a third party may want to change the input format, and a fourth party may want to run the program on another system.

The point is that software changes often and in all phases of its life cycle. Knowing this, software engineers try to develop programs that are easily modifiable. If you think it is easy to change a program, try to make a "small change" in the last program you wrote. It's difficult to remember all the details of a program after some time has passed. Modifications to programs often are not even made by the original authors but by subsequent maintenance programmers. (Someday you may be the one making the modifications to someone else's program.)

What makes a program easily modifiable? First, it should meet Goal 2: it should be readable and understandable to humans. Second, it should be able to withstand small changes easily. The design methodologies reviewed later in this chapter should help you write programs that meet this goal.

Goal 4: Quality Software Is Completed on Time and Within Budget   You know what happens in school when you turn your program in late. You probably have grieved over an otherwise perfect program that received only half credit—or no credit at all—because you turned it in one day late. "But the network was down five hours last night!" you protest.

Although the consequences of tardiness may seem arbitrary in the academic world, they are significant in the business world. The software for controlling a space launch must be developed and tested before the launch can take place. A patient data-base system for a new hospital must be installed before the hospital can open. In such cases the program doesn't meet its requirements if it isn't ready when needed.

"Time is money" may sound trite but failure to meet deadlines is *expensive*. A company generally budgets a certain amount of time and money for the development of a piece of software. As a programmer, you are paid a salary or an hourly wage. If your part of the project is only 80% complete when the deadline arrives, the company must pay you—or another programmer—to finish the work. The extra expenditure in salary is not the only cost, however. Other workers may be waiting to integrate your part of the program into the system for testing. If the program is part of a contract with a customer, there may be monetary penalties for missed deadlines. If the program is being developed for commercial sales, your company may lose money if another firm puts a similar product on the market first.

Once you know what your goals are, what can you do to meet them? Where should you start? There are many tools and techniques that software engineers use. In the next few sections of this chapter, we focus on a review of techniques to help you understand, design, and code programs.

Specification: Understanding the Problem

No matter what programming design technique you use, the first steps are the same. Imagine the following all-too-familiar situation. On the third day of class, you are given a 12-page description of Programming Assignment 1, which must be running perfectly and turned in by noon, a week from yesterday. You read the assignment and realize that this program is three times larger than any program you have ever written. Now, what is your first step?

The responses listed here are typical of those given by a class of computer science students in such a situation:

1. Panic   39%
2. Sit down at the computer and begin typing   30%
3. Drop the course   27%
4. Stop and think   4%

Response 1 is a predictable reaction from students who have not learned good programming techniques. Students who adopt Response 3 will find their education progressing rather slowly. Response 2 may seem to be a good idea, especially considering the deadline looming ahead. Resist the temptation, though; the first step is to *think*. Before you can come up with a program solution, you must understand the problem. Read the assignment, and then read it again. Ask questions of your instructor (or manager, or client). Starting early affords you many opportunities to ask questions; starting the night before the program is due leaves you no opportunity at all.

The problem with writing first is that it tends to lock you into the first solution you think of, which may not be the best approach. We have a natural tendency to believe that once we've put something in writing, we have invested too much in the idea to toss it out and start over.

On the other hand, don't agonize about all the possibilities until the day before your deadline. (Chances are that a disk drive, network, or printer will fail that day!) When you think you understand the problem you should begin writing your design.

Writing Detailed Specifications

Many writers experience a moment of terror when faced with a blank piece of paper—where to begin? As a programmer, however, you don't have to wonder about where to begin. Using the assignment description (your "requirements"), first write a complete definition of the problem, including the details of the expected inputs and outputs, the necessary processing and error handling, and all the assumptions about the problem. When you finish this task, you have a *detailed specification*—a formal definition of the problem your program must solve, which tells you exactly what the program should do. In addition, the process of writing the specifications brings to light any holes in the requirements. For instance, are embedded blanks in the input significant or can they be ignored? Do you need to check for errors in the input? On what computer system(s) is your program to run? If you get the answers to these questions at this stage, you can design and code your program correctly from the start.

Many software engineers make use of user/operational *scenarios* to understand the requirements. In software design, a scenario is a sequence of events for *one* execution of the program. Here, for example, is a scenario that a designer might consider when developing the software for a bank's automated teller machine (ATM).

1. The customer inserts bank card.
2. The ATM reads the account number on the card.
3. The ATM requests a PIN (personal identification number) from the customer.
4. The customer enters 5683.
5. The ATM successfully verifies the account number PIN combination.
6. The ATM asks the customer to select a transaction type (deposit, show balance, withdrawal, or quit).
7. The customer selects show balance.
8. The ATM obtains the current account balance ($1,204.35) and displays it.
9. The ATM asks the customer to select a transaction type (deposit, show balance, withdrawal, or quit).
10. The customer selects quit.
11. The ATM returns the customer's bank card.

Scenarios allow us to get a feel for the behavior expected from the system. A single scenario cannot show all possible behaviors, however, so software engineers typically prepare many different scenarios in order to gain a full understanding of the system's requirements.

You must know some details in order to write and run the program. Other details, if not explicitly stated in the program's requirements, may be handled according to the programmer's preference. Assumptions about unstated or ambiguous specifications should always be written explicitly in the program's documentation.

The detailed specification clarifies the problem to be solved. But it does more than that: it also serves as an important piece of written documentation about the program. There are many ways in which specifications may be expressed and a number of different sections that may be included, depending on the nature of the problem. Our recommended program specification includes the following sections:

- inputs,
- outputs,
- processing requirements, and
- assumptions.

If special processing is needed for unusual or error conditions, it too should be specified. Sometimes it is helpful to include a section containing definitions of terms used in the specification. It is also useful to list any testing requirements so that the method for verifying the program is taken into consideration early in the development process. (See Figure 4.15 for an example of a Program Specification.)

Program Design

The detailed specification of the program tells *what* the program must do, but not *how* it does it. Once you have fully clarified the goals of the program, you can begin to develop and record a strategy for meeting them; in other words, you can begin the design phase of the software life cycle.

Abstraction   The universe is filled with complex systems. We learn about such systems through *models*. A model may be mathematical, like equations describing the motion of satellites around the earth. A physical object such as a model airplane used in wind-tunnel tests is another form of model. In this approach to understanding complex systems, the important concept is that only the essential characteristics of the system are considered; minor or irrelevant details are ignored. For example, although the earth is an oblate ellipsoid, globes (models of the earth) are spheres. The small difference between the earth's equatorial diameter and polar diameter is not important to us in studying the political divisions and physical landmarks on the earth. Similarly, in-flight movies are not included in the model airplanes used for wind-tunnel testing.

An **abstraction** is a model of a complex system that includes only the essential details. Abstractions are the fundamental way that we manage complexity. Different abstractions of a particular system are used by different viewers of the system. Thus, while we see a car as a means to transport us and our friends, the automotive brake engineer may see it as a large mass with a small contact area between it and the road (Figure 1.1).

FIGURE 1.1   *An abstraction includes the essential details relative to the perspective of the viewer.*

Abstraction   A model of a complex system that includes only the details essential to the perspective of the viewer of the system

---

What does abstraction have to do with software development? The programs we write are abstractions. The spreadsheet program used by an accountant models the books used to record debits and credits. The autopilot program used by a pilot models the flight characteristics of the aircraft. Writing software is difficult because both the systems we model and the processes we use to develop the software are complex. Abstraction is our most powerful tool for dealing with this complexity. One of our major goals is to show you how abstractions are used to manage the complexity of developing software and to convince you to use them. In nearly every chapter we make use of abstraction to simplify our work.

Information Hiding   In the next sections we briefly look at two program design methods. Both are based on decomposing the problem into clear-cut levels of abstraction. One important feature of any design method is that the details that are specified in lower levels of the program design are hidden from the higher levels. The programmer sees only the details that are relevant at a particular level of the design. This **information hiding** makes certain details inaccessible to the programmer at higher levels.

Information Hiding   The practice of hiding the details of a function or data structure with the goal of controlling access to the details of a module or structure

---

Why is hiding the details desirable? Shouldn't the programmer know everything? *No!* This truly is a situation in which a certain amount of ignorance is advantageous. Information hiding prevents the high levels of the design from becoming dependent on low-level design details that are more likely to be changed. For example, you can stop a car without knowing whether it has disc brakes or drum brakes. You don't need to know these lower level details of the car's brake subsystem in order to stop it.

Furthermore, you don't want to require a complete understanding of the complicated details of low-level routines for the design of higher level routines. Such a requirement would introduce a greater risk of confusion and error throughout the whole program. For example, it would be disastrous if every time we wanted to stop our car, we had to think, "The brake pedal is a lever with a mechanical advantage of 10.6 coupled to a hydraulic system with a mechanical advantage of 7.3 that presses a semimetallic pad against a steel disc. The coefficient of friction of the pad/disc contact is . . . ."

Information hiding is not limited to driving cars and programming computers. Try to list *all* the operations and information required to make a peanut butter and jelly sandwich. We normally don't consider the details of planting, growing, and harvesting peanuts, grapes, and wheat as part of making a sandwich. Information hiding lets us deal only with the operations and information needed at a particular level in the solution of a problem.

The concepts of abstraction and information hiding are fundamental principles of software engineering. We come back to them again and again throughout this book.

The software design approach we use must help us divide a complex problem into smaller, more manageable modules that are easier to build and understand. These modules should be good abstractions with strong *cohesion*; that is, each module should have a single purpose or identity and the modules should stick together well. A cohesive module can usually be described by a simple sentence. If you have to use several sentences or one very convoluted sentence to describe your module, it is probably *not* cohesive. Each module should also exhibit information hiding so that changes within it do not result in changes in the modules that use it. This independent quality of modules is known as *loose coupling*. If your module depends on many other modules, it is *not* loosely coupled.

But what should these modules be? One approach is to break the problem into *functional* subproblems (do this, then do this, then do that). Another approach is to divide the problem into the "things" or objects that interact to solve the problem. We examine both these approaches.

Functional Decomposition   One method for designing software is called *functional decomposition*. It also is called *top-down design*. You may have learned this method in your introductory class. First the problem is broken into several large tasks. Each of these tasks is in turn divided into sections, then the sections are subdivided, and so on. The important feature is that *details are deferred as long as possible* as we move from a general to a specific solution.

The development of a computer program by functional decomposition begins with a "big picture" solution to the problem defined in the specification. We then devise a general strategy for solving the problem by dividing it into manageable functional modules. Next, each of the large functional modules is subdivided into several tasks. We do not need to write the top level of the functional design in source code (such as C++); we can write it in English or "pseudocode." (Some software development projects even use special design languages that can be compiled.) This divide-and-conquer activity continues until we reach a level that can be easily translated into lines of code.

Once it has been divided into modules, the problem is simpler to code into a well-structured program. The functional decomposition approach encourages programming in logical units, using functions. The main module of the design becomes the main program (also called the main function), and subsections develop into functions. This *hierarchy of tasks* forms the basis for functional decomposition, with the main program or function controlling the processing.

As an example, let's start the functional design for making a cake.

Make Cake

> Get ingredients
> Mix cake ingredients
> Bake
> Cool
> Apply icing

The problem now is divided into five logical units, each of which might be further decomposed into more detailed functional modules. Figure 1.2 illustrates the hierarchy of such a functional decomposition.

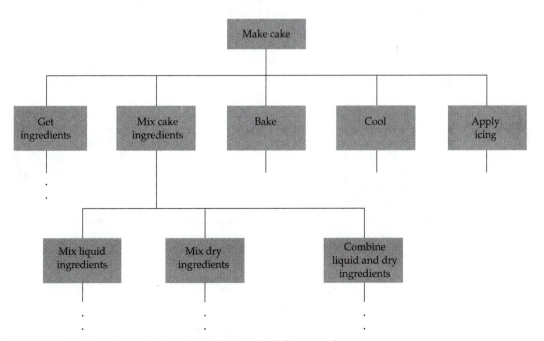

FIGURE 1.2   *A portion of a functional design for baking a cake.*

In functional decomposition, information hiding is accomplished primarily through deferring the details of algorithms. This form of information hiding is based on *procedural* or *functional abstraction*.

Object-Oriented Design   Another approach to designing programs is called *object-oriented design* (OOD). This methodology originated with the development of programs to simulate physical objects and processes in the real world. For example, to simulate an electronic circuit, you could develop a module for simulating each type of component in the circuit and then "wire-up" the simulation by having the modules pass information among themselves in the same pattern that wires connect the electronic components.

In a simulation, the top-down decomposition of the problem has already taken place. An engineer has designed a circuit or a mechanical device, a physicist has developed a model of a physical system, a biologist has developed an experimental model, an economist has designed an economic model, and so on. Your job as a programmer is to take this problem decomposition and implement it.

In object-oriented design, the first step is to identify the simplest and most widely used objects and processes in the decomposition and implement them faithfully. Once you have completed this stage, you often can reuse these objects and processes to implement more complex objects and processes. This *hierarchy of objects* is the basis for object-oriented design.

Object-oriented design, like functional decomposition, takes a divide-and-conquer approach. However, instead of decomposing the problem into functional modules, we divide it into entities or things that make sense in the context of the problem being solved. These entities, called *objects*, collaborate and interact to solve the problem. The code that allows these objects to interact is called a *driver program*.

Let's list some of the objects in our baking problem. There are, of course, all of the various ingredients: eggs, milk, flour, butter, and so on. We also need certain pieces of equipment such as pans, bowls, measuring spoons, and an oven. The baker is another important entity. All of these entities must collaborate to create a cake. For example, a spoon measures individual ingredients and a bowl holds a mixture of ingredients.

Groups of objects with similar properties and behaviors are described by an **object class** (usually shortened to *class*). Each oven in the world is a unique object. We cannot hope to describe every oven, but we can group oven objects together into a class called oven that has certain properties and behaviors.

Object Class (Class)   The description of a group of objects with similar properties and behaviors; a pattern for creating individual objects

---

An object class is similar to a C++ `class` (which we review in Chapter 2). C++ types are templates for variables; classes are templates for objects. Like types, object classes have attributes and operations associated with them. For example, an oven class might have an attribute to specify whether it is gas or electric and operations to turn it on or off and to set it to maintain a desired temperature.

With object-oriented design, we determine the classes from the things in the problem as described in the specification. We also describe how those classes are related to each other and how they interact with each other. From this work, we determine a set of properties (attributes) and a set of responsibilities (operations) to associate with each class. With object-oriented design, the *functionality* of the program is distributed among a set of collaborating objects. Table 1.1 illustrates some of the object classes that participate in baking a cake.

TABLE 1.1   Example of Object Classes That Participate in Baking a Cake

Class	Attributes	Responsibilities (Operations)
Oven	Energy source	Turn on
	Size	Turn off
	Temperature	Set desired temperature
	Number racks	
Bowl	Capacity	Add to
	Current amount	Dump
Egg	Size	Crack
		Separate (white from yolk)

Once we have defined an oven class, it can be reused in other cooking problems, such a roasting a turkey. Reuse of classes is an important aspect of modern software development. One of the major purposes of this text is to introduce you to a number of classes that are particularly important in the development of software—*abstract data types*. We discuss the concept of the abstract data type in detail in Chapter 2. In the remaining chapters we fully develop many abstract data types, and we describe others leaving you to develop them yourself. As these classes are fundamental to computer science, the C++ code for them can often be obtained from a public or private repository or purchased from vendors who market C++ components. In fact, the new C++ language standard includes such components in the Standard Template Library (STL). You may wonder why, if they are already available, we spend so much time on their development. Our goal is to teach you how to develop software. As with any skill, you need to practice the fundamentals before you can become a virtuoso.

The detailed techniques of object-oriented design are beyond the scope of this text. Object-oriented design was developed for large problems and often appears trivial when applied on a small scale. For small problems, a combination of top-down design and object-oriented design is a useful strategy that permits you to think of the data in terms of objects while continuing to functionally decompose the problem. When the decomposition reaches the level of operations on data, you can switch to active mode and implement the data and associated operations as objects.

To summarize, top-down design methods focus on the *process* of transforming the input into the output, resulting in a hierarchy of tasks. Object-oriented design focuses on the *data objects* that are to be transformed, resulting in a hierarchy of objects. Grady Booch puts it this way: "Read the specification of the software you want to build. Underline the verbs if you are after procedural code, the nouns if you aim for an object-oriented program."[1]

We propose that you circle the nouns and underline the verbs. The nouns become objects; the verbs become operations. In a functional design, the verbs are the primary focus; in an object-oriented design, the nouns are the primary focus.

Verification of Software Correctness

At the beginning of this chapter, we discussed some characteristics of good programs. The first of these was that a good program works—it accomplishes its intended function. How do you know when your program meets that goal? The simple answer is, *test it*.

Let's look at **testing** as it relates to the rest of the software development process. As programmers, we first make sure that we understand the requirements, and then we come up with a general solution. Next we design the solution in terms of a computer program, using good design principles, and finally we implement the solution, using good structured coding, with classes, functions, self-documenting code, and so on.

Once we have the program coded, we compile it repeatedly until the syntax errors are gone. Then we run the program, using carefully selected test data. If the program doesn't work, we say that it has a "bug" in it. We try to pinpoint the error and fix it, a process called **debugging**. Notice the distinction between testing and debugging. Testing is running the program with data sets designed to discover any errors; debugging is removing errors once they are discovered.

---

1. Grady Booch, "What Is and Isn't Object Oriented Design." *American Programmer*, special issue on object orientation, vol. 2, no. 7–8, Summer 1989.

Testing   The process of executing a program with data sets designed to discover errors

Debugging   The process of removing known errors

When all the bugs are out, the program is correct. Well, maybe it is. Testing is useful in revealing the presence of bugs in a program, but it doesn't prove their absence. We can only say for sure that the program worked correctly for the cases we tested. This approach seems somewhat haphazard. How do we know which tests or how many of them to run? Debugging a whole program at once isn't easy. And fixing the errors found during such testing can sometimes be a messy task. Too bad we couldn't have detected the errors earlier—while we were designing the program, for instance. They would have been much easier to fix then.

We know how program design can be improved by using a good design methodology. Is there something similar that we can do to improve our program verification activities? Yes, there is. Program verification activities don't need to start when the program is completely coded; they can be incorporated into the whole software development process, from the requirements phase on. **Program verification** is more than just testing.

Program Verification   The process of determining the degree to which a software product fulfills its specifications

Can we really "debug" a program before it has ever been run—or even before it has been written? In this section we review a number of topics related to satisfying the criterion "quality software works." The topics include

- designing for correctness
- performing code and design walk-throughs and inspections
- using debugging methods
- choosing test goals and data
- writing test plans
- structured integration testing

Origin of Bugs

When Sherlock Holmes goes off to solve a case, he doesn't start from scratch every time; he knows from experience all kinds of things that help him find solutions. Suppose Holmes finds a victim in a muddy field. He immediately looks for footprints in the mud, for he can tell from a footprint what kind of shoe made it. The first print he finds matches the shoes of the victim, so he keeps looking. Now he finds another, and from his vast knowledge of footprints he can tell that it was made by a certain type of boot. He deduces that such a boot would be worn by a particular type of laborer, and from the size and depth of the print he guesses the suspect's height and weight. Now, knowing something about the habits of laborers in this town, he guesses that at 6:30 p.m. the suspect might be found in Clancy's Pub.

In software verification we are often expected to play detective. Given certain clues, we have to find the bugs in programs. If we know what kinds of situations produce program errors, we are more likely to be able to detect and correct problems. We may even be able to step in and prevent many errors entirely, just as Sherlock Holmes sometimes intervenes in time to prevent a crime that is about to take place.

Let's look at some types of software errors that show up at various points in program development and testing and see how they might be avoided.

Specifications and Design Errors   What would happen if, shortly before you were supposed to turn in a major class assignment, you discovered that some details in the professor's program description were incorrect? To make matters worse, you also found out that the corrections were discussed at the beginning of class on the day you got there late, and somehow you never knew about the problem until your tests of the class data set came up with the wrong answers. What do you do now?

Writing a program to the wrong specifications is probably the worst kind of software error. How bad can it be? Let's look at a true story. Some time ago, a computer company contracted to replace a government agency's obsolete system with new hardware and software. A large and complicated program was written, based on specifications and algorithms provided by the customer.

The new system was checked out at every point in its development to ensure that its functions matched the requirements in the specifications document. When the system was complete and the new software was executed, it was discovered that the results of its calculations did not match those of the old system. A careful comparison of the two systems showed that the specifications of the new software were erroneous because they were based on algorithms taken from the old system's inaccurate documentation. The new program was "correct" in that it accomplished its specified functions, but the program was useless to the customer because it didn't accomplish its intended functions—it didn't work. The cost of correcting the errors measured in the millions of dollars.

How could correcting the error be so expensive? First of all, much of the conceptual and design effort, as well as the coding, was wasted. It took a great deal of time to pinpoint which parts of the specification were in error and then to correct this document before the program could be redesigned. Then much of the software development activity (design, coding, and testing) had to be repeated. This case is an extreme one, but it illustrates how critical specifications are to the software process. In general, programmers are more expert in software development techniques than in the "application" areas of their programs, such as banking, city planning, satellite control, or medical research. Thus correct program specifications are crucial to the success of program development.

The process of determining that software accomplishes its intended task is called **program validation**. Program verification asks "Are we doing the job right?"; program validation asks "Are we doing the right job?"[2]

Program Validation   The process of determining the degree to which software fulfills its intended purpose

---

Finally, **acceptance tests** on the whole system are run. Then, when these tests have been completed, the software is put into use—that is, if the system passes the acceptance tests, which it did not in this case. If the acceptance tests are passed, is the verification process finished? Hardly! More than half of the total life-cycle costs and effort generally occur *after* the program becomes operational, in the maintenance phase. Some changes are made to correct errors in the original program; others are introduced to add new capabilities to the software system. In either case, testing must be done after any program modification. This is called **regression testing**.

---

2. B. W. Boehm, *Software Engineering Economics* (Englewood Cliffs, N.J.: Prentice-Hall, 1981).

Acceptance Tests   The process of testing the system in its real environment with real data

Regression Testing   Re-execution of program tests after modifications have been made in order to ensure that the program still works correctly

---

The case of the government agency also illustrates a basic principle about software costs: the earlier in the development cycle a problem is detected, the cheaper it is to fix. "Cost" may mean dollars to pay programmers, monetary penalties for missed schedules, or points off for turning in a course assignment late. Because the development of the specifications for a software assignment precedes its design and implementation, an undetected error at this point can become very expensive. The longer the problem goes without detection, the higher the cost of fixing it rises.

Figure 1.3 shows how fast the costs rise in subsequent phases of software development. The vertical axis represents the relative cost of fixing an error; this cost might be in units of hours, or hundreds of dollars, or "programmer months" (the amount of work one programmer can do in a month). The horizontal axis represents the stages in the development of a software product. As you can see, an error that would have taken one unit to fix when you first started designing might take a hundred units to correct when the product is actually in operation!

Many specification errors can be prevented by good communication between the programmers (you) and the party who originated the problem (the professor, manager, or customer). In general, it pays to ask questions when you don't understand something in the program specifications. And the earlier you ask, the better.

A number of questions should come to mind as you first read a programming assignment. What error checking is necessary? What algorithm or data structure is supposed to be used in the solution? What assumptions are reasonable? If you obtain answers to these questions when you first begin working on an assignment, you can incorporate them into your design and implementation of the program. Later in the program's development, unexpected answers to these questions can cost you time and effort. In short, in order to write a program that is correct, you must understand precisely what it is that your program is supposed to do.

Sometimes specifications change during the design or implementation of a program. In such cases, a good design helps you to pinpoint which sections of the program have to be redone. For instance, if a program defines and uses type StringType to implement strings, changing the implementation of StringType does not require that the whole program be rewritten. We should be able to see from the design—either functional or object-oriented—that the offending code

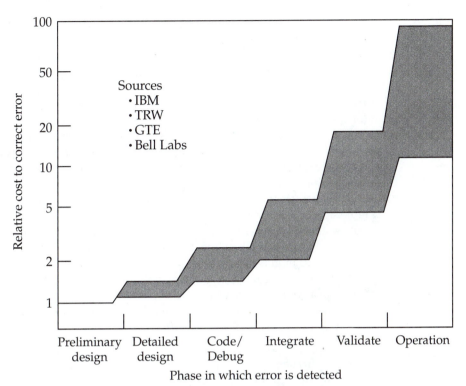

FIGURE 1.3 *This graph demonstrates the importance of early detection of software errors.*

is restricted to the module where StringType is defined. The parts of the program that require changes can usually be located more easily from a design than from the code itself.

Compile-Time Errors   In the process of learning your first programming language, you probably made a number of syntax errors. These resulted in error messages (for example, "TYPE MISMATCH," "ILLEGAL ASSIGNMENT," "SEMICOLON EXPECTED," and so on) when you tried to compile the program. Now that you are more familiar with the programming language, you can save your debugging skills for tracking down really important logical errors. *Try to get the syntax right the first time.* Having your program compile cleanly on the first attempt is not an unreasonable goal. A syntax error wastes computing time and money, as well as programmer time, and it is preventable. Although some programmers argue that looking for syntax errors is a waste of their time, that it is faster to let the compiler catch all the typos and syntax errors, don't believe it. Sometimes a coding error turns out to be a legal statement, syntactically correct but semantically wrong. This situation may cause very obscure, hard-to-locate errors.

As you progress in your college career or move into a professional computing job, learning a new programming language is often the easiest part of a new software assignment. This does not mean, however, that the language is the least important part. In this book we discuss abstract data types and algorithms that we believe are language independent. This means that they can be implemented in almost any general-purpose programming language. The success of the implementation, however, depends on a thorough understanding of the features of the programming language. What is considered acceptable programming practice in one language may be inadequate in another, and similar syntactic constructs may be just different enough to cause serious trouble.

It is, therefore, worthwhile to develop an expert knowledge of both the control and data structures and the syntax of the language in which you are programming. In general, if you have a good knowledge of your programming language—and are careful—you can avoid syntax errors. The ones you might miss are relatively easy to locate and correct. Most are flagged by the compiler with an error message. Once you have a "clean" compilation, you can execute your program.

Run-Time Errors   Errors that occur during the execution of a program are usually harder to detect than syntax errors. Some run-time errors stop execution of the program. When this happens, we say that the program "crashed" or "abnormally terminated."

Run-time errors often occur when the programmer makes too many assumptions. For instance,

```
result = dividend / divisor;
```

is a legitimate assignment statement, if we can assume that `divisor` is never zero. If `divisor` *is* zero, however, a run-time error results.

Sometimes run-time errors occur because the programmer does not fully understand the programming language. For example, in C++ the assignment operator is =, and the equality test operator is ==. Because they look so much alike, they often are miskeyed one for the other. You might think that this would be a syntax error that the compiler would catch, but it is not. Technically an assignment in C++ is an expression with two parts: the expression on the right of the assignment operator (=) is evaluated and the result is returned and stored in the place named on the left. The key word here is *returned*; the result of evaluating the right-hand side is the result of the expression. Therefore, if the assignment operator is miskeyed for the equality test operator or vice versa, the code executes with surprising results.

Let's look at an example. Consider the following two statements.

```
count == count + 1;
if (count = 10)
    .
    .
    .
```

The first statement returns false; `count` can never be equal to `count + 1`. The semicolon ends the statement, so nothing happens to the value returned; `count` has not been changed. In the next statement, the expression (`count = 10`) is evaluated. 10 is returned and stored in `count`. Because a nonzero value (10) is returned, the If expression always evaluates to true.

Run-time errors also occur because of unanticipated user errors. For instance, if `newValue` is declared to be of type `int`, the statement

```
cin >> newValue;
```

causes a stream failure if the user inputs a nonnumeric character.

Stream Input and Output

In C++, input and output are considered streams of characters. The keyboard input stream is `cin`; the screen output stream is `cout`. Important declarations relating to these streams are supplied in the library file `<iostream.h>`. If you are going to use the standard input and output streams, you must include this file in your program.

```
#include <iostream.h>
int main()
{
    int intValue;
    float realValue;

    cout  << "Enter an integer number followed by return."
          << endl;
    cin   >> intValue;
    cout  << "Enter a real number followed by return."
          << endl;
    cin   >> realValue;
    cout  << "You entered "  << intValue  << " and "
          << realValue
          << endl;
    return 0;
}
```

<< is called the *insertion* operator: the expressions on the right describe what is inserted into the output stream. >> is called the *extraction* operator: values are extracted from the input stream and stored in the places named on the right. endl is a special language feature called a *manipulator*; it terminates the current output line.

If you are reading or writing to a file, you include <fstream.h>. This gives you access to the data types ifstream (for input) and ofstream (for output). Declare variables of these types, use the open function to associate each with the external file name, and use the variable names in place of cin and cout, respectively.

```
#include <fstream.h>

int main()
{
    int intValue;
    float realValue;
    ifstream inData;
    ofstream outData;

    inData.open("input.dat");
    outData.open("output.dat");

    inData  >> intValue;
    inData  >> realValue;
    outData << "The input values are "
            << intValue    << " and "
            << realValue   << endl;
    return 0;
}
```

On input—whether from the keyboard or from a file—the >> operator skips leading whitespace characters (blank, tab, line feed, form feed, carriage return) before extracting the input value. To avoid skipping whitespace characters, you can use the get function. It is invoked by giving the name of the input stream, a dot, and then the function name and parameter list:

```
cin.get(inputChar);
```

The get function inputs the next character waiting in the input stream, even if it is a whitespace character.

Stream Failure

The key to reading data in correctly (from either the keyboard or a file) is to make sure that the order and the form in which the data are keyed are consistent with the order and type of the identifiers on the input statement. If an error occurs while accessing an I/O stream, the stream enters the *fail state*, and any further references to the stream are ignored. For example, if you misspell the name of the file that is the parameter to function open (In.dat instead of Data.In, for example), the file input stream enters the fail state. Or if you try to input a value when the stream is at the end of the file, the stream enters the fail state. Your program continues to execute when the stream is in the fail state, but all further references to the stream are ignored.

C++ gives you a way to test the state of a stream: the stream name used in an expression returns a nonzero value (true) if the state is okay and a zero (false) if the stream is in the fail state. For example, the following code segment prints an error message and halts execution if the proper input file is not found.

```
#include <fstream.h>
#include <iostream.h>

int main()
{
    ifstream inData;

    inData.open("myData.dat");
    if (!inData)
    {
        cout << "File myData.dat was not found." << endl;
        return 1;
    }
    .
    .
    .
    return 0;
}
```

Note that, by convention, the main function returns an *exit status* of 0 if execution completed normally, whereas it returns a nonzero value (above, we used 1) otherwise.

There are many places in a program where potential errors can be predicted. As software designers, we can add checks to a program to handle these errors. For example, if a program asks for a file name from the user and the user mistypes the name of the file, the program continues, but the file stream is in the fail state. Subsequent attempts to read from the file are silently ignored.

Some languages check for the errors in input data and terminate processing when they occur. C++ does not check for them but does provide ways that the user can perform the check. One way is to use *executable assertions* available in file `<assert.h>`. If an executable assertion is not true, the program halts. For example,

```
// Gain access to code that evaluates assertions.
#include <assert.h>
cin  >> newValue;
assert(cin);              // cin is not in the fail state.
inFile.open("data.in");
assert(inFile);           // inFile is not in the fail state.
```

halts execution if the data keyed for `newValue` are not correct or if file `data.in` cannot be found.

Although executable assertions can be valuable tools, there is one serious drawback to their use: the program halts when the assertion is not true. A message is printed that includes the assertion, the name of the program file, and the line number. For debugging purposes, this is often acceptable. In general, however, you must not allow conditions that stop your program from executing; your program should stay in control until the user is ready to quit. A program should not crash when it tries to open a file that doesn't exist. You can include checks for such conditions, followed by appropriate error recovery.

The ability of a program to recover when an error occurs is called **robustness**. If a commercial program is not robust, people do not buy it. Who wants a word processor that crashes if the user says "SAVE" when there is no disk in the drive? We want the program to tell us, "Put your disk in the drive, and press Enter." For some types of software, robustness is a critical requirement. An airplane's automatic pilot system or an intensive care unit's patient-monitoring program just cannot afford to crash. In such situations a defensive posture produces good results.

Robustness   The ability of a program to recover following an error; the ability of a program to continue to operate within its environment

In general, you should actively check for error-creating conditions rather than let them abort your program. For instance, it is generally unwise to make too many assumptions about the correctness of input, especially interactive input from a keyboard. A better approach is to check explicitly for the correct type and bounds of such input. The programmer can then decide how an error should be handled (request new input, print a message, or go on to the next data) rather than leave the decision to the system. Even the decision to quit should be made by a program that is in control of its own execution. If worse comes to worst, let your program die gracefully.

This does not mean that everything that the program inputs must be checked for errors. Sometimes inputs are known to be correct—for instance, input from a file that has been verified. The decision to include error checking must be based upon the requirements of the program.

Some run-time errors do not stop execution but produce the wrong results. You may have incorrectly implemented an algorithm or used a variable before it was assigned a value. You may have inadvertently swapped two parameters of the same type on a function call or forgotten to designate a function's output data as a reference parameter. (See Parameter Passing sidebar, page 67.) These logical errors are often the hardest to prevent and locate. Later we talk about debugging techniques to help pinpoint run-time errors. We also discuss structured testing methods that isolate the part of the program being tested. But knowing that the earlier we find an error the easier it is to fix, we turn now to ways of catching run-time errors before run time.

Designing for Correctness

It would be nice if there were some tool that would locate the errors in our design or code without our even having to run the program. That sounds unlikely, but consider an analogy from geometry. We wouldn't try to prove the Pythagorean Theorem by proving that it worked on every triangle; that would only demonstrate that the theorem works for every triangle we tried. We prove theorems in geometry mathematically. Why can't we do the same for computer programs?

The verification of program correctness, independent of data testing, is an important area of theoretical computer science research. The goal of this research is to establish a method for proving programs that is analogous to the method for proving theorems in geometry. The necessary techniques exist, but the proofs are often more complicated than the programs themselves. Therefore, a major focus of verification research is the attempt to build automated program provers—verifiable programs that verify other programs. In the meantime, the formal verification techniques can be carried out by hand.[3]

---

3. We do not go into this subject in detail here. For students who are interested in this topic, see David Gries, *The Science of Programming* (New York: Springer-Verlag, (1981)).

Assertions   An assertion is a logical proposition that can be true or false. We can make assertions about the state of the program. For instance, following the assignment statement

```
sum = part + 1 ;        // sum and part are integers.
```

we might assert: "The value of sum is greater than the value of part." That assertion might not be very useful or interesting by itself, but let's see what we can do with it. We can demonstrate that the assertion is true by making a logical argument: no matter what value part has (negative, zero, or positive), when it is increased by 1, the result is a larger value. Now note what we didn't do. We didn't have to run a program containing this assignment statement to verify that the assertion was correct.

Assertion   A logical proposition that can be true or false

The general concept behind formal program verification is that we can make assertions about what the program is intended to do, based on its specifications, and then prove through a logical argument (rather than through execution of the program) that a design or implementation satisfies the assertions. Thus the process can be broken down into two steps: (1) correctly asserting the intended function of the part of the program to be verified, and (2) proving that the actual design or implementation does what is asserted. The first step, making assertions, sounds as if it might be useful to us in the process of designing correct programs. After all, we already know that we cannot write correct programs unless we know what they are supposed to do.

Preconditions and Postconditions   Let's take the idea of making assertions down a level in the design process. Suppose we want to design a module (a logical chunk of the program) to perform a specific operation. To ensure that this module fits into the program as a whole, we must clarify what happens at its boundaries—what must be true when we enter the module and what is true when we exit.

To make the task more concrete, picture the design module as it is eventually coded, as a function that is called within a program. To be able to call the function, we must know its exact interface: the name and the parameter list, which indicates its inputs and outputs. But this isn't enough: we must also know any assumptions that must be true for the operation to function correctly.

We call the assertions that must be true on entry into the function **preconditions**. The preconditions are like a product disclaimer:

WARNING: If you try to execute this operation when the preconditions are not true, the results are not guaranteed.

For instance, when we said that following the execution of

```
sum = part + 1;
```

we can assert that `sum` is greater than `part`, we made an assumption—a precondition—that `part` is not `INT_MAX`. If this precondition were violated, our assertion would not be true.

We must also know what conditions are true when the operation is complete. The **postconditions** are assertions that describe the results of the operation. The postconditions do not tell us how these results are accomplished; they merely tell us what the results should be.

Preconditions   Assertions that must be true on entry into an operation or function for the postconditions to be guaranteed

Postconditions   Assertions that state what results are to be expected at the exit of an operation or function, assuming that the preconditions are true

---

Let's consider what the preconditions and postconditions might be for a simple operation: a function that deletes the last element from a list and returns its value as an output. (We are using "list" in an intuitive sense; we formally define it in Chapter 3.) The specification for GetLast is as follows:

GetLast(ListType list, int length, ValueType lastValue)

Function:　　　Removes the last element in the list and returns its value in lastValue.

Precondition:　　The list is not empty.

Postconditions:　lastValue is the value of the last element in list, the last element has been removed, and length has been decremented.

What do these preconditions and postconditions have to do with program verification? By making explicit assertions about what is expected at the interfaces between modules, we can avoid making logical errors based on misunderstandings. For instance, from the precondition we know that we must check outside of this operation for the empty condition; this module *assumes* that there is at least one element. The postcondition tells us that when the value of the last list element is retrieved, that element is deleted from the list. This fact is an important one for the list user to know. If we just want to take a peek at the last value without affecting the list, we cannot use GetLast.

Experienced software developers know that misunderstandings about interfaces to someone else's modules are one of the main sources of program problems. We use preconditions and postconditions at the module or function level in this book, because the information they provide helps us to design programs in a truly modular fashion. We can then use the modules we've designed in our programs, confident that we are not introducing errors by making mistakes about assumptions and about what the modules actually do.

Design Review Activities   When an individual programmer is designing and implementing a program, he or she can find many software errors with pencil and paper. **Deskchecking** the design solution is a very common method of manually verifying a program. The programmer writes down essential data (variables, input values, parameters of subprograms, and so on) and walks through the design, marking changes in the data on the paper. Known trouble spots in the design or code should be double-checked. A checklist of typical errors (such as loops that do not terminate, variables that are used before they are initialized, and incorrect order of parameters on function calls) can be used to make the deskcheck more effective. A sample checklist for deskchecking a C++ program appears in Figure 1.4.

Deskchecking   Tracing an execution of a design or program on paper

---

Have you ever been really stuck trying to debug a program and showed it to a classmate or colleague who detected the bug right away? It is generally acknowledged that someone else can detect errors in a program better than the original author can. In an extension of deskchecking, two programmers can trade code listings and check each other's programs. Universities, however, frequently discourage students from examining each other's programs for fear that this exchange leads to cheating. Thus many students become experienced in writing programs but don't have much opportunity to practice reading them.

Most sizable computer programs are developed by *teams* of programmers. Two extensions of deskchecking that are effectively used by programming teams are design or code **walk-throughs** and **inspections**. These are formal team activities, the intention of which is to move the responsibility for

The Design

1. Does each module in the design have a clear function or purpose?
2. Can large modules be broken down into smaller pieces? (A common rule of thumb is that a C++ function should fit on one page.)
3. Are all the assumptions valid? Are they well documented?
4. Are the preconditions and postconditions accurate assertions about what should be happening in the module they specify?
5. Is the design correct and complete as measured against the program specification? Are there any missing cases? Is there faulty logic?
6. Is the program designed well for understandability and maintainability?

The Code

7. Has the design been clearly and correctly implemented in the programming language? Are features of the programming language used appropriately?
8. Are all output parameters of functions assigned values?
9. Are parameters that return values marked as reference parameters (have & to the right of the type if the parameter is not an array)?
10. Are functions coded to be consistent with the interfaces shown in the design?
11. Are the actual parameters on function calls consistent with the parameters declared in the function prototype and definition?
12. Is each data object to be initialized set correctly at the proper time? Is each data object set before its value is used?
13. Do all loops terminate?
14. Is the design free of "magic" numbers? (A "magic" number is one whose meaning is not immediately evident to the reader.)
15. Does each constant, type, variable, and function have a meaningful name? Are comments included with the declarations to clarify the use of the data objects?

FIGURE 1.4   *Checklist for deskchecking a C++ program.*

uncovering bugs from the individual programmer to the group. Because testing is time-consuming and errors cost more the later they are discovered, the goal is to identify errors before testing begins.

In a *walk-through* the team performs a manual simulation of the design or program with sample test inputs, keeping track of the program's data by hand on paper or a blackboard. Unlike thorough program testing, the walk-through is not intended to simulate all possible test cases. Instead, its purpose is to stimulate discussion about the way the programmer chose to design or implement the program's requirements.

At an *inspection*, a reader (not necessarily the program's author) goes through the design or code line by line. Inspection participants point out errors, which are recorded on an inspection report. Some errors are uncovered just by the process of reading aloud. Others may have been noted by team members during their preinspection preparation. As with the walk-through, the chief benefit of the team meeting is the discussion that takes place among team members. This interaction among programmers, testers, and other team members can uncover many program errors long before the testing stage begins.

Walk-through   A verification method in which a *team* performs a manual simulation of the program or design

Inspection   A verification method in which one member of a team reads the program or design line by line and the others point out errors

---

At the high-level design stage, the design should be compared to the program requirements to make sure that all required functions have been included and that this program or module correctly interfaces with other software in the system. At the low-level design stage, when the design has been filled out with more details, it should be reinspected before it is implemented. When the coding has been completed, the compiled listings should be inspected again. This inspection (or walk-through) ensures that the implementation is consistent with both the requirements and the design. Successful completion of this inspection means that testing of the program can begin.

Walk-throughs and inspections should be carried out in as nonthreatening a way as possible.

Program Testing

Eventually, after all the design verification, deskchecking, and inspections have been completed, it is time to execute the code. At last, we are ready to start testing with the *intention of finding any errors that may still remain.*

The testing process is made up of a set of test cases that, taken together, allow us to assert that a program works correctly. We say "assert" rather than "prove" because testing does not generally provide a proof of program correctness.

The goal of each test case is to verify a particular program feature. For instance, we may design several test cases to demonstrate that the program correctly handles various classes of input errors. Or we may design cases to check the processing when a data structure (such as an array) is empty, or when it contains the maximum number of elements.

Within each test case, we must perform a series of component tasks:

- We determine inputs that demonstrate the goal of the test case.
- We determine the expected behavior of the program for the given input. (This task is often the most difficult one. For a math function, we might use a chart of values or a calculator to figure out the expected result. For a function with complex processing, we might use a deskcheck type of simulation or an alternative solution to the same problem.)
- We run the program and observe the resulting behavior. (This behavior may be observed by looking at either regular program output [something that happens on the screen or is written on a printer] or output used just for testing.)
- We compare the expected behavior and the actual behavior of the program. If they are the same, the test case is successful. If not, an error exists. In the latter case, we begin debugging.

For now we are talking about test cases at a module, or function, level. It's much easier to test and debug modules of a program one at a time, rather than trying to get the whole program solution to work all at once. Testing at this level is called **unit testing**.

Unit Testing   Testing a module or function by itself

How do we know what kinds of unit test cases are appropriate, and how many are needed? Determining the set of test cases that is sufficient to validate a unit of a program is in itself a difficult task. There are two approaches to specifying test cases: cases based on testing possible data inputs and cases based on testing aspects of the code itself.

Data Coverage   In those limited cases where the set of valid inputs, or the **functional domain**, is extremely small, one can verify a subprogram by testing it against every possible input element. This approach, known as "exhaustive" testing, can prove conclusively that the software meets its specifications. For instance, the functional domain of the following function consists of the values true and false.[4]

---

4. Here and in the rest of the book, we assume that bool is a defined data type. If your compiler does not recognize bool, put the following code in a header file "bool.h" and include it in your programs.

```
typedef int bool;
const bool true = 1;
const bool false = 0;
```

```
void PrintBoolean(bool error)
// Prints the Boolean value on the screen.
{
    if (error)
        cout  <<  ''true'';
    else
        cout  <<  ''false'';
    cout  << endl;
}
```

Functional Domain   The set of valid input data for a program or function

---

It makes sense to apply exhaustive testing to this function, because there are only two possible input values. In most cases, however, the functional domain is very large, so exhaustive testing is almost always impractical or impossible. What is the functional domain of the following function?

```
void PrintInteger(int intValue)
// Prints the integer value intValue on the screen.
{
    cout  << intValue;
}
```

It is not practical to test this function by running it with every possible data input; the number of elements in the set of int values is clearly too large. In such cases we do not attempt exhaustive testing. Instead, we pick some other measurement as a testing goal.

You can attempt program testing in a haphazard way, entering data randomly until you cause the program to fail. Guessing doesn't hurt (except possibly by wasting time), but it may not help much either. This approach is likely to uncover some bugs in a program, but it is very unlikely to find them all. Fortunately, however, there are strategies for detecting errors in a systematic way.

One goal-oriented approach is to cover general classes of data. You should test at least one example of each category of inputs, as well as boundaries and other special cases. For instance, in function PrintInteger there are three basic classes of int data: negative values, zero, and positive values. So you should plan three test cases, one for each of these classes. You could try more than three, of course. For example, you might want to try INT_MAX and INT_MIN, but as all the program does is print the value of its input, the additional test cases don't accomplish much.

There are other cases of data coverage. For example, if the input consists of commands, you must test each command. If the input is a fixed-sized array containing a variable number of values, you should test the maximum number of values; this is the boundary condition. A way to test for robustness is to try one more than the maximum number of values. It is also a good idea to try an array in which no values have been stored or one that contains a single element. Testing based on data coverage is called **black box testing**. The tester must know the external interface to the module—its inputs and expected outputs—but does not need to consider what is being done inside the module (the inside of the black box). (See Figure 1.5.)

Black Box Testing   Testing a program or function based on the possible input values, treating the code as a "black box"

Code Coverage   A number of testing strategies are based on the concept of code coverage, the execution of statements or groups of statements in the program. This testing approach is called **clear** (or **white**) **box testing**. The tester must look inside the module (through the clear box) to see the code that is being tested.

FIGURE 1.5   *Testing approaches.*

Clear (White) Box Testing   Testing a program or function based on covering all of the branches or paths of the code

One approach, for instance, requires that every statement in the program be executed at least once. Another approach requires that the test cases cause every **branch**, or code section, in the program to be executed. (A simple If-Then-Else statement has two branches.)

A similar type of code-coverage goal is to test program **paths.** A path is a combination of branches that might be traveled when the program is executed. In path testing, we try to execute all the possible program paths in different test cases.

Branch   A code segment that is not always executed; for example, a Switch statement has as many branches as there are case labels

Path   A combination of branches that might be traversed when a program or function is executed

Path Testing   A testing technique whereby the tester tries to execute all possible paths in a program or function

The code-coverage approaches are analogous to the ways forest rangers might check out the trails through the woods before the hiking season opens. If the rangers wanted to test to make sure that all the trails were clearly marked and not blocked by fallen trees, they would check each branch of the trails (see Figure 1.6a). Alternatively, if they wanted to classify each of the various trails (which may be interwoven) according to its length and difficulty from start to finish, they would use path testing (see Figure 1.6b).

To create test cases based on code-coverage goals, we select inputs that drive the execution into the various program paths. How can we tell whether a branch or a path is executed? One way to trace execution is to put debugging output statements at the beginning of every branch, indicating that this particular branch was entered. Software projects often use tools that help programmers track program execution automatically.

These strategies lend themselves to measurements of the testing process. We can count the number of paths in a program, for example, and keep track of how many paths have been covered in our test cases. The numbers provide statistics about the current status of testing; for instance, we could say that 75% of the branches of a program have been executed or 50% of the paths have been tested. When a single programmer is writing a single program, such numbers may be superfluous. In a software development environment with many

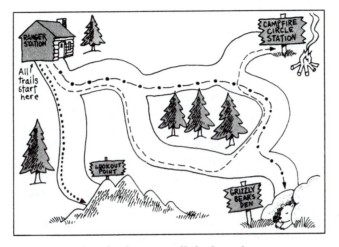

FIGURE 1.6   *(a) Checking out all the branches.*

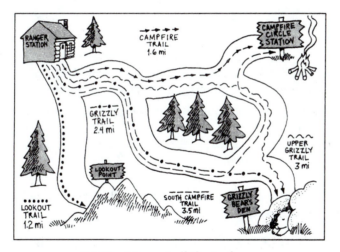

FIGURE 1.6   *(b) Checking out all the trails.*

programmers, however, statistics like these are very useful for tracking the progress of testing.

These measurements can also be used to indicate when a certain level of testing has been completed. Achieving 100% path coverage is often not a feasible goal. A software project might have a lower standard (say, 80% branch coverage) that the programmer who writes the module is required to reach before turning the module over to the project's testing team. Testing in which goals are based on certain measurable factors is called **metric based testing**.

Metric Based Testing   Testing based on measurable factors

Test Plans   Deciding on the goal of the test approach—data coverage, code coverage, or (most often) a mixture of the two—precedes the development of a **test plan**. Some test plans are very informal—the goal and a list of test cases, written by hand on a piece of paper. Even this type of test plan may be more than you have ever been required to write for a class programming project. Other test plans (particularly those submitted to management or to a customer for approval) are very formal, containing the details of each test case in a standardized format.

Implementing a **test plan** involves running the program with the input values listed in the plan and observing the results. If the answers are incorrect, the program is debugged and rerun until the observed output is the expected output. The process is complete when all the test cases listed in the plan give the desired output.

Test Plan   A document showing the test cases planned for a program or module, their purposes, inputs, expected outputs, and criteria for success

Implementing a Test Plan   Running the program with the test cases listed in the test plan

Let's develop a test plan for a function called `Divide`, which was coded from the following specifications:

■ **Divide(int dividend, int divisor, bool& error, float& result)**

Function: Divides one number by another and tests for divisor of zero.
Preconditions: None.
Postconditions: error is true if divisor is 0.
                   result is dividend / divisor, if error is false.
                   result is undefined, if error is true.

Should we use code coverage or data coverage for this test plan? Because the code is so short and straightforward, we can use either. Let's begin with code coverage. A code-coverage test plan is based on an examination of the code itself. Here is the code to be tested.

```
void Divide(int dividend, int divisor, bool& error,
    float& result)
// Set error to indicate if divisor is zero.
// If no error, set result to dividend / divisor.
{
    if (divisor = 0)
        error = true;
    else
        result = float(dividend) / float(divisor);
}
```

There is one If statement with two branches; therefore, we can do complete path testing. There is a case where `divisor` is zero and the true branch is taken and a case where `divisor` is nonzero and the else branch is taken.

Reason for Test Case	Input Values	Expected Output	Observed Output
`divisor` is zero	`dividend` is 8 `divisor` is 0	`error` is true `result` is undefined	
`divisor` is nonzero	`dividend` is 8 `divisor` is 2	`error` is false `result` is 4.0	

To implement this test plan, we run the program with the listed input values and mark the results in the Observed Output column. The function is called from a **test driver**, a program that sets up the parameter values and calls the functions to be tested. A simple test driver is listed here. It is designed to execute both test cases: it assigns the parameter values for Test 1, calls `Divide`, and prints the results; then it repeats the process with new test inputs for Test 2. We run the test, and compare the values output from the test driver with the expected values.

Test Driver A program that sets up the testing environment by declaring and assigning initial values to variables, then calls the subprogram to be tested

```
#include <iostream.h>

void Divide(int, int, bool&, float&);
// Function to be tested.

void Print(int, int, bool, float);
// Prints results of test case.

int main()
{
    bool error;
    float result;
    int dividend = 8;        // Test 1
    int divisor = 0;

    Divide(dividend, divisor, error, result);
    cout << "Test 1: " << endl;
    Print(dividend, divisor, error, result);
    divisor = 2;             // Test 2
    Divide(dividend, divisor, error, result);
    cout << "Test 2: " << endl;
    Print(dividend, divisor, error, result);
    return 0;
}
    .
    .
    .
```

For Test 1, the expected value for error is true, and the expected value
for result is undefined, but the division is carried out anyway! How can that
be when divisor is zero? If the result of an If statement is not what you
expect, the first thing to check is the relational operator: did we by any chance
use a single = rather than ==? Yes, we did. After fixing this mistake, we ran the
program again.

For Test 2, the expected value for error is false, yet the value printed is
true! Our testing has uncovered another error, so we begin debugging. We
discover that the value of error, set to true in Test 1, was never reset to false in
Test 2. We leave the final correct version of this function as an exercise.

Now let's design a data-coverage test plan for the same function. In a data-
coverage plan, we know nothing about the internal working of the function; we
only know the interface that is represented in the documentation of the
function heading.

```
void Divide(int dividend, int divisor, bool& error, float& result)
// Set error to indicate if divisor is zero.
// If no error, set result to dividend / divisor.
```

There are two input parameters, both of type int. A complete data-coverage plan would require that we call the function with all possible values of type int for each parameter—clearly overkill. The interface tells us that one thing happens if divisor is zero and another thing happens if divisor is nonzero. So clearly we must have at least two test cases: one where divisor is zero and one where divisor is nonzero. When divisor is zero, error is set to true and nothing else happens, so one test case should verify this. When divisor is nonzero, a division takes place. How many test cases does it take to verify that the division is correct? What are the end cases? There are five possibilities:

- divisor and dividend are both positive,
- divisor and dividend are both negative,
- divisor is positive and dividend is negative,
- divisor is negative and dividend is positive, and
- dividend is zero.

In this case the data-coverage test plan is more complex than the code-coverage plan: there are seven cases (two of which can be combined) rather

Reason for Test Case	Input Values	Expected Output	Observed Output
divisor is zero	dividend is 8 divisor is 0	error is true result is undefined	
divisor is nonzero (also serves as case where dividend and divisor are positive)	dividend is 8 divisor is 2	error is false result is 4.0	

divisor is nonzero
  divisor is negative
  dividend is negative
	divisor is -2
	dividend is -8
		error is false
		result is 4.0	

divisor is nonzero
  divisor is positive
  dividend is negative
	divisor is 2
	dividend is -8
		error is false
		result is -4.0	

divisor is nonzero
  divisor is negative
  dividend is positive
	divisor is -2
	dividend is 8
		error is false
		result is -4.0	

divisor is nonzero dividend is zero	divisor is 2 dividend is 0	error is false result is 0.0	

than just two. One case covers a zero divisor and the others check if the division is working correctly with a nonzero divisor and alternating signs. If we knew that the function uses the built-in division operator, we would not need to check these—but we don't. This is a data-coverage plan, and we cannot see the body of the function.

For program testing to be effective, *it must be planned*. You must design your testing in an organized way, and you must put your design in writing. You should determine the required or desired level of testing, and plan your general strategy and test cases before testing begins. In fact, you should start planning for testing before writing a single line of code.

Planning for Debugging   In the previous section we talked about checking the output from our test and debugging when errors were detected. We can debug "on the fly" by adding output statements in suspected trouble spots when problems are found. But in an effort to predict and prevent problems as early as possible, can we also plan our debugging before we even run the program?

By now you know that the answer is going to be yes. When you write your design, you should identify potential trouble spots. Then temporary debugging output statements can be inserted into your code in places where errors are likely to occur. For example, to trace the program's execution through a complicated sequence of function calls, you might add output statements that indicate when you are entering and leaving each function. The debugging output is even more useful if it also indicates the values of key variables, especially parameters of the function. The following example shows a series of debugging statements that execute at the beginning and end of function `Divide`:

```
void Divide(int dividend, int divisor, bool& error, float& result)
// Set error to indicate if divisor is zero.
// If no error, set result to dividend / divisor.
{
    // For debugging
    cout  << "Function Divide entered."  << endl;
    cout  << "Dividend = "  << dividend << endl;
    cout  << "Divisor = "  << divisor << endl;
    //*************************
    // Rest of code goes here.
    //*************************
    // For debugging
    if (error)
        cout  << "Error = true ";
    else
        cout  << "Error = false ";
    cout  << "and Result = "  << result  << endl;
    cout  << "Function Divide terminated."  << endl;
}
```

If hand testing doesn't reveal all the bugs before you run the program, well-placed debugging lines at least help you locate the rest of the bugs during execution. Note that this output is only for debugging; these output lines are meant to be seen only by the tester, not by the user of the program. But it's annoying for debugging output to show up mixed with your application's real output, and it's difficult to debug when the debugging output isn't collected in one place. One way to separate the debugging output from the "real" program output is to declare a separate file to receive these debugging lines, as shown in the following example.

```
#include <fstream.h>
ofstream debugFile;

debugFile << "This is the debug output from Test 1." << endl;
```

Usually the debugging output statements are removed from the program, or "commented out," before the program is delivered to the customer or turned in to the professor. (To "comment out" means to turn the statements into comments by preceding them with // or enclosing them between /* and */.) An advantage of turning the debugging statements into comments is that you can easily and selectively turn them back on for later tests. A disadvantage of this technique is that editing is required throughout the program to change from the testing mode (with debugging) to the operational mode (without debugging).

Another popular technique is to make the debugging output statements dependent on a Boolean flag, which can be turned on or off as desired. For instance, a section of code known to be error-prone may be flagged in various spots for trace output by using the Boolean value debugFlag:

```
// Set debugFlag to control debugging mode.
const bool debugFlag = true;
.
.
.
if (debugFlag)
    debugFile << "Function Divide entered." << endl;
```

This flag may be turned on or off by assignment, depending on the programmer's need. Changing to an operational mode (without debugging output) merely involves redefining debugFlag as false and then recompiling the program. If a flag is used, the debugging statements can be left in the program; only the if checks are executed in an operational run of the program. The disadvantage of this technique is that the code for the debugging is always there, making the compiled program larger. If there are a lot of debugging statements, they may waste needed space in a large program. The debugging statements can also clutter up the program, making it harder to read. (This is another example of the trade-offs we face in developing software.)

Some systems have on-line debugging programs that provide trace outputs, making the debugging process much simpler. If the system at your school or workplace has a run-time debugger, use it! Any tool that makes the task easier should be welcome, but remember that no tool replaces thinking.

A warning about debugging: Beware of the quick fix! Program bugs often travel in swarms, so when you find a bug, don't be too quick to fix it and run your program again. Often as not, fixing one bug generates another. A superficial guess about the cause of a program error usually does not produce a complete solution. In general, the time that it takes to consider all the ramifications of the changes you are making is time well spent.

If you constantly need to debug, there's a deficiency in your design process. The time that it takes to consider all the ramifications of the design you are making is time spent best of all.

Integration Testing   In the last two sections we discussed unit testing and planned debugging. In this section we discuss many concepts and tools that can help you put your test cases for individual units together for structured testing of your whole program. The goal of this type of testing is to integrate the separately tested pieces, so it is called **integration testing**.

Integration Testing   Testing performed to integrate program modules that have already been independently unit tested

---

You can test a large, complicated program in a structured way using a method very similar to the top-down approach to program design. The central idea is one of divide and conquer: to test pieces of the program independently and then to use the parts that have been verified as the basis for the next test. The testing can use either a *top-down* or a *bottom-up* approach, or a combination of the two.

When we use a top-down approach, we begin testing at the top levels. The purpose of the test is to ensure that the overall logical design works and the interfaces between modules are correct. At each level of testing, the top-down approach is based on the assumption that the lower levels work correctly. We implement this assumption by replacing the lower level subprograms with "placeholder" modules called **stubs**. A stub may consist of a single trace output statement, indicating that we have reached the function, or a group of debug output statements, showing the current values of the parameters. It may also assign values to output parameters if values are needed by the calling function (the one being tested).

Stub   A special function that can be used in top-down testing to stand in for a lower level function

---

As an example, consider writing a program FractionCalc, which reads in operation commands and pairs of values of type FractionType (each fraction value consists of a numerator part and a denominator part), executes the appropriate operation on them, and prints the result. To test the top level of the design, we run the main function.

```
enum ComType {ADD, SUB, MULTIPLY, DIVIDE, STOP};
struct FractionType
{
    int numerator;
    int denominator;
};

// Prototypes of GetValues, Operate, PrintResult,
// and GetCommand go here.

int main()
{
    ComType command;
    FractionType fraction1;
    FractionType fraction2;
    FractionType result;

    GetCommand(command);
    while (command != STOP)
    {
        GetValues(fraction1, fraction2);
        Operate(command, fraction1, fraction2, result);
        PrintResult(command, fraction1, fraction2, result);
        GetCommand(command);
    }
    return 0;
}
```

Stubs are used to stand in for the functions GetCommand, GetValues, Operate, and PrintResult. A stub for PrintResult, which doesn't have any output parameters, could simply contain a trace output statement:

```
void PrintResult(ComType command, FractionType value1,
    FractionType value2, FractionType result)
// This is a stub for function PrintResult.
{
    debugFile << "PrintResult executed." << endl;
}
```

A stub for function `Operate`, which takes the command and two fractions as input and then sends back the result, should contain a statement to assign a value to `result`, because the calling code might try to use this result. The value assigned to `result` in the stub must be legal, but we aren't too concerned with the particular data. The stub for `Operate` might look as follows:

```
void Operate(ComType command, FractionType value1,
    FractionType value2, FractionType& result)
// This is a stub for function Operate.
{
    debugFile << "Operate executed." << endl;
    result.numerator = 1;
    result.denominator = 1;
}
```

We would write similar stubs for `GetCommand` and `GetValues`. Then we would run the program with the stubs in place, checking for correct execution of the highest level code.

At the next level of testing, the actual functions are substituted for the stubs, and new stubs are created to stand in for functions called from the second-level modules. For instance, the real function `Operate` contains a Switch statement based on the command.

```
switch (command)
{
    case ADD      : Add(value1, value2, result);
                    break;
    case SUB      : Subtract(value1, value2, result);
                    break;
    case MULTIPLY : Multiply(value1, value2, result);
                    break;
    case DIVIDE   : Divide(value1, value2, result);
                    break;
}
```

To support the testing of function `Operate`, four new stubs are created to stand in for the untested functions `Add`, `Subtract`, `Multiply`, and `Divide`. Finally, at the lowest level, these stubs are replaced with real functions.

It seems like a lot of work to test such a small program. The benefit, however, is that we can now control which module we want to test in any run of the program. In addition, the effort expended to create the stubs is not wasted. When it is time to replace the stub, we can use the stub as a template for editing the real function.

An alternative testing approach is to test from the bottom up. With this approach, we unit test the lowest level subprograms first. A bottom-up approach can be useful in testing and debugging a critical module, one in which an error would have significant effects on other modules. "Utility" subprograms, such as mathematical functions, can also be tested with test drivers, independently of the programs that eventually call them. A bottom-up integration testing approach can also be effective in a group-programming environment, where each programmer writes and tests separate modules. The smaller, tested pieces of the program are later verified together in tests of the whole program.

As an example, let's assume that your assignment is to write the program `FractionCalc` from the previous section with a partner. After working together on the design, the two of you decide to split the effort of coding and testing: your partner takes care of the I/O (input/output) routines (`GetCommand`, `GetValues`, and `PrintResult`) and function `Operate`, while you write and debug the functions that calculate the result (`Add`, `Subtract`, `Multiply`, and `Divide`). Your assignment is not as trivial a task as it seems. You can't add two values of `FractionType` with a simple assignment statement such as

```
result = value1 + value2;
```

You must first calculate the values' lowest common denominator, then adjust and add the numerators, and finally simplify the result.

You must code and test these low-level functions bottom up, because your partner won't have the rest of the program finished by the time you are ready to test. You decide to write a simple test driver. The final completed program must provide prompts to ask the user for data and must check the input values for correctness. At this point, however, it is not important how the real data are input to the program; you just need to feed your subprograms data of the correct type as conveniently as possible. For instance, your test data might be a line of input containing an operator (such as '+' or '*') followed by four integers representing the numerators and denominators of the two operands.

Here is a very simple program that you can use to "drive" your tests. Each time the program is run, a single test case is executed.

```
// Program TestDriver tests the calculation part

#include <iostream.h>
#include <fstream.h>

// Prototypes for functions Add, Multiply, Subtract, and Divide
// go here.

struct FractionType
{
    int  numerator;
    int  denominator;
};

int main()
{
    char operation;
    FractionType value1;
    FractionType value2;
    FractionType result;
    ofstream testOutput;
    testOutput.open("test.out");

    cout  << "Input operation character (+, -, *, or /) "
          << endl  << " followed by four integers, representing "
          << endl  << " the numerators and denominators. "  << endl;
    cin  >> operation  >> value1.numerator  >> value1.denominator
          >> value2.numerator  >> value2.denominator;

    // Echo print inputs.
    testOutput  << "Operation    = "  << operation  << endl;
    testOutput  << "First value  = "  << value1.numerator  << "/"
                << value1.denominator  << endl;
    testOutput  << "Second value = "  << value2.numerator  << "/"
                << value2.denominator  << endl;

    // This section calls the routines to be tested.
    switch (operation)
    {
        case '+' : Add(value1, value2, result);
                   break;
        case '-' : Subtract(value1, value2, result);
                   break;
        case '*' : Multiply(value1, value2, result);
                   break;
        case '/' : Divide(value1, value2, result);
                   break;
    }
    testOutput  << value1.numerator
```

```
            << "/"  << value1.denominator  << " "
            << operation  << " " << value2.numerator  << "/"
            << value2.denominator  << " = " << result.numerator
            << "/"  << result.denominator   << endl;
    return 0;
}


// Function definitions for Add, Subtract, Multiply, and Divide
// go here.
```

Note that the test driver gets the test data and calls the functions to be tested. It also provides written output to verify the inputs and outputs. This test driver does not do any error checking to make sure that the inputs are valid, however. For instance, it doesn't verify that the operator (type char) is really an operator character, as opposed to an 'A' or a '%' character. Remember that the goal of the test driver is to act as a skeleton of the real program, not to be the real program. Therefore, the test driver does not need to be as robust as the program it simulates.

You could also have the test driver process multiple test cases by adding a loop around the current processing.

It is often necessary to combine the top-down and bottom-up methods. Critical functions and utility subprograms (math functions, data input or conversion routines, and so on) can be tested with drivers, and then a top-down approach can be applied to integrate the whole program.

Let's look at how a mixed testing approach could be used to integrate the whole program FractionCalc. While you are testing your part of the program with a test driver, your partner is writing and testing the rest of it independently, using stubs to stand in for your modules. After your subprograms have been tested, they can be added to your partner's program, which includes the real routines that read the operands and write the results. Now when you run the program, you can verify that the I/O functions actually input and set up the data correctly for your functions. This level of testing verifies that the independently tested subprograms work together correctly; that is, it integrates the program pieces.

By now you are probably protesting that these testing approaches are a lot of trouble and that you barely have time to write your programs, let alone "throwaway code" like stubs and drivers. Structured testing methods do require extra work. Test drivers and stubs are software items; they must be written and debugged themselves, even though they seldom are turned in to a professor or delivered to a customer. These programs are part of a class of software development tools that take time to create but are invaluable in simplifying the testing effort.

Programs like these are like the scaffolding that a contractor erects around a building. It takes time and money to build the scaffolding, which is not part of the final product, but without it, the building could not be constructed. In a large program, where verification plays a major role in the software development process, creating these extra tools may be the only way to test the program.

Practical Considerations

It is obvious from this chapter that program verification techniques are time-consuming and, in a job environment, expensive. It would take a long time to do all of the things discussed in this chapter, and a programmer has only so much time to work on any particular program. Certainly not every program is worthy of such cost and effort. How can you tell how much and what kind of verification effort is necessary?

A program's requirements may provide an indication of the level of verification needed. In the classroom your professor may specify the verification requirements as part of a programming assignment. For instance, you may be required to turn in a written, implemented test plan. Part of your grade may be determined by the completeness of your plan. In the work environment, the verification requirements are often specified by a customer in the contract for a particular programming job. For instance, a contract with a military customer may specify that formal reviews or inspections of the software product be held at various times during the development process.

A higher level of verification effort may be indicated for sections of a program that are particularly complicated or error-prone. In these cases it is wise to start the verification process in the early stages of program development in order to prevent costly errors in the design.

A program whose correct execution is critical to human life is obviously a candidate for a high level of verification. For instance, a program that controls the return of astronauts from a space mission would require a higher level of verification than a program that generates a grocery list. As a more down-to-earth example, consider the potential for disaster if a hospital's patient data-base system had a bug that caused it to lose information about patients' allergies to medications. A similar error in a data-base program that manages a Christmas card mailing list, however, would have much less severe consequences.

▉▍ *Summary*

How are our quality software goals met by the strategies of abstraction and information hiding? When details are hidden at each level, the code becomes simpler and more readable, which makes the program easier to write and modify. Both functional decomposition and object-oriented design processes produce modular units that are also easier to test, debug, and maintain.

One positive side effect of modular design is that modifications tend to be localized in a small set of modules, and thus the cost of modifications is reduced. Remember that whenever a module is modified it must be retested to make sure that it still works correctly in the program. By localizing the modules affected by changes to the program, we limit the extent of retesting needed.

Finally, reliability is increased by making the design conform to our logical picture and delegating confusing details to lower levels of abstraction. An understanding of the wide range of activities involved in software development—from requirements analysis through the maintenance of the resulting program—leads to an appreciation of a disciplined software engineering approach. Everyone knows some programming wizard who can sit down and hack out a program in an evening, working alone, coding without a formal design. But we cannot depend on wizardry to control the design, implementation, verification, and maintenance of large, complex software projects that involve the efforts of many programmers. As computers grow larger and more powerful, the problems that people want to solve on them also become larger and more complex. Some people refer to this situation as a software *crisis*. We'd like you to think of it as a software *challenge*.

It should be obvious by now that program verification is not something you begin the night before your program is due. Design verification and program testing go on throughout the software life cycle.

Verification activities begin when the software specifications are developed. At this point, the overall testing approach and goals are formulated. Then, as program design work begins, these goals are applied. Formal verification techniques may be used for parts of the program, design inspections are conducted, and test cases are planned. During the implementation phase, the test cases are developed and test data to support them are generated. Code inspections give the programmer extra support in debugging the program before it is ever run. When the code has been compiled and is ready to be run, unit (module-level) testing is done, with stubs and drivers used for support. After these units have been completely tested, they are put together in integration tests. Once errors have been found and corrected, some of the earlier tests are rerun to make sure that the corrections have not introduced any new problems. Finally, acceptance tests of the whole system are run. Figure 1.7 shows how the various types of verification activities fit into the software development cycle. Throughout the life cycle one thing remains the same: the earlier in this cycle program errors are detected, the easier (and less costly in time, effort, and money) they are to remove. Program verification is a serious subject; a program that doesn't work isn't worth the disk it's stored on.

Analysis	Make sure that specifications are completely understood.
	Understand testing requirements.
Design	Design for correctness (using assertions such as preconditions and postconditions).
	Perform design inspections.
	Plan testing approach.
Code	Understand programming language well.
	Perform code inspections.
	Add debugging output statements to the program.
	Write test plan.
	Construct test drivers and/or stubs.
Test	Unit test according to test plan.
	Debug as necessary.
	Integrate tested modules.
	Retest after corrections.
Delivery	Execute acceptance tests of complete product.
Maintenance	Execute regression test whenever delivered product is changed to add new functions or to correct detected problems.

FIGURE 1.7   *Life-cycle verification activities.*

▉‖ *Exercises*

1. Explain what we mean by "software engineering."

2. Which of these statements is always true?
   (a) All of the program requirements must be completely defined before design begins.
   (b) All of the program design must be complete before any coding begins.
   (c) All of the coding must be complete before any testing can begin.
   (d) Different development activities often take place concurrently, overlapping in the software life cycle.

3. Name three computer hardware tools that you have used.

4. Name two software tools that you have used in developing computer programs.

5. Explain what we mean by "ideaware."

6. Explain why software might need to be modified
   (a) in the design phase.
   (b) in the coding phase.
   (c) in the testing phase.
   (d) in the maintenance phase.

7. Goal 4 says, "Quality software is completed on time and within budget."
   (a) Explain some of the consequences of not meeting this goal for a student preparing a class programming assignment.
   (b) Explain some of the consequences of not meeting this goal for a team developing a highly competitive new software product.
   (c) Explain some of the consequences of not meeting this goal for a programmer who is developing the user interface (the screen input/output) for a spacecraft launch system.

8. For each of the following, describe at least two different abstractions for different viewers (see Figure 1.1).
   (a) A dress   (d) A key
   (b) An aspirin   (e) A saxophone
   (c) A carrot   (f) A piece of wood

9. Functional decomposition is based on a hierarchy of _____, and object-oriented design is based on a hierarchy of _____.

10. What is the difference between an object and an object class? Give some examples.

11. Make a list of potential objects from the description of the automated-teller-machine scenario given in this chapter.

12. Have you ever written a programming assignment with an error in the specifications? If so, at what point did you catch the error? How damaging was the error to your design and code?

13. Explain why the cost of fixing an error is higher the later in the software cycle the error is detected.

14. Explain how an expert understanding of your programming language can reduce the amount of time you spend debugging.

15. Give an example of a run-time error that might occur as the result of a programmer's making too many assumptions.

16. Define "robustness." How can programmers make their programs more robust by taking a defensive approach?

17. The following program has three separate errors, each of which would cause an infinite loop. As a member of the inspection team, you could save the programmer a lot of testing time by finding the errors during the inspection. Can you help?

```
void Increment(int);
int main()
{
    int count = 1;
    while(count < 10)
        cout << " The number after " << count;  /* Function Increment
        Increment(count);                            adds 1 to count */
        cout << " is " << count << endl;
        return 0;
}
```

```
void Increment (int nextNumber)
// Increment the parameter by one.
{
    nextNumber++;
}
```

18. Is there any way a single programmer (for example, a student working alone on a programming assignment) can benefit from some of the ideas behind the inspection process?

19. When is it appropriate to start planning a program's testing?
    (a) During design or even earlier
    (b) While coding
    (c) As soon as the coding is complete

20. Differentiate between unit testing and integration testing.

21. Explain the advantages and disadvantages of the following debugging techniques:
    (a) Inserting output statements that may be turned off by commenting them out
    (b) Using a Boolean flag to turn debugging output statements on or off
    (c) Using a system debugger

22. Describe a realistic goal-oriented approach to data-coverage testing of the function specified below:

    FindElement(list, targetItem, index, found)

    Function: Searches list for targetItem.
    Preconditions: Elements of list are in no particular order; list may be empty.
    Postcondition: found is true if targetItem is in list; otherwise, found is false. index is the position of targetItem if found is true.

23. A program is to read in a numeric score (0 to 100) and display an appropriate letter grade (A, B, C, D, or F).
    (a) What is the functional domain of this program?
    (b) Is exhaustive data coverage possible for this program?
    (c) Devise a test plan for this program.

24. Explain how paths and branches relate to code coverage in testing. Can we attempt 100% path coverage?

25. Differentiate between "top-down" and "bottom-up" integration testing.

26. Explain the phrase "life-cycle verification."

27. Write the corrected version of function `Divide`.

28. Why did we type case `dividend` and `divisor` in function `Divide`?

Data Design and Implementation

GOALS

- To be able to explain what is meant by "abstract data type" and "data encapsulation"

- To be able to describe a data structure from three perspectives: logical level, application level, and implementation level

- To be able to explain how a specification can be used to record an abstract data type

- To be able, at the logical level, to describe the component selector, and to describe appropriate applications for the C++ built-in types: structs, classes, one-dimensional arrays, and two-dimensional arrays

- To be able to declare a class object

- To be able to implement the member functions of a class

- To be able to manipulate instances of a class (objects)

- To be able to define the three ingredients of an object-oriented programming language: encapsulation, inheritance, and polymorphism

- To be able to define input/output operations for the abstract data type String from three perspectives: logical, application, and implementation

■|| *Different Views of Data*

What Do We Mean by Data?

When we talk about the function of a program, we use words like "add," "read," "multiply," "write," "DO," and so on. The function of a program describes what it does in terms of the verbs in the programming language.

The data are the nouns of the programming world: the objects that are manipulated, the information that is processed by a computer program. In a sense, this information is just a collection of bits that can be turned on or off. The computer itself needs to have data in this form. Human beings, however, tend to think of information in terms of somewhat larger units like numbers and lists, and thus we want at least the human-readable portions of our programs to refer to data in a way that makes sense to us. To separate the computer's view of data from our own, we use **data abstraction** to create another view. Whether we use functional decomposition producing a hierarchy of tasks or object-oriented design producing a hierarchy of cooperating objects, data abstraction is essential.

Data Abstraction   The separation of a data type's logical properties from its implementation

---

Data Abstraction

Lots of people feel more comfortable with things that they perceive as real than with things that they think of as abstract. Thus "data abstraction" may seem more forbidding than a more concrete entity like "integer." Let's take a closer look, however, at that very concrete—and very abstract—integer you've been using since you wrote your earliest programs.

Just what is an integer? Integers are physically represented in different ways on different computers. In the memory of one machine, an integer may be a binary-coded decimal. In a second machine, it may be a sign-and-magnitude binary. And in a third one, it may be represented in one's complement or two's complement notation. Although you probably don't know what any of these terms mean, that hasn't stopped you from using integers. (You learn about these terms in an assembly language course, so we do not explain them here.) Figure 2.1 shows some different representations of an integer number.

The way that integers are physically represented determines how they are manipulated by the computer. As C++ programmers, however, you don't usually get involved at this level; you simply use integers. All you need to know is how to declare an `int` type variable and what operations are allowed

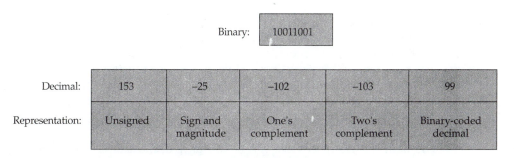

FIGURE 2.1   *The decimal equivalents of an 8-bit binary number.*

on integers: assignment, addition, subtraction, multiplication, division, and modulo arithmetic.

Consider the statement

```
distance = rate * time;
```

It's easy to understand the concept behind this statement. The concept of multiplication doesn't depend on whether the operands are, say, integers or real numbers, despite the fact that integer multiplication and floating point multiplication may be implemented in very different ways on the same computer. Computers would not be so popular if every time we wanted to multiply two numbers we had to get down to the machine-representation level. But we don't have to: C++ has surrounded the `int` data type with a nice neat package and has given us just the information we need to create and manipulate data of this type.

Another word for "surround" is "encapsulate." Think of the capsules surrounding the medicine you get from the pharmacist when you're sick. You don't have to know anything about the chemical composition of the medicine inside to recognize the big blue-and-white capsule as your antibiotic or the little yellow capsule as your decongestant. Data encapsulation means that the physical representation of a program's data is surrounded. The user of the data doesn't see the implementation, but deals with the data only in terms of its logical picture—its abstraction.

Data Encapsulation   The separation of the representation of data from the applications that use the data at a logical level; a programming language feature that enforces information hiding

But if the data are encapsulated, how can the user get to them? Operations must be provided to allow the user to create, access, and change the data. Let's look at the operations C++ provides for the encapsulated data type `int`. First of all, you can create ("construct") variables of type `int` using declarations in your program. Then you can assign values to these integer variables by using the assignment operator or by reading values into them and performing arithmetic operations using +, -, *, /, and %. Figure 2.2 shows how C++ has encapsulated the type `int` in a nice neat package.

The point of this discussion is that you have been dealing with a logical data abstraction of "integer" since the very beginning. The advantages of doing so are clear: you can think of the data and the operations in a logical sense and can consider their use without having to worry about implementation details. The lower levels are still there—they're just hidden from you.

Remember that the goal in design is to reduce complexity through abstraction. We extend this goal with another: to protect our data abstraction through encapsulation. We refer to the set of all possible values (the *domain*) of an encapsulated data "object," plus the specifications of the operations that are provided to create and manipulate the data, as an **abstract data type** (**ADT** for short).

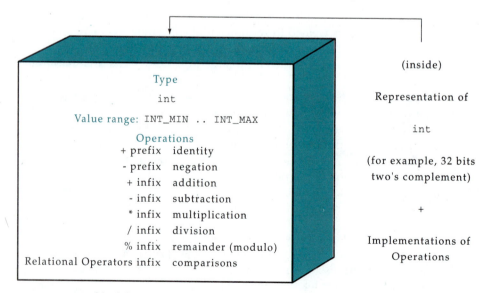

FIGURE 2.2 *A black box representing an integer.*

Abstract Data Type   A data type whose properties (domain and operations) are specified independently of any particular implementation

Data Structures

A single integer can be very useful if we need a counter, a sum, or an index in a program, but generally we must also deal with data that have lots of parts, such as a list. We describe the logical properties of this collection of data as an abstract data type; we call the concrete implementation of the data a **data structure**. When a program's information is made up of component parts, we have to consider an appropriate data structure.

Data structures have a few features worth noting. First, they can be "decomposed" into their component elements. Second, the arrangement of the elements is a feature of the structure that affects how each element is accessed. Third, both the arrangement of the elements and the way they are accessed can be encapsulated.

Let's look at a real-life example: a library. A library can be decomposed into its component elements—books. The collection of individual books can be arranged in a number of ways, as shown in Figure 2.3. Obviously, the way the books are physically arranged on the shelves determines how one would go about looking for a specific volume. The particular library we're concerned with doesn't let its patrons get their own books, however; if you want a book, you must give your request to the librarian, who gets the book for you.

The library "data structure" is composed of elements (books) in a particular physical arrangement; for instance, it might be ordered on the basis of the Dewey decimal system. Accessing a particular book requires knowledge of the arrangement of the books. The library user doesn't have to know about the structure, though, because it has been encapsulated: users access books only through the librarian. The physical structure and abstract picture of the books in the library are not the same. The card catalog provides logical views of the library—ordered by subject, author, or title—that are different than its physical arrangement.

We use this same approach to data structures in our programs. A data structure is defined by (1) the logical arrangement of data elements, combined with (2) the set of operations we need to access the elements.

Data Structure   A collection of data elements whose organization is characterized by accessing operations that are used to store and retrieve the individual data elements; the implementation of the composite data members in an abstract data type

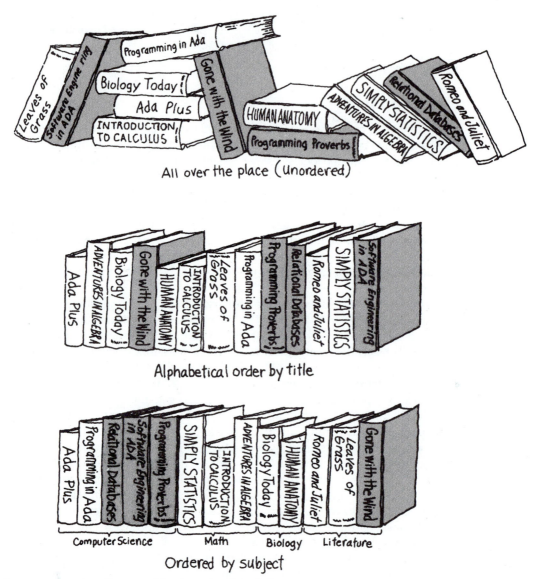

FIGURE 2.3   *A collection of books ordered in different ways.*

Notice the difference between an abstract data type and a data structure. The former is a high-level description: the logical picture of the data and the operations that manipulate them. The latter is concrete: a collection of data elements and the operations that store and retrieve individual elements. An abstract data type is implementation independent but a data structure is implementation dependent. A data structure is how we implement the data in an abstract data type whose values have component parts. The operations on an abstract data type are translated into algorithms on the data structure.

A third view of data is how they are used in a program to solve a particular problem; that is, their application. If we were writing a program to keep track of student grades, we would need a list of students and a way to record the grades for each student. We might take a by-hand grade book and model it in our program. The operations on the grade book might include adding a name, adding a grade, averaging a student's grades, etc. Once we have written a specification for our grade book data type, we must choose an appropriate data structure to use to implement it and design the algorithms to implement the operations on the structure.

In modeling data in a program, we wear many hats. We must determine the logical picture of the data, choose the representation of the data, and develop the operations that encapsulate this arrangement. During this process, we consider data from three different perspectives, or levels:

1. *Application (or user) level:* A way of modeling real-life data in a specific context; also called the problem domain.
2. *Logical (or abstract) level:* An abstract view of the data values (the domain) and the set of operations to manipulate them.
3. *Implementation level:* A specific representation of the structure to hold the data items, and the coding of the operations in a programming language (if the operations are not already provided by the language).

In our discussion, we refer to the second perspective as the "abstract data type." Because an abstract data type can be a simple type such as an integer or character, as well as a structure that contains component elements, we also use the term "composite data type" to refer to abstract data types that may contain component elements. The third level is how we actually represent and manipulate the data in memory: the data structure and the algorithms for the operations that manipulate the items on the structure.

Let's see what these different viewpoints mean in terms of our library analogy. At the application level, there are entities like the Library of Congress, the Dimsdale Collection of Rare Books, and the Austin City Library.

At the logical level, we deal with the "what" questions. What is a library? What services (operations) can a library perform? The library may be seen abstractly as "a collection of books" for which the following operations are specified:

- Check out a book.
- Check in a book.
- Reserve a book that is currently checked out.
- Pay a fine for an overdue book.
- Pay for a lost book.

How the books are organized on the shelves is not important at the logical level, because the patrons don't actually have direct access to the books. The abstract viewer of library services is not concerned with how the librarian actually organizes the books in the library. The library user only needs to know the correct way to invoke the desired operation. For instance, here is the user's view of the operation to check in a book: present the book at the check-in window of the library from which the book was checked out, and receive a fine slip if the book is overdue.

At the implementation level, we deal with the answers to the "how" questions. How are the books cataloged? How are they organized on the shelf? How does the librarian process a book when it is checked in? For instance, the implementation information includes the fact that the books are cataloged according to the Dewey decimal system and arranged in four levels of stacks, with 14 rows of shelves on each level. The librarian needs such knowledge to be able to locate a book. This information also includes the details of what happens when each of the operations takes place. For example, when a book is checked back in, the librarian may use the following algorithm to implement the check-in operation:

CheckInBook

Examine due date to see whether the book is late.
IF book is late
    Calculate fine.
    Issue fine slip.
Update library records to show that the book has been returned.
Check reserve list to see if someone is waiting for the book.
IF book is on reserve list
    Put the book on the reserve shelf.
ELSE
    Replace the book on the proper shelf, according to the library's shelf
    arrangement scheme.

All this, of course, is invisible to the library user. The goal of our design approach is to hide the implementation level from the user.

Picture a wall separating the application level from the implementation level, as shown in Figure 2.4. Imagine yourself on one side and another programmer on the other side. How do the two of you, with your separate views of the data, communicate across this wall? Similarly, how do the library user's view and the librarian's view of the library come together? The library user and the librarian communicate through the data abstraction. The abstract view provides the specification of the accessing operations without telling how the operations work. It tells *what* but not *how*. For instance, the abstract view of checking in a book can be summarized in the following specification:

FIGURE 2.4   *Communication between the application level and implementation level.*

■ **CheckInBook (library, book, fineSlip)**

Function: Checks in a book.
Preconditions: book was checked out of this library; book is presented at the check-in desk.
Postconditions: fineSlip is issued if book is overdue; contents of library is the original contents + book

The only communication from the user into the implementation level is in terms of input specifications and allowable assumptions—the preconditions of the accessing routines. The only output from the implementation level back to the user is the transformed data structure described by the output specifications, or postconditions, of the routines. The abstract view hides the data structure, but provides windows through the specified accessing operations.

When you write a program as a class assignment, you often deal with data at all three levels. In a job situation, however, you may not. Sometimes you may program an application that uses a data type that has been implemented by another programmer. Other times you may develop "utilities" that are called by other programs. In this book we ask you to move back and forth between these levels.

Abstract Data Type Operator Categories

In general, the basic operations that are performed on an abstract data type fall into four categories: *constructors*, *transformers* (also called *mutators*), *observers*, and *iterators*.

A constructor is an operation that creates a new instance (object) of an abstract data type. A constructor is almost always invoked at the language level by some sort of declaration. Transformers (sometimes called *mutators*) are operations that change the state of one or more of the data values, such as inserting an item into an object, deleting an item from an object, or making an object empty. An operation that takes two objects and merges them into a third object is a binary transformer.[1]

An observer is an operation that allows us to observe the state of one or more of the data values without changing them. Observers come in several forms: *predicates* that ask if a certain property is true, *accessor* or *selector* functions that return a copy of an item in the object, and *summary* functions that return information about the object as a whole. A Boolean function that returns true if an object is empty and false if it contains any components is an example of a predicate. A function that returns a copy of the last item put into the structure is an example of an accessor function. A function that returns the number of items in the structure is a summary function.

An iterator is an operation that allows us to process all the components in a data structure sequentially. Operations that print the items in a list or return successive list items are iterators. Iterators are only defined on structured data types.

In later chapters, we use these ideas to define and implement some useful

---

1. In some of the literature, operations that create new instances are called primitive constructors, and transformers are called nonprimitive constructors.

data types that may be new to you. But first let's explore the built-in composite data types C++ provides for us.

▋▌▏ *Abstraction and Built-in Types*

In the last section, we suggested that a built-in simple type such as int or float could be viewed as an abstraction whose underlying implementation is in terms of machine-level operations. The same perspective applies to built-in **composite data types** provided in programming languages to build data objects. A composite data type is one in which a name is given to a collection of data items. Composite data types come in two forms: unstructured and structured. An *unstructured* composite type is a collection of components that are not organized with respect to one another. A *structured* data type is an organized collection of components in which the organization determines the method used to access individual data components.

Composite Type   A data type that allows a collection of values to be associated with an object of that type

---

For instance, C++ provides the following composite types: records (structs), classes, and arrays of various dimensions. Classes and structs can have member functions as well as data, but it is the organization of the data we are considering here. Classes and structs are logically unstructured; arrays are structured.

Let's look at each of these from our three perspectives. First, we examine the abstract view of the structure—how we construct variables of that type and how we access individual components in our programs. Then, from an application perspective, we discuss what kinds of things can be modeled using each structure. These two points of view are important to you as a C++ programmer. Finally, we look at how some of the structures may be implemented—how the "logical" accessing function is turned into a location in memory. For built-in constructs, the abstract view is the syntax of the construct itself, and the implementation level is hidden within the compiler. So long as you know the syntax, you as a programmer do not need to understand the implemetation view of predefined composite data types. As you read through the implementation sections and see the formulas that are needed to access an element of a composite type, you should appreciate why information hiding and encapsulation are necessary.

Records

The record is not available in all programming languages. FORTRAN, for instance, does not support records; however, COBOL, a business-oriented language, uses records extensively. In C++, records are implemented by structs. C++ classes are another implementation of a record. For the purposes of the following discussion, we use the generic term record, but structs and classes behave as records.

Logical Level   A record is a composite data type made up of a finite collection of not necessarily homogeneous elements called *members* or *fields*. Accessing is done directly through a set of named member or field selectors.

We illustrate the syntax and semantics of the component selector within the context of the following struct declarations:

```
struct CarType
{
    int year;
    char maker[10];
    float price;
};
CarType myCar;
```

The record variable `myCar` is made up of three components. The first, `year`, is of type `int`. The second, `maker`, is an array of characters. The third, `price`, is a `float` number. The names of the components make up the set of member selectors. A picture of `myCar` appears in Figure 2.5.

The syntax of the component selector is the record variable name, followed by a period, followed by the member selector for the component you are interested in.

If this expression is on the right-hand side of an assignment statement, a value is being extracted from that place (for example, `pricePaid = myCar.price`). If it is on the left-hand side, a value is being stored in that member of the struct (for example, `myCar.price = 20009.33`).

FIGURE 2.5 `MyCar`.

The `myCar.maker` is an array whose elements are of type `char`. You can access that array member as a whole (for example, `myCar.maker`), or you can access individual characters by using an index.

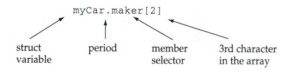

```
struct        period    member      3rd character
variable                selector    in the array
```

In C++, a struct may be passed as a parameter to a function (either by value or by reference), one struct may be assigned to another of the same type, and a struct may be a function return value.

Parameter Passing

C++ supports two types of formal parameters: value parameters and reference parameters. A value parameter is a formal parameter that receives a *copy* of the contents of the corresponding actual parameter. Because the formal parameter holds a copy of the actual parameter, the actual parameter cannot be changed by the function to which it is a parameter. On the other hand, a reference parameter is a formal parameter that receives the *location* (memory address) of the corresponding actual parameter. Because the formal parameter holds the memory address of the actual parameter, the contents of the actual parameter can be changed by the function. By default in C++, arrays are passed by reference, and nonarray paramerters are passed by value.

To specify that a formal nonarray parameter is a reference parameter, append an ampersand (&) to the right of the type name on the formal parameter list. Look at the following examples.

```
void AdjustForInflation(CarType& car, float perCent)
// Increases price by the amount specified in perCent.
{
    car.price = car.price * perCent + car.price;
}
bool LateModel(CarType car, int date)
// Returns true if the car's model year is later than or
// equal to date; returns false otherwise.
{
    return car.year >= date;
}
```

Function `AdjustForInflation` changes the `price` data member of formal parameter `car`, so `car` must be a reference parameter. Within the body of the function, `car.price` is the `price` member of the actual parameter. Function `LateModel` only examines `car` without changing it, so `car` should be a value parameter. Within the function, `car.year` is a copy of the caller's actual parameter.

Application Level   Records (structs) are very useful for modeling objects that have a number of characteristics. This data type allows us to collect various types of data about an object and to refer to the whole object by a single name. We also can refer to the different members of the object by name. You probably have seen many examples of records used in this way to represent objects.

Records are also useful for defining other data structures, allowing programmers to combine information about the structure with the storage of the elements. We make extensive use of records in this way when we develop representations of our own programmer-defined data structures.

Implementation Level   Two things must be done to achieve the implementation of a built-in composite data type: (1) memory cells must be reserved for the data, and (2) the *accessing function* must be determined. An accessing function is a rule that tells the compiler and run-time system where an individual element is located within the data structure. Before we go on to a concrete example, let's look at memory. The unit of memory that is assigned to hold a value is machine dependent. Figure 2.6 shows several different memory configurations. In practice, how memory is configured is a consideration for the compiler writer. In order to be as general as possible, however, we use the generic term *cell* to represent a location in memory rather than "word" or "byte." In the examples that follow, we assume that an integer or character is stored in one cell and a floating point number in two cells. (This assumption is not accurate in C++, but we use it to simplify the discussion.)

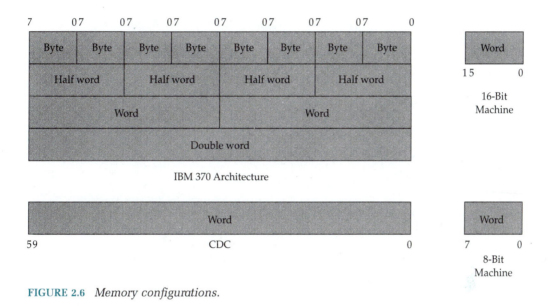

FIGURE 2.6 *Memory configurations.*

The declaration statements in a program tell the compiler how many cells are needed to represent the record. The name of the record then is associated with the characteristics of the record. These characteristics include:

1. the location in memory of the first cell in the record, called the *base address* of the record;
2. a table containing the number of memory locations needed for each member of the record.

A record occupies a block of consecutive cells in memory.[2] The record's accessing function calculates the location of a particular cell from a named member selector. The basic question is: which cell (or cells) in this consecutive block do you want?

The base address of the record is the address of the first member in the record. To access any member, we need to know how much of the record to skip to get to the desired member. A reference to a record member causes the compiler to examine the characteristics table to determine the member's offset from the beginning of the record. The compiler then can generate the member's address by adding the offset to the base. Figure 2.7 shows such a table for CarType. If the base address of myCar were 8500, the fields or members of this record would be at the addresses shown.

---

2. In some machines this may not be exactly true, for boundary alignment (full- or half-word) may require that some space in memory be skipped so that the next member starts on an address that is divisible by 2 or 4. See Figure 2.6.

Member	Length	Offset
year	1	0
maker	10	1
price	2	11

Address

Address	
8500	year member (length = 1)
8501	
8502	
.	
.	maker member (length = 10)
.	
8905	
8510	
8511	price member (length = 2)
8512	

FIGURE 2.7   *Implementation-level view of* `CarType`.

Address of `myCar.year` = 8500 + 0 = 8500
Address of `myCar.maker` = 8500 + 1 = 8501
Address of `myCar.price` = 8500 + 11 = 8511

We said that the record is a nonstructured data type, yet the component selector is dependent on the relative positions of the members of the record. This is true, a record is a structured data type if viewed from the implementation perspective. However, from the user's view, it is unstructured. The user accesses the members by name, not by position. For example, if we had defined CarType as

```
struct CarType
{
    char maker[10];
    float price;
    int year;
};
```

the code that manipulates instances of `CarType` would not change.

One-Dimensional Arrays

Logical level   A one-dimensional array is a structured composite data type made up of a finite, fixed-size collection of ordered homogeneous elements to which there is direct access. *Finite* indicates that there also is a last element. *Fixed size* means that the size of the array must be known at compile time; but it doesn't mean that all the slots in the array must contain meaningful values. *Ordered* means that there is a first element, a second element, and so on. (It is the relative position of the elements that is ordered, not necessarily the values stored there.) Because the elements in an array must all be of the same type, they are physically *homogeneous*; that is, they are all of the same data type. In general, it is desirable for the array elements to be logically homogeneous, as well—that is, for all the elements to have the same purpose. (If we kept a list of numbers in an array of integers, with the length of the list [an integer] kept in the first array slot, the array elements would be physically, but not logically, homogeneous.)

The component selection mechanism of an array is *direct access*, which means we can access any element directly, without first accessing the preceding elements. The desired element is specified using an index, which gives its relative position in the collection. We talk later about how C++ uses the index and some characteristics of the array to figure out exactly where in memory to find the element. That's part of the implementation view, and the application programmer using an array doesn't need to be concerned with it. (It's encapsulated.)

What operations are defined for the array? If the language we were using didn't have predefined arrays and we were defining arrays ourselves, we would want to specify at least the following three operations (shown as C++ function calls):

```
CreateArray(anArray, numberOfSlots);
// Create array anArray with numberOfSlots locations.
```

```
Store(anArray, value, index);
// Store value into anArray at position index.
```

```
Retrieve(anArray, value, index);
// Retrieve into value the array element found at position index.
```

Because arrays are predefined data types, however, the C++ programming language supplies a special way to perform each of these operations. C++'s syntax provides a primitive constructor for creating arrays in memory, and indexes as a way to directly access an element of an array.

In C++, the declaration of an array serves as a primitive constructor operation. For example, a one-dimensional array can be declared with this statement:

```
int numbers[10];
```

The type of the elements in the array comes first, followed by the name of the array with the number of elements (the array size) in brackets to the right of the name. This declaration defines a linearly ordered collection of ten integer items. Abstractly, we can picture `numbers` as follows:

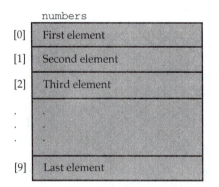

Each element of `numbers` can be accessed directly by its relative position in the array. The syntax of the component selector is described as follows:

array-name[index-expression]

The index expression must be of an integral type (`char`, `short`, `int`, `long`, or an enumeration type). The expression may be as simple as a constant or a variable name, or as complex as a combination of variables, operators, and function calls. Whatever the form of the expression, it must result in an integer value.

In C++, the index range is always 0 through the array size minus 1; in the case of `numbers`, the value must be between 0 and 9. In some other languages, the user may explicitly give the index range.

The semantics (meaning) of the component selector is "Locate the element associated with the index expression in the collection of elements identified by array-name." The component selector can be used in two ways:

1. to specify a place into which a value is to be copied, such as

```
numbers[2] = 5;
```

or

```
cin >> numbers[2];
```

2. to specify a place from which a value is to be retrieved such as

```
value = numbers[4];
```

or

```
cout << numbers[4];
```

If the component selector is used on the left-hand side of the assignment statement, it is being used as a transformer: the data structure is changing. If the component selector is used on the right-hand side of the assignment statement, it is being used as an observer: it returns the value stored in a place in the array without changing it. Declaring an array and accessing individual array elements are operations predefined in nearly all high-level programming languages.

In C++, arrays may be passed as parameters (by reference only), but cannot be assigned to one another, nor can they be the return value type of a function.

One-Dimensional Arrays as Parameters

In C++, arrays can only be *reference* parameters; it is not possible to pass an array by value. Therefore, the ampersand (&) to the right of the type is omitted. What is actually passed to a function, when an array is the formal parameter, is the base address of the array (the memory address of the first slot in the array). This is true whether the array has one or more dimensions. When declaring a one-dimensional array parameter, the compiler only needs to know that the parameter is an array; it does not need to know its size. If the size of the formal parameter is listed, the compiler ignores it. The code in the function that processes the array is responsible for ensuring that only legitimate array slots are referenced. Therefore, a separate parameter often is passed to the function to specify how many array slots are to be processed.

```
int SumValues(int values[], int numberOfValues)
// Returns the sum of values[0] through
// values[numberOfValues-1].
{
    int sum = 0;

    for (int index = 0; index < numberOfValues; index++)
        sum = sum + values[index];
    return sum;
}
```

If arrays are always passed as reference parameters, how can we protect the actual parameter from inadvertent changes? For example, in SumValues the parameter values is only to be inspected but not modified; how can we protect it from being changed? We can declare it to be a const parameter as follows:

```
int SumValues(const int values[], int numberOfValues)
```

Within the function body, trying to change the contents of values now causes a syntax error.

Application Level   A one-dimensional array is the natural structure for the storage of lists of like data elements. Some examples are grocery lists, price lists, lists of phone numbers, lists of student records, and lists of characters (a string). You have probably used one-dimensional arrays in similar ways in some of your programs.

Implementation Level   Of course, when you use an array in a C++ program you do not have to be concerned with all of the implementation details. You have been dealing with an abstraction of the array from the time the construct was introduced, and you will never have to consider all the messy details that we describe in this section.

An array declaration statement tells the compiler how many cells are needed to represent that array. The name of the array then is associated with the characteristics of the array. These characteristics include:

1. the number of elements (Number);
2. the location in memory of the first cell in the array, called the *base address* of the array (Base); and
3. the number of memory locations needed for each element in the array (SizeOfElement).

The information about the array characteristics is often stored in a table called an *array descriptor* or *dope vector*. When the compiler comes across a reference to an array element, it uses this information to generate code that calculates the element's location in memory at run time.

How are the array characteristics used to calculate the number of cells needed and to develop the accessing functions for the following arrays? As before, we assume for simplicity that an integer or character is stored in one cell and a floating point number in two cells.

```
int data[10];
float money[6];
char letters[26];
```

These arrays have the following characteristics:

	data	money	letters
Number	10	6	26
Base	unknown	unknown	unknown
SizeOfElement	1	2	1

Let's assume that the C++ compiler assigns memory cells to variables in sequential order. If, when the three declarations above are encountered, the next memory cell available to be assigned is, say, 100, the memory assignments are as follows. (We have used 100 to make the arithmetic easier.)

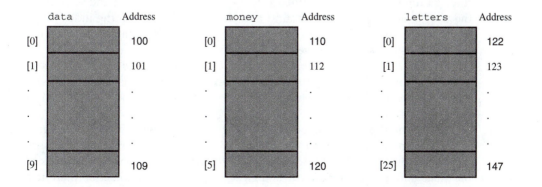

Now we have determined the base address of each array: data is 100, money is 110, and letters is 122. The arrangement of these arrays in memory gives us the following relationships:

Given	The program must access
data[0]	100
data[8]	108
letters[1]	123
letters[25]	147
money[0]	110
money[3]	116

In C++ the accessing function that gives us the position of an element in a one-dimensional array associated with the expression Index is

$$\text{Address(Index)} = \text{Base} + \text{Offset of the element at position Index}$$

How do we calculate the offset? The general formula is

$$\text{Offset} = \text{Index} * \text{SizeOfElement}$$

The whole accessing function becomes

$$\text{Address(Index)} = \text{Base} + \text{Index} * \text{SizeOfElement}$$

Let's apply this formula and see if we do get what we claimed we should.

	Base + Index * SizeOfElement	Address
data[0]	100 + (0 * 1)	= 100
data[8]	100 + (8 * 1)	= 108
letters[1]	122 + (1 * 1)	= 123
letters[25]	122 + (25 * 1)	= 147
money[0]	110 + (0 * 2)	= 110
money[3]	110 + (3 * 2)	= 116

The calculation of an array element address in C++ is much simpler than in many other languages because C++ assumes that the index range is from 0 through the maximum size minus 1. Languages such as Pascal and Ada allow the user to specify the lower bound and the upper bound on the index range rather than giving the size. This extra flexibility complicates the indexing process considerably but leaves the abstraction cleaner.

We said that an array is a structured data type. Unlike a record whose logical view is unstructured but whose implementation view is structured, both views of an array are structured. The structure is inherent in the logical component selector.

As we mentioned at the beginning of this section, when you use an array in a C++ program you do not have to be concerned with all of these implementation details. The advantages of this are very clear: you can think of the data and the operations in a logical sense and can consider their use without having to worry about implementation details. The lower levels are still there—they're just hidden from you. We strive for this same sort of separation of the abstract and implementation views in the programmer-defined classes discussed in the remainder of this book.

Two-Dimensional Arrays

Logical Level   Most of what we have said about the abstract view of a one-dimensional array applies as well to a two-dimensional (or multidimensional) array. It is a composite data type made up of a finite, fixed-size collection of ordered homogeneous elements. Its component selector is direct access: a pair of indexes specifies the desired element by giving its relative position in the collection.

A two-dimensional array is a natural way to represent data that is logically viewed as a table with columns and rows. The following example illustrates the syntax for declaring a two-dimensional array in C++.

```
int table[10][6];
```

The abstract picture of this structure is a grid with rows and columns.

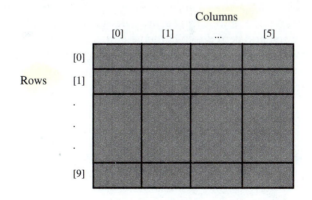

The component selector for the two-dimensional array is as follows:

```
table [row] [col]
```

specifies which row
(first dimension)

specifies which column
(second dimension)

Two-Dimensional Arrays as Parameters

Two-dimensional arrays are stored in row order in C++. This means that all of the elements in one row are stored together followed by all of the elements in the next row. In order to be able to access any row other than the first, the compiler must be able to calculate where each row begins, and this calculation depends on how many elements there are in each row. The second row begins at the base address plus the number of elements in each row, and each succeeding row begins at the address of the previous row plus the number of elements in each row. The second dimension—the number of columns—tells us how many elements are in each row; therefore the size of the second dimension *must* be included in the declaration of the formal parameter for a two-dimensional array.

```
int ProcessValues(int values[][5])
{
    .
    .
    .
}
```

ProcessValues works for an array with any number of rows as long as it has exactly five columns. That is, the size of the second dimension of the actual and formal array parameters must be identical. To ensure that formal and actual two-dimensional array parameters have the same size, use the Typedef statement to define a two-dimensional array type and then declare both the actual and the formal parameters to be of that type. For example,

```
const int NUM_ROWS = 5;
const int NUM_COLS = 4;
typedef float TableType[NUM_ROWS][NUM_COLS];

int ProcessValues(TableType table);


TableType mine;
TableType yours;
```

The Typedef statement associates a two-dimensional float array with five rows and four columns with the type name TableType: mine and yours are two such arrays. Any actual parameter for ProcessValues should be of type TableType. By setting up the types this way, no possible mismatch can occur.

Application Level　As mentioned in the previous section, a two-dimensional array is the ideal data structure for modeling data that are logically structured as a table with rows and columns. The first dimension represents rows, and the second dimension represents columns. Each element in the array contains a value, and each dimension represents a relationship. As with the one-dimensional array, the operations available for a two-dimensional array object are so limited (only creation and direct access) that the major application is the implementation of higher level objects.

Implementation Level　The implementation of two-dimensional arrays involves the mapping of two indexes to a particular memory cell. The mapping functions are more complicated than those for one-dimensional arrays. We do not give them here. You will learn to write these accessing functions in later courses. Our goal is not to teach you to be compiler writers but to give you an appreciation of the value of information hiding and encapsulation.

◼ ‖ *Higher Level Abstraction and the C++ Class Type*

In the last section, we examined C++'s built-in data types from the logical view, the application view, and the implementation view. Now we move our focus to data types that are needed in a program but not provided by the programming language. In this section, we review the syntax and semantics of the C++ class type, which is a mechanism that allows us to create programmer-defined types and encapsulate their implementations.

The **class** type is a construct in which the members of the class can be functions as well as data; that is, the data members and the code that manipulates them are bound together within the class itself. Because the data are bound together with the operations, we can use one object to build another object; that is, a data member of an object can be another object.

Class　An unstructured type that encapsulates a fixed number of data components with the functions that manipulate them; the predefined operations on an instance of a class are whole assignment and component access

---

When we design an abstract data type, we want to bind the operations of the data type with the data that are being manipulated. Therefore, the class is the perfect mechanism to implement an abstract data type because it enforces encapsulation. The class is like the case around a watch that prevents us from accessing the works. The case is provided by the watchmaker who can easily open it when repairs become necessary.

Classes are written in two parts, the specification and the implementation. The specification defines the interface to the class. It is like the face and knobs on a watch. The specification describes what *resources* the class can supply to the program. Resources supplied by a watch might include the value of the current time and operations to set the current time. In a class, resources include data and operations on the data. The implementation section provides the implementation of the resources defined in the specification—the insides of the watch.

There are significant advantages to separating the specification from its implementation. A clear interface is important, particularly when a class is used by other members of a programming team or is part of a software library. Any ambiguity in an interface results in problems. By separating the specification from its implementation, we are given the opportunity to concentrate our efforts on the design of a class without needing to worry about implementation details.

Another advantage of this separation is that we can change the implementation at any time without affecting the programs that use the class (**clients** of the class). We can make changes when a better algorithm is discovered or there is a change in the environment in which the program is run. For example, suppose we need to control how text is displayed on a screen. Text control operations may include moving the cursor to a particular location and setting text characteristics like bold, blink, and underline. The algorithms required for controlling these characteristics usually differ from one computer system to another. By defining an interface and encapsulating the algorithms as member functions, we can easily move our program to a different system simply by rewriting the implementation. We do not have to change the rest of the program.

Client   Software that declares and manipulates objects (instances) of a
        particular class

Class Specification

Although the class specification and implementation can be in the same file, the two parts to a class are usually separated into two files: the specification goes into a header file (.h extension), and the implementation goes into a file with the same name but a `.cpp` extension. This physical separation of the two parts of a class reinforces the logical separation.[3]

We describe the syntax and semantics of the class type within the context of defining an abstract data type Date.

```
// Declare a class to represent the Date ADT
// This is file DateType.h.

class DateType
{
public:
    void Initialize(int newMonth, int newDay, int newYear);
    int YearIs() const;        // returns year
    int MonthIs() const;       // returns month
    int DayIs() const;         // returns day
private:
    int  year;
    int  month;
    int  day;
};
```

The data members of the class are `year`, `month`, and `day`. The scope of a class includes the parameters on the member functions, so we must use names other than `month`, `year`, and `day` for our formal parameters. The data members are marked `private`. This means that although they are visible to the human user, they cannot be accessed by client code. Private members can be accessed only by the code in the implementation file.

The member functions of the class are `Initialize`, `YearIs`, `MonthIs`, and `DayIs`. The member functions of the class are marked `public`. This means that client code can access these functions. `Initialize` is a transformer operation; it takes values for the year, month, and day and stores these values into the appropriate data members of an object (an instance of the class).[4] `YearIs`, `MonthIs`, and `DayIs` are accessor functions; they are member functions that access the data members of the class. The `const` beside the accessor function names guarantees that these functions do not change any of the data members of the objects to which they are applied.

---

3. Your system may use extensions different from `.h` and `.cpp` for these files—for example, `.hpp` or `.hxx` (or no extension at all) for header files and `.cxx`, `.c`, or `.C` for implementation files.

4. At the implementation level from here on, we use the word *object* to refer to a class object, an instance of a class type.

Scope Rules in C++

The rules of C++ that govern who knows what, where, and when are called *scope rules*. There are three main categories of scope for an identifier in C++: class scope, local scope, and global scope. Class scope refers to identifiers declared within a class definition. Local scope is the scope of an identifier declared within a block (statements enclosed within { }). Global scope is the scope of an identifier declared outside all functions and classes.

- All identifiers declared within a class are local to the class (class scope).
- The scope of a formal parameter is the same as the scope of a local variable declared in the outermost block of the function body (local scope).
- The scope of a local identifier includes all statements following the declaration of the identifier to the end of the block in which it is declared and includes any nested blocks unless a local identifier of the same name is declared in a nested block (local scope).
- The name of a function that is not a member of a class has global scope; once a global function name has been declared, any subsequent function can call it (global scope).
- When a function declares a local identifier with the same name as a global identifier, the local identifier takes precedence (local scope).
- The scope of a global variable or constant extends from its declaration to the end of the file in which it is declared, subject to the condition in the last rule (global scope).
- The scope of an identifier does not include any nested block that contains a locally declared identifier with the same name (local identifiers have name precedence).

Class Implementation

Only the member functions of class `DateType` can access the data members, so we must associate the class name with the function definitions. We do this by placing the class name before the function name, separated by the scope resolution operator (`::`). The implementations of the member functions go into file `DateType.cpp`. In order to access the specifications, file `DateType.h` must be inserted by using an `#include` directive.

```
// Define member functions of class DateType.
// This is file DateType.cpp.

#include "DateType.h"  // gain access to specification of class

void DateType::Initialize
     (int newMonth, int newDay, int newYear)
// Post: year is set to newYear.
//       month is set to newMonth.
//       day is set to newDay.
{
    year = newYear;
    month = newMonth;
    day = newDay;
}

int DateType::MonthIs() const
// Accessor function for data member month.
{
    return month;
}

int DateType::YearIs() const
// Accessor function for data member year.
{
    return year;
}

int DateType::DayIs() const
// Accessor function for data member day.
{
    return day;
}
```

A client of class DateType must have an #include ''DateType.h''
directive for the specification (header) file of the class. Note that system
supplied header files are enclosed in angle brackets (<iostream.h>), but
user-defined header files are enclosed in double quotes. Then the client
declares a variable of type DateType just as it would any other variable.

```
#include "DateType.h"
DateType today;
DateType anotherDay;
```

Member functions of a class are invoked in the same way that data
members of a struct are accessed: with the dot notation. The following code
segment initializes two objects of type DateType and then prints the dates on
the screen.

```
today.Initialize(9, 24, 1997);
anotherDay.Initialize(9, 25, 1997);
cout  << " Today is "  << today.MonthIs()  << "/"
      << today.DayIs()  << "/"
      << today.YearIs()  << endl;
cout  << " Another date is "  << anotherDay.MonthIs()
      << "/"   << anotherDay.DayIs()  << "/"
      << anotherDay.YearIs()  << endl;
```

Member Functions with Object Parameters

A member function applied to a class object uses the dot notation. What if we want to have a member function that operates on more than one object—for example, a function that compares the data members of two instances of the class? The following code compares two instances of the class DateType.

```
enum RelationType {LESS, EQUAL, GREATER};

// Prototype of member function in the specification file.
RelationType ComparedTo(DateType someDate);
// Compares self with someDate.


// Implementation of member function in the implementation file.

RelationType DateType::ComparedTo(DateType aDate)
// Pre:  Self and aDate have been initialized.
// Post: Function value = LESS, if self comes before aDate.
//                      = EQUAL, if self is the same as aDate.
//                      = GREATER, if self comes after aDate.
{
    if (year < aDate.year)
        return LESS;
    else if (year > aDate.year)
        return GREATER;
    else if (month < aDate.month)
        return LESS;
    else if (month > aDate.month)
        return GREATER;
    else if (day < aDate.day)
        return LESS;
    else if (day > aDate.day)
        return  GREATER;
    else return EQUAL;
}
```

year refers to the year data member of the object to which the function is applied; aDate.year refers to the data member of the object passed as a parameter. The object to which a member function is applied is called **self**. In the function definition, the data members of self are referenced directly without using dot notation. If an object is passed as a parameter, the parameter name must be attached to the data member being accessed using dot notation. For example, here is some client code:

```
switch (today.ComparedTo(anotherDay))
{
    case LESS :
        cout << "today comes before anotherDay";
        break;
    case GREATER :
        cout << "today comes after anotherDay";
        break;
    case EQUAL :
        cout << "today and anotherDay are the same";
        break;
}
```

Now look back at the ComparedTo function definition. year in the function refers to the year member of today, whereas aDate.year in the function refers to the year member of anotherDay, the actual parameter to the function.

Self The object to which a member function is being applied

Why are we using LESS, GREATER, and EQUAL when COMES_BEFORE, COMES_AFTER, and SAME would be more meaningful in the context of dates? We use the more general words here, because in other places we use functions of type RelationType when comparing numbers and strings.

Difference Between Classes and Structs

In C++, the technical difference between classes and structs is that, without the use of the reserved words public and private, member functions and data are private by default in classes and public by default in structs. In practice, structs and classes are often used differently. Because the data in a struct is public by default, we think of a struct as a *passive* data structure. The operations that are performed on a struct are usually global functions to which the struct is passed as a parameter. Although a struct may have member functions, they are seldom defined. In contrast, a class is an *active* data structure where the operations defined on the data members are member functions of the class.

In object-oriented programming, an object is viewed as an active structure with control residing in the object through the use of member functions. For this reason, it is the C++ class type that is used to represent the concept of an object.

Object-Oriented Programming

In Chapter 1, we said that functional design results in a hierarchy of tasks and object-oriented design results in a hierarchy of objects. Structured programming is the implementation of a functional design and object-oriented programming (OOP) is the implementation of an object-oriented design. However, these approaches are not entirely distinct. The implementation of an operation on an object often requires a functional design of the algorithm. You probably are familiar with structured programming from your first semester; let's spend a few moments looking at object-oriented programming, beginning with its own unique vocabulary.

The vocabulary of object-oriented programming (OOP) has its roots in the programming languages Simula and Smalltalk and can be very bewildering. Such phrases as "sending a message to," "methods," and "instance variables" are sprinkled throughout the OOP literature. Although this vocabulary can seem daunting, don't panic. There is a straightforward translation between these terms and familiar C++ constructs.

First of all, an *object* is a class object or class instance; that is, an instance of a class type. A *method* is a public member function, and an *instance variable* is a private data member. *Sending a message* is a call to a public member function. In the rest of this book, we tend to mix object-oriented terms with their C++ counterparts.

There are three essential ingredients in object-oriented programming: encapsulation, **inheritance**, and **polymorphism**. We have already talked about data abstraction and encapsulation and its representation in the C++ class type. To complete the separation of the representation of data from the applications that use it, the specification of the class and the implementation of the member functions are separated into different files.

Many of the objects in the hierarchy of objects that results from an object-oriented design have a special relationship with one another: the "is-a" relationship. In this relationship, the objects get more specialized the lower in the hierarchy you go. Each new object inherits the characteristics of the parent object. For example, Maggie the brown pet is an instance of the class Labrador, a Labrador is a dog, a dog is a mammal, and a mammal is an animal. Therefore Maggie can inherit all the characteristics of animals, mammals, dogs, and

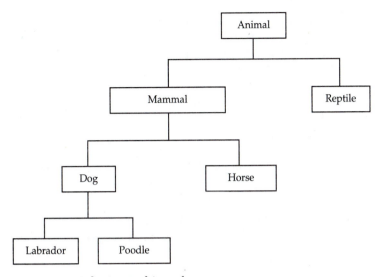

FIGURE 2.8 *Inheritance hierarchy.*

Labradors: she is an affectionate, big, brown animal that nursed her puppies. (See Figure 2.8.) In an OOP language, the object hierarchy becomes a class hierarchy because every object must be an instance of a class type.

The third essential ingredient, polymorphism, is the ability to determine either statically or dynamically which of several methods with the same name (within the class hierarchy) is to be invoked. **Overloading** means giving the same name to several different functions (or using the same operator symbol for different operations). You have already worked with overloaded operators in C++. The arithmetic operators are overloaded because they can be applied to integral values or floating point values, and the compiler selects the correct operation according to the operand types. The time at which a function name or symbol is associated with code is called **binding time** (the name is bound to the code). With overloading, the determination of which particular implementation to use occurs statically (at compile time). Determining which implementation to use at compile time is called **static binding.**

Dynamic binding, on the other hand, is the ability to postpone the decision of which operation is appropriate until run time. Many programming languages support overloading; only a few, including C++, support dynamic binding. Polymorphism is a combination of both static and dynamic binding.

Throughout the rest of this book, we stress both programming paradigms— functional and object-oriented. Because the focus is on data objects, specifically container objects, we analyze them and code them as objects but use functional design to code the member function algorithms. Many of our case studies use functional decomposition at the top level to analyze the problem and determine what objects are needed. The data objects needed in the cases are (of course) the ones developed in the chapter.

We introduce the three ingredients of object-oriented programming in stages. We concentrate first on encapsulation through the use of classes and separate compilation files. We then introduce inheritance and, finally, polymorphism.

Inheritance   A mechanism used with a hierarchy of classes by which each descendant class inherits the properties (data and operations) of its ancestor classes

Polymorphism   The ability to determine which of several operations with the same name is appropriate; a combination of static and dynamic binding

Overloading   Giving the same name to more than one function or using the same operator symbol for more than one operation; usually associated with static binding

Binding Time   The time at which a name or symbol is bound to the appropriate code

Static Binding   The compile-time determination of which implementation of an operation is appropriate

Dynamic Binding   The run-time determination of which implementation of an operation is appropriate

CASE STUDY |||

USER-DEFINED STRING I/O CLASS

Strings are lists of characters; they represent text in a program. Strings are used extensively in all kinds of programs. They label output, they are read from a file and sent to an output stream, or they can be the data that a program processes. Many languages have strings as a built-in data type. At present, standard C++ does not. A string in C++ is simply an array of type `char`, with the null character (`\0`) used to signal the end of the string. Additionally, C++ provides a set of string-handling functions in `<string.h>`, and input/output functions in `<iostream.h>` and `<fstream.h>`. Let's create our own abstract data type String that has general-purpose input and output functions and encapsulate it into a class.

Logical Level

At the logical level, a string is a finite sequence of alphanumeric characters, characterized by a property called *length*. The length is the number of characters in the string.

What are the operations that we want defined on strings? At a minimum we need a primitive constructor that creates a string by initializing it to the empty state, a transformer that reads values from a file or the keyboard into a string, and an observer that sends a copy of the string to the output stream or a file.

If a string has the property of length, we can define initializing a string as setting the length of the string to zero. Reading values into a string is more difficult. We must decide what we mean by a string in an input stream or a file. Do we mean the characters from the current point in the stream until the next whitespace character is encountered (blank, tab, newline, and so forth)? Until the end of the line is encountered? Until a special character is encountered? What do we do if the character at the current position of a stream is a whitespace character? Let's review the operations for string handling available in <iostream.h> before we decide. We assume that string in the following examples is an array of characters.

cin >> string: Whitespace is skipped and characters are collected and stored in string until whitespace is encountered. The stream is left positioned at the first whitespace character encountered. Using the extraction operator (>>) is not appropriate if the string you are trying to enter contains blanks (which are whitespace).

cin.getline(string, max): Whitespace is not skipped; the characters from the current position of the stream up to end-of-line are read and stored into string; the newline character is read but not stored in string. If max-1 characters are read and stored before encountering the newline character, the processing stops with the stream positioned at the next character.

Intermingling these two methods of inputting strings can cause serious problems. The >> operator leaves the stream positioned at whitespace. If that whitespace character is the newline character and the next operation is cin.getline(string, max), no characters are input because the newline character stops the reading. Therefore, string is the empty string. We want our string-input operation to avoid this problem and to work consistently in all situations.

Let's let the user of our string class decide what is meant by an input string by providing two parameters: a Boolean flag that determines if inappropriate characters should be skipped before inputting the string and a parameter that specifies which characters are legal in the string (anything else ends the input process). If no appropriate characters are found, the string should be set to the empty string.

The only question concerning output is whether or not the user wants the output to begin on a new line. We can provide a parameter for the user that indicates which is wanted.

Before we present our first ADT Specification, a word about notation is in order. Because we want the specification to be as programming language independent as possible, we use the general word Boolean for the type name of Boolean variables rather than the C++ word `bool`. On the other hand, there is no general word for input and output file types, so we use the C++ `ifstream` and `ofstream`, respectively. We also use the C++ symbol ampersand (&) to indicate reference parameters. In order to distinguish identifiers in running text, we put them in monospace type, but we do not do so in a specification.

■ String ADT Specification

Structure: A sequence of alphanumeric characters.

Operations:

MakeEmpty
  Function: Initializes string to empty.
  Precondition: None
  Postcondition: String is empty.

GetString(Boolean skip, InType charsAllowed)
  Function: Gets a string from the standard input stream.
  Assumptions: (1) InType is a data type consisting of the following constants:
                    ALPHA: only alphabetic characters are stored.
                    ALPHA_NUM: only alphanumeric characters are stored.
                    NON_WHITE: all non-whitespace characters are stored.
                    NOT_NEW: all characters excluding the newline character are stored.
                    (2) If skip is true, characters not allowed are skipped until the first allowed character is found. Reading and storing begins with this character and continues until a character not allowed is encountered. This character is read but not stored. If skip is false, reading and storing begins with the current character in the stream.
  Precondition: None.

Postconditions: If no allowable characters are found, the empty string is returned; else, a string has been input according to the skip and charsAllowed parameters.

Input stream is left positioned following last character read, which is a nonallowed character.

GetStringFile(Boolean skip, InType charsAllowed, ifstream& inFile)

Function: Gets a string from file inFile.

Assumptions: Same as those for GetString.

Precondition: inFile has been opened.

Postconditions: String has been input according to the skip and charsAllowed parameters.

inFile is left positioned following last character read.

PrintToScreen(Boolean newLine)

Function: Prints end-of-line character if needed before printing the string to the screen.

Precondition: String has been initialized.

Postcondition: If newLine is true, string has been printed on the screen starting on a new line; otherwise, string has been printed on the current line.

PrintToFile(Boolean newLine, ofstream& outFile)

Function: Prints end-of-line character if needed before printing the string to outFile.

Preconditions: String has been initialized.

outFile has been opened.

Postconditions: If newLine is true, string has been printed on outFile starting on a new line; otherwise string has been printed on the current line of outFile.

outFile is left positioned after the last character written.

int LengthIs()

Function: Returns the number of characters in the string.

Precondition: String has been initialized.

Postcondition: Function value = number of characters in the string.

CopyString(StrType& newString)

Function: Copies self into newString.

Precondition: Self has been initialized.

Postcondition: Self has been copied into newString.

Application Level

Let's use this very simple set of operations to read words from a file, store them into an array, and print them on the screen, one per line. The input is ordinary text; only alphanumeric characters are allowed in the string. Thus, any non-alphanumeric character acts as a word (string) delimiter.

```
#include <fstream.h>
#include "StrType.h"
#include <iostream.h>

const int MAX_WORDS = 10;

int main()
{
    StrType word;
    ifstream inFile;
    StrType words[MAX_WORDS];
    int numWords = 0;
    inFile.open("inData");

    word.MakeEmpty();
    word.GetStringFile(true, ALPHA_NUM, inFile);
    while (inFile && numWords < MAX_WORDS)
    {
        word.CopyString(words[numWords]);
        numWords++;
        word.GetStringFile(true, ALPHA_NUM, inFile);
    }

    if (inFile)
        cout << "First " << MAX_WORDS << " words on the file: ";
    else
        cout << " Words on the file: ";
    for (int index = 0; index < numWords; index++)
        words[index].PrintToScreen(true);
    return 0;
}
```

A slight change in the parameters allows us to consider only alphabetic characters as making up a word and all other characters act as delimiters: `word.GetStringFile(true, ALPHA, inFile)`. We could add a function that would check to see if `word` was in the `words` array and only add it if it were not there, giving us a list of unique words.

We use the String ADT as defined by the previous specification many times throughout the rest of this book.

Implementation Level

Now we must determine how we are going to represent our strings. Recall that C++ implements strings as one-dimensional `char` arrays with the *null* character (`\0`) indicating the end of the string. Another way of implementing a string would be a struct or class with two data members: an array of type `char` and an integer variable representing the length. The string characters would be between position 0 and position length-1 in the array.

Which shall we use? The amount of storage required for both array-based designs is nearly the same, and the amount of processing is approximately the same although the algorithms differ somewhat. Let's use the null-terminated method here. To accommodate the null character, we must remember to allocate one more position than the maximum number of characters expected—*maximum number of characters*, where does this number come from? There is nothing in the specification about a limit on the number of characters allowed in a string, but our array-based implementation requires us to specify the array size at compile time.

Let's arbitrarily choose a reasonably large number, say 200, for the maximum string length. In the specification file, `StrType.h`, we define a constant `MAX_CHARS` to be 200, letting the user know that this is the maximum length allowed. In Chapter 4, we look at a more flexible technique that lets us specify an array size dynamically (at run time) rather than statically (at compile time).

Should the client be responsible for making sure that the string is within the allowable length or should the code of `GetString` and `GetStringFile` check for this and discard any characters that cannot be stored? Both approaches have merit. We choose the latter and do the checking within `StrType`. The specifications need to be changed to reflect this decision.

The specification for class `StrType` is contained in the following header file. Note that the postconditions for `GetString` and `GetStringFile` have been expanded to describe what happens if the number of characters is too large. Here is file `StrType.h`.[5]

```
// Header file for class StrType, a specification for the
// String ADT.
#include <fstream.h>
#include <iostream.h>
```

---

5. In the interests of brevity, we do not repeat the preconditions and postconditions on the member function prototypes unless they have changed from those listed in the Specification of the ADT. The code available on the publisher's Web site is completely documented.

```
const int MAX_CHARS = 200;

enum RelationType {LESS, EQUAL, GREATER};
enum InType {ALPHA_NUM, ALPHA, NON_WHITE, NOT_NEW};

class StrType
{
public:
// Assumptions:
    // InType is a data type consisting of the following constants:
    //    ALPHA:     only alphabetic characters are stored;
    //    ALPHA_NUM: only alphanumeric characters are stored;
    //    NON_WHITE: all non-whitespace characters are stored;
    //    NOT_NEW:   all characters excluding the newline character
    //                  are stored.
    // If skip is true, characters not allowed are skipped until the
    //    first allowed character is found.  Reading and storing
    //    begins with this character and continues until a character
    //    not allowed is encountered.  This character is read but not
    //    stored.  If skip is false, reading and storing begins with
    //    the current character in the stream.

    void MakeEmpty();
    void GetString(bool skip, InType charsAllowed);
    //Post: If the number of allowable characters exceeds
    //       MAX_CHARS, the remaining allowable characters have
    //       been read and discarded.

    void GetStringFile(bool skip, InType charsAllowed,
        ifstream& inFile);
    //Post: If the number of allowable characters exceeds
    //       MAX_CHARS, the remaining allowable characters have been
    //       read and discarded.

    void PrintToScreen(bool newLine);
    void PrintToFile(bool newLine, ofstream& outFile);
    int LengthIs();
    void CopyString(StrType& newString);
private:
    char letters[MAX_CHARS + 1];
};
```

Now we must design the algorithms for our member functions and code them. In Chapter 1, we discussed the testing process and suggested that planning for testing should be done in parallel with the design. Let's practice what we preach and consider testing as we code the member functions. Our strategy is clear-box testing, because we are planning our testing as we design and code the algorithms.

MakeEmpty

When called prior to any other processing, MakeEmpty serves as a primitive constructor that takes the storage structure assigned to a variable of the class type and initializes whatever data members must be initialized. We also can use MakeEmpty to return a structure to the empty state after it has been used. In the case of the null-terminated implementation, storing '\0' in letters [0] changes the instance of StrType from undefined to the empty string. To test this function, we must take a variable of type StrType, apply the function to it, and determine if the string is empty.

```
void StrType::MakeEmpty()
// Post:  letters is empty string.
{
    letters[0] = '\0';
}
```

GetString

If skip is true, then characters are read and discarded until one is encountered that is in the set of allowed characters. This character becomes the first character in data member letters. Characters are read and stored in letters until a character is read that is not allowed. This character is then discarded. If MAX_CHARS characters are read and stored before a character not allowed is encountered, characters are read and discarded until such a character is encountered or the stream fails (due to end-of-file). The last step is to store the null-terminator following the last character stored in letters. If skip is false, no characters are skipped before reading and storing characters. How do we determine what to skip and what to store? The constants of InType tell us. We use them as labels on a Switch statement.

▬ Character and String Library Functions

C++ provides many character and string-handling facilities in its standard library. Operations available through <ctype.h> include testing to see whether a character is a letter, number, control character, uppercase, or lowercase. Operations available through <string.h> include concatenating two strings, comparing two strings, and copying one string into another. See Appendix C for more details.

GetString(Boolean skip, InType charsAllowed)

```
SWITCH (charsAllowed)
    case ALPHA_NUM    :   GetAlphaNum(skip, letters)
    case ALPHA        :   GetAlpha(skip, letters)
    case NON_WHITE    :   GetNonWhite(skip, letters)
    case NOT_NEW      :   GetTilNew(skip, letters)
```

We can use the functions available in `<ctype.h>` to control our reading in each of the auxiliary functions. If `charsAllowed` is `ALPHA_NUM`, we skip characters until function `isalnum` returns true, and store them until `isalnum` returns false or `cin` goes into the fail state. If `charsAllowed` is `ALPHA`, we skip characters until function `isalpha` returns true, and store them until `isalpha` returns false or `cin` goes into the fail state. If `charsAllowed` is `NON_WHITE`, we skip characters until function `isspace` returns false, and store them until `isspace` returns true or `cin` goes into the fail state. If `charsAllowed` is `NOT_NEW`, we skip characters until the character is not '\n', and store them until the character is '\n' or `cin` goes into the fail state.

Each of the four cases has a Boolean parameter that controls processing. Our test driver must call each of the cases with `skip` set to true and with `skip` set to false. In addition, each of the alternatives must be examined to determine what characters should be within the test data to test that alternative. We must be sure that each behaves properly when encountering end-of-file within the skip phase, and we must be sure to have words that are longer than the maximum length `MAX_CHARS`.

These algorithms are coded as shown here. We code `GetAlphaNum` and `GetTilNew` here and leave `GetAlpha` and `GetNonWhite` as exercises.

```
#include <ctype.h>
// Prototypes of auxiliary functions.
// Note: If skip is true, non-allowable leading characters are
//       skipped.  If end-of-file is encountered while skipping
//       characters, the empty string is returned. If the number
//       of allowable characters exceeds MAX_CHARS, the rest are
//       read and discarded.

void  GetAlphaNum(bool skip, char letters[]);
// Post: letters array contains only alphanumeric characters.

void  GetAlpha(bool skip, char letters[]);
// Post: letters array contains only alphabetic characters.
```

```
void  GetNonWhite(bool skip, char letters[]);
// Post: letters array contains only non-whitespace characters.

void  GetTilNew(bool skip, char letters[]);
// Post: letters array contains everything up to newline character.

void StrType::GetString(bool skip, InType charsAllowed)
{
    switch (charsAllowed)
    {
        case ALPHA_NUM : GetAlphaNum(skip, letters);
                         break;
        case ALPHA     : GetAlpha(skip, letters);
                         break;
        case NON_WHITE : GetNonWhite(skip, letters);
                         break;
        case NOT_NEW   : GetTilNew(skip, letters);
                         break;
    }
}

void  GetAlphaNum(bool skip, char letters[])
// Post: If skip is true, non-alphanumeric letters are skipped.
//       Alphanumeric characters are read and stored until a
//       non-alphanumeric character is read or MAX_CHARS characters
//       have been stored. If the stream is not in the fail state,
//       the last character read was a non-alphanumeric character.
{
    char letter;
    int count = 0;

    if (skip)
    {// skip non-alphanumeric characters
        cin.get(letter);
        while (!isalnum(letter) && cin)
            cin.get(letter);
    }
    else
        cin.get(letter);
    if (!cin || !isalnum(letter))
        // No legal character found; empty string returned.
        letters[0] = '\0';
    else
    {// Read and collect characters.
        do
```

```
        {
            letters[count] = letter;
            count++;
            cin.get(letter);
        } while (isalnum(letter) && cin && (count < MAX_CHARS));
        letters[count] = '\0';
        // Skip extra characters if necessary.
        if (count == MAX_CHARS && isalnum(letter))
            do
            {
                cin.get(letter);
            } while (isalnum(letter) && cin);
    }
}


void  GetTilNew(bool skip, char letters[])
// Post: If skip is true, newline characters are skipped.
//       All characters are read and stored until a newline
//       character is read or MAX_CHARS characters have been
//       stored. If the stream is not in the fail state, the
//       last character read was a newline character.

{
    char letter;
    int count = 0;

    if (skip)
    {// skip newlines.
        cin.get(letter);
        while ((letter == '\n') && cin)
            cin.get(letter);
    }
    else
        cin.get(letter);
    if (!cin || letter == '\n')
        letters[0] = '\0';
    else
    {// Read and collect characters.
        do
        {
            letters[count] = letter;
            count++;
            cin.get(letter);
        } while ((letter != '\n') && cin && (count < MAX_CHARS));
        letters[count] = '\0';
        // Skip extra characters if necessary.
        if (count == MAX_CHARS && letter != '\n')
```

```
        do
        {
            cin.get(letter);
        } while ((letter != '\n') && cin);
    }
}
```

GetStringFile

This operation is nearly identical to `GetString`, with `cin` changed to `inFile`. We must write new auxiliary functions like those for `GetString`, but replacing `cin` with `inFile` and adding the file name as a parameter. The same test cases apply to this operation as to `GetString`. We leave the coding of this function to you.

PrintToScreen and PrintToFile

Because we have implemented our string using the same technique C++ uses, we can use `cout` to print to the screen. If `newLine` is true, we print a newline character before printing `letters`. We must test this function with `newLine` both true and false.

```
void StrType::PrintToScreen(bool newLine)
// Post:  letters has been sent to the output stream.
{
    if (newLine)
        cout << endl;
    cout << letters;
}
```

`PrintToFile` is nearly identical to `PrintToScreen`, with `cout` replaced with `outFile`.

LengthIs and CopyString

Because our implementation of a string is the same as C++'s, we can use the `strlen` and `strcpy` functions provided by the standard library for both of these operations. Alternatively we can write loops to count characters until the null terminator is found for `LengthIs` and to copy characters from self to `newString` until the null terminator has been copied for `CopyString`. We use `strcpy` here and leave the other implementation as an exercise.

```
#include <string.h>
void StrType::CopyString(StrType& newString)
// Post: letters has been copied into newString.letters.
{
    strcpy(newString.letters, letters);
}

int StrType::LengthIs()
// Post: Function value = length of letters string
{
    return strlen(letters);
}
```

Test Plan

We must unit test each member function in the class representing the String ADT. We need to go back through our design and collect the tests outlined during the design process. Below is a portion of the test plan that deals with GetString. It is assumed that each call to GetString is followed by a call to PrintToScreen with a parameter of true (to start each word on a new line).

Member Function/ Reason for Test Case (parameters)	Input Values	Expected Output (one word per line) (I stands for newline)	Observed Output
GetString true, ALPHA_NUM	now is the time a1,a3, ##,\n ABCE,\n	now|is|the|time| a1|a3|ABCE|	
GetString false, ALPHA_NUM	same	||now|is|the|time|a 1|a3|||||ABCE||	
GetString true, ALPHA	same	now|is|the|time|a |a|ABCE|	
GetString false, ALPHA	same	||now|is|the|time |a||a||||||ABCE||	
GetString true, NON_WHITE	same	now|is|the|time| a1,a3,##,|ABCE,|	

Member Function/ Reason for Test Case (parameters)	Input Values	Expected Output (one word per line) (| stands for newline)	Observed Output
GetString false, NON_WHITE	same	||now|is|the|time|a 1,a3|##,||ABCE,|	
GetString true, NOT_NEW	now is the time a1,a3, ##,\n\n ABCE,\n	now is the time a1,a3,##,| ABCE,|	
GetString false, NOT_NEW	same	now is the time a1,a3,##,|ABCE,|	
GetString true, ALPHA_NUM true, ALPHA true, NON_WHITE true, NOT_NEW	just an end-of-file	| | | |	
GetString true, ALPHA_NUM true, ALPHA true, NON_WHITE true, NOT_NEW	a file with a string longer than MAX_CHARS followed by at least one other string	The characters beyond MAX_CHARS have been read and not stored.	

▄|| *Summary*

We have discussed how data can be viewed from multiple perspectives, and we have seen how C++ encapsulates the implementations of its predefined types and allows us to encapsulate our own class implementations.

As we create data structures, using built-in data types such as arrays, structs, and classes to implement them, we see that there are actually many levels of data abstraction. The abstract view of an array might be seen as the implementation level of the programmer-defined data structure List, which uses an array to hold its elements. At the logical level, we do not access the elements of List through their array indexes but through a set of accessing operations defined especially for objects of List type. A data type that is

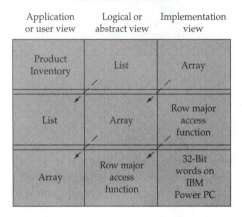

PERSPECTIVES ON DATA

Application or user view	Logical or abstract view	Implementation view
Product Inventory	List	Array
List	Array	Row major access function
Array	Row major access function	32-Bit words on IBM Power PC

designed to hold other objects is called a *container* or *collection type*. Moving up a level, we might see the abstract view of List as the implementation level of another programmer-defined data type, `ProductInventory`, and so on.

What do we gain by separating the views of the data? First, we reduce complexity at the higher levels of the design, making the program easier to understand. Second, we make the program more easily modifiable: the implementation can be completely changed without affecting the program that uses the data structure. We use this advantage in this text, developing various implementations of the same objects in different chapters. Third, we develop software that is *reusable*: the structure and its accessing operations can be used by other programs, for completely different applications, as long as the correct interfaces are maintained. You saw in the first chapter of this book that the design, implementation, and verification of high-quality computer software is a very laborious process. Being able to reuse pieces that are already designed, coded, and tested cuts down on the amount of work we have to do.

In the chapters that follow we extend these ideas to build other container classes that C++ does not provide: lists, stacks, queues, priority queues, trees, and graphs. We consider them from the logical view: what is our abstract picture of the data, and what accessing operations can we use to create, assign to, and manipulate the data elements? We express our logical view as an abstract data type (ADT) and record its description in a data specification.

Next, we take the application view of the data, using an instance of the data type in a short example.

Finally, we change hats and turn to the implementation view of the data type. We consider the C++ type declarations that represent the data structure, as well as the design of the functions that implement the specifications of the abstract view. Data structures can be implemented in more than one way, so we often look at alternative representations and methods for comparing them. In some of the chapters, we include a longer Case Study in which instances of the data type are used to solve a problem.

▉❙❙ *Exercises*

1. Explain what we mean by "data abstraction."

2. What is data encapsulation? Explain the programming goal "to protect our data abstraction through encapsulation."

3. Name three different perspectives from which we can view data. Using the logical data structure "a list of student academic records," give examples of what each perspective might tell us about the data.

4. Consider the abstract data type GroceryStore
   (a) At the application level, describe GroceryStore.
   (b) At the logical level, what grocery store operations might be defined for the customer?
   (c) Specify (at the logical level) the operation CheckOut.
   (d) Write an algorithm (at the implementation level) for the operation CheckOut.
   (e) Explain how parts (c) and (d) represent information hiding.

5. What composite types are predefined in the C++ language?

6. Describe the component selectors for structs and classes at the logical level.

7. Describe the accessing functions for structs and classes at the implementation level.

8. Describe the component selectors for one-dimensional arrays at the logical level.

9. Describe the accessing functions for one-dimensional arrays at the implementation level.

10. (a) Declare a one-dimensional array, name, that contains 20 characters.
    (b) If each character occupies one "cell" in memory, and the base address of name is 1000, what is the address of the cell referenced in the following statement?

    ```
    name[9] = 'A';
    ```

Use the following declarations for Exercises 11 and 12:

```
enum MonthType {JAN, FEB, MAR, APR, MAY, JUN, JUL, AUG, SEP, OCT,
  NOV,DEC};
struct WeatherType
{
    int avgHiTemp;
    int avgLoTemp;
    float actualRain;
    float recordRain;
};
```

Assume that an `int` requires one cell in memory, that a `float` number requires two cells, and that the struct members are in contiguous memory locations with no gaps.

11. (a) Declare a one-dimensional array type, `weatherListType`, of `WeatherType` components, to be indexed by values of type `MonthType`. Declare a variable, `yearlyWeather`, of `weatherListType`.
    (b) Assign the value 1.05 to the actual rainfall member of the July record in `yearlyWeather`.
    (c) If the base address of `yearlyWeather` is 200, what is the address of the member that you assigned in part (b)?

12. (a) Declare a two-dimensional array, `decadeWeather`, of `WeatherType` components, to be indexed by values of type `MonthType` in the first dimension.
    (b) Draw a picture of `decadeWeather`.
    (c) Assign the value 26 to the `avgLoTemp` member of the March 1989 entry.

13. (a) Define a three-dimensional array at the logical level.
    (b) Suggest some applications for three-dimensional arrays.

Use the following declarations for Problems 14–16.

```
typedef char String[10];
struct StudentRecord
{
    String firstName;
    String lastName;
    int id;
    float gpa;
    int currentHours;
    int totalHours;
};
StudentRecord student;
StudentRecord students[100];
```

Assume that an `int` requires one cell in memory, that a `float` number requires two cells, and that the struct members are in contiguous memory locations with no gaps.

14. Construct a member-length-offset table for `StudentRecord`.

15. If the base address of `student` is 100, what address does the compiler generate as the target of the following assignment statement?

```
student.gpa = 3.87;
```

16. How much space does the compiler set aside for `students`?

17. Indicate which predefined C++ types would most appropriately model each of the following (more than one may be appropriate for each):
    (a) a chessboard

(b) information about a single product in an inventory-control program

(c) a list of famous quotations

(d) the casualty figures (number of deaths per year) for highway accidents in Texas from 1954 to 1974

(e) the casualty figures for highway accidents in each of the states from 1954 to 1974

(f) the casualty figures for highway accidents in each of the states from 1954 to 1974, subdivided by month

(g) an electronic address book (name, address, and phone information for all your friends)

(h) a collection of hourly temperatures for a 24-hour period

18. What C++ construct is used to represent abstract data types?

19. Explain the difference between a C++ struct and class.

20. How is the client prevented from directly accessing the details of an instance of a class?

21. (a) The details of a private member can be *seen* by the user of a class. (True or False)

(b) The details of a private member may be *accessed* by a client program. (True or False)

22. Why is it good practice to put a class declaration in one file and the implementation in another?

23. (a) Write the specification for an ADT SquareMatrix. (A square matrix can be represented by a two-dimensional array with N rows and N columns.) You may assume a maximum size of 50 rows and columns. Include the following operations:

MakeEmpty(n), that sets the first n rows and columns to zero,
StoreValue(i, j, value), that stores value into the position at row i, column j.
Add, that adds two matrices together,
Subtract, that subtracts one matrix from another, and
Copy, that copies one matrix into another.

(b) Convert your specification to a C++ class declaration.

(c) Implement the member functions.

(d) Write a test plan for your class.

24. Enhance StrType by adding a ComparedTo function with the following specification.

RelationType ComparedTo(StrType& otherString)

  Function: Compares self to otherString in terms of alphabetic order.
  Precondition: Self and otherString have been initialized.
  Postcondition: Function value = LESS if self comes before otherString
            = GREATER if self comes after otherString;
            = EQUAL if self and otherString are equal

(a) Write member function ComparedTo using strcmp in <string.h>.

(b) Rewrite member function `ComparedTo` without using the `strcmp` library function.

25. Rewrite member function `CopyString` in class `StrType` without using the `strcpy` library function.

26. Rewrite the specification for the String ADT to include the changes that were made during the implementation phase.

27. Complete member functions `GetAlpha` and `GetNonWhite` in class `StrType`.

ADTs Unsorted List and Sorted List

- To be able to describe the abstract data type List at a logical level

- To be able to use the list operations to implement utility routines to do the following application-level tasks:

    Print the list of elements
    Create a list of elements from a file

- To be able to implement the following list operations for both unsorted lists and sorted lists:

    Create and destroy a list
    Determine whether the list is full
    Insert an element
    Retrieve an element
    Delete an element

- To be able to write and execute a test plan for an abstract data type

- To be able to explain the use of Big-O notation to describe the amount of work done by an algorithm

- To be able to compare the unsorted list operations and the sorted list operations in terms of Big-O approximations

- To be able to define class constructors and class destructors

- To be able to overload the relational operators less than (<) and equality (==)

▮ ‖ *Lists*

We all know intuitively what a "list" is; in our everyday lives we use lists all the time—grocery lists, lists of things to do, lists of addresses, lists of party guests. In computer programs, lists are very useful and common abstract data types. There are languages in which the list is a built-in structure. In Lisp, for example, the list is the main data structure provided in the language. In C++, however, lists are not built in, so we must provide our own.

From a programming point of view, a list is a homogeneous collection of elements, with a **linear relationship** between elements. Linear means that, at the logical level, each element in the list except the first one has a unique predecessor, and each element except the last one has a unique successor. (At the implementation level, there is also a relationship between the elements, but the physical relationship may not be the same as the logical one.) The number of items in the list, which we call the **length** of the list, is a property of a list. That is, every list has a length.

Lists can be **unsorted**—their elements may be placed into the list in no particular order—or they can be **sorted** in a variety of ways. For instance, a list of numbers can be sorted by value, a list of strings can be sorted alphabetically, and a list of grades can be sorted numerically. When the elements in a sorted list are of composite types, their logical (and often physical) order is determined by one of the members of the structure, the **key** member. For example, a list of students on the Honor Roll can be sorted alphabetically by name or numerically by student identification number. In the first case, the name is the key; in the second case, the identification number is the key. Such sorted lists are also called *key-sorted lists*.

If a list cannot contain items with duplicate keys, it is said to have *unique keys*. This chapter deals with both unsorted lists and lists of elements with unique keys, sorted from smallest to largest key value.

Linear Relationship   Each element except the first has a unique predecessor, and each element except the last has a unique successor

Length   The number of items in a list; the length can vary over time

Unsorted List   A list in which data items are placed in no particular order; the only relationship between data elements is the list predecessor and successor relationships

Sorted List   A list that is sorted by the value in the key; there is a semantic relationship among the keys of the items in the list

Key   A member of a record (struct or class) whose value is used to determine the logical and/or physical order of the items in a list

---

■ ǁ *Abstract Data Type Unsorted List*

Logical Level

There are many different operations that programmers can provide for lists. For different applications we can imagine all kinds of things users might need to do to a list of elements. In this chapter we formally define a list and develop a set of general-purpose operations for creating and manipulating lists. By doing this, we are building an abstract data type.

To complete the definition of a list as an abstract data type, we must add a set of operations that allow us to access and manipulate the list. In the next section we design the specifications for a List ADT where the items in the list are unsorted; that is, there is no semantic relationship between an item and its predecessor or successor. They simply appear next to one another in the list.

Abstract Data Type Operations   The first step in designing any abstract data type is to stand back and consider what a user of the data type would want it to provide. Recall that there are four kinds of operations: constructors, transformers, observers, and iterators. We begin by reviewing each type and consider each kind of operation with respect to the List ADT.

Constructors   A constructor creates an instance of the data type. It is usually implemented with a language-level declaration.

Transformers   Transformers are operations that change the structure in some way: they may make the structure empty, put an item into the structure, or remove a specific item from the structure. For our Unsorted List ADT, let's call these transformers `MakeEmpty`, `InsertItem`, and `DeleteItem`.

`MakeEmpty` needs only the list, no other parameters. As we implement our operations as member functions, the list is the object to which the function is applied. `InsertItem` and `DeleteItem` need an additional parameter: the item to be inserted or removed. For this Unsorted List ADT, let's assume that the item to be inserted is *not* currently in the list and the item to be deleted *is* in the list.

A transformer that takes two sorted lists and merges them into one sorted list or appends one list to another would be a binary transformer. The specification for such an operation is given in the exercises, where you are asked to implement it.

Observers   Observers also come in several forms. They ask true/false questions about the data type (Is the structure empty?), select or access a particular item (Give me a copy of the last item.), or return a property of the structure (How many items are in the structure?). The Unsorted List ADT needs at least two observers: `IsFull` and `LengthIs`. `IsFull` returns true if the list is full; `LengthIs` tells us how many items there are in the list. Another useful observer is one that searches the list for an item with a particular key and returns a copy of the associated information if it is found. Let's call this one `RetrieveItem`.

If an abstract data type places limits on the component type, we could define other observers. For example, if we know that our abstract data type is a list of numerical values, we could define statistical observers such as Minimum, Maximum, and Average. Here, we are interested in generality; we know nothing about the type of the items on the list, so we use only general observers.

In most of our discussions of error checking, we put the responsibility of checking for error conditions on the user through the use of preconditions that prohibit the operation's call if these conditions exist. In making the client responsible for checking for error conditions, however, we must make sure that the ADT gives the user the tools with which to check for the conditions. In contrast, we could keep an error variable in our list, have each operation record whether an error occurs, and provide operations that test this variable. The operations that test to see if an error has occurred would be observers. However, in the Unsorted List ADT we are specifying, let's let the user prevent error conditions by obeying the preconditions of the ADT operations.

Iterators   Iterators are used with composite types to allow the user to process an entire structure, component by component. To give the user access to each item in sequence, we provide two operations: one to initialize the iteration process (analogous to Reset or Open with a file) and one to return a copy of the "next component" each time it is called. The user can then set up a loop that processes each component. Let's call these operations ResetList and GetNextItem. Note that ResetList is not an iterator itself, but is an auxiliary operation that supports the iteration. Another type of iterator is one that takes an operation and applies it to every element in the list.

Declarations and Definitions

In general programming terminology, a declaration associates an identifier with a data object, an action (such as a function), or a data type. C++ terminology distinguishes between a declaration and a definition. A declaration becomes a definition when it binds storage to the identifier. Hence, all definitions are declarations, but not all declarations are definitions. For example, a function prototype is a declaration only, but a function heading with a body is a function definition. On the other hand, declarations such as typedef's can never be definitions, because they are never bound to storage. An exception to this terminology occurs with classes. C++ refers to a class specification as a definition rather than declaration, so we do the same.

Generic Data Types   A **generic data type** is one for which the operations are defined but the types of the items being manipulated are not. Some programming languages have a built-in mechanism for defining generic data types; some do not. Although C++ does have such a mechanism (called a template), we postpone its description until the next chapter. Here we are going to present a simple, general-purpose way of simulating generics that works in any programming language. We let the user define the type of the items on the list in a class named `ItemType` and have our Unsorted List ADT include the class definition.

Generic Data Type   A type for which the operations are defined but the types of the items being manipulated are not

---

Two of the list operations (`DeleteItem` and `RetrieveItem`) are going to involve the comparison of the keys of two list components (as does `InsertItem` if the list is sorted by key value). We could require the user to name the key data member "key" and compare the key data members using the C++ relational operators. However, this isn't a very satisfactory solution for two reasons: "key" is not always a meaningful identifier in an application program, and the keys would be limited to values of simple types. C++ does have a way to change the meaning of the relational operators (called overloading them), but for the time being we present a general solution rather than a language-dependent one.

We let the user define a member function `ComparedTo` in the class `ItemType`. This function compares two items and returns LESS, GREATER, or EQUAL depending on whether the key of one item comes before the key of the other item, comes after it, or the keys of the two items are equal. If the keys are of a simple type such as an identification number, `ComparedTo` would be implemented using the relational operators. If the keys are strings, function `ComparedTo` would use the string-comparison functions supplied in <`string.h`>. If the keys are people's names, both last name and first name would be compared. Therefore, our specification assumes that `ComparedTo` is a member of `ItemType`.

There is one more piece of information that our ADT needs from the client: the maximum number of items to be on the list. As this information varies from application to application, it is logical for the client to have to provide it. Now we can formalize the specification for the Unsorted List ADT.

■ **Unsorted List ADT Specification**

Structure:	The list elements are of ItemType. The list has a special property called the *current position*—the position of the last element accessed by GetNextItem during an iteration through the list. Only ResetList and GetNextItem affect the current position.

Definitions   (provided by user):

MAX_ITEMS:	A constant specifying the maximum number of items to be on the list.
ItemType:	Class encapsulating the type of the items in the list
RelationType:	An enumeration type that consists of LESS, GREATER, EQUAL

Member function of ItemType that must be included:

RelationType ComparedTo(ItemType item)

Function:	Determines the ordering of two ItemType objects based on their keys.
Precondition:	Self and item have their key members initialized.
Postcondition:	
Function value	= LESS if the key of self is less than the key of item.
	= GREATER if the key of self is greater than the key of item.
	= EQUAL if the keys are equal.
Operations	(provided by Unsorted List ADT):

MakeEmpty

Function:	Initializes list to empty state.
Precondition:	None
Postcondition:	List is empty.

Boolean IsFull

Function:	Determines whether list is full.
Precondition:	List has been initialized.
Postcondition:	Function value = (list is full)

int LengthIs

Function:	Determines the number of elements in list.
Precondition:	List has been initialized.
Postcondition:	Function value = number of elements in list

RetrieveItem (ItemType& item , Boolean& found)

Function:	Retrieves list element whose key matches item's key (if present).

Preconditions:	List has been initialized.
	Key member of item is initialized.
Postconditions:	If there is an element someItem whose key matches item's key, then found = true and item is a copy of someItem; otherwise found = false and item is unchanged. List is unchanged.

InsertItem (ItemType item)

Function:	Adds item to list.
Preconditions:	List has been initialized.
	List is not full.
	item is not in list.
Postcondition:	item is in list.

DeleteItem (ItemType item)

Function:	Deletes the element whose key matches item's key.
Preconditions:	List has been initialized.
	Key member of item is initialized.
	One and only one element in list has a key matching item's key.
Postcondition:	No element in list has a key matching item's key.

ResetList

Function:	Initializes current position for an iteration through the list.
Precondition:	List has been initialized.
Postcondition:	Current position is prior to first element in list.

GetNextItem (ItemType& item)

Function:	Gets the next element in list.
Preconditions:	List has been initialized and has not been changed since last call.
	Current position is defined.
	Element at current position is not last in list.
Postconditions:	Current position is updated to next position.
	item is a copy of element at current position.

Because we do not know the makeup of the key member in the `ItemType`, we have to pass an entire object of `ItemType` as the parameter to both `RetrieveItem` and `DeleteItem`. Notice that the preconditions for both operations state that the key member of the parameter `item` is initialized. `RetrieveItem` fills in the rest of the members of `item` if a list component with the same key is found, and `DeleteItem` removes from the list the component whose key matches that of `item`.

The specifications of the operations are somewhat arbitrary. For instance, we specified in the preconditions of `DeleteItem` that the element to delete must exist in the list and it must be unique. It would be just as legitimate to specify an operation that does not require the element to be in the list and leaves the list unchanged if the item is not there. This is a design choice. If we were designing a specification for a specific application, then the design choice would be based on the requirements of the problem. In this case, we made an arbitrary decision. In the exercises, you are asked to examine the effect of different design choices.

The operations defined in this specification are a sufficient set to create and maintain an unsorted list of elements. Notice that no operation is dependent on the type of the items in the structure. This data independence is what makes the Unsorted List ADT truly abstract. Each program that uses the Unsorted List ADT defines ItemType within the context of the application and provides a comparison member function defined on two items of type ItemType.

Application Level

The set of operations that we are providing for the Unsorted List ADT may seem rather small and primitive. However, this set of operations gives you the tools to create other special-purpose routines that require a knowledge of ItemType. For instance, we have not included a print operation. Why? Because to write a print routine, we must know what the data members look like. The user (who does know what the data members look like) can use the LengthIs, ResetList, and GetNextItem operations to iterate through the list printing each data member. In the code that follows, we assume the user has defined a member function for ItemType that prints the data members of one item. We also assume that the Unsorted List ADT is itself implemented as a class with the operations as member functions.

```
void PrintList(ofstream& dataFile, UnsortedType list)
// Pre:   list has been initialized.
//        dataFile is open for writing.
// Post: Each component in list has been written to dataFile.
//        dataFile is still open.
{
    int length;
    ItemType item;

    list.ResetList();
    length = list.LengthIs();
    for (int counter = 1; counter <= length; counter++)
    {
        list.GetNextItem(item);
        item.Print(dataFile);
    }
}
```

Note that we defined a local variable `length`, stored the result of `list.LengthIs` in it, and used the local variable in the loop. We did this for efficiency reasons. This way the function is called only once, saving the overhead of extra function calls.

Another operation that is application dependent is one to read data (of type `ItemType`) from a file and create a list containing these elements. Without knowing how the list is implemented, the user can write a function `CreateListFromFile`, using the operations specified in the Unsorted List ADT. We assume a function `GetData`, which accesses the individual data members from the file and returns them in `item`.

```
void CreateListFromFile(ifstream& dataFile, UnsortedType& list)
// Pre:  dataFile exists and is open.
// Post: list contains items from dataFile.
//       dataFile is in the fail state due to end-of-file.
//       Items read after the list becomes full are discarded.
{
    ItemType item;

    list.MakeEmpty();
    GetData(dataFile, item);  // reads one item from dataFile
    while (dataFile)
    {
        if (!list.IsFull())
            list.InsertItem(item);
        GetData(dataFile, item);
    }
}
```

In these two functions we have made calls to the list operations specified for the List ADT, creating and printing a list *without knowing how the list is implemented*. At an application level, these are logical operations on a list. At a lower level, these operations are implemented as C++ functions that manipulate an array or other data-storing medium holding the list's elements. There are multiple functionally correct ways to implement an abstract data type. Between the user picture and the eventual representation in the computer's memory, there are intermediate levels of abstraction and design decisions. For instance, how is the logical order of the list elements reflected in their physical ordering? We address questions like this as we now turn to the implementation level of our ADT.

Implementation Level

The logical order of the list elements may or may not mirror the way that we actually store the data. If we implement a list in an array, the components are arranged so that the predecessor and the successor of a component are physically before and after it. In Chapter 5, we introduce a way of implementing a list in which the components are sorted logically rather than physically. However, the way that the list elements are physically arranged certainly affects the way that we access the elements of the list. This arrangement may have implications for how efficient the list operations are. For instance, there is nothing in the specification of the Unsorted List ADT that requires us to implement the list with the elements stored in random order. If we stored the elements in an array, completely sorted, we could still implement all the Unsorted List operations. Does it make a difference if the items are stored unsorted or sorted? At the end of this chapter, we introduce Big-O notation as a way of comparing the efficiency of algorithms, and we answer the question then.

There are two ways to implement a list that preserves the order of the list items; that is, that stores the elements physically in such a way that, from one list element, we can access its logical successor directly. We look at a *sequential array-based* list representation in this chapter. The distinguishing feature of this implementation is that the elements are stored sequentially, in adjacent slots in an array. The order of the elements is implicit in their placement in the array.

The second approach, which we introduce in Chapter 5, is a *linked-list* representation. In a linked implementation, the data elements are not constrained to be stored in physically contiguous, sequential order; rather, the individual elements are stored "somewhere in memory," and their order is maintained by explicit links between them.

Before we go on, let's establish a design terminology that we can use in our algorithms, independent of the eventual list implementation.

List Design Terminology   Assuming that `location` "accesses" a particular list element,

Node(location)	refers to all the data at `location`, including implementation-specific data.
Info(location)	refers to the user's data at `location`.
Info(last)	refers to the user's data at the last location in the list.
Next(location)	gives the location of the node following Node(location).

What then is `location`? For an array-based implementation, `location` is an index, because we access array slots through their indexes. For example, the design statement

Print element Info(location)

means "Print the user's data in the array slot at index `location`"; eventually it might be coded in C++ as

```
list.info[location].Print(dataFile);
```

When we look at a linked implementation in a later chapter the translation is quite different, but the algorithms remain the same. That is, our code implementing the operations changes, but the algorithms do not. Thus, using this design notation, we define implementation-independent algorithms for our List ADT.

But what does Next(location) mean in an array-based sequential implementation? To answer this question, consider how we access the next list element stored in an array: we increment the location, that is, the index. The design statement

Set location to Next(location)

might be coded in C++ as

```
location++;        // location is an array index
```

We have not introduced this list design terminology just to force you to learn the syntax of another computer "language." We simply want to encourage you to think of the list, and the parts of the list elements, as *abstractions*. We have intentionally made the design notation similar to the syntax of function calls to emphasize that, at the design stage, the implementation details can be hidden. There is a lower level of detail that is encapsulated in the "functions" Node, Info, and Next. Using this design terminology, we hope to record algorithms that can be coded for both array-based and linked implementations.

Member Functions   In our implementation, the elements of a list are stored in an array of class objects.

```
ItemType info[MAX_ITEMS];
```

We need a `length` data member in order to keep track of both the number of items we have stored in the array and where the last item was stored. Because the list items are unsorted, we place the first item put into the list into the first slot, the second item into the second slot, and so forth. Because our language is C++, we must remember that the first slot is indexed by 0, the second slot by 1, and

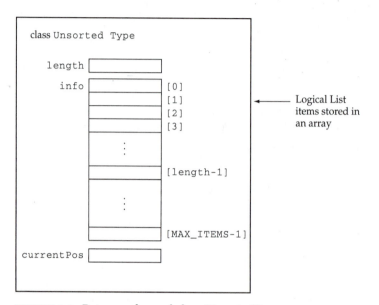

FIGURE 3.1 *Data members of class UnsortedType.*

the last slot by MAX_ITEMS-1. Now we know where the list begins—in the first array slot. Where does the list end? The *array* ends at the slot with index MAX_ITEMS-1, but the *list* ends in the slot with index length-1.

Is there any other information about the list that we must include? Both operations ResetList and GetNextItem refer to a "current position." What is this current position? It is the index of the last element accessed in an iteration through the list. Let's call it currentPos. ResetList initializes currentPos to -1. GetNextItem increments currentPos and returns the value in info[currentPos]. The ADT specification states that only ResetList and GetNextItem affect the current position. Figure 3.1 illustrates the data members of our class UnsortedType.

```
#include "ItemType.h"
// File ItemType.h must be provided by the user of this class.
// ItemType.h must contain the following definitions:
//    MAX_ITEMS:      the maximum number of items on the list
//    ItemType:       the definition of the objects on the list
//    RelationType:   {LESS, GREATER, EQUAL}
//    Member function ComparedTo(ItemType item) which returns
//              LESS, if self "comes before" item
//              GREATER, if self "comes after" item
//              EQUAL, if self and item are the same
```

```
class UnsortedType
{
public:
    void MakeEmpty();
    bool IsFull() const;
    int LengthIs() const;
    void RetrieveItem(ItemType& item, bool& found);
    void InsertItem(ItemType item);
    void DeleteItem(ItemType item);
    void ResetList();
    void GetNextItem(ItemType& item);
private:
    int length;
    ItemType info[MAX_ITEMS];
    int currentPos;
};
```

Now let's look at the operations that we have specified for the Unsorted List ADT. The first operation is MakeEmpty. The postcondition states that the list is empty. Any array cannot be "empty"; the slots exist. A list, however, is only those values that we have stored in the array, that is, from location zero through location length - 1. An empty list, then, is one where the length is 0. Therefore, MakeEmpty sets the length member to zero.

```
void UnsortedType::MakeEmpty()
{
    length = 0;
}
```

Notice that we do *not* have to do anything to the array that holds the list items to make a list empty. If length is zero, the list is empty. If length is not zero, we must have stored items in the array through length - 1 position covering up what was there. What is in the array from the length position to the end is of no interest to us. *This is a very important distinction: the list is between positions 0 and length - 1; the array is between positions 0 and MAX_ITEMS - 1.*

The third function, IsFull, just checks to see if length is equal to MAX_ITEMS.

```
bool UnsortedType::IsFull() const
{
    return (length == MAX_ITEMS);
}
```

The body of the observer member function `LengthIs` is also just one statement.

```
int UnsortedType::LengthIs() const
{
    return length;
}
```

So far we have not used our special design terminology. The algorithms have all been one (obvious) statement long. The next operation, `RetrieveItem`, is more complex.

RetrieveItem Operation   The `RetrieveItem` operation allows the list user to access the list item with a specified key, if that element exists in the list. `item` (with the key initialized) is input to this operation; `item` and a flag (`found`) are returned. If the key of `item` matches a key in the list, `found` is true and `item` is set equal to the element with the same key. Otherwise `found` is false and `item` is unchanged. Notice that `item` is used for both input and output to and from the function. Conceptually, the key member is input; the other data members are output because they are filled in by the function.

To retrieve an element, we first must find it. Because the items are unsorted, we must use a linear search. We begin at the first component in the list and loop until either we find an item with the same key or there are no more items to examine. Recognizing a match is easy: `item.ComparedTo(info[location])` returns `EQUAL`. But how do we know when to stop searching? If we have examined the last element, we can stop. Thus, in our design terminology, we keep looking as long as we have not examined Info(last). So our looping statement is a While statement with the expression (moreToSearch AND NOT found). The body of the loop is a Switch statement based on the results of function `ComparedTo`. We summarize these observations in the algorithm below.

RetrieveItem

Initialize location to position of first item
Set found to false
Set moreToSearch to (have not examined Info(last))
WHILE moreToSearch AND NOT found
    SWITCH (item.ComparedTo(Info(location)))
        case LESS   :
        case GREATER : Set location to Next(location)
                        Set moreToSearch to (have not examined Info(last))
        case EQUAL   : Set found to true
                        Set item to Info(location)

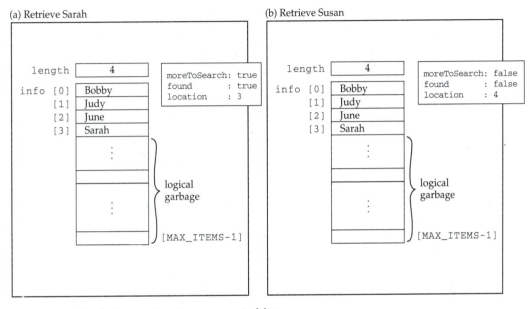

FIGURE 3.2 *Retrieving an item in an unsorted list.*

Before we code this algorithm, let's look at the cases where we find the item in the list and where we examine Info(last) without finding it. We represent these cases in Figure 3.2 in an Honor Roll list. We first retrieve Sarah. Sarah is in the list, so moreToSearch is true, found is true, and location is 3. That's as it should be (see Figure 3.2a). Next, we retrieve Susan. Susan is not in the list so moreToSearch is false, found is false, and location is equal to length (see Figure 3.2b).

Now we are ready to code the algorithm replacing the general design notation with the equivalent array notation. The substitutions are straightforward except for initializing location and determining if we have examined Info(last). To initialize location in an array-based implementation in C++, we set it to 0. We know we have not examined Info(last) as long as location is less than length. Be careful: because C++ indexes arrays from 0, the last item in the list is at index length-1. Here is the coded algorithm.

```
void UnsortedType::RetrieveItem(ItemType& item, bool& found)
// Pre:  Key member(s) of item is initialized.
// Post: If found, item's key matches an element's key in the
//       list and a copy of that element has been stored in item;
//       otherwise, item is unchanged.
{
    bool moreToSearch;
    int location = 0;
    found = false;
```

```
moreToSearch = (location < length);
while (moreToSearch && !found)
{
    switch (item.ComparedTo(info[location]))
    {
        case LESS    :
        case GREATER : location++;
                       moreToSearch = (location < length);
                       break;
        case EQUAL   : found = true;
                       item = info[location];
                       break;
    }
}
```

Note that a *copy* of the list element is returned. The caller cannot access directly any data that are in the list.

InsertItem Operation   Because the list elements are unsorted by key value, we can put the new item anywhere. A straightforward strategy is to place the item in the `length` position and increment `length`.

InsertItem

> Set Info(length) to item
> Increment length

This algorithm is translated easily into C++.

```
void UnsortedType::InsertItem(ItemType item)
// Post: item is in the list.
{
    info[length] = item;
    length++;
}
```

DeleteItem Operation   The `DeleteItem` function takes an item with the key member indicating which item to delete. There are clearly two parts to this operation: finding the item to delete and removing it. We can use the `RetrieveItem` algorithm to search the list: when `ComparedTo` returns `GREATER` or `LESS`, we increment `location`; when `ComparedTo` returns `EQUAL`, we exit the loop and remove the element.

How do we "remove the element from the list"? Let's look at the example in Figure 3.3. Removing Sarah from the list is easy, for hers is the last element in the list (see Figures 3.3a and 3.3b). If Bobby is deleted from the list, however, we need to move up all the elements that follow to fill in the space—or do we? See Figure 3.3(c). If the list is sorted by value, we would have to move all the elements up as shown in Figure 3.3(c), but because the list is unsorted, we can just swap the item in the `length-1` position with the item being deleted (see Figure 3.3d). In an array-based implementation, we do not actually remove the element; instead we cover it up with the elements that previously followed it (if the list is sorted) or the element in the last position (if the list is unsorted). Finally, we decrement `length`.

Because the preconditions for `DeleteItem` state that an item with the same key is definitely in the list, we do not need to test for reaching the end of the list. This simplifies the algorithm so much that we give the code with no further discussion.

```
void UnsortedType::DeleteItem(ItemType item)
// Pre:  item's key has been initialized.
//       An element in the list has a key that matches item's.
// Post: No element in the list has a key that matches item's.
{
    int location = 0;

    while (item.ComparedTo(info[location]) != EQUAL)
        location++;

    info[location] = info[length - 1];
    length--;
}
```

ResetList and GetNextItem Operations The `ResetList` function is analogous to the open operation for a file in which the file pointer is positioned at the beginning of the file so that the first input operation accesses the first component of the file. Each successive call to an input operation gets the next item in the file. Therefore `ResetList` must initialize `currentPos` to point to the predecessor of the first item in the list.

The `GetNextItem` operation is analogous to an input operation; it accesses the next item by incrementing `currentPos` and returning Info(currentPos).

ResetList

Initialize currentPos

(a) Original list

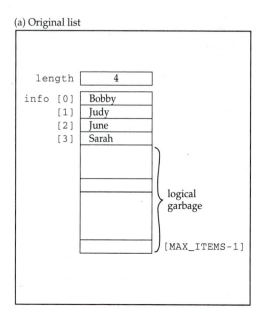

(b) Deleting Sarah

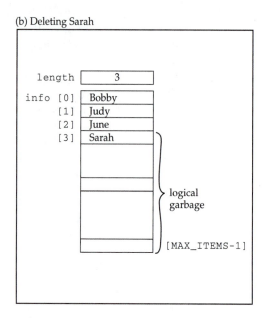

(c) Deleting Bobby (move up)

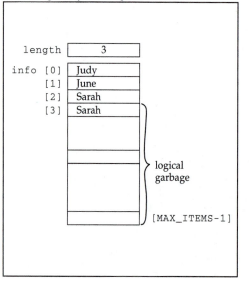

(d) Deleting Bobby (swap)

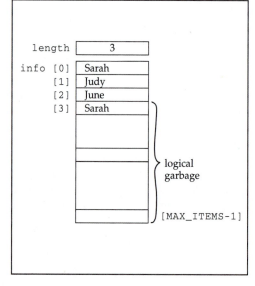

FIGURE 3.3   *Deleting an item in an unsorted list.*

GetNextItem

> Set currentPos to Next(currentPos)
> Set item to Info(currentPos)

currentPos is undefined until it is initialized by ResetList. After the first call to GetNextItem, currentPos is the location of the last item accessed by GetNextItem. Therefore, to implement this algorithm in an array-based list in C++, currentPos must be initialized to -1. These operations are coded as follows:

```
void UnsortedType::ResetList()
// Post: currentPos has been initialized.
{
    currentPos = -1;
}

void UnsortedType::GetNextItem(ItemType& item)
// Post: currentPos has been updated.
//       item is the list item at the updated currentPos position.
{
    currentPos++;
    item = info[currentPos];
}
```

ResetList and GetNextItem are designed to be used in a loop in the client program that iterates through all of the items in the list. The precondition in the specifications for GetNextItem protects against trying to access an array element that is not in the list. This precondition requires that, before a call to GetNextItem, the element at the current position is not the last in the list. Notice that this precondition places the responsibility for accessing only defined items on the client rather than on GetNextItem. Recall that the preconditions tell the user the assumptions that the member functions make. The user is then responsible for ensuring that these assumptions are true.

Notes on the Array-Based List Implementation   In several of the list operations, we have declared local variable location, which contains the array index of the list item being processed. The values of array indexes are never revealed outside of the list operations; this information is internal to the implementation of the Unsorted List ADT. If the list user wants an item in the list, the RetrieveItem operation does not give the user the index of the item; instead it returns a copy of the item itself. If the user wants to change values of data members in an item, those changes are not reflected in the list unless the user deletes the original and inserts the modified version. The list user is never allowed to see or manipulate the physical structure in which the list is stored. These details of the list implementation are encapsulated by the ADT.

Test Plan   Class `UnsortedType` has eight member functions: `MakeEmpty`, `InsertItem`, and `DeleteItem` (transformers); `IsFull`, `LengthIs`, and `RetrieveItem` (observers); and `ResetList` and `GetNextItem` (iterators). Because our operations are independent of the type of the objects on the list, we can define `ItemType` to be `int` and know that if our operations work with this data, they work with any other `ItemType`. Here, then, is the definition of `ItemType` that we use in our test plan. We set the maximum number of items to 5. We include a member function to print an item of type `ItemType`. We need this function in the driver program to see the value in a list item. (Recall that a driver program in a testing environment is one whose sole purpose is to test other functions.)

```cpp
// The following declarations and definitions go into file
// ItemType.h.
const int MAX_ITEMS = 5;
enum RelationType {LESS, GREATER, EQUAL};
class ItemType
{
public:
    RelationType ComparedTo(ItemType) const;
    void Print() const;
    void Initialize(int number);
private:
    int value;
};
// The following definitions go into file ItemType.cpp.
#include <iostream.h>

RelationType ItemType::ComparedTo(ItemType otherItem) const
{
    if (value < otherItem.value)
        return LESS;
    else if (value > otherItem.value)
        return GREATER;
    else return EQUAL;
}
```

```
void ItemType::Initialize(int number)
{
    value = number;
}

void ItemType::Print() const
{
    cout << value << endl;
}
```

The preconditions and postconditions in our specification determine the tests necessary for a black-box testing strategy. The code of the functions determines a clear-box testing strategy. To test the ADT Unsorted List implementation, we use a combination of the two strategies. Because a precondition on all the other operations is that the list has been initialized, we test MakeEmpty first by invoking it and testing to see if the list is empty (a call to LengthIs returns 0).

LengthIs, InsertItem, and DeleteItem must be tested together. That is, we insert several items and check the length; we delete several items and check the length. How do we know that InsertItem and DeleteItem work correctly? We write an auxiliary function PrintList that uses LengthIs, ResetList, and GetNextItem to iterate through the list printing out the values. We call PrintList to check the status of the list after a series of insertions and deletions. To test the IsFull operation, we must insert four items and print the result of the test, and then insert the fifth item and print the result of the test. To test RetrieveItem, we must search for items that we know are in the list and for items that we know are not in the list. To test MakeEmpty, we invoke it when we know that there are values in the list and then print out the number of values (which should be zero).

How do we choose the values to use in our test plan? We look at the end cases. What are the end cases in a list? The item is in the first position in the list, the item is in the last position in the list, and the item is somewhere else in the list. So we must be sure that our DeleteItem can correctly delete items in these positions. We must also check that RetrieveItem can find items in these same positions and can correctly determine that values that are less than the one in the first position or greater than the one in the last position are not there. Notice that this test plan is mostly a black-box strategy. We are looking at the list as described in the interface, not the code.

These observations are summarized in the following test plan. The tests are shown in the order in which they should be preformed.

Operation to Be Tested and Description of Action	Input Values	Expected Output	Observed Output
MakeEmpty: invoke and print LengthIs		length is 0	
InsertItem: insert four items and print insert item and print	5, 7, 6, 9 1	5 7 6 9 5 7 6 9 1	
RetrieveItem: retrieve 4 and print whether found retrieve 5 and print whether found retrieve 9 and print whether found retrieve 10 and print whether found		item is not found item is found item is found item is not found	
IsFull: invoke (list is full) delete 5 and invoke		list is full list is not full	
DeleteItem: print delete 1 and print delete 6 and print		7 6 9 1 7 6 9 7 9	
MakeEmpty: invoke and print LengthIs()		length is 0	

But what about testing `LengthIs`, `ResetList`, and `GetNextItem`? They do not appear explicitly in the test plan, but they are tested each time the auxiliary function `PrintList` is called to print the contents of the list.

To implement this test plan, we must construct a test driver that carries out the tasks outlined in the first column of the plan. We can either make the test plan a document separate from the driver with the last column filled in and initialed by the person running the program and observing the screen output, or we can incorporate the test plan into the driver as comments and have the output go to a file. The key to properly testing any software is in the plan: it must be carefully thought out and it must be written.

■‖ *Abstract Data Type Sorted List*

At the beginning of this chapter, we said that a list is a linear sequence of items; from any item (except the last) you can access the next one. We looked at the specifications and implementation for the operations that manipulate a list and guarantee this property.

We now want to add an additional property: the key member of any item (except the first) comes before the key member of the next one. We call a list with this property a *sorted list.*

Logical Level

When we defined the specifications for the Unsorted List ADT, we commented that there was nothing in the specifications to prevent the list from being stored and maintained in sorted order. Now, we have to change the specifications to guarantee that the list is sorted. We must add preconditions to those operations for which order is relevant. For example, the observer functions do not change the state of the list, so they do not have to be changed. The algorithm for RetrieveItem can be improved but works on a sorted list. The algorithms for ResetList and GetNextItem are not changed by the additional property. What then must be changed? InsertItem and DeleteItem.

■‖ Sorted List ADT Specification (partial)

InsertItem (ItemType item)

Function:	Adds item to list.
Preconditions:	List has been initialized.
	List is not full.
	item is not in list.
	List is sorted by key member using function ComparedTo.
Postconditions:	item is in list.
	List is still sorted.

DeleteItem (ItemType item)

Function:	Deletes the element whose key matches item's key.
Preconditions:	List has been initialized.
	Key member of item is initialized.
	List is sorted by key member using function ComparedTo.
	One and only one element in list has a key matching item's key.
Postconditions:	No element in list has key matching item's key.
	List is still sorted.

Application Level

The application level for the Sorted List ADT is the same as for the Unsorted List ADT. As far as the user is concerned, the interfaces are the same. The only difference is that when `GetNextItem` is called in the Sorted List ADT, the element returned is the next one in order by key. If the user wants that property, the client code includes the file containing class `SortedType` rather than `UnsortedType`.

Implementation Level

InsertItem Operation   To add an element to a sorted list, we must first find the place where the new element belongs, which depends on the value of its key. We use an example to illustrate the insertion operation. Let's say that Becca has made the Honor Roll. To add the element Becca to the sorted list pictured in Figure 3.4(a), maintaining the alphabetic ordering, we must accomplish three tasks:

1. Find the place where the new element belongs.
2. Create space for the new element.
3. Put the new element in the list.

The first task involves traversing the list comparing the new item to each item in the list until we find an item where the new item is less (in this case, Becca). We set `moreToSearch` to `false` when we reach a point where `item.ComparedTo(Info(location))` is `LESS`. At this point, `location` is where the new item should go (see Figure 3.4b). If we don't find a place where `item.ComparedTo(Info(location))` is `LESS`, then the item should be put at the end of the list. This is true when `location` equals `length`.

Now that we know where the element belongs, we need to create space for it. Because the list is sequential, Becca must be put into the list at Info(location). But this position may be occupied. To "create space for the new element," we must move down all the list elements that follow it, from `location` through `length-1`. Now we just assign item to Info(location) and increment `length`. Figure 3.4(c) shows the resulting list.

Let's summarize these observations in algorithmic form before we write the code.

InsertItem

Initialize location to position of first item
Set moreToSearch to (have not examined Info(last))
WHILE moreToSearch
　　SWITCH (item.ComparedTo(Info(location)))
　　　　case LESS　　　:　Set moreToSearch to false
　　　　case EQUAL　　:　// Cannot happen because item is not in list
　　　　case GREATER :　Set location to Next(location)
　　　　　　　　　　　　 Set moreToSearch to (have not examined
　　　　　　　　　　　　 Info(last))
FOR index going from length DOWNTO location + 1
　　Set Info(index) to Info(index-1)
Set Info(location) to item
Increment length

Remember that the preconditions on `InsertItem` state that item does not exist in the list, so we do not need to have `EQUAL` as a label in the Switch statement. Translating the design notation into the array-based implementation gives us the following function.

```
void SortedType::InsertItem(ItemType item)
{
    bool moreToSearch;
    int location = 0;

    moreToSearch = (location < length);

    while (moreToSearch)
    {
        switch (item.ComparedTo(info[location]))
        {
            case LESS    : moreToSearch = false;
                           break;
            case GREATER : location++;
                           moreToSearch = (location < length);
                           break;
        }
    }
    for (int index = length; index > location; index--)
        info[index] = info[index - 1];
    info[location] = item;
    length++;
}
```

Does this function work if the new element belongs at the beginning or end of the list? Draw yourself a picture to see how the function works in each of these cases.

DeleteItem Operation   When discussing function `DeleteItem` for the Unsorted List ADT, we commented that if the list is sorted, we would have to move the elements up one position to cover the one being removed. Moving the

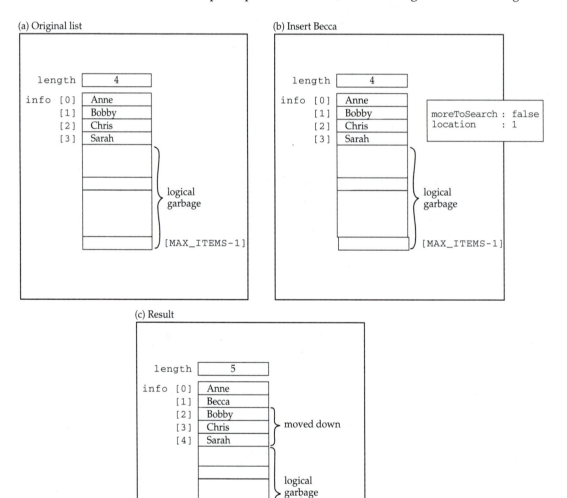

FIGURE 3.4 *Inserting into a sorted list.*

elements up one position is the mirror image of moving the elements down one position. The loop control for finding the item to delete is the same as for the unsorted version.

Initialize location to position of first item
Set found to false
WHILE NOT found
   SWITCH (item.ComparedTo(Info(location)))
      case GREATER　:　Set location to Next(location)
      case LESS　　　:　// Cannot happen because list is sorted.
      case EQUAL　　:　Set found to true
FOR index going from location +1 TO length -1
   Set Info(index - 1) to Info(index)
Decrement length

Examine this algorithm carefully and convince yourself that it is correct. Try cases where you are deleting the first item and the last one.

```
void SortedType::DeleteItem(ItemType item)
{
    int location = 0;

    while (item.ComparedTo(info[location]) != EQUAL)
        location++;
    for (int index = location + 1; index < length; index++)
        info[index - 1] =  info[index];
    length--;
}
```

Improving the RetrieveItem Operation   If the list is not sorted, the only way to search for a value is to start at the beginning and look at each item in the list comparing the key member of the one for which we are searching to the key member of each item in the list in turn. This was the algorithm used in the RetrieveItem operation in the Unsorted List ADT.

If the list is sorted by key value, there are two ways to improve the searching algorithm. The first way is to stop when we pass the place where the item would be if it were there. Look at Figure 3.5(a). If you are searching for Chris, a comparison with Judy would show that Chris is LESS. This means that you have passed the place where Chris would be if it were there. At this point you can stop and return found as false. Figure 3.5(b) shows what happens when you are searching for Susy. location is equal to 4 , moreToSearch is false, and found is false.

If the item we are looking for is in the list, the search is the same for the unsorted list and the sorted list. It is when the item is *not* there that this algorithm is better. We do not have to search all of the items in order to know that the one we want is not there. When the list is sorted, however, we can improve the algorithm even more.

Binary Search Algorithm   Think of how you might go about finding a name in a phone book, and you can get an idea of a faster way to search. Let's look for the name "Dale." We open the phone book to the middle and see that the names there begin with M. M is larger than D, so we search the first half of the phone book, the section that contains A to M. We turn to the middle of the first half and see that the names there begin with G. G is larger than D, so we search the first half of this section, from A to G. We turn to the middle page of this section, and find that the names there begin with C. C is smaller than D, so we search the second half of this section—that is, from C to G—and so on, until we are down to the single page that contains the name Dale. This algorithm is illustrated in Figure 3.6.

We begin our search with the whole list to examine; that is, our current search area goes from `info[0]` through `info[length-1]`. In each iteration, we split the current search area in half at the midpoint, and if the item is not found there, we search the appropriate half. The part of the list being searched at any time is the *current search area*. For instance, in the first iteration of the loop, if a comparison shows that the item comes before the element at the midpoint, the new current search area goes from index 0 through the midpoint-1. If the item comes after the element at the midpoint, the new current search area goes from the midpoint+1 through index `length-1`. Either way, the current search area has been split in half. It looks like we can keep track

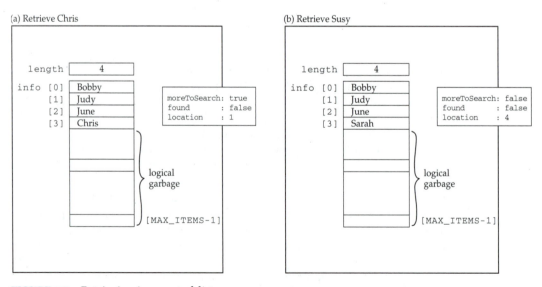

FIGURE 3.5   *Retrieving in a sorted list.*

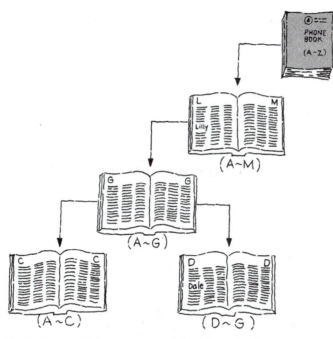

FIGURE 3.6 *A binary search of the phone book.*

of the boundaries of the current search area with a pair of indexes, first and last. In each iteration of the loop, if an element with the same key as item is not found, one of these indexes is reset to shrink the size of the current search area.

How do we know when to quit searching? There are two possible terminating conditions: item is not in the list and item has been found. The first terminating condition occurs when there's no more to search in the current search area. The second terminating condition occurs when item has been found.

```
Set first to 0
Set last to length - 1
Set found to false
Set moreToSearch to (first <= last)
WHILE moreToSearch AND NOT found
    Set midPoint to (first + last) / 2
    SWITCH (item.ComparedTo(info[midPoint]))
        case LESS       :  Set last to midPoint - 1
                           Set moreToSearch to (first <= last)
        case GREATER    :  Set first to midPoint + 1
                           Set moreToSearch to (first <= last)
        case EQUAL      :  Set found to true
```

Notice that when we look in the lower half or upper half, we can ignore the midpoint because we know it is not there. Therefore, `last` is set to `midPoint-1`, or `first` is set to `midPoint+1`. The coded version of our algorithm follows.

```cpp
void SortedType::RetrieveItem(ItemType& item, bool& found)
{
    int midPoint;
    int first = 0;
    int last = length - 1;
    bool moreToSearch = first <= last;

    found = false;
    while (moreToSearch && !found)
    {
        midPoint = ( first + last) / 2;
        switch (item.ComparedTo(info[midPoint]))
        {
            case LESS    : last = midPoint - 1;
                           moreToSearch = first <= last;
                           break;
            case GREATER : first = midPoint + 1;
                           moreToSearch = first <= last;
                           break;
            case EQUAL   : found = true;
                           item = info[midPoint];
                           break;
        }
    }
}
```

Let's walk through the code for this algorithm. The value being searched for is 24. Figure 3.7(a) shows the values of `first`, `last`, and `midPoint` during the first iteration. In the first iteration, 24 is compared with 103, the value in `info[midPoint]`. Because 24 is less than 103, `last` becomes `midPoint-1` and `first` stays the same. Figure 3.7(b) illustrates the situation during the second iteration. This time 24 is compared with 72, the value in `info[midPoint]`. Because 24 is less than 72, `last` becomes `midPoint-1` and `first` again stays the same.

In the third iteration (Figure 3.7c), `midPoint` and `first` are both 0. The value 24 is compared with 12, the value in `info[midPoint]`. Because 24 is greater than 12, `first` becomes `midPoint + 1`. In the fourth iteration (Figure 3.7d), `first`, `last`, and `midPoint` are all the same. Again 24 is compared with the value in `info[midPoint]`. Because 24 is less than 64, `last` becomes

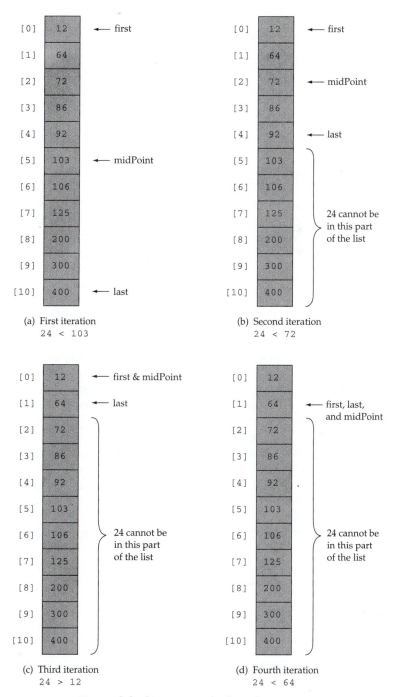

FIGURE 3.7 *Trace of the binary search algorithm.*

TABLE 3.1   **Iteration Trace of the Binary Search Algorithm**

Iteration	first	last	midPoint	info[midPoint]	Terminating Condition
item: 106					
First	0	10	5	103	
Second	6	10	8	200	
Third	6	7	6	106	found is true
item: 400					
First	0	10	5	103	
Second	6	10	8	200	
Third	9	10	9	300	
Fourth	10	10	10	400	found is true
item: 406					
First	0	10	5	103	
Second	6	10	8	200	
Third	9	10	9	300	
Fourth	10	10	10	400	
Fifth	11	10			last < first

midPoint-1. This step makes last less than first, and the process stops. found is false.

The binary search algorithm is the most complex algorithm that we have examined so far. Table 3.1 shows the values for first, last, midPoint, and info[midPoint] during each iteration of the loop for searches for 106, 400, and 406. You should review the results carefully.

Notice that the loop never executes more than four times. It never executes more than four times in a list of eleven components because the list is being cut in half each time through the loop. Table 3.2 compares a linear search and a binary search in terms of the average number of iterations needed to find an item.

If the binary search is so much faster, why not use it all the time? It is certainly faster in terms of the number of times through the loop, but more

TABLE 3.2   **Comparison of Linear and Binary Search**

Length	Average Number of Iterations	
	Linear Search	Binary Search
10	5.5	2.9
100	50.5	5.8
1,000	500.5	9.0
10,000	5000.5	12.0

computations are executed within the binary search loop than in the other search algorithms. So if the number of components in the list is small (say, under 20), the linear search algorithms are faster because they perform less work at each iteration. As the number of components in the list increases, the binary search algorithm becomes relatively more efficient. Remember, however, that the binary search requires the list to be sorted and sorting takes time.

Test Plan   We can use the same test plan that we used for the unsorted list with the expected outputs changed to reflect the ordering. We also need to change the items to be deleted to reflect where the items fall in the list.

Operation to Be Tested and Description of Action	Input Values	Expected Output	Observed Output
MakeEmpty: invoke and print LengthIs	length is 0		

InsertItem:
  insert 4 items and print
  insert item and print
	5, 7, 6, 9
	1
		5 6 7 9
		1 5 6 7 9	

RetrieveItem:
  retrieve 4 and print whether found
  retrieve 1 and print whether found
  retrieve 9 and print whether found
  retrieve 10 and print whether found
		item is not found
		item is found
		item is found
		item is not found	

IsFull:
  invoke (list is full)
  delete 1 and invoke
		list is full
		list is not full	

DeleteItem:
  print
  delete 9 and print
  delete 6 and print
		5 6 7 9
		5 6 7
		5 7	

■ ∥ *Comparison of Algorithms*

As we have shown in this chapter, there is more than one way to solve most problems. If you were asked for directions to Joe's Diner (see Figure 3.8), you could give either of two equally correct answers:

1. "Go east on the big highway to the Y'all Come Inn, and turn left," or
2. "Take the winding country road to Honeysuckle Lodge, and turn right."

The two answers are not the same, but because following either route gets the traveler to Joe's Diner, both answers are *functionally correct.*

If the request for directions contained special requirements, one solution might be preferable to the other. For instance, "I'm late for dinner. What's the quickest route to Joe's Diner?" calls for the first answer, whereas "Is there a pretty road that I can take to get to Joe's Diner?" suggests the second. If no special requirements are known, the choice is a matter of personal preference—which road do you like better?

In this chapter, we have presented many algorithms. How we choose between two algorithms that do the same task often depends on the

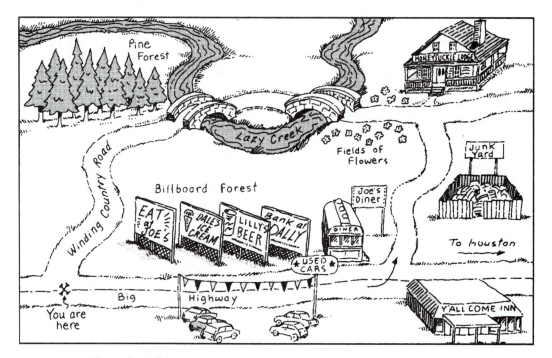

FIGURE 3.8 *Map to Joe's Diner.*

requirements of a particular application. If no relevant requirements exist, the choice may be based on the programmer's own style.

Often the choice between algorithms comes down to a question of efficiency. Which one takes the least amount of computing time? Which one does the job with the least amount of work? We are talking here of the amount of work that the *computer* does. Later we also compare algorithms in regard to how much work the *programmer* does. (One is often minimized at the expense of the other.)

To compare the work done by competing algorithms, we must first define a set of objective measures that can be applied to each algorithm. The *analysis of algorithms* is an important area of theoretical computer science; in advanced courses students undoubtedly see extensive work in this area. In this text you learn about a small part of this topic, enough to let you determine which of two algorithms requires less work to accomplish a particular task.

How do programmers measure the work that two algorithms perform? The first solution that comes to mind is simply to code the algorithms and then compare the execution times for running the two programs. The one with the shorter execution time is clearly the better algorithm. *Or is it?* Using this technique, we really can determine only that program A is more efficient than program B *on a particular computer*. Execution times are specific to a particular computer. Of course, we could test the algorithms on all possible computers, but we want a more general measure.

A second possibility is to count the number of instructions or statements executed. This measure, however, varies with the programming language used, as well as with the style of the individual programmer. To standardize this measure somewhat, we could count the number of passes through a critical loop in the algorithm. If each iteration involves a constant amount of work, this measure gives us a meaningful yardstick of efficiency.

Another idea is to isolate a particular operation fundamental to the algorithm and count the number of times that this operation is performed. Suppose, for example, that we are summing the elements in an integer list. To measure the amount of work required, we could count the integer addition operations. For a list of 100 elements, there are 99 addition operations. Note, however, that we do not actually have to count the number of addition operations; it is some *function* of the number of elements (N) in the list. Therefore, we can express the number of addition operations in terms of N: for a list of N elements, there are $N-1$ addition operations. Now we can compare the algorithms for the general case, not just for a specific list size.

If we wanted to compare algorithms for multiplying two real matrices together, we could use a measure that combines the real multiplication and addition operations required for matrix multiplication. This example brings up an interesting consideration: sometimes an operation so dominates the algorithm that the other operations fade into the background "noise." If we want to buy elephants and goldfish, for example, and we are considering two pet suppliers, we only need to compare the prices of elephants; the cost of the goldfish is trivial in comparison. Similarly, on many computers floating point multiplication is so much more expensive than addition in terms of computer time that the addition operation is a trivial factor in the efficiency of the whole matrix multiplication algorithm; we might as well count only the multiplication operations, ignoring the addition. In analyzing algorithms, we often can find one operation that dominates the algorithm, effectively relegating the others to the "noise" level.

Big-O

We have been talking about work as a function of the size of the input to the operation (for instance, the number of elements in the list to be summed). We can express an approximation of this function using a mathematical notation called **order of magnitude**, or **Big-O notation**. (This is a letter O, not a zero.) The order of magnitude of a function is identified with the term in the function that increases fastest relative to the size of the problem. For instance, if

$$f(N) = N^4 + 100N^2 + 10N + 50,$$

then $f(N)$ is of order N^4—or, in Big-O notation, $O(N^4)$. That is, for large values of N, some multiple of N^4 dominates the function for sufficiently large values of N.

Big-O Notation   A notation that expresses computing time (complexity) as the term in a function that increases most rapidly relative to the size of a problem

---

How is it that we can just drop the low-order terms? Remember the elephants and goldfish that we talked about earlier? The elephants were so much bigger that we could just ignore the goldfish. Similarly, for large values of N, N^4 is so much larger than 50, $10N$, or even $100N^2$ that we can ignore these other terms. This doesn't mean that the other terms do not contribute to the computing time; it only means that they are not significant in our approximation when N is "large."

What is this value N? N represents the size of the problem. Most of the rest of the problems in this book involve data structures—lists, stacks, queues, and trees. Each structure is composed of elements. We develop algorithms to add an element to the structure and to modify or delete an element from the structure. We can describe the work done by these operations in terms of N, where N is the number of elements in the structure. Yes, we know. We have called the number of elements in a list the length of the list. However, mathematicians talk in terms of N, so we use N for the length when we are comparing algorithms using Big-O notation.

Suppose that we want to write all the elements in a list into a file. How much work is that? The answer depends on how many elements are in the list. Our algorithm is

---

Open the file

WHILE more elements in list DO
  Write the next element

If N is the number of elements in the list, the "time" required to do this task is

$$(N * \text{time-to-write-one-element}) + \text{time-to-open-the-file}$$

This algorithm is $O(N)$ because the time required to perform the task is proportional to the number of elements (N)—plus a little to open the file. How can we ignore the open time in determining the Big-O approximation? Assuming that the time necessary to open a file is constant, this part of the algorithm is our goldfish. If the list only has a few elements, the time needed to open the file may seem significant, but for large values of N, writing the elements is an elephant in comparison with opening the file.

The order of magnitude of an algorithm does *not* tell you how long in microseconds the solution takes to run on your computer. Sometimes we need that kind of information. For instance, a word processor's requirements state that the program must be able to spell-check a 50-page document (on a particular computer) in less than 120 seconds. For information like this, we do not use Big-O analysis; we use other measurements. We can compare different implementations of a data structure by coding them and then running a test, recording the time on the computer's clock before and after. This kind of "benchmark" test tells us how long the operations take on a particular computer, using a particular compiler. The Big-O analysis, however, allows us to compare algorithms without reference to these factors.

Common Orders of Magnitude

O(1) is called *bounded time*. The amount of work is bounded by a constant and is not dependent on the size of the problem. Assigning a value to the ith element in an array of N elements is O(1), because an element in an array can be accessed directly through its index. Although bounded time is often called constant time, the amount of work is not constant. It is bounded by a constant.

O($\log_2 N$) is called *logarithmic time*. The amount of work depends on the log of the size of the problem. Algorithms that successively cut the amount of data to be processed in half at each step typically fall into this category. Finding a value in a list of sorted elements using the binary search algorithm is O($\log_2 N$).

O(N) is called *linear time*. The amount of work is some constant times the size of the problem. Printing all the elements in a list of N elements is O(N). Searching for a particular value in a list of unsorted elements is also O(N), because you (potentially) must search every element in the list to find it.

O($N \log_2 N$) is called (for lack of a better term) $N \log_2 N$ *time*. Algorithms of this type typically involve applying a logarithmic algorithm N times. The better sorting algorithms, such as Quicksort, Heapsort, and Mergesort discussed in Chapter 10, have $N \log_2 N$ complexity. That is, these algorithms can transform an unsorted list into a sorted list in O($N \log_2 N$) time.

O(N^2) is called *quadratic time*. Algorithms of this type typically involve applying a linear algorithm N times. Most simple sorting algorithms are O(N^2) algorithms. (See Chapter 10.)

O(N^3) is called *cubic time*. An example of an O(N^3) algorithm is a routine that increments every element in a three-dimensional table of integers.

O(2^N) is called *exponential time*. These algorithms are costly. As you can see in Table 3.3, exponential times increase dramatically in relation to the size of N. (It also is interesting to note that the values in the last column grow so quickly that the computation time required for problems of this order may exceed the estimated life span of the universe!)

Note that throughout this discussion we have been talking about the amount of work the computer must do to execute an algorithm. This determination does not necessarily relate to the size of the algorithm, say, in lines of code. Consider the following two algorithms to initialize to zero every element in an N-element array.

```
Algorithm Init 1      Algorithm Init2
items[0] = 0;         for (index = 0; index < N; index++)
items[1] = 0;             items[index] = 0;
items[2] = 0;
items[3] = 0;

   .

   .

items[N-1] = 0;
```

TABLE 3.3 **Comparison of Rates of Growth**

N	$\log_2 N$	$N \log_2 N$	N^2	N^3	2^N
1	0	1	1	1	2
2	1	2	4	8	4
4	2	8	16	64	16
8	3	24	64	512	256
16	4	64	256	4,096	65,536
32	5	160	1,024	32,768	4,294,967,296
64	6	384	4,096	262,114	About 5 years' worth of instructions on a super computer
128	7	896	16,384	2,097,152	About 600,000 times greater than the age of the universe in nanoseconds (for a 6-billion-year estimate)
256	8	2,048	65,536	16,777,216	Don't ask!

Both algorithms are O(N), even though they greatly differ in the number of lines of code.

Now let's look at two different algorithms that calculate the sum of the integers from 1 to N. Algorithm Sum1 is a simple For loop that adds successive integers to keep a running total:

Algorithm Sum1

```
sum = 0;
for (count = 1; count <= n; count++)
    sum = sum + count;
```

That seems simple enough. The second algorithm calculates the sum by using a formula. To understand the formula, consider the following calculation when $N = 9$.

$$1 + 2 + 3 + 4 + 5 + 6 + 7 + 8 + 9$$
$$+ \ 9 + 8 + 7 + 6 + 5 + 4 + 3 + 2 + 1$$

$$10 + 10 + 10 + 10 + 10 + 10 + 10 + 10 + 10 = 10 * 9 = 90$$

We pair up each number from 1 to N with another, such that each pair adds up to $N + 1$. There are N such pairs, giving us a total of $(N + 1) * N$. Now, because each number is included twice, we divide the product by 2. Using this formula, we can solve the problem: $((9 + 1) * 9)/2 = 45$. Now we have a second algorithm:

Algorithm Sum2

```
sum = ((n + 1) * n) / 2;
```

Both of the algorithms are short pieces of code. Let's compare them using Big-O notation. The work done by Sum1 is a function of the magnitude of N; as N gets larger, the amount of work grows proportionally. If N is 50, Sum1 works 10 times as hard as when N is 5. Algorithm Sum1, therefore, is $O(N)$.

To analyze Sum2, consider the cases when $N = 5$ and $N = 50$. They should take the same amount of time. In fact, whatever value we assign to N, the algorithm does the same amount of work to solve the problem. Algorithm Sum2, therefore, is $O(1)$.

Does this mean that Sum2 is always faster? Is it always a better choice than Sum1? That depends. Sum2 might seem to do more "work," because the formula involves multiplication and division, whereas Sum1 is a simple running total. In fact, for very small values of N, Sum2 actually might do more work than Sum1. (Of course, for very large values of N, Sum1 does a proportionally larger amount of work, whereas Sum2 stays the same.) So the choice between the algorithms depends in part on how they are used, for small or large values of N.

Another issue is the fact that Sum2 is not as obvious as Sum1, and thus it is harder for the programmer (a human) to understand. Sometimes a more efficient solution to a problem is more complicated; we may save computer time at the expense of the programmer's time.

So, what's the verdict? As usual in the design of computer programs, there are trade-offs. We must look at our program's requirements and then decide which solution is better. Throughout this text we examine different choices of algorithms and data structures. We compare them using Big-O, but we also examine the program's requirements and the "elegance" of the competing solutions. As programmers, we design software solutions with many factors in mind.

Family Laundry: An Analogy

How long does it take to do a family's weekly laundry? We might describe the answer to this question with the function

$$f(N) = c * N$$

where N represents the number of family members and c is the average number of minutes that each person's laundry takes. We say that this function is $O(N)$ because the total laundry time depends on the number of people in the family. The "constant" c may vary a little for different families—depending on the size of their washing machine and how fast they can fold clothes, for instance. That is, the time to do the laundry for two different families might be represented with these functions:

$$f(N) = 100 * N$$

$$g(N) = 90 * N$$

But overall, we describe these functions as $O(N)$.

Now what happens if Grandma and Grandpa come to visit the first family for a week or two? The laundry time function becomes

$$f(N) = 100 * (N + 2)$$

We still say that the function is $O(N)$. How can that be? Doesn't the laundry for two extra people take any time to wash, dry, and fold? Of course it does! If N is small (the family consists of Mother, Father, and Baby), the extra laundry for two people is significant. But as N grows large (the family consists of Mother, Father, 12 kids, and a live-in baby-sitter), the extra laundry for two people doesn't make much difference. (The family's laundry is the elephant; the guest's laundry is the goldfish.) When we compare algorithms using Big-O, we are concerned with what happens when N is "large."

If we are asking the question "Can we finish the laundry in time to make the 7:05 train?" we want a precise answer. The Big-O analysis doesn't give us this information. It gives us an approximation. So, if 100 * N, 90 * N, and 100 * $(N + 2)$ are all $O(N)$, how can we say which is "better"? We can't—in Big-O terms, they are all roughly equivalent for large values of N. Can we find a better algorithm for getting the laundry done? If the family wins the state lottery, they can drop all their dirty clothes at a professional laundry 15 minutes' drive from their house (30 minutes round trip). Now the function is

$$f(N) = 30$$

This function is $O(1)$. The answer is not dependent on the number of people in the family. If they switch to a laundry 5 minutes from their house, the function becomes

$$f(N) = 10$$

This function is also $O(1)$. In terms of Big-O, the two professional-laundry solutions are equivalent: no matter how many family members or house guests you have, it takes a constant amount of the family's time to do the laundry. (We aren't concerned with the professional laundry's time.)

▪▎ *Comparison of Unsorted and Sorted List ADT Algorithms*

In order to determine the Big-O notation for the complexity of these functions, we must first determine the size factor. Here we are considering algorithms to manipulate items in a list. Therefore the size factor is the number of items in the list: `length`.

Many of our algorithms are identical for the Unsorted List ADT and the Sorted List ADT. Let's examine these first. `MakeEmpty` contains one line: `length` is set to 0. `LengthIs` and `IsFull` each contain only one statement: `return length` and `return (length == MAX_ITEMS)`. As none of these functions are dependent on the number of items in the list, they have O(1) complexity. `ResetList` contains one assignment statement and `GetNextItem` contains two assignment statements. Neither of these functions is dependent on the number of items in the list, so they have O(1) complexity.

The other functions are different for the two implementations.

Unsorted List ADT

The algorithm for `RetrieveItem` requires that the list be searched until an item is found or the end of the list is reached. We might find the item in any position in the list, or we might not find it at all. How many places must we examine? At best only one, at worst `length`. If we took the best case as our measure of complexity, then all of the operations would have O(1) complexity. But this is a rare case. What we want is the average case or worst case, which in this instance are the same: O(length). True, the average case would be O(length/2), but when we are using order notation, O(length) and O(length/2) are equivalent. In some cases that we discuss later, the average and the worst cases are not the same.

`InsertItem` has two parts: find the place to insert the item and insert the item. In the unsorted list, the item is put in the `length` position and `length` is incremented. Neither of these operations is dependent on the number of items in the list, so the complexity is O(1).

`DeleteItem` has two parts: find the item to delete and delete the item. Finding the item uses the same algorithm as `RetrieveItem`, so the complexity of that part is O(length). To delete the item, we put the value in the `length-1` position into the location of the item to be deleted and decrement `length`. This store and decrement are not dependent on the number of items in the list, so this part of the operation has complexity O(1). The entire delete algorithm has complexity O(length) because O(length) plus O(1) is O(length). (Remember, the O(1) is the goldfish.)

Sorted List ADT

We looked at three different algorithms for `RetrieveItem`. We said that the Unsorted List ADT algorithm would work for a sorted list but that there were two more efficient algorithms: a linear search in the sorted list that exits when the place where the item would be is passed and a binary search.

A linear search in a sorted list is faster than in an unsorted list when searching for an item that is *not* in the list, but is the same when searching for an item that is in the list. Therefore, the complexity of the linear search in a sorted list is the same as the complexity in an unsorted list: O(length). Does that mean that we shouldn't bother taking advantage of the ordering in our search? No, it just means that the Big-O complexity measures are the same.

What about the binary search algorithm? We showed a table comparing the number of items searched in a linear search versus a binary search for certain sizes of lists. How do we describe this algorithm using Big-O notation? To figure this out, let's see how many times we can split a list of N items in half. Assuming that we don't find the item we are looking for at one of the earlier midpoints, we have to divide the list $\log_2 N$ times at the most, before we run out of elements to split. In case you aren't familiar with logs,

$$2^{\log_2 N} = N$$

That is, if $N = 1024$, $\log_2 N = 10$ ($2^{10} = 1024$). How does that apply to our searching algorithms? The sequential search is O(N); in the worst case, we would have to search all 1024 elements of the list. The binary search is O($\log_2 N$); in the worst case we would have to make $\log_2 N + 1$, or 11, search comparisons. A heuristic (a rule of thumb) tells us that a problem that is solved by successively splitting it in half is an O($\log_2 N$) algorithm. Figure 3.9 illustrates the relative growth of the linear and binary searches, measured in number of comparisons.

`InsertItem` still has the same two parts: finding the place to insert the item and inserting the item. Because the list must remain sorted, we must search for the position into which the new item must go. Our algorithm used a

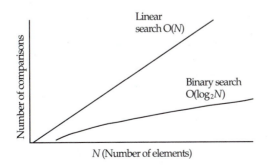

FIGURE 3.9 *Comparison of linear and binary searches.*

linear search to find the appropriate location: O(length). Inserting requires that we move all those elements from the insertion point down one place in the array. How many items must we move? At most length, giving us O(length). O(length) plus O(length) is O(length) because we disregard the constant two. Note, however, that the constant two does not actually occur here. We actually access each item in the list only once except for the item at the insertion point: we access those to the place of insertion and we move those items stored from length - 1 through that place. Therefore, only the element in the insertion location is accessed twice: once to find the insertion point and once to move it.

DeleteItem also still has the same two parts: finding the item to delete and deleting the item. The algorithm for finding the item is the mirror image of finding the insertion point: O(length). Deleting the item in a sorted list requires that all the elements from the deletion location to the end of the list must be moved forward one position. This shifting algorithm is the reverse of the shifting algorithm in the insertion and, therefore, has the same complexity: O(length). Hence the complexity of the insertion and deletion algorithms are the same in the Sorted List ADT.

Table 3.4 summarizes these complexities. We have replaced length with *N*, the generic name for the size factor.

In the deletion operation, we could improve the efficiency by using the binary search algorithm to find the item to delete. Would this change the

TABLE 3.4   Big-O Comparison of List Operations

Operation	Unsorted List	Sorted List
MakeEmpty	O(1)	O(1)
LengthIs	O(1)	O(1)
IsFull	O(1)	O(1)
ResetList	O(1)	O(1)
GetNextItem	O(1)	O(1)
RetrieveItem	O(N)	O(N) linear search
		O($\log_2 N$) binary search
InsertItem		
Find	O(1)	O(N)
Put	O(1)	O(N)
Combined	O(1)	O(N)
DeleteItem		
Find	O(N)	O(N)
Remove	O(1)	O(N)
Combined	O(N)	O(N)

complexity? No, it would not. The find would be O(log$_2$N), but the removal would still be O(N) because O(log$_2$N) combined with O(N) is O(N). (Recall that the term with the largest power of N dominates.) Does this mean that we should not use the binary search algorithm? No, it just means that as the length of the list grows, this cost of the removal dominates the cost of the find.

Think of the common orders of complexity as being bins into which we sort algorithms (Figure 3.10). For small values of the size factor, an algorithm in one bin may actually be faster than the equivalent algorithm in the next-more-efficient bin. As the size factor increases, the differences among algorithms in the different bins gets larger. When choosing between algorithms within the same bin, you look at the constants to determine which to use.

Class Constructors, Class Destructors, and Overloading Operators

In this chapter, we have looked at a general implementation of two abstract data types that represent what we normally think of as lists. We have used a sequential array-based implementation where the user is responsible for providing the description of the items on the list and initializing the structure using function `MakeEmpty`. The techniques we have presented work in most programming languages. In this section, we cover three C++ constructs that make these implementations simpler and more robust.

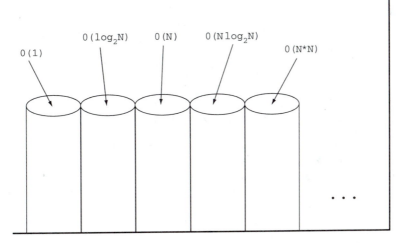

FIGURE 3.10 *Complexity bins.*

Class Constructors

In the unsorted list implementation, MakeEmpty set the length data member to 0. The preconditions for all of the other list operations state that the list has been initialized. What happens if the client program forgets to call MakeEmpty? The results are undefined; the contract between the client and the function implementation is broken. Because the class is an active rather than a passive construct, C++ provides a mechanism to let the class object initialize itself: the **class constructor**. A class constructor is a member function of the class *implicitly* invoked whenever a class object is created. When we are implementing a list ADT in C++, the class itself can guarantee the "list has been initialized" precondition by having a class constructor that automatically initializes each class object.

Class Constructor   A special member function of a class that is implicitly invoked when a class object is defined

---

Class constructors come in two varieties: parameterized and default (which has no parameters). Their name is the name of the class, and they are distinguished by their parameter lists. A class may have none, one, or both defined for it. Let's define both kinds of constructor for the sorted list implementation. (The following class definition also includes a class destructor, which we discuss later.)

```
class SortedType
{
public:
    SortedType();                       // Default constructor.
    SortedType(ItemType initialValue);  // Parameterized constr.
    ~SortedType();                      // Destructor.
    void MakeEmpty();
    bool IsFull() const;
    int LengthIs() const;
    void RetrieveItem(ItemType& item, bool& found);
    void InsertItem(ItemType item);
    void DeleteItem(ItemType item);
    void ResetList();
    void GetNextItem(ItemType& item);
private:
    int length;
    ItemType info[MAX_ITEMS];
    int currentPos;
};
```

The prototype of the constructor seems strange: it has no return value type, nor does it have the word `void` before it. The reason is that the constructor cannot return a function value. Its purpose is only to initialize a class object's private data. In other words, a constructor logically creates an object by initializing necessary storage cells allocated to an instance of a class. In the case of an array-based list, the constructor must set the `length` data member to 0— exactly what our original `MakeEmpty` method did.

The implementation of a constructor looks strange as well. Because the name of the class is the name of the member function, the class name is repeated twice.

```
SortedType::SortedType()
// Default constructor.
{
    length = 0;
}
```

Perhaps the user wants to initialize all of the possible elements in the list of items to a single value. A parameterized constructor allows the user to do so. The client can pass a parameter of the same type as the items to be on the list, and the constructor can store this value into each place in the array.

```
SortedType::SortedType(ItemType initialValue)
// Parameterized constructor.
{
    length = 0;
    for (int counter = 0; counter < MAX_ITEMS; counter++)
        info[counter] = initialValue;
}
```

The following client definitions create two objects of type `SortedType` (`initialValue` is of type `ItemType`):

```
SortedType myList;
SortedType yourList(initialValue);
```

Both `myList` and `yourList` have the `length` data member set to 0; `yourList` also has all of the positions in array `info` set to `initialValue`. Remember, the list is between the beginning of the array and the `length-1` position; setting the values to some initial value is not necessary, but this example does demonstrate how to define and use a parameterized constructor. Note that there are no parentheses after the variable name when using the default constructor.

Note that in our class definition, we did not replace `MakeEmpty` with the class constructor; we added the class constructor. The class constructor is *implicit*: it is automatically executed when a variable of the class is defined. We still leave the *explicit* operation `MakeEmpty` should the client need to set the list to empty after it has been used.

▬ Rules for Using Class Constructors

C++ has intricate rules about using constructors. The following guidelines are especially pertinent.

1. A constructor cannot return a function value, so the function is declared without a return value type. Although not necessary, `return` statements with no expressions are allowed at the end of a constructor. Thus `return;` is legal in a constructor, but `return 0;` is not.
2. A class may provide several constructors. When a class object is declared, the compiler chooses the appropriate constructor according to the number and data types of the parameters to the constructor.
3. Parameters to a constructor are passed by placing the actual parameter list immediately after the name of the class object being declared:

```
SortedType myList(initialValue);
```

4. If a class object is declared without a parameter list, as in the statement

```
SortedList yourList;
```

then the effect depends upon what constructors (if any) the class provides. If the class has no constructors at all, memory is allocated for `yourList` but its private data members are in an uninitialized state. If the class does have constructors, then the default (parameterless) constructor is invoked if there is one. If there is no default constructor, a syntax error occurs.
5. If a class has at least one constructor, and an array of class objects is declared as in the statement

```
SortedType lists[5];
```

then one of the constructors must be the default (parameterless) constructor. This constructor is invoked for each element in the array. There is no way to pass parameters to a constructor when creating an array of class objects.

Class Destructor

Before leaving the topic of constructors, we give a brief preview of another special member function supported by C++: the **class destructor**. Just as a constructor is implicitly invoked when a class object is created (defined), a destructor is implicitly invoked when a class object goes out of scope—for example, when control leaves the block in which an object is declared. A class destructor is named the same as a class constructor except that the destructor has a tilde (~) in front of the type name. The prototype of the destructor is illustrated in the preceding definition of `SortedType`. However, in this array-based implementation, there is no reason to use a destructor. In Chapter 4, we first encounter a situation where a destructor should be used; in Chapter 6, we explore destructors in detail and describe the situations in which you need to use them.

Class Destructor   A special member function of a class that is implicitly invoked when a class object goes out of scope

---

Note that a destructor is not the same as the `MakeEmpty` operation listed in our specification. `MakeEmpty` is specified to return a list to the empty state. As we shall see, a destructor is used most often to return memory no longer needed to the run-time support system.

Overloading an Operator

We required class `ItemType` to have a member function `ComparedTo`. Our list operations all invoked `ComparedTo` when a comparison was needed between an item on the list and another item of `ItemType`. C++ allows us to redefine the meaning of the relational operators in terms of the data members of a class. This redefining of an operator symbol is called *overloading* the operator. We discuss overloading the relational operators in this chapter; we discuss overloading other operators in Chapter 6.

Let's describe the mechanism in terms of our `StrType` class defined in the last chapter. As an exercise, you were asked to add a comparison operation to this class. We also need this operation in our Case Study. The expanded definition of class `StrType` is shown here.

```
enum InType {ALPHA_NUM, ALPHA, NON_WHITE, NOT_NEW};
const int MAX_CHARS = 200;

class StrType
{
public:
    StrType();
    void MakeEmpty();
    void GetString(bool skip, InType charsAllowed);
    void GetStringFile(bool skip, InType charsAllowed,
        ifstream inFile);
    void PrintToScreen(bool newLine);
    void PrintToFile(bool newLine, ofstream& outFile);
    bool operator<(StrType otherString) const;
    bool operator == (StrType otherString) const;
private:
    char letters[MAX_CHARS];
};
```

The syntax for overloading a symbol is the word `operator` followed by the symbol to be overloaded. These functions are member functions and are known in C++ as *operator functions*. Because we store the characters the same way that C++ does, we can use the string functions provided in `<string.h>` to implement these operator functions.

```
bool StrType::operator<(StrType otherString) const
{
    int result;

    result = strcmp(letters, otherString.letters);
    if (result < 0)
        return true;
    else
        return false;
}

bool StrType::operator == (StrType otherString) const
{
    int result;

    result = strcmp(letters, otherString.letters);
    if (result == 0)
        return true;
    else
        return false;
}
```

When the client code includes

```
if (myString < yourString)
```

or

```
if (myString == yourString)
```

the respective member functions from class `StrType` are invoked.

For our Unsorted ADT and Sorted ADT, we required `ItemType` to be a class with a member function `ComparedTo`. Now that we know how to overload the relational operators, we could overload "<" and "==" in the `ItemType` class and then rewrite the code for `InsertItem`, `RetrieveItem`, and `DeleteItem` using the relational operators. We could, but should we? We cannot use the relational operators as labels on a Switch statement, so the code would have to be a series of `if-else` clauses. Some programmers find Switch statements more self-documenting, and others like to use the relational operators. The choice is a matter of personal style.

Notice that in enhancing the `StrType` class, we added a class constructor. The class constructor must do exactly what `MakeEmpty` does: set the string to the empty string. We did not add a class destructor because it is not needed with this array-based implementation.

```
StrType::StrType()
{
    letters[0] = '\0';
}
```

CASE STUDY III

REAL ESTATE LISTINGS, AN OBJECT-ORIENTED DESIGN

Problem: Write a program to keep track of a real estate company's residential listings. The program needs to input and keep track of all the listing information, which is currently stored on 3×5 cards in a box in their office. The real estate sales people must be able to perform a number of tasks using this data: add or delete a house listing, print the information about a particular house given the owner's name, and print a list of home owners sorted alphabetically.

Discussion: We said that nouns in the problem statement represent objects and that verbs describe actions. Let's approach this problem by analyzing the problem statement in terms of nouns and verbs. Let's circle nouns and underline verbs. The relevant nouns in the first paragraph are *listings, information, cards, box,* and *office:* circle them. The verbs that describe possible program actions are *keep track of, input,* and *stored:* underline them. In the second paragraph, the nouns are *people, listing, data, information, house, name, list,* and *owners:* circle them. Possible action verbs are *perform, add, delete,* and *print:* underline them. Figure 3.11 shows the problem statement with the nouns circled and the verbs underlined.

We did not circle *program* or underline *write* because these are instructions to the programmer and not part of the problem to be solved. Now, let's examine these nouns and verbs and see what insights they give us into the solution of this problem.

The first paragraph describes the current system: the objects are cards that contain information. These cards are stored in a box. Therefore, there are two objects in the office that we are going to have to simulate: 3 x 5 cards and a box to put them in. In the second paragraph, we see what processing must be done with the cards and the box in which they are stored. The noun *people* represents the outside world interacting with the program, so the rest of the paragraph describes the processing options that must be provided to the user of the program. In terms of the box of cards, the user must be able to add a new card, delete a card, print the information on the card given the owner's name, and print a list of all of the owners' names in the box alphabetically.

We can represent the cards by a class whose data members are the information written on the 3 × 5 cards. Let's call this class `HouseType`. How

Write a program to <u>keep</u> track of a real estate company's residential ⟨listings⟩ The program needs to <u>input</u> and <u>keep track of</u> all the listing ⟨information⟩ which is currently <u>stored</u> on 3 x 5 ⟨cards⟩ in a ⟨box⟩ in their ⟨office⟩

The real estate sales ⟨people⟩ must be able <u>to perform</u> a number of tasks using this ⟨data⟩ <u>add</u> or <u>delete</u> a house ⟨listing⟩ <u>print</u> the ⟨information⟩ about a particular ⟨house⟩ given the owner's name, and <u>print</u> a ⟨list⟩ of home ⟨owners⟩ sorted alphabetically.

FIGURE 3.11   *Problem statement with nouns circled and verbs underlined.*

do we represent the box of cards? We have just written two versions of the abstract data type List. A list is a good candidate to simulate a box and the information on the list can be objects of type HouseType. So far, we have ignored the noun *office*. A box of cards is stored permanently in the office. A list is a structure that exists only as long as the program in which it is defined is running. But how do we keep track of the information between runs of the program? That is, how do we simulate the office in which the box resides? A file is the structure that is used for permanent storage of information. Hence, there are two representations of the box of cards. When the program is running, the box is represented as a list. When the program is not running, the box is represented as a file. The program must move the information on the cards from a file to a list as the first action, and from a list to a file as the last action.

Input: Let's assume that the information on the 3×5 cards includes the owner's first and last names, the address, price, number of square feet, and number of bedrooms. The company never accepts more than one listing per customer, so there are no duplicates names. If an agent attempts to insert a duplicate listing, an error message is printed to the screen. As all the processing is by owner's name, the combined first and last name should be the object's key.

We must give the user, the real estate agent, a menu of the tasks that can be performed on the list of houses. After a consultation with the agents, the following commands were decided upon:

A   Add a house listing.
D   Delete a house listing.
P   Print all of the information about a house on the screen, given the name of the owner.
L   Print the names of all of the owners in alphabetical order on the screen.
Q   Quit.

The user continues to manipulate the list of houses until he or she enters a Q.

Notice that there are three kinds of input: the file of houses saved from the last run of the program, the commands, and data entered from the keyboard in conjunction with implementing the commands.

Output: There are two kinds of output: the file of houses saved at the end of the run of the program, and screen output directed by one or more of the commands.

Data Objects: There are house objects, represented in the program as HouseType class objects. There are two container objects: the file of house objects retained from one run of the program to the next and the list into which the house objects are stored when the program is running (houseList). The collection of house listings is called our *data base*.

We name the physical file in which we retain the house objects house.mf. However, within our program we use two separate file stream objects: masterIn (of type ifstream) and masterOut (of type ofstream). The object `masterIn` reads data from physical file `house.mf`, and `masterOut` writes to `house.mf`.

The diagrams in Figures 3.12 and 3.13 show the general flow of the processing and what the data objects look like. Note that we know the internal workings of the List ADT because we have just written the code earlier in the chapter. However, we write the program only using the interface as represented in the header file of the class. But which class shall we use? The unsorted version or the sorted version? Because one of the operations prints the names of the owners in order, the sorted version is a better choice.

Where do we go from here? Do we determine the methods (member functions) for `HouseType` or do we design the main function next? At this stage we do not know exactly what operations need to be applied to objects of type `HouseType`, but we do know the general processing required, so let's design the main function making notes of the methods needed as we go along.

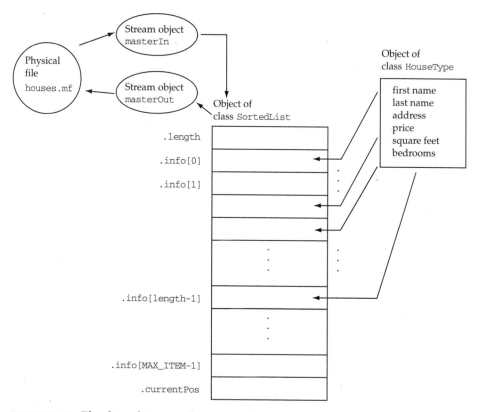

FIGURE 3.12 *The data objects in the case study.*

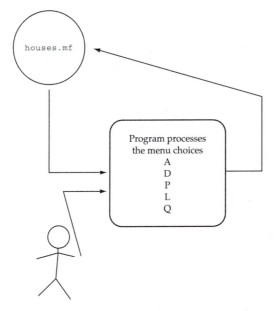

FIGURE 3.13   *The high-level processing of the case study.*

We must first decide on the interface that we give the user for manipulating the data base. The operations are to add a house, delete a house, print information about one house, and print a listing of all the owners. Let's define an enumeration type with these commands.

Driver (Main)

Read file data into houseList

Get a command
WHILE command != Quit
  SWITCH (command)
    case ADD   : AddHouse(houseList)
    case DELETE   : DeleteHouse(houseList)
    case PRINT_ONE : PrintHouse(houseList)
    case PRINT_ALL : PrintOwners(houseList)
  Get a command

Write houseList to file

The first time the program is run, `houses.mf` is empty, but it must exist; that is, we need to create an empty file and name it `houses.mf`. The data base (the list of houses) must be built by the user entering the information about the houses from the 3 × 5 cards. For example, suppose the 3 × 5 cards contain the following information:

John Jones
304 Spider Hollow, 78744
$96,000.00
1200 sq. feet, 3 bedrooms

Susan Smith
111 Lark Lane, 78712
$105,000.00
1500 sq. feet, 3 bedrooms

Claire Clear
123 Shallow Cove
$160,000
2000 sq. feet, 4 bedrooms

The first task for the user would be to signal that a new house is to be added to the list (enter A at the prompt). The program would prompt for the information necessary, and the user would key it from the 3 × 5 cards. Each house would be put into the list of houses as it is entered. If the user then enters a Q, the information on these three houses would be written to the file `houses.mf`. At the next run of the program, `houses.mf` now has three listings that are read in at the beginning of the run. The user is prompted to enter one of the commands to add a new listing, delete a listing, print a particular listing, print all the owners, or quit.

Now, let's complete the design of the driver.

FileToList(SortedType& houseList, ifstream& masterIn)

```
Open file masterIn
houseList.MakeEmpty()
item.GetFromFile(masterIn)          // Reads one item from masterIn.
WHILE more data
    houseList.InsertItem(item)
    item.GetFromFile(masterIn)
Close file masterIn
```

ListToFile(SortedType houseList, ofstream& masterOut)

Open file masterOut
houseList.ResetList()
Set length to houseList.LengthIs()
FOR count going from 1 to length
    houseList.GetNextItem(item)
    Write item to masterOut
Close file masterOut

AddHouse(SortedType& houseList)

item.GetFromUser()
houseList.RetrieveItem(item, found)
IF (NOT found)
    houseList.InsertItem(item)
ELSE
    Write "Duplicate name; operation aborted."

DeleteHouse(SortedType& houseList)

item.GetNameFromUser()
houseList.RetrieveItem(item, found)
IF (found)
    houseList.DeleteItem(item)
ELSE
    Write "Person not in list."

Note that we have to check to be sure the house to be deleted is in the list because the precondition on `DeleteItem` in the `SortedType` class is that the item is there. Because the input/output is interactive, we should write a message to the user if the item is not there.

PrintHouse(SortedType houseList)

---

item.GetNameFromUser()
houseList.RetrieveItem(item, found)
IF (found)
    item.PrintHouseToScreen()
ELSE
    Write "Owner not in list."

PrintOwners(SortedType houseList)

---

houseList.ResetList()
Set length to houseList.LengthIs()
FOR count going from 1 to length
    houseList.GetNextItem(item)
    item.PrintNameToScreen()

GetCommand(CommandType& command)

Write "Operations are listed below. "
    "Enter the appropriate uppercase letter and press return."
    "A : Add a house to the list of houses."
    "D : Delete a specific owner's house."
    "P : Print all the information about an owner's house."
    "L : Print all the names on the screen."
    "Q : Quit processing."

// Input command.
Get a letter
Set ok to false
WHILE NOT ok
    Set ok to true
    SWITCH (letter)
        case 'A' : Set command to ADD
        case 'D' : Set command to DELETE
        case 'P' : Set command to PRINT_ONE
        case 'L' : Set command to PRINT_ALL
        case 'Q' : Set command to QUIT
        default   : Write "Letter entered is not one of the specified "
                     "uppercase commands. Reenter and press return."
                     Get a letter
                     Set ok to false

All of the second-level tasks are simple enough to code directly. We do not have to code the member functions of `HouseType` yet. That is the last task in preparing this program.

```cpp
// CLIENT PROGRAM
// This program manipulates real estate property listings.
#include <iostream.h>
#include "Sorted.h"        // Gain access to Sorted List ADT.
#include <fstream.h>

enum CommandType {ADD, DELETE, PRINT_ONE, PRINT_ALL, QUIT};
    // Each constant represents a task.
void FileToList(SortedType&, ifstream&);
    // moves houses from file to list
void ListToFile(SortedType, ofstream&);
    // moves houses from list to file
void AddHouse(SortedType&);
    // adds a house to the list
void DeleteHouse(SortedType&);
    // removes a house from the list
void PrintHouse(SortedType);
    // prints a specific owner listing
void PrintOwners(SortedType);
    // prints a sorted list of owners
void GetCommand(CommandType&);
    // prompts for and gets next command
int main()
{
    ifstream masterIn;      // master file of houses (input)
    ofstream masterOut;     // master file of houses (output)
    CommandType command;
    SortedType houseList;

    FileToList(houseList, masterIn);
    GetCommand(command);
    // Read and process commands until user enters a quit command.
    while (command != QUIT)
    {
        switch (command)
        {
            case ADD       : AddHouse(houseList);
                             break;
            case DELETE    : DeleteHouse(houseList);
                             break;
            case PRINT_ONE : PrintHouse(houseList);
                             break;
```

```
                    case PRINT_ALL : PrintOwners(houseList);
                                     break;
            }
          GetCommand(command);
      }

    ListToFile(houseList, masterOut);

    return 0;
}


// *************************************************************
// *************** Second Level Functions *********************

void FileToList(SortedType& houseList, ifstream& masterIn)
// Pre:  masterIn has not been opened.
// Post: houseList contains items from masterIn.
//       masterIn has been closed.
{
    ItemType item;
    masterIn.open("houses.mf");
    houseList.MakeEmpty();
    item.GetFromFile(masterIn);  // Reads one item from masterIn.
    while (masterIn)
    {
        houseList.InsertItem(item);
        item.GetFromFile(masterIn);
    }
    masterIn.close();
}


void ListToFile(SortedType houseList, ofstream& masterOut)
// Pre:  masterOut has not been opened.
//       houseList has been initialized.
// Post: houseList has been written on masterOut.
//       masterOut has been closed.
{

    ItemType item;
    int length;

    masterOut.open("houses.mf");
    houseList.ResetList();
    length = houseList.LengthIs();
    for (int count = 1; count <= length; count++)
    {
        houseList.GetNextItem(item);
        item.WriteToFile(masterOut);
    }
```

```
        masterOut.close();
}

void AddHouse(SortedType& houseList)
// Pre:  houseList has been initialized.
// Post: A house has been added to the list if the names are
//       not duplicated; otherwise the operation is aborted with
//       a message to user.
{
    bool found;
    ItemType item;

    item.GetFromUser();
    houseList.RetrieveItem(item, found);
    if (!found)
    {
        houseList.InsertItem(item);
        cout << "Operation completed." << endl;
    }
    else
        cout << "Duplicate name; operation aborted" << endl;
}

void DeleteHouse(SortedType& houseList)
// Pre:  houseList has been initialized.
// Post: A house, specified by user input, is no longer in the list.
{
    bool found;
    ItemType item;

    item.GetNameFromUser();
    houseList.RetrieveItem(item, found);
    if ( found)
    {
        houseList.DeleteItem(item);
        cout << "Operation completed." << endl;
    }
    else
        cout << "Person not in list." << endl;
}

void PrintHouse(SortedType houseList)
// Pre:  houseList has been initialized.
// Post: If owner, specified by user input, is in houseList,
//       house info is printed on the screen.
{
    bool found;
    ItemType item;
```

```
        item.GetNameFromUser();
        houseList.RetrieveItem(item, found);
        if (found)
            item.PrintHouseToScreen();
        else
            cout << "Owner not in list." << endl;
    }


void PrintOwners(SortedType houseList)
// Pre:  houseList has been initialized.
// Post: Owners' names are printed on the screen.

    {
        ItemType item;
        int length;

        houseList.ResetList();
        length = houseList.LengthIs();
        for (int count = 1; count <= length; count++)
        {
            houseList.GetNextItem(item);
            item.PrintNameToScreen();
        }
        cout << "Operation completed." << endl;
    }


void GetCommand(CommandType& command)
// Pre:  None
// Post: User command has been prompted for and input; a valid
//       command has been found.
    {
        // Prompt.
        cout << "Operations are listed below.  "
             << "Enter the appropriate uppercase letter and "
             << "press return." << endl;
        cout << "A : Add a house to the list of houses." << endl;
        cout << "D : Delete a specific owner's house." << endl;
        cout << "P : Print the information about an owner's house."
             << endl;
        cout << "L : Print all the names on the screen." << endl;
        cout << "Q : Quit processing." << endl;

        // Input command.
        char letter;
        cin >> letter;

        bool ok = false;
        while (!ok)
```

```
      {
        ok = true;
        switch (letter)
        {
            case 'A' : command = ADD;
                       break;
            case 'D' : command = DELETE;
                       break;
            case 'P' : command = PRINT_ONE;
                       break;
            case 'L' : command = PRINT_ALL;
                       break;
            case 'Q' : command = QUIT;
                       break;
            default  : cout  << "Letter entered is not one of the "
                             << "specified uppercase commands. "
                             << "Reenter and press return."
                             << endl;
                       cin  >> letter;
                       ok = false;
                       break;
        }
    }
}
```

Now we must design the data members and collect the operations that should be made member functions of class `HouseType`. Three of the data members are strings: last name, first name, and address. We can use `StrType` defined in Chapter 2. The other three data members (price, square feet, and bedrooms) are of simple types. We incorporate these data members into the following header file, `ItemType.h`, along with the prototypes of the member functions required by the program.

Note that the header file is named `ItemType.h`, not `HouseType.h`, because the code for our Sorted List ADT uses the directive `#include ''ItemType.h''`. Note also the Typedef statement at the bottom of the header file. Because the Sorted List ADT expects the list items to be of type `ItemType`, we use the `typedef` to make `ItemType` an alias for `HouseType`.

```
// ItemType.h contains the specifications for the data for the real
// estate manipulation program.

const int MAX_ITEMS = 200;

#include <fstream.h>
#include "StrType.h"                    // Gain access to String ADT.
```

```
class HouseType
{
public:
    void GetFromFile(ifstream&);
    void WriteToFile(ofstream&) const;
    void GetFromUser();
    void PrintHouseToScreen() const;
    void GetNameFromUser();
    void PrintNameToScreen() const;
    RelationType ComparedTo(HouseType) const;
private:
    StrType lastName;
    StrType firstName;
    StrType address;
    float price;
    int squareFeet;
    int bedRooms;
};
// Make ItemType an alias for HouseType.
typedef HouseType ItemType;
```

Each of the member functions is short and straightforward. The operations in StrType help with the input/output and the comparison of two HouseType objects. We assume that StrType overloads the "<" operator.

```
// IMPLEMENTATION FILE FOR HouseType
#include "ItemType.h"
#include <iostream.h>
#include <fstream.h>

void HouseType::GetFromFile(ifstream& file)
{
    lastName.GetStringFile(true, NOT_NEW, file);
    firstName.GetStringFile(true, NOT_NEW, file);
    address.GetStringFile(true, NOT_NEW, file);
    file >> price  >> squareFeet >> bedRooms;
}

void HouseType::WriteToFile(ofstream& file) const
{
    lastName.PrintToFile( false, file);
    firstName.PrintToFile(true, file);
    address.PrintToFile(true, file);
    file << endl  << price  << endl;
    file << squareFeet  << endl;
```

```
        file  << bedRooms  << endl;
}

void HouseType::GetFromUser()
{
    cout  << "Enter last name; press return."  << endl;
    lastName.GetString(true, NOT_NEW);
    cout  << "Enter first name; press return."  << endl;
    firstName.GetString(true, NOT_NEW);
    cout  << "Enter address; press return."  << endl;
    address.GetString(true, NOT_NEW);
    cout  << "Enter price, square feet, number of bedrooms;"
          << " press return." << endl;
    cin >> price  >> squareFeet >> bedRooms;
}

void HouseType::PrintHouseToScreen() const
{
    firstName.PrintToScreen(false);
    cout  << " ";
    lastName.PrintToScreen(false);
    address.PrintToScreen(true);
    cout  << endl  << "Price: "  << price  << endl;
    cout  << "Square Feet: "  << squareFeet  << endl;
    cout  << "Bedrooms: "  << bedRooms  << endl;
}

void HouseType::GetNameFromUser()
{
    cout  << "Enter last name; press return."  << endl;
    lastName.GetString(true, NOT_NEW);
    cout  << "Enter first name; press return."  << endl;
    firstName.GetString(true, NOT_NEW);
}

void HouseType::PrintNameToScreen() const
{
    firstName.PrintToScreen(false);
    cout  << " ";
    lastName.PrintToScreen(false);
    cout  << endl;
}

RelationType HouseType::ComparedTo(HouseType house) const
{
    if (lastName < house.lastName)
        return LESS;
    else if (house.lastName < lastName)
```

```
        return GREATER;
    else if ( firstName < house.firstName)
        return LESS;
    else if (house.firstName < firstName)
        return GREATER;
    else return EQUAL;
}
```

In this extended example, we have walked through the design process from the informal problem statement through the coding phase. We have not, however, written a formal specification. We leave the writing of the formal specification as an exercise.

TEST PLAN

Classes `SortedType` and `StrType` have been thoroughly tested. This leaves class `HouseType` and the main function to test. To test `HouseType`, we would need to create a test driver program to call the member functions. But recall that the member functions were determined to be those the main function (or driver) needs. Therefore, we can use the main function as the test driver to test `HouseType`. In other words, we can test them both together.

The first task is to create a master file of houses by using the Add command to input several houses and quit. We then need to input a variety of commands to add more houses, delete houses, print the list of owners, and print the information about a particular owner's house. All of the error conditions must be thoroughly tested. The program must be run several times in order to test the access and preservation of the data base (file `houses.mf`). We leave the final test plan as a programming assignment (Chapter 3, Programming Assignment 3).

In the discussion of object-oriented design in Chapter 1, we said that the code responsible for coordinating the objects is called a driver. Now, we can see why. A driver program in testing terminology is a program whose role is to call various subprograms and observe their behavior. In object-oriented terminology, a program is a collection of collaborating objects. Therefore, the role of the main function is to invoke operations on certain objects, i.e., get them started collaborating, so the term driver is appropriate. In subsequent chapters, when we use the term driver, the meaning should be clear from the context.

■‖ *Summary*

In this chapter, we have created two abstract data types that represent lists. The Unsorted List ADT assumes that the list elements are not sorted by key; the Sorted List ADT assumes that the list elements are sorted by key. We have viewed each from three perspectives: the logical level, the application level, and the implementation level. The extended Case Study uses the Sorted List ADT in a problem. Figure 3.14 shows the relationships among the three views of the list data in the Case Study.

In order to make the software as reusable as possible, the specification of each ADT states that the user of the ADT must prepare a class that defines the objects to be in each container class. A member function Compa redTo that compares two objects of this class must be included in the definition. This function returns one of the constants in RelationType: LESS, EQUAL, GREATER. By requiring the user to provide this information about the objects on the list, the code of the ADTs is very general. The Unsorted List or Sorted List ADT can process items of any kind; they are completely context independent. The value of this independence was shown in the Case Study.

The operations on the two ADTs were compared using Big-O notation. Insertion into an unsorted list has $O(1)$; insertion into a sorted list has $O(N)$. Deletions from both have $O(N)$. Searching in the unsorted list has $O(N)$; searching in a sorted list has order $O(\log_2 N)$ if a binary search is used.

Because a class object is an active structure, class constructor and destructor operations can be written so that the object is responsible for both its creation and destruction. A class constructor that converts storage space allocated to the object into a specific type by initializing the necessary variables is implicitly invoked each time an object of the class is defined. A class

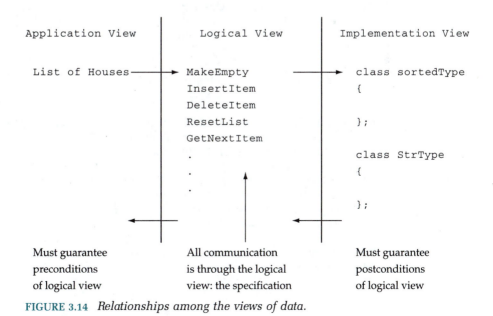

```
Application View              Logical View              Implementation View


List of Houses ────────►  MakeEmpty        ──────────►   class sortedType
                          InsertItem                     {
                          DeleteItem
                          ResetList                       };
                          GetNextItem

                               •                         class StrType
                               •                         {
                               •

                                                          };
```

Must guarantee   All communication   Must guarantee
preconditions   is through the logical   postconditions
of logical view   view: the specification   of logical view

FIGURE 3.14 *Relationships among the views of data.*

destructor is implicitly called each time an object of the class goes out of scope.

We have demonstrated how to write test plans by preparing them for the List ADTs.

■|| *Exercises*

1. The Unsorted List ADT is to be extended with a Boolean member function, IsThere, which takes as a parameter an item of type ItemType and determines whether there is an element with this key in the list.
   (a) Write the specifications for this function.
   (b) Write the prototype for this function.
   (c) Write the function definition.
   (d) Describe this function in terms of Big-O.

2. The Sorted List ADT is to be extended with a Boolean member function, IsThere, which takes as a parameter an item of type ItemType and determines whether there is an element with this key in the list.
   (a) Write the specifications for this function.
   (b) Write the prototype for this function.
   (c) Write the function definition using the binary search algorithm.
   (d) Describe this function in terms of Big-O.

3. Write a paragraph comparing your answers in Exercises 1 and 2.

4. Rather than enhancing the Unsorted List ADT by adding a member function IsThere, you decide to write a client function to do the same task.
   (a) Write the specifications for this function.
   (b) Write the function definition.
   (c) Describe this function in terms of Big-O.
   (d) Write a paragraph comparing the client function and the member function (Exercise 1) for the same task.

5. Rather than enhancing the Sorted List ADT by adding a member function IsThere, you decide to write a client function to do the same task.
   (a) Write the specifications for this function.
   (b) Write the function definition.
   (c) Were you able to use the binary search algorithm? Explain your answer.
   (d) Describe this function in terms of Big-O.
   (e) Write a paragraph comparing the client function and the member function (Exercise 2) for the same task.

6. Write a client function that merges two instances of the Sorted List ADT using the following specification.

MergeLists(SortedType list1, SortedType list2, SortedType& result)

Function:	Merges two sorted lists into a third sorted list.
Preconditions:	list1 and list2 have been initialized and are sorted by key using function `ComparedTo`.
	list1 and list2 do not have any keys in common.
Postcondition:	result is a sorted list that contains all of the items from list1 and list2.

(a) Write the prototype for `MergeLists`.
(b) Write the code for the function.
(c) Describe the algorithm in terms of Big-O.

7. Rewrite Exercise 6, making `MergeLists` a member function of the Sorted List ADT.

8. A List ADT is to be extended by the addition of function `SplitLists`, which has the following specifications where ListType is either class `UnsortedType` or `SortedType`:

SplitLists(ListType list, ItemType item, ListType& list1, ListType& list2)

Function:	Divides list into two lists according to the key of item.
Preconditions:	list has been initialized and is not empty.
Postconditions:	list1 contains all the items of list whose keys are less than or equal to item's key.
	list2 contains all the items of list whose keys are greater than item's key.

(a) Implement `SplitLists` as a member function of the Unsorted List ADT.
(b) Implement `SplitLists` as a member function of the Sorted List ADT.
(c) Compare the algorithms used in (a) and (b).
(d) Implement `SplitLists` as a client function of the Unsorted List ADT.
(e) Implement `SplitLists` as a client function of the Sorted List ADT.

9. The specifications for the Unsorted List ADT state that the item to be deleted is in the list.
   (a) Rewrite the specification for `DeleteItem` so that the list is unchanged if the item to be deleted is not in the list.
   (b) Implement `DeleteItem` as specified in (a).
   (c) Rewrite the specification for `DeleteItem` so that all copies of the item to be deleted are removed if they exist.
   (d) Implement `DeleteItem` as specified in (c).

10. The specifications for the Sorted List ADT state that the item to be deleted is in the list.
   (a) Rewrite the specification for `DeleteItem` so that the list is unchanged if the item to be deleted is not in the list. (There is at most one such item.)
   (b) Implement `DeleteItem` as specified in (a).
   (c) Rewrite the specification for `DeleteItem` so that all copies of the item to be deleted are removed if they exist.
   (d) Implement `DeleteItem` as specified in (c).

11. Write a formal specification for the problem explored in the Case Study.

12. Give an example of an algorithm (other than the examples discussed in the chapter) that is
    (a) O(1) (b) O(N) (c) O(N²)

13. A routine to calculate the sum of the results of applying `int` function X to the values in array `data` contains the following code segment:

```
sumOfX = 0;
for (int index = 0; index < numberOfElements; index++)
    sumOfX = sumOfX + X(data[index]);
```

If the function X is O(N), what is the order of the algorithm with respect to `numberOfElements`?

14. Algorithm 1 does a particular task in a "time" of N^3 where N is the number of elements processed. Algorithm 2 does the same task in a "time" of $3N + 1000$.
    (a) What are the Big-O requirements of each algorithm?
    (b) Which algorithm is more efficient by Big-O standards?
    (c) Under what conditions, if any, would the "less efficient" algorithm execute more quickly than the "more efficient" algorithm?

15. Replace function `ComparedTo` in the Unsorted List ADT by assuming that member functions of `ItemType` overload the relational operators.

16. Replace function `ComparedTo` in the Sorted List ADT by assuming that member functions of `ItemType` overload the relational operators.

ADTs Stack and Queue

GOALS

- To be able to describe a stack and its operations at a logical level
- To be able to demonstrate the effect of stack operations using a particular implementation of a stack
- To be able to implement the Stack ADT in an array-based implementation
- To be able to declare variables of pointer types
- To be able to access the variables to which pointers point
- To be able to create and access dynamically allocated data
- To be able to explain the difference between static and dynamic allocation of the space in which the elements of an abstract data type are stored
- To be able to use the C++ template mechanism for defining generic data types
- To be able to define and use an array in dynamic storage
- To be able to describe the structure of a queue and its operations at a logical level
- To be able to demonstrate the effect of queue operations using a particular implementation of a queue
- To be able to implement the Queue ADT using an array-based implementation

■ ‖ *Stacks*

In Chapter 2, we looked at the built-in structures in C++ from the logical view, the application view, and the implementation view. We saw that at the language level, the logical view is the syntax of the construct itself, and the implementation view is hidden within the compiler. In Chapter 3, we defined the ADTs Unsorted List and Sorted List. For these user-defined ADTs, the logical view is the class definition where the documentation on the prototypes of the member functions becomes the interface between the client program and the ADT. In this chapter, we examine two very useful ADTs: the stack and the queue. We begin with the stack.

Logical Level

Consider the items pictured in Figure 4.1. Although the objects are all different, each illustrates a common concept—the **stack**. At the logical level, a stack is an ordered group of homogeneous items or elements. The removal of existing items and the addition of new ones can take place only at the top of the stack. For instance, if your favorite blue shirt is underneath a faded, old, red one in a stack of shirts, you must first remove the red shirt (the top item) from the stack. Only then can you remove the desired blue shirt, which is now the top item in the stack. The red shirt may then be replaced on the top of the stack or thrown away.

The stack may be considered an "ordered" group of items because elements occur in a sequence according to how long they've been in the stack.

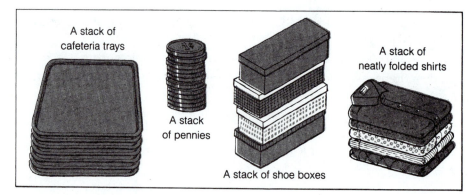

FIGURE 4.1   *Real-life stacks.*

The items that have been in the stack the longest are at the bottom; the most recent are at the top. At any time, given any two elements in a stack, one is higher than the other. (For instance, the red shirt was higher in the stack than the blue shirt.)

Because items are added and removed only from the top of the stack, the last element to be added is the first to be removed. There is a handy mnemonic to help you remember this rule of stack behavior: a stack is a LIFO (**L**ast **In**, **F**irst **Out**) structure.

Stack   An abstract data type in which elements are added and removed from only one end; a "last in, first out" (LIFO) structure

---

The accessing protocol for a stack is summarized as follows: both to retrieve elements and to store new elements, access only the top of the stack.

Operations on Stacks

The logical picture of the structure is only half the definition of an abstract data type. The other half is a set of operations that allows the user to access and manipulate the elements stored in the structure. Given the logical view of a stack, what kinds of operations do we need in order to use a stack?

The operation that adds an element to the top of a stack is usually called *Push*, and the operation that takes the top element off the stack is referred to as *Pop*. When we begin using a stack, it should be empty, so from here on, we assume that each ADT is implemented with at least a default class constructor. We also need a client operation that sets the stack to empty: *MakeEmpty*. We must also be able to tell whether a stack contains any elements before we pop it, so we need a Boolean operation *IsEmpty*. As a logical data structure, a stack is never conceptually "full," but for a particular implementation you may need to test whether a stack is full before pushing. We call this Boolean operation *IsFull*. Figure 4.2 shows how a stack, envisioned as a stack of building blocks, is modified by several Push and Pop operations.

We now have a logical picture of a stack and are almost ready to use the stack in a program. The part of the program that uses the stack, of course, won't be concerned with how the stack is actually implemented—we want the implementation level to be hidden, or encapsulated. The accessing operations such as Push and Pop are the windows into the stack encapsulation, through which the stack's data are passed. The interfaces to the accessing operations are described in the following specification for the Stack ADT.

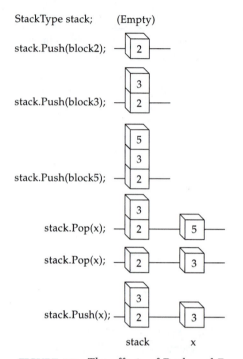

StackType stack;   (Empty)

stack.Push(block2);

stack.Push(block3);

stack.Push(block5);

stack.Pop(x);

stack.Pop(x);

stack.Push(x);

stack   x

FIGURE 4.2   *The effects of Push and Pop operations.*

Stack ADT Specification

Structure:	Elements are added to and removed from the top of the stack.
Definitions	(provided by user):
MAX_ITEMS:	Maximum number of items that might be on the stack.
ItemType:	Data type of the items on the stack.
Operations	(provided by the ADT):

MakeEmpty
Function:	Sets stack to an empty state.
Preconditions:	None
Postcondition:	Stack is empty.

Boolean IsEmpty
Function:	Determines whether the stack is empty.
Precondition:	Stack has been initialized.
Postcondition:	Function value = (stack is empty)

Boolean IsFull

Function:	Determines whether the stack is full.
Precondition:	Stack has been initialized.
Postcondition:	Function value = (stack is full)

Push(ItemType newItem)

Function:	Adds newItem to the top of the stack.
Preconditions:	Stack has been initialized and is not full.
Postcondition:	newItem is at the top of the stack.

Pop(ItemType& item)

Function:	Removes top item from stack and returns it in item.
Preconditions:	Stack has been initialized and is not empty.
Postconditions:	Top element has been removed from stack. item is a copy of removed element.

Application Level

Now let's look at an example of how the stack operations might be used in a program. To this point, you have used the extraction operator (>>) to input values of type `float`. Let's look behind this abstraction and see what the code to input floating point numbers might look like.

ReadReal (ifstream& inFile, float& realNumber, Boolean& error)

Function:	Reads characters representing a real number from inFile and converts them to type float. A number terminates with a whitespace character; any other nonnumeric characters (except a decimal point) generate an error.
Preconditions:	inFile has been opened and is ready for reading.
Postconditions:	error is true if realNumber terminates with a nonwhitespace character. If error, realNumber is undefined; otherwise, realNumber is the floating point representation of the input characters. inFile is left positioned after the terminating character.

This function reads in the characters representing a real number and converts them into a value of type `float`. Postponing the error processing momentarily, we use the following algorithm:

ReadReal

> Convert the "whole" part of the number
>
> IF decimal point found
>   Convert the "decimal" part of the number
>
> Add the whole and decimal parts

To convert the whole part of the number, we read and process characters until a nonnumeric character is encountered.

ConvertWholePart

> Skip whitespace
> Set number to 0
> Get numeral from inFile
>
> WHILE numeral is a digit
>   Set number to number * 10 + numeric equivalent of numeral
>   Get next numeral from inFile

In each iteration, the numeric conversion of the characters previously read is multiplied by 10, and the product is added to the numeric equivalent of numeral. Let's walk through this loop with the input 1234.567.

Before loop (after "priming" read):
        number = 0   numeral = '1'
After first iteration:
        number = (10 * 0) + 1 = 1   numeral = '2'
After second iteration:
        number = (10 * 1) + 2 = 12   numeral = '3'
After third iteration:
        number = (10 * 12) + 3 = 123   numeral = '4'
After fourth iteration:
        number = (10 * 123) + 4 = 1234   numeral = '.'
numeral is not a digit. *Stop!*

When the loop terminates, number contains the conversion of all the characters we have read, except for the last one. numeral still contains the last character read. At this point, there are three possible scenarios:

1. numeral is a whitespace character, in which case the real number ended with no decimal part (realNumber is number converted to floating point and error is false).
2. numeral is a decimal point ('.'), in which case we need to read and convert the decimal part of the number (error is false so far). Or
3. numeral is any other character, in which case error is true.

Scenarios 1 and 3 terminate the function and need no further decomposition, but scenario 2 needs more work. To convert the characters that follow the decimal point, we need to read characters until a nonnumeric character is encountered. In each iteration of the reading loop, the numeric conversion of the characters that were previously read is divided by 10, and the result is added to the numeric equivalent of numeral.

ConvertDecimalPart

Set decimal to 0.0
Get numeral from inFile

WHILE numeral is a digit
    Set decimal to (decimal/10) + numeric equivalent of numeral
    Get next numeral from inFile

Let's walk through this algorithm with the input 567 (the part that follows the decimal point in our original input 1234.567):

Before loop (after "priming" read):
    decimal = 0.0   numeral = '5'
After first iteration:
    decimal = (0/10) + 5 = 5   numeral = '6'
After second iteration:
    decimal = (5/10) + 6 = 6.5   numeral = '7'
After third iteration:
    decimal = (6.5/10) + 7 = 7.65   numeral = ' '

Whoops—our digits are coming out backward! What we need to do is to start at the last digit of the number and move toward the decimal point. That is, we need to process the digits in the reverse order from the order in which they were read.

A stack is great for reversing data, because the last element put into the stack is the first one out (LIFO). Our reading loop must be modified to read until a nonnumeric character is encountered, pushing each numeral onto a stack. To simplify the processing, we assume that the stack is large enough to contain all the numerals in the decimal part:

ConvertDecimalPart (Read and Push)

> CreateStack
> Get numeral from inFile
> WHILE numeral is a digit
>   Push numeral onto stack
>   Get next numeral from inFile

Let's trace this loop with the input 567 (following the decimal point):

Before loop (after "priming" read):
            stack: (empty)   numeral = '5'
After first iteration:
            stack: '5'   numeral = '6'
After second iteration:
            stack: '6' '5'   numeral = '7'
After third iteration:
            stack: '7' '6' '5'   numeral = ' '

After we have read and pushed all the numeric characters, we enter a second loop. In each iteration of the loop body, we pop the stack, putting the top item into numeral, and process it: the numeric conversion of the characters that were previously popped is divided by 10, and the result is added to the numeric equivalent of numeral.

ConvertDecimalPart (Pop and Calculate)

> WHILE stack is not empty
>   Pop stack into numeral
>   Set decimal to (decimal/10) + numeric equivalent of numeral.

Before loop
            stack: '7' '6' '5'   numeral = ' '   decimal = 0.0
After first iteration:
            stack: '6' '5'   numeral = '7'   decimal = (0/10) + 7 = 7
After second iteration:
            stack: '5'   numeral = '6'   decimal = (7/10) + 6 = 67
After third iteration:
            stack: (empty)   numeral = '5'   decimal = (6.7/10) + 5 = 5.67

Now the digits are in the correct order, but the result is off by one decimal point.

In setting the output parameter, realNumber, we correct this situation as follows:

AddWholeAndDecimalParts

> Set realNumber to number + (decimal/10)

To complete our example, realNumber = 1234 + (5.67/10) = 1234.567.

There is one more possibility to consider. The number might be negative. To determine the sign of the result, we check the first nonwhitespace character; if it is a minus sign, we need to multiply the answer by -1 to get the correct sign.

In coding this function we insert additional error checking into the ConvertDecimalPart algorithm to set error to true if the decimal part terminates in a nonnumeric, nonwhitespace character. If this error occurs, we must empty the stack, which may still contain items.

```
void ReadReal(ifstream& inFile, float& realNumber, bool& error)
// Function: Reads characters representing a real number from
//           inFile and converts them to type float.  A number
//           terminates with a whitespace character; any other
//           nonnumeric characters (except a decimal point) generate
//           an error.
// Pre:  inFile has been opened and is ready for reading.
// Post: error is true if realNumber terminates with a nonwhitespace
//           character.  If error, realNumber is undefined; otherwise,
//           realNumber is the floating point representation of the
//           input characters.  inFile is left positioned after the
//           terminating character.
{
    int number = 0;
    float decimal = 0.0;
    float signFactor;    // Determines the sign of the result
    char numeral;
    StackType stack;     // Assumes a StackType class exists

    error = false;
    inFile >> numeral;   // Automatically skips whitespace
    if (numeral == '-')  // Number is negative
    {
        signFactor = -1.0;
        inFile.get(numeral);
    }
```

```
    else                    // Number is nonnegative
        signFactor = 1.0;


// Calculate the whole part
while (isdigit(numeral))
{
    number = (10 * number) + int(numeral) - int ('0');
    inFile.get(numeral);
}

if (isspace(numeral))
    realNumber = number * signFactor;  // No decimal part
else
{
    if (numeral == '.')
    {
        inFile.get(numeral);
        while (isdigit(numeral))    // Put digits on the stack
        {
            stack.Push(numeral);
            inFile.get(numeral);
        }
        if (isspace(numeral))
        {
            while (!stack.IsEmpty())
            {
                stack.Pop(numeral);
                decimal = int(numeral)- int('0') + decimal/10;
            };
            realNumber = (number + decimal/10) * signFactor;
        }
        else
        {
            error = true;
            stack.MakeEmpty();
        }
    }
    else
        error = true;
}
}
```

In writing function ReadReal, we have been acting as stack users. We have written an interesting stack application, without even considering how the stack is implemented. The stack user doesn't need to know the implementation! The details of the implementation are hidden inside the StackType class.

Implementation Level

We now consider the implementation of our Stack ADT. After all, our functions Push and Pop are not magically available to the C++ programmer. We need to write these routines in order to include them in a program.

Because all the elements of a stack are of the same type, an array seems like a reasonable structure to contain them. We can put elements into sequential slots in the array, placing the first element pushed into the first array position, the second element pushed into the second array position, and so on. The floating "high-water" mark is the top element in the stack. Why this sounds just like our Unsorted List ADT implementation! info[length - 1] is the top of the stack.

Be careful: we are not saying that a stack is an unsorted list. A stack and an unsorted list are two entirely different abstract data types. What we are saying is that we can use the same implementation strategy.

Definition of Stack Class We implement our Stack ADT as a C++ class. Just as we did for the various versions of the List ADT, we require the user to provide us with a class ItemType, which defines the items on the stack. However, we do not need a comparison function because none of the operations require comparing two items on the stack.

What data members does our Stack ADT need? We need the stack items themselves and a variable indicating the top of the stack (which behaves the same as length in the List ADT). What about error conditions? Our specifications leave the error checking to the user by means of preconditions on the stack operations.

```
#include ItemType.h
// ItemType.h must be provided by the user of this class.
// This file must contain the following definitions:
//    MAX_ITEMS:    the maximum number of items on the stack
//    ItemType:     the class definition of the objects on the stack

class StackType
{
public:
    StackType();
    void MakeEmpty();
    bool IsEmpty() const;
    bool IsFull() const;
    void Push(ItemType item);
    void Pop(ItemType& item);
private:
    int top;
    ItemType items[MAX_ITEMS];
};
```

Definitions of Stack Operations   In the List ADT, length indicated how many items were on the list. In the Stack ADT, top indicates which is the top element. So our analogy to the List ADT is off by one. MakeEmpty and the class constructor should set top to -1 rather than 0. IsEmpty should compare top to -1 and IsFull should compare top with MAX_ITEMS -1.

```
StackType::StackType()
{
    top = -1;
}

void StackType::MakeEmpty()
{
    top = -1;
}

bool StackType::IsEmpty() const
{
    return (top == -1);
}

bool StackType::IsFull() const
{
    return (top == MAX_ITEMS-1);
}
```

Now, we have to write the algorithm to Push an item on the top of the stack and Pop an item from the top of the stack. Push must increment top and store the new item into items[top].

```
void StackType::Push(ItemType newItem)
{
    top++;
    items[top] = newItem;
}
```

Before we call Push in a program, we must make sure that the stack is not already full.

```
if (!stack.IsFull())
    stack.Push(item);
```

If the stack is already full when we invoke Push, the resulting condition is called **stack overflow**. Error checking for overflow conditions may be handled in a number of different ways. We could check for overflow inside Push, instead of making the calling program do the test. In that case we would need to tell the caller whether or not the Push was possible, which we could do by adding a Boolean variable overFlow to the parameter list. Here is the revised algorithm.

Push (Checks for Overflow)

IF stack is full
    Set overFlow to true
ELSE
    Set overFlow to false
    Increment top
    Set items[top] to newItem

Which version of Push we decide to use in a program depends on the specifications. Our Stack ADT specification uses the first version because the precondition for Push states that the stack is not full. If the member functions and their calling programs are being written by different programmers, as often happens, or we are writing a routine to put into a software library, it is important to establish whose responsibility it is to check for overflow, for this decision determines the number of parameters in the interface. (The second version of Push is left as an exercise.)

Stack Overflow   The condition resulting from trying to push an element onto a full stack

Pop is essentially the reverse of Push: we must return items [top] and decrement top.

```
void StackType::Pop(ItemType& item)
{
    item = items[top];
    top--;
}
```

To invoke Pop as implemented here, the caller must first test for an empty stack:

```
if (!stack.IsEmpty())
    stack.Pop(item);
```

If the stack is empty when we try to pop it, the resulting condition is called **stack underflow**. Just as we can test for overflow within the Push operation, we could test for underflow inside the Pop function. The algorithm for Pop would have to be modified slightly to return a Boolean value underFlow in addition to the popped item.

Stack Underflow   The condition resulting from trying to pop an empty stack

---

Figure 4.3 shows the result of pushing and popping where the stack items are characters.

Test Plan

The test plan for the Stack ADT is much like the test plan for the List ADT. Because we are testing the implementation of an abstract data type that we have just written, we use a clear-box strategy, checking each operation. Unlike the List ADT, we do not have an iterator that allows us to cycle through the items and print them. We must Push items onto the stack and then Pop and print them rather than printing the contents of the stack.

Because the type of data stored in the stack has no effect on the operations that manipulate the stack, we can define ItemType to represent int values and set MAX_ITEMS to 5, knowing that the code works the same whether MAX_ITEMS is 5 or 1000.

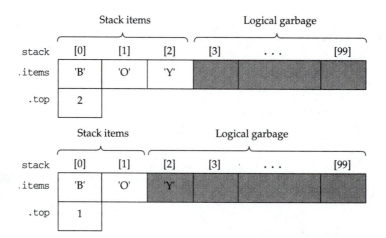

FIGURE 4.3   *The effect of a Pop following a series of Pushes.*

Operation to Be Tested and Description of Action	Input Values	Expected Output	Observed Output
Class constructor: apply IsEmpty immediately		Stack is empty	

Push and Pop:
  push 4 items, pop, and print
  push with duplicates and
  pop and print
	5, 7, 6, 9
	
	2, 3, 3, 4
		9, 6, 7, 5
		
		4, 3, 3, 2	

IsEmpty:
  invoke when empty
  push and invoke
		Stack is empty
		Stack is not empty	

IsFull: push 4 items and invoke push another item and invoke	1, 2, 3, 4 5	Stack is not full Stack is full.	
MakeEmpty: invoke and apply IsEmpty		Stack is empty	

■ll *More about Generics: C++ Templates*

In Chapter 3 we defined a generic data type as a type for which the operations are defined but the types of the items being manipulated are not. We have demonstrated how the list and the stack types can be generic by defining the type of items to be on the structure in a separate file `ItemType.h` and having the files containing the specifications for the list and stack types include that file. This technique works for any language that allows you to include or access other files. However, some languages have special language constructs that allow you to define generic data types. C++ is one of these. The construct is called a **template**. A template allows you to write a description of a class type with "blanks" left in the description to be filled in by the client code. Just as variables are the parameters to functions, types are the parameters to templates.

Template   A C++ language construct that allows the compiler to generate multiple versions of a class type or a function by allowing parameterized types

---

Let's look at how this construct works using the Stack ADT.

```
template<class ItemType>
class StackType
{
public:
    StackType();
    void MakeEmpty();
    bool IsEmpty() const;
    bool IsFull() const;
    void Push(ItemType item);
    void Pop(ItemType& item);
private:
    int top;
    ItemType items[MAX_ITEMS];
};
```

This code is known as a *class template*. The definition of `StackType` begins with `template<class ItemType>`, and `ItemType` is called the *formal parameter* to the template. (You could use any identifier for the formal parameter; we use `ItemType` in this example.) The client program uses code like the following to create several stacks whose components are of different data types:

```
// Client code
StackType<int> myStack;
StackType<float> yourStack;
StackType<StrType> anotherStack;

myStack.Push(35);
yourStack.Push(584.39);
```

In the definitions of `myStack`, `yourStack`, and `anotherStack`, the data type name enclosed in angle brackets is called the *actual parameter* to the template. At compile time, the compiler generates (*instantiates*) three distinct class types and gives its own internal name to each of the types. You might imagine that the definitions are transformed internally into something like this:

```
StackType_int myStack;
StackType_flo yourStack;
StackType_str anotherStack;
```

In C++ terminology, the three new class types are called *template classes* (as opposed to the *class template* from which they were created).

When the compiler instantiates a template, it literally substitutes the actual parameter for the formal parameter throughout the class template, just as you would do a search-and-replace operation in a word processor or text editor. For example, when the compiler encounters `StackType<float>` in the client code, it generates a new class by substituting `float` for every occurrence of `ItemType` in the class template. The result is the same as if we had written

```
class StackType_float
{
    .

    .

    .

    void Push( float item);
    void Pop( float& item);
private:
    int top;
    float items[MAX_ITEMS];
};
```

A useful perspective on templates is this: whereas an ordinary class definition is a pattern for stamping out individual variables or objects, a class template is a pattern for stamping out individual data types.

There are two things to note about parameters to templates. First, the class template uses the word `class` in its formal parameter list: `template<class ItemType>`. However, the word `class` is simply required syntax and does not mean that the client's actual parameter must be the name of a class. The actual parameter can be the name of any data type, built-in or user-defined. In the client code just shown, we used `int`, `float`, and `StrType` as actual parameters. Second, observe that when the client passes a parameter to the `StackType` template (as in `StackType<int>`), the parameter is a data type name, not a variable name. This seems strange at first, because when we pass parameters to functions, we always pass variable names or expressions, not data type names. Furthermore, note that passing a parameter to a template has an effect at *compile time*, whereas passing a parameter to a function has an effect at *run time*.

Now that we've seen how to write the definition of a class template, what do we do about the definitions of the member functions? We need to write them as *function templates* so that the compiler can associate each one with the proper template class. For example, we code the `Push` function as the following function template:

```
template<class ItemType>
StackType<ItemType>::Push(ItemType newItem)
{
    top++;
    items[top] = newItem;
}
```

Just as with the class template, we begin the function definition with
`template<class ItemType>`. Following this, every occurrence of the word
`StackType` must have `<ItemType>` appended to it. If the client has declared a
type `StackType<float>`, the compiler generates a function definition similar
to the following:

```
StackType_float::Push( float newItem)
{
    top++;
    items[top] = newItem;
}
```

Finally, when working with templates, we also change the ground rules
regarding which file(s) we put the source code into. Previously, we placed the
class definition into a header file `StackType.h` and the member function
definitions into `StackType.cpp`. As a result, `StackType.cpp` could be
compiled into object code independently of any client code. This strategy won't
work with templates. The compiler cannot instantiate a function template
unless it knows the actual parameter to the template, and this actual parameter
is found in the client code. Different compilers use different mechanisms to
solve this problem. One general solution is to compile the client code and the
member functions at the same time. A common technique is to place *both* the
class definition and the member function definitions into the same file:
`StackType.h`. Another technique is to give the `include` directive for the
implementation file at the end of the header file. Either way, when the client
code specifies `#include "StackType.h"`, the compiler has all the source
code—both the member functions and the client code—available to it at once.
The following is a listing of the contents of both the class definition and the
function implementations. Pay close attention to the required syntax of the
member function definitions.

```
// The class definition for StackType using templates

#include "MaxItems.h"
// MaxItems.h must be provided by the user of this class.
// This file must contain the definition of MAX_ITEMS,
// the maximum number of items on the stack.

template<class ItemType>
class StackType
{
public:
    StackType();
```

```cpp
    void MakeEmpty();
    bool IsEmpty() const;
    bool IsFull() const;
    void Push(ItemType item);
    void Pop(ItemType& item);
private:
    int top;
    ItemType items[MAX_ITEMS];
};

// The function definitions for class StackType.
template<class ItemType>
StackType<ItemType>::StackType()
{
    top = -1;
}

template<class ItemType>
void StackType<ItemType>::MakeEmpty()
{
    top = -1;
}

template<class ItemType>
bool StackType<ItemType>::IsEmpty() const
{
    return (top == -1);
}

template<class ItemType>
bool StackType<ItemType>::IsFull() const
{
    return (top ==  MAX_ITEMS-1);
}

template<class ItemType>
void StackType<ItemType>::Push(ItemType newItem)
{
    top++;
    items[top] = newItem;
}

template<class ItemType>
void StackType<ItemType>::Pop(ItemType& item)
{
    item = items[top];
    top--;
}
```

■‖ *Pointer Types*

Logical Level

Pointers are simple—not composite—types, but they do allow us to *create* composite types at run time. We describe the creation, accessing function, and one use in this chapter. In Chapter 5 we discuss another use in detail and use pointers in alternate implementations of the abstract data types defined in Chapters 3 and 4.

A pointer variable does not contain a data value in the ordinary sense; it contains the *memory address* of another variable. To declare a pointer that can point to an integer value, you use the following syntax.

```
int* intPointer;
```

The asterisk (*) as a postfix symbol on the type says that the variable being defined is a pointer to an object of that type: intPointer can point to a place in memory that can contain a value of type int. (Alternatively, the asterisk may be used as a prefix symbol on the variable name.) The contents of intPointer, like all newly defined variables, are undefined. Memory after this statement has been executed is shown in the following diagram. (For illustrative purposes, we assume that the compiler has allocated location 10 to intPointer.)

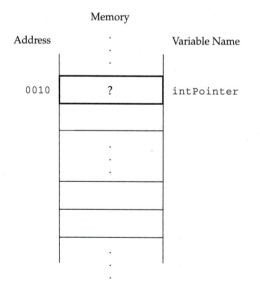

How do we get intPointer something to point to? One way is to use the prefix & operator, which is called the *address-of* operator. Given the declarations

```
int alpha;
int* intPointer;
```

the assignment statement

```
intPointer = &alpha;
```

takes the address of alpha and stores it into intPointer. If alpha is at address 33, memory looks like this:

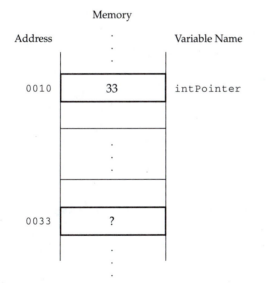

We have a pointer, we have a place to which the pointer points, but how do we access that place? An asterisk (*) as a prefix to the pointer name accesses the place to which the pointer points. The asterisk is called the **dereference operator**. Let's store 25 in the place to which intPointer points.

```
*intPointer = 25;
```

Dereference Operator   An operator that when applied to a pointer variable denotes the variable to which the pointer points

Memory now looks like this:

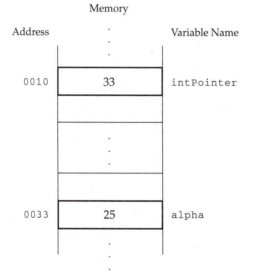

Because intPointer points to alpha, the statement

```
*intPointer = 25;
```

represents *indirect addressing* of alpha; the machine first accesses intPointer, then uses its contents to find alpha. In contrast, the statement

```
alpha = 10;
```

represents *direct addressing* of alpha. Direct addressing is like opening a post office box (P.O. Box 15, for example) and finding a package, whereas indirect addressing is like opening P.O. Box 15 and finding a note telling you that your package is sitting in P.O. Box 23.

A second method for getting `intPointer` something to point to is called **dynamic allocation**. In the previous example, the memory space for both `intPointer` and `alpha` was allocated *statically* (at compile time). Alternatively, our programs can allocate memory *dynamically* (at run time).

Dynamic Allocation   Allocation of memory space for a variable at run time (as opposed to static allocation at compile time)

To achieve dynamic allocation of a variable, we use the C++ operator `new`, followed by the name of a data type:

```
intPointer = new int;
```

At run time, the `new` operator allocates a variable capable of holding an `int` value and returns its memory address, which is then stored into `intPointer`. If the `new` operator returns the address 90 as a result of executing the preceding statement, memory looks like this:

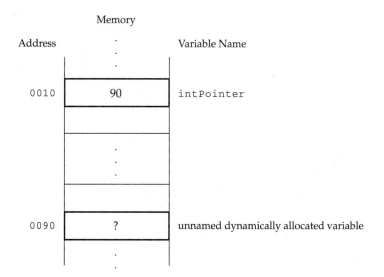

Variables created by `new` are said to be on the **free store** (or **heap**), a region of memory set aside for dynamic allocation. A dynamically allocated variable has no name and cannot be directly addressed. It must be indirectly addressed through the pointer returned by `new`.

Free Store (Heap)   A pool of memory locations reserved for dynamic allocation of data

---

There are times when we want a pointer to point to nothing. By definition in C++, a pointer value of 0 is called the *null* pointer; it points to nothing. To help distinguish the null pointer from the integer value 0, `<stddef.h>` contains the definition of a named constant `NULL` that we use instead of referring directly to 0. Let's look at a few more examples.

```
bool* truth = NULL;
float* money = NULL;
```

When drawing pictures of pointers, we use a diagonal line from upper right to lower left to indicate that the value is `NULL`.

Let's examine memory after a few more pointer manipulations.

```
truth = new bool;
*truth = true;
money = new float;
*money = 33.46;
float* myMoney = new float;
```

When drawing pictures of pointers and the objects to which they point, we use boxes and arrows.

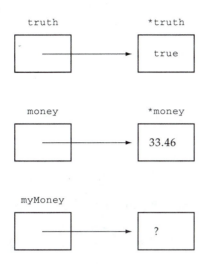

Any operation that can be applied to a constant or variable of type int can be applied to *intPointer. Any operation that can be applied to a constant or variable of type float can be applied to *money. Any operation that can be applied to a constant or variable of type bool can be applied to *truth. For example, we can read a value into *myMoney with the following statement.

```
cin >> *myMoney;
```

If the current value in the input stream is 99.86, then *myMoney contains 99.86 after the execution of the preceding statement.

Pointer variables can be compared for equality and can be assigned one to another as long as they point to variables of the same data type. Examine the following two statements.

```
*myMoney = *money;
myMoney = money;
```

The first statement copies the value in the place pointed to by money into the place pointed to by myMoney.

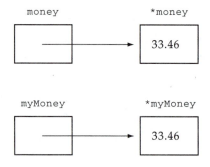

The second statement copies the value in money into myMoney, giving the following configuration:

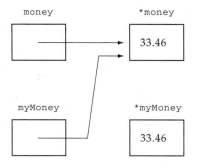

At this point the location that holds the second copy of 33.46 cannot be accessed; there is no longer any pointer that points to it. This situation is called a **memory leak**, and the memory cells that can no longer be accessed are called **garbage.** Some programming languages, such as Java, provide garbage collection; that is, the run-time support system periodically goes through memory and reclaims the memory locations for which there is no access path.

Memory Leak   The loss of available memory space that occurs when memory locations are allocated dynamically but never deallocated

Garbage   Memory locations that can no longer be accessed

To avoid memory leaks, C++ provides operator delete, which returns to the free store a memory location allocated previously by the new operator. It may be allocated again if need be. The following code segment prevents our memory leak.

```
delete myMoney;
myMoney = money;
```

The location originally pointed to by `myMoney` is no longer allocated. Note that `delete` does not delete the pointer variable, but the variable to which the pointer points.

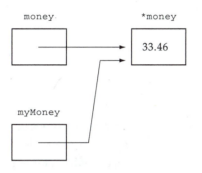

Notice the difference between assigning one pointer to another (`myMoney = money`) and assigning the pointed-to locations (`*myMoney = *money`). *Always be careful to distinguish between the pointer and the object to which it points!*

Application Level

Have you passed an array as a parameter? If so, you have used a *pointer constant*. The name of an array without any index brackets is a constant pointer expression: the base address of the array. Look at the following code segment.

```
char alpha[20];
char* alphaPtr;
char* letterPtr;
void Process(char[]);
    .
    .
    .
alphaPtr = alpha;
letterPtr = &alpha[0];
Process(alpha);
```

`alphaPtr` is assigned the constant pointer expression `alpha`; `letterPtr` is assigned the address of the first position in the array `alpha`. `alphaPtr` and `letterPtr` both contain the address of the first position in the array `alpha`. When the prototype for function `Process` says that it takes a `char` array as a parameter, it is expecting a pointer expression (the base address of the array) as an actual parameter. The calling statement therefore sends the name of the array without any index brackets to the function.

Pointers can be used with composite types as well.

```
struct MoneyType
{
    int dollars;
    int cents;
};

MoneyType* moneyPtr = new MoneyType;
moneyPtr->dollars = 3245;
moneyPtr->cents = 33;
```

The arrow operator `(->)` is a shortcut for dereferencing a pointer and accessing a struct or class member. That is, `moneyPtr->cents` is shorthand for `(*moneyPtr).cents`. (The dereferencing operator has a lower precedence than the dot operator, so the parentheses are necessary.)

In Chapter 5, we use the idea of a pointer pointing to a variable of a composite type in which one of the data members is a pointer to another variable of the same composite type. Using this technique, we can build *linked structures*. There is one named pointer called the *external pointer* to the structure, and the structure is chained together by having a data member in each variable in the chain be a pointer that points to the next one in the chain. The last variable in the chain has NULL in its pointer member.

Implementation Level

A pointer variable simply contains a memory address. The operating system controls memory allocation and grants memory to your program on request.

■ ▌▌ *Dynamically Allocated Arrays*

The template is a nice feature: it allows the client program to specify the type of the items on the structure at the time that an object of the data type is defined. Now, if we could just find a technique for the client to be able to specify the maximum number of items on the stack at the same time, we would not need to use an auxiliary file—and of course there is a way in C++. We can let the maximum number of items be a parameter to a class constructor. But the implementation structure is an array, and doesn't the compiler need to know at compile time what the size of an array is to be? Yes, it does if the array is in static storage, but memory for the array can be allocated at run time *if we let it be in dynamic storage (the free store or heap)*. This change requires the following changes in the class definition:

```cpp
template<class ItemType>
class StackType
{
public:
    StackType(int max);  // max is stack size.
    StackType();         // Default size is 500.
    // Rest of the prototypes go here.
private:
    int top;
    int maxStack;        // Maximum number of stack items.
    ItemType* items;     // Pointer to dynamically allocated memory.
};
```

When declaring a class object, the client can specify the maximum number of stack items by using the parameterized constructor:

```cpp
StackType<int> myStack(100);
// Integer stack of at most 100 items.

StackType<float> yourStack(50);
// Floating point stack of at most 50 items
```

Or the client can accept the default size of 500 by using the default constructor:

```cpp
StackType<char> aStack;
```

Within the function definition for each constructor, the idea is to use the new operator to allocate an array of exactly the desired size. Earlier we saw that the expression new SomeType allocates a single variable of type SomeType on the free store and returns a pointer to it. To allocate an array, you attach to the data type name the array size in brackets: new AnotherType[size]. In this case, the new operator returns the base address of the newly allocated array. Here are the implementations of the StackType constructors:

```
template<class ItemType>
StackType<ItemType>::StackType(int max)
{
    maxStack = max;
    top = -1;
    items = new ItemType[max];
}

template<class ItemType>
StackType<ItemType>::StackType()
{
    maxStack = 500;
    top = -1;
    items = new ItemType[500];
};
```

Notice that `items` is now a pointer variable, not an array name. It points to the first element of a dynamically allocated array. However, a basic fact in C++ is that you can attach an index expression to any pointer—not only an array name—as long as the pointer points to an array. Therefore `items` can be indexed exactly as it was when it was defined as an array of type `ItemType` (see Figure 4.4). Thus, only one member function needs to be changed: `IsFull`.

```
template<class ItemType>
bool StackType<ItemType>::IsFull() const
{
    return (top == maxStack-1);
}
```

We do, however, need to use a class destructor. If the stack is a local variable (and not declared as `static`), the memory allocated to the stack object is deallocated when the stack goes out of scope. That means that the memory allocated to `top`, `maxStack`, and `items` is deallocated, *but the array that* `items` *points to is not.* Therefore, we must include a class destructor that deallocates the array when the stack object goes out of scope. We include the following prototype in the `public` part of the class definition:

```
~StackType(); // Destructor.
```

and implement the function as follows:

```
template<class ItemType>
StackType<ItemType>::~StackType()
{
    delete [] items;
}
```

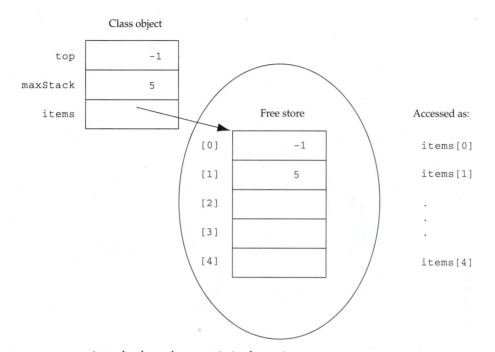

FIGURE 4.4 *A stack where the array is in dynamic storage.*

Note that to deallocate an array, you insert brackets between the word delete and the name of the pointer. See how this class destructor differs from the MakeEmpty operation? MakeEmpty resets the top data member so that the stack can be used again within the same scope. The class destructor releases the space that was allocated to the array. There is another distinction between the two: the MakeEmpty operation is a logical operation defined in the ADT specification, but the class destructor is an implementation level operation. Implementations that do not use dynamically allocated space usually do not need destructors.

Before we leave this StackType implementation, let's ask if it's necessary to provide both a parameterized constructor and a default constructor. Isn't the parameterized constructor good enough? In most cases, yes. However, the user may want to declare an array of stack objects, in which case the parameterized constructor cannot be used. (Remember the rule: if a class has any constructors at all and an array of class objects is declared, one of the constructors must be the default constructor, and it is invoked for each element in the array.) Therefore, it's wisest to include a default constructor in the StackType class to allow client code like this:

```
StackType<float> stackGroup[10];
// 10 stacks, each of size 500.
```

Lifetime of a Variable

The *lifetime* of a variable is the time during program execution when the variable has storage assigned to it.

- The lifetime of a global variable is the entire execution of the program.
- The lifetime of a local variable is the execution of the block in which it is declared.
- The lifetime of a dynamically allocated variable is from the time it is allocated (using `new`) until the time it is deallocated (using `delete`).

There are times when it is useful for a local variable to retain its value, so C++ lets the user extend the lifetime of a local variable to the entire run of the program. To do this, you preface the data type identifier with the reserved word `static` when the variable is defined. Otherwise, the default storage category for a local variable is *automatic*, meaning that storage is allocated on entry and deallocated on exit from a block.

CASE STUDY |||

POSTFIX EXPRESSION EVALUATION

Problem: *Postfix notation* is a notation for writing arithmetic expressions in which the operands appear before their operators. There are no precedence rules to learn, and parentheses are never needed. Because of this simplicity, some popular hand-held calculators use postfix notation to avoid the complications of the multiple parentheses required in nontrivial infix expressions (Figure 4.5). You are to write a computer program that simulates how these postfix calculators evaluate expressions.

Discussion: In elementary school you learned how to evaluate simple expressions that involve the basic binary operators: addition, subtraction, multiplication, and division. (These are called *binary* operators because they each operate on two operands.) It is easy to see how a child would solve the following problem:

$$2 + 5 = ?$$

As expressions become more complicated, the pencil-and-paper solutions require a little more work. A number of tasks must be performed to solve the following problem:

$$(((13 - 1) / 2)((3 + 5))) = ?$$

FIGURE 4.5 *A calculator that evaluates postfix expressions.*

These expressions are written using a format known as *infix* notation. This same notation is used for writing arithmetic expressions in C++. The operator in an infix expression is written in between its operands. When an expression contains multiple operators such as the one shown here, we need to use a set of rules to determine which operation to carry out first. You learned in your mathematics classes that multiplication is done before addition. You learned C++'s operator-precedence rules in your first programming class. In both situations, we use parentheses to override the normal ordering rules. It is easy to make a mistake writing or interpreting an infix expression containing multiple nested sets of parentheses.

EVALUATING POSTFIX EXPRESSIONS

Postfix notation is another format for writing arithmetic expressions. In this notation, the operator is written after the two operands. (We look at *prefix* notation, a third way to write expressions, in Chapter 9.) Here are some simple postfix expressions and their results.

Postfix Expression	Result
4 5 +	9
9 3 /	3
17 8 -	9

The rules for evaluating postfix expressions with multiple operators are much simpler than those for evaluating infix expressions; simply evaluate the operations from left to right. Now, let's look at a postfix expression containing two operators.

6 2 / 5 +

We evaluate the expression by scanning from left to right. The first item, 6, is an operand, so we go on. The second item, 2, is also an operand, so again we continue. The third item is the division operator. We now apply this operator to the two previous operands. Which of the two saved operands is the divisor? The one we saw most recently. We divide 6 by 2 and substitute 3 back into the expression replacing 6 2 / . Our expression now looks like this:

3 5 +

We continue our scanning. The next item is an operand, 5, so we go on. The next (and last) item is the operator +. We apply this operator to the two previous operands, obtaining a result of 8.

Here's another example.

4 5 + 7 2 - *

Scanning from left to right, the first operator we encounter is +. Applying this to the two preceding operands, we obtain the expression

9 7 2 - *

The next operator we encounter is -, so we subtract 2 from 7 obtaining

9 5 *

Finally, we apply the last operator, *, to its two preceding operands and obtain our final answer, 45.

Here are some more examples of postfix expressions containing multiple operators and the results of evaluating them. See if you get the same results when you evaluate them.

Postfix Expression	Result
4 5 7 2 + - *	-16
3 4 + 2 * 7 /	2
5 7 + 6 2 - *	48
4 2 3 5 1 - * + *	56
4 2 + 3 5 1 - * +	18

Our task is to write a program that evaluates postfix expressions entered interactively from the keyboard. (The algorithm for converting from infix notation to postfix notation is given in Chapter 4, Programming Assignment 2.) Before we specify our input exactly, let's look at the data objects involved in the problem solution.

DATA OBJECTS

As so often happens, our by-hand algorithm can be used as a guideline for our computer algorithm. From the previous discussion, we see that there are two basic objects: numbers and operators. We get items (a number or an operator) one at a time from the input stream. When the item we get is an operator, we apply it to the last two operands. Because we can't back up on the input line, we must save previously scanned operands in a container object of some kind. A stack is the ideal place to store the previous operands, because the top item is always the most recent operand and the next item on the stack is always the second most recent operand—just the two operands required when we find an operator. The following algorithm uses a stack in this manner to evaluate a postfix expression entered from the keyboard.

EvaluateExpression

```
WHILE more input items exist
    Get an item
    IF item is an operand
        stack.Push(item)
    ELSE
        stack.Pop(operand2)
        stack.Pop(operand1)
        Set result to operand1 item operand2
        stack.Push(result)
stack.Pop(result)
```

Each iteration of this loop processes one operator or one operand from the input line. When an operand is found, there is nothing to do with it (we haven't yet found the operator to apply to it) so we save it on the stack until later. When an operator is found, we get the two operands from the stack, do the operation, and put the result back on the stack; the result may be an operand for a future operator.

Let's trace this algorithm. Before we enter the loop, the input that has not yet been processed and the stack look like this.

```
5 7 + 6 2 - *
```

After one iteration of the loop, we have processed the first operand and pushed it onto the stack.

```
5 7 + 6 2 - *

           5
```

After the second iteration of the loop, the stack contains two operands.

```
5 7 + 6 2 - *

           7
           5
```

We encounter the + operator in the third iteration. We pop the two operands from the stack, perform the operation, and push the result onto the stack.

```
5 7 + 6 2 - *

          12
```

In the next two iterations of the loop, we push two operands onto the stack.

5 7 + 6 2 - *

```
  2
  6
 12
```

When we find the - operator, we pop the top two operands, subtract, and push the result onto the stack.

5 7 + 6 2 - *

```
  4
 12
```

When we find the * operator, we pop the top two operands, multiply, and push the result onto the stack.

5 7 + 6 2 - *

```
 48
```

Now that we have processed all of the items on the input line, we exit the loop. We pop the final result, 48, from the stack.

5 7 + 6 2 - *

Result
48

Of course, we have glossed over a few "minor" details, such as how we recognize an operator and how we know when we are finished. All the input values were one-digit numbers. Clearly, this is too restrictive. Let's look at the specifications shown in Figure 4.6.

Specification: Program Postfix Evaluation

Function

The program evaluates arithmetic expressions containing real numbers and the operators +, -, *, and /.

Input

The input is a series of arithmetic expressions entered interactively from the keyboard in postfix notation. The user is prompted to enter an expression made up of operators (the characters '+', '-', '*', and '/') and real numbers. The end of the expression is marked by the expression terminator character, '='. Operators and operands must be terminated by at least one blank.

Real numbers must be expressed in decimal format: the whole part, followed by a decimal point ('.'), followed by the decimal part. The decimal point and the decimal part are optional. Exponential notation (that is, 3.2E3) is not valid.

The user terminates the program by entering the character "#" instead of a new expression.

Output

The user is prompted for each new expression to be evaluated with the following prompt:

"Enter expression to evaluate or a # to quit."

After the evaluation of each expression, the results are printed to the screen:
"Result = *value*"

where *value* is a real number in decimal format, with a field width of 8 and a decimal field of 4.

Processing Requirements

1. This program must read real-number inputs as characters and make the appropriate conversions.

Assumptions

1. The expressions are correctly entered in postfix notation.
2. Each expression is terminated by '='.
3. The operations in expressions are valid at run time. This means that we do not try to divide by zero.

FIGURE 4.6   *Specification for postfix evaluator.*

The specification tells us that the end of an expression is recognized when the operator is an equal sign. It also tells us that the data values are real and that the program must read them as characters. That's easy: we just wrote a function that read real numbers in character format from a file. We may have to modify it somewhat, but we have the basic algorithm.

Unions

A union is like a struct except that it holds only *one* of its members at a time while the program is executing. Given the declaration

```
union
{
    int i;
    float x;
    char ch;
};
```

all of i, x, and ch share the same memory space, *one at a time*. In the sequence of statements

```
i = 24;
x = 6.05;    // Previous int value is lost
```

the second assignment statement is probably not what the programmer wanted to do, because both i and x use the same memory location.

The union declared here is called an *anonymous union* because we have not given it a name.

The specification does *not* tell us how to determine if we have an operand or an operator; we are going to have to decide how to do that ourselves. In our algorithm we used the expression "Get an item" where the item could be either an operator or an operand. How can we represent two different objects in the same variable? C++ provides a data type that is ideal for this situation: the *union*. The union allows us to use a variable for multiple purposes. Using a union, we can declare a *variant record*. A variant record is a struct consisting of a type field and one or more anonymous unions. Here is what the item type would look like.

```
enum OpType {OPERATION, OPERAND};
struct ItemType
{
    OpType whichType;
    union
    {
        char operation;
        float operand;
    };
};
```

Variables `operation` and `operand` occupy the same space. (`operator` is a reserved word, so we used `operation` for our identifier.) We use member `whichType` to determine whether we have an operator or an operand.

GetAnItem

> Skip leading blanks
> IF first nonblank character is '0' ... '9' or a '-'
>   ReadReal(item.operand, character)
>   Set item.whichType to OPERAND
> ELSE
>   Set item.operation to character
>   Set item.whichType to OPERATION

Now all we need is to write the main function.

Main

> Write "Enter expression to evaluate or a # to quit:"
> GetAnItem(item)
> WHILE item.operation != '#'
>   EvaluateExpression(item)
>   Write "Enter expression to evaluate or # to quit:"
>   GetAnItem(item)

`EvaluateExpression` needs to be refined in light of our later design decisions.

EvaluateExpression (revised)

Set finished to false
WHILE !finished
   SWITCH (item.whichType)
      case OPERAND : stack.Push(item)
                        GetAnItem(item)
      case OPERATION :
        IF item.operator = '='
           Set finished to true
        ELSE
           stack.Pop(operand2)
           stack.Pop(operand1)
           Set result to operand1 operation operand2
           stack.Push(result)
           GetAnItem(item)
stack.Pop(result)
cout << "Result = " << result

The only task left is to modify the function that we wrote to read a real number. Because our specification states that the input expression is correct, we can remove the error checking. As we are reading the first digit outside the function, we must pass it as a parameter. Here is the code for the revised input routine.

```
void ReadReal( float& realNumber, char numeral)
// Function: Reads characters representing a real number from cin
//        and converts them to type float.  The first character is
//        passed as parameter numeral.  A number terminates with a
//        whitespace character.
// Pre:  numeral contains the first character of an input number.
// Post: realNumber is the floating point representation of the
//        input characters.
{
    int number = 0;
    float decimal = 0.0;
    float signFactor;        // Determines the sign of the result
    StackType<char> stack;   // Assumes a StackType class exists

    if (numeral == '-')      // Number is negative
    {
        signFactor = -1.0;
        cin.get(numeral);
    }
```

```
else                          // Number is not negative
    signFactor = 1.0;

// Calculate the whole part
while (isdigit(numeral))
{
    number = (10 * number) + int(numeral) - int ('0');
    cin.get(numeral);
}

if (isspace(numeral))
    realNumber = number * signFactor;     // No decimal part
else      // It's a '.'
{
    cin.get(numeral);
    while (isdigit(numeral))      // Put digits on the stack
    {
        stack.Push(numeral);
        cin.get(numeral);
    }
    while (!stack.IsEmpty())
    {
        stack.Pop(numeral);
        decimal = int(numeral)- int('0') + decimal/10;
    }
    realNumber = (number + decimal/10) * signFactor;
}
}
```

We leave the coding of the rest of the algorithms as Chapter 4, Programming Assignment 1.

Queues

Logical Level

A stack is an abstract data structure with the special property that elements are always added to and removed from the top. We know from experience that many collections of data elements operate in the reverse manner: items are added at one end and removed from the other. This structure, called a FIFO (First In, First Out) queue, has many uses in computer programs. We consider the FIFO queue data structure at three levels: logical, implementation, and application. In the rest of this chapter, "queue" refers to a FIFO queue. (Another queue-type abstract data type, the priority queue, is discussed in Chapter 9. The accessing protocol of a priority queue is different from that of a FIFO queue.)

A **queue** (pronounced like the letter Q) is an ordered, homogeneous group of elements in which new elements are added at one end (the "rear") and elements are removed from the other end (the "front"). As an example of a queue, consider a line of students waiting to pay for their textbooks at a university bookstore (see Figure 4.7). In theory, if not in practice, each new student gets in line at the rear. When the cashier is ready for a new customer, the student at the front of the line is served.

To add elements to a queue we access the rear of the queue; to remove elements we access the front. The middle elements are logically inaccessible, even if we physically store the queue elements in a random-access structure such as an array. It is convenient to picture the queue as a linear structure with the front at one end and the rear at the other end. However, we must stress that the "ends" of the queue are abstractions; they may or may not correspond to any physical characteristics of the queue's implementation. The essential property of the queue is its FIFO access.

Queue   A data structure in which elements are added to the rear and removed from the front; a "first in, first out" (FIFO) structure

---

FIGURE 4.7   *A FIFO queue.*

Like the stack, the queue is a holding structure for data that we use later. We put a data item onto the queue, and then when we need it we remove it from the queue. If we want to change the value of an element, we must take that element off the queue, change its value, and then return it to the queue. We do not directly manipulate the values of items that are currently in the queue.

Operations on Queues   The bookstore example suggests two operations that can be applied to a queue. First, new elements can be added to the rear of the queue, an operation that we call *Enqueue*. We can also take elements off the front of the queue, an operation that we call *Dequeue*. Unlike the stack operations Push and Pop, the adding and removing operations on a queue do not have standard names. Enqueue is sometimes called Enq, Enque, Add, or Insert; Dequeue is also called Deq, Deque, Remove, or Serve.

Another useful queue operation is checking whether the queue is empty. The *IsEmpty* function returns true if the queue is empty and false otherwise. We can only dequeue when the queue is not empty. Theoretically we can always enqueue, for in principle a queue is not limited in size. We know from our experience with stacks, however, that certain implementations (an array representation, for instance) require that we test whether the structure is full before we add another element. This real-world consideration applies to queues as well, so we define an *IsFull* operation. We also need an operation to initialize a queue to an empty state, which we call *MakeEmpty*. Figure 4.8 shows how a series of these operations would affect a queue. We have briefly described a set of accessing operations for a queue. Before we talk about its use and implementation, let's define the specification for the Queue ADT.

We continue to leave the statements in the specifications defining what the user must provide. However, as we are using C++, we assume that this information is provided when a class object is declared (in the form of a template parameter and a constructor parameter).

■ Queue ADT Specification

Structure:	Elements are added to rear and removed from the front of the queue.
Definitions	(provided by user):
MAX_ITEMS: ItemType:	Maximum number of items that might be on the queue. Data type of the items on the queue.

Operations   (provided by ADT):

MakeEmpty
 Function: Initializes the queue to an empty state.
 Preconditions: None
 Postcondition: Queue is empty.

Boolean IsEmpty
 Function: Determines whether the queue is empty.
 Precondition: Queue has been initialized.
 Postcondition: Function value = (queue is empty)

Boolean IsFull
 Function: Determines whether the queue is full.
 Precondition: Queue has been initialized.
 Postcondition: Function value = (queue is full)

Enqueue(ItemType newItem)
 Function: Adds newItem to the rear of the queue.
 Preconditions: Queue has been initialized and is not full.
 Postcondition: newItem is at rear of queue.

Dequeue(ItemType& item)
 Function: Removes front item from queue and returns it in item.
 Preconditions: Queue has been initialized and is not empty.
 Postconditions: Front element has been removed from queue.
       item is a copy of removed element.

Note that in this specification we made the caller of `Enqueue` and `Dequeue` responsible for checking for overflow and underflow conditions. As discussed in relation to stacks, these conditions could be checked inside the routines and a Boolean flag returned. The specifications of the `Enqueue` and `Dequeue` routines would have to be changed, of course. One of the exercises at the end of this chapter asks you to design and implement this version of the queue operations.

Application Level

Let's see how the queue operations might be used in a program. Suppose that we need a Boolean utility function that takes two files as input and returns true if they are identical except for formatting and punctuation and false otherwise. Function `FilesTheSame` is specified as follows:

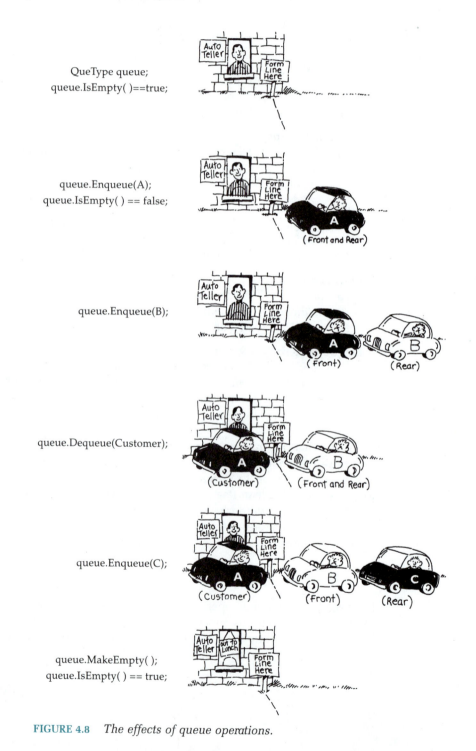

QueType queue;
queue.IsEmpty( )==true;

queue.Enqueue(A);
queue.IsEmpty( ) == false;

queue.Enqueue(B);

queue.Dequeue(Customer);

queue.Enqueue(C);

queue.MakeEmpty( );
queue.IsEmpty( ) == true;

FIGURE 4.8   *The effects of queue operations.*

■ **Boolean FilesTheSame(ifstream& inFile1, ifstream& inFile2)**

Function:	Determines if inFile1 and inFile2 are the same except for formatting and punctuation.
Preconditions:	Both files have been opened and are positioned at the beginning.
Postcondition:	Function value = (files are identical except for formatting and punctuation)

If all the strings made up of only alphanumeric characters are the same in both files, then the files are the same except for formatting and punctuation. The algorithm for this function uses two queues. The objects on the queues are of type StrType, defined in Chapter 2. We use function GetStringFile with the parameters set so that alphanumeric characters are allowed and leading non-alphanumeric characters are skipped.

Boolean FilesTheSame(ifstream& inFile1, ifstream& inFile2)

```
WHILE (inFile1)
    string1.GetStringFile(true, ALPHA_NUM, infile1)
    q1.Enqueue(string1)
WHILE (inFile2)
    string2.GetStringFile(true, ALPHA_NUM, infile2)
    q2.Enqueue(string2)

Set same to true
WHILE !(q1.IsEmpty()) AND !(q2.IsEmpty()) AND same
    q1.Dequeue(string1)
    q2.Dequeue(string2)
    IF string1.ComparedTo(string2) != EQUAL
        Set same to false
return (same AND q1.IsEmpty() AND q2.IsEmpty())
```

Does this algorithm work in all cases? The algorithm works when the files are the same length and are identical except for formatting. It works when the files do not have the same data or one file has more data than the other—no, we missed a case. Non-alphanumeric characters are discarded before reading if they exist, but what happens if one of the files has extra non-alphanumeric characters at the end of the file and the other doesn't? In this case, the file with the extra characters returns the empty string, making that queue longer. Our algorithm would return false in this case. Therefore, we need to check for this case and change what is returned.

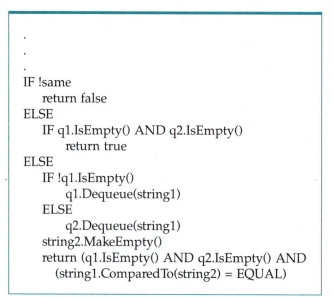

```
        .
        .
        .
IF !same
    return false
ELSE
    IF q1.IsEmpty() AND q2.IsEmpty()
        return true
ELSE
    IF !q1.IsEmpty()
        q1.Dequeue(string1)
    ELSE
        q2.Dequeue(string1)
    string2.MakeEmpty()
    return (q1.IsEmpty() AND q2.IsEmpty() AND
      (string1.ComparedTo(string2) = EQUAL)
```

Note that `string1` in the second else-clause can only be assigned a value once, so the comparison is correct. As is often the case, those pesky end cases require more code than the basic algorithm. We have to be sure that the files are both empty or if not, that the last item on the queue is the empty string. In the following client function, we assume that each file holds no more than 100 words.

```
bool FilesTheSame(ifstream& inFile1, ifstream& inFile2)
// Pre:   Each file holds at most 100 words.
//        Both files are opened and positioned at the beginning of
//        the file.
// Post: Function value = (inFile1 and inFile2 are the same except
//        for formatting and punctuation)
{
    QueType<StrType> q1(100), q2(100);
    StrType string1, string2;
    bool same = true;

    while (inFile1)     // Read and enqueue strings from inFile1.
    {
        string1.GetStringFile(true, ALPHA_NUM, inFile1);
        q1.Enqueue(string1);
    }

    while (inFile2)     // Read and enqueue strings from inFile2.
    {
        string2.GetStringFile(true, ALPHA_NUM, inFile2);
```

```
        q2.Enqueue(string2);
}

while (!q1.IsEmpty() && !q2.IsEmpty() && same)
// Compare strings.
{
    q1.Dequeue(string1);
    q2.Dequeue(string2);
    if (string1.ComparedTo(string2) != EQUAL)
        same = false;
}
if (!same)
    return false;
else if (q1.IsEmpty() && q2.IsEmpty())
    return true;
else
{    // One queue is not empty.
    if (!q1.IsEmpty())
        q1.Dequeue(string1);
    else
        q2.Dequeue(string1);
    string2.MakeEmpty();
    return
        (q1.IsEmpty() && q2.IsEmpty() &&
         string1.ComparedTo(string2) ==  EQUAL);
}
}
```

Implementation Level

Now that we've had the opportunity to be queue users, let's take a look at how a queue might be implemented in C++. As with a stack, the queue can be stored in a static array with its size fixed at compile time or in a dynamically allocated array with its size determined at run time. We look at the dynamic implementation here.

Definition of Queue Class   We implement our Queue ADT as a C++ class template. We again require the user to specify the data type of the items on the queue. Like the stack class, we do not need a comparison function because none of the operations require comparing items on the queue.

What data members does our Queue ADT need? We need the items themselves, but at this stage we do not know what else we need. As we described in the previous section, we allow the user to determine the type of items on the queue and the maximum size by using a template and a parameterized constructor.

```
template<class ItemType>
class QueType
{
public:
    QueType(int max);          // max is the size of the queue.
    QueType();                 // Default size of 500.
    ~QueType();
    void MakeEmpty();
    bool IsEmpty() const;
    bool IsFull() const;
    void Enqueue(ItemType item);
    void Dequeue(ItemType& item);
private:
    ItemType* items;
    int maxQue;
    // Whatever else we need.
};
```

Implementations of Queue Operations   The first question to consider is how we order the items in the array. In implementing the stack, we began by inserting an element into the first array position and then let the top float with subsequent `Push` and `Pop` operations. The bottom of the stack, however, was fixed at the first slot in the array. Can we use a similar solution for a queue, keeping the front of the queue fixed in the first array slot and letting the rear move down as we add new elements?

Let's see what happens after a few `Enqueue`s and `Dequeue`s if we insert the first element into the first array position, the second element into the second position, and so on. After four calls to `Enqueue` with parameters 'A', 'B', 'C', and 'D', the queue would look like this:

A	B	C	D	
[0]	[1]	[2]	[3]	[4]

Remember that the front of the queue is fixed at the first slot in the array, whereas the rear of the queue moves down with each `Enqueue`. Now we `Dequeue` the front element in the queue:

	B	C	D	
[0]	[1]	[2]	[3]	[4]

This operation deletes the element in the first array slot and leaves a hole. To keep the front of the queue fixed at the top of the array, we need to move every element in the queue up one slot:

B	C	D		
[0]	[1]	[2]	[3]	[4]

Let's summarize the queue operations corresponding to this queue design. The Enqueue operation would be the same as Push. The Dequeue operation would be more complicated than Pop, because all the remaining elements of the queue would have to be shifted up in the array, to move the new front of the queue up to the first array slot. The class constructor, MakeEmpty, IsEmpty, and IsFull operations could be the same as the equivalent stack operations.

Before we go any further, we want to stress that this design would work. It may not be the best design for a queue, but it could be successfully implemented. There are multiple *functionally correct* ways to implement the same abstract data structure. One design may not be as good as another (because it uses more space in memory or takes longer to execute) and yet may still be correct. Though we don't advocate the use of poor designs for programs or data structures, the first requirement must always be program correctness.

Now let's evaluate this design. Its strengths are its simplicity and ease of coding; it is almost exactly like the stack implementation. Though the queue is accessed from both ends rather than just one (as in the stack), we only have to keep track of the rear, because the front is fixed. Only the Dequeue operation is more complicated. What is the weakness of the design? The need to move all the elements up every time we remove an element from the queue increases the amount of work needed to dequeue.

How serious is this weakness? To make this judgment, we have to know something about how the queue is to be used. If this queue is used for storing large numbers of elements at one time, or if the elements in the queue are large (class objects with many data members, for instance), the processing required to move up all the elements after the front element has been removed makes this solution a poor one. On the other hand, if the queue generally contains only a few elements and they are small (integers, for instance), all this data movement may not amount to much processing. Further, we need to consider whether performance—how fast the program executes—is of importance in the application that uses the queue. Thus the complete evaluation of the design depends on the requirements of the client program.

In the real programming world, however, you don't always know the exact uses or complete requirements of programs. For instance, you may be working on a very large project with a hundred other programmers. Other programmers may be writing the specific application programs for the project while you are producing some utility programs that are used by all the different applications.

If you don't know the requirements of the various users of your queue operations, you must design general-purpose utilities. In this situation the design described here is not the best one possible.

Another Queue Design   The need to move the elements in the array was created by our decision to keep the front of the queue fixed in the first array slot. If we keep track of the index of the front as well as the rear, we can let both ends of the queue float in the array.

Figure 4.9 shows how several Enqueues and Dequeues would affect the queue. (For simplicity, these figures show only the elements that are in the queue. The other slots contain logical garbage, including values that have been dequeued.) The Enqueue operations have the same effect as before; they add elements to subsequent slots in the array and increment the index of the rear indicator. The Dequeue operation is simpler, however. Instead of moving elements up to the beginning of the array, it merely increments the front indicator to the next slot.

Letting the queue elements float in the array creates a new problem when the rear indicator gets to the end of the array. In our first design, this situation told us that the queue was full. Now, however, it is possible for the rear of the

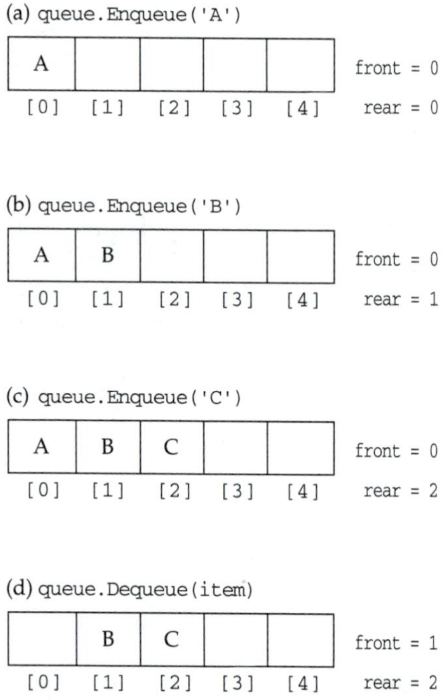

(a) queue.Enqueue('A')

A				
[0]	[1]	[2]	[3]	[4]

front = 0
rear = 0

(b) queue.Enqueue('B')

A	B			
[0]	[1]	[2]	[3]	[4]

front = 0
rear = 1

(c) queue.Enqueue('C')

A	B	C		
[0]	[1]	[2]	[3]	[4]

front = 0
rear = 2

(d) queue.Dequeue(item)

	B	C		
[0]	[1]	[2]	[3]	[4]

front = 1
rear = 2

FIGURE 4.9   *The effect of Enqueue and Dequeue.*

queue to reach the end of the (physical) array when the (logical) queue is not yet full (Figure 4.10a).

Because there may still be space available at the beginning of the array, the obvious solution is to let the queue elements "wrap around" the end of the array. In other words, the array can be treated as a circular structure, in which the last slot is followed by the first slot (Figure 4.10b). To get the next position for the rear indicator, for instance, we can use an If statement:

```
if (rear == maxQue - 1)
    rear = 0;
else
    rear = rear + 1;
```

Another way to reset `rear` is to use the remainder (%) operator:

```
rear = (rear + 1) % maxQue;
```

This solution leads us to a new problem: how do we know if a queue is empty or full? In Figure 4.11 we remove the last element, leaving the queue empty. In Figure 4.12 we add an element to the last free slot in the queue, leaving the queue full. The values of `front` and `rear`, however, are identical in the two situations. We cannot distinguish between a full queue and an empty queue.

The first solution that comes to mind is to add another data member to our queue class, in addition to `front` and `rear`—a count of the elements in the queue. When the count member is 0, the queue is empty; when the count is equal to the maximum number of array slots, the queue is full. Note that keeping this count adds work to the `Enqueue` and `Dequeue` routines. If the

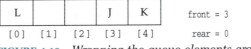

FIGURE 4.10   *Wrapping the queue elements around.*

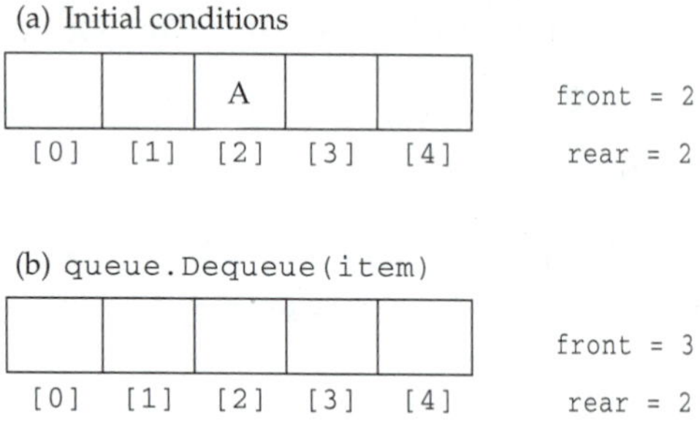

(a) Initial conditions

		A			front = 2
[0]	[1]	[2]	[3]	[4]	rear = 2

(b) queue.Dequeue(item)

					front = 3
[0]	[1]	[2]	[3]	[4]	rear = 2

FIGURE 4.11 *An empty queue.*

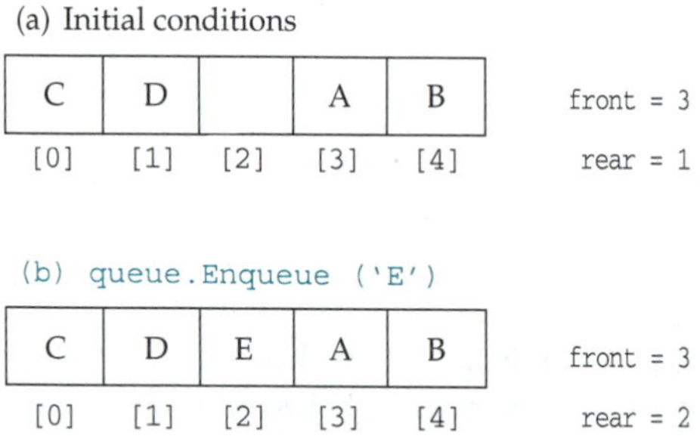

(a) Initial conditions

C	D		A	B	front = 3
[0]	[1]	[2]	[3]	[4]	rear = 1

(b) queue.Enqueue ('E')

C	D	E	A	B	front = 3
[0]	[1]	[2]	[3]	[4]	rear = 2

FIGURE 4.12 *A full queue.*

queue user frequently needed to know the number of elements in the queue, however, this solution would certainly be a good one. We leave the development of this solution as an exercise.

Another common but less intuitive approach is to let front indicate the index of the array slot *preceding* the front element in the queue, rather than the index of the front element itself. (The reason for this may not be immediately clear, but keep reading.) If rear still indicates the index of the rear element in the queue, the queue is empty when front is equal to rear. To dequeue, front is incremented to indicate the true location of the front queue element, and the value in that array slot is assigned to item. (Note that updating front precedes assigning the value in this design, for front does not point to the actual front element at the beginning of Dequeue.) After this Dequeue operation, IsEmpty finds that front is equal to rear, indicating that the queue is empty (see Figure 4.13).

An additional convention that we must establish to implement this scheme is that the slot indicated by front (the slot preceding the true front element) is reserved. It cannot contain a queue element. Thus, if there are 100 array positions, the maximum size of the queue is 99 elements. To test for a full

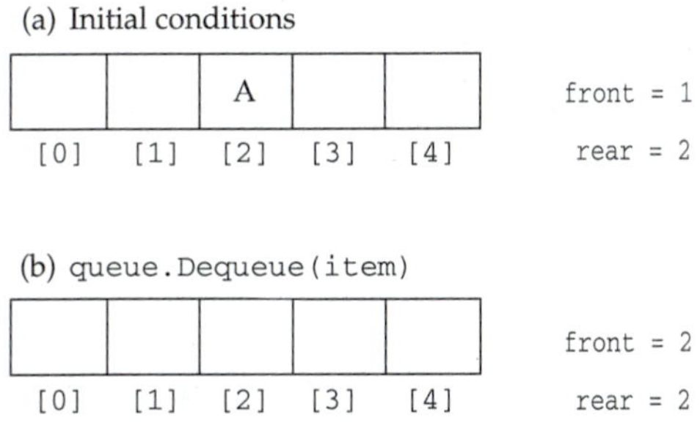

(a) Initial conditions

		A		
[0]	[1]	[2]	[3]	[4]

front = 1

rear = 2

(b) `queue.Dequeue(item)`

[0]	[1]	[2]	[3]	[4]

front = 2

rear = 2

FIGURE 4.13 *Testing for an empty queue.*

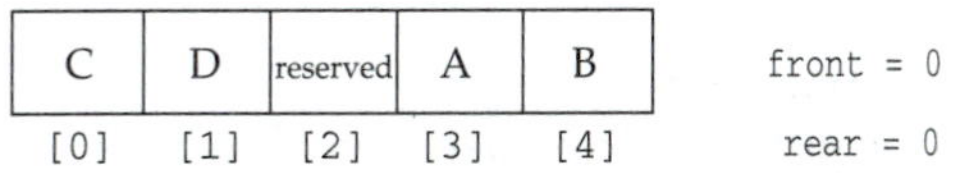

C	D	reserved	A	B
[0]	[1]	[2]	[3]	[4]

front = 0

rear = 0

FIGURE 4.14 *Testing for a full queue.*

queue, we look to see whether the next space available (after rear) is the special reserved slot indicated by front (see Figure 4.14).

To enqueue, we must first increment rear so that it contains the index of the next free slot in the array. We can then insert the new element into this space.

Using this scheme, how do we initialize a queue to its empty state? We want front to indicate the array index that precedes the front of the queue, so that when we first call Enqueue the front of the queue is in the first slot of the array. What is the position that precedes the first array slot? Because the array is circular, the first slot is preceded by the last slot. Thus we initialize front to maxQue - 1. Because our test for an empty queue is front is equal to rear, we initialize rear to front, or maxQue - 1.

Now we see that we must add two data members to the QueType class: front and rear. The header file follows. Through the parameterized constructor we are letting the user determine the maximum size of the queue when a class object is declared. Because implementation takes one more array slot, we must increment max (the parameter to the constructor) before we save it in maxQue. (This implementation is called a circular or ring queue.)

```
template<class ItemType>
class QueType
{
public:
    QueType(int max);
    QueType();
    ~QueType();
    void MakeEmpty();
```

```
    bool IsEmpty() const;
    bool IsFull() const;
    void Enqueue(ItemType newItem);
    void Dequeue(ItemType& item);
private:
    int front;
    int rear;
    ItemType* items;
    int maxQue;
};


template<class ItemType>
QueType<ItemType>::QueType(int max)
// Paramaterized class constructor
// Post: maxQue, front, and rear have been initialized.
//        The array to hold the queue elements has been dynamically
//        allocated.
{
    maxQue = max + 1;
    front = maxQue - 1;
    rear = maxQue - 1;
    items = new ItemType[maxQue];
}
template<class ItemType>
QueType<ItemType>::QueType()              // Default class constructor
// Post: maxQue, front, and rear have been initialized.
//        The array to hold the queue elements has been dynamically
//        allocated.
{
    maxQue = 501;
    front = maxQue - 1;
    rear = maxQue - 1;
    items = new ItemType[maxQue];
}
template<class ItemType>
QueType<ItemType>::~QueType()              // Class destructor
{
    delete [] items;
}
template<class ItemType>
void QueType<ItemType>::MakeEmpty()
// Post: front and rear have been reset to the empty state.
{
    front = maxQue - 1;
    rear = maxQue - 1;
```

```
}
template<class ItemType>
bool QueType<ItemType>::IsEmpty() const
// Returns true if the queue is empty; false otherwise.
{
    return (rear == front);
}
template<class ItemType>
bool QueType<ItemType>::IsFull() const
// Returns true if the queue is full; false otherwise.
{
    return ((rear + 1) % maxQue == front);
}
template<class ItemType>
void QueType<ItemType>::Enqueue(ItemType newItem)
// Post: newItem is at the rear of the queue.
{
    rear = (rear +1) % maxQue;
    items[rear] = newItem;
}
template<class ItemType>
void QueType<ItemType>::Dequeue(ItemType& item)
// Post: The front of the queue has been removed and a copy returned
//       in item.
{
    front = ( front + 1) % maxQue;
    item = items[front];
}
```

Note that Dequeue, like the stack Pop operation, does not actually remove the value of the item from the array. The value that has just been dequeued still physically exists in the array. It no longer exists in the queue, however, and cannot be accessed because of the change in front. That is, the dequeued data element exists in the implementation but not in the abstraction.

Test Plan   To make sure that you have tested all the necessary cases, make a test plan, listing all the queue operations and what tests are needed for each, as we did for stacks. (For example, to test function IsEmpty, you must call it at least twice, once when the queue is empty and once when it is not.)

We want to enqueue elements until the queue is full and then to call functions IsEmpty and IsFull to see whether they correctly judge the state of the queue. We can then dequeue all the elements in the queue, printing them out as we go, to make sure that they are correctly removed. At this point we can call the queue status functions again to see if the empty condition is correctly detected. We also want to test out the "tricky" part of the array-based algorithm: enqueue until the queue is full, dequeue an element, then enqueue again, forcing the operation to circle back to the beginning of the array.

Comparing Array Implementations   The circular array solution is not nearly as simple or intuitive as our first queue design. What did we gain by adding some amount of complexity to our design? By using a more efficient `Dequeue` algorithm, we achieved better performance. To find out how much better, let's analyze the first design: because the amount of work needed to move all the remaining elements is proportional to the number of elements, this version of `Dequeue` is an O(N) operation. The second array-based queue design only requires `Dequeue` to change the value of the front indicator and to put the value into `item` to be returned. The amount of work never exceeds some fixed constant, no matter how many elements are in the queue, so the algorithm has O(1).

All the other operations have O(1). No matter how many items are in the queue, they do (essentially) a constant amount of work.

CASE STUDY ||||

SIMULATION

Problem: Write a general-purpose simulation program that determines how long items (people, jobs, cars, ...) must wait in line before being served. The simulation must vary the number of servers and the time between arrivals of the items.

Discussion: Before astronauts go up into space, they spend many hours in a spaceship simulator, a physical model of a space vehicle in which they can experience all the things that will happen to them in space. The spaceship simulator is a physical model of another object. The technique that is used to make the model behave as the real object is called simulation. We can use similar techniques to build computer models of objects and events rather than physical models.

A model can be thought of as a series of rules that describe the behavior of a real-world system. We change the rules and watch the effects of these changes on the behavior we are observing.

Let's look at a very useful type of simulation that uses queues as the basic data structure. In fact, the real-world system is called a *queuing system*. A queuing system is made up of servers and queues of objects to be served. We deal with queuing systems all the time in our daily lives. When you stand in line to check out at the grocery store or to cash a check at the bank, you are dealing with a queuing system. When you submit a batch "job" (such as a compilation) on a mainframe computer, your job must wait in line until the CPU finishes the jobs scheduled ahead of it. The operating system is a queuing system. When you make a phone call to reserve an airline ticket and get a recording that says, "Thank you for calling Air Busters. Your call will be answered by the next available operator. Please wait."—you are dealing with a queuing system.

Please wait. Waiting is the critical element. The objective of a queuing system is to utilize the servers (the tellers, checkers, CPU, operators, and so on) as fully as possible, while keeping the wait time within a reasonable limit. These goals usually require a compromise between cost and customer satisfaction.

To put this on a personal level, no one likes to stand in line. If there were one checkout counter for each customer in a supermarket, the customers would be delighted. The supermarket, however, would not be in business very long. So a compromise is made: the number of cashiers is kept within the limits set by the store's budget, and the average customer is not kept waiting *too* long.

How does a company determine the optimal compromise between the number of servers and the wait time? One way is by experience; the company tries out different numbers of servers and sees how things work out. There are two problems with this approach: it takes too long and it is too expensive. Another way of examining this problem is by using a computer simulation. To simulate a queuing system, we must know four things:

1. The number of events and how they affect the system
2. The number of servers
3. The distribution of arrival times
4. The expected service time

The simulation program uses these parameters to predict the average wait time. The interactions of these parameters are the rules of the model. By changing these parameters, we change the rules. The average wait times are then examined to determine what a reasonable compromise would be.

Before we start designing a simulation program, let's walk through a simple simulation of a real-life example. Consider the case of a drive-in bank with one teller. How long does the average car have to wait? If business gets better and cars start to arrive more frequently, what would be the effect on the average wait time? When would the bank need to open a second drive-in window?

This problem has the characteristics a queuing problem. We have a *server* (the teller) and *objects being served* (customers in cars), and the *average wait time* is what we are interested in observing.

The events in this system are the arrivals and the departures of customers. Suppose that the number of servers is 1, the average transaction takes 5 minutes, and a new customer arrives about every 3 minutes. Let's look at how we can solve this problem as a time-driven simulation. A *time-driven simulation* is one in which the program has a counter that represents a clock. To simulate the passing of a unit of time (a minute, for example), we increment the clock. We run the simulation for a predetermined amount of time, say, 100 minutes. (Of course, simulated time usually passes much more quickly than real time; 100 simulated minutes pass in a flash on the computer.)

From a software point of view, the simulation is a big loop that executes a set of rules for each value of the clock—from 1 to 100, in our example. Here are the rules that are processed in the loop body:

Rule 1. If a customer arrives, he or she gets in line.
Rule 2. If the teller is free and if there is anyone waiting, the first customer in line leaves the line and advances to the teller's window. The service time is set to 5 minutes.
Rule 3. If a customer is at the teller's window, the time remaining for that customer to be serviced is decremented.
Rule 4. If there are customers in line, the additional minute that they have remained in the queue is recorded.

The output from the simulation is the average wait time. We calculate this value using the following formula:

Average wait time = total wait time for all customers / number of customers

Given this output, the bank can see whether their customers have an unreasonable wait in a one-teller system. If so, the bank can repeat the simulation with two tellers.

We have described this example in terms of a single teller and a specific arrival rate and transaction time. In fact, these simulation parameters should be varied to see what effect the changes have on the average wait time. Therefore these values are read as inputs to the program.

Because there are so many different applications that might use this program—modeling bank queues, phone call-waiting systems, CPU "job queues," doctor's office waiting room, and so on—we write our program as a *generic* time-driven queuing system simulator. That is, the same program can be used to simulate many different real-world systems. We refer to the bank tellers, phone operators, etc., as *servers* and the objects to be serviced (customers, patients, etc.) as *jobs*. This program simulates a *multiple*-server/ *single*-queue system. That is, the jobs waiting to be served are stored in a single queue. (In contrast, grocery stores are usually multiple-server/multiple-queue systems.) The specifications of this program are listed in Figure 4.15.

Specification: Program Simulation

Function

The program simulates a queuing system, using the following simulation parameters: length of simulation, average time between arrivals, number of servers, and average transaction time.

Input

The simulation parameters are entered interactively and include:

1. the length of the simulation,
2. the average transaction time,
3. the number of servers, and
4. the distribution of arrival times (average time between job arrivals).

The program must prompt the user for each input, and each input (a positive integer) is entered on a separate line.

At the end of each simulation, the program asks if another simulation is desired. If the user responds positively, the program prompts the user to input a new set of simulation parameters.

Output

The outputs are printed both to the screen and to a report file. The screen output is the resulting average wait time for the current simulation properly labeled. Following the execution of the last simulation, the following message is printed to the screen:

"Simulation is complete. Summary in file Report.sim."

The output in file Report.sim consists of the set of simulation parameters, the resulting average wait time, and the number of jobs that are still waiting when the simulation runs out. The output for each set of parameters should be printed on a single line, resulting in a tabular listing. A header line should be written to the file at the beginning of the program to label the columns, and a trailer section should be written to the end of the file, describing the meaning of the columns in the table.

Processing Requirements

1. The program must include processing to guard against range errors in the user's inputs. The maximum values allowed for each parameter must be described as constants, so that they can be "tuned" if necessary. Use the following initial values:

Maximum Servers	10
Maximum Simulation Length	10000

Maximum Transaction Length	1000
Maximum Time Between Arrivals	1000
Maximum Size of the Queue	100

2. Real-number output should be specified to two decimal places.
3. If a job arrives when the queue is full, abort the simulation with an error message to both the screen and the report file.

Assumptions

1. No more than one job arrives per time unit.
2. User inputs can be assumed to be numeric.

FIGURE 4.15   *Specification for simulation program.*

OBJECT-ORIENTED DESIGN

In a computer simulation, each physical object in the real-world system can be represented as a class object. Actions in the real world are represented as functions that manipulate the data members of these objects. In Chapter 2, we said that object-oriented design is ideal for simulation problems. An object-oriented design begins by looking for potential objects in the problem specification.

Low-Level Objects

What, then, are the objects in our problem that we must model? In Chapter 1, we suggested that a good strategy was to circle the nouns. Go back and look at the problem statement. The operational nouns are items (jobs in this case) and servers. These should be the fundamental, low-level, objects in the simulation.

What are the characteristics of a job that must be recorded? That is, what are the data members associated with job objects? As we are interested in the average time that a job spends waiting to be served, we must have a timer that records the number of time units each job has to wait. What are the operations that must be performed on the job object? We must be able to initialize the timer to zero when a job arrives, and we must be able to increment the timer for each clock cycle that the job remains in the queue. If each job had a different transaction time, we would have to record it as part of the job object. However, in this simulation all the jobs have the same transaction time. So it seems that the only information associated with a job is the time it waits in line.

What about a server? A server can be free or busy, so we should have a data member that keeps track of whether the server is free or busy. We need functions to set the server's status to busy or free and to interrogate the status. We also need to be able to determine when the job being served is completed. Therefore, we need a timer associated with each server that is set to the transaction time when a job arrives and is decremented at each clock cycle. When this timer reaches zero, the job has been completed and the server is free.

A review of the last two paragraphs shows us that there is an object more fundamental than either a job or a server. Both of these objects need to include a timer object. The job object needs to initialize the timer to zero and increment it; the server object needs to initialize the timer to a nonzero value and decrement it. Here are the definitions of our three fundamental objects.

```cpp
class TimerType
{
public:
    TimerType();                // Class constructor
    // Sets count to zero.
    void SetTimer(int value);
    // Sets count to value.
    void Increment();
    // Increments count.
    void Decrement();
    // Decrements count.
    int TimeIs() const;
    // Returns count.
private:
    int count;
};

class JobType
{
public:
    JobType();                  // Class constructor
    int WaitTimeIs() const;
    // Returns the value of waitTime.
private:
    TimerType waitTime;
};

enum StatusType {BUSY, FREE};
class ServerType
{
public:
    ServerType();               // Class constructor
    // Initializes status to FREE.
    bool IsFree() const;
```

```
    // Returns true if status is FREE; false otherwise.
    void SetBusy();
    // Sets status to BUSY.
    void SetFree();
    // Sets status to FREE.
    void SetTimeRemaining(int time);
    // Sets timeRemaining to time.
private:
    StatusType status;
    TimerType timeRemaining;
};
```

Now, we need to look back at the specification and determine other objects—the objects that contain our servers and jobs.

CONTAINER OBJECTS

From the abstract perspective, we have a *list of servers*. Can we use either our Unsorted List ADT or our Sorted List ADT to hold the servers? Let's look at the operations that must be performed on the list of servers and see. Looking back at the rules to be processed in the loop body, we see that we need an operation to determine if a server is free and one to engage a free server, thus changing its status flag (Rule 2). We also need an operation to decrement the timers of the busy servers. Both List ADTs allow us to iterate through the list items, but *not to change them*. Decrementing the timers and changing the status flags require access to the server objects themselves not just to copies of the objects. We can make the items on the list pointers to our server objects, thus gaining access to the objects themselves or we can write a problem-dependent list ourselves. Let's write a specialized ServerList ADT.

Let's call the operation to engage a server `EngageServer`. How do we know which, if any, server is free? We need another operation `GetFreeServerID` to tell us which server is available or to indicate that no server is free. Finally, we need an operation to decrement the timers of all the active servers to indicate that a clock unit has passed (Rule 3). We call this operation `UpdateServers`. The ADT can be described with the following specification:

■ ServerList ADT Specification

Structure: List of server items, each of which has an associated server ID and a timer.

Operations:

InitServers(int numServers)
Function: Initializes numServers items to "free" status.
Precondition: 1 <= numServers <= maximum number of servers allowed.
Postcondition: List contains numServers free servers.

GetFreeServerId(int& serverId, Boolean& found)
Function: Searches list for a free server; if found, returns serverId.
Precondition: List has been initialized.
Postconditions: found = (free server was found).
                   If found, serverId = ID of free server; otherwise, serverId is undefined.
                   (Note: This operation only identifies a free server; it does not engage the server.)

EngageServer(int serverID, int transactionTime)
Function: Engages the designated server for transactionTime
Preconditions: List has been initialized.
                   Server with serverID is free.
Postcondition: Timer of server with serverID = transactionTime.

UpdateServers
Function: Decrements the timer of each server that is currently engaged.
Precondition: List has been initialized.
Postcondition: Timer of each engaged server = previous timer value -1.

At the abstract level, the jobs waiting in line to be processed can be described as a queue of jobs. Let's see if we can use the Queue ADT that we discussed in this chapter. Rule 1 tells us that if a job arrives, it should be put in line; this is the Enqueue operation. Rule 2 suggests two queue operations: we need to know if there is a job waiting in line (the IsEmpty operation), and we need to be able to remove the first job from the queue (the Dequeue operation). Finally, Rule 4 says that the wait timers of all the jobs still in line must be incremented to show the passing of a clock unit. This is an operation that is not supported by the Queue ADT that we developed in the chapter, but we can certainly implement it using operations that are supported. Here is the specification for the client function `UpdateQue`.

■| **UpdateQue(waitQue)**

Function: Increments the time of every job waiting.
Precondition: waitQue has been initialized.
■| *Postcondition*: The timer of each job in the queue has been incremented.

With the addition of `UpdateQueue`, we can use the Queue ADT that we discussed in this chapter. Just to prove how committed we are to the idea of data encapsulation, we are not going to discuss the implementation of the ServerList ADT and `UpdateQue` until we finish designing the driver program for the simulation. We believe that the information in the specifications tells us enough that we can use these modules without knowing anything more. In fact, we give these modules to another programmer to implement however she wishes, and we write the rest of our program without knowing the implementations. When we finish our design, we get the implementations of these modules from our friend.

DRIVER DESIGN

Now we're ready to design the driver program, the code that allows these objects to interact. The specification tells us that the program must continue to run simulations and print results with different sets of parameters until the user is ready to quit. This suggests a loop, each iteration of which invokes an `ExecuteSimulation` function. Before we can process the first simulation, we must do some initialization—opening the report file and writing the report header. After we finish the last simulation, we must do some termination processing—writing the report trailer, for example. Here is the top level of the driver design.

Driver

```
Open reportFile for writing
Write title and headings to reportFile
DO
    ExecuteSimulation
    Write to screen "Enter an S to stop or another letter to continue;
        press return."
    Read letter
    Set finished to (letter = "S" or "s")
WHILE NOT finished
Write trailer to reportFile
```

The main work of the program is in `ExecuteSimulation`. It must get the simulation parameters, run the simulation, and print out the result to the screen and the report file. Here is the design for this important module.

ExecuteSimulation

```
GetParameters (timeLimit, numServers, transactionTime, timeBetween)
Initialize simulation variables
WHILE more time to run
    UpdateClock
    servers.UpdateServers()
    UpdateQue(waitQue)
    IF JobArrives()
        waitQue.Enqueue(job)
    servers.GetFreeServerId(serverId, found)
    IF (found AND !waitQue.IsEmpty())
        StartJob
Clean up wait queue
Calculate average wait time
PrintResults
```

This design gives an overall view of a simulation but leaves many questions unanswered. Clearly more levels of the design are needed.

The `GetParameters` function gets all the parameters for this execution of the simulation. Because it returns so many different values, we decide to make it send back a single parameter, a struct that contains a data member for each simulation parameter.

```
struct ParametersType
{
    int timeLimit;
    int numServers;
    int transactionTime;
    int timeBetween;
};
```

`GetParameters` must prompt the user for each parameter value, read the response, check the response to make sure that it falls within the bounds listed in the program specifications, and—if the response is not valid—ask for another value. Clearly this is a lot of work, and we do not want to get distracted right now. We really want to get on to the main processing of this program, the execution of the simulation using these parameters, so we decide to *postpone the design and coding of this module* until we've had a chance to test the simulation processing. But this module returns the simulation parameters. How can we postpone coding it? We code a *stub* to stand in its place. The stub simply assigns sample simulation parameters to the struct.

```
void GetParameters(ParametersType& parameters)
// Stub used for testing; sets simulation parameters.
{
    parameters.timeLimit = 100;
    parameters.transactionTime = 5;
    parameters.numServers = 2;
    parameters.timeBetween = 3;
}
```

We use this stub until we're convinced that our main simulation processing works; then we come back and code this module to get real values from the user. This means that we are coding and testing our program *incrementally*.

Our next job is to initialize the simulation variables. What are these variables? As we saw in reference to the bank-teller example, we must keep track of two values: (1) the total wait time for all jobs and (2) the number of jobs that are served. These are the values that are used to calculate the average wait time. The last variable to initialize is the clock.

InitializeSimulationVariables

> Set totalWait to 0
> Set numJobs to 0
> Set clock to 0

Now we come to activities in the While loop in `ExecuteSimulation`. Updating the clock is just incrementing `clock`; `UpdateServers` and `UpdateQue` have already been specified and can be coded directly from the specifications. Our next activity inside the loop is to determine if a new job arrives. How do we know whether or not a job has arrived in this particular clock unit? The answer is a function of two factors: the simulation parameter `timeBetween` (the average time between job arrivals) and luck.

Luck? We're writing a computer program that bases calculations on sheer luck? Well, not exactly. Let's express `timeBetween` another way—as the *probability* that a job arrives in any given clock unit. Probabilities range from 0.0 (no chance) to 1.0 (a sure thing). If on the average a new job arrives every five minutes, then the chance of a customer arriving in any given minute is 0.2 (1 chance in 5). Therefore, the probability of a new job arriving in this iteration of the loop body is 1.0 divided by `timeBetween`. Let's call this value `arrivalProb`. Now what about luck? In computer terms, luck can be represented by the use of a *random-number generator*. We simulate the arrival of a customer by writing a function `JobArrives`, which generates a random number between 0.0 and 1.0 and applies the following rules.

1. If the random number is between 0.0 and `arrivalProb` (inclusive), a job has arrived and `JobArrives` returns true.
2. If the random number is greater than `arrivalProb`, no job arrived in this clock unit and `JobArrives` returns false.

Where do we get a random-number generator? You can find the formula in a statistics book and code it yourself. However, there is an easier way. C++ compilers have one available in the standard library—the `rand` function.

```
#include <stdlib.h>
    .
    .
    .
randomInt = rand();
```

`rand` returns a random integer in the range of 0 through RAND_MAX, a constant defined in `<stdlib.h>`. (RAND_MAX is typically the same as INT_MAX.) To convert this number to one between 0.0 and 1.0, cast it to a floating point number and divide it by `float(RAND_MAX)`:

```
float(rand())/float(RAND_MAX)
```

Boolean JobArrives

> Set value to float (rand()) / float(RAND_MAX)
> Return (value <= arrivalProb)

Finally we come to the last activity in the `ExecuteSimulation` loop body: if a server is free and a job is waiting, start a job. What parameters does `StartJob` need? To be able to engage the server, it must have the list of servers, the index of the free server, and the transaction time (from `parameters`). If a job starts, two other variables are changed: the number of jobs served (numJobs) and the total wait time of jobs served (totalWait).

StartJob(servers, waitQue, serverId, parameters, numJobs, totalWait)

```
waitQue.Dequeue(job)
Increment numJobs
Set totalWait to totalWait + job.WaitTimeIs()
servers.EngageServer(serverID, parameters.transactionTime)
```

When the loop terminates (after the clock hits the timeLimit), this version of the simulation is finished. Now we need to clean up the wait queue, calculate the average wait time, and print out the results.

CleanUp(waitQue, jobsLeftInQue)

```
Set jobsLeftInQue to 0
WHILE NOT waitQue.IsEmpty()
    waitQue.Dequeue(job)
    Increment jobsLeftInQue
```

Finally we are ready to calculate the average wait time—the information that we have been waiting for:

```
Set averageWait to totalWait / numJobs
```

What happens if no jobs were ever received? If the simulation was run for a short timeLimit, with a relatively large timeBetween parameter, it is possible that numJobs is zero. Division by zero causes the program to crash at run time, so it is better to check for this condition explicitly:

```
IF numJobs > 0
    Set averageWait to totalWait / numJobs
ELSE
    Set averageWait to 0
```

All that is left in the ExecuteSimulation design is to print the results. The output that is specified to be printed to the screen can be generated with a simple output statement. Printing the reportFile output, however, requires us to know how the columns in the table were set up. This reminds us that there are two other file output operations—one to print the report "header" (the title and column headings) and one to print the report "trailer" (text regarding the meaning of the columns).

The work required to get the output printed with title centered and the columns straight is not important to developing and testing the simulator. Like GetParameters, these print operations can be coded in the second development iteration. Our final program needs these operations, of course, but we just don't need them *now*. Straight tabular output is irrelevant to testing whether the simulation works. So we put the coding of these three operations on hold, and replace them for now with stubs:

```cpp
void PrintResults(ofstream& reportFile,
    ParametersType parameters, float averageWait,
    int jobsLeftInQue)
{
    reportFile << "Average wait time is "  << averageWait
            << endl;
}

void PrintReportHeader(ofstream& reportFile)
{
    reportFile << "Starting Simulation" << endl;
}

void PrintReportTrailer(ofstream& reportFile)
{
    reportFile << "Ending Simulation" << endl;
}
```

This completes the design of the driver for our simulation (except for the input/output functions that we are postponing to the second development iteration).

As we promised earlier, we developed the design for the driver of this program without ever knowing how the ServerList ADT and the UpdateQue function were implemented. Meanwhile, our friend has been busy developing these modules for us. Let's see what she came up with.

THE SERVER ADT

The list of servers is represented as a class with two data members: the number of servers (numServers) and an array of ServerType items. Recall that ServerType objects have a data member timeRemaining of type TimerType that indicates how much time is left on the current job and a data member status that contains either BUSY or FREE. Here is the definition for the class ServerList.

```
class ServerList
{
public:
    ServerList();                  // class constructor
    ServerList(int number);        // parameterized constructor
    ~ServerList();                 // class destructor
    void GetFreeServerId(int& serverID, bool& found);
    void EngageServer(int serverId, int transactionTime);
    void UpdateServers();
private:
    int numServers;
    ServerType* servers;
};
```

The InitServers operation is implemented as a class constructor for class ServerList. It sets numServers to the input parameter number and uses the new operator to allocate the array of servers. GetFreeServerId searches the array of servers for one that is free. If one is found, found is set to true and serverID is set to the index of its array slot; otherwise found is false. EngageServer is the simplest of all: it merely sets the server's timer to transactionTime and status to BUSY. Finally, the UpdateServers operation loops through the servers, decrementing the timers of the active servers and changing a server's status if the timer is zero.

We have only the client function UpdateQue left to discuss. We need to cycle through the queue, incrementing the timer for each job object. Because we do not have access to the items on the queue, we must dequeue one job at a time, increment the timer, and put the job back into the queue. How do we know that we have processed each job in the queue? Let's enqueue an extra dummy job with the timer set to a negative number. When this job is dequeued, we have incremented all the timers in the queue.

The design is now finished. The completion of the program is left as Chapter 4, Programming Assignment 3.

SIMULATION RESULTS

We ran our version of the program, letting it execute four simulations. The average wait times printed to the screen are 3.21, 0.88, 7.03, and 0.52. How can that be? The program inputs are now coming from the GetParameters stub, not from the tester. Each time ExecuteSimulation calls GetParameters, the same parameters are returned. So how can the simulation come up with different results for each simulation? It is the random-number generator supplying a little "luck," just as in real life, a bank teller might be really busy one Thursday morning and bored the next. Let's try using a bigger time limit. We change the timeLimit member in the GetParameters stub to 1000 clock units, recompile, and run the program again. This time the four executions of the simulation are much more alike: 2.01, 2.92, 2.27, and 4.40.

We start the program again, and let it run four more executions of the simulation with the same time limit. This time we get exactly the same results as the previous run! How can that be? Aren't the random numbers random? Much theoretical work has gone into the development of algorithms to produce random numbers. Given a particular function to produce random numbers and the current result of the function, however, the next value is completely predictable—not random at all! Random-number generators use an initial *seed* value from which to start the sequence of random numbers. Because function rand initializes this seed to the same value each time, each run of the program produces the same sequence of "random" numbers. Therefore the numbers from such a function are called *pseudo-random*. For simulation purposes, however, pseudo-random numbers are sufficient. If a simulation is run for a long enough period of time, the theory of random numbers says that the wait times converge no matter what kind of random-number generator you use. As we saw, with a larger timeLimit value, the results were more alike. However, the C++ standard library does provide a function srand that allows the user to specify an initial seed before the first call to rand. The prototype for srand is

```
void srand(unsigned int);
```

How do we know whether the program is working? The results seem more or less "reasonable," but how do we know they are *correct*? A good way to see what the program is doing is to trace its execution using debugging outputs. We add output lines throughout the program—when we enqueue and dequeue, when we engage a server, and so on. Then we walk through the debug output, comparing what the program is doing to what we expect it to do.

Another way to test out this program is to run it with different values of input parameters and to see if the results change in predictable ways. To make this test, however, we need to code the real GetParameters routine.

The output from file Report.sim for a sample test of the program is shown in Table 4.1. (The blank lines have been deleted between some output lines to enhance readability.) We want to answer our original question about the drive-in bank. Is one teller enough? The test demonstrates cases where the transaction time is five minutes, new jobs arrive every three minutes, and the number of servers varies from one to four. We have run each set of parameters for 100, 500, 1000, and 5000 clock units (minutes in this case), respectively.

When testing most programs, we have a test plan in which we calculate and record what the results should be with certain input data values. We run the test data and check the actual results with the predicted results. As you can see, testing programs involving a random-number generator are much more complex because the results are not easily predicted.

TABLE 4.1   Output from One Run of Program Simulation

SIMULATION

Simulation Length	Number of Servers	Average Transaction	Time Between Arrivals	Average Wait	Jobs Left
100	1	5	3	18.0	14
500	1	5	3	106.65	58
1000	1	5	3	202.55	132
5000	1	5	3	1042.11	686
100	2	5	3	2.19	3
500	2	5	3	1.41	1
1000	2	5	3	3.89	0
5000	2	5	3	2.99	2
100	3	5	3	0.09	0
500	3	5	3	0.28	0
1000	3	5	3	0.28	1
5000	3	5	3	0.22	0
100	4	5	3	0.00	0
500	4	5	3	0.03	0
1000	4	5	3	0.01	0
5000	4	5	3	0.01	0

All times are expressed in clock units. Average wait time reflects the wait time of jobs served; it does not reflect the wait time of jobs that were not yet served. Jobs Left reflects the number of jobs that were waiting to be served when the simulation time limit was reached.

■‖ *Summary*

We have defined a stack at the logical level as an abstract data type, discussed its use in an application, and presented an implementation encapsulated in a class. Though our logical picture of a stack is a linear collection of data elements with the newest element (the top) at one end and the oldest element at the other end, the physical representation of the stack class does not have to recreate our mental image. The implementation of the stack class must support the last in, first out (LIFO) property; how this property is supported, however, is another matter. For instance, the Push operation could "time stamp" the stack elements and put them into an array in any order. To pop, we would have to search the array, looking for the newest time stamp. This representation is very different from the stack implementation we developed in this chapter, but to the user of the stack class they are functionally equivalent. The implementation is transparent to the program that uses the stack because the stack is encapsulated by the operations in the class that surrounds it.

Rather than requiring the user to provide a file containing information about the size of a structure and the type of the items on the structure, C++ provides a way to provide this information when a structure is declared in a program. Templates are a C++ construct that allows the client to specify the type of the items to be on the structure in angle brackets beside the type name in the declaration statement. Because class constructors can be parameterized, the client can pass the size of the structure by placing it in parentheses beside the variable name in the declaration statement. Additionally, a class constructor can use the new operator to get an array of the proper size in dynamic storage.

We also examined the definition and operations of a queue. We discussed some of the design considerations encountered when an array is used to contain the elements of a queue. Though the array itself is a random-access structure, our logical view of the queue as a structure limits us to accessing only the elements in the front and rear positions of the queue stored in the array.

There usually is more than one functionally correct design for the same data structure. When multiple correct solutions exist, the requirements and specifications of the problem may determine which solution is the best design.

In the design of data structures and algorithms, you find that there are often trade-offs. A more complex algorithm may result in more efficient execution; a solution that takes longer to execute may save memory space. As always, we must base our design decisions on what we know about the problem's requirements.

∎∥ *Exercises*

1. Indicate whether a stack would be a suitable data structure for each of the following applications.
   (a) A program to evaluate arithmetic expressions according to the specific order of operators.
   (b) A bank simulation of its teller operation to see how waiting times would be affected by adding another teller.
   (c) A program to receive data that are to be saved and processed in the reverse order.
   (d) An address book to be maintained.
   (e) A word processor to have a PF key that causes the preceding command to be redisplayed. Every time the PF key is pressed, the program is to show the command that preceded the one currently displayed.
   (f) A dictionary of words used by a spelling checker to be built and maintained.
   (g) A program to keep track of patients as they check into a medical clinic, assigning patients to doctors on a first-come, first-served basis.
   (h) A data structure used to keep track of the return addresses for nested functions while a program is running.

2. Describe the accessing protocol of a stack at the abstract level.

3. Show what is written by the following segments of code, given that `item1`, `item2`, and `item3` are `int` variables..
   (a)
   ```
   StackType<int> stack;
   item1 = 1;
   item2 = 0;
   item3 = 4;
   stack.Push(item2);
   stack.Push(item1);
   stack.Push(item1 + item3);
   stack.Pop(item2);
   stack.Push(item3*item3);
   stack.Push(item2);
   stack.Push(3);
   stack.Pop(item1);
   cout << item1 << endl << item2 << endl << item3 << endl;
   while (!stack.IsEmpty())
   {
       stack.Pop(item1);
       cout << item1 << endl;
   }
   ```
   (b)
   ```
   StackType<int> stack;
   item1 = 4;
   item3 = 0;
   item2 = item1 + 1;
   ```

```
stack.Push(item2);
stack.Push(item2 + 1);
stack.Push(item1);
stack.Pop(item2);
item1 = item2 + 1;
stack.Push(item1);
stack.Push(item3);
while (!stack.IsEmpty())
{
    stack.Pop(item3);
    cout << item3  << endl;
}
cout << item1 << endl   << item2  << endl   << item3  << endl;
```

Use the following information for Exercises 4–7: the stack is implemented as a class containing an array of items, a data member indicating the index of the last item put on the stack (`top`), and two Boolean data members, `underFlow` and `overFlow`, as discussed in this chapter. The stack items are characters and MAX_ITEMS is 5. In each exercise, show the result of the operation on the stack. Put a 'T' or 'F' for true or false in the Boolean data members.

4. `stack.Push(letter);`

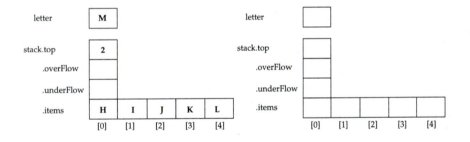

5. `stack.Push(letter);`

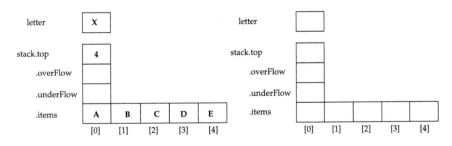

6. `stack.Pop(letter);`

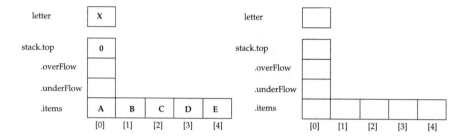

7. `stack.Pop(letter);`

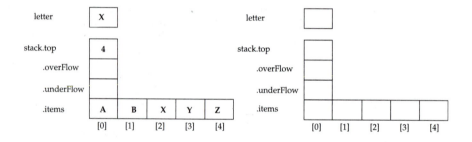

8. Write a segment of code to perform each of the following operations. You may call any of the member functions of `StackType`. The details of the stack type are encapsulated; you may only use the stack operations in the specification to perform the operations. (You may declare additional stack objects.)

   (a) Set `secondElement` to the second element in the stack, leaving the stack without its original top two elements.

   (b) Set `bottom` equal to the bottom element in the stack, leaving the stack empty.

   (c) Set `bottom` equal to the bottom element in the stack, leaving the stack unchanged.

   (d) Make a copy of the stack, leaving the stack unchanged.

9. (Multiple choice) The statement

   `stack.items[0] = stack.items[1];`

   (setting the top element equal to the second element) in a client program of the stack class

   (a) would cause a syntax error at compile time.

   (b) would cause a run-time error.

   (c) would not be considered an error by the computer, but would violate the encapsulation of the stack data type.

   (d) would be a perfectly legal and appropriate way to accomplish the intended task.

10. (Multiple choice) The statements

    ```
    stack.Push(item1 + 1);
    stack.Pop(item1 + 1);
    ```

    in the client program
    (a) would cause a syntax error at compile time.
    (b) would cause a run-time error.
    (c) would be legal, but would violate the encapsulation of the stack.
    (d) would be perfectly legal and appropriate.

11. Given the following specification of the Top operation:

    ItemType Top

Function:	Returns a copy of the last item put onto the stack.
Precondition:	Stack is not empty.
Postconditions:	Function value = copy of item at top of stack.
	Stack is not changed.

    (a) Write this function as client code, using operations from the nontemplate version of the StackType class. Remember, the client code has no access to the private members of the class.
    (b) Write this function as a new member function of the StackType class.

12. Two stacks of positive integers are needed, one containing elements with values less than or equal to 1000 and the other containing elements with values larger than 1000. The total number of elements in the small-value stack and the large-value stack combined are not more than 200 at any time, but we cannot predict how many are in each stack. (All the elements could be in the small-value stack, they could be evenly divided, both stacks could be empty, etc.) Can you think of a way to implement both stacks in one array?
    (a) Draw a diagram of how the stack might look.
    (b) Write the definitions for such a double-stack structure.
    (c) Implement the Push operation; it should store the new item into the correct stack according to its value (compared to 1000).

13. A stack of integer elements is implemented as an array. The index of the top element is kept in position 0 in the array, and the stack elements are stored in stack[1] . . . stack[stack[0]].
    (a) How does this implementation fare with the idea of an array as a homogeneous collection of data elements?
    (b) How would this implementation change the stack specifications? How would it change the implementations of the functions?

14. Using one or more stacks, write a code segment to read in a string of characters and determine whether it forms a palindrome. A palindrome is a sequence of characters that reads the same both forward and backward; for example: ABLE WAS I ERE I SAW ELBA.

The character '.' ends the string. Write a message indicating whether the string is a palindrome. You may assume that the data are correct and that the maximum number of characters is 80.

15. Write the body for a function that replaces each copy of an item in a stack with another item. Use the following specification. (This function is in the *client* program.)

    ReplaceItem(StackType& stack, ItemType oldItem, ItemType newItem)

Function:	Replaces all occurrences of oldItem with newItem.
Precondition:	stack has been initialized.
Postcondition:	Each occurrence of oldItem in stack has been replaced by newItem.

    (You may use any of the member functions of the nontemplate version of `StackType`, but you may not assume any knowledge of how the stack is implemented.)

16. In each plastic container of Pez candy, the colors are stored in random order. Your little brother only likes the yellow ones, so he painstakingly takes out all the candies, one by one, eats the yellow ones, and keeps the others in order, so that he can return them to the container in exactly the same order as before—minus the yellow candies, of course. Write the algorithm to simulate this process. (You may use any of the stack operations defined in the Stack ADT, but may not assume any knowledge of how the stack is implemented.)

17. The specifications for the Stack ADT have been changed. The class representing the stack must check for overflow and underflow. (See the discussion on pages 188–189.)
    (a) Rewrite the specifications incorporating this change.
    (b) What new data members must be added to the class?
    (c) What new member functions must be added to the class?

18. Implement the following specification for a client Boolean function that returns true if two stacks are identical and false otherwise.

    Boolean Identical(StackType stack1, StackType stack2)

Function:	Determines if two stacks are identical.
Preconditions:	stack1 and stack2 have been initialized.
Postconditions:	stack1 and stack2 are unchanged.
	Function value = (stack1 and stack2 are identical)

    (You may use any of the member functions of `StackType`, but you may not assume any knowledge of how the stack is implemented.)

The following code segment (used for Exercises 19-20) is a count-controlled loop going from 1 through 5. At each iteration, the loop counter is either printed or put on a stack depending on the result of Boolean function `RanFun()`. (The behavior of `RanFun()` is immaterial.) At the end of the loop, the items on the stack are popped and printed. Because of the logical properties of a stack, this code segment cannot print certain sequences of the values of the loop counter. You are given an output and asked to determine if the code segment could generate the output.

```
for (count = 1; count <= 5; count++)
    if (RanFun())
        cout << count;
    else
        stack.Push(count);
while (!stack.IsEmpty())
{
    stack.Pop(number);
    cout << number;
}
```

19. The following output is possible using a stack: 1 3 5 2 4
    (a) True   (b) False   (c) Not enough information

20. The following output is possible using a stack: 1 3 5 4 2
    (a) True   (b) False   (c) Not enough information

21. Based on the following declarations, tell whether each statement below is syntactically legal (yes) or illegal (no).

```
int* p;
int* q;
int* r;
int a;
int b;
int c;
```

	yes/no		yes/no		yes/no
(a) p = new int;	____	(f) r = NULL;	____	(k) delete r;	____
(b) q* = new int;	____	(g) c = *p;	____	(l) a = new p;	____
(c) a = new int;	____	(h) p = *a;	____	(m) q* = NULL;	____
(d) p = r;	____	(i) delete b;	____	(n) *p = a;	____
(e) q = b;	____	(j) q = &c;	____	(o) c = NULL;	____

22. The following program has careless errors on several lines. Find and correct the errors and show the output where requested.

```
#include <iostream.h>
int main ()
{
    int* ptr;
    int* temp;
    int x;

    ptr = new int;
    *ptr = 4;
    *temp = *ptr;
```

```
cout  <<  ptr  <<  temp;
x = 9;
*temp = x;
cout  <<  *ptr  <<  *temp;
ptr = new int;
ptr = 5;
cout  <<  *ptr  <<  *temp; // output:_____
return 0;
}
```

23. Describe the accessing protocol of a queue at the abstract level.

24. Show what is written by the following segments of code, given that `item1`, `item2`, and `item3` are `int` variables.

(a)

```
QueType<int> queue;

item1 = 1;
item2 = 0;
item3 = 4;
queue.Enqueue(item2);
queue.Enqueue(item1);
queue.Enqueue(item1 + item3);
queue.Dequeue(item2);
queue.Enqueue(item3*item3);
queue.Enqueue(item2);
queue.Enqueue(3);
queue.Dequeue(item1);
cout  <<  item1  <<  endl  <<  item2  <<  endl  <<  item3  <<  endl;
while (!queue.IsEmpty())
{
    queue.Dequeue(item1);
    cout  <<  item1  <<  endl;
}
```

(b)

```
QueType<int> queue;

item1 = 4;
item3 = 0;
item2 = item1 + 1;
queue.Enqueue(item2);
queue.Enqueue(item2 + 1);
queue.Enqueue(item1);
queue.Dequeue(item2);
item1 = item2 + 1;
queue.Enqueue(item1);
```

```
queue.Enqueue(item3);
while (!queue.IsEmpty())
{
    queue.Dequeue(item3);
    cout << item3  << endl;
}
cout << item1 << endl  << item2  << endl  << item3  << endl;
```

25. The specifications for the Queue ADT have been changed. The class representing the queue must check for overflow and underflow.
    (a) Rewrite the specifications incorporating this change.
    (b) What new data members must be added to the class?
    (c) What new member functions must be added to the class?

Use the following information for Exercises 26-31: the queue is implemented as a class containing an array of items, a data member indicating the index of the last item put on the queue (`rear`), a data member indicating the index of the location before the first item put on the queue (`front`), and two Boolean data members `underFlow` and `overFlow` as discussed in this chapter. The item type is `char` and `maxQue` is 5. In each exercise below, show the result of the operation on the queue. Put a 'T' or 'F' for true or false in the Boolean data members.

26. `queue.Enqueue(letter);`

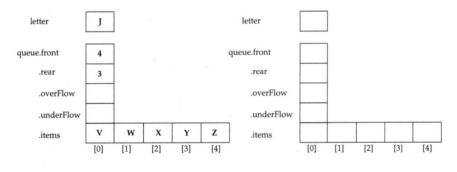

27. `queue.Enqueue(letter);`

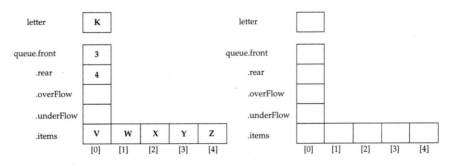

28. `queue.Enqueue(letter);`

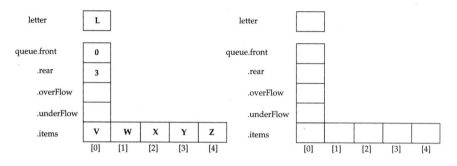

29. `queue.Dequeue(letter);`

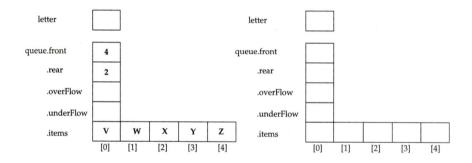

30. `queue.Dequeue(letter);`

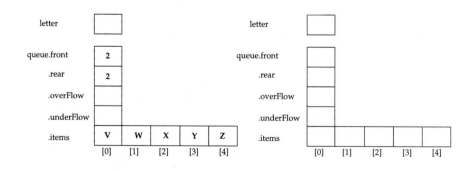

31. `queue.Dequeue(letter);`

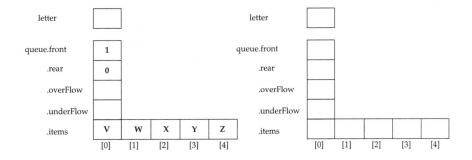

32. Write a segment of code to perform each of the following operations. You may call any of the member functions of `QueType`. The details of the queue are encapsulated; you may only use the queue operations in the specification to perform the operations. (You may declare additional queue objects).
    (a) Set `secondElement` to the second element in the queue, leaving the queue without its original front two elements.
    (b) Set `last` equal to the rear element in the queue, leaving the queue empty.
    (c) Set `last` equal to the rear element in the queue, leaving the queue unchanged.
    (d) Make a copy of the queue, leaving the queue unchanged.

33. (Multiple choice) The statement

    `queue.items[1] = queue.items[2];`

    (setting one element equal to the next element) in a client program of the queue class
    (a) would cause a syntax error at compile time.
    (b) would cause a run-time error.
    (c) would not be considered an error by the computer, but would violate the encapsulation of the queue data type.
    (d) would be a perfectly legal and appropriate way to accomplish the intended task.

34. (Multiple choice) The statements

    `queue.Enqueue(item1 + 1);`
    `queue.Dequeue(item1 + 1);`

    in the client program
    (a) would cause a syntax error at compile time.
    (b) would cause a run-time error.
    (c) would be legal, but would violate the encapsulation of the queue.
    (d) would be perfectly legal and appropriate.

35. Given the following specification of a `Front` operation:

    ItemType Front

Function:	Returns a copy of the front item on the queue.
Precondition:	Queue is not empty.
Postconditions:	Function value = copy of the front item on the queue.
	Queue is not changed.

    (a) Write this function as client code, using operations from the `QueType` class. (Remember, the client code has no access to the private members of the class.)

    (b) Write this function as a new member function of the `QueType` class.

36. Write the body for a function that replaces each copy of an item in a queue with another item. Use the following specification. (This function is in the client program.)

    ReplaceItem(QueType<int>& queue, int oldItem, int newItem)

Function:	Replaces all occurrences of oldItem with newItem.
Preconditions:	queue has been initialized.
Postcondition:	Each occurrence of oldItem in queue has been replaced by newItem.

    (You may use any of the member functions of `QueType`, but you may not assume any knowledge of how the queue is implemented.)

37. Indicate whether each of the following applications would be suitable for a queue.

    (a) An ailing company wants to evaluate employee records in order to lay off some workers on the basis of service time (the most recently hired employees are laid off first).

    (b) A program is to keep track of patients as they check into a clinic, assigning them to doctors on a first-come, first-served basis.

    (c) A program to solve a maze is to backtrack to an earlier position (the last place where a choice was made) when a dead-end position is reached.

    (d) An inventory of parts is to be processed by part number.

    (e) An operating system is to process requests for computer resources by allocating the resources in the order in which they are requested.

    (f) A grocery chain wants to run a simulation to see how average customer wait time would be affected by changing the number of checkout lines in the stores.

    (g) A dictionary of words used by a spelling checker is to be initialized.

    (h) Customers are to take numbers at a bakery and be served in order when their numbers come up.

    (i) Gamblers are to take numbers in the lottery and win if their numbers are picked.

38. Implement the following specification for a Boolean function in the client program that returns true if two queues are identical and false otherwise.

Boolean Identical(QueType<float> queue1, QueType<float> queue2)

Function: Determines if two queues are identical.
Preconditions: queue1 and queue2 have been initialized.
Postconditions: Queues are unchanged.
                   Function value = (queue1 and queue2 are identical)

(You may use any of the member functions of QueType, but you may not assume any knowledge of how the queue is implemented.)

39. Implement the following specification for an integer function in the client program that returns the number of items in a queue. The queue is unchanged.

int Length(QueType<char> queue)

Function: Determines the number of items in the queue.
Precondition: queue has been initialized.
Postconditions: queue is unchanged.
                   Function value = number of items in queue.

40. One queue implementation discussed in this chapter dedicated an unused cell before the front of the queue in order to distinguish between a full queue and an empty queue. Write another queue implementation that keeps track of the length of the queue in a data member length.
    (a) Write the class definition for this implementation.
    (b) Implement the member functions for this implementation. (Which of the member functions have to be changed and which do not?)
    (c) Compare this new implementation with the previous one in terms of Big-O notation.

41. In the queue application (function FilesTheSame) we stated that string1 in the second else-clause would only be assigned a value once. Explain. (Clearly it's because of the nested if-else; but why is the nested if-else appropriate?)

42. Discuss the difference between the MakeEmpty operation in the specification and a class constructor.

The following code segment (used for Exercises 43-44) is a count-controlled loop going from 1 through 5. At each iteration, the loop counter is either printed or put on a queue depending on the result of Boolean function RanFun(). (The behavior of RanFun() is immaterial.) At the end of the loop, the items on the queue are dequeued and printed. Because of the logical properties of a queue, this code segment cannot print certain sequences of the values of the loop counter. You are given an output and asked to determine if the code segment could generate the output.

```
for (count = 1; count <= 5; count++)
    if (RanFun())
        cout << count;
    else
        queue.Enqueue(count);
while (!queue.IsEmpty())
{
    queue.Dequeue(number);
    cout << number;
}
```

43. The following output is possible using a queue: 1 2 3 4 5
    (a) True   (b) False   (c) Not enough information

44. The following output is possible using a queue: 1 3 5 4 2
    (a) True   (b) False   (c) Not enough information

Linked Structures

GOALS

- To be able to implement the Stack ADT as a linked data structure
- To be able to implement the Queue ADT as a linked data structure
- To be able to implement the Unsorted List ADT as a linked data structure
- To be able to implement the Sorted List ADT as a linked data structure
- To be able to compare alternative implementations of an abstract data type with respect to performance

▪ ‖ *Implementing a Stack as a Linked Structure*

The implementation of a stack in an array is very simple, but it has a serious drawback: the size of a stack must be determined when a stack object is declared. When we declare a variable of class `StackType`, the maximum number of stack items is passed as a parameter to the constructor, and an array of that size is allocated on the free store. If we use fewer elements, space is wasted; if we need to push more elements than the array can hold, we cannot. It would be nice if we could just get space for stack elements as we need it.

Dynamic allocation of each stack element—one at a time—allows us to do just that. Let's see how we might use this concept to build a stack.

Function Push

We can modify function `Push` to allocate space for each new element dynamically.

Push

```
Allocate space for new item
Put new item into the allocated space
Put the allocated space into the stack
```

Implementing the first part of this operation is simple. We use the built-in C++ operator `new` to allocate space dynamically:

```
// Allocate space for new item.
itemPtr = new ItemType;
```

The `new` operator allocates a block of memory big enough to hold a value of type `ItemType` (the type of data contained in the stack) and returns the block's address, which is copied into the variable `itemPtr`. Let's say for the moment that `itemPtr` has been declared to be of type `ItemType*`. Now we can use the dereference operator (*) to put `newItem` into the space that was allocated: `*itemPtr = newItem`. The situation at this point is pictured in Figure 5.1, with `newItem` being 'E'.

The third part of the `Push` operation is to "put the allocated space into the stack." How do we do this? Let's think for a minute what happens after we have pushed a few characters. Space is allocated for each new element, and each character is put into the space. Figure 5.2 shows the results of calling `Push` to add the characters 'D', 'A', and 'L' to the stack.

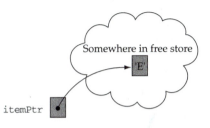

FIGURE 5.1 *Putting new element into the allocated space.*

Whoops—we see our data in the dynamically allocated space, but it's not a stack! There's no order. Even worse, because we haven't returned the pointers to the dynamically allocated space from function `Push`, we have no way to access any of the elements any more. Clearly, the third part of the `Push` operation needs to do something to fix this situation. Where can we store the pointers to our data?

One possibility that comes to mind is to declare the stack as an array of pointers and to put the pointer to each new item into this array, as shown in Figure 5.3. This solution would keep track of the pointers to all the elements in the correct order, but it wouldn't solve our original problem: we still need to declare an array of a particular size. Where else could we put the pointers? It would be nice if we could just chain all the elements together somehow, as shown in Figure 5.4. We call each element in this "linked" stack a *node*.

This solution looks promising. Let's see how we might use this idea to implement the stack. First we push the character 'D'. `Push` uses operator `new` to allocate space for the new node, and puts 'D' into the space. There's now one element in the stack. We don't want to lose the pointer to this element, so we need a data member in our stack class in which to store the pointer to the top of the stack (`topPtr`). The first `Push` operation is illustrated in Figure 5.5.

Now we call `Push` to add the character 'A' to the stack. `Push` applies `new` to allocate space for the new element and puts 'A' into the space. Next we want to chain 'A' to 'D', the old stack element. We can establish a link between the two elements by letting one element "point" to the next; that is, we can store into each stack element the address of the next element. To do this, we need to modify the stack node type. Let's make each node in the stack contain two

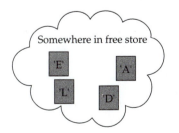

FIGURE 5.2 *After four calls to* Push.

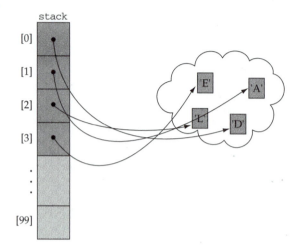

FIGURE 5.3   *One way to keep track of the pointers.*

parts: `info` and `next`. The `info` member contains the stack user's data—a character, for instance. The `next` member contains the address of the next element in the stack. A single node is pictured in Figure 5.6.

As you can see in the figure, the `next` member of each node points to the next node in the stack. What about the `next` member of the last node? We cannot leave it unassigned. The `next` member of the last node in the stack must contain some special value that is not a valid address. NULL, a special pointer constant available in <`stddef.h`>, says, "This pointer doesn't point to anything." We can put NULL in the `next` member of the last node, to mark the end of the stack. Graphically, we use a slash across the `next` member to represent a NULL pointer.

In fact, in Chapter 3 we introduced a list design terminology that incorporated the abstraction of a node. Let's review this terminology that allows us to refer to the parts of a node in our algorithms (see Figure 5.7).

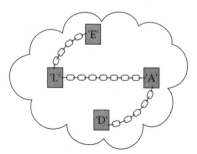

FIGURE 5.4   *Chaining the stack elements together.*

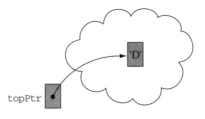

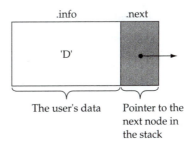

FIGURE 5.5 *Pushing the first element.*

FIGURE 5.6 *A single node.*

Node(location)	refers to all the data at `location`, including implementation-specific data.
Info(location)	refers to the user's data at `location`.
Info(last)	refers to the user's data at the last location in the list.
Next(location)	gives the location of the node following Node(location).

`location` in the array-based implementation is an index; in our pointer-based implementation it must be a pointer to a record that contains both the user's information and a pointer to the next node on the stack.

Now let's return to our Push algorithm. We have allocated a node to contain the new element 'A' using operator new (Figure 5.8a). Let's revert to our design terminology, and call the pointer `location`.

Set location to address of a new node of type ItemType // Allocate space
// for new item

Then the new value, 'A', is put into the node (Figure 5.8b):

Set Info(location) to newItem // Put new item into the allocated space

---

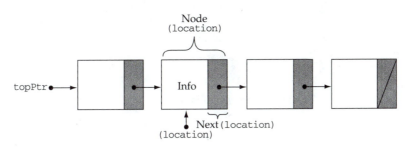

FIGURE 5.7 *Node terminology.*

(a) new(location)

(b) info(location) <- newElement

(c) Make next (location) point to Stack's top node

(d) Make Stack point to the new node

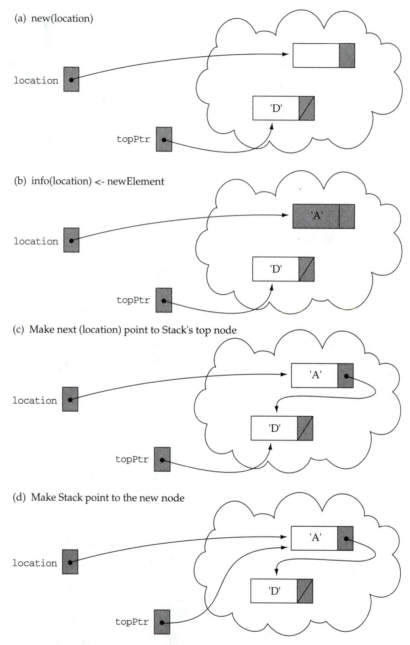

FIGURE 5.8   *The second Push operation.*

Now we are ready to link the new node to the stack. Where should we link it? Should the new node come before or after the node containing 'D'? To answer that question, let's look at how the stack is accessed: we add elements to the top (`Push`) and remove elements from the top (`Pop`). Last in, first out. Therefore, it would be a good idea to have the new node come first, so that we can access it directly. Linking the new node to the (previous) top node in the stack is a two-step process:

Make Next(location) point to the stack's top node // (Figure 5.8c)
Make topPtr point to the new node   // (Figure 5.8d)

Note that the order of these tasks is critical. If we changed the `topPtr` pointer before making Next(`location`) point to the top of the stack, we would have lost access to the stack nodes! (See Figure 5.9.) This situation is generally true when we are dealing with a linked structure: you must be very careful to change the pointers in the correct order, so that you do not lose access to any of the data.

Before we code this algorithm, let's see how the stack data are declared. Remember that from the stack user's point of view, nothing has changed; the prototype for member function `Push` is the same as it was for the array-based implementation.

```
void Push(ItemType newItem);
```

`ItemType` is still the type of data that the user wants to put in the stack. Class `StackType`, however, needs new definitions. It no longer is a class with a `top` member and an array member to hold the items; its only data member is `topPtr`, the pointer to a single node, the top of the stack. The node to which

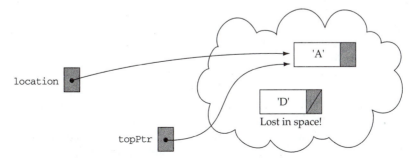

FIGURE 5.9 *Be careful when you change pointers.*

topPtr points has two parts, info and next, which suggests a C++ struct or class representation. We choose to make NodeType a struct rather than a class, because the nodes in the structure are passive. They are acted upon by the member functions of StackType.

```cpp
// Header file for Stack ADT.
template<class ItemType>
struct NodeType;

template<class ItemType>
class StackType
{
public:
    StackType();
    ~StackType();
    void MakeEmpty();
    void Push(ItemType);
    void Pop(ItemType&);
    bool IsEmpty() const;
    bool IsFull() const;
private:
    NodeType<ItemType>* topPtr;
};
          .
          .
          .
```

As mentioned before, ItemType stays the same (it is the formal parameter to the class template). NodeType is to be a struct containing the user's data, as well as a pointer to the next node. We alert the compiler that we are going to use a pointer to NodeType before we have defined NodeType by using the statement

```cpp
template<class ItemType>
struct NodeType;
```

This statement, called a *forward declaration*, is analogous to a function prototype: the compiler is told the nature of an identifier before the identifier is fully defined. The definition of NodeType (shown below) comes later in either the header file or the implementation file. Note that NodeType has to be templated because the data member info is of type ItemType.

```
template <class ItemType>
struct NodeType
{
    ItemType info;
    NodeType* next;
};
```

To summarize, StackType is a class with only one data member: a pointer to the top node in the stack. We also omit the parametrized constructor that allowed the client to specify a maximum stack size. With our dynamically allocated linked structure, there is no specific limit on the size of the stack.

Now let's code the Push algorithm. We use a local variable, location, of type NodeType*. The first two tasks are simple:

```
// Allocate space for new item.
location = new NodeType<ItemType>;
// Put new item into the allocated space.
location->info = newItem;
```

location is a pointer to a node containing an info member and a next member. *location is the way that we reference this node; it is a struct with two members. Because *location is a struct, we can access its members in the usual way—by adding a period, followed by the desired member name. So (*location).info refers to the info member of the struct on the free store pointed to by location. The parentheses are necessary because the dot operator has higher precedence than the dereferencing operator (*). Because we so often want to access the members of the struct or class to which a pointer points, C++ provides the -> operator, which both dereferences the pointer and accesses a member. So the expression (*location).info is equivalent to location->info. The shaded area in Figure 5.10(a) corresponds to location, the shaded area in (b) corresponds to *location, and the shaded area in (c) corresponds to location->info.

location->info is the same type as the user's data, so we can assign newItem to it. So far, so good.

Now for the linking task:

Make Next(location) point to the stack's top node // [Figure 5-8(c)]
Make topPtr point to the new node   // [Figure 5-8(d)]

Next(location) is the next member of the node pointed to by

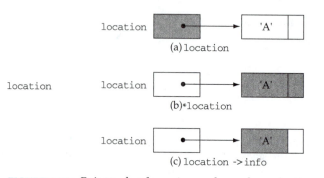

FIGURE 5.10   *Pointer dereferencing and member selection.*

location. We can access it just as we accessed the info member: location->next. What can we put into this field? It is declared as a pointer, so we can assign it another value of the same pointer type. We want to make this member point to the stack's top node. Because we have a pointer to the stack's top node (topPtr), this assignment is simple.

```
location->next = topPtr;
```

Finally, we need to complete the linking by making topPtr point to the new node. topPtr is declared as a pointer, so we can assign another value of the same pointer type to it. Because we have a pointer to the new node (the local variable location), this assignment can be made:

```
topPtr = location;
```

Here is the complete function Push. Note that, because we declared NodeType as a struct template, every occurrence of the word NodeType must have an actual parameter attached to it (in this case ItemType).

```
template <class ItemType>
void StackType<ItemType>::Push(ItemType newItem)
// Adds newItem to the top of the stack.
// Pre:  Stack has been initialized and is not full.
// Post: newItem is at the top of the stack.
{
    NodeType<ItemType>* location;
```

```
location = new NodeType<ItemType>;
location->info = newItem;
location->next = topPtr;
topPtr = location;
}
```

You have seen how this code works on a stack that contains at least one value. What happens if this function is called when the stack is empty? Space is allocated for the new element and the element is put into the space (Figure 5.11a). Does the function correctly link the new node to the top of an empty stack? Let's see. The `next` member of the new node is assigned the value of `topPtr`. What is this value when the stack is empty? It is NULL, which is exactly what we want to put into the `next` member of the last node of a linked stack (Figure 5.11b). Then `topPtr` is reset to point to the new node (Figure 5.11c). So this function works for an empty stack, as well as a stack that contains at least one element.

The coded version of function `Push` uses pointer-variable terminology where our algorithm used our special node terminology. Table 5.1 summarizes the relationship between the design and code terminology.

TABLE 5.1   Comparing Node Design Notation to C++ Code

Design Notation	C++ Code
Node(location)	`*location`
Info(location)	`location->info`
Next(location)	`location->next`
Set location to Next(location)	`location = location->next`
Set Info(location) to value	`location->info = value`

Function Pop

Now let's look at the `Pop` operation. The algorithm for `Pop` is as follows:

Pop

> Set item to Info(top node)
> Unlink the top node from the stack
> Deallocate the old top node

Let's try out this algorithm on the stack in Figure 5.12. We first put the value from the top node into `item`. How do we "unlink" the top node from the stack?

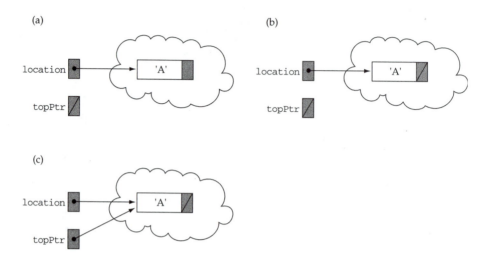

FIGURE 5.11   *Pushing onto an empty stack.*

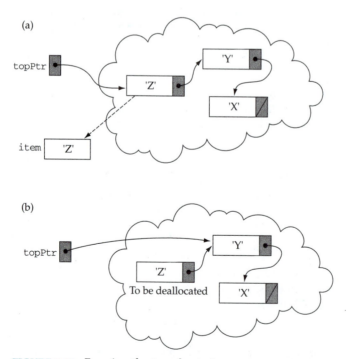

FIGURE 5.12   *Popping the top element.*

If we reset `topPtr` to point to the node following the top node, the resulting stack should be correct. Now we can free the space occupied by the old top node by using the C++ `delete` operation.

Whoops! The problem with this algorithm is that it leaves the old top node inaccessible—we no longer have a pointer to this node. Without a pointer, we cannot use the `delete` operation to free the space. When we code the function, let's add a local pointer variable to save the address of this node before we reset `topPtr`.

```
template<class ItemType>
void StackType<ItemType>::Pop(ItemType& item)
// Removes top item from stack and returns it in item.
// Pre:  Stack has been initialized and is not empty.
// Post: Top element has been removed;item is a copy of
//       removed element.
{
    NodeType<ItemType>* tempPtr;

    item = topPtr->info;
    tempPtr = topPtr;
    topPtr = topPtr->next;
    delete tempPtr;
}
```

Let's walk through this function, using the stack in Figure 5.13. `item` is set to the value in the `info` member of the first (top) node (Figure 5.13a). We save a pointer to the first node, so that we can access it later to delete it (Figure 5.13b). Then the external pointer to the stack is advanced to jump over the first node, making the second node the new top item. How do we know the address of the second node? We get it from the `next` member of the first node (`topPtr->next`). This value is assigned to `topPtr` to complete the unlinking task (Figure 5.13c). Finally, we free the space occupied by the old top node by using the `delete` operator, giving it the address we saved in `tempPtr` (Figure 5.13d).

Does this function work if there is only one node in the stack when Pop is called? Let's see. `item` is assigned the last value in the stack, then we unlink the first/last node from the stack. We save a pointer to the node, as before, and then try to assign `topPtr->next` to `topPtr` (Figure 5.14). What is the value of `topPtr->next`? Because this is the last node in the list, its `next` member should contain NULL. This value is assigned to `topPtr`, which is exactly what we want, because a NULL stack pointer means that the stack is empty. So the function works for a stack of one element.

(a)

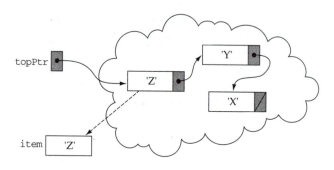

(b)

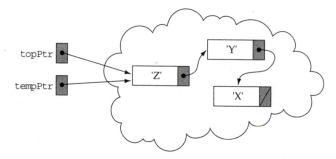

(c)

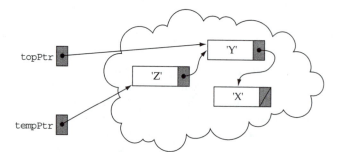

(d)

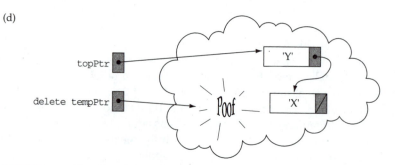

FIGURE 5.13 *Popping the stack.*

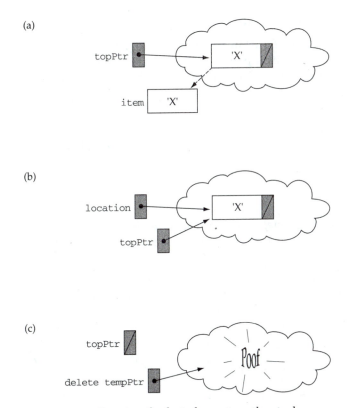

(a)

(b)

(c)

FIGURE 5.14 *Popping the last element on the stack.*

What happens if the stack is empty when Pop is called? If topPtr contains NULL, then the assignment statement

```
topPtr = topPtr->next;
```

results in a run-time error. On some systems you get the message ATTEMPT TO DEREFERENCE NULL POINTER; on other systems the screen freezes. But this is not our problem. The precondition in the specification of this function explicitly states that the stack is *not* empty. So the Pop function is not required or expected to protect the client from this situation. The client is responsible for checking for an empty stack before the call to Pop. In fact, that is why we provided the IsEmpty function.

Other Stack Functions

In the explanation of pushing the first element, it was noted that an empty stack is indicated by a NULL pointer. This fact has implications for the other stack operations. To initialize a stack to the empty state, we merely need to set topPtr to NULL:

```
template <class ItemType>
StackType<ItemType>::StackType()     // Class constructor.
{
    topPtr = NULL;
}
```

That was simple; function IsEmpty is correspondingly simple. If we initialize an empty stack by setting topPtr to NULL, then we can detect an empty stack by checking for a NULL pointer.

```
template <class ItemType>
bool StackType<ItemType>::IsEmpty() const
// Returns true if there are no elements on the stack;
// false otherwise.
{
    return (topPtr == NULL);
}
```

What about function IsFull? Using dynamically allocated nodes rather than an array, we no longer have an explicit limit on the stack size. We can continue to get more nodes until we run out of memory on the free store. The new operator in C++ returns a NULL pointer when there is no more space to allocate. We can test to see if there is more space by trying to allocate a node and testing the resulting pointer against NULL.

```
template<class ItemType>
bool StackType<ItemType>::IsFull() const
// Returns true if there is no room for another NodeType node
// on the free store; false otherwise.
{
    NodeType<ItemType>* location;

    location = new NodeType<ItemType>;
    if (location == NULL)
        return true;
```

```
    else
    {
        delete location;
        return false;
    }
}
```

Finally, we come to function `MakeEmpty`. In the array implementation, this function was virtually identical to the class constructor. We could make the two functions the same here also—just set `topPtr` to NULL to leave the stack empty—but that leaves all the space occupied by the nodes still allocated but inaccessible (a memory leak). We must free the node space.

Our `MakeEmpty` operation loops through all the elements in the stack, removing them one by one and deallocating the space.

MakeEmpty

WHILE more nodes in the stack
    Unlink top node
    Deallocate the node

This process is very much like putting function `Pop` inside a loop. In fact, we could just write the loop as

```
while (!IsEmpty())
    Pop(dummy);
```

But for the sake of efficiency (avoiding all the function calls), not to mention getting some extra practice using pointers, we write the function from scratch. How do we know when there are "more nodes in the stack"? As long as `topPtr` is not NULL, the stack is not empty. So the resulting condition on the loop is `while(topPtr != NULL)`. The inside of the loop is virtually the same as the unlinking code in `Pop`, so let's just "borrow" it. Here is the resulting function.

```
template <class ItemType>
void StackType<ItemType>::MakeEmpty()
// Post: stack is empty; all items have been deallocated.
{
    NodeType<ItemType>* tempPtr;
```

```
    while (topPtr != NULL)
    {
        tempPtr = topPtr;
        topPtr = topPtr->next;
        delete tempPtr;
    }
}
```

Our class definition also provides a class destructor. Do we need one? Yes, we do. If the stack is a local variable, the space for the data member `topPtr` is deallocated when the stack goes out of scope, but the nodes that `topPtr` points to do not. The class destructor must do exactly as `MakeEmpty` does: loop through the stack returning the nodes to the free store with the `delete` operator. Does this mean that `MakeEmpty` is not needed? No, they have different purposes. `MakeEmpty` is called explicitly by the client and resets the stack to the empty state without destroying the class object; the class destructor is called implicitly just before the class object goes out of scope and is destroyed. In fact, we can simply code the destructor as a call to `MakeEmpty`.

```
template <class ItemType>
StackType<ItemType>::~StackType()      // Class destructor
{
    MakeEmpty();
}
```

The linked implementation of the Stack ADT can be tested using the same test plan that was written for the array-based version.

Comparing Stack Implementations

We have looked at two very different implementations of the Stack ADT. We can compare these implementations in terms of storage requirements and efficiency of the algorithms. An array variable of the maximum stack size takes the same amount of memory, no matter how many array slots are actually used; we need to reserve space for the maximum possible. The linked implementation using dynamically allocated storage only requires space for the number of elements actually on the stack at run time. Note, however, that the elements are larger because we must store the link as well as the user's data.

We compare the relative "efficiency" of the two implementations in terms of Big-O notation. In both implementations, the class constructor, `IsFull`, and `IsEmpty` clearly have O(1). They always take a constant amount of work. What about `Push` and `Pop`? Does the number of elements in the stack affect the amount of work done by these operations? No, it does not. In both implementations, we directly access the top of the stack, so these operations also take a constant amount of work. They too have O(1) complexity. Only `MakeEmpty` differs from one implementation to the other. The array implementation simply sets the `top` data member to -1, so it is clearly an O(1) operation. The pointer implementation must process every node in the stack, in order to free the node space. This operation, therefore, has O(N) complexity, where N is the number of nodes in the stack. The array-based implementation in static storage did not need a destructor, but the array-based implementation in dynamic storage did need one. The class destructor in the array-based implementation in dynamic storage has a single statement that executes the `delete` operator, so is not dependent on the number of items in the stack (has O(1)). The class destructor in the dynamically linked version executes `MakeEmpty` so it has the same complexity, O(N).

Overall the two stack implementations are roughly equivalent in terms of the amount of work they do, only differing in one of the six operations and the class destructor. Note that if the difference had been in the `Push` or `Pop` operation, rather than the less frequently called `MakeEmpty`, it would be more significant. Table 5.2 summarizes the Big-O comparison of the stack operations. Those operations that differ between the two implementations are in boldface.

TABLE 5.2   Big-O Comparison of Stack Operations

	Array Implementation	Linked Implementation
Class constructor	O(1)	O(1)
MakeEmpty	O(1)	O(N)
IsFull	O(1)	O(1)
IsEmpty	O(1)	O(1)
Push	O(1)	O(1)
Pop	O(1)	O(1)
Destructor	O(1)	O(N)

So which is better? The answer, as usual, is: it depends on the situation. The linked implementation certainly gives more flexibility, and in applications where the number of stack items can vary greatly, it wastes less space when the stack is small. In situations where the stack size is totally unpredictable, the linked implementation is preferable, because size is largely irrelevant. Why then would we ever want to use the array-based implementation? Because it is short, simple, and efficient. If pushing and popping occur frequently, the array-based implementation executes faster because it does not incur the run-time overhead of the `new` and `delete` operations. When `maxStack` (MAX_ITEMS in the ADT specification) is small and we can be sure that we do not need to exceed the declared stack size, the array-based implementation is a good choice. Also, if you are programming in a language that does not support dynamic storage allocation, an array implementation may be the only good choice.

Implementing a Queue as a Linked Structure

The major weakness of the array-based implementation of a FIFO queue is identical to that of a stack: the need to create an array big enough for a structure of the maximum expected size. This size is set once and cannot change. If a much smaller number of elements is actually needed, we have wasted a lot of space. If a larger number of elements is unexpectedly needed, we are in trouble. We cannot extend the size of the array. We would have to allocate a larger array, copy the elements into it, and deallocate the smaller array.

We know, however, from our discussion of stacks, that we can get around this problem by using dynamic storage allocation to get space for each queue element only as needed. This implementation relies on the idea of linking the elements one to the next to form a chain.

Function Enqueue

In the array-based implementation of a queue, we decided to keep track of two indexes that pointed to the front and rear boundaries of the data in the queue. In a linked representation we can use two pointers, qFront and qRear, to mark the front and the rear of the queue. (See Figure 5.15. By now you realize that dynamically allocated nodes in linked structures exist "somewhere on the free store," rather than in adjacent locations like array slots, but we are going to show the nodes arranged linearly for clarity.)

We can dequeue elements from the queue using an algorithm similar to our stack Pop algorithm, with qFront pointing to the first node in the queue. Because we add new elements to the queue by inserting after the last node, however, we need a new Enqueue algorithm (see Figure 5.16).

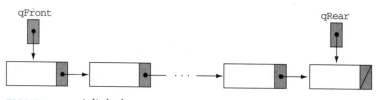

FIGURE 5.15   *A linked queue representation.*

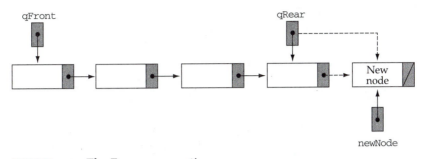

FIGURE 5.16 *The Enqueue operation.*

Enqueue

> Get a node for the new item
> Insert the new node at the rear of the queue
> Update pointer to the rear of the queue

The first of these tasks is familiar from the stack `Push` operation. We get the space using C++'s `new` operator and then store the new item into the node's `info` member. The new node is inserted at the rear end of the queue, so we also need to set the node's `next` member to NULL.

> // Get a node for the new item
> Set newNode to the address of a newly allocated node
> Set Info(newNode) to newItem
> Set Next(newNode) to NULL

The second part of the `Enqueue` algorithm, updating the `next` member of Node(qRear) to make it point to the new node, is simple:

> // Insert the new node at the rear of the queue.
> Set Next(qRear) to newNode

What happens if the queue is empty, when we enqueue the first element? In this case, there is no Node(qRear); we must set `qFront` to point to the new node. We modify the algorithm to take this condition into account:

```
//Insert the new node at the rear of the queue.
IF the queue is empty
    Set qFront to newNode
ELSE
    Set Next(qRear) to newNode
```

The last task in the `Enqueue` algorithm, updating the `qRear` pointer, simply involves the assignment `qRear = newNode`. Does this work if this is the first node in the queue? Sure; we always want `qRear` to be pointing to the rear node following a call to `Enqueue`, regardless of how many items are in the queue.

Note the relative positions of `qFront` and `qRear`. Had they been reversed (as in Figure 5.17), we could have used our stack `Push` algorithm for the `Enqueue` operation. But how could we dequeue? To delete the last node of the linked queue, we need to be able to reset `qFront` to point to the node preceding the deleted node. Because our pointers all go forward, we can't get back to the preceding node. To accomplish this task, we would either have to traverse the whole list (an O(N) solution—very inefficient, especially if the queue is long) or else keep a list with pointers in both directions. Use of this kind of a *doubly linked* structure is not necessary if we set up our queue pointers correctly to begin with.

Function Dequeue

In writing the `Enqueue` algorithm we noticed that inserting into an empty queue is a special case because we need to make `qFront` point to the new node also. Similarly, in our `Dequeue` algorithm we need to allow for the case of deleting the last node in the queue, leaving the queue empty. If `qFront` is NULL after we have deleted the front node, we know that the queue is now empty. In this case we need to set `qRear` to NULL also. The algorithm for removing the front element from a linked queue is illustrated in Figure 5.18. This algorithm

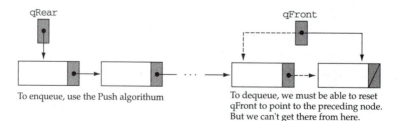

To enqueue, use the Push algorithum

To dequeue, we must be able to reset qFront to point to the preceding node. But we can't get there from here.

FIGURE 5.17 *A bad queue design.*

assumes that the test for an empty queue was performed before the `Dequeue` routine was entered, so we know that the queue contains at least one node. (We can make this assumption because this is the precondition for `Dequeue` in our FIFO Queue ADT specification.) As in `Pop`, we need to keep a local pointer to the node being removed, so that we can access it for the `delete` operation after the `qFront` pointer change.

Dequeue

```
Set tempPtr to qFront            //Save it for deallocating
Set item to Info(qFront)
Set qFront to Next(qFront)
IF queue is now empty
    Set qRear to NULL
Deallocate Node(tempPtr)
```

How do we know when the queue is empty? Both `qFront` and `qRear` should then be `NULL` pointers. This makes the class constructor and `IsEmpty` extremely simple. What about function `IsFull`? We can use the same `IsFull` we wrote for the Stack ADT.

In the array-based implementation, operation `MakeEmpty` merely changed the front and rear indexes to make the queue appear to be empty. There was no need to do anything to the data slots in the array; they became logical garbage, inaccessible through the queue operations. In the linked implementation, `MakeEmpty` must result in an empty queue, but there's more to this operation than just setting `qFront` and `qRear` to `NULL`. We must also free the dynamically allocated space in which the queue elements reside as we did for the stack items. In fact, the algorithm for destroying the queue is exactly the same as the algorithm for destroying the stack.

As in the case of changing the stack implementation to a linked structure, we change only the declarations and the insides of the queue operations. For a queue-using program, the interfaces to the operations remain the same. Let's

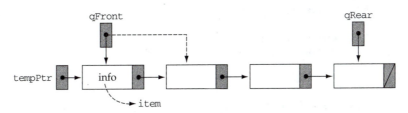

FIGURE 5.18 *The Dequeue operation.*

look at the declarations first. In our design, we referred to the two queue pointers as qFront and qRear. These become the data members in our class QueType. Each of these pointers points to a node in the linked queue (or are NULL pointers if the queue is empty). Each queue node has two members, info (containing the user's data) and next (containing the pointer to the next node, or in the case of the last node, NULL). We can implement the FIFO Queue ADT with the following code.

```
// Header file for Queue ADT.
template <class ItemType>
struct NodeType;

template <class ItemType>
class QueType
{
public:
    QueType();
    ~QueType();
    void MakeEmpty();
    void Enqueue(ItemType);
    void Dequeue(ItemType&);
    bool IsEmpty() const;
    bool IsFull() const;
private:
    NodeType<ItemType>* qFront;
    NodeType<ItemType>* qRear;
};
```

The implementation of the member functions requires only the translation from the design notation to the linked notation. This translation is so straightforward that we give the code with no further explanation.

```
#include <stddef.h>              // For NULL

template <class ItemType>
struct NodeType
{
    ItemType info;
    NodeType* next;
};


template <class ItemType>
QueType<ItemType>::QueType()          // Class constructor.
```

```
// Post:   qFront and qRear are set to NULL.
{
    qFront = NULL;
    qRear = NULL;
}

template <class ItemType>
void QueType<ItemType>::MakeEmpty()
// Post: Queue is empty; all elements have been deallocated.
{
    NodeType<ItemType>* tempPtr;

    while (qFront != NULL)
    {
        tempPtr = qFront;
        qFront = qFront->next;
        delete tempPtr;
    }
    qRear = NULL;
}

template <class ItemType>                  // Class destructor.
QueType<ItemType>::~QueType()
{
    MakeEmpty();
}

template <class ItemType>
bool QueType<ItemType>::IsFull() const
// Returns true if there is no room for another NodeType node
// on the free store; false otherwise.
{
    NodeType<ItemType>* ptr;

    ptr = new NodeType<ItemType>;
    if (ptr == NULL)
        return true;
    else
    {
        delete ptr;
        return false;
    }
}

template <class ItemType>
bool QueType<ItemType>::IsEmpty() const
// Returns true if there are no elements on the queue;
// false otherwise.
```

```
{
    return (qFront == NULL);
}


template <class ItemType>
void QueType<ItemType>::Enqueue(ItemType newItem)
// Adds newItem to the rear of the queue.
// Pre:  Queue has been initialized and is not full.
// Post: newItem is at rear of queue.
{
    NodeType<ItemType>* newNode;

    newNode = new NodeType<ItemType>;
    newNode->info = newItem;
    newNode->next = NULL;
    if (qRear == NULL)
        qFront = newNode;
    else
        qRear->next = newNode;
    qRear = newNode;
}


template <class ItemType>
void QueType<ItemType>::Dequeue(ItemType& item)
// Removes front item from the queue and returns it in item.
// Pre:  Queue has been initialized and is not empty.
// Post: Front element has been removed from queue.
//       item is a copy of removed element.
{
    NodeType<ItemType>* tempPtr;

    tempPtr = qFront;
    item = qFront->info;
    qFront = qFront->next;
    if (qFront == NULL)
        qRear = NULL;
    delete tempPtr;
}
```

A Circular Linked Queue Design

Our QueType class contains two pointers, one to each end of the queue. This design is based on the linear structure of the linked queue: given only a pointer to the front of the queue, we could follow the pointers to get to the rear, but this makes accessing the rear (to enqueue an item) an O(*N*) operation. With a pointer only to the rear of the queue, we could not access the front because the pointers only go from front to rear.

However, we could access both ends of the queue from a single pointer, if we made the queue *circularly linked*. That is, the `next` member of the rear node would point to the front node of the queue (see Figure 5.19). Now `QueType` has only one data member, rather than two. One interesting thing about this queue implementation is that it differs from the logical picture of a queue as a linear structure with two ends. This queue is a circular structure with no ends. What makes it a queue is its support of FIFO access.

In order to enqueue, we access the "rear" node directly through the pointer `qRear`. To dequeue, we must access the "front" node of the queue. We don't have a pointer to this node, but we do have a pointer to the node preceding it— `qRear`. The pointer to the "front" node of the queue is in Next(qRear). An empty queue would be represented by qRear = NULL. Designing and coding the queue operations using a circular linked implementation is left as a programming assignment (Chapter 5, Programming Assignment 4).

Both linked implementations of the Queue ADT can be tested using the same test plan that was written for the array-based version.

Comparing Queue Implementations

We have now looked at several different implementations of the Queue ADT. How do they compare? As we compared stack implementations, we look at two different factors: the amount of memory required to store the structure and the amount of "work" the solution requires, as expressed in Big-O notation. Let's compare the two implementations that we have coded completely: the array-based implementation and the dynamically linked implementation.

An array variable of the maximum queue size takes the same amount of memory, no matter how many array slots are actually used; we need to reserve space for the maximum possible number of elements. The linked implementation using dynamically allocated storage space only requires space for the number of elements actually in the queue at run time. Note, however, that the node elements are larger, because we must store the link (the `next` member) as well as the user's data.

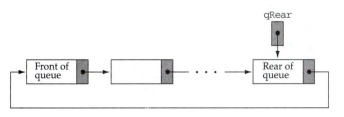

FIGURE 5.19 *A circular linked queue.*

Let's see how these implementations would compare if the queue contains strings (each requiring, say, 80 bytes). If the maximum number of queue elements is 100 strings, maxQue must be 101 to account for the reserved space before front. On our sample system, an array index (type int) takes 2 bytes and a pointer takes 4 bytes. The storage requirements of the array-based implementation are

(80 bytes * 101 array slots) + (2 bytes * 2 indexes) = 8084 bytes

no matter how many elements are in the queue at any time. The linked queue implementation requires

80 bytes (the string) + 4 bytes (the "next" pointer) = 84 bytes

per queue node, plus 8 bytes for the two external queue pointers. The storage requirements of these queue implementations are graphed in Figure 5.20(a). Note that the linked implementation does not always take less space than the array; when the number of elements in the queue exceeds 96, the linked queue requires more memory, due to the need to store the pointers.

If the queue item type were small, like a character or an integer, the pointer member could be larger than the user's data member. In this case, the space used by the linked representation exceeds that of the array-based representation much faster. Consider a queue that may contain up to 100 integer elements (2 bytes each). The storage requirements for the array-based queue are

(2 bytes (per element) * 101 array slots) + (2 bytes * 2 indexes) = 206 bytes

no matter how many elements are in the queue at any time. The linked queue implementation requires

2 bytes (the info member) + 4 bytes (the next member) = 6 bytes

per queue node, plus 8 bytes for the two external queue pointers. The storage requirements for this queue are graphed in Figure 5.20(b). When the number of elements in this queue exceeds 33, the linked queue requires more memory, due to the need to store pointers that are twice as big as the ItemType!

We can also compare the relative "efficiency" of the two implementations, in terms of Big-O. In both implementations, the class constructor, IsFull, and IsEmpty operations are clearly O(1). They always take the same amount of

(a) Queue contains 80-byte strings

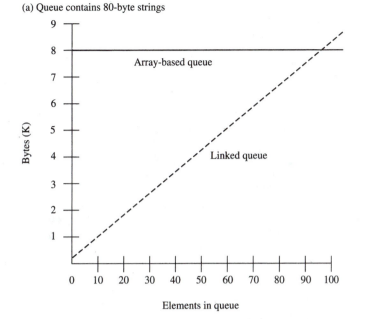

(b) Queue contains 2-byte integers

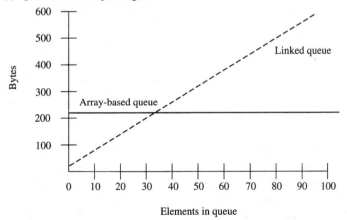

FIGURE 5.20 *Comparison of storage requirements.*

work regardless of how many items are on queue. What about `Enqueue` and `Dequeue`? Does the number of elements in the queue affect the amount of work done by these operations? No, it does not; in both implementations, we can directly access the front and rear of the queue. The amount of work done by these operations is independent of the Queue size, so these operations also have O (1).

TABLE 5.3   **Big-O Comparison of Queue Operations**

	Array Implementation	*Linked Implementation*
Class constructor	O(1)	O(1)
MakeEmpty	O(1)	O(N)
IsFull	O(1)	O(1)
IsEmpty	O(1)	O(1)
Enqueue	O(1)	O(1)
Dequeue	O(1)	O(1)
Destructor	O(1)	O(N)

Only the `MakeEmpty` operation differs from one implementation to the other. The array-based implementation merely sets the `front` and `rear` indexes, so it is clearly an O(1) operation. The linked implementation must process every node in the queue in order to free the node space. This operation, therefore, has O(N), where N is the number of nodes in the queue. The class destructor was not needed in the statically allocated array-based structure but was in the dynamically allocated array-based structure. The class destructor in the array-based implementation in dynamic storage has only one statement, so it has O(1). The class destructor in the dynamically allocated linked structure contains a loop executing as many times as there are items on the queue. Thus the dynamically linked version has O(N). As with the array-based and linked implementations of stacks, these two queue implementations are roughly equivalent in terms of the amount of work they do, only differing in one of the six operations and in the class destructor. Table 5.3 summarizes the Big-O comparison of the queue operations.

▪▮‖ *Implementing the Unsorted List as a Linked Structure*

Just as in the implementations of the Stack and Queue ADTs, each node in a linked list must have at least two data members. The first contains the user's data; the second is a pointer to the next element in the list. In order to implement the Unsorted List ADT, we need to record two pieces of information about the structure in addition to the list of items. The `LengthIs` operation returns the number of items in the list. In the array-based implementation, the `length` member defines the extent of the list within the array. *Therefore, the `length` member must be present.* In a link-based list we have a choice: we can keep a `length` member or we can count the number of elements each time the `LengthIs` operation is called. Keeping a `length` member requires an addition operation each time `InsertItem` is called and a subtraction operation each time `DeleteItem` is called. Which is better? We cannot determine in the abstract; it depends on the relative frequency of use of the `LengthIs`,

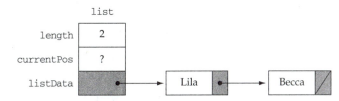

FIGURE 5.21 *Honor roll list with two items (ResetList has not been called).*

`InsertItem`, and `DeleteItem` operations. Here, let's explicitly keep track of the length of the list by including a `length` member in the `UnsortedType` class.

ResetList and GetNextItem require that we keep track of the current position during an iteration, so we need a `currentPos` member. In the array-based implementation, `currentPos` is an array index. What is the logical equivalent within a linked list? A *pointer*. Figure 5.21 pictures this structure.

The function headings (prototypes) that complete the specification are identical to those in the array-based implementation. Remember that the specification of the class is the interface that the user sees. The interface documentation tells the user what the operations do and this doesn't change with the implementation. Because the specification was given two chapters ago, we include them in the class documentation. We have removed the precondition that the list be initialized as we have included a class constructor. However, because we use templates to implement the list in a generic fashion, we do not need to have the client prepare an auxiliary file `ItemType.h` defining `ItemType`. What about a member function `ComparedTo`? We no longer need `ItemType` to have such a function. We assume that the relational operators "<" and "==" are defined for `ItemType`.

Here is the beginning of the header file for our linked version of the unsorted list.

```
// Header file for Unsorted List ADT.
template <class ItemType>
struct NodeType;

// Assumption: ItemType is a type for which the operators "<"
// and "==" are defined—either an appropriate built-in type or
// a class that overloads these operators.

template <class ItemType>
class UnsortedType
{
public:
    UnsortedType();     // Class constructor
    ~UnsortedType();    // Class destructor
```

```
bool IsFull() const;
// Determines whether list is full.
// Post: Function value = (list is full)

int  LengthIs() const;
// Determines the number of elements in list.
// Post: Function value = number of elements in list.

void MakeEmpty();
// Initializes list to empty state.
// Post:  List is empty.

void RetrieveItem(ItemType& item, bool& found);
// Retrieves list element whose key matches item's key
// (if present).
// Pre:  Key member of item is initialized.
// Post: If there is an element someItem whose key matches
//       item's key, then found = true and item is a copy
//       of someItem; otherwise found = false and item is
//       unchanged.
//       List is unchanged.

void InsertItem(ItemType item);
// Adds item to list.
// Pre:  List is not full.
//       item is not in list.
// Post: item is in list.

void DeleteItem(ItemType item);
// Deletes the element whose key matches item's key.
// Pre:  Key member of item is initialized.
//       One and only one element in list has a key matching
//       item's key.
// Post: No element in list has a key matching item's key.

void ResetList();
// Initializes current position for an iteration through the
// list.
// Post: Current position is prior to first element in list.

void GetNextItem(ItemType& item);
// Gets the next element in list.
// Pre:  Current position is defined.
//       Element at current position is not last in list.
// Post: Current position is updated to next position.
//       item is a copy of element at current position.
```

```
private:
    NodeType<ItemType>* listData;
    int length;
    NodeType<ItemType>* currentPos;
};
```

.
.
.

As with the stack and the queue, the UnsortedType class template is preceded by a forward declaration of the NodeType struct. Now we must give the full definition of NodeType:

```
template<class ItemType>
struct NodeType
{
    ItemType info;
    NodeType* next;
};
```

From the List ADT implementor's perspective, the algorithms for the list operations are very similar to the ones developed for the sequential (array-based) implementation. To initialize an empty list we merely set listData (the external pointer to the linked list) to NULL and set length to 0. Here is the class constructor to implement this operation:

```
template <class ItemType>
UnsortedType<ItemType>::UnsortedType()     // Class constructor
{
    length = 0;
    listData = NULL;
}
```

The IsFull operation is identical to the ones in the Stack and Queue ADT. We use operator new to get a node and check to see if the pointer to the node is NULL.

```
template <class ItemType>
bool UnsortedType<ItemType>::IsFull() const
// Returns true if there is no room for another NodeType node
// on the free store; false otherwise.
{
    NodeType<ItemType>* ptr;
    ptr = new NodeType<ItemType>;
    if (ptr == NULL)
        return true;
```

```
else
{
    delete ptr;
    return false;
}
}
```

As in the array-based implementation, the `LengthIs` operation just returns the `length` data member.

```
template <class ItemType>
int UnsortedType<ItemType>::LengthIs() const
// Post: Function value = number of items in the list.
{
    return length;
}
```

Function MakeEmpty

The MakeEmpty operation for a linked list is more complicated than its sequential list counterpart, because the dynamically allocated space used by the elements must be freed, one node at a time. The easiest approach is just to unlink each successive node in the list and free it. As this is exactly like our `MakeEmpty` functions for the Stack and Queue, we just "borrow" the code, changing the references from `topPtr` or `qFront` to `listData`. We must also set `length` to zero.

```
template <class ItemType>
void UnsortedType<ItemType>::MakeEmpty()
// Post: List is empty; all items have been deallocated.
{
    NodeType<ItemType>* tempPtr;

    while (listData != NULL)
    {
        tempPtr = listData;
        listData = listData->next;
        delete tempPtr;
    }
    length = 0;
}
```

The body of the class destructor is identical to `MakeEmpty` with the exception that we do not need to set `length` to 0. When the list object goes out of scope, all members of the object (including `length`) are returned to the system to be used again.

Function RetrieveItem

The algorithm for the linked implementation is the same as the one for the array-based implementation. Given the parameter `item`, we traverse the list looking for a location where `item` equals Info(location). The difference is in how we traverse the list and how we access Info(location). The equivalent expressions for our list design notation using an index and a pointer are shown in Table 5.4.

When we coded the array-based function, we directly substituted the index notation for the list notation. Can we directly substitute the pointer notation for the list notation in the linked list? Let's try it and see. The algorithm follows; the substitutions are marked in boldface for emphasis.

RetrieveItem

Initialize location to **listData**
Set found to false
Set moreToSearch to (**location != NULL**)
WHILE moreToSearch AND NOT found
    SWITCH (item.ComparedTo(**location -> info**))
        case LESS   :
        case GREATER   :   Set location to **location -> next**
                           Set moreToSearch to (**location != NULL**)
        case EQUAL   :   Set found to true
                           Set item to **location -> info**

TABLE 5.4   Comparing List Notation to C++ Code

List Notation	Index Expression	Pointer Expression
Initialize location	`location = 0`	`location = listData`
Set location to Next(location)	`location ++`	`location = location->next`
Have not examined Info(last)	`location < length`	`location != NULL`
Info(location)	`info[location]`	`location -> info`

Let's look at this algorithm and be sure that the substitutions do what we want by examining the value of `location` at the end. There are two cases:

1. *location = NULL.* If we reach the end of the list without finding an item whose key is equal to `item`'s key, then the item is not in the list. `location` correctly has the value NULL (see Figure 5.22a).
2. *item.ComparedTo(location->info) = EQUAL.* In this case, we have found the element within the list and have copied it into `item` (see Figure 5.22b).

We can now code this algorithm being reasonably confident that it is correct. We now have a choice: we can write a `ComparedTo` function that uses "<" and "==", or we can replace the Switch statement in the algorithm with an If statement. Because the code within each case of the Switch statement is very simple, let's use the relational operators.

```
template <class ItemType>
void UnsortedType<ItemType>::RetrieveItem(ItemType& item,
    bool& found)
// Pre:   Key member(s) of item is initialized.
// Post:  If found, item's key matches an element's key in the
//        list and a copy of that element has been stored in item;
//        otherwise, item is unchanged.
{
    bool moreToSearch;
    NodeType<ItemType>* location;

    location = listData;
    found = false;
    moreToSearch = (location != NULL);

    while (moreToSearch && !found)
```

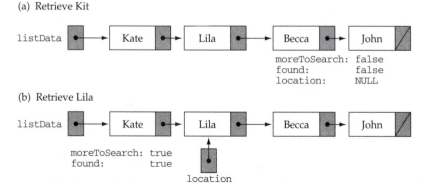

(a) Retrieve Kit

(b) Retrieve Lila

FIGURE 5.22 *Retrieving an item in an unsorted linked list.*

```
    {
        if (item == location->info)
        {
            found = true;
            item = location->info;
        }
        else
        {
            location = location->next;
            moreToSearch = (location != NULL);
        }
    }
}
```

Function InsertItem

In the array-based implementation, we put the new item at the end because that was the easiest place to put it. What is the analogous place in the linked implementation? At the beginning of the list. Because the list is unsorted, we can put the new item wherever we choose, and we choose the easiest place: at the front of the list. In fact, InsertItem is nearly identical to Push in the linked stack implementation. Note, we are *not* saying that inserting an item into an unsorted list is the same as pushing an item on a stack. The unsorted list and the stack are two entirely different ADTs. We are saying, however, that the algorithms for the respective operations are the same.

```
template <class ItemType>
void UnsortedType<ItemType>::InsertItem(ItemType item)
// Post: item is in the list; length has been incremented.
{
    NodeType<ItemType>* location;

    location = new NodeType<ItemType>;
    location->info = item;
    location->next = listData;
    listData = location;
    length++;
}
```

Function DeleteItem

In order to delete an item, we must first find it. In Figure 5.22(b), we see that location is left pointing to the node that contains the item for which we are searching, the one to be removed. In order to remove it, we must change the pointer in the *previous* node. That is, the next data member of the previous node must be changed to the next data member of the one being deleted (see Figure 5.23a).

Because we know from the specifications that the item to be deleted is in the list, we can change our search algorithm slightly. Rather than compare the item for which we are searching with the information in Info(location), we compare it with Info(location->next). When we find a match, we have pointers to both the previous node (location) and the one containing the item to be deleted (location->next). Note that removing the first node must be a special case because the external pointer to the list (listData) must be changed. Is removing the last node a special case? No. The next data member of the node being deleted is NULL and it is stored into the next data member of Node(location), where it belongs.

```
template <class ItemType>
void UnsortedType<ItemType>::DeleteItem(ItemType item)
// Pre:  item's key has been initialized.
//       An element in the list has a key that matches item's.
// Post: No element in the list has a key that matches item's.
{
    NodeType<ItemType>* location = listData;
    NodeType<ItemType>* tempLocation;

    // Locate node to be deleted.
    if (item == listData->info)
    {
        tempLocation = location;
        listData = listData->next;          // Delete first node.
    }
    else
    {
        while (!(item == (location->next)->info))
            location = location->next;
        // Delete node at location->next
```

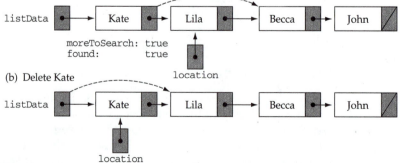

(a) Delete Lila

(b) Delete Kate

FIGURE 5.23 *Deleting the nodes containing Lila and Kate.*

```
        tempLocation = location->next;
        location->next = (location->next)->next;
    }
    delete tempLocation;
    length--;
}
```

Functions ResetList and GetNextItem

The Unsorted List ADT specification defines the "current position" to mean the location of the last item accessed during an iteration through the list. In the array-based implementation, ResetList initialized currentPos to -1, and GetNextItem incremented currentPos and returned info[currentPos]. For currentPos, we used the special value -1 to mean "prior to the first item in the list." In the linked implementation, what special pointer value can we use for "prior to the first item in the list"? We can use the special pointer value NULL. Therefore UnsortedList sets the currentPos member to NULL, and GetNextItem sets currentPos either to listData (in case currentPos was NULL) or to currentPos->next (in case it was not NULL) before returning currentPos->info.

```
template <class ItemType>
void UnsortedType<ItemType>::ResetUnsortedList()
// Post: Current position has been initialized.
{
    currentPos = NULL;
}
```

```
template <class ItemType>
void UnsortedType<ItemType>::GetNextItem(ItemType& item)
// Post:  Current position has been updated; item is current item.
{
    if (currentPos == NULL)
        currentPos = listData;
    else
        currentPos = currentPos->next;
    item = currentPos->info;
}
```

Notice that the body of GetNextItem is not required to check for running off the end of the list. That is the responsibility of the caller. A precondition of GetNextItem is that the item at the current position is not the last in the list.

The linked implementation of the Unsorted List ADT can be tested using the same test plan that was written for the array-based implementation.

Comparing Unsorted List Implementations

Now let's compare the sequential and linked implementations of the Unsorted List ADT. Just as we compared Stack and Queue ADT implementations, we look at two different factors: the amount of memory required to store the structure and the amount of work the solution does.

An array variable of the maximum list size takes the same amount of memory, no matter how many array slots are actually used, because we need to reserve space for the maximum possible. The linked implementation using dynamically allocated storage space requires only enough space for the number of elements actually in the list at run time. However, as we discussed in detail when evaluating queue implementations, each node element is larger, because we must store the link (the `next` member) as well as the user's data.

Again we use Big-O notation to compare the efficiency of the two implementations. As mentioned before, most of the operations are nearly identical in the two implementations. The class constructor, `IsFull`, `ResetList`, and `GetNextItem` functions in both implementations clearly have O(1) complexity. As in the stack and queue operations, `MakeEmpty` is a O(1) operation for a sequential list but becomes a O(N) operation for a linked list in dynamic storage. The sequential implementation merely marks the list as empty, while the linked implementation must actually access each list element to free its dynamically allocated space.

We did not introduce the concept of an array in dynamic storage until the chapter following the statically allocated array-based list. If the list had been implemented using an array in dynamic storage, a class destructor would have been necessary and its complexity would have been O(1). The class destructor for the dynamically linked version has the same complexity as `MakeEmpty`: O(N)

`LengthIs` is always O(1) in an array-based implementation, but we have a choice in the linked version. We chose to make it O(1) by keeping a counter of the number of elements we insert and delete. If we had chosen to implement `LengthIs` by counting the number of elements each time the function is called, the operation would be O(N). The moral here is that you must know how `LengthIs` is implemented in a linked implementation in order to specify its Big-O measure.

The `RetrieveItem` operations are virtually identical for the two implementations. Beginning at the first element, they examine one element after another until the correct element is found. Because they must potentially search through all the elements in a list, the loops in both implementations are O(N).

Because the list is unsorted, we can choose to put the new item into a directly accessible place: the last position in the array-based implementation or the front in the linked version. Therefore, the complexity of `InsertItem` is the same in both implementations: O(1). In both implementations, `DeleteItem` has O(N) because the list must be searched for the item to delete. These observations are summarized in Table 5.5. For those operations that require an initial search, we break the Big-O into two parts: the search and what is done following the search.

TABLE 5.5   **Big-O Comparison of Unsorted List Operations**

	Array Implementation	Linked Implementation
Class constructor	O(1)	O(1)
Destructor	O(1)	O(N)
MakeEmpty	O(1)	O(N)
IsFull	O(1)	O(1)
LengthIs	O(1)	O(1)
ResetList	O(1)	O(1)
GetNextItem	O(1)	O(1)
RetrieveItem		
Find	O(N)	O(N)
Process	O(1)	O(1)
Combined	O(N)	O(N)
InsertItem		
Find	O(1)	O(1)
Insert	O(1)	O(1)
Combined	O(1)	O(1)
DeleteItem		
Find	O(N)	O(N)
Delete	O(1)	O(1)
Combined	O(N)	O(N)

Implementing the Sorted List as a Linked Structure

When writing the array-based implementation of the Sorted List ADT, we found that only `InsertItem` and `DeleteItem` had to be changed from the unsorted version, but that `RetrieveItem` could be made more efficient. Because both `InsertItem` and `DeleteItem` have to search the list, let's look at `RetrieveItem` first.

Function RetrieveItem

For the unsorted version, we took the array-based algorithm and changed the array notation to linked notation. Let's try that again.

RetrieveItem

```
Set location to listData
Set found to false
Set moreToSearch to (location != NULL)
WHILE moreToSearch AND NOT found
    SWITCH (item.ComparedTo(location->info))
        case GREATER   :   Set location to location->next
                           Set moreToSearch to (location != NULL)
        case EQUAL      :   Set found to true
                           Set item to location->info
        case LESS       :   Set moreToSearch to false
```

Let's look at this algorithm and be sure that the substitutions do what we want by examining the value of `location` at the end. There are three cases here instead of two:

1. *location=NULL.* If we reach the end of the list without finding an item whose key is equal to `item`'s key, then the item is not in the list. `location` correctly has the value NULL (see Figure 5.22a, assuming the people's names are in alphabetical order).
2. *item.ComparedTo(location->info)=EQUAL.* In this case, we have found the element within the list and have copied it into `item` (see Figure 5.22b, assuming the people's names are in alphabetical order).
3. *item.ComparedTo(location->info)=LESS.* In this case, we have passed the location where the item belongs, so it isn't in the list (see Figure 5.24).

The first two cases remain the same as for the unsorted list. Figure 5.24 shows the third case.

Retrieve Kit

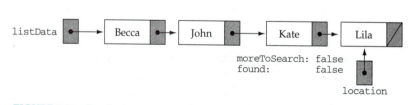

FIGURE 5.24 *Retrieving an item that is not there.*

Having looked at all three cases, we can again code this algorithm being reasonably confident that it is correct. We use the relational operators here also.

```cpp
template <class ItemType>
void SortedType<ItemType>::RetrieveItem(ItemType& item,
    bool& found)
{
    bool moreToSearch;
    NodeType<ItemType>* location;

    location = listData;
    found = false;
    moreToSearch = (location != NULL);

    while (moreToSearch && !found)
    {
        if (location->info < item)
        {
            location = location->next;
            moreToSearch = (location != NULL);
        }
        else if (item == location->info)
        {
            found = true;
            item = location->info;
        }
        else
            moreToSearch = false;
    }
}
```

Function InsertItem

We only had to substitute the pointer expressions for the corresponding index expressions in `RetrieveItem`. Does this work for `InsertItem`? Well, we know we don't have to shift any elements as we did in an array, so let's make the substitutions up to that point and see.

InsertItem

Set location to **listData**
Set moreToSearch to (**location != NULL)**
WHILE moreToSearch
    SWITCH (item.ComparedTo(**location->info**))
       case GREATER : Set location to **location->next**
                         Set moreToSearch to (**location != NULL)**
       case LESS   : Set moreToSearch to false
    .
    .
    .

When we exit the loop, `location` is pointing to the location where `item` goes. That's correct. (See figure 5.24.) We just need to get a new node, put `item` into the `info` member, put `location` into the `next` member, and put the address of the new node in the `next` member of the node before it (the node containing Kate). *Oops! We don't have a pointer to the node before it.* We must keep track of the previous pointer as well as the current pointer. When we had a similar problem in `DeleteItem` in the unsorted version, we compared one item ahead (`(location->next)->info`). Can we do that here? No. We were able to use that technique because we knew that the item for which we were searching was in the list. Here we know that the item for which we are searching is *not* in the list. If the new item were to go at the end of the list, this algorithm would crash because `location->next` would be NULL. (See Figure 5.25.)

We could change the way of determining `moreToSearch`, but there is an easier method for handling this situation. We use two pointers to search the list with one pointer always trailing one node behind. We call the previous pointer `predLoc` and let it trail one node behind `location`. When `ComparedTo` returns GREATER, we advance both pointers. As Figure 5.26 shows, the process resembles the movement of an inchworm. `predLoc` (the tail of the inchworm) catches up with `location` (the head), and then `location` advances. Because there is not a node before the first one, we initialize `predLoc` to NULL. Now let's summarize these thoughts into an algorithm.

Insert Sarah

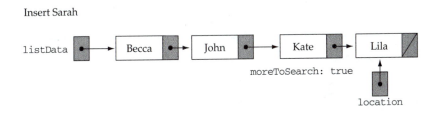

moreToSearch: true

location

FIGURE 5.25 *Inserting at the end of the list.*

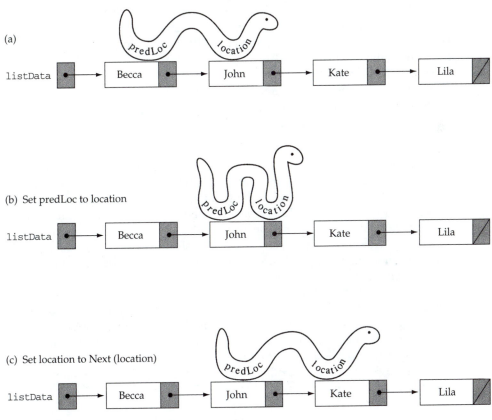

(a)

listData   Becca   John   Kate   Lila

(b) Set predLoc to location

listData   Becca   John   Kate   Lila

(c) Set location to Next (location)

listData   Becca   John   Kate   Lila

FIGURE 5.26 *The inchworm effect.*

InsertItem(item)

```
Set location to listData
Set predLoc to NULL
Set moreToSearch to (location != NULL)
WHILE moreToSearch
    SWITCH (item.ComparedTo(location->info))
        case GREATER  :  Set predLoc to location
                         Set location to location->next
                         Set moreToSearch to (location != NULL)
        case LESS  :     Set moreToSearch to false
Set newNode to the address of a newly allocated node
Set newNode->info to item
Set newNode->next to location
Set predLoc->next to newNode
Increment length
```

Let's do an algorithm walk-through before we code it. There are four cases: the new item goes before the first element, between two other elements, comes after the last element, or is inserted into an empty list. (See Figure 5.27.) If we insert at the first (Figure 5.27a), Alex compared to Becca returns LESS, and we exit the loop. We store `location` into `newNode->next` and `newNode` into `predLoc->next`. Whoops! The program crashes because `predLoc` is NULL. We must check to see if `predLoc` is NULL, and if it is, we must store `newNode` into `listData` rather than `predLoc -> next`.

What about the in-between case? Inserting Kit (Figure 5.27b) leaves `location` pointing to the node with Lila and `predLoc` pointing to the node with Kate. `newNode->next` points to the node with Lila; the node with Kate points to the new node. That's fine. What about when we insert at the end? Inserting Kate (Figure 5.27c) leaves `location` equal to NULL, and `predLoc` pointing to the node with Chris. NULL is stored into `newNode->next`; `newNode` is stored in the `next` member of the node containing Chris.

Does the algorithm work when the list is empty? Let's see. `location` and `predLoc` are both NULL, but we must store `newNode` into `listData` when `predLoc` is NULL, so there isn't a problem. (See Figure 5.27d.) Now we can code function `InsertItem`.

(a) Insert Alex (goes at the beginning)

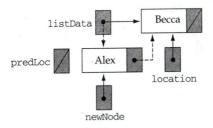

(b) Insert Kit (goes in the middle)

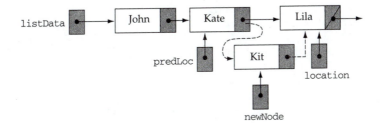

(c) Insert Kate (goes at the end)

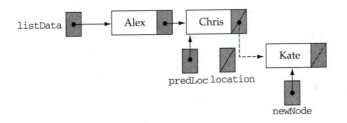

(d) Insert John (into an empty list)

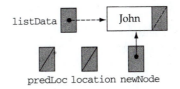

FIGURE 5.27 *Four insertion cases.*

```cpp
template <class ItemType>
void SortedType<ItemType>::InsertItem(ItemType item)
{
    NodeType<ItemType>* newNode;   // pointer to node being inserted
    NodeType<ItemType>* predLoc;   // trailing pointer
    NodeType<ItemType>* location;  // traveling pointer
    bool moreToSearch;

    location = listData;
    predLoc = NULL;
    moreToSearch = (location != NULL);

    // Find insertion point.
    while (moreToSearch)
    {
        if (location->info < item)
        {
            predLoc = location;
            location = location->next;
            moreToSearch = (location != NULL);
        }
        else
            moreToSearch = false;
    }

    // Prepare node for insertion
    newNode = new NodeType<ItemType>;
    newNode->info = item;

    // Insert node into list.
    if (predLoc == NULL)           // Insert as first
    {
        newNode->next = listData;
        listData = newNode;
    }
    else
    {
        newNode->next = location;
        predLoc->next = newNode;
    }
    length++;

}
```

Function DeleteItem

As in the case of `RetrieveItem` and `InsertItem`, the `DeleteItem` algorithm begins with a search. In this case we exit the searching loop when `item.ComparedTo(location->info)` returns `EQUAL`. Once we have found the item, we delete it. Because our precondition states that the item to be deleted is in the list, we have a choice. We can use the unordered list algorithm exactly as it is or we can write an algorithm that is the mirror image of the insertion. We leave the coding of the new algorithm to you as an exercise. The four cases that occur are represented in Figure 5.28.

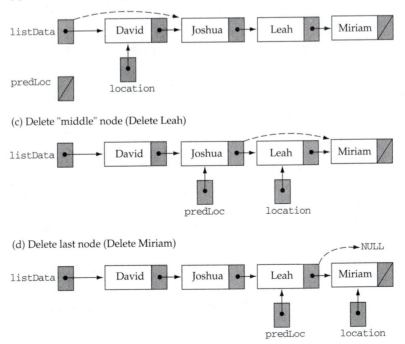

FIGURE 5.28   *Deleting from a linked list.*

Comparing Sorted List Implementations

We developed three algorithms for `RetrieveItem` in an array-based list: a sequential search, a sequential search with an exit when the place is passed where the item would be if present, and a binary search. The first two have order $O(N)$; the binary search has order $O(\log_2 N)$. The first two searches can be implemented in a linked list but a binary search cannot. (How do you get directly to the middle of a linked list?) Therefore, the array-based algorithm for searching a list is faster than the linked version if the binary search algorithm is used.

In both list implementations, the `InsertItem` function uses a sequential search to find the insertion position; therefore, the search parts of the algorithms have $O(N)$ complexity. The array-based list must also move down all the elements that follow the insertion position to make room for the new element. The number of elements to be moved ranges from 0, when we insert at the end of the list, to `length`, when we insert at the beginning of the list. So the insertion part of the algorithm also has $O(N)$ complexity for the array-based list. Because $O(N) + O(N) = O(N)$, the sequential list's `InsertItem` operation has $O(N)$. Even if we used the binary search to find where the item belongs ($O(\log_2 N)$), the items would have to be moved to make room for the new one ($O(N)$). $O(\log_2 N) + O(N)$ is $O(N)$.

The insertion part of the algorithm for the linked list representation simply requires the reassignment of a couple of pointers. This makes the insertion task $O(1)$ for a linked list, which is one of the main advantages of linking. However, adding the insertion task to the search task gives us $O(N) + O(1) = O(N)$—the same Big-O approximation as for the sequential list! Doesn't the linking offer any advantage in efficiency? Perhaps. But remember that the Big-O evaluations are only rough approximations of the amount of work that an algorithm does.

The `DeleteItem` function is similar to `InsertItem`. In both implementations, the search task is performed, an $O(N)$ operation. Then the sequential list's delete operation "deletes" the element by moving up all the subsequent elements in the list, which adds $O(N)$. The whole function is $O(N) + O(N)$, or $O(N)$. The linked list deletes the element by unlinking it from the list, which adds $O(1)$ to the search task. The whole function is $O(N) + O(1)$, or $O(N)$. Thus both `DeleteItem` operations are $O(N)$; for large values of N, they are roughly equivalent.

The fact that two operations have the same Big-O measure does not mean that they take the same amount of time to execute, however. The sequential implementation requires, on average, a great deal of data movement for both `InsertItem` and `DeleteItem`. Does all this data movement really make any difference? It doesn't matter too much in our Honor Roll example; the list is very small. If there are 1000 students on the Honor Roll, however, the data movement starts to add up.

Table 5.6 summarizes the Big-O comparison of the sorted list operations for sequential and linked implementations.

TABLE 5.6   Big-O Comparison of Sorted List Operations

	Array Implementation	*Linked Implementation*
Class constructor	O(1)	O(1)
Destructor	O(1)	O(N)
MakeEmpty	O(1)	O(N)
IsFull	O(1)	O(1)
LengthIs	O(1)	O(1)
ResetList	O(1)	O(1)
GetNextItem	O(1)	O(1)
RetrieveItem		
Find	O(N)*	O(N)
Process	O(1)	O(1)
Combined	O(N)	O(N)
InsertItem		
Find	O(N)*	O(**N**)
Insert	O(N)	O(1)
Combined	O(N)	O(N)
DeleteItem		
Find	O(N)*	O(N)
Delete	O(N)	O(1)
Combined	O(N)	O(N)

*$O(\log_2 N)$ if a binary search is used.

∎‖ *Summary*

We have seen how stacks, queues, unsorted lists, and sorted lists may be represented in an array-based or linked representation. The specifications for each ADT didn't mention any of these design issues, so we were free to implement them in any way we choose. There was nothing in the specification of these ADTs to say that the structures should be array-based or linked, or that the elements were stored in statically or dynamically allocated storage.

We could specify a number of other operations for a List ADT. Some operations, such as one to find the preceding node in a list, are easy to implement for an array-based list but would be difficult to implement using a list that is linked in one direction (like the lists in this chapter). This operation would be simpler if the list had links going both forward and backward. We can think of many variations for representing a linked list in order to simplify the kinds of operations that are specified for the list: doubly linked lists, circular lists, lists that are accessed from both the beginning and the end. We look at some of these alternative implementation structures in the next chapter.

The idea of linking the elements in a data structure is not specific to stacks, queues, and lists. We use this powerful tool to implement many other data structures in this book.

■‖ *Exercises*

1. Given the following specification of the `top` operation:

ItemType Top

Function:	Returns copy of the last item put onto the stack.
Precondition:	Stack is not empty.
Postconditions:	Function value = copy of item at top of stack.
	Stack is not changed.

   (a) Write this function as client code, using operations from the `StackType` class. Remember, the client code has no access to the private members of the class.

   (b) Write this function as a new member function of the `StackType` class.

2. Implement the following operation as a member function of the `StackType` class.

ReplaceItem(ItemType oldItem, ItemType newItem)

Function:	Replaces all occurrences of oldItem with newItem.
Precondition:	Stack has been initialized.
Postcondition:	Each occurrence of oldItem in stack has been changed to newItem.

3. Implement the following operation as a member function of the `StackType` class.

Boolean Identical(StackType& stack1)

Function:	Determines if stack1 and self are identical.
Precondition:	stack1 and self have been initialized.
Postconditions:	stack1 and self are unchanged.
	Function value = (self and stack1 are identical)

4. Given the following specification of a `Front` operation:

ItemType Front

Function:	Returns copy of the front item on the queue.
Precondition:	Queue is not empty.
Postconditions:	Function value = copy of the front item on the queue.
	Queue is not changed.

   (a) Write this function as client code, using operations from the `QueType` class. (Remember, the client code has no access to the private members of the class.)

(b) Write this function as a new member function of the QueType class.

5. Implement the following operation as a member function of the QueType class.

ReplaceItem(ItemType oldItem, ItemType newItem)

    Function: Replaces all occurrences of oldItem with newItem.
    Precondition: Queue has been initialized.
    Postcondition: Each occurrence of oldItem in queue has been changed to
                      newItem.

6. Implement the following specification for an integer function that returns the number of items in a queue. This function is a member function of the QueType class.

int Length

    Function: Returns the number of items in the queue.
    Precondition: Queue has been initialized.
    Postconditions: Function value = number of items in the queue.
                      Queue is unchanged.

7. Exercise 1 in Chapter 3 asks you to add a member function IsThere to the Unsorted List ADT. Rewrite the function definition using a linked structure. You may assume a templated class where ItemType has the == operator defined.

8. Exercise 2 in Chapter 3 asks you to add a member function IsThere to the Sorted List ADT. Rewrite the function definition using a linked structure. You may assume a templated class where ItemType has the == and > operators defined.

9. Write a member function that merges two instances of the Sorted List ADT using the following specification.

MergeLists(SortedType& list, SortedType& result)

    Function: Merges two sorted lists into a third sorted list.
    Preconditions: Self and list are in ascending order by key.
                      Self and list do not have any keys in common; self and list
                      are not empty.
    Postcondition: result is a sorted list that contains all of the items from self
                      and list.

You may assume that SortedType is a templated class and that the relational operators are defined for ItemType.
(a) Write the prototype for MergeLists.
(b) Write the code for the function.
(c) Describe the algorithm in terms of Big-O.

10. A list ADT is to be extended by the addition of member function SplitLists, which has the following specification:

SplitLists(ListType& list1, ListType& list2, ItemType item)

Function: Divides self into two lists according to the key of item.

Precondition: Self has been initialized.

Postconditions: list1 contains all the elements of self whose keys are less than or equal to item's.

                        list2 contains all the elements of self whose keys are greater than item's.

You may assume that `ListType` is a templated class and that the relational operators are defined for `ItemType`.

(a) Implement `SplitLists` as a member function of the Unsorted List ADT.

(b) Implement `SplitLists` as a member function of the Sorted List ADT.

(c) Compare the algorithms used in (a) and (b).

11. The specifications for the Unsorted List ADT state that the item to be deleted is in the list. You may assume that `UnsortedType` is a templated class and that the relational operators are defined for `ItemType`.

(a) Rewrite the specification for `DeleteItem` so that the list is unchanged if the item to be deleted is not in the list.

(b) Implement `DeleteItem` as specified in (a).

(c) Rewrite the specification for `DeleteItem` so that all copies of the item to be deleted are removed if they exist; otherwise, the list is unchanged.

(d) Implement `DeleteItem` as specified in (c).

12. The specifications for the Sorted List ADT state that the item to be deleted is in the list.

(a) Rewrite the specification for `DeleteItem` so that the list is unchanged if the item to be deleted is not in the list.

(b) Implement `DeleteItem` as specified in (a).

(c) Rewrite the specification for `DeleteItem` so that all copies of the item to be deleted are removed if they exist; otherwise, the list is unchanged.

(d) Implement `DeleteItem` as specified in (c).

13. (a) Explain the difference between a sequential and a linked representation of a list.

(b) Give an example of a problem for which a sequential list would be the better solution.

(c) Give an example of a problem for which a linked list would be the better solution.

14. True or False? If you answer False, correct the statement.

(a) An array is a random-access structure.

(b) A sequential list is a random-access structure.

(c) A linked list is a random-access structure.

(d) A sequential list is always stored in a statically allocated structure.

(e) A stack is not a random-access structure.

(f) A queue is a random-access structure.

Use the linked list pictured below in Exercises 15 through 18.

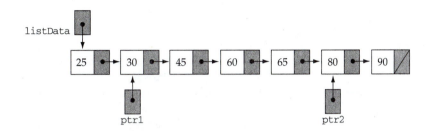

15. Give the values of the following expressions:
    (a) `ptr1->info`
    (b) `ptr2->next->info`
    (c) `listData->next->next->info`

16. Are the following expressions true or false?
    (a) `listdata->next == ptr1`
    (b) `ptr1->next->info == 60`
    (c) `ptr2->next == NULL`
    (d) `listData->info == 25`

17. Decide whether the *syntax* of the each of the following statements is valid or invalid. If it is valid, mark it OK; if it is invalid, explain what is wrong.
    (a) `listData->next = ptr1->next;`
    (b) `listData->next = *(ptr2->next);`
    (c) `*listData = ptr2;`
    (d) `ptr2 = ptr1->next->info;`
    (e) `ptr1->info = ptr2->info;`
    (f) `ptr2 = ptr2->next->next;`

18. Write *one* statement to do each of the following:
    (a) Make `listData` point to the node containing 45.
    (b) Make `ptr2` point to the last node in the list.
    (c) Make `listData` point to an empty list.
    (d) Set the `info` member of the node containing 45 to 60.

If memory locations are allocated as shown in the second column of the following table, what is printed by the statements in the first column? Fill in the last column in the following table for Exercises 19 through 24 . The Exercise number is in the first column in comments.

Statements	Memory Allocated	What Is Printed?
`int value;`	value is at location 200	
`value = 500;`		
`char*charPtr;`	charPtr is at location 202	
`char string[10] = "Good luck";`	string[0] is at location 300	
`charPtr = string;`		
`cout << &value;` `// Exercise 19`	& means "the address of"	
`cout << value;` `// Exercise 20`		
`cout << &charPtr;` `// Exercise 21`	& means "the address of"	
`cout << charPtr;` `// Exercise 22`		
`cout << *charPtr;` `// Exercise 23`		
`cout << &string[2];` `// Exercise 24`	& means "the address of"	

CHAPTER

6

Lists Plus

This chapter is a combination of alternate implementations of lists and new theoretical material accompanied by the C++ implementations of the constructs. It begins with three new implementations of lists: circular linked lists, doubly linked lists, and lists with headers and trailers. We then introduce the concepts of shallow copying and deep copying, and demonstrate how to force deep copying with the class copy constructor and overloading the assignment operation.

We return to lists and discuss a List ADT with different operations, which we later use in the Case Study. Our last linked list implementation uses an array of records rather than pointers. This implementation is widely used in operating systems software. Finally we introduce two new features provided by C++ to support object-oriented programming: inheritance and dynamic binding.

■ⅠⅠ *Circular Linked Lists*

The linked list data structures that we implemented in Chapter 5 are characterized by a *linear* (line-like) relationship between the elements: each element (except the first one) has a unique predecessor, and each element (except the last one) has a unique successor. There is a problem with using linear linked lists: given a pointer to a node anywhere in the list, we can access all the nodes that follow but none of the nodes that precede it. With a singly linked linear list structure (a list with all its pointers in one direction) we must always have a pointer to the beginning of the list to be able to access all the nodes in the list.

In addition, it is not uncommon for the data we want to add to a sorted list to already be in order. Sometimes people manually sort raw data before turning it over to a data entry clerk. Data produced by other programs are often in some order. Given a Sorted List ADT and sorted input data, we always insert at the end of the list. It is ironic that the work done manually to order the data now results in maximum insertion times.

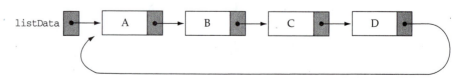

FIGURE 6.1   *A circular linked list.*

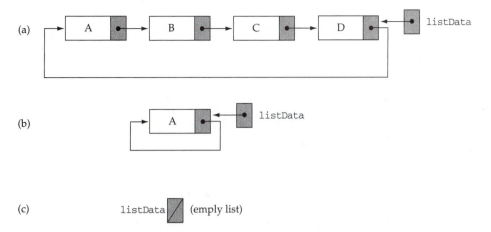

FIGURE 6.2 *Circular linked lists with the external pointer pointing to the rear element.*

We can, however, change the linear list slightly, making the pointer in the `next` member of the last node point back to the first node instead of containing NULL (Figure 6.1). Now our list is a **circular linked list** rather than a linear linked list. We can start at any node in the list and traverse the whole list. If we let our external pointer point to the last item in the list rather than the first, we have direct access to both the first and the last elements in the list (Figure 6.2). `listData->info` references the item in the last node, and `listData->next->info` references the item in the first node. We mentioned this type of list structure in Chapter 5, in discussing circular linked queues.

Circular Linked List   A list in which every node has a successor; the "last" element is succeeded by the "first" element

---

There is no need to change any of the declarations in class `SortedType` to make the list circular, rather than linear. After all, the members in the nodes are the same, only the value of the `next` member of the last node has changed. How does the circular nature of the list change the implementations of the list operations? Because an empty circular list is one with a NULL pointer, the `IsEmpty` operation is not changed at all. However, using a circular list requires an obvious change in algorithms that traverse the list. We no longer stop when the traversing pointer becomes NULL. Unless the list is empty, the pointer never becomes NULL. Instead we must look for the external pointer itself as a stop sign. Let's examine these changes in the Sorted List ADT.

(a) For a linear linked list

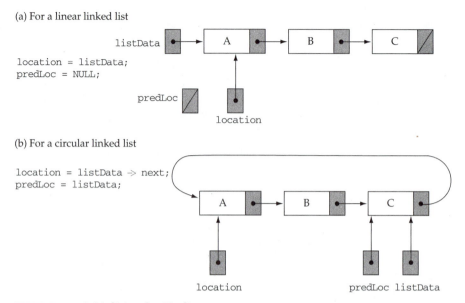

```
location = listData;
predLoc = NULL;
```

(b) For a circular linked list

```
location = listData -> next;
predLoc = listData;
```

FIGURE 6.3 *Initializing for FindItem.*

Finding a List Item

`RetrieveItem`, `InsertItem`, and `DeleteItem` all require a search. Rather than rewriting each of these with minor variations, let's write a general `FindItem` routine that takes `item` as a parameter and returns `location`, `predLoc`, and `found`. `InsertItem` and `DeleteItem` need the location of the predecessor node (`predLoc`); `RetrieveItem` can just ignore it.

In the linear list implementation, we searched the list using a pair of pointers, `location` and `predLoc`. (Remember the inchworm?) We modify this approach slightly for the circular list. In the linear list version, we initialized `location` to point to the first node in the list and set `predLoc` to NULL (Figure 6.3a). For the circular list search, we initialize `location` to point to the first node and `predLoc` to point to its "predecessor"—the last node in the list (Figure 6.3b).

The search loop executes until (1) a key greater than or equal to the `item`'s key is encountered, or (2) we reach the "end" of the list. In a linear list, the end of the list is detected when `location` equals NULL. In a circular list, because the external pointer to the list points to the last element, we know we have processed all of the items and not found a match when `location` points to the first element again: `location` equals `listData->next`. Because it makes no sense to search an empty list, let's make it a precondition that the list is not empty. Because we now have overloaded the relational operators "<" and "==", we use them in our algorithm.

FindItem

Set location to Next(listData)
Set predLoc to listData
Set found to false
Set moreToSearch to true
WHILE moreToSearch AND NOT Found DO
    IF item < Info(location)
        Set moreToSearch to false
    ELSE IF item = Info(location)
        Set found to true
    ELSE
        Set predLoc to location
        Set location to Next(location)
        Set moreToSearch to (location != Next(listData))

Following the execution of the loop, if a matching key is found, location points to the list node with that key and predLoc points to its predecessor in the list (Figure 6.4a). Note that if item's key is the smallest key in the list, predLoc is pointing to its predecessor—the last node in the circular list (Figure 6.4b). If item's key is not in the list, predLoc points to its logical predecessor in the list and location points to its logical successor (Figure 6.4c). Notice that predLoc is correct even if item's key is greater than any element in the list (Figure 6.4d). This leaves predLoc set correctly for inserting an element whose key is larger than any currently in the list.

The following C++ code implements our FindItem algorithm as a *function template*. Notice two things in the function heading. First, NodeType was defined in Chapter 5 as a struct template, so each declaration using NodeType must include an actual parameter (the name of a data type) in angle brackets. For example, listData is declared in the code that follows to be of type NodeType<ItemType>* and not simple NodeType*. Second, observe the syntax for the declarations of location and predLoc. You see an asterisk (*) and an ampersand (&) next to each other. Although this syntax may look strange at first, it is consistent with the usual way we indicate pass-by-reference: place an & after the data type of the parameter. Here we place an & after the data type NodeType<ItemType>*, which is a pointer to a node.

```
template<class ItemType>
void FindItem(NodeType<ItemType>* listData, ItemType item,
    NodeType<ItemType>*& location, NodeType<ItemType>*& predLoc,
    bool& found)
// Assumption:  ItemType is a type for which the operators "<" and
```

(a) The general case (Find B)

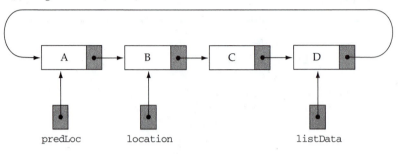

(b) Searching for the smallest item (Find A)

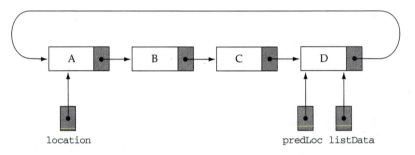

(c) Searching for item that isn't there (Find C)

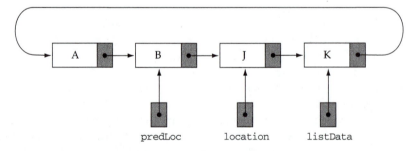

(d) Searching for item bigger than any in the list (Find E)

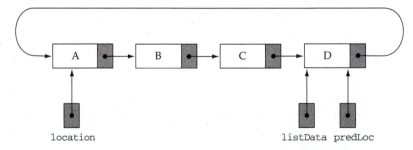

FIGURE 6.4   *The FindItem operation for a circular list.*

```
//          "==" are defined—either an appropriate built-in type or a
//          class that overloads these operations.
// Pre:   List is not empty.
// Post:  If there is an element someItem whose key matches item's
//          key, then found = true; otherwise, found = false.
//          If found, location contains the address of someItem and
//          predLoc contains the address of someItem's predecessor;
//          otherwise, location contains the address of item's logical
//          successor and predLoc contains the address of item's
//          logical predecessor.
{
    bool moreToSearch = true;

    location = listData->next;
    predLoc = listData;
    found = false;
    while (moreToSearch && !found)
    {
        if (item < location->info)
            moreToSearch = false;
        else if (item == location->info)
            found = true;
        else
        {
            predLoc = location;
            location = location->next;
            moreToSearch = (location != listData->next);
        }
    }
}
```

It is important to note that `FindItem` is not a member function of class `SortedType`. It is an auxiliary or "helper" operation, hidden within the implementation, that is used by `SortedType` member functions.

Inserting into a Circular List

The algorithm to insert an element into a circular linked list is similar to that for the linear list insertion.

InsertItem

> Set newNode to address of newly allocated node
> Set Info(newNode) to item
> Find the place where the new element belongs
> Put new element into the list

The task of allocating space is the same as for the linear list. We allocate space for the node using the new operator and then store item into newNode->info. The next task is equally simple; we just call FindItem:

```
FindItem(listData, item, location, predLoc, found);
```

Of course, we do not find the element because it isn't there; it is the predLoc pointer that interests us. The new node is linked into the list immediately after Node(predLoc). To put the new element into the list we store predLoc->next into newNode->next and newNode into predLoc->next.

The general case is illustrated in Figure 6.5(a). What are the special cases? First, we have the case of inserting the first element into an empty list. In this case, we want to make listData point to the new node, and to make the new node point to itself (Figure 6.5b). In the insertion algorithm for the linear linked list we also had a special case when the new element key was smaller than any other key in the list. Because the new node became the first node in the list, we had to change the external pointer to point to the new node. The external pointer to a circular list, however, doesn't point to the first node in the list—it points to the last node. Therefore, inserting the smallest list element is not a special case for a circular linked list (Figure 6.5c). However, inserting the largest list element at the end of the list is a special case. In addition to linking the node to its predecessor (previously the last list node) and its successor (the first list node), we must modify the external pointer to point to Node(newNode)— the new last node in the circular list (Figure 6.5d).

The statements to link the new node to the end of the list are the same as the general case, plus the assignment of the external pointer, listData. Rather than checking for this special case before the search, we can treat it together with the general case: search for the insertion place and link in the new node. Then, if we detect that we have added the new node to the end of the list, we reassign listData to point to the new node. To detect this condition, we compare item to listData->info.

The resulting implementation of InsertItem is shown here.

```
template<class ItemType>
void SortedType<ItemType>::InsertItem(ItemType item)
{
    NodeType<ItemType>* newNode;
    NodeType<ItemType>* predLoc;
    NodeType<ItemType>* location;
    bool found;

    newNode = new NodeType<ItemType>;
    newNode->info = item;
```

(a) The general case (Insert C)

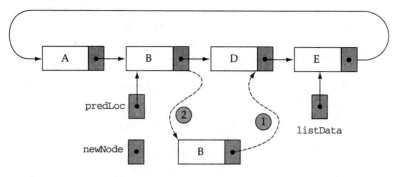

(b) Special case: the empty list (Insert A)

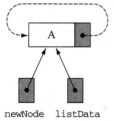

(c) Special case: (?): inserting to front of list (Insert A)

(d) Special case: inserting to end of list (Insert E)

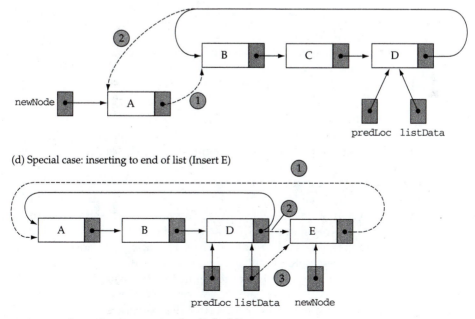

FIGURE 6.5 *Inserting into a circular linked list.*

```
if (listData != NULL)
{
    FindItem(listData, item, location, predLoc, found);
    newNode->next = predLoc->next;
    predLoc->next = newNode;

    // If this is last node in list, reassign listData.
    if (listData->info < item)
        listData = newNode;
}
else        // Inserting into an empty list.
{
    listData = newNode;
    newNode->next = newNode;
}
length++;
}
```

Deleting from a Circular List

To delete an element from the circular linked list, we use the same general algorithm we developed for the linear list:

DeleteItem

Find the element in the list
Remove the element from the list
Deallocate the node

For the first task, we use FindItem. On return from FindItem, location is pointing to the node we wish to delete, and predLoc is pointing to its predecessor in the list. To remove Node(location) from the list, we simply reset predLoc->next to jump over the node we are deleting. That works for the general case, at least (see Figure 6.6a). What kind of special cases do we have to consider? In the linear list version, we had to check for deleting the first (or first-and-only) element. From our experience with the insertion operation, we might surmise that deleting the smallest element (the first node) of the circular list is *not* a special case; Figure 6.6(b) shows that guess to be correct. However, deleting the only node in a circular list *is* a special case, as we see in Figure 6.6(c). The external pointer to the list must be set to NULL to indicate that the list is now empty. We can detect this situation by checking to see if predLoc equals location after the execution of FindItem; if so, the node we are deleting is the only one in the list.

(a) The general case (Delete B)

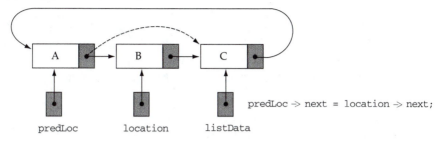

predLoc → next = location → next;

(b) Special case (?): deleting the smallest item (Delete A)

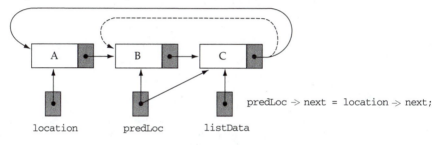

predLoc → next = location → next;

(c) Special case: deleting the only item (Delete A)

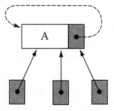

listData = NULL;

(b) Special case: deleting the largest item (Delete C)

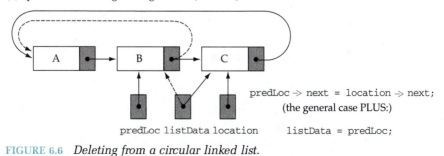

predLoc → next = location → next;
(the general case PLUS:)

listData = predLoc;

FIGURE 6.6 *Deleting from a circular linked list.*

We might also guess that deleting the largest list element (the last node) from a circular list is a special case. As Figure 6.6(d) illustrates, when we delete the last node, we first do the general-case processing to unlink Node(location) from the list, then we reset listData to point to its predecessor, Node(predLoc). We can detect this situation by checking whether location equals listData after the search.

```
template<class ItemType>
void SortedType<ItemType>::DeleteItem(ItemType item)
{
    NodeType<ItemType>* location;
    NodeType<ItemType>* predLoc;
    bool found;

    FindItem(listData, item, location, predLoc, found);
    if (predLoc == location)            // Only node in list?
        listData = NULL;
    else
    {
        predLoc->next = location->next;
        if (location == listData)       // Deleting last node in list?
            listData = predLoc;
    }
    delete location;
    length--;
}
```

Having worked through a number of the list operations in detail, we leave the circular implementation of the other Sorted List ADT operations as a programming assignment (Chapter 6, Programming Assignment 5). None of the operations we have looked at so far have become shorter or much simpler by changing the implementation to a circular list. Why then might we want to use a circular, rather than linear, linked list? Circular lists are good for applications that require access to both ends of the list. (The circular linked version of the queue in Chapter 5 is a good example of this.)

■|| *Doubly Linked Lists*

We have discussed using circular linked lists to enable us to reach any node in the list from any starting point. Although this structure has advantages over a simple linear linked list, it is still too limited for certain types of applications. Suppose we want to delete a particular node in a list, given only a pointer to that node (location). This task involves changing the next member of the node preceding Node(location). As we saw in the previous chapter, however, given only the pointer location, we cannot access its predecessor in the list.

Another task that is difficult to perform on a linear linked list is traversing the list in reverse. For instance, suppose we have a list of student records, sorted by grade point average (GPA) from lowest to highest. The Dean of Students might want a printout of the students' records, sorted from highest to lowest, to use in preparing the Dean's List.

In cases like these, where we need to be able to access the node that precedes a given node, a doubly linked list is useful. In a doubly linked list, the nodes are linked in both directions. Each node of a doubly linked list contains three parts:

Info: the data stored in the node
Next: the pointer to the following node
Back: the pointer to the preceding node

Doubly Linked List   A linked list in which each node is linked to both its successor and its predecessor

---

A linear doubly linked list is pictured in Figure 6.7. Note that the back member of the first node, as well as the next member of the last node, contains a NULL. The following definition might be used to declare the nodes in such a list:

```
template<class ItemType>
struct NodeType
{
    ItemType info;
    NodeType<ItemType>* next;
    NodeType<ItemType>* back;
};
```

Using this definition, let's write member functions InsertItem and DeleteItem using the auxiliary function FindItem.

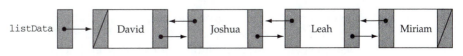

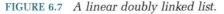
FIGURE 6.7   *A linear doubly linked list.*

Finding an Item in a Doubly Linked List

In the `FindItem` function, we no longer need to use the inchworm search; instead we can get the predecessor to any node through its `back` member. We change the `FindItem` interface slightly; because we no longer need `predLoc`, we return one pointer, `location`. If found is true, `location` points to the node with the same key as `item`; otherwise, `location` points to the node that is the logical successor of `item`. (Recall that `FindItem` is a function template.)

```
template<class ItemType>
void FindItem(NodeType<ItemType>* listData, ItemType item,
    NodeType<ItemType>*& location, bool& found)
// Assumption:  ItemType is a type for which the operators "<" and
//        "==" are defined—either an appropriate built-in type or a
//        class that overloads these operations.
// Pre:  List is not empty.
// Post: If there is an element someItem whose key matches item's
//        key, then found = true; otherwise, found = false.
//        If found, location contains the address of someItem;
//        otherwise, location contains the address of the logical
//        successor of item.
{
    bool moreToSearch = true;

    location = listData;
    found = false;
    while (moreToSearch && !found)
    {
        if (item < location->info)
            moreToSearch = false;
        else if (item == location->info)
            found = true;
        else
        {
            location = location->next;
            moreToSearch = (location != NULL);
        }
    }
}
```

Operations on a Doubly Linked List

The algorithms for the insertion and deletion operations on a doubly linked list are somewhat more complicated than those for operations on a singly linked list. The reason is clear: there are more pointers to keep track of in a doubly linked list.

For example, consider the `InsertItem` operation. To link the new node, Node(`newNode`), after a given node, Node(`location`), in a singly linked list, we need to change two pointers: `newNode->next` and `location->next` (see Figure 6.8a). The same operation on a doubly linked list requires four pointer changes (see Figure 6.8b).

We allocate space for the new node and call `FindItem` to find the insertion point:

```
FindItem(listData, item, location, found);
```

(a) Inserting into a singly linked list (Insert Leah)

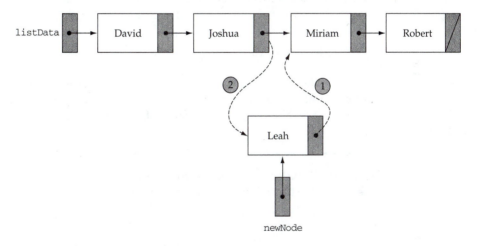

(b) Inserting into a doubly linked list

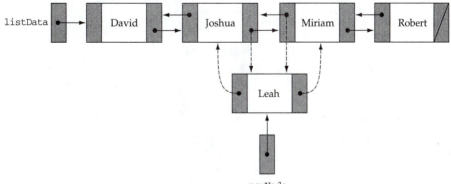

FIGURE 6.8 *Insertions into singly and doubly linked lists.*

On return from `FindItem`, `location` is pointing to the node that should follow the new node. Now we are ready to link Node(`newNode`) into the list. Because of the complexity of the operation, it is important to be careful about the order in which you change the pointers. For instance, when inserting Node(`newNode`) before Node(`location`), if we change the pointer in `location->back` first, we lose our pointer to Node(`location`)'s predecessor. The correct order for the pointer changes is illustrated in Figure 6.9.

Set Back(newNode) to Back(location)
Set Next(newNode) to location
Set Next(Back(location)) to newNode
Set Back(location) to newNode

We do have to be careful about inserting into an empty list, as it is a special case.

One of the useful features of a doubly linked list is that we don't need a pointer to a node's predecessor in order to delete the node. Through the `back` member we can alter the `next` member of the preceding node to make it jump

Set Next(Back(location)) to Next(location)
Set Back(Next(location)) to Back(location)

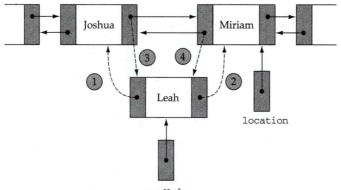

FIGURE 6.9 *Linking the new node into the list.*

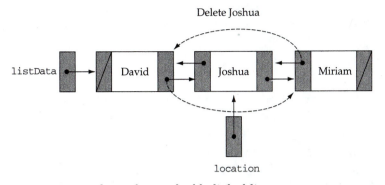

FIGURE 6.10 *Deleting from a doubly linked list.*

over the unwanted node. Then we make the `back` pointer of the succeeding node point to the preceding node.

We do, however, have to be careful about the end cases. If `location->back` is NULL, we are deleting the first node; if `location->next` is NULL, we are deleting the last node. If both `location->back` and `location->next` are NULL, we are deleting the only node. This operation is pictured in Figure 6.10.

We leave the coding of `SortedType` as a programming assignment (Chapter 6, Programming Assignment 6).

Linked Lists with Headers and Trailers

In writing the insert and delete algorithms for all implementations of linked lists, we see that special cases arise when we are dealing with the first node or the last node. One way to simplify these algorithms is to make sure that we never insert or delete at the ends of the list.

How can this be accomplished? Recall that the elements in the sorted linked list are arranged according to the value in some key—for example, numerically by identification number or alphabetically by name. If the range of possible values for the key can be determined, it is often a simple matter to set up dummy nodes with values outside of this range. A **header node**, containing a value smaller than any possible list element key, can be placed at the beginning of the list. A **trailer node**, containing a value larger than any legitimate element key, can be placed at the end of the list.

The header and the trailer are regular nodes of the same type as the real data nodes in the list. They have a different purpose, however; instead of storing list data, they act as place holders.

> **Header Node**   A placeholder node at the beginning of a list; used to simplify list processing
>
> **Trailer Node**   A placeholder node at the end of a list; used to simplify list processing

If a list of students is sorted by last name, for example, we might assume that there are no students named "AAAAAAAAAA" or "ZZZZZZZZZZ." We could therefore initialize our linked list to contain header and trailer nodes with these values as the keys. See Figure 6.11. How can we write a general list algorithm if we must know the minimum and maximum key values? We can use a parameterized class constructor and let the user pass as parameters elements containing the dummy keys. Alternatively, we can just leave the keys undefined and start the search with the second node in the list.

■‖ *Copy Structures*

In this section, we reverse the usual order of presentation. We show an example of a problem, and then we show the solution to the general problem. Let's look at an example where a client of the Stack ADT needs a `CopyStack` operation.

CopyStack(StackType oldStack, StackType& copy)

Function: Makes a copy of a stack.
Precondition: oldStack has been initialized.
Postconditions: copy is a duplicate of oldStack.
                   oldStack is unchanged.

The client has access to all the public member functions of `StackType` but cannot access any of the private data members. To make a copy of a stack, we must take all the items off `oldStack` and store them in a temporary stack. We can then copy the temporary stack back into `copy`.

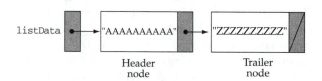

FIGURE 6.11   *An "empty" list with a header and a trailer.*

```
template<class ItemType>
void CopyStack(StackType<ItemType> oldStack,
    StackType<ItemType>& copy)
{
    StackType<ItemType> tempStack;
    ItemType item;

    while (!oldStack.IsEmpty())
    {
        oldStack.Pop(item);
        tempStack.Push(item);
    }

    // oldStack is now empty; tempStack is reverse of oldStack.
    while (!tempStack.IsEmpty())
    {
        tempStack.Pop(item);
        copy.Push(item);
    }
}
```

This seems quite straightforward. We realize that `oldStack` is empty because all of the items have been popped, but because `oldStack` is a value parameter, the original stack is not affected. Right? Wrong! If the static, array-based implementation of `StackType` is used, this function works correctly. The array is physically located within a class object. The class object is copied into the value parameter `oldStack` and the original object is protected from change. But what happens if the dynamically linked implementation is used? The external pointer to the stack is copied into `oldStack` and is not changed, *but the items to which it points are changed; they are not protected* (Figure 6.12).

Can't we solve this problem by copying `tempStack` back into `oldStack`? Let's consider the code for the `Push` operation and see what happens in the linked implementation. The first item is pushed onto the stack, and its address is stored into the data member `topPtr` of the parameter `oldStack`. As each

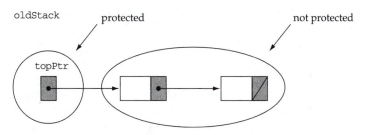

FIGURE 6.12 *Stack is a value parameter.*

successive item is put onto the stack, its address is stored into data member `topPtr`. Therefore, the `topPtr` data member of `oldStack` should contain the address of the last item put onto the stack, which is what we want. But because the stack is passed by value, only the *copy* of the external pointer to the stack (data member `topPtr` of `oldStack`) is passed to the function and the original is not changed. We have recreated the stack, but its external pointer is not transmitted back to the calling code.

There are two solutions to this problem: we can make the first parameter a reference parameter and recreate the stack, or we can provide a *copy constructor* as described in the next section.

Shallow vs. Deep Copies

The problem described in the previous section occurred because when a class object is passed by value, a **shallow copy** of the parameter is made. A shallow copy is one where only the data members in the parameter are copied. In the case of `CopyStack`, only a copy of the external pointer to the stack was passed as the parameter. When pointers are involved, we need a **deep copy**, one where the data members of the parameter and everything to which the data members point are copied. Figure 6.13 shows the difference.

Shallow Copy   An operation that copies one class object to another without copying any pointed-to data

Deep Copy   An operation that not only copies one class object to another but also makes copies of any pointed-to data

---

If the calling code passes an actual parameter `callerStack` to the `CopyStack` function, a shallow copy causes the data member `callerStack.topPtr` to be copied into `oldStack.topPtr`. Both pointers now point to the same linked structure (Figure 6.13a). When the `CopyStack` function removes the items from the stack, it is destroying the caller's stack! What we want is a deep copy of the stack so that `CopyStack` works with an identical but *separate* copy of the caller's stack (Figure 6.13b). In this case the caller's stack is completely unchanged by any manipulations within the function.

Class Copy Constructors

C++ uses shallow copying in the following cases: passing parameters by value, initializing a variable in a declaration (`StackType<int> myStack = yourStack;`), returning an object as the value of a function (`return thisStack;`), and implementing the assignment operation (`stack1 =`

(a) A shallow copy

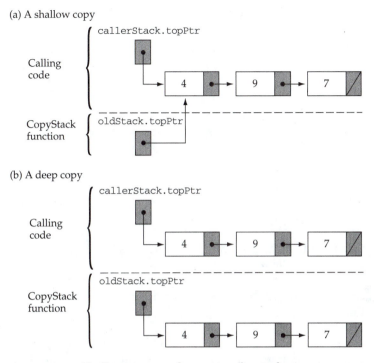

(b) A deep copy

FIGURE 6.13   *Shallow copy vs. deep copy of a stack.*

`stack2;`). Again because of the active stance of a class object, C++ supports another special class operation called the **copy constructor,** which we describe shortly. If present, the copy constructor is used implicitly when a class object is passed by value, when a class object is initialized in a declaration, and when an object is a function return value. (What about the assignment operation? No, if you want to assign one object to another using a deep copy, you have to (a) write a member function to perform the deep copy and explicitly invoke it rather than use the assignment operator, or (b) overload the assignment operator. We discuss the first alternative in this section and the second alternative in the next section.)

Copy Constructor   A special member function of a class that is implicitly invoked when passing parameters by value, initializing a variable in a declaration, and returning an object as the return value of a function

---

The copy constructor has a special syntax. Like the class constructor and destructor, it has no return type, just the class name.

```
template <class ItemType>
class StackType
{
public:
    .
    .
    .
    // Copy constructor.
    StackType(const StackType<ItemType>& anotherStack);
    .
    .
    .
};
```

The pattern that signals a copy constructor is the single reference parameter of the class type. The word `const` protects the parameter from being altered even though it is being passed by reference. Because the copy constructor is a class member function, the implementation has direct access to the class data. To copy a linked structure, we must cycle through the structure one node at a time making a copy of the node's content as we go. Therefore we need two running pointers, one pointing to successive nodes in the structure being copied and one pointing to the last node of the new structure. Remember, the deep copy of a linked structure is one where the `info` members are the same but the `next` members are not. In writing the algorithm, we must be sure to take care of the case where the stack being copied is empty.

Copy Constructor

IF anotherStack.topPtr is NULL
    Set topPtr to NULL
ELSE
    Set topPtr to the address of a newly allocated node
    Set Info(topPtr) to Info(anotherStack.topPtr)
    Set ptr1 to Next(anotherStack.topPtr)
    Set ptr2 to topPtr
WHILE ptr1 is not NULL
    Set Next(ptr2) to the address of a newly allocated node
    Set ptr2 to Next(ptr2)
    Set Info(ptr2) to Info(ptr1)
    Set ptr1 to Next(ptr1)
Set Next(ptr2) to NULL

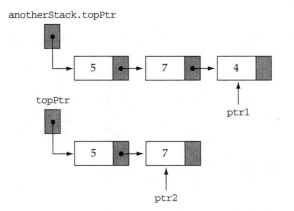

FIGURE 6.14 *Relative position of pointers at the beginning of each iteration.*

Notice that our algorithm avoids using an extra pointer to the new node being inserted by storing its address directly into the structure where the new node is to go. `ptr1` points to the node to be copied; `ptr2` points to the last node copied. (See Figure 6.14.)

```
template <class ItemType>
StackType<ItemType>::StackType(const StackType<ItemType>&
anotherStack)
{
    NodeType<ItemType>* ptr1;
    NodeType<ItemType>* ptr2;

    if (anotherStack.topPtr == NULL)
        topPtr = NULL;
    else
    {
        topPtr = new NodeType<ItemType>;
        topPtr->info = anotherStack.topPtr->info;
        ptr1 = anotherStack.topPtr->next;
        ptr2 = topPtr;
        while (ptr1 != NULL)
        {
            ptr2->next = new NodeType<ItemType>;
            ptr2 = ptr2->next;
            ptr2->info = ptr1->info;
            ptr1 = ptr1->next;
        }
        ptr2->next = NULL;
    }
}
```

Copy Function

We saw how the client program could write a function `CopyStack` to copy one stack into another, provided a class copy constructor is defined to maintain the integrity of the original stack passed as a value parameter. Alternatively, could we include a member function to copy one stack into another and let the client invoke it explicitly? Sure, but first we must decide whether we are copying self into another object or another object into self. That is, member functions are always applied to an object of the class type. One stack would be the object to which the function is applied, and the other stack would be a parameter of the function. Given the following statement

```
myStack.Copy(yourStack);
```

is `myStack` being copied into `yourStack` or the other way around? Of course, we can't answer the question until we see the function declaration. If `yourStack` is being copied into `myStack`, then the code for `Copy` would be nearly identical to the class copy constructor. The difference is that self already points to a dynamic structure, and we must deallocate all the nodes of this structure by applying `MakeEmpty` before the copying begins. On the other hand, if `myStack` is being copied into `yourStack`, then the algorithm would have to be rethought. We leave this change as an exercise.

There is a third way to implement a copy function. Suppose that we'd like to write a function in which both stacks are parameters to the function.

```
Copy(myStack, yourStack);
```

Compared to dot notation, this syntax is more familiar (and therefore more comfortable) to some programmers. But we just said that member functions are applied to an object of the class type. How can we do this? C++ provides a syntactic device called a *friend function* that allows this type of construction. A friend function is *not* a member of the class, yet it has permission to access private class members directly. Here is how this friend function would be declared and implemented.

```
template<class ItemType>
class StackType
{
public:
    .
    .
    .
```

```
        friend void Copy(StackType<ItemType>, StackType<ItemType>&);
        .
        .
        .
};

template<class ItemType>
void Copy(StackType<ItemType> original, StackType<ItemType>& copy)
{
    if (original.topPtr == NULL)
        copy.topPtr = NULL;
    else
    {
        NodeType<ItemType>* ptr1;
        NodeType<ItemType)* ptr2;

        copy.topPtr = new NodeType<ItemType>;
        copy.topPtr->info = original.topPtr->info;
        ptr1 = original.topPtr->next;
        ptr2 = copy.topPtr;
        while (ptr1 != NULL)
        {
            ptr2->next = new NodeType<ItemType>;
            ptr2 = ptr2->next;
            ptr2->info = ptr1->info;
            ptr1 = ptr1->next;
        }
        ptr2->next = NULL;
    }
}
```

Notice that the name of the function is not prefaced with the class name and :: operator. This is because Copy is a friend function, not a member function. However, Copy does have access to the private data members of its parameters, but access to them must be qualified by the parameter name and a dot. There is no implicit *self* in a friend function. The friend function is declared within a class definition, but it is not a member function of the class.

Overloading the Assignment Operator

In the last section we pointed out that the assignment operator (=) normally causes shallow copying. It would be nice if we could write

```
myStack = yourStack;
```

but if the stack is implemented as a dynamic linked structure, we would have two pointers pointing to the same stack rather than two distinct stacks. We can solve the problem of shallow copying with the assignment operator by overloading its meaning. In Chapter 3 we showed how to overload the relational operators. We can do the same thing for the assignment operator.

```
template<class ItemType>
class StackType
{
public:

    .
    .
    .

    void operator=(StackType<ItemType>);
    .
    .
    .

};
```

The function definition looks like this:

```
template<class ItemType>
void StackType<ItemType>::operator=
    (StackType<ItemType> anotherStack)
{
    .
    .
    .
}
```

The function body is identical to that of the Copy member function that we discussed (but left as an exercise) earlier. Therefore, if we have already written a Copy member function, then to overload the assignment operator we have to make only one small change: change the function name from Copy to operator=.

With an operator= function provided by the StackType class, the client code can use a statement like

```
myStack = yourStack;
```

The compiler implicitly translates this statement into the function call

```
myStack.operator = (yourStack);
```

Thus, the class object to the left of the equal sign in the client code is the object to which the `operator=` function is applied, and the object to the right of the equal sign becomes the parameter to the function.

The assignment operator can be overloaded for any number of classes. When the compiler sees an assignment operator, it looks at the types of the operands and uses the appropriate code. If the operands are objects of a class that has not overloaded the assignment operator, the default meaning of assignment is used—copying of data members only, yielding a shallow copy.

▬▬ Guidelines for Operator Overloading

1. All C++ operators may be overloaded except `::`, `.`, `sizeof`, and `?:`.
2. At least one operand of the overloaded operator must be a class instance.
3. You cannot change the standard order of operator precedence, define new operator symbols, or change the number of operands of an operator.
4. Overloading unary operators: If `data` is of type `SomeClass`, and you want to overload, say, the unary minus operator, then `-data` is equivalent to `data.operator-()` if `operator-` is a member function and `operator-(data)` if `operator-` is a friend function.
5. Overloading binary operators: If `data` is of type `SomeClass` and you want to overload, say, the addition operator (+), then `data+otherData` is equivalent to `data.operator+(otherData)` if `operator+` is a member function and `operator+(data, otherData)` if `operator+` is a friend function.
6. Overloading the `++` and `--` operators requires client code to use the preincrement form: `++someObject` or `-- someObject`. There is a mechanism for allowing postincrement as well, but we do not discuss it here.
7. Operator functions must be member functions when overloading `=`, `()`, and `[]`. Other restrictions apply as well. See a C++ reference book before attempting to overload `()` and `[]`.
8. Many meanings for an operator can coexist as long as the compiler can distinguish among the data types of the operands.

One final comment before we leave the problems involved with classes in which at least one of the data members is a pointer. If one of the three—class destructor, copy constructor, or overloaded assignment operator—is necessary, then most likely all three are necessary. This is sometimes called the "Rule of the big 3."

■‖ *A Specialized List ADT*

So far our List ADTs have been either unsorted (elements are inserted at the front in the linked implementation or at the back in the array-based implementation) or sorted by key value. We have examined various ways of implementing the same member functions using different implementation structures. In the Case Study at the end of the chapter, we are going to need a List ADT with different operations. We are going to need to process items from left-to-right and from right-to-left. In addition, we are going to need to insert items at the front and at the back.

One advantage of a doubly linked structure is the ability to traverse a structure in both directions. When a structure is linked only in one direction, it is not simple to traverse it in the other direction. Because a doubly linked list is linked in both directions, traversing the list forward or backward is equally simple. On the other hand, a circular structure with the external pointer pointing to the last item in the structure gives direct access to both the front element and the last element. A doubly linked circular structure would be ideal (see Figure 6.15).

Let's practice using these new implementation structures by defining a class that incorporates the operations that we need in the Case Study. Because this is a special-purpose ADT, we combine the specification and the class definition and give the class type a different name. Because we are processing from both ends, let's call it List2Type

```
template<class ItemType>
struct NodeType;

template<class ItemType>
class List2Type
{
public:
    List2Type();                        // Class constructor
    ~List2Type();                       // Class destructor
```

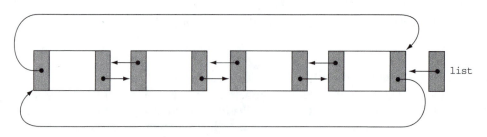

FIGURE 6.15   *A circular doubly linked list.*

```
    List2Type(const List2Type& someList); // Copy constructor
    void operator=(List2Type someList);

    void ResetForward();
    // Initializes current position for an iteration
    // through the list from first item to last item.

    void GetNextItem(ItemType& item, bool& finished);
    // Gets the next item in the structure.
    // finished is true if all the items have been accessed.
    // GetNextItem and GetPriorItem are independent; a forward
    // iteration and a backward iteration may be in progress
    // at the same time.

    void ResetBackward();
    // Initializes current position for an iteration
    // through the list from last item to first item.

    void GetPriorItem(ItemType& item, bool& finished);
    // Gets the previous item in the structure.
    // finished is true if all the items have been accessed.

    void InsertFront(ItemType item);
    // Inserts item as the first item in the structure.

    void InsertEnd(ItemType item);
    // Inserts item as the last item in the structure.

    int LengthIs();
    // Returns the number of items in the structure.
private:
    NodeType<ItemType>* list;
    NodeType<ItemType>* currentNextPos;
    NodeType<ItemType>* currentBackPos;
    int length;
};
    .
    .

    .
template<class ItemType>
struct NodeType
{
    NodeType<ItemType>* next;
    NodeType<ItemType>* back;
    ItemType info;
};
```

Although we are providing a length operation, we give the user another way of determining when the last item has been accessed: `GetNextItem` and `GetPriorItem` both have an extra parameter, a Boolean flag. This flag is set to true when the last item has been returned. These operations are all very general and require no knowledge of `ItemType`.

`ResetForward` sets `currentNextPos` to NULL, and `GetNextItem` returns the next item in the structure, setting `finished` to true when `currentNextPos` equals `list`. `ResetBackward` sets `currentBackPos` to NULL, and `GetPriorItem` returns the previous item in the structure, setting `finished` to true when `currentBackPos` equals `list->next`.

```
template<class ItemType>
void List2Type<ItemType>::ResetForward()
// Post: currentNextPos has been initialized for a forward
//       traversal.
{
    currentNextPos = NULL;
}

template<class ItemType>
void List2Type<ItemType>::GetNextItem(ItemType& item,
    bool& finished)
// Pre:  ResetForward has been called before the first call to
//       this function.
// Post: item is a copy of the next item in the list.
//       finished is true if item is the last item in the list;
//       false otherwise.
{
    if (currentNextPos == NULL)
        currentNextPos = list->next;
    else
        currentNextPos = currentNextPos->next;
    item = currentNextPos->info;
    finished = (currentNextPos == list);
}

template<class ItemType>
void List2Type<ItemType>::ResetBackward()
// Post: currentBackPos has been initialized for a backward
//       traversal.
{
    currentBackPos = NULL;
}

template<class ItemType>
void List2Type<ItemType>::GetPriorItem(ItemType& item,
    bool& finished)
```

```
// Pre:   ResetBackward has been called before the first call to
//            this function.
// Post: item is a copy of the previous item in the list.
//        finished is true if item is the first item in the list;
//        false otherwise.
{
    if (currentBackPos == NULL)
        currentBackPos = list;
    else
        currentBackPos = currentBackPos->back;
    item = currentBackPos->info;
    finished = (currentBackPos == list->next);
}
```

InsertFront inserts the new item as the first item in the list (see Figure 6.16a). InsertEnd inserts the new item as the last item in the list (see Figure 6.16b). The results look quite different in the diagram, but a careful examination reveals that they are identical *except for the external pointer list*. Inserting at the beginning does not change list; inserting at the end does. We can use the same insertion routine for both, but have InsertEnd move list.

```
template<class ItemType>
void List2Type<ItemType>::InsertFront(ItemType item)
// Post: item has been inserted at the front of the list.
```

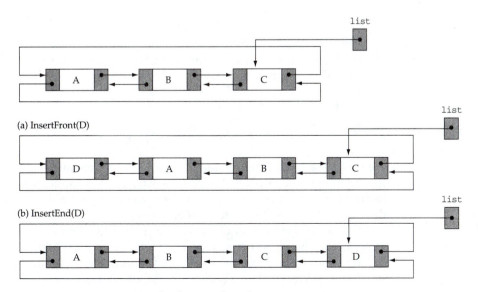

(a) InsertFront(D)

(b) InsertEnd(D)

FIGURE 6.16 *Inserting at the front and at the rear.*

```
{
    NodeType<ItemType>* newNode;

    newNode = new NodeType<ItemType>;
    newNode->info = item;
    if (list == NULL)
    { // list is empty.
        newNode->back = newNode;
        newNode->next = newNode;
        list = newNode;
    }
    else
    {
        newNode->back = list;
        newNode->next = list->next;
        list->next->back = newNode;
        list->next = newNode;
    }
    length++;
}

template<class ItemType>
void List2Type<ItemType>::InsertEnd(ItemType item)
// Post: item has been inserted at the end of the list.
{
    InsertFront(item);
    list = list->next;
}
```

We leave the implementations of the class constructor, destructor, copy constructor and overloaded assignment operator plus function LengthIs as a programming assignment (Chapter 6, Programming Assignment 9).

▪❚❚ *A Linked List as an Array of Records*

We have used both statically allocated arrays and dynamically allocated arrays for our array-based implementations. We have used dynamic memory allocation to obtain the necessary memory for the nodes making up the linked structures developed in this and the previous chapters.

The choice between array-based and linked-list representations is not the same as the choice between static and dynamic storage allocation. These are separate issues. We typically store arrays in variables that have been declared statically, as illustrated in Figure 6.17(a), but an array-based implementation does not necessarily use static storage. The whole array could exist in a

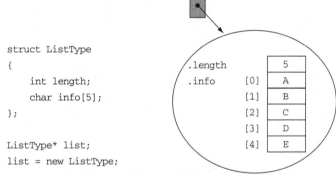

(a) A sequential list in static storage

```
struct ListType
{
    int length;
    char info[5];
};

ListType list;
```

(b) A sequential list in dynamic storage

```
struct ListType
{
    int length;
    char info[5];
};

ListType* list;
list = new ListType;
```

FIGURE 6.17 *Array-based lists in static and dynamic storage.*

dynamically allocated area of memory; that is, we could get space for the whole structure at once using the new operator, as illustrated in Figure 6.17(b).

We tend to think of linked structures as being in dynamically allocated storage, as illustrated in Figure 6.18(a), but this is not a requirement. A linked list could be implemented in an array; the elements might be stored in the array in any order, and "linked" by their indexes (see Figure 6.18b). In the following sections, we develop the array-based linked-list implementation.

Why Use an Array?

We have seen that dynamic allocation of list nodes has many advantages, so why would we even discuss using an array-of-records implementation instead? We have said that dynamic allocation is only one advantage of choosing a linked implementation; another advantage is the efficiency of the insert and delete algorithms. Most of the algorithms that we have discussed for operations on a linked structure can be used for either an array-based or a dynamic implementation. The main difference is the requirement that we manage our

(a) A linked list in dynamic storage

```
struct NodeType
{
    char info;
    NodeType* next;
};

NodeType* list;
list = new NodeType;
```

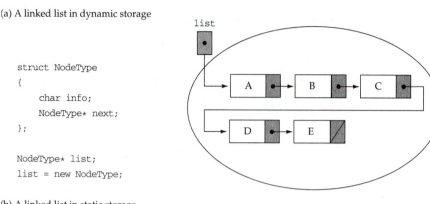

(b) A linked list in static storage

```
struct NodeType
{
    char info;
    int next;
};
struct ListType
{
    NodeType nodes[5];
    int first;
};
ListType list;
```

	list	
	.nodes	
[0]	C	4
[1]	B	0
[2]	E	-1
[3]	A	1
[4]	D	2
.first	3	

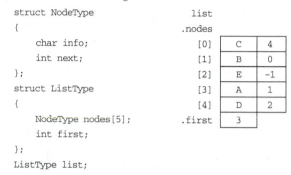

FIGURE 6.18 *Linked lists in static and dynamic storage.*

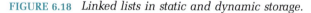

own free space in an array-based implementation. Managing the free space ourselves gives us greater flexibility.

Another reason to use an array of records is that there are a number of programming languages that do not have dynamic allocation or pointer types. You can still use linked structures if you are programming in one of these languages, but you would have to represent pointer values as array indexes.

Using pointer variables presents a problem when we need to save the information in a data structure between runs of a program. Suppose we want to write all the nodes in a list to a file and then use this file as input the next time we run the program. If the links are pointer values—containing memory addresses—they are meaningless on the next run of the program because the program may be placed somewhere else in memory the next time. We must save the user data part of each node in the file and then rebuild the linked structure the next time we run the program. An array index, however, is still valid on the next run of the program. We can store the whole array, including the next data members (indexes), and then read it back in the next time we run the program.

Most importantly, there are times when dynamic allocation isn't possible or feasible, or when dynamic allocation of each node, one at a time, is too costly in terms of time—especially in system software such as operating system code.

How Is an Array Used?

Let's get back to our discussion of how a linked list can be implemented in an array. As we have said, the `next` member of each node tells us the array index of the succeeding node. The beginning of the list is accessed through a "pointer" that contains the array index of the first element in the list. Figure 6.19 shows how a sorted list containing the elements David, Joshua, Leah, Miriam, and Robert might be stored in an array of records called `nodes`. Do you see how the order of the elements in the list is explicitly indicated by the chain of `next` indexes?

What goes in the `next` member of the last list element? Its "null" value must be an invalid address for a real list element. Because the `nodes` array indexes begin at 0, the value -1 is not a valid index into the array; that is, there is

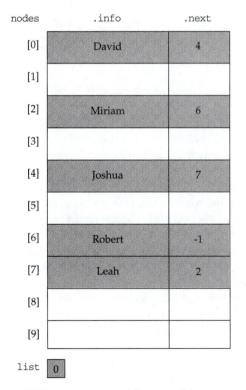

FIGURE 6.19   *A sorted list stored in an array of records.*

no nodes [-1] . Therefore -1 makes an ideal value to use as a "null" address. However, let's use the constant identifier NUL rather than NULL to keep the distinction clear. We could use the literal value -1 in our programs:

```
while (location != -1)
```

but it is better programming style to declare a named constant. In fact, we can define NUL to be -1.

```
const int NUL = -1;
```

When an array-of-records implementation is used to represent a linked list, the programmer must write routines to manage the free space available for new list elements. Where is this free space? Look again at Figure 6.19. All of the array elements that do not contain values in the list constitute free space. Instead of the built-in allocator new, which allocates memory dynamically, we must write our own function to allocate nodes from the free space. We call this function GetNode.

When elements are deleted from the list, we need to free the node space. We can't use delete, because it only works for dynamically allocated space. We write our own function, FreeNode, to put a node back into the pool of free space.

This collection of unused array elements can be linked together into a second list, a linked list of free nodes. Figure 6.20 shows the array nodes with both the list of values and the list of free space linked through their next members. list is the external pointer to a list that begins at index 0 (containing the value David). Following the links in the next member, we see that the list continues with the array slots at index 4 (Joshua), 7 (Leah), 2 (Miriam), and 6 (Robert), in that order. The free list begins at free, at index 1. Following the links in the next member, we see that the free list also includes the array slots at index 5, 3, 8, and 9. You see two NUL values in the next column because there are two linked lists contained in the nodes array.

There are two approaches to using an array-of-records implementation for linked structures. The first is to simulate dynamic memory. One array is used to store many different linked lists, just as the nodes on the free store can be dynamically allocated for different lists. In this approach the external pointers to the lists are not part of the storage structure, but the external pointer to the list of free nodes is part of the structure. Figure 6.21 shows an array that contains two different lists. The list indicated by list1 contains the values John, Nell, Susan, and Suzanne and the list indicated by list2 contains the values Mark, Naomi, and Robert. The remaining three array slots in Figure 6.21 are linked together in the free list.

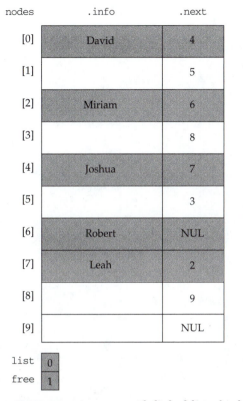

nodes	.info	.next
[0]	David	4
[1]		5
[2]	Miriam	6
[3]		8
[4]	Joshua	7
[5]		3
[6]	Robert	NUL
[7]	Leah	2
[8]		9
[9]		NUL

list 0
free 1

FIGURE 6.20 *An array with linked list of values and free space.*

Another approach is to have one array of records for each list. In this approach, the external pointer is part of the storage structure itself (see Figure 6.22). The list constructor takes a parameter that specifies the maximum number of items to be on the list. This parameter is used to dynamically allocate an array of the appropriate size. Note that the array itself is in dynamic storage, but the linked structure uses array indexes as "pointers." If the list is to be saved between runs, the contents of the array are saved, and the indexes (links) are still valid.

Here we implement this second approach. In implementing our class functions, we need to keep in mind that there are two distinct processes going on within the array of records: bookkeeping relating to the space (such as initializing the array of records, getting a new node, and freeing a node) and the operations on the list that contains the user's data. The bookkeeping operations are transparent to the user. The prototypes of the member functions stay the same, including both a parameterized and a default constructor. The private data members, however, change. We need to include the array of records. Let's call the array `nodes` and place it in dynamic storage. `MemoryType`, then, is

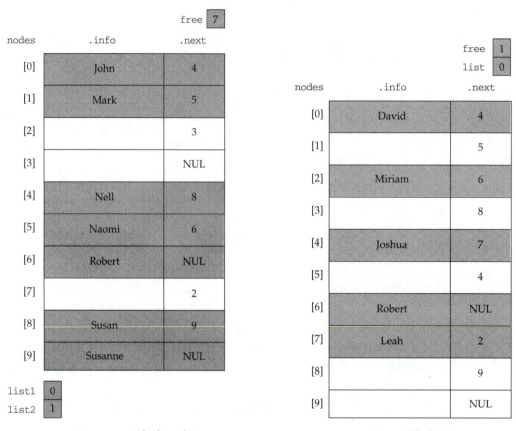

FIGURE 6.21 *An array with three lists (including the free list).*

FIGURE 6.22 *List and linked structure are together.*

a struct containing two items: an integer "pointer" to the first free node and a true pointer to the dynamically allocated array of nodes.

To simplify the following discussion and code, we assume the items on the list are integers rather than using a template class.

```
struct MemoryType;

class ListType
{
public:
    // Member function prototypes go here.
private:
    int listData;
    int currentPos;
```

```
    int length;
    int maxItems;
    MemoryType storage;
};
        .
        .
        .
```

The functions that do the bookkeeping are auxiliary ("helper") functions, not class member functions. Member functions are those functions that the user invokes; auxiliary functions are those that help to implement the member functions. First let's look at these bookkeeping functions. The nodes are all free initially, so they must be chained together and the index of the first node stored into free. GetNode must return the index of the next free node and update free. FreeNode must take the node index received as a parameter and insert it into the list of free nodes. As the first item in the list is the one that is directly accessible, we have GetNode return the first free item, and we have FreeNode insert the node being returned at the beginning of the free list. (Yes, we are keeping the free list as a stack—not because we need the LIFO property but because the code is the simplest for what we need.)

Here is the code that defines MemoryType and implements these auxiliary functions.

```
// Prototypes of auxiliary functions.
void GetNode(int& nodeIndex, MemoryType& storage);
// Returns the index of a free node in nodeIndex.
void FreeNode(int nodeIndex, MemoryType& storage);
// Returns the node at nodeIndex to storage.
void InitializeMemory(int maxItems, MemoryType&);
// Initializes all memory to the free list.

// Define end-of-list symbol.
const int NUL = -1;

struct NodeType
{
    int info;
    int next;
};

struct MemoryType
{
    int free;
    NodeType* nodes;
};
```

```
void InitializeMemory(int maxItems, MemoryType& storage)
{
    for (int index = 1; index < maxItems; index++)
        storage.nodes[index-1].next = index;
    storage.nodes[maxItems-1] = NUL;
    storage.free = 0;
}

void GetNode(int& nodeIndex, MemoryType& storage)
{
    nodeIndex = storage.free;
    storage.free = storage.nodes[free].next;
}

void FreeNode(int nodeIndex, MemoryType& storage)
{
    storage.nodes[nodeIndex].next = storage.free;
    storage.free = nodeIndex;
}
```

The class constructors for class ListType must allocate the storage for the array of records and call InitializeMemory. For the default constructor, we arbitrarily choose an array size of 500.

```
ListType::ListType(int max)
{
    length = 0;
    maxItems = max;
    storage.nodes = new NodeType[max];
    InitializeMemory(maxItems, storage);
    listData = NUL;
}

ListType::ListType()
{
    length = 0;
    maxItems = 500;
    storage.nodes = new NodeType[500];
    InitializeMemory(500, storage);
    listData = NUL;
}

ListType:: ~ListType()
{
    delete [] storage.nodes;
}
```

Let's look at our design notation, the dynamic pointer-based equivalent, and the array-of-records equivalent. We also need to look at the bookkeeping equivalent of the dynamic pointer-based operations and the array-of-records version. Once we understand all these relationships, coding the member functions of ListType is quite straightforward. In fact, it is so straightforward, we leave the code as a programming assignment (Chapter 6, Programming Assignment 7).

Design Notation/ Algorithm	Dynamic Pointers	Array-of-Records "Pointers"
Node(location)	*location	storage.nodes[location]
Info(location)	location->info	storage.nodes[location].info
Next(location)	location->next	storage.nodes[location].next
Set location to Next(location)	location = location->next	location = storage.nodes[location].next
Set Info(location) to value	location->info = value	storage.nodes[location].info = value
Allocate a node	nodePtr = new NodeType	GetNode(nodePtr)
Deallocate a node	delete nodePtr	FreeNode(nodePtr)

■II *Object-Oriented Design: Composition and Inheritance*

In an object-oriented design of a program, classes typically exhibit one of the following relationships: they are independent of one another, they are related by composition, or they are related by inheritance. **Composition** (or **containment**) is the relationship that we have demonstrated so far: a class contains a data member that is an object of another class type. For example, in our various implementations of lists, the user's data that are stored on the list are of class ItemType. C++ does not need any special language notation for composition. You simply declare a data member of one class to be of another class type.

Composition (Containment)   A mechanism by which an internal data member of one class is defined to be an object of another class type

---

Containment can be used to build an abstract data type in which a data member is of another abstract data type. For example, we can implement the Set ADT by having a data member be of type `UnsortedList` or `SortedList`. The list would contain the elements in the set. The set operations would be implemented as list operations. Chapter 6, Programming Assignment 8 in the back of the book asks you to implement the ADT Set and includes a further discussion of this topic.

In the world at large, it is often possible to arrange concepts into an *inheritance hierarchy*—a hierarchy in which each concept inherits the properties of the concept immediately above it in the hierarchy. For example, we might classify different kinds of vehicles according to the inheritance hierarchy in Figure 6.23. Moving down the hierarchy, each kind of vehicle is more specialized than its *parent* (and all of its *ancestors*) and is more general than its *children* (and all of its *descendants*). A wheeled vehicle inherits properties common to all vehicles (it holds one or more people and carries them from place to place) but has an additional property that makes it more specialized (it has wheels). A car inherits properties common to all wheeled vehicles, but also has additional, more specialized properties (four wheels, an engine, a body, and so forth).

As we stated in Chapter 2, the inheritance relationship can be viewed as an *is-a relationship*. Every two-door car is a car, every car is a wheeled vehicle, and every wheeled vehicle is a vehicle.

Object-oriented languages provide a way for creating inheritance relationships among classes. In these languages, **inheritance** is the mechanism by which one class acquires the properties of another class. You can take an

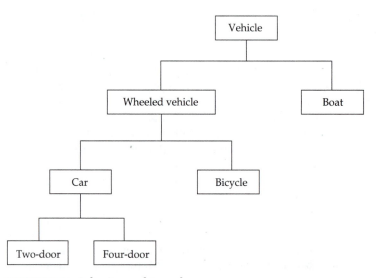

FIGURE 6.23 *Inheritance hierarchy.*

existing class (called the **base class**) and create a new class from it (called the **derived class**). The derived class inherits all the properties of its base class. In particular, the data and operations defined for the base class are now defined for the derived class. Note the is-a relationship—every object of a derived class is also an object of the base class.

Inheritance   The language mechanism by which one class acquires the properties—data and operations—of another class

Base Class   The class being inherited from

Derived Class   The class that inherits

Deriving One Class from Another

Our Queue ADT did not have an operation that determined the number of items on the queue. Let's define a new class CountedQue that is derived from class QueType and has a data member length that records the number of items on the queue.

```
template<class ItemType>
class CountedQue : public QueType<ItemType>
{
public:
    CountedQue();
    void Enqueue(ItemType newItem);
    void Dequeue(ItemType& item);
    int LengthIs() const;
    // Returns the number of items on the queue.
private:
    int length;
};
        .
        .
        .
```

The line

```
class CountedQue : public QueType<ItemType>
```

states that `CountedQue` is derived from `QueType`; that is, `CountedQue` is the derived class and `QueType` is the base class.[1]

The reserved word `public` declares `QueType` to be a *public base class* of `CountedQue`. This means that all public members of `QueType` are also public members of `CountedQue`. In other words, `QueType`'s member functions `Enqueue`, `Dequeue`, `IsEmpty`, and `IsFull` can also be invoked for objects of type `CountedQue`. However, the public part of class `CountedQue` specializes the base class by redefining the inherited functions `Enqueue` and `Dequeue` and by adding another data member `length`, an operation that returns the value of `length`, and its own class constructor.

Every object of type `CountedQue` has an object of type `QueType` as a subobject. That is, an object of type `CountedQue` is an object of type `QueType` and more. Figure 6.24 displays a *class interface diagram* for the `CountedQue` class. The public interface, shown as ovals at the side of the large circles, consists of the operations available to the client code. The private data items shown in the interior are inaccessible to clients. A dashed line between ovals indicates that the two operations are the same. For example, `IsEmpty` applied to an object of type `CountedQue` is the `IsEmpty` member function defined in type `QueType`. However, `Enqueue` applied to an object of type `CountedQue` is not the `Enqueue` defined in `QueType` but the one defined in `CountedQue`.

C++ uses the terms *base class* and *derived class*; *superclass* and *subclass* are also used in the literature. However, the use of *superclass* and *subclass* can be confusing because the prefix *sub* usually implies something smaller than the original (for example, a subset of a mathematical set). In contrast, a subclass is often "bigger" than its superclass—that is, it has more data and/or functions.

Implementation of the Derived Class

The implementation of the `CountedQue` class needs to deal only with the new features that are different from those in `QueType`. Specifically, we must write the code to redefine the `Enqueue` and `Dequeue` functions, and we must write the `LengthIs` function and the class constructor. The new `Enqueue` and `Dequeue` functions just need to increment or decrement the `length` data member and call the `QueType` functions of the same name. `LengthIs` just returns the value of `length`. The class constructor sets `length` to zero and can use the `QueType` class constructor to initialize the rest of the class data members. Here is the code. A discussion of the syntactic details follows.

---

1. To make the discussion easier to follow, we take the liberty of referring to `QueType` and `CountedQue` as classes. In fact, they are class templates, not classes. So if the client code uses `int` as the parameter to the template, then `QueType<int>` is the base class and `CountedQue<int>` is the derived class.

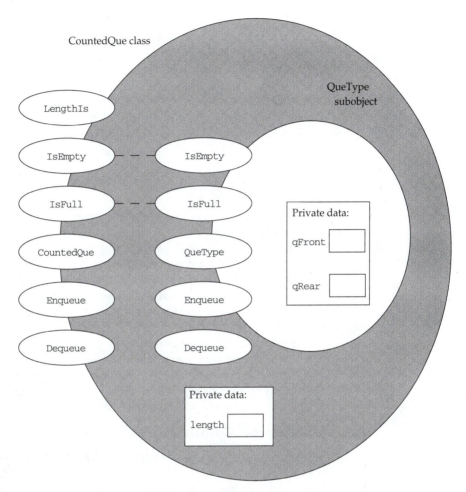

FIGURE 6.24 *Class interface diagram for CountedQue class.*

```
template<class ItemType>
void CountedQue<ItemType>::Enqueue(ItemType newItem)
{
    length++;
    QueType<ItemType>::Enqueue(newItem);
}

template<class ItemType>
void CountedQue<ItemType>::Dequeue(ItemType& item)
{
    length --;
    QueType<ItemType>::Dequeue(item);
}
```

```
template<class ItemType>
int CountedQue<ItemType>::LengthIs() const
{
    return length;
}

template<class ItemType>
CountedQue<ItemType>::CountedQue() : QueType<ItemType>()
{
    length = 0;
}
```

There are two points of syntax to note here. In order for `Enqueue` to invoke the `Enqueue` defined in `QueType`, the name of the class must precede the function name with the scope resolution operator (`::`) between. The same is true for `Dequeue`. In the class constructor, `length` is set to zero, but how are `qFront` and `qRear` set? The colon followed by `QueType<ItemType>()` after the parameter list of the derived-class constructor causes the invocation of the base-class constructor. This construct (colon followed by a call to the base-class constructor) is called a *constructor initializer*.

A class such as `QueType` can be used as-is in many different contexts or can be adapted to a particular context by using inheritance. Inheritance allows us to create *extensible* data abstractions—a derived class typically extends the base class by including additional private data or public operations or both.

Application of the CountedQue Class

FIFO queues are commonly used as "waiting lines." Such waiting lines are common on multiuser computer systems and networked systems of workstations. If you are using a multiuser or networked computer system, you probably share a printer with other users. When you request a printout of a file, your request is added to a print queue. When your request gets to the front of the print queue, your file is printed. The print queue ensures that only one person at a time has access to the printer and that this access is on a first-come first-served basis. Similarly, queues are used to schedule use of other shared resources like disks and tapes.

Another application area in which queues figure as the prominent data structure is the computer simulation of real-world situations. For instance, consider a bank that is planning to set up drive-in teller windows. There should be enough tellers to service each car within a "reasonable" wait time, but not too many tellers for the number of customers. The bank may want to run a computer simulation of typical customer transactions, using objects to represent the real-world physical objects like tellers, cars, and the clock. The queue is used to represent the waiting line of customers.

As we said in the simulation Case Study in Chapter 4, queuing simulations usually involve servers (the bank tellers), the items in the queue (people, cars, or whatever is waiting to be served), and the amount of time each item in the queue is expected to take. By varying these parameters and keeping track of the average lengths of the queues, management can determine how many servers must be employed to keep the customers happy. Therefore, in simulations using queues, the number of items on each queue is important information. Of course, this information can be calculated by the client program by dequeueing, counting, and enqueueing again, but a derived counted queue is a better choice.

Inheritance and Accessibility

Inheritance is a logical issue, not an implementation one. A class inherits the behavior of another class and enhances it in some way. Inheritance does *not* mean inheriting access to another class's private variables. Although some languages do allow access to the base class's private members, such access often defeats the concepts of encapsulation and information hiding. With C++, access to the private data members of the base class is not allowed. Neither external client code nor derived class code can directly access the private members of the base class.

Virtual Functions

In addition to *encapsulation* and *inheritance*, the third capability that must be available in an object-oriented programming language is *polymorphism*. In Chapter 2, we defined polymorphism as the ability to determine which function to call for a particular object. The determination can be done at compile time (static binding) or at run time (dynamic binding). Therefore, for a language to be a true object-oriented language, it must support both static and dynamic binding; that is, support polymorphism. C++ uses *virtual functions* to implement run-time binding.

The basic C++ rule for passing class objects as parameters is that the actual parameter and its corresponding formal parameter must be of an identical type. With inheritance, C++ relaxes this rule somewhat. The type of the actual parameter may be a class derived from the class of the formal parameter. To force the compiler to generate code that guarantees dynamic binding of a member function to a class object, the word `virtual` appears before the function declaration in the definition of the base class. Virtual functions work in the following way. If a class object is passed *by reference* to some function, and if the body of that function contains a statement

```
formalParameter.MemberFunction(...);
```

then

1. If MemberFunction is not a virtual function, the type of the *formal parameter* determines which function to call. (Static binding is used.)
2. If MemberFunction is a virtual function, the type of the *actual parameter* determines which function to call. (Dynamic binding is used.)

Let's look at an example. Suppose that ItemType is declared as follows.

```
class ItemType
{
public:
    .
    .
    .
    virtual RelationType ComparedTo(ItemType) const;
private:
    StrType lastName;
    .
    .
    .
};


RelationType ItemType::ComparedTo(ItemType item) const
{
    int result;

    result = strcmp(lastName, item.lastName);
    if (result < 0)
        return LESS;
    else if (result > 0)
        return GREATER;
    else return EQUAL;
}
```

Now let's derive a class NewItemType, where there are two StrType data members and we want ComparedTo to use both of them in the comparison.

```
class NewItemType : public ItemType
{
public:
    .
    .
    .
    RelationType ComparedTo(NewItemType) const;
private:
```

```
        // In addition to the inherited lastName member
        StrType firstName;
        .

        .

        .

};


RelationType NewItemType::ComparedTo(NewItemType item) const
{
    int result;

    result = strcmp(lastName, item.lastName);
    if (result < 0)
        return LESS;
    else if (result > 0)
        return GREATER;
    else
    {
        result = strcmp( firstName, item.firstName);
        if (result < 0)
            return LESS;
        else if (result > 0)
            return GREATER;
        else return EQUAL;
    }
}
```

Function `ComparedTo` is marked virtual in the base class (`ItemType`), and, according to the C++ language, `ComparedTo` is a virtual function in all derived classes as well. Whenever an object of type `ItemType` or `NewItemType` is passed by reference to a formal parameter of type `ItemType`, the determination of which `ComparedTo` to use within that function is postponed until run time. Let's assume that the client program includes the following function:

```
void PrintResult(ItemType& first, ItemType& second)
{
    if ( first.ComparedTo(second) == LESS)
        cout << "First comes before second";
    else
        cout << "First does not come before second";
}
```

and then executes the following code:

```
ItemType item1, item2;
NewItemType item3, item4:
       .
       .

       .
PrintResult(item1, item2);
PrintResult(item3, item4);
```

Because `item3` and `item4` are objects of a class derived from `ItemType`, both of the calls to `PrintResult` are valid. `PrintResult` invokes `ComparedTo`. Which one? Is it `ItemType::ComparedTo` or `NewItemType::ComparedTo`? Because `ComparedTo` is a virtual function and the class objects are passed by reference to `PrintResult`, the type of the actual parameter—not the formal parameter—determines which version of `ComparedTo` is called. In the first call to `PrintResult`, `ItemType::ComparedTo` is invoked; in the second, `NewItemType::ComparedTo` is invoked. This is illustrated in the following diagram.

Run-time Execution of `PrintResult`:
      `PrintResult(one, two)`

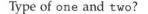

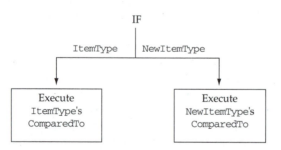

This example demonstrates an important benefit of dynamic binding. The client does not need to have multiple versions of the `PrintResult` function, one for each type of parameter that is passed to it. If new classes are derived from `ItemType` (or even from `NewItemType`), objects of those classes can be passed to `PrintResult` without modifying `PrintResult` whatsoever.

If you have a pointer defined as a pointer to a base class and dynamically allocate storage using the base type, the pointer points to a base-class object. If you dynamically allocate storage using the derived type, the pointer points to a derived-class object. Take for example the following short program with a base class `One` and a derived class `Two`. Here we allocate an object of type (base) class `One` and an object of (derived) class `Two`.

```
#include <iostream.h>
class One
{
public:
    virtual void Print();
};

class Two : public One
{
public:
    void Print();
};

void PrintTest(One*);

int main()
{
    One* onePtr;
    onePtr = new One;

    cout << "Result of passing an object of class One: " ;
    PrintTest(onePtr);

    onePtr = new Two;

    cout << "Result of passing an object of class Two: ";

    PrintTest(onePtr);
    return 0;
}

void PrintTest(One* ptr)
{
    ptr->Print();
}

void One::Print()
{
    cout  << "Print member function of class One" << endl;
}

void Two::Print()
{
    cout  << "Print member function of class Two" << endl;
}
```

onePtr points first to an object of class One and then to an object of class Two. When the parameter to PrintTest points to an object of class One, the class One member function is applied. When the parameter points to an object of class Two, the class Two member function is applied. The fact that the type of the run-time object determines which member function is executed is verified by the following output.

```
Result of passing an object of class One: Print member function of
class One
Result of passing an object of class Two: Print member function of
class Two
```

Dynamic binding occurred because we declared Print to be a virtual function.

We must issue one word of caution about passing a parameter of a derived type to any function whose formal parameter is of the base type. If the parameter is passed by reference, there is no problem, but if the parameter is passed by value, only the subobject that is of the base type is actually passed. For example, if the base type has two data members and the derived type has two additional data members, only the two data members of the base type are passed to a function if the formal parameter is a value parameter of the base type and the actual parameter is of the derived type. This is called the *slicing problem* (any additional data members declared by the derived class are "sliced off") and also can occur if we assign an object of the derived type to an object of the base type.

Look back at Figure 6.24 which shows the relationship of objects of QueueType and CountedQue type. If a CountedQue object is passed as a value parameter to a function SomeFunc, in which the formal parameter is of type QueType, only those data members of the QueueType subobject are copied; length, a member of CountedQue, is not.

CASE STUDY ‖‖

IMPLEMENTING A LARGE INTEGER ADT

The range of integer values that can be supported varies from one computer to another. In most C++ environments, file <limits.h> shows you the limits. For example long integers range from -2,147,483,648 to +2,147,483,647 on many machines. However long they may be on a particular machine, some user is bound to want to represent integers with larger values. Let's design and implement a class LargeInt that allows the user to manipulate integers where the number of digits is only limited by the size of the free store.

Because we are providing an alternate implementation for a mathematical object, an integer number, most of the operations are already specified: addition, subtraction, multiplication, division, assignment, and the relational operators. For this Case Study, we limit our attention to addition, subtraction, equality, and less than. Chapter 6, Programming Assignment 10 asks you to enhance this ADT with the other operations.

In addition to the standard mathematical operations, we need an operation that constructs a number one digit at a time. This operation cannot be a parameterized constructor because the integer parameter might be too large to represent in the machine—after all, that is the idea of this ADT. So we must have a special member function that can be called within a loop that inserts the digits one at a time. We also need an operation that writes the integer to a file, one digit at a time from most significant digit to least significant digit.

Before we can begin to look at the algorithms for these operations, we need to decide on our representation. Because we said earlier that we were designing class List2Type to use in this Case Study, you know that we are going to use a circular, doubly linked list. Why doubly linked? Because we need to access the digits from most significant to least significant to write them to a file, and we need to access them from least significant to most significant to manipulate them arithmetically. Why circular? Because the user needs to insert digits from most significant to least significant when constructing an object, and we need to insert digits from least significant to most significant when constructing an object that is the result of an arithmetic operation. (Figure 6.25 shows several examples of numbers in a singly linked list and an addition.) Figure 6.25(a) and (c) show one digit per node; Figure 6.25(b) shows several digits per node. We develop the algorithms for a single digit per node. You are asked in the exercises to explore the necessary changes to include more than one digit in each node.

Here is the first approximation of class LargeInt.

```cpp
#include "List2Type.h"
#include <fstream.h>
class LargeInt
{
public:
    LargeInt();
    ~LargeInt();
    LargeInt(const LargeInt&);
    bool operator<(LargeInt second);
    bool operator==(LargeInt second);
    LargeInt operator+(LargeInt second);
    LargeInt operator-(LargeInt second);
    void InsertDigit(int);
    void Write(ofstream&);
private:
    List2Type<int> number;
};
```

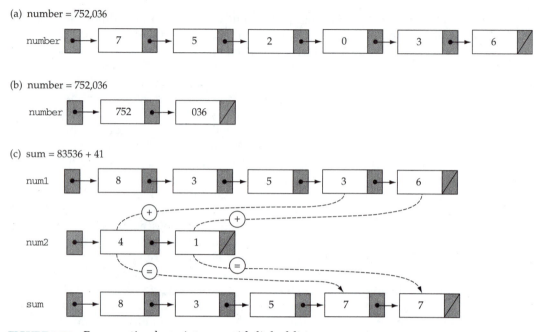

FIGURE 6.25   *Representing large integers with linked lists.*

Earlier we said that classes in a program typically exhibit one of the following relationships: they are independent of each other, they are related by composition, or they are related by inheritance. Class `LargeInt` and class `List2Type<int>` are related by composition. As you see in the private part of the class definition, a `LargeInt` object is composed of (or contains) a `List2Type<int>` object. Just as inheritance expresses an *is-a* relationship (a `CountedQue` object is a `QueType` object [and more]), composition expresses a *has-a* relationship (a `LargeInt` object has a `List2Type<int>` object inside it).

ADDITION AND SUBTRACTION

Let's look at addition of positive integers first, and then look at the role of the sign. We begin by adding the two least significant digits (the units position). Next, we add the digits in the tens position (if present) plus the carry from the sum of the least significant digits (if any). This process continues until one of three things happens: the first operand runs out of digits, the second operand runs out of digits, or they both run out of digits simultaneously. Rather than try to determine which operand is self at this stage, let's summarize these observations in an algorithm with three parameters of type `List2Type`:

first (the large number), second, and result where, abstractly, result = first + second.

Add(first, second, result)

Set carry to 0
Set finished1 to false
Set finished2 to false

first.ResetBackward()
second.ResetBackward()
WHILE (!finished1 AND !finished2)
    first.GetPriorItem(digit1, finished1)
    second.GetPriorItem(digit2, finished2)
    Set temp to digit1 + digit2 + carry
    Set carry to temp / 10
    result.InsertFront(temp % 10)
Finish up digits in first, adding carries as necessary
Finish up digits in second, adding carries as necessary
IF (carry != 0)
    result.InsertFront(carry)

Apply the algorithm to the following examples.

322	388	399	999	3	1	988	0
44	108	1	11	44	99	100	0
366	496	400	1010	47	100	1088	0

Now let's examine subtraction in the simplest case: both integers are positive and the smaller one is being subtracted from the larger one. Again we begin with the digits in the units position. Let's call the digit in the larger number digit1 and the digit in the smaller one digit2. If digit2 is less than digit1, we subtract and insert the resulting digit at the front of the result. If digit2 is greater than digit1, we borrow 10 and subtract. Then we access the digits in the tens position. If we have borrowed, we subtract 1 from the new digit1 and proceed as before. Because we have limited our problem to the case where the smaller number is being subtracted from the larger one, they either run out of digits together or the larger number still contains digits when the smaller number has been processed. Also note that this constraint guarantees that borrowing does not extend beyond the most significant digit of the larger number. We again express the algorithm with three parameters of type List2Type: first, second, and result where second is being subtracted from first.

Sub(first, second, result)

```
Set borrow to false
Set finished1 to false
Set finished2 to false

first.ResetBackward()
second.ResetBackward()
WHILE ( !finished1 AND ! finished2)
    first.GetPriorItem(digit1, finished1)
    IF (borrow)
        IF (digit1 != 0)
            Set digit1 to digit1 - 1
            Set borrow to false
        ELSE
            Set digit1 to 9
            Set borrow to true
    second.GetPriorItem(digit2, finished2)
    IF (digit2 <= digit1)
        result.InsertFront(digit1 - digit2)
    ELSE
        Set borrow to true
        result.InsertFront(digit1 + 10 - digit2)
WHILE ( !finished1)
    first.GetPriorItem(digit1, finished1)
    IF (borrow)
        IF (digit1 != 0)
            Set digit1 to digit1 - 1
            Set borrow to false
        ELSE
            Set digit1 to 9
            Set borrow to true
    result.InsertFront(digit1)
```

By now you are wondering what good is a subtraction algorithm that is so restricted. Well, it turns out that with these restricted subtraction and addition algorithms, we can implement addition and subtraction with all combinations of signs. Here are the rules where first is the first operand and second is the second operand.

Addition Rules

1. If both operands are positive, use the addition algorithm.
2. If one operand is negative and one operand is positive, subtract the smaller absolute value from the larger absolute value and give the result the sign of the larger absolute value.
3. If both operands are negative, use the addition algorithm and give the result a minus sign.

Subtraction Rules

1. If both operands are positive, subtract the smaller value from the larger value. Give the result a minus sign if second is larger.
2. If both operands are negative, change the sign of second and add.
3. If first is negative and second is positive, change the sign of second and add.
4. If first is positive and second is negative, change the sign of second and add.

Here are some examples showing the various cases.

Addition					Subtraction			
322	388	-399	-999		3	-1	-988	105
44	-108	1	-11		44	-99	100	-34
366	280	-398	-1010		-41	98	-1088	139

These rules indicate that the signs should be manipulated separately from the actual addition or subtraction. Therefore, we must add a sign data member to our LargeInt class. How shall we represent the sign? Let's define an enumeration type SignType having two constants (MINUS and PLUS) and adopt the convention that zero has the sign PLUS. Let's encode our simplified addition and subtraction algorithms into auxiliary functions Add and Sub that take three arguments, each of type List2Type. The code for each overloaded arithmetic symbol applies the rules for its operation and calls either Add or Sub. Sub should not be called, however, if the two operands are the same as the result would be zero. Here is the algorithm for function operator+.

operator+(LargeInt second)

```
// self is first operand
IF sign = second.sign
    Add(number, second.number, result.number)
    Set result.sign to sign
ELSE
    IF |self| < |second|
        Sub(second.number, number, result.number)
        Set result.sign to second.sign
    ELSE IF |second| < |self|
        Sub(number, second.number, result.number)
        Set result.sign to sign
Return result
```

RELATIONAL OPERATORS

When comparing strings, we compare the characters in each character position one at a time from left to right. The first characters that do not match determine which string comes first. When comparing numbers we only have to compare the numbers digit by digit if they have the same sign and are the same length (have the same number of digits). Here are the rules.

1. A negative number is less than a positive number.
2. If the signs are positive and one has more digits than the other, the one with fewer digits is the smaller value.
3. If the signs are both minus and one has more digits than the other, then the number with more digits is the smaller value.
4. If the signs are the same and the number of digits is the same, compare the digits from left to right. The first unequal pair determines the result.

Look at the following examples carefully and convince yourself that all the cases for "less than" are represented.

```
   true              false

   -1 < 1            1 < -1
    5 < 10          10 < 5
  -10 < -5           -5 < -10
   54 < 55          55 < 54
  -55 < -54         -54 < -55
                    -55 < -55
                     55 < 55
```

Let's summarize these observations for the "less than" operation. Notice that because we have only one digit per node, class `List2Type`'s `LengthIs` function gives us the number of digits in the number. This is a member function, so the first operand is self and the second operand is `second`.

operator<(second)

```
IF (sign is MINUS AND second.sign is PLUS)
    return true
ELSE IF (sign is PLUS AND second.sign is MINUS)
    return false
ELSE IF (sign is PLUS AND number.LengthIs() <
        second.number.LengthIs())
    return true
ELSE IF (sign is PLUS AND number.LengthIs() >
        second.number.LengthIs())
    return false
ELSE IF (sign is MINUS AND number.LengthIs() >
        second.number.LengthIs())
    return true
ELSE IF (sign is MINUS AND number.LengthIs() <
        second.number.LengthIs())
    return false
ELSE      // Must compare digit by digit
    Set relation to CompareDigits(number, second.number)
    IF (sign is PLUS AND relation is LESS)
        return true
    ELSE IF (sign is PLUS AND relation is GREATER)
        return false
    ELSE IF (sign is MINUS AND relation is GREATER)
        return true
    ELSE    return false
```

Function `LengthIs` of class `List2Type` is called eight times in this algorithm. We should make the number of digits a data member of class `LargeInt` and avoid these function calls. This means that each operation that defines a new large integer must call `LengthIs` once and store this value in the `LargeInt` object. Let's call this new data member `numDigits`. We now need to specify an operation that compares the digits in two equal-length lists and returns `LESS`, `GREATER`, or `EQUAL` depending on the relationship of its two arguments. We pass the lists of digits only, so this function is comparing the absolute values of its two arguments.

RelationType CompareDigits(operand1, operand2)

```
operand1.ResetForward()
operand2.ResetForward()
Set same to true
Set finished to false
WHILE !finished
     operand1.GetNextItem(digit1, finished)
     operand2.GetNextItem(digit2, finished)
     IF (digit1 < digit2)
          return LESS
     IF (digit 1 > digit2)
          return GREATER
return EQUAL
```

The algorithm for `operator==` also makes use of `CompareDigits`. If the two large integers have different signs or a different number of digits, `false` is returned. Otherwise, `CompareDigits` must be called.

operator==(second)

```
IF (sign != second.sign) OR (numDigits != second.numDigits)
     return false
ELSE
     return (CompareDigits(number, second.number)==EQUAL)
```

OTHER OPERATIONS

We have now examined all of the algorithms for the linked long integer representation except for `Write` and `InsertDigit` and the class constructors and destructor. Before we look at which implicit operations we need, we should examine the relationship between classes `LargeInt` and `List2Type`. The only data member in class `LargeInt` that contains dynamic pointers is `number`, which is of type `List2Type`. Because class `List2Type` has a destructor, we do not need one for class `LargeInt`. For the same reason, we do not need a class copy constructor. We can delete these from our preliminary class definition. However, we should retain the default class constructor to set the object to 0. Figure 6.26 shows our final objects and how they interact.

LargeInt value
containing
53653

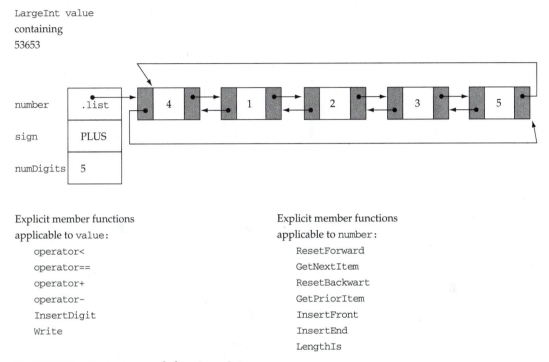

Explicit member functions
applicable to value:

    operator<

    operator==

    operator+

    operator-

    InsertDigit

    Write

Explicit member functions
applicable to number:

    ResetForward

    GetNextItem

    ResetBackwart

    GetPriorItem

    InsertFront

    InsertEnd

    LengthIs

FIGURE 6.26 *An instance of class LargeInt.*

The following code shows the revised class definition, the complete
addition operation, and the "less than" operator. We have implemented the
changes that were made in the algorithm discussions. We leave the completion
of the other operations as Chapter 6, Programming Assignment 9.

```
// Gain access to List2Type
#include "List2Type.h"
#include <fstream.h>
enum SignType {PLUS, MINUS};

class LargeInt
{
public:
    LargeInt();
    bool operator<(LargeInt second);
    bool operator==(LargeInt second);
    LargeInt operator+(LargeInt second);
    LargeInt operator-(LargeInt second);
```

```
    void InsertDigit(int);
    void Write(ofstream&);
private:
    List2Type<int> number;
    SignType sign;
    int numDigits;
};


void Add(List2Type<int> first, List2Type<int> second,
    List2Type<int>& result)
// Post:  result = first + second.
{
    int carry = 0;
    bool finished1 = false;
    bool finished2 = false;
    int temp;
    int digit1;
    int digit2;

    first.ResetBackward();
    second.ResetBackward();

    while ( !finished1 && !finished2)
    {
        first.GetPriorItem(digit1, finished1);
        second.GetPriorItem(digit2, finished2);
        temp = digit1 + digit2 + carry;
        carry = temp / 10;
        result.InsertFront(temp % 10);
    }
    while ( !finished1)
    {// Adds remaining digits (if any) in first to the sum.
        first.GetPriorItem(digit1, finished1);
        temp = digit1 + carry;
        carry = temp / 10;
        result.InsertFront(temp % 10);
    }
    while ( !finished2)
    {// Adds remaining digits (if any) in second to the sum.
        second.GetPriorItem(digit2, finished2);
        temp = digit2 + carry;
        carry = temp / 10;
        result.InsertFront(temp % 10);
    }
    if (carry != 0)       // Adds in carry (if any)
        result.InsertFront(carry);
}
```

```
LargeInt LargeInt::operator+(LargeInt second)
// self is first operand
{
    SignType selfSign;
    SignType secondSign;
    LargeInt result;

    if (sign == second.sign)
    {
        Add(number, second.number, result.number);
        result.sign = sign;
    }
    else
    {
        selfSign = sign;
        secondSign = second.sign;
        sign = PLUS;
        secondSign = PLUS;
        if (*this < second)
        {
            Sub(second.number, number, result.number);
            result.sign = secondSign;
        }
        else if (second < *this)
        {
            Sub(number, second.number, result.number);
            result.sign = selfSign;
        }
        sign = selfSign;
    }
    result.numDigits = result.number.LengthIs();
    return result;
}

enum RelationType {LESS, GREATER, EQUAL};
RelationType CompareDigits(List2Type<int> first,
    List2Type<int> second);
    .
    .
    .
bool LargeInt::operator<(LargeInt second)
{
    RelationType relation;

    if (sign == MINUS && second.sign == PLUS)
        return true;
    else if (sign == PLUS && second.sign == MINUS)
        return false;
```

```
        else if (sign == PLUS && numDigits < second.numDigits)
            return true;
        else if (sign == PLUS && numDigits > second.numDigits)
            return false;
        else if (sign == MINUS && numDigits > second.numDigits)
            return true;
        else if (sign == MINUS && numDigits < second.numDigits)
            return false;
        else // Must compare digit by digit
        {
            relation = CompareDigits(number, second.number);
            if (sign == PLUS && relation == LESS)
                return true;
            else if (sign == PLUS && relation == GREATER)
                return false;
            else if (sign == MINUS && relation == GREATER)
                return true;
            else return false;
        }
    }
}


RelationType CompareDigits(List2Type<int> first,
    List2Type<int> second)
{
    bool same = true;
    bool finished = false;
    int digit1;
    int digit2;

    first.ResetForward();
    second.ResetForward();
    while ( !finished)
    {
        first.GetNextItem(digit1, finished);
        second.GetNextItem(digit2, finished);
        if (digit1 < digit2)
            return LESS;
        if (digit1 > digit2)
            return GREATER;
    }
    return EQUAL;
}
```

▬ Explicit Reference to Self

The object to which a member function is applied can reference its data members directly. There are occasions when an object needs to refer to itself as a whole, not just to its data members. An example occurs in the code for overloading the plus operator. Within this function, we have to determine if self is less than the other operand. Here is that segment of the algorithm.

IF |self| < |second|
    Sub(second.number, number, result.number)
    Set result.sign to second.sign

We need to apply the relational operator "less than" to two `LargeInt` objects from within a member function. How do we reference self? C++ has a hidden pointer `this`. When a class member function is invoked, `this` points to the object to which the function is applied. `this` is available for the programmer to use. The algorithm segment shown here can be implemented by substituting `*this` for self.

```
secondSign = second.sign;
sign = PLUS;
second.sign = PLUS;
if (*this < second)
{
    Sub(second.number, number, result.number);
    result.sign = secondSign;
}
```

Test Plan

Each `LargeInt` operation must be unit tested. The complexity of the code for each operation is evident in the number of If statements in the algorithms. The more complex the code, the more test cases are necessary to test it. A white-box strategy would require going through the code of each operation and determining data that test at least all branches. A black-box strategy involves choosing data that test the varieties of possible input. This would involve varying combinations of signs and relative relationships between operands. In the case of "less than," addition, and subtraction, the examples used in the discussion would serve as test data for those operations. However, other end cases should be included, such as cases where one of the operands is zero or both of the operands are zero.

Of course this discussion presupposes that `List2Type` has been thoroughly tested!

∎∥ *Summary*

This chapter is a collection of theoretical material and implementation techniques. The idea of linking the elements in a list has been extended to include lists with header and trailer nodes, circular lists, and doubly linked lists. The idea of linking the elements is a possibility to consider in the design of many types of data structures. In addition to using dynamically allocated nodes to implement a linked structure, we looked at a technique for implementing linked structures in an array of records. In this technique the links are not pointers into the free store but indexes into the array of records. This type of linking is used extensively in systems software.

While a linked list can be used to implement almost any list application, its real strength is in applications that largely process the list elements in order. This is not to say that we cannot do "random access" operations on a linked list. Our specifications include operations that logically access elements in random order—for instance, member functions `RetrieveItem` and `DeleteItem` manipulate an arbitrary element in the list. However, at the implementation level the only way to find an element is to search the list, beginning at the first element and continuing sequentially to examine element after element. This search is $O(N)$, because the amount of work required is directly proportional to the number of elements in the list. A particular element in a sequentially sorted list in an array, in contrast, can be found with a binary search, decreasing the search algorithm to $O(\log_2 N)$. For a large list, the $O(N)$ sequential search can be quite time-consuming. There is a linked structure that supports $O(\log_2 N)$ searches: the binary search tree. We discuss this data structure in detail in Chapter 8.

The theoretical concepts examined in this chapter included inheritance and polymorphism and the C++ techniques with which to implement these concepts. We also examined the concept of deep versus shallow copying and assignment operator overloading.

The Case Study at the end of the chapter designed a Large Integer ADT. The number of digits is bounded only by the size of memory. Several relational and arithmetic operators were overloaded to work with objects of this type.

■|| *Exercises*

1. Dummy nodes are used to simplify list processing by eliminating some "special case."
   (a) What special case is eliminated by a header node in a linear linked list?
   (b) What special case is eliminated by a trailer node in a linear linked list?
   (c) Would dummy nodes be useful in implementing a linked stack? That is, would their use eliminate a special case?
   (d) Would dummy nodes be useful in implementing a linked queue with a pointer to both head and rear elements?
   (e) Would dummy nodes be useful in implementing a circular linked queue?

2. Implement the class constructor, destructor, and copy constructor for the circular linked list class.

3. If you were going to implement the FIFO Queue ADT as a circular linked list, with the external pointer accessing the "rear" node of the queue, which member functions would require changing?

4. Write a member function `PrintReverse` that prints the elements in reverse order. For instance, for the list X Y Z, `list.PrintReverse()` would output Z Y X. The list is implemented as a circular list with `listData` pointing to the first element in the list. You may assume that the list is not empty.

5. Can you derive a type `DLList` from class `List2Type` that has a member function `InsertItem` that inserts the item into its proper place in the list? If so, derive the class and implement the function. If not, explain why not.

6. If you were to rewrite the implementation of the Sorted List ADT using a doubly linked list, would the class definition have to be changed? If so, how?

7. Outline the changes to the member functions that would be necessary to implement the Sorted List as a doubly linked list.

8. Write a member function `Copy` of the Stack ADT, assuming that the stack named in the parameter list is copied into self.

9. Write a member function `Copy` of the Stack ADT, assuming that self is copied into the stack named in the parameter list.

10. Using the circular doubly linked list below, give the expression corresponding to each of the following descriptions.

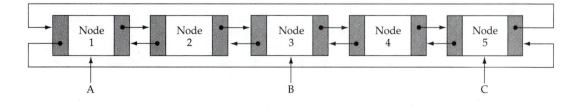

(For example, the expression for the `info` member of Node 1, referenced from pointer A, would be `A->info`.)

(a) The `info` member of Node 1, referenced from pointer C
(b) The `info` member of Node 2, referenced from pointer B
(c) The `next` member of Node 2, referenced from pointer A
(d) The `next` member of Node 4, referenced from pointer C
(e) Node 1, referenced from pointer B
(f) The `back` member of Node 4, referenced from pointer C
(g) The `back` member of Node 1, referenced from pointer A

11. The text edited by a line editor is represented by a doubly linked list of nodes, each containing an 80-column line of text (type `LineType`). There is one external pointer (type `LineType*`) to this list, which points to the "current" line in the text being edited. The list has a header node, which contains the string "- - - Top of File - - -" and a trailer node, which contains the string "- - - Bottom of File - - -".

(a) Draw a sketch of this data structure.
(b) Write the type declarations to support this data structure.
(c) Write the class constructor, which sets up the header and trailer nodes.
(d) Code the following operations as class member functions:

GoToTop

Function: Goes to top of the list.
Postcondition: currentLine is set to access the first line of text.

GoToBottom

Function: Goes to bottom of the list.
Postcondition: currentLine is set to access the last line of text.

(e) Describe the operations in (d) in terms of Big-O. How could the list be changed to make these operations O(1)?
(f) Code the `InsertLine` operation, using the following specification:

InsertLine(LineType newLine)

Function: Inserts newLine at the current line.
Postcondition: newLine has been inserted after currentLine, after which currentLine points to newLine.

(g) What other member functions should be included?

12. Of the three variations of linked lists (circular, with header and trailer nodes, and doubly linked) which would be most appropriate for each of the following applications?

(a) Search a list for a key and return the keys of the two elements that come before it and the keys of the two elements that come after it.
(b) A text file contains integer elements, one per line, *sorted* from smallest to largest. You must read the values from the file and create a sorted linked list containing the values.

(c) A list that is short and frequently becomes empty. You want a list that is optimum for inserting an element into the empty list and deleting the last element from the list.

13. What is the Big-O measure for initializing the free list in the array-based linked implementation? For the function GetNode and FreeNode?

14. Use the linked lists contained in the array pictured in Figure 6.21 to answer the following questions:
    (a) What elements are in the list pointed to by list1?
    (b) What elements are in the list pointed to by list2?
    (c) What array positions (indexes) are part of the free space list?
    (d) What would the array look like after the deletion of Nell from the first list?
    (e) What would the array look like after the insertion of Anne into the second list? Assume that before the insertion the array is as pictured in Figure 6.21.

15. An array of records (nodes) is used to contain a doubly linked list, with the next and back members indicating the indexes of the linked nodes in each direction.
    (a) Show how the array would look after it was initialized to an empty state, with all the nodes linked into the free-space list. (Note that the free-space nodes only have to be linked in one direction.)

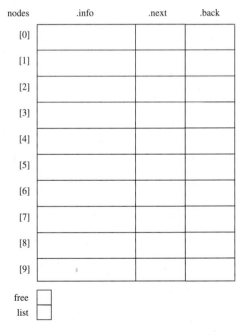

(b) Draw a box-and-arrow picture of a doubly linked list into which the following numbers are inserted into their proper places in the doubly linked list: 17, 4, 25.

(c) Fill in the contents of the array below after the following numbers are inserted into their proper places in the doubly linked list: 17, 4, 25.

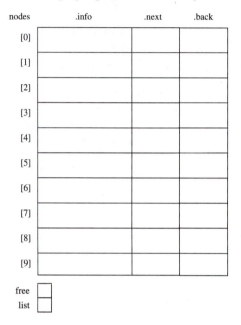

(d) Show how the array in part (c) would look after 17 is deleted.

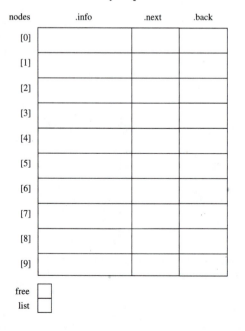

16. Name three ways that classes can relate to each other.

17. Distinguish between composition and inheritance.

18. Dintinguish between a base class and a derived class.

19. Does a derived class have access to the private data members of the base class?

20. Does a derived class have access to the public member functions of the base class?

21. Define and implement a `CountedStack` class which inherits from `StackType`.

22. Discuss the changes that would be necessary if more than one digit is stored per node in our `LargeInt` class.

23. Distinguish between static and dynamic binding of functions.

Programming with Recursion

- To be able to discuss recursion as another form of repetition
- To be able to do the following, given a recursive routine:

    Determine whether the routine halts
    Determine the base case(s)
    Determine the general case(s)
    Determine what the routine does
    Determine whether the routine is correct and, if it is not, correct it

- To be able to do the following, given a simple recursive problem:

    Determine the base case(s)
    Determine the general case(s)
    Design and code the solution as a recursive void function or value-returning function

- To be able to verify a recursive routine, according to the Three-Question Method
- To be able to decide if a recursive solution is appropriate for a problem
- To be able to compare and contrast dynamic storage allocation and static storage allocation in relation to using recursion
- To be able to explain how recursion works internally by showing the contents of the run-time stack
- To be able to replace a recursive solution with iteration and/or the use of a stack
- To be able to explain why recursion may or may not be a good choice to implement the solution of a problem

■‖ *What Is Recursion?*

In C++, any function can call another function. A function can even call itself! When a function calls itself, it is making a *recursive call*. The word *recursive* means "having the characteristic of coming up again, or repeating." In this case, a function call is being repeated by the function itself. Recursion is a powerful technique that can be used in place of iteration (looping).

Recursive solutions are often less efficient than iterative solutions to the same problem. However, some problems lend themselves to simple, elegant, recursive solutions and are exceedingly cumbersome to solve iteratively. Some programming languages, like early versions of FORTRAN, BASIC, and COBOL, did not allow recursion. Other languages are especially oriented to recursive algorithms—LISP is one of these. C++ lets us take our choice: we can implement both iterative and recursive algorithms in C++.

■‖ *The Classic Example of Recursion*

Mathematicians often define concepts in terms of the process used to generate them. For instance, $n!$ (read "n factorial") is used to calculate the number of permutations of n elements. One mathematical description of $n!$ is

$$n! = \begin{cases} 1, & \text{if } n = 0 \\ n * (n-1) * (n-2) * \ldots * 1, & \text{if } n > 0 \end{cases}$$

Consider the case of 4!. Because $n > 0$, we use the second part of the definition:

$$4! = 4 * 3 * 2 * 1 = 24$$

This description of $n!$ provides a different definition for each value of n, for the three dots stand in for the intermediate factors. That is, the definition of 2! is $2 * 1$, the definition of 3! is $3 * 2 * 1$, and so forth.

We can also express $n!$ with a single definition for any nonnegative value of n:

$$n! = \begin{cases} 1. & \text{if } n = 0 \\ n * (n-1)! & \text{if } n > 0 \end{cases}$$

This definition is *recursive*, because we express the factorial function in terms of itself.

Let's consider the recursive calculation of 4! intuitively. Because 4 is not equal to 0, we use the second half of the definition:

4! = 4 * (4-1)! = 4 * 3!

Of course, we can't do the multiplication yet, because we don't know the value of 3!. So we call up our good friend Sue Ann, who has a Ph.D. in math, to find the value of 3!.

Sue Ann has the same formula we have for calculating the factorial function, so she knows that

3! = 3 * (3-1)! = 3 * 2!

She doesn't know the value of 2!, however, so she puts you on hold and calls up her friend Max, who has an M.S. in math.

Max has the same formula Sue Ann has, so he quickly calculates that

$$2! = 2 * (2-1)! = 2 * 1!$$

But Max can't complete the multiplication because he doesn't know the value of 1!. He puts Sue Ann on hold and calls up his mother, who has a B.A. in math education.

Max's mother has the same formula Max has, so she quickly figures out that

$$1! = 1 * (1-1)! = 1 * 0!$$

Of course, she can't perform the multiplication, because she doesn't have the value of 0!. So Mom puts Max on hold and calls up her colleague Bernie, who has a B.A. in English literature.

Bernie doesn't need to know any math to figure out that 0! = 1 because he can read that information in the first clause of the formula (*n*! = 1, if *n* = 0). He reports the answer immediately to Max's mother. She can now complete her calculations:

1! = 1 * 0! = 1 * 1 = 1.

She reports back to Max, who now performs the multiplication in his formula and learns that

2! = 2 * 1! = 2 * 1 = 2.

He reports back to Sue Ann, who can now finish her calculation:

3! = 3 * 2! = 3 * 2 = 6.

Sue Ann calls you with this exciting bit of information. You can now complete your calculation:

4! = 4 * 3! = 4 * 6 = 24.

■ ∥ *Programming Recursively*

Of course, the use of recursion is not limited to mathematicians with telephones. Computer languages such as C++ that support recursion give the programmer a powerful tool for solving certain kinds of problems by reducing the complexity or hiding the details of the problem.

We consider recursive solutions to several simple problems. In our initial discussion, you may wonder why a recursive solution would ever be preferred to an iterative, or nonrecursive one, for the iterative solution may seem simpler and more efficient. Don't worry. There are, as you see later, situations in which the use of recursion produces a much simpler—and more elegant—program.

Coding the Factorial Function

A recursive function is one that calls itself. In the previous section Sue Ann, Max, Max's mom, and Bernie all had the same formula for solving the factorial function. When we construct a recursive C++ function `Factorial` for solving $n!$, we know where we can get the value of $(n-1)!$ that we need in the formula. We already have a function for doing this calculation: `Factorial`. Of course, the actual parameter (`number-1`) in the recursive call is different from the parameter in the original call (`number`). (The recursive call is the one within the function.) As we see, this is an important and necessary consideration.

```
int Factorial(int number)
// Pre:   number is nonnegative.
// Post: Function value = factorial of number.
{
    if (number == 0)                            // line 1
        return 1;                               // line 2
    else
        return number * Factorial(number-1);    // line 3
}
```

Notice the use of `Factorial` in line 3. `Factorial` is a recursive call to the function, with the parameter `number-1`.

Let's walk through the calculation of 4! using function `Factorial`. The original value of `number` is 4. Table 7.1 shows the steps in the calculation.

For purposes of comparison, let's look at the recursive and iterative solutions to this problem side by side:

```
int Factorial(int number)          int Factorial(int number)
{                                  {
    if (number == 0)                   int fact = 1;
        return 1;
    else                               for (int count = 2;
        return number *                    count <= number; count++)
            Factorial(number - 1);             fact = fact * count;
}                                      return fact;
                                   }
```

TABLE 7.1   **Walk-Through of Factorial(4)**

Recursive Call	Line	Action
	1	4 is not 0, so skip to else-clause.
	3	return number * Factorial(4 - 1)
		First recursive call returns us to the beginning of the function with number = 3.
1	1	3 is not 0, so skip to else-clause.
	3	return number * Factorial(3 - 1)
		Second recursive call returns us to the beginning of the function with number = 2.
2	1	2 is not 0, so skip to else-clause.
	3	return number * Factorial(2 - 1)
		Third recursive call returns us to the beginning of the function with number = 1.
3	1	1 is not 0, so skip to else-clause.
	3	return number * Factorial(1 - 1)
		Fourth recursive call returns us to the beginning of the function with number = 0.
4	1	0 is 0, so go to line 2.
	2	return 1
3	3	1 replaces call to Factorial; number is 1.
		return 1
2	3	1 replaces call to Factorial; number is 2.
		return 2
1	3	2 replaces call to Factorial; number is 3.
		return 6
	3	6 replaces call to Factorial; number is 4.
		return 24

These two versions of Factorial illustrate a couple of differences between recursive and iterative functions. First, an iterative algorithm uses a *looping construct* such as the For loop (or While or Do . . While) to control the execution. The recursive solution uses a *branching structure* (If or Switch statement). The iterative version needs a couple of local variables, whereas the recursive version uses the parameters of the function to provide all its information. Sometimes, as we see later, the recursive solution needs more parameters than the equivalent iterative one. Data values used in the iterative solution are usually initialized inside the routine, above the loop. Similar data values used in a recursive solution are usually initialized by the choice of parameter values in the initial call to the routine.

Let's summarize the vocabulary of recursive solutions. A **recursive definition** is a definition that defines something in terms of smaller versions of itself. The definition of the factorial function certainly fits this definition. A

recursive call is a call made to the function from within the function itself. Line 3 in function `Factorial` is an example of a recursive call.

In a recursive definition (and recursive algorithm) there is always at least one case for which the answer is known; the solution is not stated in terms of smaller versions of itself. In the case of the factorial, the answer is known if the number is 0. The case(s) for which the answer is known is called the **base case**. The case that is stated recursively is the **general** or **recursive case.**

Recursive Definition   A definition in which something is defined in terms of smaller versions of itself

Recursive Call   A function call in which the function being called is the same as the one making the call

Base Case   The case for which the solution can be stated nonrecursively

General (Recursive) Case   The case for which the solution is expressed in terms of a smaller version of itself

---

■|| *Verifying Recursive Functions*

The kind of walk-through we did in the previous section, to check the validity of a recursive function, is time-consuming, tedious, and often confusing. Furthermore, simulating the execution of `Factorial(4)` tells us that the function works when `number = 4`, but it doesn't tell us whether the function is valid for *all* nonnegative values of `number`. It would be useful to have a technique that would help us determine inductively whether a recursive algorithm works.

The Three-Question Method

We use the Three-Question Method of verifying recursive functions. To verify that a recursive solution works, you must be able to answer yes to all three of these questions.

1. *The Base-Case Question:* Is there a nonrecursive way out of the function, and does the routine work correctly for this base case?
2. *The Smaller-Caller Question:* Does each recursive call to the function involve a smaller case of the original problem, leading inescapably to the base case?
3. *The General-Case Question:* Assuming that the recursive call(s) works correctly, does the whole function work correctly?

Let's apply these three questions to function `Factorial`. (We use the mathematical N rather than the variable `number`.)

1. *The Base-Case Question:* The base case occurs when $N = 0$. `Factorial` then returns the value 1, which is the correct value of 0!, and no further (recursive) calls to `Factorial` are made. The answer is yes.

2. *The Smaller-Caller Question:* To answer this question we must look at the parameters passed in the recursive call. In function `Factorial`, the recursive call passes `N-1`. Each subsequent recursive call sends a decremented value of the parameter, until the value sent is finally 0. At this point, as we verified with the base-case question, we have reached the smallest case, and no further recursive calls are made. The answer is yes.

3. *The General-Case Question:* In the case of a function like `Factorial`, we need to verify that the formula we are using actually results in the correct solution. Assuming that the recursive call `Factorial(N-1)` gives us the correct value of $(N-1)!$, the `return` statement computes $N * (N-1)!$. This is the definition of a factorial, so we know that the function works for all positive integers. In answering the first question, we have already ascertained that the function works for $N = 0$. (The function is defined only for nonnegative integers.) So the answer is yes.

Those of you who are familiar with *inductive proofs* should recognize what we have done. Having made the assumption that the function works for some base case $(n-1)$, we can now show that applying the function to the next value, $(n-1) + 1$, or n, results in the correct formula for calculating $n!$.

▪‖ *Writing Recursive Functions*

The questions used for verifying recursive functions can also be used as a guide for *writing* recursive functions. You can use the following approach to write any recursive routine:

1. Get an exact definition of the problem to be solved. (This, of course, is the first step in solving any programming problem.)

2. Determine the *size* of the problem to be solved on this call to the function. On the initial call to the function, the size of the whole problem is expressed in the value(s) of the parameter(s).

3. Identify and solve the *base case(s)* in which the problem can be expressed nonrecursively. This ensures a yes answer to the base-case question.

4. Identify and solve the *general case(s)* correctly in terms of a smaller case of the same problem—a recursive call. This ensures yes answers to the smaller-caller and general-case questions.

In the case of `Factorial`, the definition of the problem is summarized in the definition of the factorial function. The size of the problem is the number of values to be multiplied: N. The base case occurs when $N = 0$, in which case we take the nonrecursive path. Finally, the general case occurs when $N > 0$, resulting in a recursive call to `Factorial` for a smaller case: `Factorial (N-1)`.

Writing a Boolean Function

Let's apply this approach to writing a Boolean function, `ValueInList`, that searches for a value in a list of integers and returns true or false according to whether the value is found. The list is declared as follows and is passed as a parameter to `ValueInList`.

```
struct ListType
{
    int length;
    int info[MAX_ITEMS];
};


ListType list;
```

The recursive solution to this problem is as follows:

> Return (value is in the first position?) OR
> (value is in the rest of the list?)

We can answer the first question just by comparing the value to `list.info[0]`. But how do we know if the value is in the rest of the list? If only we had a function that would search the rest of the list. *But we do have one!* Function `ValueInList` searches for a value in a list. We simply need to start searching at position one, instead of position zero (a smaller case). To do this, we pass the search starting place to `ValueInList` as a parameter. We know the end of the list is at position `list.length-1` so we can stop searching if the value isn't there. Thus we use the following function specification:

■ **Boolean ValueInList (list, value, startIndex)**

Function: Searches list for value between positions startIndex and list.length-1.

Precondition: list.info[startIndex]..list.info[list.length - 1] contain values to be searched.

Postcondition: Function value = (value exists in list.info[startIndex]..list.info[list.length - 1]).

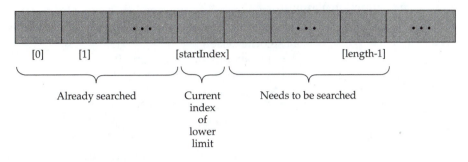

FIGURE 7.1 *Function ValueInList in midexecution.*

To search the whole list, we would invoke the function with the statement

```
if (ValueInList(list, value, 0))
    .
    .
    .
```

The general case of this algorithm is the part that searches the rest of the list. This case involves a recursive call to `ValueInList`, specifying a smaller part of the array to be searched:

```
return ValueInList(list, value, startIndex + 1);
```

By using the expression `startIndex + 1` as the parameter, we have effectively diminished the size of the problem to be solved by the recursive call. That is, searching the list from `startIndex + 1` to `list.length-1` is a smaller task than searching from `startIndex` to `list.length-1`. Figure 7.1 shows function `ValueInList` frozen in midexecution.

Finally, we need to know when to stop searching. In this problem we have two base cases: (1) when the value is found (return true), and (2) when we have reached the end of the list without finding the value (return false). In either case we can stop making recursive calls to `ValueInList`.

Let's summarize what we have discussed and then write function `ValueInList`.

Function ValueInList

Definition:	Searches list for value. Returns true if value is found; returns false otherwise.
Size:	The number of slots to search in list.info[startIndex]..list.info[list.length-1].
Base Cases:	(1) If list.info[startIndex] equals value, return true.
	(2) If startIndex equals list.length-1 and list.info[list.length-1] does not equal value, return false.

General Case: Search the rest of the list for value. This is a recursive invocation of ValueInList with a parameter startIndex+1 (smaller caller).

The code for function `ValueInList` follows.

```
bool ValueInList(ListType list, int value, int startIndex)
{
    if (list.info[startIndex] == value)
        return true;                          // Base case 1
    else if (startIndex == list.length-1)
        return false;                         // Base case 2
    else return ValueInList(list, value, startIndex + 1);
}
```

Note that it is the parameter `startIndex` that acts as an index through the array; it is initialized in the original invocation of `ValueInList` and incremented on each recursive call. The equivalent iterative solution would use a local counter, initialized inside the function above the loop and incremented inside the loop.

Let's use the Three-Question Method to verify this function.

1. *Base Case:* One base case occurs when the value is found on this call and the function is exited without any further calls to itself. A second base case occurs when the end of the list is reached without the value being found and the function is exited without any further recursive calls. The answer is yes.
2. *Smaller Caller:* The recursive call in the general case increments the value of `startIndex`, making the part of the list left to be searched smaller. The answer is yes.
3. *General Case:* Let's assume that the recursive call in the general case correctly tells us whether the value is found in the second through last elements in the list. Then Base Case 1 gives us the correct answer of true if the value is found in the first element in the list, and Base Case 2 gives us the correct answer of false if the value is not in the first element and the first element is the *only* element in the list. The only other possible case is that the value exists somewhere in the rest of the list. Assuming that the general case works correctly, the whole function works, so the answer to this question is also yes.

■|| *Using Recursion to Simplify Solutions*

So far the examples we have looked at could just as easily (or more easily) have been written as iterative routines. At the end of the chapter, we talk more about choosing between iterative and recursive solutions. There are many problems, however, in which using recursion simplifies the solution.

The first problem we look at is a function, Combinations, that tells us how many combinations of a certain size can be made out of a total group of elements. For instance, if we have twenty different books to pass out to four students, we can easily see that—to be equitable—we should give each student five books. But how many combinations of five books can be made out of a group of twenty books?

There is a mathematical formula that can be used for solving this problem. Given that C is the total number of combinations, *group* is the total size of the group to pick from, *members* is the size of each subgroup, and group >= *members*,

C(group, members) =
$$\begin{cases} \text{group,} & \text{if members = 1} \\ 1, & \text{if members = group} \\ C\,(group - 1, members - 1) + C(group - 1, members), & \text{if group > members > 1} \end{cases}$$

Because this definition of C is recursive, it is easy to see how a recursive function could be used to solve the problem.

Let's summarize our problem.

■| **Function Combinations**

Definition: Calculates how many combinations of members size can be made from the total group size.
Size: Sizes of group, members.
Base Cases: (1) If members = 1, return group.
(2) If members = group, return 1.
General Case: If group > members > 1, return
Combinations(group-1, members-1) +
Combinations(group-1, members)

The resulting recursive function, Combinations, is listed here.

```
int Combinations(int group, int members)
// Pre:  group and members are positive.
// Post: Function value = number of combinations of members size
//       that can be constructed from the total group size.
{
```

```
if (members == 1)
    return group;              // Base case 1
else if (members == group)
    return 1;                  // Base case 2
else
    return (Combinations(group-1, members-1)  +
            Combinations(group-1, members));
}
```

The processing of this function to calculate the number of combinations of three elements that can be made from a set of four is shown in Figure 7.2.

Returning to our original problem, we can now find out how many combinations of five books can be made from the original set of twenty books with the statement

```
cout  << "Number of combinations = "  << Combinations(20, 5)
      << endl;
```

Writing a recursive solution to a problem that is characterized by a recursive definition, like Combinations or Factorial, is fairly straightforward.

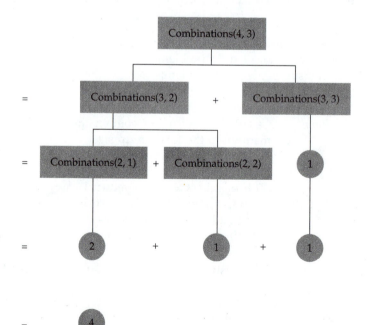

FIGURE 7.2 *Calculating Combinations(4, 3).*

■∥ *Recursive Linked List Processing*

Let's look next at a different kind of problem, a function that prints out the elements in a dynamically allocated linked list. The list has been implemented using the following declarations. For this example, `SortedType` is a class rather than a class template. `NodeType` is a struct rather than a struct template, and the `info` member of type `NodeType` is of type `int`.

```
struct NodeType;
class SortedType
{
public:
    // Prototypes of member functions
private:
    NodeType* listData;
};
```

By now you are probably protesting that this task is so simple to accomplish iteratively (`while (ptr != NULL)`) that it does not make any sense to write it recursively. So let's make the task more fun: print out the elements in the list in *reverse order*. This problem is much more easily and "elegantly" solved recursively.

What is the task to be performed? The algorithm follows (Figure 7.3).

RevPrint

Print out the second through last elements in the list in reverse order
Then print the first element in the list

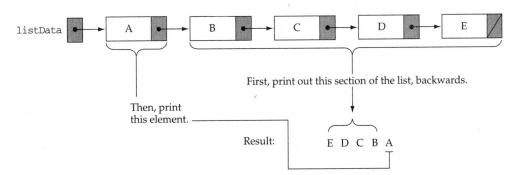

FIGURE 7.3   *Recursive RevPrint.*

The second part of the task is simple. If `listPtr` points to the first node in the list, we can print out its contents with the statement `cout << listPtr->info`. The first part of the task—printing out all the other nodes in the list in reverse order—is also simple, because we have a routine that prints out lists in reverse order: we just call function `RevPrint` recursively. Of course, we have to adjust the parameter somewhat, to `RevPrint(listPtr->next)`. This call says "Print, in reverse order, the linked list pointed to by `listPtr->next`." This task in turn is accomplished recursively in two steps:

> RevPrint the rest of the list (third through last elements)
> Then print the second element in the list

And of course the first part of this task is accomplished recursively. Where does it all end? We need a base case. We can stop calling `RevPrint` when we have completed its smallest case: `RevPrint`-ing a list of one element. Then the value of `listPtr->next` is NULL, and we can stop making recursive calls. Let's summarize the problem.

Function RevPrint

Definition   Prints out the list in reverse order.
Size: Number of elements in the list pointed to by listPtr.
Base Case: If the list is empty, do nothing.
General Case: RevPrint the list pointed to by listPtr->next,
                 then print listPtr->info.

The other recursive routines that we have written have been value-returning functions; `RevPrint` is a void function. `RevPrint` is a void function because each function call simply performs an action (printing the contents of a list node) without returning a value to the calling code.

```
void RevPrint(NodeType* listPtr)
{
    if (listPtr != NULL)
    {
        RevPrint(listPtr->next);
        cout << listPtr->info << endl;
    }
}
```

Given our `SortedType` class, can we make `RevPrint` a public member function of the class? The answer is no, and here is the reason. To print the whole linked list, the client's initial call to `RevPrint` must pass as a parameter the pointer to the first node in the list. But in the `SortedType` class, this pointer (`listData`) is a *private* member of the class, so the following client code is not permitted:

```
list.RevPrint(list.listData);    // Not allowed—listData is private
```

Therefore, we must treat `RevPrint` as an auxiliary, nonmember function and define a member function, say, `PrintReversed` that calls `RevPrint`:

```
void PrintReversed();    // Prototype in SortedType class declaration
  .
  .
  .
void ListType::PrintReversed()
{
    RevPrint(listData);
}
```

Given this design, the client can print the entire list with the following function call:

```
list.PrintReversed();
```

Let's verify `RevPrint` using the Three-Question Method.

1. *The Base-Case Question:* The base case is implied. When `listPtr` is equal to NULL, we return to the statement following the last recursive call to `RevPrint`, and no further recursive calls are made. The answer is yes.
2. *The Smaller-Caller Question:* The recursive call passes the list pointed to by `listPtr->next`, which is one node smaller than the list pointed to by `listPtr`. The answer is yes.
3. *The General-Case Question:* We assume that `RevPrint(listPtr->next)` correctly prints out the rest of the list in reverse order; this call, followed by the statement printing the value of the first element, gives us the whole list, printed in reverse order. So the answer is yes.

How would you change function `RevPrint` (in addition to changing its name) to make it print out the list in forward rather than reverse order? We leave this as an exercise.

■‖ *A Recursive Version of Binary Search*

In the chapter on array-based lists (Chapter 3), we developed the binary search algorithm for the member function `RetrieveItem` in our Sorted List ADT. Let's review the algorithm:

BinarySearch

Set first to 0
Set last to length-1
Set found to false
Set moreToSearch to (first <= last)
WHILE moreToSearch AND NOT found
  Set midPoint to (first + last) / 2
  SWITCH (item.ComparedTo(info[midPoint]))
    case LESS   : Set last to midPoint - 1
                    Set moreToSearch to (first <= last)
    case GREATER : Set first to midPoint + 1
                    Set moreToSearch to (first <= last)
    case EQUAL   : Set found to true

Though the function that we wrote in Chapter 3 was iterative, this really is a *recursive algorithm*. The solution is expressed in smaller versions of the original problem: if the answer isn't found in the middle position, perform `BinarySearch` (a recursive call) to search the appropriate half of the list (a smaller problem). Let's summarize the problem in terms of a Boolean function that simply returns true or false according to whether the desired item is found. We assume that it is not a public member function of class `SortedType` but an auxiliary function of the class that takes the array `info` as a parameter.

■‖ **Boolean BinarySearch**

Definition:	Searches the list to see if item is present.
Size:	The number of elements in list.info[fromLocation]..list.info[toLocation].
Base Cases:	(1) If fromLocation>toLocation, return false.
	(2) If item.ComparedTo(list.info[midPoint]) = EQUAL, return true.
General Case:	If item.ComparedTo(list.info[midPoint]) = LESS, BinarySearch the first half of the list.
	If item.ComparedTo(list.info[midPoint]) = GREATER, BinarySearch the second half of the list.

The recursive version of the function follows. Because there is only one statement on each branch of the Switch statement, we use the relational operators. Notice that we had to make `fromLocation` and `toLocation` parameters to the function rather than local index variables. An initial call to the function would be of the form `BinarySearch(info,item,0,length-1)`.

```
template<class ItemType>
bool BinarySearch
    (ItemType info[], ItemType item,
     int fromLocation, int toLocation)
{
    if (fromLocation > toLocation)        // Base case 1
        return false;
    else
    {
        int midPoint;
        midPoint = (fromLocation + toLocation) / 2;
        if (item < info[midPoint])
            return
                BinarySearch(info, item, fromLocation, midPoint-1);
        else if (item == info[midPoint])
            return true;
        else
            return
                BinarySearch(info, item, midPoint + 1, toLocation);
    }
}
```

▪▍ *Recursive Versions of InsertItem and DeleteItem*

The InsertItem Operation

Inserting an item into a linked implementation of a sorted list requires two pointers: one pointing to the node being examined and one pointing to the node behind it. We need this trailing pointer because by the time we discover where to insert a node, we are beyond the node that needs to be changed. The recursive version is actually simpler because we let the recursive process take care of the trailing pointer. We develop the algorithm here, and in the next section, we demonstrate why it works.

Let's begin by looking at an example where the item type is `int`.

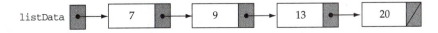

If we insert 11, we begin by comparing 11 to the value in the first node of the list, 7. Eleven is greater than 7, so we look for the insertion point in the list pointed to by the `next` member of the first node. This new list is one node shorter than the original list. We compare 11 to the value in the first node in this list, 9. Eleven is greater than 9, so we look for the insertion point in the list pointed to by the `next` member of the first node. This new list is one node shorter than the current list. We compare 11 with the value in the first node of this new list, 13. Eleven is less than 13, so we have found the insertion point: we insert a new node with 11 as the value of the first node in the list we are examining.

What happens if the value we are inserting is greater than the value in the last node of the list? In this case, the list is empty and we insert the value into the empty list. `Insert` is not a member function of `SortedType`; it is an auxiliary function called by `InsertItem` with the pointer to the list as a parameter.

Function Insert

Definition: Inserts item into a sorted list.
Size: The number of items in the list
Base Cases: (1) If the list is empty, insert item into the empty list.
                 (2) If item.ComparedTo(listPtr->info) = LESS, insert item as the
                     first node.
General Case: Insert(listPtr->next, item)

The function is coded below. Note that the pointer to the list is a reference parameter; that is, the function receives the actual address of the pointer to the current node, not just a copy of the pointer. We show why this must be true in the next sections.

```
template<class ItemType>
void Insert(NodeType<ItemType>*& listPtr, ItemType item)
{
    if (listPtr == NULL || item < listPtr->info)
    {
        // Save current pointer.
        NodeType<ItemType>* tempPtr = listPtr;
        // Get a new node.
        listPtr = new NodeType<ItemType>;
        listPtr->info = item;
        listPtr->next = tempPtr;
    }
    else Insert(listPtr->next, item);
}
```

The DeleteItem Operation

The Delete function is a mirror image of the Insert function. In the iterative version, we find the node to delete only after we have gone past the node containing a pointer to it. We solved that problem in the recursive Insert by passing the address of the pointer to the list. Does it work for the deletion operation? Let's delete 13 from the same list.

The precondition to the operation is that the item is in the list, so we compare 13 with the value in the first node in the list, 7. They are not equal, so we look for 13 in the list pointed to by the next member of the first node in the

list. We compare 13 with 9; they are not equal so we look for 13 in the list pointed to by the next member of the first node. We compare 13 with the value in the first node in the list and they are equal. We save the pointer to the node containing 13 (to deallocate the node later) and set the pointer to the list equal to the next member of the first node.

Function Delete

Definition: Deletes item from list.
Size: The number of items in the list
Base Case: If item.ComparedTo(listPtr->info) = EQUAL, delete node pointed to by listPtr.
General Case: Delete(listPtr->next, item)

Again the function must receive the address in the structure where the pointer to the current node is stored.

```
template<class ItemType>
voidDelete(NodeType<ItemType>*& list Ptr, ItemType item)
{
    if (item == listPtr->info)
    {
        NodeType<ItemType>* tempPtr = listPtr;
        listPtr = listPtr->next;
        delete tempPtr;
    }
    else
        Delete(listPtr->next,item);
}
```

■|| *How Recursion Works*

In order to understand how recursion works and why some programming languages allow it and some do not, we have to take a detour and look at how languages associate places in memory with variable names. The association of a memory address with a variable name is called *binding*. The point in the compile/execute cycle when binding occurs is called the *binding time*. We want to stress that binding time refers to a point of time in a process, not the amount of clock time that it takes to bind a variable.

Static storage allocation associates variable names with memory locations at compile time; dynamic storage allocation associates variable names with memory locations at execution time. As we look at how static and dynamic storage allocation work, consider the following question: *When are the parameters of a function bound to a particular address in memory?* The answer to this question tells something about whether recursion can be supported.

Static Storage Allocation

As a program is being translated, the compiler creates a table called a *symbol table*. When a variable is declared, it is entered into the symbol table, and a memory location—an address—is assigned to it. For example, let's see how the compiler would translate the following C++ global declarations:

```
int girlCount, boyCount, totalKids;
```

To simplify this discussion, we assume that integers take only one memory location. This statement causes three entries to be made in the symbol table. (The addresses used are arbitrary.)

Symbol	Address
girlCount	0000
boyCount	0001
totalKids	0002

That is, *at compile time,*

girlCount is *bound* to address 0000.
boyCount is *bound* to address 0001.
totalKids is *bound* to address 0002.

Whenever a variable is used later in the program, the compiler searches the symbol table for its actual address and substitutes that address for the variable name. After all, meaningful variable names are for the convenience of the human reader; addresses, however, are meaningful to computers. For example, the assignment statement

```
totalKids = girlCount + boyCount;
```

is translated into machine instructions that execute the following actions:

- Get the contents of address 0000.
- Add it to the contents of address 0001.
- Put the result into address 0002.

The object code itself is then stored in a different part of memory. Let's say that the translated instructions begin at address 1000. At the beginning of execution, control is transferred to address 1000. The instruction stored there is executed, then the instruction in 1001 is executed, and so on.

Where are the parameters of functions stored? With static storage allocation, the formal parameters of a function are assumed to be in a particular place; for instance, the compiler might set aside space for the parameter values immediately preceding the code for each function. Consider a function with two int parameters, girlCount and boyCount, as well as a local variable totalKids. Let's assume that the function's code begins at an address we call CountKids. The compiler leaves room for the two formal parameters and the local variable at addresses CountKids - 1, CountKids - 2, and CountKids - 3, respectively. Given this function heading and declaration:

```
void CountKids(int girlCount, int boyCount)
{
    int totalKids;
    .
    .
    .
}
```

the statement

```
totalKids = girlCount + boyCount;
```

in the body of the function would generate the following actions:

- Get the contents of address CountKids - 1.
- Add it to the contents of address CountKids - 2.
- Store the result in address CountKids - 3.

Figure 7.4 shows how a program with three functions might be arranged in memory.

This discussion has been simplified somewhat, because the compiler sets aside space not only for the parameters and local variables, but also for the return address (the location in the calling code of the next instruction to process, following the completion of the function) and the computer's current register values. However, we have illustrated the main point: the function's formal parameters and local variables are bound to actual addresses in memory at compile time.

We can compare the static allocation scheme to one way of allocating seats in an auditorium where a lecture is to be held. A finite number of invitations are issued for the event, and the exact number of chairs needed are set up before the lecture. Each invited guest has a reserved seat. If anyone brings friends, however, there is nowhere for them to sit.

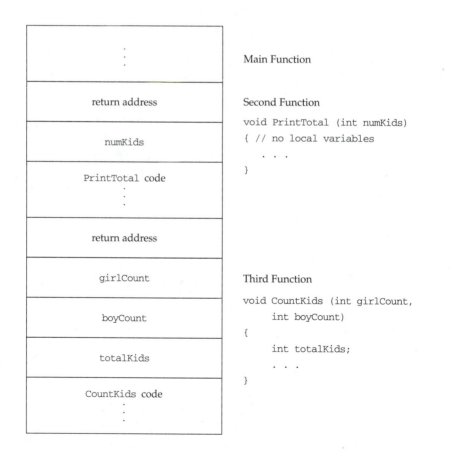

FIGURE 7.4   *Static allocation of space for a program with three functions.*

What is the implication of binding variable names to memory locations before the program executes? Each parameter and local variable has but a single location assigned to it at compile time. (They are like invited guests with reserved seats.) If each call to a function is an independent event, there is no problem. But in the case of recursion, each recursive call is dependent on the state of the values in the previous call. Where is the storage for the multiple versions of the parameters and local variables generated by recursive calls? Because the intermediate values of the parameters and local variables must be retained, the recursive call cannot store its arguments in the fixed number of locations that were set up at compile time. The values from the previous recursive call would be overwritten and lost. Thus a language that uses only static storage allocation *cannot* support recursion.

Dynamic Storage Allocation

The situation we have described is like a class of students that must share one copy of a workbook. Joe writes his exercise answers in the space provided in the workbook, then Mary erases his answers and writes hers in the same space. This process continues until each student in the class writes his or her answers into the workbook, obliterating all the answers that came before. Obviously this situation is not practical. Clearly what is needed is for each student to read from the single copy of the workbook, then to write his or her answers on a separate piece of paper. In computer terms, what each invocation of a function needs is its own work space. Dynamic storage allocation provides this solution.

With dynamic storage allocation, variable names are not bound to actual addresses in memory until *run time*. The compiler references variables not by their actual addresses, but by relative addresses. Of particular interest to us, the compiler references the parameters and local variables of a function relative to some address known at run time, not relative to the location of the function's code.

Let's look at a simplified version of how this might work in C++. (The actual implementation depends on the particular machine and compiler.) When a function is invoked, it needs space to keep its formal parameters, its local variables, and the return address (the address in the calling code to which the computer returns when the function completes its execution). Just like students sharing one copy of a workbook, each invocation of a function needs its own work space. This work space is called an **activation record** or **stack frame**. A simplified version of an activation record for function Factorial might have the following "declarations":

Activation Record (Stack Frame)   A record used at run time to store information about a function call, including the parameters, local variables, register values, and return address

```
struct ActivationRecordType
{
    AddressType returnAddr;     // return address
    int result;                 // returned value
    int number;                 // formal parameter
    .
    .
    .
};
```

Each call to a function, including recursive calls, generates a new activation record. Within the function, references to the parameters and local variables use the values in the activation record. When the function ends, the activation record is released. How does this happen? Your source code doesn't need to allocate and free activation records; the compiler adds a "prologue" to the beginning of each function and an "epilogue" to the end. Table 7.2 compares the source code for Factorial with a simplified version of the "code" executed at run time. (Of

TABLE 7.2   Run-Time Version of Factorial (Simplified)

What Your Source Code Says	What the Run-time System Does

```int Factorial(int number)```
```{```
	```// function prologue```
	```actRec = new ActivationRecordType;```
	```actRec->returnAddr = retAddr;```
	```actRec->number = number;```
	```// actRec->result is undefined```

```   if (number == 0)```
```   return 1;```
```   else```
```   return number *```
```   Factorial(number - 1);```
```}```
	```if (actRec->number == 0)```
	``` actRec->result = 1;```
	```else```
	``` actRec->result =```
	``` actRec->number *```
	``` Factorial(actRec->number-1);```
	```// function epilogue```
	```returnValue = actRec->result;```
	```retAddr = actRec->returnAddr;```
	```delete actRec;```
	```Jump (goto) retAddr```

course the code executed at run time is object code, but we are listing the source code "equivalent" so that it makes sense to the reader.)

What happens to the activation record of one function when a second function is invoked? Consider a program whose main function calls Proc1, which then calls Proc2. When the program begins executing, the "main" activation record is generated. (The main function's activation record exists for the entire execution of the program.) At the first function call an activation record is generated for Proc1:

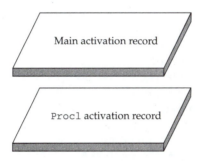

When Proc2 is called from within Proc1, its activation record is generated. Because Proc1 has not finished executing, its activation record is still around; just like the mathematicians with telephones, one waits "on hold" until the next call is finished:

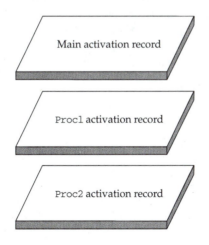

When Proc2 finishes executing, its activation record is released. But which of the other two activation records becomes the active one: Proc1's or main's? Proc1's activation record should now be active, of course. The order of activation follows the Last-In-First-Out rule. We know of a structure that supports LIFO access—the stack—so it should come as no surprise that the structure that keeps track of the activation records at run time is called the **run-time stack**. Note that our drawing shows the top of the stack at the bottom of the picture.

Run-time Stack   A data structure that keeps track of activation records during the execution of a program

---

When a function is invoked, its activation record is pushed onto the run-time stack. Each nested level of function calls adds another activation record to the stack. As each function completes its execution, its activation record is popped from the stack. Recursive function calls, like calls to any other functions, cause a new activation record to be generated. The level of recursive calls in a program determines how many activation records for this function are pushed onto the run-time stack at any one time.

Using dynamic allocation might be compared to another way of allocating seats in an auditorium where a lecture has been scheduled. A finite number of invitations is issued, but each guest is asked to bring his or her own chair. In addition, each guest can invite an unlimited number of friends, as long as they all bring their own chairs. Of course, if the number of extra guests gets out of hand, the space in the auditorium runs out, and there may not be enough room for any more friends or chairs. Similarly, the level of recursion in a program must eventually be limited by the amount of memory available in the run-time stack.

Let's walk through function `Factorial` again, to see how its execution affects the run-time stack. Here is the function:

```
int Factorial(int number)
{
    if (number == 0)
        return 1;
    else
        return number * Factorial(number - 1);
}
```

Let's say that the main function is loaded in memory beginning at location 5000, and that the initial call to `Factorial` is made in a statement at memory location 5200. Suppose also that the `Factorial` function is loaded in memory at location 1000, with the recursive call made in the statement at location 1010. Figure 7.5 shows a simplified version of how this example program is loaded in

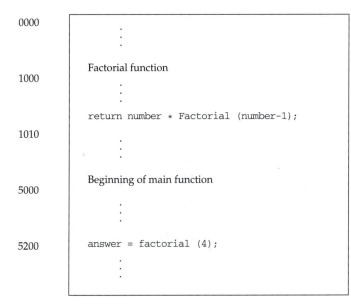

0000

Factorial function

1000

return number * Factorial (number-1);

1010

Beginning of main function

5000

5200   answer = factorial (4);

FIGURE 7.5 *The sample program loaded in memory.*

memory. (These numbers have been picked arbitrarily, so that we have actual numbers to show in the return address field of the activation record.)

When `Factorial` is called the first time from the statement in the main function at address 5200:

```
answer = Factorial(4);
```

an activation record is pushed onto the run-time stack to hold three pieces of data: the return address (5200), the formal parameter `number` (4), and the value to be returned from the function (`result`), which has not yet been evaluated. Rather than showing our activation records as pictures, we show them as a table. Each new activation record is a new row of the table. This activation record in the last row of the table is now on the top of the run-time stack. We have added a column on the left that identifies which call it is.

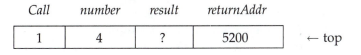

Call	number	result	returnAddr
1	4	?	5200	← top

The code is now executed. Is `number` (the `number` value in the top activation record) equal to 0? No, it is 4, so the `else` branch is taken:

```
return number * Factorial(number - 1);
```

This time the function `Factorial` is called from a different place. It is called recursively from within the function, from the statement at location 1010. After the value of `Factorial(number-1)` has eventually been calculated, we are going to return to this location to multiply the result times `number`. A new activation record is pushed onto the run-time stack:

Call	number	result	returnAddr	
1	4	?	5200	
2	3	?	1010	← top

The code for the new invocation of `Factorial` begins executing. Is `number` (the `number` value in the top activation record) equal to 0? No, it is 3, so the `else` branch is taken

```
return number * Factorial(number - 1);
```

So the function `Factorial` is again called recursively from the instruction at location 1010. This process continues until the situation looks as shown below with the fifth call.

Call	number	result	returnAddr	
1	4	?	5200	
2	3	?	1010	
3	2	?	1010	
4	1	?	1010	
5	0	?	1010	← top

Now, as the fifth call is executed, we again ask the question: is `number` (the `number` value in the top activation record) equal to 0? *Yes*. This time we perform the then-clause, storing the value 1 into `result` (the `result` in the top activation record, that is). The fifth invocation of the function has executed to completion, and the value of `result` in the top activation record is returned from the function. The run-time stack is popped to release the top activation record, leaving the activation record of the fourth call to `Factorial` at the top of the run-time stack. We don't restart the fourth function call from the beginning, however. As with any function call, we return to the place where the function was called. This place was the return address (location 1010) stored in the activation record.

Next, the returned value (1) is multiplied by the value of `number` in the top activation record (1) and the result (1) is stored into `result` (the instance of `result` in the top activation record, that is). Now the fourth invocation of the function is complete, and the value of `result` in the top activation record is returned from the function. Again the run-time stack is popped to release the top activation record, leaving the activation record of the third call to `Factorial` at the top of the run-time stack.

Call	number	result	returnAddr
1	4	?	5200
2	3	?	1010
3	2	2	1010

← top

We return to the place where we made the recursive call to `Factorial`.

This process continues until we are back to the first call:

Call	number	result	returnAddr
1	4	?	5200

← top

and 6 has just been returned as the value of `Factorial(number-1)`. This value is multiplied by the value of `number` in the top activation record (that is, 4) and the result, 24, is stored into the `result` field of the top activation record. This assignment completes the execution of the initial call to function `Factorial`. The value of `result` in the top activation record (24) is returned to the place of the original call (address 5200), and the activation record is popped. This leaves the main activation record at the top of the run-time stack. The final value of `result` is stored into the variable `answer`, and the statement following the original call is executed.

The number of recursive calls is the *depth* of the recursion. Notice the relationship between the complexity of the iterative version in terms of Big-O notation and the depth of recursion for the factorial: both are based on the parameter `number`. Is it a coincidence that the depth of recursion is the same as the complexity of the iterative version? No. Recursion is another way of doing repetition, so you would expect that the depth of recursion would be approximately the same as the number of iterations for the iterative version of same problem. In addition, they are both based on the *size* of the problem.

Tracing the Execution of Recursive Function Insert

Earlier we wrote a recursive `Insert` function that inserts a new node into a dynamically allocated linked list. In order to follow the execution of `Insert`, let's put addresses on the nodes in the list. In the following diagram, the number above a node is the base address of the node. The number under the `next` member is the address of the `next` data member only. The external pointer to the list is stored in location 010.

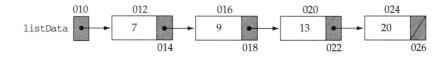

Here is the function we trace.

```
template<class ItemType>
void Insert(NodeType<ItemType>*& listPtr, ItemType item)
{
    if (listPtr == NULL || item < listPtr->info)
    {
        // Save current pointer.
        NodeType<ItemType>* tempPtr = listPtr;
        // Get a new node.
        listPtr = new NodeType<ItemType>;
        listPtr->info = item;
        listPtr->next = tempPtr;
    }
    else Insert(listPtr->next, item);
}
```

Our trace must keep track of `listPtr`, `item`, and the return address. The local variable `tempPtr` also has a place in the activation record. Rather than give a specific return address, however, we use the convention that R0 is the return address from the nonrecursive call and R1 is the return address from the recursive call. We trace `Insert(listData, item)` where `item` is 11. Recall that the formal parameter `listPtr` is passed by reference and `item` by value. This is what the activation record looks like after the nonrecursive call.

Call	listPtr	item	tempPtr	returnAddr
1	010	11	?	R0

← top

As the code begins execution, the value stored in the place named in `listPtr` (location 010) is examined (because `listPtr` is a reference parameter). This value is not NULL so `item` is compared with the `info` data member of the node pointed to by location 010. Eleven is greater than 7, so the function is called again recursively.

Call	listPtr	item	tempPtr	returnAddr
1	010	11	?	R0
2	014	11	?	R1

← top

The value stored in the place named in `listPtr` (i.e., location 014) is not NULL and 11 is greater than 9, so the function is called again recursively.

Call	listPtr	item	tempPtr	returnAddr
1	010	11	?	R0
2	014	11	?	R1
3	018	11	?	R1

← top

The value stored in the place named in `listPtr` is not NULL but 11 is less than 13, so the then-clause is executed and the following steps are performed. The value in the place named in `listPtr` is copied into `tempPtr`. The `new` operator is executed and the address of a node of type `NodeType` is stored into the place named in `listPtr`. The stack now looks as follows if the address of the new node is 028:

Call	listPtr	item	tempPtr	returnAddr
1	010	11	?	R0
2	014	11	?	R1
3	018	11	020	R1

← top

`listPtr` has not changed! Didn't we just store the address 028 there? No, we stored 028 into the place *named* in `listPtr`: in location 018, the `next` member of the previous node. Our list now looks like this:

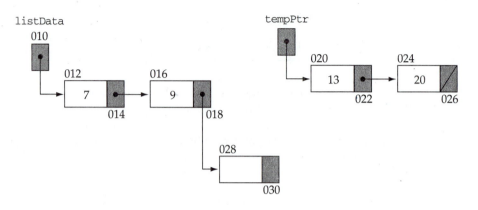

The next two statements store `item` into `listPtr->info` and `tempPtr` into `listPtr->next`, completing the insertion.

Let's see what the activation records would look like at this point if we had passed `listPtr` as a value parameter.

Call	listPtr	item	tempPtr	returnAddr	
1	012	11	?	R0	
2	016	11	?	R1	
3	028	11	020	R1	← top

When the `new` operator is executed, the address of a node of type `NodeType` is stored into `listPtr`—not the place *named* in `listPtr`. Therefore 028 is stored into the activation record member `listPtr`, not into the `next` data member of the preceding node as is the case when `listPtr` is a reference parameter. The `next` data member of the new node gets set properly, but the pointer to the new node is stored in the activation record that is removed when the function exits. Thus the rest of the list is lost. In fact, if you use this incorrect version to build the list, the list is empty. (Can you explain why?)

Our recursive `Insert` works properly because the first parameter is the *address* in memory of either the external pointer to the list or the `next` data member of a node in the list.

■‖ *Debugging Recursive Routines*

Because of their nested calls to themselves, recursive routines can be confusing to debug. The most serious problem is the possibility that the routine recurses forever. A typical symptom of this problem is an error message telling us that the system has run out of space in the run-time stack, due to the level of recursive calls. Using the Three-Question Method to verify recursive functions should help us avoid the problem of never finishing. If we can answer yes to the base-case and smaller-caller questions, we should be able to guarantee that the routine eventually ends—theoretically, at least.

That does not guarantee, however, that the program does not fail due to lack of space. We saw in the previous section that a function call requires a certain amount of overhead to save the parameters, the return address, and the local data. A call to a recursive function may generate many, many levels of function calls to itself—more than the system can handle.

One error that programmers often make when they first start writing recursive routines is to use a looping structure instead of a branching one. Because they tend to think of the problem in terms of a repetitive action, they inadvertently use a While statement rather than an If statement. The main body of the recursive routine should always be a breakdown into base and recursive cases. Hence, we use a branching statement, not a looping statement. It's a good idea to double-check your recursive functions to make sure that you used an If or Switch statement to get a branching effect.

Recursive routines are good places to put debug output statements during testing. Print out the parameters and local variables, if any, at the beginning and end of the function. Be sure to print the values of the parameters on the recursive call(s) to make sure that each call is trying to solve a problem smaller than the previous one.

▪‖ *Removing Recursion*

In cases where a recursive solution is not desired, either because the language doesn't support recursion or because the recursive solution is deemed too costly in terms of space or time, a recursive algorithm can be implemented as a nonrecursive function. There are two general techniques that are often substituted for recursion: iteration and stacking.

Iteration

When the recursive call is the last action executed in a recursive function, an interesting situation occurs. The recursive call causes an activation record to be put on the run-time stack to contain the function's parameters and local variables. When this recursive call finishes executing, the run-time stack is popped and the previous values of the variables are restored. But because the recursive call is the last statement in the function, the function terminates without using these values. The pushing and popping of activation records is superfluous. All we really need to do is to change the "smaller-caller" variable(s) on the recursive call's parameter list, and "jump" back to the beginning of the function. In other words, we really need a *loop*.

For instance, as noted later in this chapter, function `ValueInList` is a poor use of recursion. However, it is simple to remove the recursion from this function. The last statement executed in the general case is the recursive call to itself. Let's see how to replace the recursion with a loop.

The recursive solution has two base cases: one occurs if we find the value and the other occurs if we reach the end of the list without finding the value. The base cases solve the problem without further executions of the function. In the iterative solution, the base cases become the terminating conditions of the loop:

```
while (!found && moreToSearch)
```

When the terminating conditions are met, the problem is solved without further executions of the loop body.

In the general case of the recursive solution, `ValueInList` is called to search the remaining, unsearched part of the list. Each recursive execution of the function processes a smaller version of the problem. The smaller-caller question is answered affirmatively because `startIndex` is incremented, shrinking the unsearched part of the list on every recursive call. Similarly, in an iterative solution, each subsequent execution of the loop body processes a smaller version of the problem. The unsearched part of the list is shrunk on each execution of the loop body by incrementing `startIndex`.

IF value = list.info[startIndex]
  Set found to true
ELSE
  Increment startIndex

Here is the iterative version of the function:

```
bool ValueInList(ListType list, int value, int startIndex)
{
    bool found = false;

    while (!found && startIndex < list.length)
        if (value == list.info[startIndex])
            found = true;
        else startIndex++;
    return found;
}
```

Cases where the recursive call is the last statement executed are called **tail recursion**. Note that the recursive call is not necessarily the last statement in the function. For instance, the recursive call in the following version of ValueInList is still tail recursion, even though it is *not* the last statement in the function:

```
bool ValueInList(ListType list, int value, int startIndex)
{
    if (list.info[startIndex] == value)
        return true;
    else if (startIndex != list.length-1)
        return ValueInList(list, value, startIndex + 1);
    else return false;
}
```

The recursive call is the last statement *executed* in the general case—thus it is tail recursion. Tail recursion is usually replaced by iteration to remove recursion from the solution. In fact, many compilers catch tail recursion and automatically replace it with iteration.

Tail Recursion   The case in which a function contains only a single recursive invocation and it is the last statement to be executed in the function

---

Stacking

When the recursive call is *not* the last action executed in a recursive function, we cannot simply substitute a loop for the recursion. For instance, in function RevPrint we make the recursive call and then print the value in the current node. In cases like this, we must replace the stacking that was done by the *system* with stacking that is done by the *programmer*.

How would we write function RevPrint nonrecursively? As we traverse the list, we must keep track of the pointer to each node, until we reach the end of the list (when our traversing pointer equals NULL). When we reach the end of the list, we print the info data member of the last node. Then we back up and print again, back up and print, and so on, until we have printed the first list element.

We know of a data structure in which we can store pointers and retrieve them in reverse order: the stack. The general task for RevPrint is

RevPrint (iterative)

> Create an empty stack of pointers
> Set ptr to point to first node in list
> WHILE the list is not empty
>   Push ptr onto the stack
>   Advance ptr
> WHILE the stack is not empty
>   Pop the stack to get ptr (to previous node)
>   Print Info(ptr)

A nonrecursive `RevPrint` function may be coded as follows. Note that we now make `RevPrint` a member function of class `SortedType` instead of a helper function. Because `RevPrint` no longer has a parameter, we don't have to deal with the problem of having the client pass the (inaccessible) pointer to the beginning of the linked list.

```
#include "StackType.h"

void ListType::RevPrint()
{
    StackType<NodeType*> stack;
    NodeType* listPtr;

    listPtr = listData;

    while (listPtr != NULL)    // Put pointers onto the stack.
    {
        stack.Push(listPtr);
        listPtr = listPtr->next;
    }
    // Retrieve pointers in reverse order and print elements.
    while (!stack.IsEmpty())
    {
        stack.Pop(listPtr);
        cout << listPtr->info;
    }
}
```

Notice that the nonrecursive version of `RevPrint` is quite a bit longer than its recursive counterpart, especially if we add in the code for the stack routines `Push`, `Pop`, and `IsEmpty`. This verbosity is caused by our need to stack and unstack the pointers explicitly. In the recursive version, we just called RevPrint recursively, and let the run-time stack keep track of the pointers.

◼‖ *Deciding Whether to Use a Recursive Solution*

There are several factors to consider in deciding whether or not to use a recursive solution to a problem. The main issues are the clarity and the efficiency of the solution. Let's talk about efficiency first. In general, a recursive solution is more costly in terms of both computer time and space. (This is not an absolute decree; it really depends on the computer and the compiler.) A recursive solution usually requires more "overhead" because of the nested recursive function calls, in terms of both time (the function prologues and epilogues must be run for each recursive call) and space (an activation record must be created). A call to a recursive routine may hide many layers of internal recursive calls. For instance, the call to an iterative solution to Factorial involves a single function invocation, causing one activation record to be put on the run-time stack. Invoking the recursive version of Factorial, however, requires $N + 1$ function calls and $N + 1$ activation records to be pushed onto the run-time stack, where N represents the formal parameter number. That is, the depth of recursion is $O(N)$. For some problems, the system just may not have enough space in the run-time stack to run a recursive solution.

As an extreme example, consider the original version of the recursive function ValueInList. Every time it is invoked, it saves copies of the parameters, including the whole list that is passed as a value parameter. As we search farther and farther in the list, nesting more and more levels of recursive calls, the amount of memory needed for the run-time stack becomes considerable. If the list contains 100 elements and the one we are looking for is not in the list, we end up saving 100 copies of the 100-element list. Eventually we use up so much memory that we may run out of space altogether! This is an extreme example of one of the "overhead" problems of recursive calls. In this particular case we might make the list a reference parameter (something generally not done in value-returning functions) so that new copies of the array would not be generated on every invocation of ValueInList. (The address of the one and only copy of list would be passed instead.) Still, the level of recursion is $O(N)$ and the iterative solution is about the same length and just as clear. Thus ValueInList is a poor use of recursion.

Another problem to look for is the possibility that a particular recursive solution might just be *inherently* inefficient. Such inefficiency is not a reflection of how we choose to implement the algorithm; rather, it is an indictment of the algorithm itself. For instance, look back at function Combinations, which we discussed earlier in this chapter. The example of this function illustrated in Figure 7.2, Combinations(4,3), seems straightforward enough. But consider the execution of Combinations(6,4), as illustrated in Figure 7.6. The inherent problem with this function is that the same values are calculated over and over. Combinations(4,3) is calculated in two different places, and Combinations(3,2) is calculated in three places, as are Combinations(2,1) and Combinations(2,2). It is unlikely that we could solve a combinatorial problem of any large size using this function. The problem is that the program runs "forever"—or until it exhausts the capacity of the computer; it is an exponential-time, $O(2^N)$, solution to a linear time, $O(N)$, problem. Although our recursive function is very easy to understand, it was not a practical solution. In such cases, you should seek an iterative solution.

The issue of the clarity of the solution is still an important factor, however. For many problems a recursive solution is simpler and more natural for the programmer to write. The total amount of work required to solve a problem can be envisioned as an iceberg. By using recursive programming, the applications programmer may limit his or her view to the tip of the iceberg. The system takes care of the great bulk of the work below the surface. Compare, for example, the recursive and nonrecursive versions of function RevPrint. In the recursive version we let the system take care of the stacking that we had to do explicitly in the nonrecursive function. Thus recursion is a tool that can help reduce the complexity of a program by hiding some of the implementation details. With the cost of computer time and memory decreasing and the cost of a programmer's time rising, it is worthwhile to use recursive solutions to such problems.

To summarize, it is good to use recursion when:

- *The depth of recursive calls is relatively "shallow,"* some fraction of the size of the problem. For instance, the level of recursive calls in the BinarySearch function is $O(\log_2 N)$; this is a good candidate for recursion. The depth of recursive calls in the Factorial and ValueInList routines, however, is $O(N)$.

- *The recursive version does about the same amount of work as the nonrecursive version.* You can compare the Big-O approximations to determine this. For instance, we have determined that the $O(2^N)$ recursive version of Combinations is a poor use of recursion, compared to an $O(N)$ iterative version. Both the recursive and iterative versions of BinarySearch, however, are $O(\log_2 N)$. BinarySearch is a good example of a recursive function.

- *The recursive version is shorter and simpler than the nonrecursive solution.* By this rule, Factorial and ValueInList are not good uses of recursive programming. They illustrate how to understand and write recursive functions, but they could more efficiently be written iteratively—without any loss of clarity in the solution. RevPrint is a better use of recursion. Its recursive solution is very simple to understand, and the nonrecursive equivalent is much less elegant.

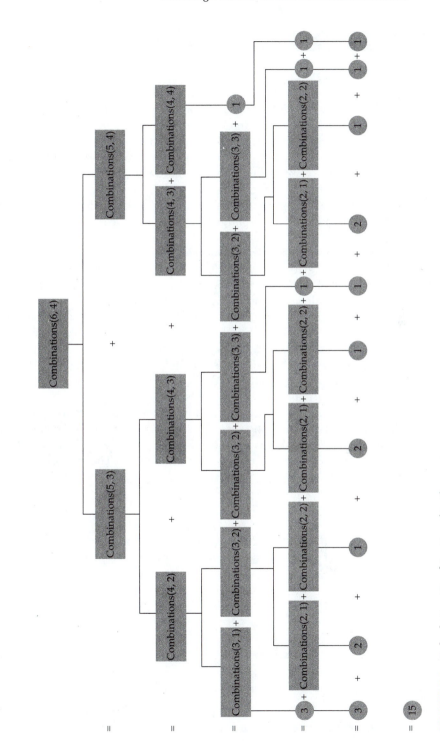

FIGURE 7.6   *Calculating Combinations(6, 4).*

QUICK SORT

In Chapter 3, we presented two versions of the List ADT: one was unsorted and one was created and maintained in sorted order by unique key. In Chapter 10, we look at a variety of sorting algorithms. At the logical level, sorting algorithms take an unsorted list object and convert it into a sorted list object. At the implementation level, sorting algorithms take an array and reorganize the values in the array so that they are in order by key.

The quick sort algorithm is based on the idea that it is faster and easier to sort two small lists than one larger one. The name comes from the fact that, in general, quick sort can sort a list of data elements quite rapidly. The basic strategy of this sort is to divide and conquer.

If you were given a large stack of final exams to sort by name, you might use the following approach: pick a splitting value, say L, and divide the stack of tests into two piles, A–L and M–Z. (Note that the two piles do not necessarily contain the same number of tests.) Then take the first pile and subdivide it into two piles, A–F and G–L. The A–F pile can be further broken down into A–C and D–F. This division process goes on until the piles are small enough to be easily sorted. The same process is applied to the M–Z pile.

Eventually all the small sorted piles can be stacked one on top of the other to produce a sorted set of tests. (See Figure 7.7.)

This strategy is based on recursion—on each attempt to sort the stack of tests the stack is divided and then the same approach is used to sort each of the smaller stacks (a smaller case). This process goes on until the small stacks do not need to be further divided (the base case). The parameter list of the

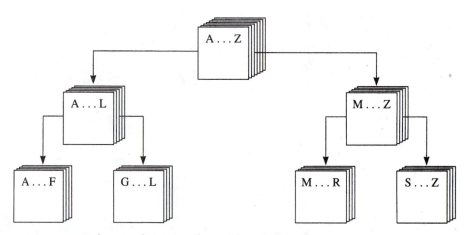

FIGURE 7.7 *Ordering a list using the quick sort algorithm.*

QuickSort function reflects the part of the list that is currently being processed: we pass the array and the first and last indexes that define the part of the array to be processed on this call. The initial call to QuickSort is

```
QuickSort(values, 0, numberOfValues-1);
```

Function QuickSort

Definition:	Sorts the items in array values.
Size:	values[first]..values[last]
Base Case:	If less than 2 items in values[first]..values[last], do nothing.
General Case:	Split the array according to splitting value.
	QuickSort the elements <= splitting value.
	QuickSort the elements > splitting value.

QuickSort

```
IF there is more than one item in values[first]..values[last]
    Select splitVal
    Split the array so that
        values[first]..values[splitPoint-1] <= splitVal
        values[splitPoint] = splitVal
        values[splitPoint+1]..values[last] > splitVal
    QuickSort the left half
    QuickSort the right half
```

How do we select splitVal? One simple solution is to use the value in values[first] as the splitting value. (We show a better value later.)

splitVal = 9

9	20	6	10	14	8	60	11

[first]   [last]

After the call to Split, all the items less than or equal to splitVal are on the left side of the array and all of those greater than splitVal are on the right side of the array.

smaller values   larger values

9	8	6	10	14	20	60	11

[first]   [last]

The two "halves" meet at `splitPoint`, the index of the last item that is less than or equal to `splitVal`. Note that we don't know the value of `splitPoint` until the splitting process is complete. We can then swap `splitVal` with the value at `splitPoint`.

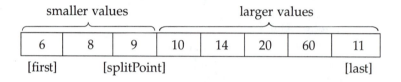

6	8	9	10	14	20	60	11

[first]   [splitPoint]   [last]

Our recursive calls to `QuickSort` use this index (`splitPoint`) to reduce the size of the problem in the general case.

`QuickSort(values, first, splitPoint-1)` sorts the left "half" of the array. `QuickSort(values,splitPoint + 1,last)` sorts the right "half" of the array. (The "halves" are not necessarily the same size.) `splitVal` is already in its correct position in `values[splitPoint]`.

What is the base case? When the segment being examined has less than two items, we do not need to go on. So "there is more than one item in `values[first]..values[last]`" can be translated into "if (`first < last`)". We can now code function `QuickSort`.

```
template<class ItemType>
void QuickSort(ItemType values[], int first, int last)
{
    if ( first < last)
    {
        int splitPoint;

        Split(values, first, last, splitPoint);
        // values[first]..values[splitPoint-1] <= splitVal
        // values[splitPoint] = splitVal
        // values[splitPoint + 1]..values[last] > splitVal

        QuickSort(values, first, splitPoint-1);
        QuickSort(values, splitPoint + 1, last);
    }
}
```

Let's verify `QuickSort` according to the Three-Question Method.

1. *Is there a nonrecursive base case?* Yes. When `first >= last` (there is at most one element in the segment), `QuickSort` does nothing.
2. *Does each recursive call involve a smaller case of the problem?* Yes. `Split` divides

the segment into two not necessarily equal pieces, and each of these smaller pieces is then QuickSort'd. Note that even if splitVal is the largest or smallest value in the segment, the two pieces are still smaller than the original one: if splitVal is smaller than all the other values in the segment, then QuickSort(values, first, splitPoint - 1) terminates immediately, because first > splitPoint - 1. QuickSort(values, splitPoint + 1, last) quick sorts a segment one element smaller than the original.

3. *Assuming that the recursive calls succeed, does the whole function work?* Yes. We assume that QuickSort(values, first, splitPoint - 1) actually sorts the first splitPoint - 1 elements, whose values are less than or equal to splitVal. values[splitPoint], containing splitVal, is in its correct place. We also assume that QuickSort (values, splitPoint + 1, last) has correctly sorted the rest of the list, whose values are all greater than splitVal. So we know that the whole list is sorted.

In good top-down fashion, we have shown that our algorithm works *if function Split works.* Now we must develop our splitting algorithm. We must find a way to get all of the elements equal to or less than splitVal on one side of splitVal and the elements greater than splitVal on the other side.

We do this by moving the indexes, first and last, toward the middle of the array, looking for items that are on the wrong side of the split point (Figure 7.8). We make first and last value parameters, so we can change their values without affecting the calling function. We save the original value of first in a local variable, saveFirst. (See Figure 7.8a.)[1]

We start out by moving first to the right, toward the middle, comparing values[first] to splitVal. If values[first] is less than or equal to splitVal, we keep incrementing first; otherwise we leave first where it is and begin moving last toward the middle. (See Figure 7.8b.)

Now values[last] is compared to splitVal. If it is greater, we continue decrementing last; otherwise we leave last in place. (See Figure 7.8c.) At this point it is clear that values[last] and values[first] are each on the wrong side of the array. Note that the elements to the left of values[first] and to the right of values[last] are not necessarily sorted; they are just on the correct side *with respect to* splitVal. To put values[first] and values[last] into their correct sides, we merely swap them, then increment first and decrement last. (See Figure 7.8d.)

Now we repeat the whole cycle, incrementing first until we encounter a value that is greater than splitVal, then decrementing last until we encounter a value that is less than or equal to splitVal. (See Figure 7.8e.)

---

1. We assume that the relational operators are defined on values of ItemType.

(a) Initialization. Note that splitVal = values[first] = 9.

9	20	6	10	14	8	60	11

[saveFirst][first]   [last]

(b) Increment first until values[first] > splitVal

9	20	6	10	14	8	60	11

[saveFirst][first]   [last]

(c) Decrement last until values[last] < = splitVal

9	20	6	10	14	8	60	11

[saveFirst][first]   [last]

(d) Swap values[first] and values[last]; move first and last
   toward each other

9	8	6	10	14	20	60	11

[saveFirst]   [first]   [last]

(e) Increment first until values[first] > splitVal or first > last.
   Decrement last until values[last] < = splitVal or first > last

9	8	6	10	14	20	60	11

[saveFirst]   [last] [first]

(f) first > last so no swap occurs within the loop.
   Swap values[saveFirst] and values[last]

6	8	9	10	14	20	60	11

[saveFirst]   [last]
                  (splitPoint)

FIGURE 7.8 *Function Split.*

When does the process stop? When first and last cross, no further
swaps are necessary. splitPoint is last. This is the location where

splitVal belongs, so we swap values[saveFirst], which contains splitVal, with the element at values[splitPoint] (Figure 7.8f.) The index splitPoint is returned from the function, to be used by QuickSort to set up the next recursive call.

```cpp
template<class ItemType>
void Split(ItemType values[], int first, int last, int& splitPoint)
{
    ItemType splitVal = values[first];
    int saveFirst = first;
    bool onCorrectSide;

    first++;
    do
    {
        onCorrectSide = true;
        while (onCorrectSide)                 // Move first toward last.
            if (values[first] > splitVal)
                onCorrectSide = false;
            else
            {
                first++;
                onCorrectSide = (first <= last);
            }

        onCorrectSide = (first <= last);
        while (onCorrectSide)                 // Move last toward first.
            if (values[last] <= splitVal)
                onCorrectSide = false;
            else
            {
                last--;
                onCorrectSide = (first <= last);
            }

        if (first < last)
        {
            Swap(values[first], values[last]);
            first++;
            last--;
        }
    } while (first <= last);

    splitPoint = last;
    Swap(values[saveFirst], values[splitPoint]);
}
```

What happens if our splitting value is the largest or the smallest value in the segment? The algorithm still works correctly, but because of the lopsided splits it is not so quick.

Is this situation likely to occur? That depends on how we choose our splitting value and on the original order of the data in the array. If we use `values[first]` as the splitting value and the array is already sorted, then *every* split is lopsided. One side contains one element, while the other side contains all but one of the elements. Thus our `QuickSort` is not a quick sort. This splitting algorithm favors an array in random order.

It is not unusual, however, to want to sort an array that is already in nearly sorted order. If this is the case, a better splitting value would be the middle value,

```
values[(first + last) / 2]
```

This value could be swapped with `values[first]` at the beginning of the function.

There are many possible splitting algorithms. One that is a slight variation of the one we have just developed is given below. It uses the value in the middle of the array as the splitting value without moving it to the first slot. As a result the value in `values[splitPoint]` may or may not be in its permanent place.

```cpp
template<class ItemType>
void Split2(ItemType values[], int first, int last,
            int& splitPt1, int& splitPt2)
{
    ItemType splitVal = values[(first + last)/2];
    bool onCorrectSide;
    do
    {
        onCorrectSide = true;
        while (onCorrectSide)            // Move first toward last.
            if (values[first] >= splitVal)
                onCorrectSide = false;
            else
                first++;

        onCorrectSide = true;
        while (onCorrectSide)            // Move last toward first.
            if (values[last] <= splitVal)
                onCorrectSide = false;
            else
                last--;
        if (first <= last)
        {
            Swap(values[first], values[last]);
```

```
            first++;
            last--;
        }
    } while (first <= last);

    splitPt1 = first;
    splitPt2 = last;
}
```

If this algorithm is used, function `QuickSort` has to be adjusted slightly.

```
template<class ItemType>
void QuickSort2(ItemType values[], int first, int last)
{
    if (first < last)
    {
        int splitPt1;
        int splitPt2;

        Split2(values, first, last, splitPt1, splitPt2);
        // values[first]..values[splitPt2] <= splitVal
        // values[splitPt1 + 1]..values[last] > splitVal

        if (splitPt1 < last)
            QuickSort2(values, splitPt1, last);
        if ( first < splitPt2)
            QuickSort2(values, first, splitPt2);
    }
}
```

Notice that `QuickSort2` only makes the recursive call if there is more than one element in a segment. This makes the code more efficient. We analyze the complexity of `QuickSort` when we analyze the other sorting algorithms in Chapter 10. However, we emphasize here that the algorithm is very sensitive to the choice of the splitting value.

■‖ *Summary*

Recursion is a very powerful computing tool. Used appropriately, it can simplify the solution of a problem, often resulting in shorter, more easily understood source code. As usual in computing, there are trade-offs: recursive functions are often less efficient, in terms of both time and space, due to the overhead of many levels of function calls. How expensive this cost is depends on the computer system and compiler.

A recursive solution to a problem must have at least one base case—that is, a case where the solution is derived nonrecursively. Without a base case, the function recurses forever (or at least until the computer runs out of memory). The recursive solution also has one or more general cases that include recursive calls to the function. The recursive calls must involve a "smaller caller." One (or more) of the actual parameter values must change in each recursive call to redefine the problem to be smaller than it was on the previous call. Thus each recursive call leads the solution of the problem toward the base case(s).

A typical implementation of recursion involves the use of a stack. Each call to a function generates an activation record to contain its return address, parameters, and local variables. The activation records are accessed in a Last-In-First-Out manner. Thus a stack is the choice of data structure. Recursion can be supported by systems and languages that use dynamic storage allocation. The function parameters and local variables are not bound to addresses until an activation record is created at run time. Thus multiple copies of the intermediate values of recursive calls to the function can be supported, as new activation records are created for them.

With static storage allocation, in contrast, a single location is reserved at compile time for each parameter and local variable of a function. There is no place to store intermediate values calculated by repeated nested calls to the same function. Therefore, systems and languages with only static storage allocation cannot support recursion.

When recursion is not possible or appropriate, a recursive algorithm can be implemented nonrecursively by using a looping structure and, in some cases, by pushing and popping relevant values onto a stack. This programmer-controlled stack explicitly replaces the system's run-time stack. While such nonrecursive solutions are often more efficient in terms of time and space, there is usually a trade-off in terms of the elegance of the solution.

■|| *Exercises*

1. Explain what is meant by
   (a) base case
   (b) general (or recursive) case
   (c) run-time stack
   (d) binding time
   (e) tail recursion

2. True or False? If false, correct the statement. *Recursive functions :*
   (a) often have fewer local variables than the equivalent nonrecursive routines.
   (b) generally use While or For statements as their main control structure.
   (c) are possible only in languages with static storage allocation.
   (d) should be used whenever execution speed is critical.
   (e) are always shorter and clearer than the equivalent nonrecursive routines.

(f) must always contain a path that does not contain a recursive call.

(g) are always less "efficient," in terms of Big-O.

3. Use the Three-Question Method to verify the `ValueInList` function in this chapter.

4. Describe the Three-Question Method of verifying recursive routines in relation to an inductive proof.

5. What data structure would you most likely see in a nonrecursive implementation of a recursive algorithm?

6. Using the recursive function `RevPrint` as a model, write the recursive function `PrintList`, which traverses the elements in the list in forward order. Does one of these routines constitute a better use of recursion? If so, which one?

Use the following function in answering Exercises 7 and 8:

```
int Puzzle(int base, int limit)
{
    if (base > limit)
        return -1;
    else
        if (base == limit)
            return 1;
        else
            return base * Puzzle(base + 1, limit);
}
```

7. Identify
   (a) the base case(s) of function `Puzzle`.
   (b) the general case(s) of function `Puzzle`.

8. Show what would be written by the following calls to the recursive function `Puzzle`.
   (a) `cout << Puzzle (14, 10);`
   (b) `cout << Puzzle (4, 7);`
   (c) `cout << Puzzle (0, 0);`

9. Given the following function:

```
int Func(int num)
{
    if (num == 0)
        return 0;
    else
        return num + Func(num + 1);
}
```

   (a) Is there a constraint on the values that can be passed as a parameter in order for this function to pass the smaller-caller test?
   (b) Is `Func (7)` a good call? If so, what is returned from the function?
   (c) Is `Func (0)` a good call? If so, what is returned from the function?
   (d) Is `Func (-5)` a good call? If so, what is returned from the function?

10. Put comments on the following routines to identify the base and general cases and explain what each routine does.

    (a)

    ```
    int Power(int base, int exponent)
    {
        if (exponent == 0)
            return 1;
        else
            return base * Power(base, exponent-1);
    }
    ```

    (b)

    ```
    int Factorial(int number)
    {
        if (num > 0)
            return num * Factorial(num - 1);
        else
            if (num == 0)
                return 1;
    }
    ```

    (c)

    ```
    void Sort(int values[], int fromIndex, int toIndex)
    {
        int maxIndex;

        if (fromIndex != toIndex)
        {
            maxIndex = MaxPosition(values, fromIndex, toIndex);
            Swap(values[maxIndex], values[toIndex]);
            Sort(values, fromIndex, toIndex - 1);
        }
    }
    ```

11.

    (a) Fill in the blanks to complete the following recursive function:

    ```
    int Sum(int info[], int fromIndex, int toIndex)
    // Computes the sum of the items between fromIndex and toIndex.
    {
        if (fromIndex _____ toIndex)
            return _____;
        else
            return _____;
    }
    ```

    (b) Which is the base case and which is the general case?

(c) Show how you would call this function to sum all the elements in an array called numbers, which contains elements indexed from 0 to MAX_ITEMS -1.

(d) What run-time problem might you have with this function as it is coded?

12. You must assign the grades for a programming class. Right now the class is studying recursion, and they have been given this simple assignment: write a recursive function SumSquares that takes a pointer to a linked list of integer elements and returns the sum of the squares of the elements.

Example:

SumSquares(listPtr) yields (5 * 5) + (2 * 2) + (3 * 3) + (1 * 1) = 39

Assume that the list is not empty.

You have received quite a variety of solutions. Grade the functions below, marking errors where you see them.

(a)
```
int SumSquares(NodeType* list)
{
    return 0;
    if (list != NULL)
        return (list->info * list->info) + SumSquares(list->next));
}
```

(b)
```
int SumSquares(NodeType* list)
{
    int sum = 0;
    while (list != NULL)
    {
        sum = (list->info * list->info) + sum;
        list = list->next;
    }
return sum;
}
```

(c)
```
int SumSquares(NodeType* list)
{
    if (list == NULL)
        return 0;
    else
        return list->info* list->info + SumSquares(list-> next);
}
```

(d)

```
int SumSquares(NodeType* list)
{
    if (list->next == NULL)
        return list->info*list->info;
    else
        return list->info*list->info + SumSquares(list->next);
}
```

(e)

```
int SumSquares(NodeType* list)
{
    if (list == NULL)
        return 0;
    else
        return (SumSquares(list->next) * SumSquares(list->next));
}
```

13. The Fibonacci sequence is the series of integers

    ```
    0, 1, 1, 2, 3, 5, 8, 13, 21, 34, 55, 89 ...
    ```

    See the pattern? Each element in the series is the sum of the preceding two items. There is a recursive formula for calculating the Nth number of the sequence (the 0th number is Fib(0) = 0):

    $$\text{Fib}(N) = \begin{cases} N, & \text{if } N = 0 \text{ or } 1 \\ \text{Fib}(N-2) + \text{Fib}(N-1), & \text{if } N > 1 \end{cases}$$

    (a) Write a recursive version of function `Fibonacci`.
    (b) Write a nonrecursive version of function `Fibonacci`.
    (c) Write a driver to test the recursive and iterative versions of function `Fibonacci`.
    (d) Compare the recursive and iterative versions for efficiency. (Use words, not Big-O notation.)
    (e) Can you think of a way to make the recursive version more efficient?

14. The following defines a function that calculates an approximation of the square root of a number, starting with an approximate answer (`approx`), within the specified tolerance (`tol`).

    SqrRoot(number, approx, tol) =

    $$\begin{cases} \text{approx}, & \text{if } |\text{approx}^2 - \text{number}| <= \text{tol} \\ \text{SqrRoot(number, (approx}^2 + \text{number})/(2*\text{approx}), \text{tol}), & \text{if } |\text{approx}^2 - \text{number}| > \text{tol} \end{cases}$$

    (a) What limitations must be made on the values of the parameters if this method is to work correctly?
    (b) Write a recursive version of function `SqrRoot`.
    (c) Write a nonrecursive version of function `SqrRoot`.
    (d) Write a driver to test the recursive and iterative versions of function `SqrRoot`.

15. A sequential search member function of `SortedType` has the following prototype:

    ```
    void Search(int value, bool& found);
    ```

    (a) Write the function definition as a recursive search, assuming a linked implementation.
    (b) Write the function definition as a recursive search, assuming an array-based implementation.

16. We want to count the number of possible paths to move from row 1, column 1 to row N, column N in a two-dimensional grid. Steps are restricted to going up or to the right, but not diagonally. The illustration shows three of many paths, if N = 10:

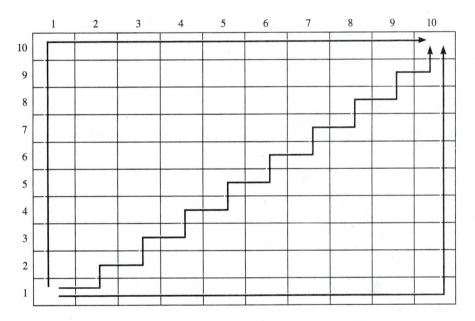

    (a) The following function, `NumPaths`, is supposed to count the number of paths, but it has some problems. Debug the function.

    ```
    int NumPaths(int row, int col, int n)
    {
        if (row == n)
            return 1;
        else
            if (col == n)
                return NumPaths + 1;
            else
                return NumPaths(row + 1, col) * NumPaths(row, col + 1);
    }
    ```

(b) After you have corrected the function, trace the execution of NumPaths with n = 4 by hand. Why is this algorithm inefficient?

(c) The efficiency of this operation can be improved by keeping intermediate values of NumPaths in a two-dimensional array of integer values. This keeps the function from having to recalculate values that it has already done. Design and code a version of NumPaths that uses this approach.

(d) Show an invocation of the version of NumPaths in Part (c), including any array initialization necessary.

(e) How do the two versions of NumPaths compare in terms of time efficiency? Space efficiency?

17. Given the following function:[2]

```
int Ulam(int num)
{
    if (num < 2)
        return 1;
    else
        if (num % 2 == 0)
            return Ulam(num / 2);
        else
            return Ulam(3 * num + 1);
}
```

(a) What problems come up in verifying this function?

(b) How many recursive calls are made by the following initial calls:

```
cout    << Ulam(7)   << endl;
cout    << Ulam(8)   << endl;
cout    << Ulam(15)  << endl;
```

18. Explain the relationship between dynamic storage allocation and recursion.

19. What do we mean by binding time, and what does it have to do with recursion?

20. Given the following values in list:

list										
.length	10									
.info	2	6	9	14	23	65	92	96	99	100
	[0]	[1]	[2]	[3]	[4]	[5]	[6]	[7]	[8]	[9]

---

2. One of our reviewers pointed out that the proof of termination of this algorithm is a celebrated open question in mathematics. See *Programming Pearls* by Jon Bentley for a discussion and further references.

show the contents of the run-time stack during the execution of this call to BinarySearch:

```
BinarySearch(info, 99, 0, 9)
```

21. The parameter to the following two recursive routines is a pointer to a singly linked list of numbers, whose elements are unique (no duplicates) and unsorted. Each node in the list contains two members, info (a number) and next (a pointer to the next node).

    (a) Write a recursive value-returning function, MinLoc, that receives a pointer to a list of unsorted numbers and returns a pointer to the node that contains the minimum value in the list.

    (b) Write a recursive void function, Sort, that receives a pointer to an unsorted list of numbers and reorders the values in the list from smallest to largest. This function may call the recursive MinLoc function that you wrote in part (a). (*Hint*: It is easier to swap the values in the info part of the nodes than to try to reorder the nodes in the list.)

22. True or False? If false, correct the statement. *A recursive solution should be used when:*

    (a) computing time is critical.

    (b) the nonrecursive solution would be longer and more difficult to write.

    (c) computing space is critical.

    (d) your instructor says to use recursion.

Binary Search Trees

GOALS

- To be able to define and use the following terminology:
  - binary tree
  - binary search tree
  - root
  - parent
  - child
  - ancestor
  - descendant
  - level
  - height
  - subtree
- To be able to define a binary search tree at the logical level
- To be able to show what a binary search tree would look like after a series of insertions and deletions
- To be able to implement the following binary search tree algorithms in C++:
  - inserting an element
  - deleting an element
  - retrieving an element
  - modifying an element
  - copying a tree
  - traversing a tree in preorder, inorder, and postorder

We have discussed some of the advantages of using a linear linked list to store sorted information. One of the drawbacks of using a linear linked list is the time it takes to search a long list. A sequential or linear search of (possibly) all the nodes in the whole list is an O(N) operation. In Chapter 3, we saw how a binary search could find an element in a sorted list stored sequentially in an array. The binary search is an $O(\log_2 N)$ operation. It would be nice if we could binary search a linked list, but there is no practical way to find the midpoint of a linked list of nodes. We can, however, reorganize the list's elements into a linked structure that is just perfect for binary searching: the *binary search tree*. The binary search tree provides us with a structure that retains the flexibility of a linked list while allowing quicker $O(\log_2 N)$ access to any node in the list.

This chapter introduces some basic tree vocabulary and then develops the algorithms and implementations of the operations needed to use a binary search tree.

■ ‖ *The Logical Level*

A binary search tree is a structure with two properties: a shape property and a property that relates the keys of the elements in the structure. We first look at the shape property.

Each node in a singly linked list may point to one other node: the one that follows it. Thus a singly linked list is a *linear* structure; each node in the list (except the last) has a unique successor. A **binary tree** is a structure in which each node is capable of having two successor nodes, called *children*. Each of the children, being nodes in the binary tree, can also have up to two child nodes, and these children can also have up to two children, and so on, giving the tree its branching structure. The "beginning" of the tree is a unique starting node called the **root**.

Binary Tree   A structure with a unique starting node (the root), in which each node is capable of having two child nodes, and in which a unique path exists from the root to every other node

Root   The top node of a tree structure; a node with no parent

---

Figure 8.1 depicts a binary tree. The root node of this binary tree contains the value A. Each node in the tree may have 0, 1, or 2 children. The node to the left of a node, if it exists, is called its *left child*. For instance, the left child of the root node contains the value B. The node to the right of a node, if it exists, is its *right child*. The right child of the root node contains the value C. The root node is the parent of the nodes containing B and C. (Earlier textbooks used the terms left son, right son, and father to describe these relationships.) If a node in the

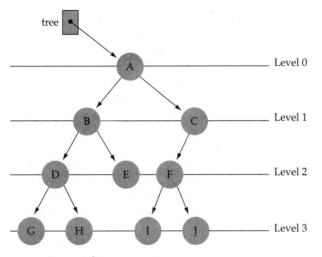

FIGURE 8.1 *A binary tree.*

tree has no children, it is called a **leaf**. For instance, the nodes containing G, H, E, I, and J are leaf nodes.

Leaf Node   A tree node that has no children

In addition to specifying that a node may have up to two children, the definition of a binary tree states that a unique path exists from the root to every other node. This means that every node (except the root) has a unique parent. In the structure pictured here, the nodes have the correct number of children, but the

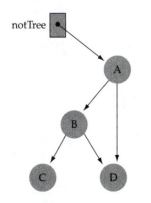

unique path rule is violated: there are two paths from the root to the node containing D. Therefore this structure is not a tree at all, let alone a binary tree.

Note, in Figure 8.1, that each of the root node's children is itself the root of a smaller binary tree, or subtree. The root node's left child, containing B, is the root of its *left subtree*, while the right child, containing C, is the root of its *right subtree*. In fact, any node in the tree can be considered the root node of a subtree. The subtree whose root node has the value B also includes the nodes with values D, G, H, and E. These nodes are the *descendants* of the node containing B. The descendants of the node containing C are the nodes with the values F, I, and J. A node is the *ancestor* of another node if it is the parent of the node, or the parent of some other ancestor of that node. (Yes, this is a recursive definition.) The ancestors of the node with the value G are the nodes containing D, B, and A. Obviously, the root of the tree is the ancestor of every other node in the tree.

The *level* of a node refers to its distance from the root. If we designate the level of the root as 0 (zero), the nodes containing B and C are Level 1 nodes, the nodes containing D, E, and F are Level 2 nodes, and the nodes containing G, H, I, and J are Level 3 nodes.

The maximum level in a tree determines its *height*. The maximum number of nodes at any level N is 2^N. Often, however, levels do not contain the maximum number of nodes. For instance, in Figure 8.1, Level 2 could contain four nodes, but because the node containing C in Level 1 has only one child, Level 2 contains three nodes. Level 3, which could contain eight nodes, has only four. We could make many differently shaped binary trees out of the ten nodes in this tree. A few variations are illustrated in Figure 8.2. It is easy to see that the maximum number of levels in a binary tree with N nodes is N. What is the minimum number of levels? If we fill the tree by giving every node in each level two children until we run out of nodes, the tree has $\log_2 N + 1$ levels (Figure 8.2a). Demonstrate this to yourself by drawing "full" trees with 8 [$\log_2(8) = 3$] and 16 [$\log_2(16) = 4$] nodes. What if there are 7, 12, or 18 nodes?

The height of a tree is the critical factor in determining how efficiently we can search for elements. Consider the maximum-height tree in Figure 8.2(c). If we begin searching at the root node and follow the pointers from one node to the next, accessing the node with the value J (the farthest from the root) is an $O(N)$ operation—no better than searching a linear list! On the other hand, given the minimum-height tree depicted in Figure 8.2(a), to access the node containing J, we only have to look at three other nodes—the ones containing E, A, and G—before we find J. Thus, if the tree is of minimum height, its structure supports $O(\log_2 N)$ access to any element.

However, the arrangement of the values in the tree pictured in Figure 8.2(a) does not lend itself to quick searching. Let's say that we want to find the value G. We begin searching at the root of the tree. This node contains E, not G, so we need to keep searching. But which of its children should we look at next, the right or the left? There is no special order to the nodes, so we have to check

(a) A 4-level tree   (b) A 5-level tree   (c) A 10-level tree

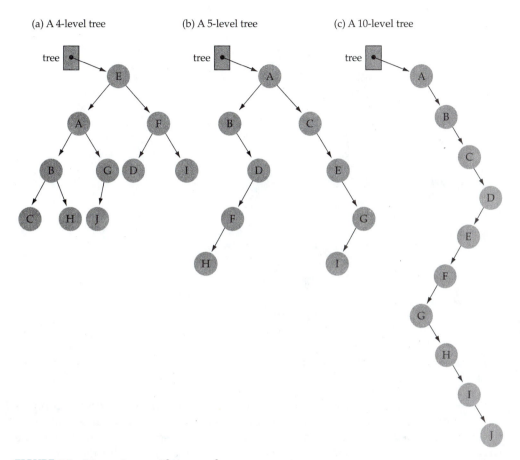

FIGURE 8.2   *Binary trees with ten nodes.*

both subtrees. We could search the tree, level by level, until we come across the value we are searching for. But that is an O(N) search operation, which is no better than searching a linked list!

To support O($\log_2 N$) searching, we add a special property based on the relationship among the keys of the items in the tree. We put all the nodes with values smaller than the value in the root into its left subtree, and all the nodes with values larger than the value in the root into its right subtree. Figure 8.3 shows the nodes from Figure 8.2(a) rearranged to satisfy this property. The root node, which contains E, accesses two subtrees. The left subtree contains all the values smaller than E and the right subtree contains all the values larger than E.

Searching for the value G, we look first in the root node. G is larger than E, so we know that G must be in the root node's right subtree. The right child of the root node contains H. Now what? Do we go to the right or to the left? This

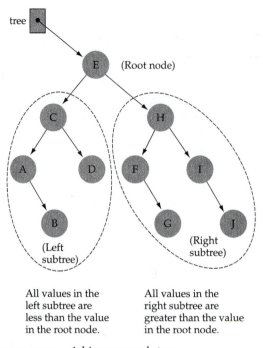

All values in the left subtree are less than the value in the root node.

All values in the right subtree are greater than the value in the root node.

FIGURE 8.3   *A binary search tree.*

subtree is also arranged according to the binary search property: the nodes with smaller values are to the left and the nodes with larger values are to the right. The value of this node, H, is greater than G, so we search to its left. The left child of this node contains the value F, which is smaller than G, so we reapply the rule and move to the right. The node to the right contains G; we have found the node we were searching for.

A binary tree with this special property is called a **binary search tree**. Like any binary tree, it gets its branching structure by allowing each node to have up to two child nodes. It gets its easy-to-search structure by maintaining the binary search property: the left child of any node (if there is one) is the root of the subtree that contains all of the values smaller than the node. The right child of any node (if there is one) is the root of the subtree that contains all of the values that are larger than the node.

Binary Search Tree   A binary tree in which the key value in any node is greater than the key value in its left child and any of its children (the nodes in the left subtree) and less than the key value in its right child and any of its children (the nodes in the right subtree)

Four comparisons instead of up to ten doesn't sound like such a big deal, but as the number of elements in the structure increases, the difference becomes impressive. In the worst case—searching for the last node in a linear linked list—you must look at every node in the list; on the average you must search half the list. If the list contains 1000 nodes, you must make 1000 comparisons to find the last node! If the 1000 nodes were arranged in a binary search tree of minimum height, you would never make more than 10 ($\log_2$ (1000) < 10) comparisons, no matter which node you were seeking!

▪‖ *Binary Search Tree ADT*

Now let's specify the operations defined for a Binary Search Tree ADT. You see that the traversal operations (`ResetTree` and `GetNextItem`) have a parameter of type `OrderType`. Because trees can be traversed in more than one way, we let the user choose the traversal order. We discuss this in much more detail later in the chapter.

▪‖ Binary Search Tree Specification

Structure   The placement of each element in the binary tree must satisfy the binary search property: the value of the key of an element is greater than the value of the key of any element in its left subtree, and less than the value of the key of any element in its right subtree.

Operations   (provided by TreeADT):

Assumption: Before any call is made to a tree operation, the tree has been declared and a constructor has been applied.

MakeEmpty
  Function: Initializes tree to empty state.
  Postconditions: Tree exists and is empty.

Boolean   **IsEmpty**
  Function: Determines whether tree is empty.
  Postcondition: Function value = (tree is empty)

Boolean   **IsFull**
  Function: Determines whether tree is full.
  Postcondition: Function value = (tree is full)

int NumberOfNodes
  Function: Determines the number of elements in tree.
  Postcondition: Function value = number of elements in tree

RetrieveItem(ItemType& item, Boolean& found)

Function:	Retrieves item whose key matches item's key (if present).
Precondition:	Key member of item is initialized.
Postconditions:	If there is an element someItem whose key matches item's key, then found = true and item is a copy of someItem; otherwise found = false and item is unchanged.
	Tree is unchanged.

InsertItem(ItemType item)

Function:	Adds item to tree.
Preconditions:	Tree is not full.
	item is not in tree.
Postconditions:	item is in tree.
	Binary search property is maintained.

DeleteItem(ItemType item)

Function:	Deletes the element whose key matches item's key.
Preconditions:	Key member of item is initialized.
	One and only one element in tree has a key matching item's key.
Postcondition:	No element in tree has key matching item's key.

PrintTree(ofstream& outFile)

Function:	Prints the values in the tree in ascending key order on outFile.
Precondition:	outFile has been opened for writing.
Postconditions:	Items in the tree have been printed in ascending key order.
	outFile is still open.

ResetTree(OrderType order)

Function:	Initializes current position for an iteration through the tree in OrderType order.
Postcondition:	Current position is prior to root of tree.

GetNextItem(ItemType& item, OrderType order, Boolean& finished)

Function:	Gets the next element in tree.
Preconditions:	Current position is defined.
	Element at current position is not last in tree.
Postconditions:	Current position is one position beyond current position at entry to GetNextItem.
	finished = (current position is last in tree)
	item is a copy of element at current position.

Application Level

Although we have changed the names of some of the operations to reflect that we are specifying tree operations, the functions are very similar to those provided to the user of the various List ADTs. There are two major differences: we have added an operation to print the items in a tree in ascending key order and a parameter on the `ResetTree` and `GetNextItem` operations. Of course, the algorithms we develop to implement the operations are different from those for the list operations.

Replace the list operations with the corresponding tree operations in any of the applications that we have written for the other List ADTs and you have an application of the Binary Search Tree ADT.

Implementation Level

We develop the algorithms for the operations specified for the Binary Search Tree ADT and represent the tree as a linked structure whose nodes are allocated dynamically. Because the binary search tree is inherently a recursive structure, we first implement the algorithms using recursive solutions. We then take the `InsertItem` and `DeleteItem` functions and show how they can be implemented iteratively. Here is the first approximation to class `TreeType`. If we find we need more data members, we can add them at a later time.

```
#include <fstream.h>

template<class ItemType>
struct TreeNode;
// Assumption:  ItemType is a type for which the operators "<"
// and "==" are defined—either an appropriate built-in type or
// a class that overloads these operators.

enum OrderType {PRE_ORDER, IN_ORDER, POST_ORDER};

template<class ItemType>
class TreeType
{
public:
    TreeType();                          // constructor
    ~TreeType();                         // destructor
    TreeType(const TreeType<ItemType>& originalTree);
    // copy constructor
    void operator=(const TreeType<ItemType>& originalTree);
    void MakeEmpty();
    bool IsEmpty() const;
```

```
    bool IsFull() const;
    int NumberOfNodes() const;
    void RetrieveItem(ItemType& item, bool& found);
    void InsertItem(ItemType item);
    void DeleteItem(ItemType item);
    void ResetTree(OrderType order);
    void GetNextItem (ItemType& item, OrderType order,
        bool& finished);
    void PrintTree(ofstream& outFile) const;
private:
    TreeNode<ItemType>* root;
};
```

Before we go on, we need to decide just what a node in the tree is going to look like. In our discussion of trees, we talked about right and left children. These are the structural pointers in the tree: they hold the tree together. We also need a place to store the user's data in the node. We might as well continue to call it `info`. Figure 8.4 shows a picture of a node.

Here is the definition of `TreeNode` that corresponds with the picture in Figure 8.4.

```
template<class ItemType>
struct TreeNode
{
    ItemType info;
    TreeNode* left;
    TreeNode* right;
};
```

■‖ *Recursive Binary Search Tree Operations*

`TreeType` is a class that contains the external pointer to the list of nodes as a data member (`root`). The recursive implementations of the tree operations

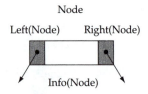

FIGURE 8.4 *Node terminology for a tree node.*

should recurse on nodes. Therefore each of the member functions calls a secondary recursive function that takes `root` as a parameter. The names of the secondary functions make it clear which operations they are helping to implement. We now develop these recursive functions.

Function NumberOfNodes

In function `Factorial` we said that we could determine the factorial of N if we knew the factorial of N-1. The analogous statement here is, we can determine the number of nodes in the tree if we know the number of nodes in the left subtree and the number of nodes in the right subtree. That is, the number of nodes in a tree is

number of nodes in left subtree + number of nodes in right subtree + 1.

This is easy. Given a function `CountNodes` and a pointer to a tree node, we know how to calculate the number of nodes in a subtree; we call `CountNodes` recursively with the pointer to the subtree as the argument! Thus we know how to write the general case. What about the base case? Well, a leaf node has no subtrees, so the number of nodes is one. How do we determine that a node has no subtrees? The pointers to its children are `NULL`. Let's try summarizing these observations into an algorithm, where `tree` is a node.

CountNodes Version 1

```
IF (Left(tree) is NULL) AND (Right(tree) is NULL)
    return 1
ELSE
    return CountNodes(Left(tree)) + CountNodes(Right(tree)) + 1
```

Let's try this algorithm on a couple of examples to be sure that it works (see Figure 8.5).

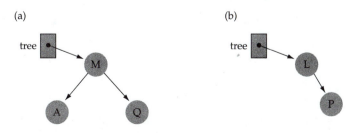

(a)   (b)

tree   tree

FIGURE 8.5 *Two binary search trees.*

We call `CountNodes` with the tree in Figure 8.5(a). The left and right children of the root node (M) are not `NULL`, so we call `CountNodes` with the node containing A as the root. Because both the left and right children are `NULL` on this call, we send back the answer 1. Now we call `CountNodes` with the tree containing Q as the root. Both of its children are `NULL`, so we send back the answer 1. Now we can calculate the number of nodes in the tree with M in the root: it is

```
1 + 1 + 1 = 3.
```

This seems okay.

The tree in Figure 8.5(b) is not balanced; let's see if this proves to be a problem. It is not true that both children of the root (L) are `NULL`, so `CountNodes` is called with the left child as the argument. OOPS; we do have a problem. The first statement checks to see if the children of the root are `NULL`, but the root itself is `NULL`. The function crashes when we try to access `tree->left` when `tree` is `NULL`. Well, we can check to see if the left or right child is `NULL`, and not call `CountNodes` if it is.

CountNodes Version 2

> IF (Left(tree) is NULL) AND (Right(tree) is NULL)
>   return 1
> ELSE IF Left(tree) is NULL
>   return CountNodes(Right(tree)) + 1
> ELSE IF Right(tree) is NULL
>   return CountNodes(Left(tree)) + 1
> ELSE return CountNodes(Left(tree)) + CountNodes(Right(tree)) + 1

Version 2 works correctly if function `CountNodes` has a precondition that the tree is not empty. However, an initially empty tree causes a crash. We must check to see if the tree is empty as the first statement in the algorithm, and if it is, return zero.

CountNodes Version 3

```
IF tree is NULL
    return 0
ELSE IF (Left(tree) is NULL) AND (Right(tree) is NULL)
    return 1
ELSE IF Left(tree) is NULL
    return CountNodes(Right(tree)) + 1
ELSE IF Right(tree) is NULL
    return CountNodes(Left(tree)) + 1
ELSE return CountNodes(Left(tree)) + CountNodes(Right(tree)) + 1
```

This certainly looks complicated; there must be a simpler solution—and there is. We can collapse the two base cases into one. There is no need to make the leaf node a special case. We can simply have one base case: an empty tree returns zero.

CountNodes Version 4

```
IF tree is NULL
    return 0
ELSE
    return CountNodes(Left(tree)) + CountNodes(Right(tree)) + 1
```

We have taken the time to work through the versions containing errors because they illustrate two important points about recursion with trees: (1) always check for the empty tree first, and (2) leaf nodes do not need to be treated as separate cases. Table 8.1 reviews the design notation and the corresponding C++ code.

TABLE 8.1   Comparing Node Design Notation to C++ Code

Design Notation	C++ Code
Node(location)	`*location`
Info(location)	`location->info`
Right(location)	`location->right`
Left(location)	`location->left`
Set Info(location) to value	`location->info = value`

Here is the function specification.

Function CountNodes

Definition:	Counts the number of nodes in tree
Size:	Number of nodes in tree
Base Case:	If tree is NULL, return 0
General Case:	Return CountNodes(Left(tree)) + CountNodes(Right(tree)) + 1

```
template<class ItemType>
int TreeType<ItemType>::NumberOfNodes() const
// Calls recursive function CountNodes to count the
// nodes in the tree.
{
    return CountNodes(root);
}

template<class ItemType>
int CountNodes(TreeNode<ItemType>* tree)
// Post: returns the number of nodes in the tree.
{
    if (tree == NULL)
        return 0;
    else
        return CountNodes(tree->left) +
                CountNodes(tree->right) + 1;
}
```

Function RetrieveItem

At the beginning of this chapter we demonstrated how to search for an element in a binary search tree. First check to see if the item searched for is in the root. If it is not, compare the element with the root and look either in the left or the right subtree. This statement looks recursive. Let's apply the general guidelines for determining recursive solutions.

We have two choices for the size of the problem: the number of nodes in the tree or the number of nodes in the path from the root to the node for which we are searching (or until we reach an empty tree). Either is acceptable. The first is easier to say; the second is more precise. One base case is when we find the element with the same key; another is when we determine that an element with the same key is not in the tree. The general case is either retrieve the element from the left subtree or retrieve it from the right subtree. Because the left or right subtree is at least one node smaller than the original tree and one level deeper, the size decreases with each call.

The only remaining question is how we know there is no item with the same key in the tree. If the tree is empty, then there cannot be an item with the same key as item's key. Let's summarize these observations. We define a recursive routine `Retrieve`, which is invoked by the `RetrieveItem` member function.

■▌ Function Retrieve

Definition:	Searches for an element with the same key as item's key. If found, store it into item.
Size:	Number of nodes in tree (or number of nodes in the path)
Base Cases:	(1) If item's key matches key in Info(tree), item is set to Info(tree) and found is true.
	(2) If tree = NULL, found is false.
General Case:	If item's key is less than key in Info(tree), Retrieve(Left(tree), item, found); else Retrieve(Right(tree), item, found).

```
template<class ItemType>
void TreeType<ItemType>::RetrieveItem(ItemType& item, bool& found)
// Calls recursive function Retrieve to search the tree for item.
{
    Retrieve(root, item, found);
}


template<class ItemType>
void Retrieve(TreeNode<ItemType>* tree,
     ItemType& item, bool& found)
// Recursively searches tree for item.
// Post: If there is an element someItem whose key matches item's,
//       found is true and item is set to a copy of someItem;
//       otherwise found is false and item is unchanged.
{
    if (tree == NULL)
        found = false;                          // item is not found.
    else if (item < tree->info)
        Retrieve(tree->left, item, found);   // Search left subtree.
    else if (item > tree->info)
        Retrieve(tree->right, item, found); // Search right subtree.
    else
    {
        item = tree->info;                      // item is found.
        found = true;
    }
}
```

Let's trace this operation, using the tree in Figure 8.6. We want to find the element with the key 18 so the nonrecursive call is

```
Retrieve(root, 18, found)
```

`root` is not NULL, and 18 > `tree->info`, so we issue the first recursive call

```
Retrieve(tree->right, 18, found)
```

`tree` now points to the node whose key is 20 so 18 < `tree->info`. The next recursive call is

```
Retrieve(tree->left, 18, found)
```

Now `tree` points to the node with the key 18 so 18 = `tree->info`. We set `found` and `item` and the recursion halts.

Next, let's look at an example where the key is not found in the tree. We want to find the element with the key 7. The nonrecursive call is

```
Retrieve(root, 7, found)
```

`tree` is not NULL and 7 < `tree->info`, so the first recursive call is

```
Retrieve(tree->left, 7, found)
```

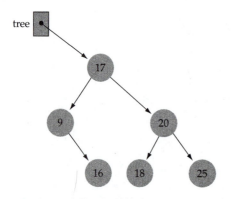

FIGURE 8.6 *Tracing the Retrieve operation.*

`tree` is pointing to the node that contains 9. `tree` is not NULL and we issue the second recursive call

```
Retrieve(tree->left, 7, found)
```

Now `tree` is NULL, and we set `found` to `false` and `item` is unchanged.

Function InsertItem

To create and maintain the information stored in a binary search tree, we must have an operation that inserts new nodes into the tree. We use the following insertion approach. A new node is always inserted into its appropriate position in the tree *as a leaf*. Figure 8.7 shows a series of insertions into a binary tree.

We want to write a function `Insert` that inserts an item into the tree, given a pointer to the root of the whole tree (which is passed as a reference parameter):

```
Insert(tree, item);
```

Before we go into the development of the algorithm, we want to reiterate that every node in a binary search tree is the root node of a binary search tree. In Figure 8.8(a), we want to insert a node with the key value 13 into the tree whose root is the node containing 7. Because 13 is greater than 7, we know that the new node belongs in the root node's right subtree. We now have redefined a smaller version of our original problem: we want to insert a node with the key value 13 into the tree *whose root is* `tree->right` (Figure 8.8b). Of course, we have a function to insert elements into a binary search tree: `Insert`. `Insert` is called recursively:

```
Insert(tree->right, item);
```

Insert begins its execution, looking for the place to insert `item` in the tree whose root is the node with the key value 15. We compare the key of `item` (13) to the key of the root node; 13 is less than 15, so we know that the new `item` belongs in the tree's left subtree. Again, we have redefined a smaller version of the problem. We want to insert a node with the key value 13 into the tree *whose root is* `tree->left` (Figure 8.8c). We call `Insert` recursively to perform this task. Remember that in this (recursive) execution of `Insert`, `tree` points to the node whose key is 15, not the original `tree` root:

```
Insert(tree->left, item);
```

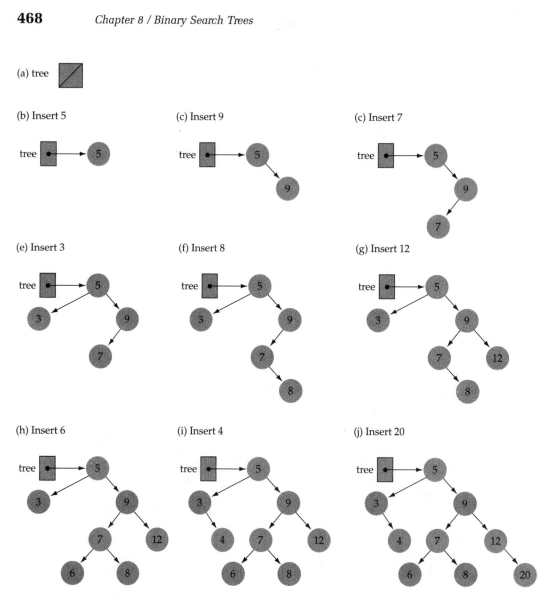

FIGURE 8.7 *Insertions into a binary search tree.*

Again we recursively execute Insert. We compare the key of item to the key of the (current) root node and then call Insert to insert item into the correct subtree—the left subtree if item's key is less than the key of the root node; the right subtree if item's key is greater than the key of the root node.

Where does it all end? There must be a base case, in which space for the new element is allocated and the value of item copied into it. This case occurs when tree is NULL, when the subtree we wish to insert into is empty.

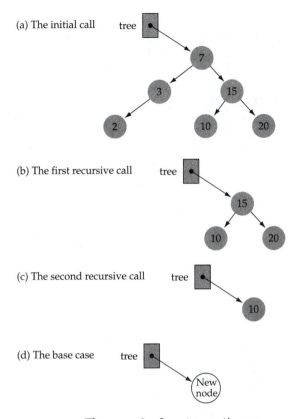

(a) The initial call

(b) The first recursive call

(c) The second recursive call

(d) The base case

FIGURE 8.8 *The recursive Insert operation.*

(Remember, we are going to add item as a leaf node.) Figure 8.8(d) illustrates the base case. We can create the new node and link it to the correct member of its logical parent with the statement

```
tree = new TreeNode<ItemType>;
```

Wait a minute! How does this execution of new link the new node to the existing tree? To understand this point, we must consider what tree is in a recursive execution of the function. The last recursive call (Figure 8.9a) is Insert(tree->right, item). Because tree is a reference parameter, in the final recursive execution of Insert, tree refers to the right data member of the node containing 10 (the logical parent of the new node). The statement executing new gets the address of the new node and stores it into tree, the right data member of the node containing 10, thus linking the new node into the tree structure (Figure 8.9b). It is critical that tree be a reference parameter. If tree is not, the pointer that is being passed to Insert is a copy of the root of the subtree and not the location of the root itself.

This technique should sound familiar. We used it in the last chapter when we inserted into a linked implementation of a sorted list recursively. The important point to remember is that passing a pointer by *value* allows the function to change only what the caller's pointer points to; passing a pointer by *reference* allows the function to change the caller's pointer, as well as to change what the pointer points to. The recursive function is summarized as follows:

(a) The last call to Insert

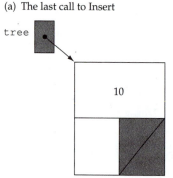

Insert(tree->right,item);

(b) Within the last execution of Insert

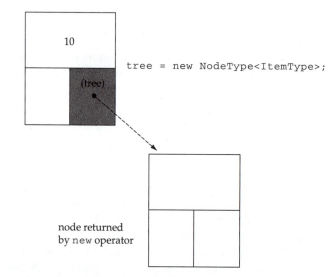

tree = new NodeType<ItemType>;

node returned
by new operator

FIGURE 8.9 *The tree parameter is a pointer within the tree.*

■ | **Function Insert**

Definition: Inserts item into binary search tree.
Size: The number of elements in path from root to insertion place
Base Case: If tree is NULL, then allocate a new leaf to contain item.
General Cases: (1) If item < Info(tree), then Insert(Left(tree), item).
                    (2) If item > Info(tree), then Insert(Right(tree), item).

Here is the code that implements this recursive algorithm.

```
template<class ItemType>
void TreeType<ItemType>::InsertItem(ItemType item)
// Calls recursive function Insert to insert item into tree.
{
    Insert(root, item);
}

template<class ItemType>
void Insert(TreeNode<ItemType>*& tree, ItemType item)
// Inserts item into tree.
// Post:  item is in tree; search property is maintained.
{
    if (tree == NULL)
    {// Insertion place found.
        tree = new TreeNode<ItemType>;
        tree->right = NULL;
        tree->left = NULL;
        tree->info = item;
    }
    else if (item < tree->info)
        Insert(tree->left, item);    // Insert in left subtree.
    else
        Insert(tree->right, item);   // Insert in right subtree.
}
```

Insertion Order and Tree Shape   Because nodes are always added as leaves, the order in which nodes are inserted determines the shape of the tree. Figure 8.10 illustrates how the same data, inserted in different orders, produce very differently shaped trees. If the values are inserted in order (or in reverse order), the tree is very skewed. A random mix of the elements produces a shorter, "bushy" tree. Because the height of the tree determines the maximum number of comparisons in a binary search, the tree's shape is very important. Obviously, minimizing the height of the tree maximizes the efficiency of the search. There are algorithms to adjust a tree to make its shape more desirable; these schemes are subjects for more advanced courses.

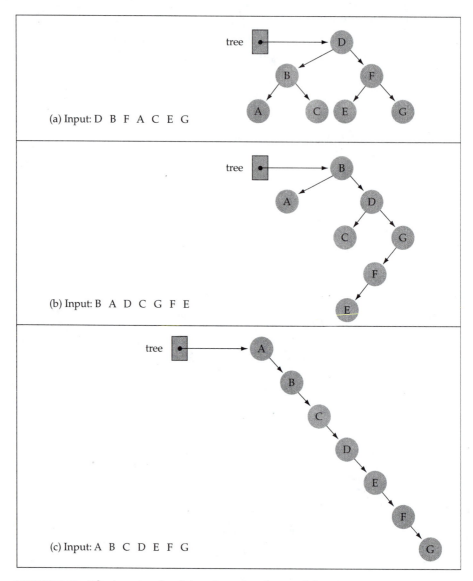

(a) Input: D B F A C E G

(b) Input: B A D C G F E

(c) Input: A B C D E F G

FIGURE 8.10 *The input order determines the shape of the tree.*

Function DeleteItem

`Delete` (the recursive helper function for `DeleteItem`) receives the external pointer to a binary search tree and an item, and finds and deletes the node matching the item's key from the tree. According to the specifications of the operation, an item with the same key exists in the tree. These specifications suggest a two-part operation:

Delete

> Find the node in the tree
> Delete the node from the tree

We know how to find the node; we did it in `Retrieve`. The second part of the operation—deleting this node from the tree—is more complicated. This task varies according to the position of the node in the tree. Obviously it is simpler to delete a leaf node than to delete the root of the tree. In fact, we can break down the deletion algorithm into three cases, depending on the number of children linked to the node we want to delete:

1. *Deleting a leaf (no children):* As shown in Figure 8.11, deleting a leaf is simply a matter of setting the appropriate link of its parent to NULL and then disposing of the unnecessary node.
2. *Deleting a node with only one child:* The simple solution for deleting a leaf does not suffice for deleting a node with a child, because we don't want to lose all of its descendants from the tree. We want to make the pointer from the parent skip over the deleted node and point instead to the child of the node we intend to delete. We then dispose of the unwanted node (see Figure 8.12).

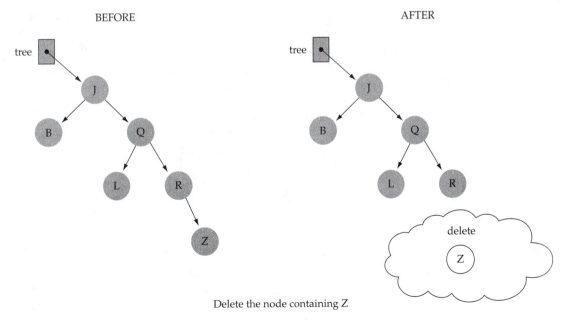

Delete the node containing Z

FIGURE 8.11 *Deleting a leaf node.*

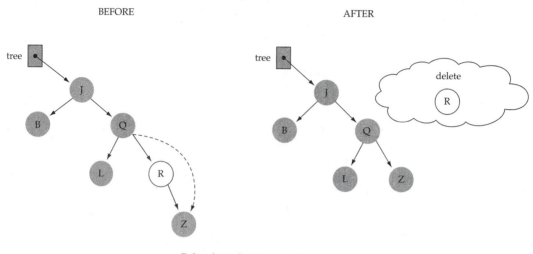

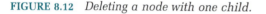

Delete the node containing R

FIGURE 8.12   *Deleting a node with one child.*

3. *Deleting a node with two children:* This case is the most complicated because we cannot make the parent of the deleted node point to *both* of the deleted node's children. The tree must remain a binary tree and the search property must remain intact. There are several ways to accomplish this deletion. The method we use does not delete the *node* but replaces its `info` data member with the `info` data member from another node in the tree that retains the search property. We then delete this other node.

What element could we replace the deleted `item` with that would maintain the search property? The elements whose keys immediately precede or follow `item`'s: `item`'s logical predecessor or successor. We replace the `info` data member of the node we wish to delete with the `info` data member of its logical predecessor—the node whose key is closest in value to, but less than, the key of the node to be deleted. Look at Figure 8.7(j) and locate the logical predecessors of nodes 5, 9, and 7. Do you see the pattern? The logical predecessor of 5 is the largest value in 5's left subtree. The logical predecessor of 9 is the largest value in 9's left subtree. The logical predecessor of 7 is 6, the largest value in 7's left subtree. This replacement value is in a node with either 0 or 1 child. We then delete the node the replacement value was in by changing one of its parent's pointers (see Figure 8.13). Examples of all of these types of deletions are shown in Figure 8.14.

It is clear that the delete task involves changing pointers of the *parent* of the node to be deleted. If our recursive algorithm passes `tree` as a reference parameter, `tree` itself is the parent that we must change. Let's look at the three cases in terms of our implementation.

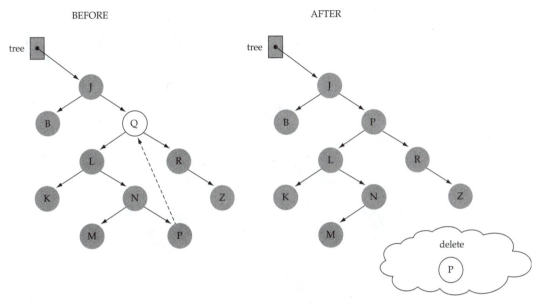

Delete the node containing Q

FIGURE 8.13 *Deleting a node with two children.*

If both child pointers are NULL the node is a leaf, and we just set `tree` to NULL. If one child pointer is NULL, we set `tree` to the other child pointer. If neither child pointer is NULL, we replace the `info` data member of `tree` with the `info` data member of the node's logical predecessor and delete the node containing the predecessor. Let's summarize this as `DeleteNode`.

DeleteNode

```
IF (Left(tree) is NULL) AND (Right(tree) is NULL)
    Set tree to NULL
ELSE IF Left(tree) is NULL
    Set tree to Right(tree)
ELSE IF Right(tree) is NULL
    Set tree to Left(tree)
ELSE
    Find predecessor
    Set Info(tree) to Info(predecessor)
    Delete predecessor
```

Now we can write the recursive definition and code for `Delete`.

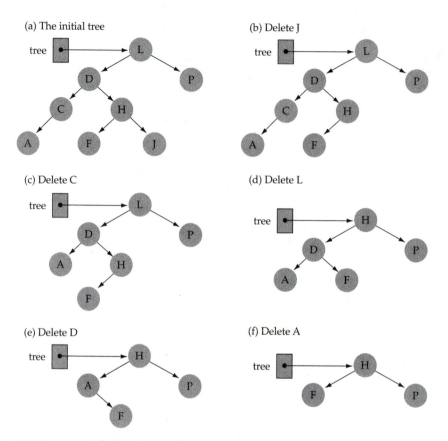

FIGURE 8.14 *Deletions from a binary search tree.*

▪▪ Function Delete

Definition:	Removes someItem from tree where item equals someItem.
Size:	The number of nodes in the path from the root to the node to be deleted.
Base Case:	If item's key matches key in Info(tree), delete node pointed to by tree.
General Case:	If item < Info(tree), Delete(Left(tree), item); else Delete(Right(tree), item).

```
template<class ItemType>
void TreeType<ItemType>::DeleteItem(ItemType item)
// Calls recursive function Delete to delete item from tree.
{
    Delete(root, item);
}
```

```
template<class ItemType>
void Delete(TreeNode<ItemType>*& tree, ItemType item)
// Deletes item from tree.
// Post:  item is not in tree.
{
    if (item < tree->info)
        Delete(tree->left, item);    // Look in left subtree.
    else if (item > tree->info)
        Delete(tree->right, item);   // Look in right subtree.
    else
        DeleteNode(tree);            // Node found; call DeleteNode.
}
```

Before we code `DeleteNode`, let's look at it again. We can remove one of the tests if we notice that the action taken when the left child pointer is NULL also takes care of the case in which both child pointers are NULL. When the left child pointer is NULL, the right child pointer is stored into `tree`. If the right child pointer is also NULL, then NULL is stored into `tree`, which is what we want if they are both NULL.

In good top-down fashion, let's now write the code for `DeleteNode` using `GetPredecessor` as the name of an operation that returns a copy of the `info` member of the predecessor of the node with two children.

```
template<class ItemType>
void DeleteNode(TreeNode<ItemType>*& tree)
// Deletes the node pointed to by tree.
// Post: The user's data in the node pointed to by tree is no
//       longer in the tree. If tree is a leaf node or has only
//       one non-NULL child pointer, the node pointed to by tree is
//       deleted; otherwise, the user's data is replaced by its
//       logical predecessor and the predecessor's node is deleted.
{
    ItemType data;
    TreeNode<ItemType>* tempPtr;

    tempPtr = tree;
    if (tree->left == NULL)
    {
        tree = tree->right;
        delete tempPtr;
    }
    else if (tree->right == NULL)
    {
        tree = tree->left;
        delete tempPtr;
    }
    else
```

```
    {
        GetPredecessor (tree->left, data);
        tree->info = data;
        Delete(tree->left, data);   // Delete predecessor node.
    }
}
```

Now we must look at the operation for finding the logical predecessor. We know that the logical predecessor is the maximum value in `tree`'s left subtree. Where is this node? The maximum value in a binary search tree is in its *right-most node*. Therefore, given `tree`'s left subtree, we just keep moving right until the right child is NULL. When this occurs, we set data to the `info` member of the node. There is no reason to look for the predecessor recursively in this case. A simple iteration until `tree->right` is NULL suffices.

```
template<class ItemType>
void GetPredecessor(TreeNode<ItemType>* tree, ItemType& data)
// Sets data to the info member of the right-most node in tree.
{
    while (tree->right != NULL)
        tree = tree->right;
    data = tree->info;
}
```

Function PrintTree

To traverse a linear linked list, we set a temporary pointer equal to the start of the list and then follow the links from one node to the other until we reach a node whose pointer value is NULL. Similarly, to traverse a binary tree, we initialize our pointer to the root of the tree. But where do we go from there—to the left or to the right? Do we access the root or the leaves first? The answer is "all of these." There are only two ways to traverse a list: forward and backward. There are many ways to traverse a tree. An *inorder traversal* is the one that accesses the nodes in such a way that the values in the nodes are accessed in order from the smallest to the largest, and it is therefore the one we want for `PrintTree`.

We first need to print the root's left subtree, all the values in the tree that are smaller than the value in the root node. Then we print the value in the root node. Finally, we print the values in the root's right subtree, all the values that are larger than the value in the root node (see Figure 8.15).

Let's describe this problem again, thinking recursively (and writing a recursive helper function named `Print`). We want to print the elements in the binary search tree rooted at `tree` in order; that is, first we print the left subtree in order, then we print the root, and finally we print the right subtree in order.

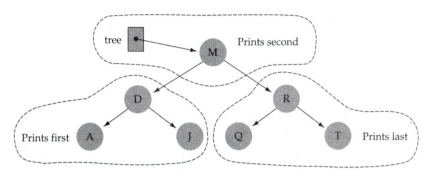

FIGURE 8.15 *Printing all the nodes in order.*

`tree->left` points to the root of the left subtree. Because the left subtree is also a binary search tree, we can call function `Print` to print it, using `tree->left` as the root parameter. When `Print` finishes printing out the left subtree, we print out the value in the root node. Then we call function `Print` to print the right subtree with `tree->right` as the root parameter.

Of course, each of these two calls to function `Print` uses the same approach to print the subtree: print the left subtree with a call to `Print`, print the root, and then print the right subtree with another call to `Print`. What happens if the incoming parameter is NULL on one of the recursive calls? This situation means that the parameter is the root of an empty tree. In this case, we just want to exit the function—clearly there's no point to printing an empty subtree.

Function Print

Definition:	Prints the items in the binary search tree in order from smallest to largest.
Size:	The number of nodes in the tree whose root is tree
Base Case:	If tree = NULL, do nothing.
General Case:	Traverse the left subtree in order.
	Then print Info(tree).
	Then traverse the right subtree in order.

This description can be coded into the following recursive function. For simplicity, we assume that `tree->info` can be output directly using the stream insertion operator.

```
template<class ItemType>
void Print(TreeNode<ItemType>* tree, ofstream& outFile)
// Prints info member of items in tree in sorted order on outFile.
{
    if (tree != NULL)
```

```
    {
        Print(tree->left, outFile);    // Print left subtree.
        outFile << tree->info;
        Print(tree->right, outFile);   // Print right subtree.
    }
}
```

This traversal is called an *inorder traversal* because it accesses each node's left subtree before it processes (prints) the information in the node itself, and then accesses the node's right subtree.

Finally, the `PrintTree` member function of the `TreeType` class invokes `Print` as follows.

```
template<class ItemType>
void TreeType<ItemType>::PrintTree(ofstream& outFile) const
// Calls recursive function Print to print items in the tree.
{
    Print(root, outFile);
}
```

Overloading << and >>

The extraction and insertion operators can be overloaded just like any other operator with one difference: `operator>>` and `operator<<` must be friend functions, not member functions. Here's the reason. When a binary operator function is a member function, the left operand is always self. For example, if `operator+` is a member of class `ItemType` and `x` and `y` are class objects, then the expression

x + y

compiles into

x.operator+(y)

If you want to overload the << operator in class `ItemType`, the expression

cout << x

is a problem, because the left operand isn't an `ItemType` class object— it's an `ostream` class object. So `operator<<` must be declared as a friend function taking two parameters, the first of type `ostream&` and the second of type `ItemType`. For `operator>>`, the first parameter is of type `istream&` and the second is a reference parameter of type `ItemType&`. Here is an example.

```
#include <iostream.h>
class ItemType
{
public:
    friend istream& operator>>(istream& is, ItemType& item);
    friend ostream& operator<<(ostream& os, ItemType item);
private:
    int data;
};
istream& operator>>(istream& is, ItemType& item)
{
    is >> item.data;
    return is;
}
ostream& operator<<(ostream& os, ItemType item)
{
    os  << item.data;
    return os;
}
```

Each of the functions `operator<<` and `operator>>` returns a function value of *reference type*: `istream&` or `ostream&`. This ensures that when a statement like

```
cout << myItem << yourItem;
```

is compiled into

```
operator<< (operator<<(cout, myItem), yourItem);
```

the first parameter in each call to `operator<<` is of the correct type (`ostream&`).

To be precise, we should have added "Further" to the heading of this sidebar. As built-in operators, `<<` and `>>` are actually the bit-wise left shift and bit-wise right shift operators. The `iostream.h` header file overloads them for stream insertion and extraction.

Class Constructor and Destructor

The default class constructor simply creates an empty tree by setting `root` to NULL. As there is no other logical way of constructing an empty tree, there is not a parameterized constructor.

```
template<class ItemType>
TreeType<ItemType>::TreeType()
{
    root = NULL;
}
```

In the same way that the class constructor takes care of each class object's initialization, the class destructor takes care of deallocating dynamic nodes when a class object goes out of scope. The operation invokes a recursive routine with the pointer to a binary search tree as a parameter and destroys all the nodes, leaving the tree empty. To delete all the elements, we have to traverse the tree. Instead of printing each element, as we did in the previous section, we remove the node from the tree. We said that there is more than one way to traverse a binary tree. Is there a way that is best for destroying the tree?

While any of the traversals would result in the function performing correctly, one traversal order is more efficient than the others. Knowing that the `DeleteNode` operation does less work to delete a leaf node than a node with children, we want to delete leaves first. The traversal that allows us to access leaf nodes first is called a *postorder traversal*: we access each node's left subtree and its right subtree before we process the node itself. If we delete the nodes in postorder, each node is a leaf by the time it is its turn to be deleted. The code for the destructor follows.

```
template<class ItemType>
TreeType<ItemType>::~TreeType()
// Calls recursive function Destroy to destroy the tree.
{
    Destroy(root);
}

template<class ItemType>
void Destroy(TreeNode<ItemType>*& tree)
// Post: Tree is empty; nodes have been deallocated.
```

```
{
    if (tree != NULL)
    {
        Destroy(tree->left);
        Destroy(tree->right);
        delete tree;
    }
}
```

The body of the MakeEmpty member function is identical to that of the class destructor, with one exception: after the call to Destroy, it must set root to NULL.

Copying a Tree

Both the copy constructor and overloading the assignment operator involve making a copy of a tree. Copying a tree may be the most interesting—and complex—algorithm associated with trees. Clearly, copying a tree is a recursive algorithm. We must do what we did with all the other member functions: call an auxiliary recursive function with root as a parameter. Both the copy constructor and the assignment operator must call this function.

```
template<class ItemType>
TreeType<ItemType>::TreeType
     (const TreeType<ItemType>& originalTree)
// Calls recursive function CopyTree to copy tree pointed to by
// originalTree into self.
{
    CopyTree(root, originalTree.root);
}
```

```
template<class ItemType>
void TreeType<ItemType>::operator=
     (const TreeType<ItemType>& originalTree)
// Calls recursive function CopyTree to copy tree pointed to by
// originalTree into self.
{
    if (&originalTree == this)
        return;                      // Ignore assigning self to self.
    Destroy(root);                   // Deallocate existing tree nodes.
    CopyTree(root, originalTree.root);
}
```

The recursive function `CopyTree` has two parameters, both pointers to tree nodes. What is the base case? If `originalTree` is NULL, then `copy` is NULL. What is `copy` if `originalTree` is not NULL? Well, we get a node for `copy` to point to and put `originalTree->info` into it. We then store a copy of `originalTree`'s left subtree into `copy`'s left child and store a copy of `originalTree`'s right subtree into `copy`'s right child. Where do we get a copy of the subtrees? We use `CopyTree` recursively, of course.

```
template<class ItemType>
void CopyTree(TreeNode<ItemType>*& copy,
     const TreeNode<ItemType>* originalTree)
// Post: copy is the root of a tree that is a duplicate
//       of tree pointed to by originalTree.
{
    if (originalTree == NULL)
        copy = NULL;
    else
    {
        copy = new TreeNode<ItemType>;
        copy->info = originalTree->info;
        CopyTree(copy->left, originalTree->left);
        CopyTree(copy->right, originalTree->right);
    }
}
```

Be sure you understand how this code works before going on to the next section. Like many recursive algorithms, this short function is elegant but not obvious. In fact, let's trace `CopyTree` on the following tree:

originalTree

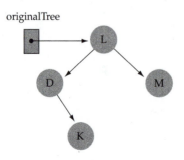

As we did in Chapter 7, we let R0 stand for the nonrecursive call, R1 stand for the first recursive call (`copy->left`), and R2 stand for the second recursive call (`copy->right`). In the trace, we let an arrow pointing to the contents of a node stand for the pointer to that node. We have added a Comment column to the table showing the trace. ``Copy'' in the Comment column refers to the parameter in the ``copy'' column.

Call #	copy	originalTree	Which call	Comment
1	external pointer to new tree	→L	R0	copy is given a node to point to; L is copied into the info member; R1 is executed
2	left of node allocated in call 1	→D	R1	copy is given a node to point to; D is copied into the info member; R1 is executed
3	left of node allocated in call 2	NULL	R1	NULL is copied into copy (i.e., left of node allocated in call 2) and call 3 is completed

At this point the third call is finished, and the copy looks like this:

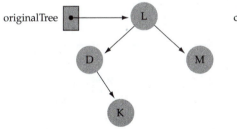
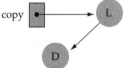

We return to finish the second call. We shade the completed calls to show that the execution of that call has finished and that activation record is no longer on the stack.

Call #	copy	originalTree	Which call	Comment
1	external pointer to new tree	→L	R0	`copy` is given a node to point to; L is copied into the `info` member; R1 is executed
2	left of node allocated in call 1	→D	R1	`copy` is given a node to point to; D is copied into the `info` member; R1 is executed
3	left of node allocated in call 2	NULL	R1	NULL is copied into `copy` (i.e., `left` of node allocated in call 2) and call 3 is completed
4	right of node allocated in call 2	→K	R2	`copy` is given a node to point to; K is copied into the `info` member; R1 is executed
5	left of `copy` allocated in call 4	NULL	R1	NULL is copied into `copy` (i.e., `left` of node allocated in call 4) and call 5 is completed

After the completion of the fifth call, control returns to the fourth call. Because the fifth call came from R1, R2 must be executed.

Call #	copy	originalTree	Which call	Comment
1	external pointer to new tree	→L	R0	`copy` is given a node to point to; L is copied into the `info` member; R1 is executed
2	left of node allocated in call 1	→D	R1	`copy` is given a node to point to; D is copied into the `info` member; R1 is executed
3	left of node allocated in call 2	NULL	R1	NULL is copied into `copy` (i.e., `left` of node allocated in call 2) and call 3 is completed
4	right of node allocated in call 2	→K	R2	`copy` is given a node to point to; K is copied into the `info` member; R1 is executed
5	left of node allocated in call 4	NULL	R1	NULL is copied into `copy` (i.e., `left` of node allocated in call 4) and call 5 is completed
6	right of node allocated in call 4	NULL	R2	NULL is copied into `copy` (i.e., `right` of node allocated in call 4) and call 6 is completed

Because the sixth call came from R2, the fourth call is now finished, and the copy looks like this:

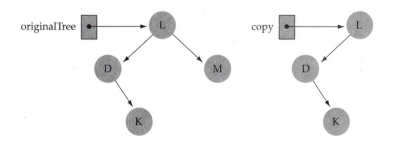

But as the fourth call came from R2, call 4 is also finished, leaving only the activation record from the original call on the stack. Execution continues with the second recursive call from call 1.

Call #	copy	originalTree	Which call	Comment
1	external pointer to new tree	→L	R0	`copy` is given a node to point to; L is copied into the `info` member; R1 is executed
2	left of node allocated in call 1	→D	R1	`copy` is given a node to point to; D is copied into the `info` member; R1 is executed
3	left of node allocated in call 2	NULL	R1	NULL is copied into `copy` (i.e., `left` of node allocated in call 2) and call 3 is completed
4	right of node allocated in call 2	→K	R2	`copy` is given a node to point to; K is copied into the `info` member; R1 is executed
5	left of node allocated in call 4	NULL	R1	NULL is copied into `copy` (i.e., `left` of node allocated in call 4) and call 5 is completed
6	right of node allocated in call 4	NULL	R2	NULL is copied into `copy` (i.e., `right` of node allocated in call 4) and call 6 is completed
7	right of node allocated in call 1	→M	R2	`copy` is given a node to point to; M is copied into the `info` member; R1 is executed
8	left of node allocated in call 7	NULL	R1	NULL is copied into `copy` (i.e., `left` of node allocated in call 7) and call 8 is completed

All we have left to do is the second recursive call from call 7.

Call #	copy	originalTree	Which call	Comment
1	external pointer to new tree	→L	R0	copy is given a node to point to; L is copied into the info member; R1 is executed
2	left of node allocated in call 1	→D	R1	copy is given a node to point to; D is copied into the info member; R1 is executed
3	left of node allocated in call 2	NULL	R1	NULL is copied into copy (i.e., left of node allocated in call 2) and call 3 is completed
4	right of node allocated in call 2	→K	R2	copy is given a node to point to; K is copied into the info member; R1 is executed
5	left of node allocated in call 4	NULL	R1	NULL is copied into copy (i.e., left of node allocated in call 4) and call 5 is completed
6	right of node allocated in call 4	NULL	R2	NULL is copied into copy (i.e., left of node allocated in call 4) and call 6 is completed
7	right of node allocated in call 1	→M	R2	copy is given a node to point to; M is copied into the info member; R1 is executed
8	left of node allocated in call 7	NULL	R1	NULL is copied into copy (i.e., left of node allocated in call 7) and call 8 is completed
9	right of node allocated in call 7	NULL	R2	NULL is copied into copy (i.e., right of node allocated in call 7) and call 9 is completed

Call 9's completion finishes up call 7, which then finishes up call 1. Because call 1 is the nonrecursive call, the process is finished. The tree pointed to by copy is a duplicate of the tree pointed to by originalTree.

More about Traversals

In the `Print` function we presented the **inorder traversal** of a binary search tree: the value in a node was printed *in* between the printing of the values in its left subtree and the values in its right subtree. An inorder traversal prints the values in a binary search tree in ascending key order. When implementing the destructor for the binary search tree, we introduced a **postorder traversal**: a node was deleted *after* destroying its left subtree and its right subtree. There is one more important traversal: the **preorder traversal**. In a preorder traversal, the values in a node are visited *before* the values in its left subtree and the values in its right subtree.

Inorder Traversal   A systematic way of visiting all the nodes in a binary tree that visits the nodes in the left subtree of a node, then visits the node, and then visits the nodes in the right subtree of the node

Postorder Traversal   A systematic way of visiting all the nodes in a binary tree that visits the nodes in the left subtree of a node, then visits the nodes in the right subtree of the node, and then visits the node

Preorder Traversal   A systematic way of visiting all the nodes in a binary tree that visits a node, then visits all the nodes in the left subtree of the node, and then visits the nodes in the right subtree of the node

---

Compare the algorithms for these three traversals to be sure you understand the difference among them.

Inorder(tree)

```
IF tree is not NULL
    Inorder(Left(tree))
    Visit Info(tree)
    Inorder(Right(tree))
```

Postorder(tree)

```
IF tree is not NULL
    Postorder(Left(tree))
    Postorder(Right(tree))
    Visit Info(tree)
```

Preorder(tree)

IF tree is not NULL
   Visit Info(tree)
   Preorder(Left(tree))
   Preorder(Right(tree))

When we say "visit," we mean that the algorithm does whatever it needs to do with the values in the node: print them, sum certain data members, or delete them, for example. Notice that the name given to each traversal specifies where the node itself is processed in relation to its subtrees. Figure 8.16 illustrates these three traversals.

An inorder traversal allows us to print the values in ascending order; the postorder traversal allows us to destroy a tree more efficiently. So, where is a preorder traversal useful? A preorder traversal is not particularly useful when dealing with binary search trees; however, there are other uses of binary trees where it is very useful. These other uses are described in the next chapter.

ResetTree and GetNextItem

`ResetTree` gets the current position ready for a traversal; `GetNextItem` moves the current position to the next node and returns the value stored there.

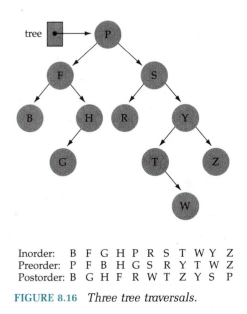

Inorder: B F G H P R S T W Y Z
Preorder: P F B H G S R Y T W Z
Postorder: B G H F R W T Z Y S P

FIGURE 8.16 *Three tree traversals.*

We have looked at three kinds of traversal, so what does "next node" mean? Both `ResetTree` and `GetNextItem` have a parameter of type `OrderType` that allows the user to specify which traversal is meant.

When traversing a linear structure, getting from one item to the next one is specified explicitly. Our tree traversals are recursive and thus the location of the next item is a function of the current item and the run-time stack. We could use an auxiliary stack to implement the traversal, thus saving the history that we need to find the next item. However, there is a simpler way: we let `ResetTree` generate a queue of node contents in the proper order and let `GetNextItem` process the node contents from the queue. Recall that `OrderType` is specified as

```
enum OrderType {PRE_ORDER, IN_ORDER, POST_ORDER};
```

We let `ResetTree` call one of three recursive functions depending on the value of the parameter `order`. Each function implements a recursive traversal storing the node contents onto a queue. This means that we must have three queues declared in the private section of `TreeType`.

```
enum OrderType {PRE_ORDER, IN_ORDER, POST_ORDER};

template<class ItemType>
class TreeType
{
public:
    // Function prototypes go here.
private:
    TreeNode<ItemType>* root;
    QueType<ItemType> preQue;
    QueType<ItemType> inQue;
    QueType<ItemType> postQue;
};


// Function prototypes for auxiliary functions.
template<class ItemType>
void PreOrder(TreeNode<ItemType>*, QueType<ItemType>&);
// Enqueues tree items in preorder.

template<class ItemType>
void InOrder(TreeNode<ItemType>*, QueType<ItemType>&);
// Enqueues tree items in inorder.

template<class ItemType>
```

```
void PostOrder(TreeNode<ItemType>*, QueType<ItemType>&);
// Enqueues tree items in postorder.

template<class ItemType>
void TreeType<ItemType>::ResetTree(OrderType order)
// Calls function to create a queue of the tree elements in
// the desired order.
{
    switch (order)
    {
        case PRE_ORDER : PreOrder(root, preQue);
                         break;
        case IN_ORDER  : InOrder(root, inQue);
                         break;
        case POST_ORDER: PostOrder(root, postQue);
                         break;
    }
}

template<class ItemType>
void PreOrder(TreeNode<ItemType>*tree,
     QueType<ItemType>& preQue)
// Post: preQue contains the tree items in preorder.
{
    if (tree != NULL)
    {
        preQue.Enqueue(tree->info);
        PreOrder(tree->left, preQue);
        PreOrder(tree->right, preQue);
    }
}

template<class ItemType>
void InOrder(TreeNode<ItemType>*tree,
     QueType<ItemType>& inQue)
// Post: inQue contains the tree items in inorder.
{
    if (tree != NULL)
    {
        InOrder(tree->left, inQue);
        inQue.Enqueue(tree->info);
        InOrder(tree->right, inQue);
    }
}

template<class ItemType>
void PostOrder(TreeNode<ItemType>*tree,
     QueType<ItemType>& postQue)
```

```
// Post: postQue contains the tree items in postorder.
{
    if (tree != NULL)
    {
        PostOrder(tree->left, postQue);
        PostOrder(tree->right, postQue);
        postQue.Enqueue(tree->info);
    }
}

template<class ItemType>
void TreeType<ItemType>::GetNextItem(ItemType& item,
    OrderType order, bool& finished)
// Returns the next item in the desired order.
// Post: For the desired order, item is the next item in the queue.
//       If item is the last one in the queue, finished is true;
//       otherwise finished is false.
{
    finished = false;
    switch (order)
    {
        case PRE_ORDER : preQue.Dequeue(item);
                if (preQue.IsEmpty())
                    finished = true;
                break;
        case IN_ORDER  : inQue.Dequeue(item);
                if (inQue.IsEmpty())
                    finished = true;
                break;
        case POST_ORDER: postQue.Dequeue(item);
                if (postQue.IsEmpty())
                    finished = true;
                break;
    }
}
```

Iterative Insertion and Deletion

Searching a Binary Search Tree

In the recursive versions of the tree operations, we embedded the search task within the function that needed it. The other alternative is to have a general search function; let's do that here. Function `FindNode` receives a pointer to a binary search tree and an item with the key initialized. It sends back a pointer to the desired node (`nodePtr`) and a pointer to the node's parent (`parentPtr`) if an item with a matching key is found.

What do we do if we do not find an item with a key that matches item's, as is the case when we are inserting a new element? We set nodePtr to NULL. In this case, parentPtr points to the node into which the new element must be inserted as a right or left child. There is one other case: what do we do if we find a matching key in the root node? In this case, there is no parent node, so we set parentPtr to NULL.

Here is the specification for the *internal* tree function, FindNode:

**FindNode(TreeNode<ItemType>* tree, ItemType item,
  TreeNode<ItemType>*& nodePtr, TreeNode<ItemType>*& parentPtr)**

Function: Searches for a node whose key matches item's key.

Precondition: tree points to the root of a binary search tree.

Postconditions: If a node is found with the same key as item's, then nodePtr points to that node and parentPtr points to its parent node. If the root node has the same key as item's, parentPtr is NULL. If no node has the same key, then nodePtr is NULL and parentPtr points to the node in the tree that is the logical parent of item.

Let's look at the search algorithm in detail. We use nodePtr and parentPtr (the outgoing parameters) to search the tree. Because we access the tree through its root, we initialize nodePtr to the external pointer, tree. We initialize parentPtr to NULL. We compare item and nodePtr->info. If the keys are equal, we have found the node we are looking for. If item's key is less, we look in the left subtree; if item's key is greater, we look in the right subtree. This is exactly like a recursive search except that we change pointer values to move left and right rather than making recursive calls.

FindNode

```
Set nodePtr to tree
Set parentPtr to NULL
Set found to false

WHILE more elements to search AND NOT found
   IF item < Info(nodePtr)
      Set parentPtr to nodePtr
      Set nodePtr to Left(nodePtr)
   ELSE IF item > Info(nodePtr)
      Set parentPtr to nodePtr
      Set nodePtr to Right(nodePtr)
   ELSE
      Set found to true
```

When does the loop terminate? There are two terminating conditions. First, we stop searching if the correct node is found. In this case, `nodePtr` points to the node containing the same key as `item`'s, and `parentPtr` points to this node's parent. Second, if no element in the tree has the same key as `item`'s, we search until we fall out of the tree. At this point, `nodePtr` = NULL, and `parentPtr` points to the node that would be the `item`'s parent—if it did exist in the tree. (We use this value of `parentPtr` when we insert into a tree.) The resulting loop condition is

```
while (nodePtr != NULL && !found)
```

The algorithm illustrates that the maximum number of comparisons in a binary search tree equals the height of the tree. As we discussed earlier, this may range from $\log_2 N$ to N (where N is the number of tree elements), depending on the shape of the tree.

The complete function follows.

```
template<class ItemType>
void FindNode(TreeNode<ItemType>* tree, ItemType item,
     TreeNode<ItemType>*& nodePtr, TreeNode<ItemType>*& parentPtr)
// Post: If a node is found with the same key as item's, then
//       nodePtr points to that node and parentPtr points to its
//       parent node. If the root node has the same key as item's,
//       parentPtr is NULL. If no node has the same key, then
//       nodePtr is NULL and parentPtr points to the node in the
//       tree that is the logical parent of item.
{
    nodePtr = tree;
    parentPtr = NULL;
    bool found = false;
    while (nodePtr != NULL && !found)
    {
        if (item < nodePtr->info)
        {
            parentPtr = nodePtr;
            nodePtr = nodePtr->left;
        }
        else if (item > nodePtr->info)
        {
            parentPtr = nodePtr;
            nodePtr = nodePtr->right;
        }
        else
            found = true;
    }
}
```

Let's trace this function, using the tree in Figure 8.6 on page 466. We want to find the element with the key 18. nodePtr is initially set to tree, the external pointer. item's key (18) is greater than nodePtr->info (17), so we advance the pointers. parentPtr now points to the root node and we move nodePtr to the right; it now points to the node with the key 20. item's key (18) is less than this key (20), so we advance the pointers. Now parentPtr points to the node with the key 20, and we move nodePtr to the left; nodePtr now points to the node with the key 18. Now 18 is equal to nodePtr->info. At this point, found is true, so we stop looping. We exit the function with nodePtr pointing to the node with the desired key, and with parentPtr pointing to this node's parent.

Next, let's look at an example where the key is not found in the tree. We want to find the element with the key 7. nodePtr is initially set to tree. Because item's key (7) is less than nodePtr->info (17), we move to the left. Now nodePtr points to the node containing 9 and parentPtr points to the root node. item's key is less than nodePtr->info, so we move again to the left. Now nodePtr is equal to NULL; it has fallen out of the tree. Because there's no more to search in this subtree, we stop looping. We exit the function with nodePtr equal to NULL and parentPtr pointing to the node with the key 9. If we were calling FindNode with the intention of subsequently inserting a node with the key 7, we would now know two things:

1. Because nodePtr is equal to NULL, we know that there is no node with the key 7 in the tree.
2. Because parentPtr points to the last node visited before we fell out of the tree, we know that the new node, with a key value of 7, must be attached to the node at parentPtr. This information is very helpful when we are developing the iterative InsertItem operation.

Function InsertItem

The algorithm for the iterative InsertItem operation has the same three tasks that any insert operation must have:

InsertItem

Create a node to contain the new item
Find the insertion place
Attach new node

Creating a node is the same as in the recursive version. Finding the insertion point and inserting the node are different. Let's see how function

`FindNode` can be used to perform the search for us. We call `FindNode`, asking it to find the node with the same key as `item`'s:

`FindNode(tree, item, nodePtr, parentPtr);`

Suppose we want to insert an element with the key value 13 into the binary search tree pictured in Figure 8.17. In function `FindNode`, `nodePtr` is initialized to point to the root of the tree, and `parentPtr` is initialized to NULL (Figure 8.17a). `item`'s key (13) is larger than the key of the root node (7), so we move `nodePtr` to the right, dragging `parentPtr` along behind it (Figure 8.17b). Now `item`'s key is less than `nodePtr->info`, so we move `nodePtr` to the left, with `parentPtr` following (Figure 8.17c). Now `item`'s key is greater than `nodePtr->info` so `parentPtr` catches up, and `nodePtr` moves to the right (Figure 8.17d). At this point, `nodePtr` is NULL, so we exit function `FindNode` with the pointers as shown in Figure 8.17(d).

Of course, a node with `item`'s key is not supposed to be found, for we are just now inserting its node. The good news is that `nodePtr` has fallen out of the tree just at the spot where the new node should be inserted. Because `parentPtr` is trailing right behind `nodePtr`, we can simply attach the new node to the node pointed to by `parentPtr` (Figure 8.17e).

Now we're ready for the third task: to fix the pointers in the node pointed to by `parentPtr` to attach the new node. In the general case we compare the key of the new element to the key of `parentPtr->info`. Either `parentPtr->left` or `parentPtr->right` must be set to point to the new node:

AttachNewNode

```
IF item < Info(parentPtr)
    Set Left(parentPtr) to newNode
ELSE
    Set Right(parentPtr) to newNode
```

In the case of inserting the first node into an empty tree, however, `parentPtr` still equals NULL and dereferencing `parentPtr` is illegal. We need to make inserting the first node into the tree a special case. We can test for `parentPtr = NULL` to determine whether the tree is empty; if so, we change `tree` to point to the new node.

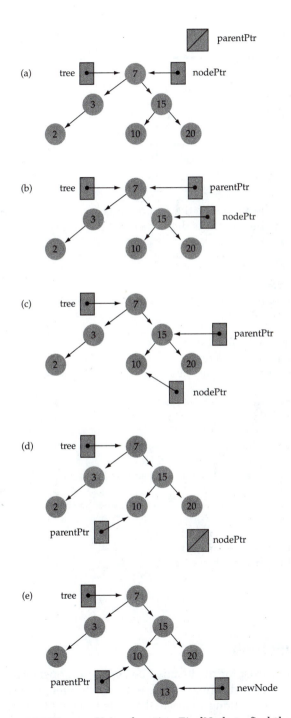

FIGURE 8.17 *Using function FindNode to find the insertion point.*

AttachNewNode (revised)

```
IF parentPtr equals NULL
    Set tree to newNode
ELSE IF item < Info(parentPtr)
    Set Left(parentPtr) to newNode
ELSE
    Set Right(parentPtr) to newNode
```

Taken together, the pieces of the insert design can be coded as function `InsertItem`, with the interface described in the Binary Search Tree ADT specification.

```cpp
template<class ItemType>
void TreeType<ItemType>::InsertItem(ItemType item)
// Post: item is in tree.
{
    TreeNode<ItemType>* newNode;
    TreeNode<ItemType>* nodePtr;
    TreeNode<ItemType>* parentPtr;

    newNode = new TreeNode<ItemType>;
    newNode->info = item;
    newNode->left = NULL;
    newNode->right = NULL;

    FindNode(root, item, nodePtr, parentPtr);

    if (parentPtr == NULL)          // Insert as root.
        root = newNode;
    else if (item < parentPtr->info)
        parentPtr->left = newNode;
    else parentPtr->right = newNode;
}
```

Function DeleteItem

The same three cases exist for the iterative `DeleteItem` operation that existed for the recursive `Delete`: deleting a node with no children, one child, or two children. We can use `FindNode` to locate the node (pointed to by `nodePtr`) to delete and its parent node (pointed to by `parentPtr`).

The actual deletion in the recursive version is done in `DeleteNode`. Can we use it to delete the node pointed to by `nodePtr`? `DeleteNode` takes only one parameter, the place in the tree where the pointer to the node to be deleted resides. We can use the `DeleteNode` developed for the recursive version if we can determine the *place in the structure* to pass to `DeleteNode`. That is, given `nodePtr` and `parentPtr`, we must determine whether the node pointed to by `nodePtr` is the right or left child of the node pointed to by `parentPtr`. If the value of `nodePtr` is the same as the value of `parentPtr->left`, we pass `parentPtr->left` to `DeleteNode`, otherwise we pass `parentPtr->right`.

```
template<class ItemType>
void TreeType<ItemType>::DeleteItem(ItemType item)
// Post: There is no node in the tree whose info member
//       matches item.
{
    TreeNode<ItemType>* nodePtr;
    TreeNode<ItemType>* parentPtr;

    FindNode(root, item, nodePtr, parentPtr);

    if (nodePtr == root)
        DeleteNode(root);
    else
        if (parentPtr->left == nodePtr)
            DeleteNode(parentPtr->left);
        else DeleteNode(parentPtr->right);
}
```

It is very important to recognize the difference between passing `nodePtr` to `DeleteNode` and passing either `parentPtr->right` or `parentPtr->left`. See Figures 8.18 and 8.19.

Recursion or Iteration?

Now that we have looked at both the recursive and the iterative versions of inserting and deleting nodes, can we determine which is better? In the last chapter, we gave some guidelines for determining when recursion is appropriate. Let's apply these to the use of recursion with binary search trees.

Is the depth of recursion relatively shallow?

Yes. The depth of recursion is dependent on the height of the tree. If the tree is well balanced (relatively short and bushy, not tall and stringy), the depth of recursion is closer to $O(\log_2 N)$ than to $O(N)$.

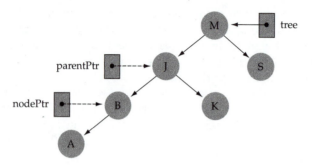

FIGURE 8.18   *Pointers nodePtr and parentPtr are external to the tree.*

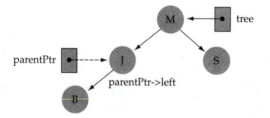

FIGURE 8.19   *Pointer parentPtr is external to the tree, but parentPtr->left is an actual pointer in the tree.*

Is the recursive solution shorter or clearer than the nonrecursive version?

Yes. The recursive solutions are certainly shorter than the combination of the nonrecursive functions plus the supporting function `FindNode`. Is it clearer? Once you accept that in every recursive execution, the parameter `tree` is actually a pointer member within a node of the tree, the recursive version becomes intuitively obvious.

Is the recursive version much less efficient than the nonrecursive version?

No. Both the recursive and the nonrecursive versions of inserting and deleting are O($\log_2 N$) operations, assuming a well-balanced tree. The only efficiency issue of concern is that of space. `item` is a value parameter; our functions pass a copy of it on each recursive call. If `item` is a large struct or class object, these copies may cause an overflow of the run-time stack. (It would be better to make `item` a `const` reference parameter if `ItemType` is large or the tree has great height.)

    We give the recursive versions of the functions an 'A'; it is a good use of recursion.

Comparing Binary Search Trees to Linear Lists

A binary search tree is an appropriate structure for many of the same applications discussed previously in conjunction with other sorted list structures. The special advantage of using a binary search tree is that it facilitates searching, while conferring the benefits of linking the elements. It provides the best features of both the sorted array-based list and the linked list: like a sorted array-based list, it can be searched quickly, using a binary search. Like a linked list, it allows insertions and deletions without having to move data. Thus it is particularly suitable for applications in which search time must be minimized or in which the nodes are not necessarily processed in sequential order.

As usual, there is a trade-off. The binary search tree, with its extra pointer in each node, takes up more memory space than a singly linked list. In addition, the algorithms for manipulating the tree are somewhat more complicated. If all of the list's uses involve sequential rather than random processing of the elements, the tree may not be as good a choice.

Suppose we have 100,000 customer records in a list. If the main activity in the application is to send out updated monthly statements to the customers and if the order in which the statements are printed is the same as the order in which the records appear on the list, a linked list would be suitable. But suppose we decide to keep a terminal available to give out account information to the customers whenever they ask. If the data are kept in a linked list, the first customer on the list can be given information almost instantly, but the last customer has to wait while the other 99,999 records are examined. When direct access to the records is a requirement, a binary search tree is a more appropriate structure.

Big-O Comparisons

Finding the node to process (FindNode), as we would expect in a structure dedicated to searching, is the most interesting operation to analyze. In the best case—if the order in which the elements were inserted results in a short and bushy tree—we can find any node in the tree with at most $\log_2 N + 1$ comparisons. We would expect to be able to locate a random element in such a tree much faster than finding an element in a sorted linked list. In the worst case—if the elements were inserted in order from smallest to largest or vice versa—the tree won't really be a tree at all; it is a linear list, linked through either the left or right data members. *This is called a "degenerate" tree.* In this case, the tree operations should perform much the same as the operations on a linked list. Therefore, if we were doing a *worst-case* analysis, we would have to say that the complexity of the tree operations is identical to the comparable linked-list operations. However, in the following analysis, we assume that the items are inserted into the tree in random order giving a balanced tree.

The `InsertItem` and `RetrieveItem` operations are basically finding the node [$O(\log_2 N)$] plus tasks that are $O(1)$—for instance, creating a node, resetting pointers, or copying data. Thus these operations are described as $O(\log_2 N)$. The `DeleteItem` operation consists of finding the node plus `DeleteNode`. In the worst case (deleting a node with two children), `DeleteNode` must find the replacement value, an $O(\log_2 N)$ operation. (Actually, the two tasks together add up to $\log_2 N$ comparisons, because if the delete node is higher in the tree, fewer comparisons are needed to find it, and more comparisons may be needed to find its replacement node.) Otherwise, if the deleted node has 0 or 1 child, `DeleteNode` is an $O(1)$ operation. So `DeleteItem` too may be described as $O(\log_2 N)$.

The `PrintTree` and destructor operations require the tree to be traversed, processing each element once. Thus these are $O(N)$ operations. The orders of magnitude for the tree and list operations as we have coded them are compared in Table 8.2. The binary search tree operations are based on a random order of the items; the find operation in the array-based implementation is based on using a binary search.

TABLE 8.2   Big-O Comparison of List Operations

	Binary Search Tree	Array-Based Linear List	Linked List
Class constructor	$O(1)$	$O(1)$	$O(1)$
Destructor	$O(N)$	$O(1)^*$	$O(N)$
IsFull operation	$O(1)$	$O(1)$	$O(1)$
IsEmpty operation	$O(1)$	$O(1)$	$O(1)$
Retrieve operation			
Find	$O(\log_2 N)$	$O(\log_2 N)$	$O(N)$
Process	$O(1)$	$O(1)$	$O(1)$
Combined	$O(\log_2 N)$	$O(\log_2 N)$	$O(N)$
Insert operation			
Find	$O(\log_2 N)$	$O(\log_2 N)$	$O(N)$
Process	$O(1)$	$O(N)$	$O(1)$
Combined	$O(\log_2 N)$	$O(N)$	$O(N)$
Delete operation			
Find	$O(\log_2 N)$	$O(\log_2 N)$	$O(N)$
Process	$O(1)$	$O(N)$	$O(1)$
Combined	$O(\log_2 N)$	$O(N)$	$O(N)$

*If there is a possibility that the items in the array-based list contain pointers, the items must be deallocated, making this an $O(N)$ operation.

CASE STUDY ▮▮▮

BUILDING AN INDEX

Problem: Our publisher has asked us to produce an index for this text. The first step in this process is to decide which words should go into the index; the second is to produce a list of the pages where each word occurs.

Instead of trying to choose words out of our heads (thin air), we decided to let the computer produce a list of all the unique words used in the manuscript and their frequency of occurrence. We could then go over the list and choose which words to put into the index.

Discussion: Clearly, the main object in this problem is a word with associated frequency. Therefore, the first thing we must do is define a "word."

Looking back over the preceding paragraphs, what is a tentative definition of word in this context? How about "something between two blanks"? Or better yet, a "character string between two blanks." That definition works for most of the words. However, all words before '.' and ',' would have the '.' and ',' attached. Also, words with quotes would cause a problem.

Does the following definition take care of the problem? A word is a string of alphanumeric characters between markers, where markers are whitespace characters and all punctuation marks. Yes, this is a good working definition of the kind of word that would be a candidate for an index term. In fact, this definition would allow us to use `StrType` defined in Chapter 2. The option `ALPHA_NUM` in `GetString` defines a string as only alphanumeric characters; anything non-alphanumeric stops the reading. If we skip all unallowed characters before getting the string, we should have exactly what we want.

This process ignores quotation marks, leaving only contractions as a problem. Let's examine a few and see if we can find a solution. "let's", "can't", "couldn't", and "that's", four very common contractions, all have only one letter after the single quote. The algorithm would return the characters up to the single quote as one word and the character between the single quote and the double quote as one word. What we really want to do is ignore the characters after the single quote. If we say that words must be at least three characters long to be considered for the index, this problem is solved. Ignoring words of fewer than three letters also removes from consideration such words as "a", "is", "to", "do", and "by" that do not belong in an index.

For each word that we find that is three characters or longer, we check to see if it is a word that we have had before. If it is, we increment its frequency; if not, we add it to the list of words with a frequency of one.

Input: The text of the manuscript on file "book.in".

Output: The list of words, written to "words.out".

Data Objects: There are word objects represented in the program as `WordType` objects. There are two data members in this class, word of type

`StrType` and `count` of type `int`. We postpone deciding on the member functions needed until we design the main function. We need a container object in which to store the unique words. We can use any of the List ADTs we have written. In order to have the output file list the words in alphabetic order, we should use Sorted List or Binary Search Tree. Because we have no idea how many unique words might be in the file, we choose the Binary Search Tree.

We are now ready to summarize our discussion in the main driver function.

Driver (Main)

```
Open input file inFile
Open output file outFile
WHILE more data in inFile
    string.GetStringFile(true, ALPHA_NUM, inFile)
    IF string.LengthIs() > 2
       Store string into word member of a wordObject
       list.RetrieveItem(wordObject, found)
       IF found
          Increment count of wordObject
       ELSE
          list.InsertItem(wordObject)
list.PrintTree(outFile)
```

OOPS! There is a major flaw in this design. `RetrieveItem` returns a *copy* of the item in the list. If we increment the count, we are only incrementing the count of the copy. Therefore, all the frequencies would end up being one. In fact, this problem really doesn't lend itself to using the Binary Search Tree ADT. The processing could be made much more efficient if we write a single function that searches the tree for a string and increments the count if it finds it and inserts a node with the string if it doesn't. When the search finds that the string is not there it is at the point where the node belongs.

This brings up a very important point: there are times when it is not appropriate to use an off-the-shelf container class. Using library classes—whether provided by C++ or your own—allows you to write more reliable software in a shorter amount of time. These classes are already tested and debugged. If they fit the needs of your problem, use them. If they do not, then write a special-purpose function to do the job. In this case, we need to write our own. Here is a revised main function.

```
Open input file inFile
Open output file outFile
WHILE more data in inFile
    string.GetStringFile(true, ALPHA_NUM, inFile)
    IF string.LengthIs() > 2
        IncrementOrInsert(tree, string)
PrintTree(tree, outFile)
```

Because `IncrementOrInsert` and `PrintTree` are designed for a special purpose there is no need to make them template functions. In fact, there is no reason why they should not have direct access to the data members of `WordType`. Therefore, let's code `WordType` as a struct rather than a class.

IncrementOrInsert

```
IF tree is NULL
    Get a new node for tree to point to
    Set word member of Info(tree) to string
    Set count member of Info(tree) to 1
    Set Left(tree) to NULL
    Set Right(tree) to NULL
ELSE IF word member of Info(tree) = string
    Increment count member of Info(tree)
ELSE IF string < word member of Info(tree)
    IncrementOrInsert(Left(tree), string)
ELSE
    IncrementOrInsert(Right(tree), string)
```

PrintTree

```
IF tree is not NULL
    PrintTree(Left(tree), outFile)
    word member of Info(tree).PrintToFile(true, outFile)
    outFile << " " << count
    PrintTree(Right(tree), outFile)
```

We are now ready to code our algorithms.

```
#include <fstream.h>
#include "StrType.h"
#include <stdlib.h>
#include <iostream.h>

struct WordType
{
    StrType word;
    int count;
};

struct TreeNode
{
    WordType info;
    TreeNode* left;
    TreeNode* right;
};

void PrintTree(TreeNode*, ofstream&);
// Prints the words in the tree and their frequency counts.

void IncrementOrInsert(TreeNode*&, StrType);
// Increments the frequency count if the string is in the tree
// or inserts the string if it is not there.

int main()
{
    TreeNode* tree = NULL;
    ifstream inFile;
    ofstream outFile;
    StrType string;

    inFile.open("book.in");
    outFile.open("words.out");
    string.GetStringFile(true, ALPHA_NUM, inFile);
    while (inFile)
    {
        if (string.LengthIs() > 2)
            IncrementOrInsert(tree, string);
        string.GetStringFile(true, ALPHA_NUM, inFile);
    }
    PrintTree(tree, outFile);
    return 0;
}

void IncrementOrInsert(TreeNode*& tree, StrType string)
{
    if (tree == NULL)
```

```
    {
        tree = new TreeNode;
        tree->info.word = string;
        tree->info.count = 1;
        tree->left = NULL;
        tree->right = NULL;
    }
    else if (tree->info.word == string)
        tree->info.count++;
    else if (string < tree->info.word)
        IncrementOrInsert(tree->left, string);
    else
        IncrementOrInsert(tree->right, string);
}

void PrintTree(TreeNode* tree, ofstream& outFile)
{
    if ( !(tree == NULL))
    {
        PrintTree(tree->left, outFile);
        tree->info.word.PrintToFile(true, outFile);
        outFile << " " << tree->info.count;
        PrintTree(tree->right, outFile);
    }
}
```

We leave the rest of the problem of creating the index as Chapter 8, Programming Problem 2.

TESTING

As a test plan for this program, we can take the first few paragraphs of the first chapter, calculate what the words and frequencies should be, and run the program with them as input data.

■‖ *Summary*

In this chapter we have seen how the binary search tree may be used to structure sorted information to reduce the search time for any particular element. For applications where direct access to the elements in a sorted structure is needed, the binary search tree is a very useful data type. If the tree is balanced, we can access any node in the tree with an $O(\log_2 N)$ operation. The binary search tree combines the advantages of quick random-access (like a binary search on a linear list) with the flexibility of a linked structure.

We also saw that the tree operations could be implemented very elegantly and concisely using recursion. This makes sense, because a binary tree is itself a "recursive" structure: any node in the tree is the root of another binary tree. Each time we moved down a level in the tree, taking either the right or left path from a node, we cut the size of the (current) tree in half, a clear case of the smaller-caller. We also saw cases of iteration that replaced recursion (InsertItem and DeleteItem).

■|| *Exercises*

1. (a) What does the level of a binary search tree mean in relation to the searching efficiency?
   (b) What is the maximum number of levels that a binary search tree with 100 nodes can have?
   (c) What is the minimum number of levels that a binary search tree with 100 nodes can have?

2. Which of these formulas gives the maximum total number of nodes in a tree that has N levels? (Remember that the root is at Level 0.)
   (a) $N^2 - 1$ (b) 2^N (c) $2^{N+1} - 1$ (d) 2^{N+1}

3. Which of these formulas gives the maximum number of nodes in the Nth level of a binary tree?
   (a) N^2 (b) 2^N (c) 2^{N+1} (d) $2^N - 1$

4. How many ancestors does a node in the Nth level of a binary search tree have?

5. (a) How many different *binary trees* can be made from three nodes that contain the key values 1, 2, and 3?
   (b) How many different *binary search trees* can be made from three nodes that contain the key values 1, 2, and 3?

6. Draw all the possible binary trees that have four leaves and all the nonleaf nodes have two children.

7. The TreeType class used a queue as an auxiliary storage structure for iterating through the elements in the tree. Discuss the relative merits of using a dynamically allocated array-based queue versus a dynamically allocated linked queue.

Answer the questions in Exercises 8–10 independently, using the following binary search tree.

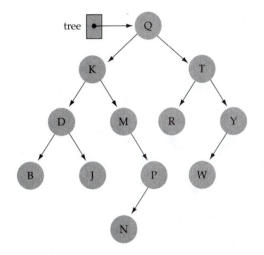

8. (a) What are the ancestors of node P?
   (b) What are the descendants of node K?
   (c) What is the maximum possible number of nodes in the tree at the level of node W?
   (d) What is the maximum possible number of nodes in the tree at the level of node N?
   (e) Insert node O. How many nodes would be in the tree if it were completely full down to and including the level of node O?

9. Show what the tree would look like after each of the following changes. (Use the original tree to answer each part.)
   (a) Add node C.
   (b) Add node Z.
   (c) Add node X.
   (d) Delete node M.
   (e) Delete node Q.
   (f) Delete node R.

10. Show the order in which the nodes in the tree are processed by
    (a) an inorder traversal of the tree.
    (b) a postorder traversal of the tree.
    (c) a preorder traversal of the tree.

11. Draw the binary search tree whose elements are inserted in the following order:
    50 72 96 94 107 26 12 11 9 2 10 25 51 16 17 95

Exercises 12–16 use the following binary search tree.

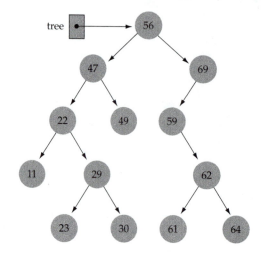

12. (a) What is the height of the tree?
    (b) What nodes are on level 3?
    (c) Which levels have the maximum number of nodes that they could contain?
    (d) What is the maximum height of a binary search tree containing these nodes? Draw such a tree.
    (e) What is the minimum height of a binary search tree containing these nodes? Draw such a tree.

13. (a) Trace the path that would be followed in searching for a node containing 61.
    (b) Trace the path that would be followed in searching for a node containing 28.

14. Show the order in which the nodes in the tree are processed by
    (a) an inorder traversal of the tree.
    (b) a postorder traversal of the tree.
    (c) a preorder traversal of the tree.

15. Show how the tree would look after the deletion of 29, 59, and 47.

16. Show how the (original) tree would look after the insertion of nodes containing 63, 77, 76, 48, 9, and 10 (in that order).

17. True or False.
    (a) Invoking the delete function in this chapter might create a tree with more levels than the original tree had.
    (b) A preorder traversal processes the nodes in a tree in the exact reverse order that a postorder traversal processes them.
    (c) An inorder traversal always processes the elements of a tree in the same order, regardless of the order in which the elements were inserted.
    (d) A preorder traversal always processes the elements of a tree in the same order, regardless of the order in which the elements were inserted.

18. If you wanted to traverse a tree, writing all the elements to a file, and later (the next time you ran the program) rebuild the trees by reading and inserting, would an inorder traversal be appropriate? Why or why not?

19. (a) One hundred integer elements are chosen at random and inserted into a sorted linked list and a binary search tree. Describe the efficiency of searching for an element in each structure, in terms of Big-O.
    (b) One hundred integer elements are inserted in order, from smallest to largest, into a sorted linked list and a binary search tree. Describe the efficiency of searching for an element in each structure, in terms of Big-O.

20. The key of each node in a binary search tree is a short character string.
    (a) Show how such a tree would look after the following words were inserted (in the order indicated):

    monkey canary donkey deer zebra yak walrus vulture penguin quail

    (b) Show how the tree would look if the same words were inserted in this order:

    quail walrus donkey deer monkey vulture yak penguin zebra canary

    (c) Show how the tree would look if the same words were inserted in this order:

    zebra yak walrus vulture quail penguin monkey donkey deer canary

21. Write a function called `PtrToSuccessor` that finds a node with the smallest key value in a tree, unlinks it from the tree, and returns a pointer to the unlinked node.

22. Modify the `DeleteNode` function from the chapter so that it uses the immediate successor (rather than the predecessor) of the value to be deleted in the case of deleting a node with two children. You should call function `PtrToSuccessor` that you wrote in the previous exercise.

23. Use the Three-Question method to verify the recursive function `Insert`.

24. Use the Three-Question method to verify the recursive function `Delete`.

25. Write `IsFull` and `IsEmpty` for class `TreeType`.

26. Add a `TreeType` member function `Ancestors` that prints the ancestors of a given node whose `info` member contains `value`. Do not print `value`.
    (a) Write the declaration.
    (b) Write the iterative implementation.

27. Write a recursive version of function `Ancestors` described in Exercise 26.

28. Write a recursive version of `Ancestors` (see Exercise 27) that prints out the ancestors in reverse order (first the parent, then the grandparent, and so on).

29. Add a Boolean member function `IsBST` to class `TreeType` that determines if a binary tree is a binary search tree.
    (a) Write the declaration of function `IsBST`. Include adequate comments.
    (b) Write a recursive implementation of this function.

30. The Binary Search Tree ADT is extended to include member function `LeafCount` that returns the number of leaf nodes in the tree. Write this function.

31. The Binary Search Tree ADT is extended to include member function `SingleParentCount` that returns the number of nodes in the tree that have only one child. Write this function.

32. Write a client function that returns a count of the number of nodes that contain a value less than the parameter `value`.

33. The Binary Search Tree ADT is extended to include a Boolean function `SimilarTrees` that receives pointers to two binary trees, and determines if the shapes of the trees are the same. (The nodes do not have to contain the same values, but each node must have the same number of children.)
    (a) Write the declaration of function `SimilarTrees` as a `TreeType` member function. Include adequate comments.
    (b) Write the body of function `SimilarTrees`.

34. `TreeType` member function `MirrorImage` creates and returns a mirror image of the tree.
    (a) Write the declaration of function `MirrorImage`. Include adequate comments.
    (b) Write the body of function `MirrorImage`.
    (c) Can the binary tree returned from this function be used for binary searching? If so, how?

35. Write a client function `MakeTree` that creates a binary search tree from the elements in a sorted list of integers. You cannot traverse the list inserting the elements in order, because that would produce a tree that would have N levels. You must create a tree with at most $\log_2 N + 1$ levels.

36. Write a client Boolean function `MatchingItems` that determines if a binary search tree and a sequential list contain the same values.

Examine the following binary search tree and answer the questions in Exercises 37–40. The numbers on the nodes are *labels* so that we can talk about the nodes; they are not key values within the nodes.

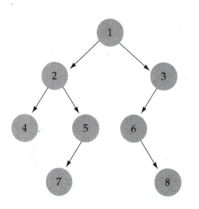

37. If an item is to be inserted whose key value is less than the key value in node 1 but greater than the key value in node 5, where would it be inserted?

38. If node 1 is to be deleted, the value in which node could be used to replace it?

39. 4 2 7 5 1 6 8 3 is a traversal of the tree in which order?

40. 1 2 4 5 7 3 6 8 is a traversal of the tree in which order?

41. In Chapter 6 we discussed how a linked list could be stored in an array of nodes using index values as "pointers" and managing our list of free nodes. We can use these same techniques to store the nodes of a binary search tree in an array, rather than using dynamic storage allocation. Free space is linked through the left member.
    (a) Show how the array would look after these elements had been inserted in this order:

    Q L W F M R N S

    Be sure to fill in all the spaces. If you do not know the contents of a space, use '?'.

nodes	.info	.left	.right
[0]			
[1]			
[2]			
[3]			
[4]			
[5]			
[6]			
[7]			
[8]			
[9]			

free [ ]

root [ ]

(b) Show the contents of the array after 'B' has been inserted and 'R' has been deleted.

nodes	.info	.left	.right
[0]			
[1]			
[2]			
[3]			
[4]			
[5]			
[6]			
[7]			
[8]			
[9]			

free ☐
root ☐

Trees Plus

- To be able to show how an arithmetic expression can be stored in a binary tree

- To be able to build a binary expression tree

- To be able to show how a binary tree can be represented as an array, with implicit positional links between the elements

- To be able to define the following terms:

    full binary tree
    complete binary tree
    heap

- To be able to describe the shape and order properties of a heap, and to implement a heap in a nonlinked tree representation in an array

- To be able to describe a priority queue at the logical level and to implement a priority queue as a list and as a heap

- To be able to compare the implementations of a priority queue using a heap, linked list, and binary search tree

- To be able to define the following terms related to graphs:

directed graph	edge	weighted graph
undirected graph	path	adjacency matrix
vertex	complete graph	adjacency list

- To be able to implement a graph using an adjacency matrix to represent the edges

- To be able to explain the difference between a depth-first and a breadth-first search and to implement these searching strategies using stacks and queues for auxiliary storage

- To be able to implement a shortest-paths operation, using a priority queue to access the edge with the minimum weight

So far we have examined several basic data types in depth, discussing their uses and operations, as well as one or more implementations of each. As we have constructed these programmer-defined data structures out of the built-in types provided by our high-level language, we have noted variations that adapt them to the needs of different applications. In Chapter 8 we looked at how a tree structure, the binary search tree, facilitates searching data stored in a linked structure. In this chapter we see how other branching structures are used to model a variety of applications.

Binary Expression Trees

Let's look at how the words *binary* and *tree* suggest that binary trees have something in common with arithmetic expressions.

Binary Expressions are made up of values on which binary operations (such as addition, subtraction, multiplication, and division) may be performed. Each node of a binary tree may have at most two children; therefore, we can represent a simple binary expression as a two-level binary tree. The root node contains the operator, and the two children contain the two operands. Following are tree representations of four such expressions:

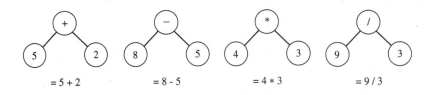

Note that the values are in the leaf nodes, and the operator is in their parent node.

Tree The various parts of a complicated expression have different levels of precedence of evaluation. For instance, when we see the expression $(A + B) * C$, we know that $(A + B)$ is evaluated before the multiplication is performed. When we write the expression in infix notation, with the operator between the operands, we must depend on some operator precedence scheme and the use of parentheses to describe an expression precisely. When we use a binary tree to represent an expression, however, parentheses are not needed to indicate precedence. The levels of the nodes in the tree indicate the relative precedence of evaluation implicitly.

The following binary tree represents the expression $(12 - 3) * (4 + 1)$.

Let's start at the root node and evaluate the expression. The root contains the operator, $*$, so we look at its children to get the two operands. The subtrees

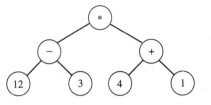

to the left and right of the root contain the two operands. Because the node to the left of the root contains another operator, –, we know that the left subtree itself consists of an expression. We must evaluate the subtraction of the value in that node's right child from the value in its left child before we can do the multiplication. Similarly, in the node to the right of the root, we find another operator, +. Therefore, we know that we must evaluate the addition of the operands in that node's left and right children before we can do the multiplication. This example illustrates that the operations at higher levels of the tree are evaluated later than those below them. The operation at the root of the tree is always the last operation performed.

See if you can determine the expressions represented by the following binary trees:

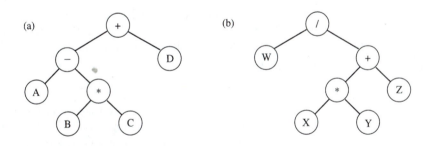

Expression Evaluation

Let's develop a function to evaluate a binary expression tree. We know that the value of the complete tree is equal to

Operand1 BinOperator Operand2

where BinOperator is one of the binary operators (+, –, *, or /) in the root node, Operand1 is the value of its left subtree, and Operand2 is the value of its right subtree. What is the value of the left subtree? If the left subtree consists of a single node containing a value, Operand1 is that value itself. If the left subtree consists of an expression, we must evaluate it. Of course, we can use our same expression evaluation function to calculate its value. That is, our function is a recursive one. The right subtree is evaluated similarly.

Let's summarize the recursive solution:

Function Eval

Definition: Evaluates the expression represented by the binary tree.
Size: The number of nodes in the tree.
Base Case: If the content of the node is an operand,
              Function value = the value of the operand.
General Case: If the content of the node is an operator BinOperator,
              Function value = Eval(left subtree) BinOperator Eval(right subtree)

This description leads us to the following algorithm for function `Eval`:

Eval(TreeNode∗ tree)

```
IF Info(tree) is an operand
    Return Info(tree)
ELSE
    SWITCH (Info(tree))
        case + : Return Eval(Left(tree)) + Eval(Right(Tree))
        case − : Return Eval(Left(tree)) − Eval(Right(Tree))
        case * : Return Eval(Left(tree)) * Eval(Right(Tree))
        case / : Return Eval(Left(tree)) / Eval(Right(Tree))
```

When we try to code this function, we notice that we are using the `info` member of the tree node to contain two different types of data—sometimes a character representing an operator, and other times a numeric value. How can we represent two data types in the same member of the node? We can use a union as we did in Chapter 4 when we used a stack to evaluate postfix expressions. For our binary expression tree, here is a variant record named `InfoNode` that defines the data type of the `info` member of a tree node:

```
enum OpType {OPERATOR, OPERAND};

struct InfoNode
{
    OpType whichType;      // Type field
    union                  // Anonymous union
```

```
    {
        char operation;
        int operand;
    };
};
```

(Notice that in the union we use the identifier `operation` rather than `operator`, as we did in Chapter 4.)

Whenever we access a node in the tree, we need to test the type field to see whether the node contains an operator or an operand. Therefore, when we first store a value into a node, we must also set the type field accordingly:

```
tree->info.whichType = OPERATOR;
tree->info.operation = '+';
          .

          .

          .
tree->info.whichType = OPERAND;
tree->info.operand = 463;
```

Given the type `InfoNode`, we now declare the nodes in our tree to be of the following type:

```
struct TreeNode
{
    InfoNode info;
    TreeNode* left;
    TreeNode* right;
};
```

We have not templated type `TreeNode` because we are using it for a specific application, not as a generic type. Now we can encode function `Eval` as follows:

```
int Eval(TreeNode* tree)
{
    switch (tree->info.whichType)
    {
        case OPERAND : return tree->info.operand;
        case OPERATOR:
            switch (tree->info.operation)
            {
                case '+' : return (Eval(tree->left)
                                    + Eval(tree->right));
                case '-' : return (Eval(tree->left)
                                    - Eval(tree->right));
                case '*' : return (Eval(tree->left) *
                                    Eval(tree->right));
```

```
                        case '/' : return (Eval(tree->left) /
                                           Eval(tree->right));
            }
        }
}
```

Printing a Binary Expression Tree

Prefix notation and postfix notation provide us with ways of writing an expression without using parentheses to denote precedence. It's very simple to print out the prefix and postfix representations of an expression stored in a binary tree. The preorder and postorder tree traversals that we discussed in Chapter 8 accomplish the task. Figure 9.1 shows an expression stored in a binary tree and its corresponding prefix, infix, and postfix notations. Note that we cannot write the infix notation directly from the tree because of the need to add parentheses.

Building a Binary Expression Tree

By now you have probably already asked the obvious question: how did the expression get into the tree? We now develop an algorithm for building a binary expression tree from an expression in prefix notation. For simplicity, we use single letters as operands in this discussion.

The basic format of the prefix expression is

BinOperator Operand1 Operand2

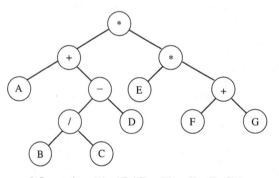

Infix notation: ((A +((B / C) − D)) ∗ (E ∗ (F +G)))
Prefix notation: ∗ + A − / B C D ∗ E + F G
Postfix notation: A B C / D − + E F G + ∗ ∗

FIGURE 9.1 *Notation for an expression stored in a binary tree.*

We know that for a simple prefix expression like + A B, the operator, +, goes in the root node, and the operands, A and B, go in its left and right child nodes, respectively. What happens if one of the operands is also an expression? For instance, how would we represent + * A Y B [equivalent to (A * Y) + B] in a tree? Again, the first operator, +, goes in the root node. The second operator, *, goes in the node to the left of the root, for it is part of Operand1. The operands of *, A and Y, are the children of this node. To put B into the tree, we must backtrack up to the root, in order to place its node as the right child of the root node:

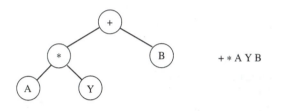

$$+ * A Y B$$

So if we have an operator, we put it in a node and set up its left operand. If we have an operand, we put it in a node and backtrack to the previous node to set up its right operand. It looks like the following general approach should work: insert new nodes, each time moving to the *left* until we have put in an operand. Then backtrack to the last operator, and put the next node to its *right*. We continue in the same pattern. If we have just inserted an operator node, we put the next node to its left; if we have just inserted an operand node, we backtrack and put the next node to the right of the last operator.

In addition to the tree we are creating, we need a temporary data structure in which to store pointers to the operator nodes, to support the backtracking we just described. Did you guess from the word *backtrack* that we would use a stack? We also use a flag, nextMove, to indicate whether our next node should be attached to the left or the right, based on whether the current node contains an operator or an operand. (We are assuming the presence of some special character to denote the end of the expression. In the figures, this character is represented as a semicolon; however, its identity is not relevant to the processing.)

A more detailed version of the algorithm appears on page 524.

This algorithm is a bit complicated, so let's trace it through a simple expression: * + A - B C D. [This expression is the same as ((A + (B – C)) * D).] We begin by getting the first symbol, *, and building the root node. At the point, before the loop, when we get the next symbol, our tree looks as shown in Figure 9.2. (In this and the following figures, we do not show whichType as it is obvious from the symbol itself.) We then get the next symbol, +, and because it is not the last symbol, we enter the loop.

BuildTree(TreeNode* tree)

```
// Build root node
Get next symbol
Get a new node, pointed to by newNode
Put symbol into newNode->info.operation   // Will be an operator
Put OPERATOR into newNode->info.whichType
Set tree to newNode

// Prepare for loop.
Set nextMove to LEFT
Get next symbol

WHILE symbol is not LAST_SYMBOL
    Set lastNode to newNode
    Get a new node, pointed to by newNode
    IF symbol is an operator
        Put OPERATOR into newNode->info.whichType
        Put symbol into newNode->info.operation
    ELSE
        Put OPERAND into newNode->info.whichType
        Put symbol into newNode->info.operand
        Set child members of Node(newNode) to NULL
    SWITCH (nextMove)
        case LEFT :   Attach Node(newNode) to left of
                      Node(lastNode) stack.Push(lastNode)
        case RIGHT : stack.Pop(lastNode)
                      Attach Node(newNode) to right of
                      Node(lastNode)
    IF newNode->info.whichType is OPERATOR
        Set nextMove to LEFT
    ELSE
        Set nextMove to RIGHT
    Get next symbol
```

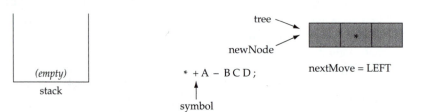

FIGURE 9.2   *Before the first iteration of the loop.*

In the loop we first set `lastNode` (a trailing pointer) to `newNode`. Then we allocate a new node and put `symbol` into it. `nextMove` is still equal to `LEFT`, so we attach the new node to the left of Node(`lastNode`). At this point it is obvious why we are keeping the pointer `lastNode`. We must have this pointer in order to access the node whose left child pointer is set to `newNode`. We do one more task when `nextMove = LEFT`: we push `lastNode` onto the stack. This allows us to return to this node eventually, in order to attach its right child node (the other operand). Next, we reset `nextMove` according to the symbol type. The symbol (+) is an operator, so `nextMove` is reset to `LEFT` to indicate that the next node must be attached to the left of Node(`newNode`). Because this node contains an operator, it must have first a left child and then a right child containing its operands, so `LEFT` is the correct value for `nextMove` at this point. The last operation in the loop is to get the next symbol. At this point the data looks as shown in Figure 9.3.

The new value for `symbol` (A) is not the last symbol, so we reenter the loop. We build a new node to contain A, setting both child members of the new node to `NULL` (remember, operands always live in leaf nodes). Because `nextMove` is still equal to `LEFT`, we attach this node to the tree exactly as we did before, saving the pointer `lastNode` in the stack. Now we must reset `nextMove`. The symbol (A) is an operand, so we execute the else-clause to set `nextMove` to `RIGHT`. We just attached the first operand to the left of the last operator; now we must get the second operand to put on its right, so `RIGHT` is the correct value for `nextMove` at this point. Then we get the next symbol. At this point the data look as shown in Figure 9.4. (Note that we continue to show previous values of `lastNode`, indicated by subscripts and in parentheses, so that it is apparent later how these values correspond to the values being popped from the stack.)

Because the next symbol (-) is not the last symbol, we reenter the loop. We build a new node to contain the symbol, and then check the value of `nextMove`. Because `nextMove` is equal to `RIGHT`, we must link the new node

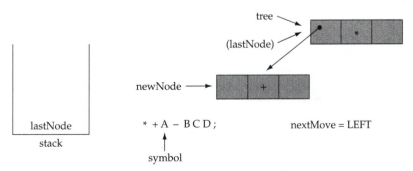

FIGURE 9.3 *At the end of the first iteration of the loop.*

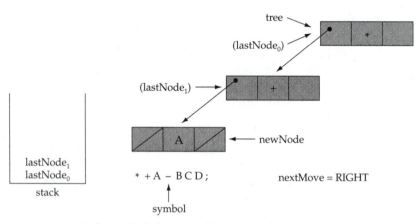

FIGURE 9.4   *At the end of the second iteration of the loop.*

to the last *operator* node, not the last node built. To get the pointer to this node, we pop the stack. Then we set the right child pointer of the last operator node to newNode. We said before that, having attached the first operand to the left of the operator node, we were ready to attach the second operand to its right. But Node(newNode) doesn't contain an operand; it contains another operator. (This means that the second operand is itself an expression.) We need to move to the left of this new node, so we reset nextMove to LEFT. We then get the next symbol. At this point the data look as shown in Figure 9.5.

Trace through the algorithm yourself to see how it progresses. The next three iterations of the loop produce the data pictured in Figures 9.6 through 9.8.

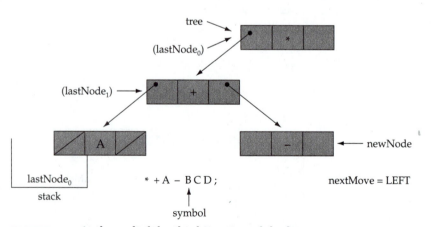

FIGURE 9.5   *At the end of the third iteration of the loop.*

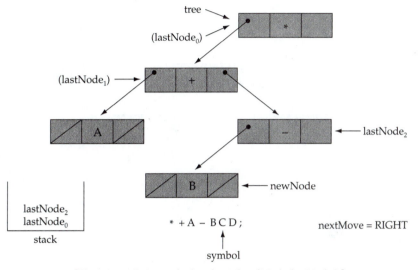

[The next node is attached to the right of Node(lastNode$_2$).]

FIGURE 9.6   *At the end of the fourth iteration of the loop.*

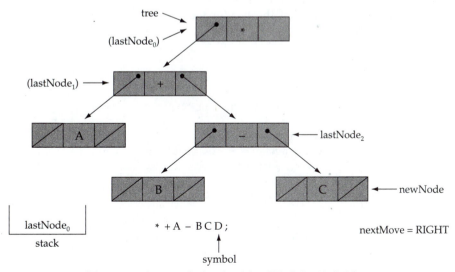

[The next node is attached to the right of Node(lastNode$_0$).]

FIGURE 9.7   *At the end of the fifth iteration of the loop.*

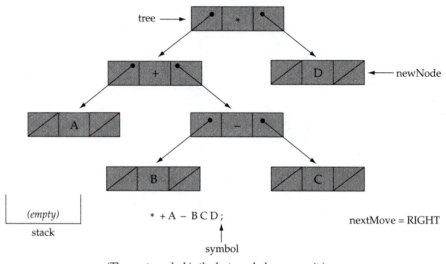

FIGURE 9.8   *At the end of the sixth (last) iteration of the loop.*

Did you get the same result? Do a preorder traversal of the resulting tree to see whether it indeed matches the original prefix expression.

Before we write function `BuildTree`, let's specify clearly what the input looks like. It is a valid prefix expression, made up of single-letter operands and the binary operators +, *, −, and /. We assume that `LAST_SYMBOL` has been defined and that the header file for the class template `StackType` has been included.

```
void BuildTree(TreeNode*& tree)
{
    enum MoveType {RIGHT, LEFT};

    MoveType nextMove = LEFT;
    TreeNode* newNode = new TreeNode;
    TreeNode* lastNode;
    char symbol;
    StackType<TreeNode*> stack;

    cin >> symbol;
    newNode->info.whichType = OPERATOR;
    newNode->info.operation = symbol;
    tree = newNode;
    cin >> symbol;
```

```
while (symbol != LAST_SYMBOL)
{
    lastNode = newNode;
    newNode = new TreeNode;
    if (!isalpha(symbol))
    {
        newNode->info.whichType = OPERATOR;
        newNode->info.operation = symbol;
    }
    else
    {
        newNode->info.whichType = OPERAND;
        newNode->info.operand = symbol;
        newNode->right = NULL;
        newNode->left = NULL;
    }
    switch (nextMove)
    {
        case LEFT    : lastNode->left = newNode;
                       stack.Push(lastNode);
                       break;
        case RIGHT   : stack.Pop(lastNode);
                       lastNode->right = newNode;
                       break;
    }
    if (newNode->info.whichType == OPERATOR)
        nextMove = LEFT;
    else
        nextMove = RIGHT;
    cin >> symbol;
}
}
```

Notice that the operands here are letters, and the operands in function `Eval` are integers. Here we are building an expression tree with, for example, variable names as operands; in function `Eval` we are evaluating an expression tree with constants as operands.

■ ∥ *A Nonlinked Representation of Binary Trees*

Our discussion of the implementation of binary trees has so far been limited to a scheme in which the pointers from parent to children are *explicit* in the data structure. A member was declared in each node for the pointer to the left child and the pointer to the right child.

A binary tree can be stored in an array in such a way that the relationships in the tree are not physically represented by link members, but are *implicit* in the algorithms that manipulate the tree stored in the array. The code is, of course, much less self-documenting, but we might save memory space because there are no pointers.

Let's take a binary tree and store it in an array in such a way that the parent-child relationships are not lost. We store the tree elements in the array, level by level, left-to-right. If the number of nodes in the tree is numElements, we can package the array and numElements into a struct as illustrated in Figure 9.9. The tree elements are stored with the root in tree.nodes[0] and the last node in tree.nodes[numElements-1].

To implement the algorithms that manipulate the tree, we must be able to find the left and right child of a node in the tree. Comparing the tree and the array in Figure 9.9, we see that

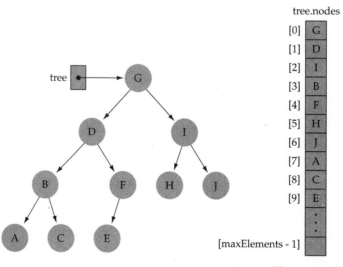

FIGURE 9.9   *A binary tree and its array representation.*

`tree.nodes[0]`'s children are in `tree.nodes[1]` and `tree.nodes[2]`.
`tree.nodes[1]`'s children are in `tree.nodes[3]` and `tree.nodes[4]`.
`tree.nodes[2]`'s children are in `tree.nodes[5]` and `tree.nodes[6]`.

Do you see the pattern? For any node `tree.nodes[index]`, its left child is in `tree.nodes[index * 2 + 1]` and its right child is in `tree.nodes[index * 2 + 2]` (provided that these child nodes exist). Notice that the nodes in the array from `tree.nodes[tree.numElements / 2]` to `tree.nodes[tree.numElements-1]` are leaf nodes.

Not only can we easily calculate the location of a node's children, we also can determine the location of its *parent* node. This task is not an easy one in a binary tree linked together with pointers from parent to child nodes, but it is very simple in our implicit link implementation: `tree.nodes[index]`'s parent is in `tree.nodes[(index-1)/2]`.

Because integer division truncates any remainder, `(index-1)/2` is the correct parent index for either a left or right child. Thus this implementation of a binary tree is linked in both directions: from parent to child, and from child to parent. We take advantage of this fact later in this chapter.

This tree representation works well for any binary tree that is full or complete. A **full binary tree** is a binary tree in which all of the leaves are on the same level and every nonleaf node has two children. The basic shape of a full binary tree is triangular:

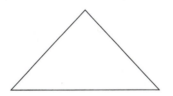

A **complete binary tree** is a binary tree that is either full or full through the next-to-last level, with the leaves on the last level as far to the left as possible. The shape of a complete binary tree is either triangular (if the tree is full) or something like the following:

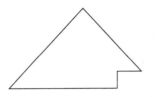

Full Binary Tree   A binary tree in which all of the leaves are on the same
level and every nonleaf node has two children

Complete Binary Tree   A binary tree that is either full or full through the
next-to-last level, with the leaves on the last level as far to the left as
possible

Figure 9.10 shows some examples of binary trees.

The array-based representation is simple to implement for trees that are full
or complete, because the elements occupy contiguous array slots. If a tree is not
full or complete, however, we must account for the gaps where nodes are
missing. To use the array representation, we must store a dummy value in those
positions in the array in order to maintain the proper parent-child relationship.
The choice of a dummy value depends on what information is stored in the
tree. For instance, if the elements in the tree are nonnegative integers, a negative
value can be stored in the dummy nodes.

Figure 9.11 illustrates a tree that is not complete and its corresponding array. Some of the array slots do not contain actual tree elements, however; they contain dummy values. The algorithms to manipulate the tree
must reflect this situation. For example, to determine whether the node
in `tree.nodes[index]` has a left child, you must check whether
`index * 2 + 1 < tree.numElements`, and then check to see if the value in
`tree.nodes[index * 2 + 1]` is the dummy value.

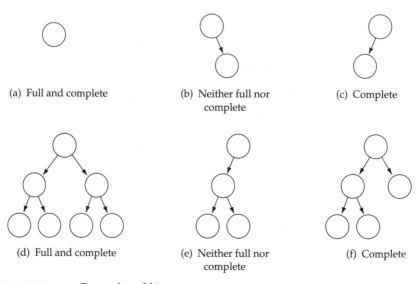

(a) Full and complete

(b) Neither full nor
complete

(c) Complete

(d) Full and complete

(e) Neither full nor
complete

(f) Complete

FIGURE 9.10   *Examples of binary trees.*

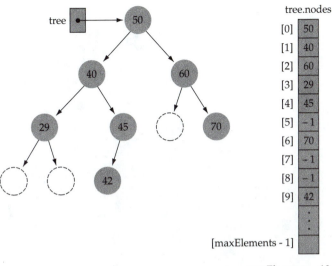

tree.numElements = 10

FIGURE 9.11   *A binary search tree stored in an array with dummy values.*

We have seen how an array can be used to represent a binary tree. We can also reverse this process, creating a binary tree from the elements in an array. In fact, we can regard *any* one-dimensional array as representing the nodes in a tree, but the data values that happen to be stored in it may not match this structure in a meaningful way.

Heaps

A **heap** is a binary tree that satisfies two properties, one concerning its shape and the other concerning the order of its elements. The *shape property* is simple: a heap must be a complete binary tree. The *order property* says that, for every node in the heap, the value stored in that node is greater than or equal to the value in each of its children. (The heap as a data structure is not to be confused with an unrelated concept of the same name. *Heap* is also a synonym for the free store—the area of memory available for dynamically allocated data.)

Heap   A complete binary tree, each of whose elements contains a value that is greater than or equal to the value of each of its children

---

Figure 9.12 shows two heaps that contain the letters 'A' through 'J'. Notice that the placement of the values differs in the two trees, but the shape is the same: a complete binary tree of ten elements. Note also that the two heaps have the same root node. A group of values can be stored in a binary tree in many

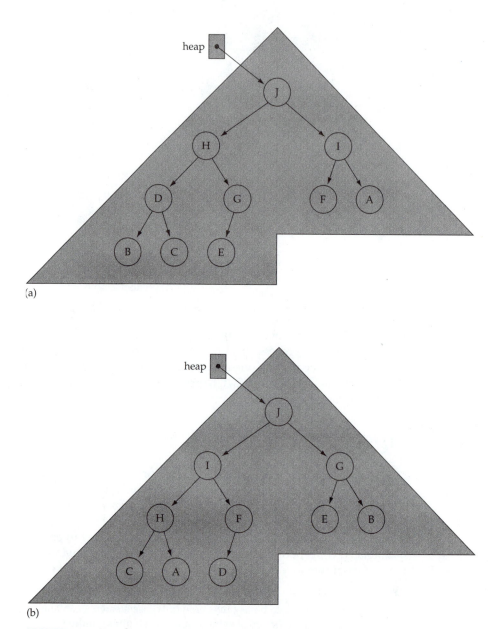

(a)

(b)

FIGURE 9.12 *Two heaps containing the letters 'A' through 'J'.*

ways and still satisfy the order property of heaps. Because of the shape property, we know that the shape of all the heaps with a given number of elements is the same. We also know, because of the order property, that the root node always contains the largest value in the heap. This fact gives us a hint as to what this data structure might be good for. The special feature of heaps is that we always know where the maximum value is: it is in the root node.

When we refer to a "heap" in this section, we are referring to the structure defined above. This might also be called a "maximum heap," because the root node contains the maximum value in the structure. It is also possible to create a "minimum heap," each of whose elements contains a value that is *less* than or equal to the value of each of its children.

Let's say that we want to remove the element with the largest value from a heap. The largest element is in the root node, so we can easily remove it, as illustrated in Figure 9.13(a). But this leaves a hole in the root position. Because the heap's tree must be complete, we decide to fill the hole with the bottom rightmost element from the heap; now the structure satisfies the shape property (Figure 9.13b). However, the replacement value came from the bottom of the tree, where the smaller values are; the tree no longer satisfies the order property of heaps.

This situation suggests one of the basic heap operations: given a complete binary tree whose elements satisfy the heap order property *except in the root position*, repair the structure so that it is again a heap. This operation, called *Reheap Down*, involves moving the element down from the root position until it ends up in a position where the order property is satisfied (see Figure 9.13c). ReheapDown has the following specification.

ReheapDown (heap, root, bottom)

Function:	Restores the order property of heaps to the tree between root and bottom.
Precondition:	The order property of heaps may be violated only by the root node of the tree.
Postcondition:	The order property applies to all elements of the heap.

We have tried to make this operation fairly general, by telling it where to find the root and the bottom rightmost element of the heap. Letting the root be a parameter, instead of just assuming that we start at the root of the whole heap, generalizes this routine, allowing us to perform the reheap operation on any subtree, as well as on the original heap.

Now let's say that we want to add an element to the heap—where do we put it? The shape property tells us that the tree must be complete, so we put the new element in the next bottom rightmost place in the tree, as illustrated in Figure 9.14(a). Now the shape property is satisfied, but the order property may be violated. This situation illustrates the need for another basic heap operation: given a complete binary tree containing N elements, whose first $N-1$ elements satisfy the order property of heaps, repair the structure so that it is again a heap. To fix this structure, we need to float the Nth element up in the tree until it is in its correct place (see Figure 9.14b). This operation is called *Reheap Up*. Here is the specification.

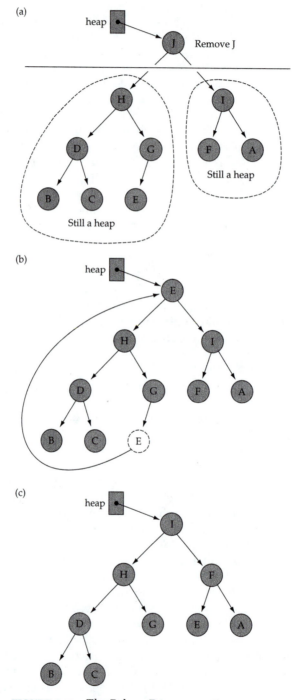

FIGURE 9.13 *The ReheapDown operation.*

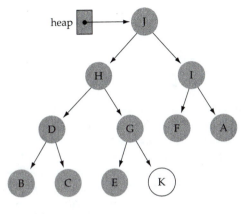

(a) Add K

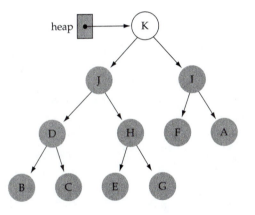

(b) ReheapUp

FIGURE 9.14   *The ReheapUp operation.*

■ **ReheapUp (heap, root, bottom)**

Function: Restores the order property to the heap between root and
                   bottom.
Preconditions: The order property is satisfied from the root of the heap
                   through the next-to-last node; the last (bottom) node may
                   violate the order property.
Postcondition: The order property applies to all the elements of the heap from
                   root through bottom.

Heap Implementation

Although we have graphically depicted heaps as binary trees with nodes and links, it would be very impractical to implement the heap operations using the usual linked-tree representation. The shape property of heaps tells us that the binary tree is complete, so we know that it never has any holes in it. Thus we can easily store the tree in an array with implicit links, as discussed earlier in this chapter. Figure 9.15 shows how the values in a heap would be stored in this array representation. If a heap with numElements elements is implemented this way, the shape property says that the heap elements are stored in numElements consecutive slots in the array, with the root element in the first slot (index 0) and the last leaf node in the slot with index numElements-1. The order property says that, for every nonleaf node heap.elements[index],

```
heap.elements[index] >= heap.elements[index * 2 + 1]
```

and, if there is a right child,

```
heap.elements[index] >= heap.elements[index * 2 + 2]
```

We use the following declarations to support this heap implementation.

```
template<class ItemType>
// Assumes ItemType is either a built-in simple type or a class
// with overloaded relational operators.
struct HeapType
{
    void ReheapDown(int root, int bottom);
    void ReheapUp(int root, int bottom);
    ItemType* elements;      // Array to be allocated dynamically
    int numElements;
};
```

This declaration is somewhat different from anything we have used so far. We are making HeapType a struct with member functions. Why not make it a class? Because heaps are seldom used alone. Like arrays, they are used as implementation structures for higher level classes. We define the functions that restore the heap property as part of the struct, but we also allow access to the data members. Common uses for a heap are to implement a Priority Queue ADT (discussed later in this chapter) and efficient sorting algorithms. Our algorithms are very general, with the positions of both the root and bottom elements passed as parameters. Additionally, we have chosen to include data member numElements to record the number of elements on the heap, although our example algorithms do not use it.

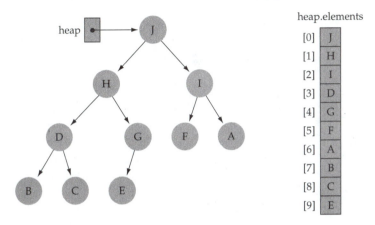

FIGURE 9.15 *Heap values in an array representation.*

We've specified the utility operations ReheapDown and ReheapUp to fix heaps that are "broken" at one end or the other. Now let's look at these operations in more detail.

When ReheapDown is first called, there are two possibilities. If the value in the root node (heap.elements[0]) is greater than or equal to the values in its children, the order property is still intact and we don't have to do anything. Otherwise we know that the maximum value of the tree is in either the root node's left child (heap.elements[1]) or the right child (heap.elements[2]). One of these values must be swapped with the smaller value in the root. Now the subtree rooted at the node that is swapped is a heap—except (possibly) for *its* root node. We apply the same process again, asking whether the value in this node is greater than or equal to the values in its children. We test smaller and smaller subtrees of the original heap, moving our original root node down until (1) the root of the current subtree is a leaf node, or (2) the value in the root of the current subtree is greater than or equal to the values in both its children.

The algorithm for this function is given here and illustrated with an example in Figure 9.16. At the start, root is the index of the node that (possibly) violates the heap order property.

ReheapDown(root, bottom)

IF elements[root] is not a leaf
    Set maxChild to index of child with larger value
    IF elements[root] < elements[maxChild]
        Swap(elements[root] , elements[maxChild])
        ReheapDown(maxChild, bottom)

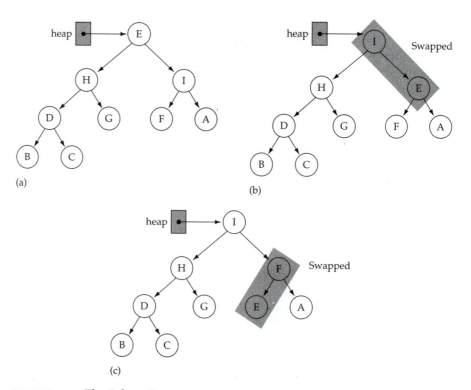

FIGURE 9.16   *The ReheapDown operation.*

maxChild to its index. Otherwise we compare the values in the two child nodes and set maxChild to the index of the node that has the larger value.

The whole function is shown in the following code. It uses a utility function, Swap, which swaps the values of its two parameters. (Because this function is trivial, we do not show its implementation here.)

```
template<class ItemType>
void HeapType<ItemType>::ReheapDown(int root, int bottom)
// Post: Heap property is restored.
{
    int maxChild;
    int rightChild;
    int leftChild;

    leftChild = root*2+1;
    rightChild = root*2+2;
    if (leftChild <= bottom)
    {
        if (leftChild == bottom)
```

```
                maxChild = leftChild;
        else
        {
            if (elements[leftChild] <= elements[rightChild])
                maxChild = rightChild;
            else
                maxChild = leftChild;
        }
        if (elements[root] < elements[maxChild])
        {
            Swap(elements[root], elements[maxChild]);
            ReheapDown(maxChild, bottom);
        }
    }
}
```

The converse operation, `ReheapUp`, takes a leaf node that violates the order property of heaps and moves it up until its correct position is found. We compare the value in the bottom node with the value in its parent node. If the parent's value is smaller, the order property is violated, so the two nodes are swapped. Then we examine the parent, repeating the process until (1) the current node is the root of the heap, or (2) the value in the current node is less than or equal to the value in its parent node. The algorithm for this function is given below and illustrated in Figure 9.17.

ReheapUp(root, bottom)

IF bottom > root
    Set parent to index of parent of bottom node
    IF elements[parent] < elements[bottom]
        Swap(elements[parent], elements[bottom])
        ReheapUp(root, parent)

This is also a recursive algorithm. In the general case, we swap the (current) "bottom" node with its parent and reinvoke the function. On the recursive call, we specify `parent` as the bottom node; this shrinks the size of the tree still to be processed, so the smaller-caller question can be answered affirmatively. There are two base cases: (1) if we have reached the root node, or (2) if the heap order property is satisfied. In either of these cases, we exit the function without doing anything.

How do we find the parent node? This is not an easy task in a binary tree

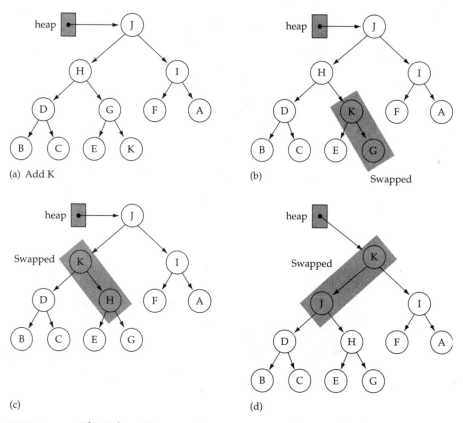

FIGURE 9.17   *The ReheapUp operation.*

linked together with pointers from parent to child nodes, but, as we saw earlier, it is very simple in our implicit link implementation:

```
parent = (index-1) / 2;
```

We can now code the whole function:

```
template<class ItemType>
void HeapType<ItemType>::ReheapUp(int root, int bottom)
// Post: Heap property is restored.
{
    int parent;

    if (bottom > root)
    {
        parent = (bottom-1) / 2;
        if (elements[parent] < elements[bottom])
        {
```

```
            Swap(elements[parent], elements[bottom]);
            ReheapUp(root, parent);
        }
    }
}
```

Application Level

In discussing FIFO queue applications in Chapter 4, we said that the operating system of a multiuser computer system may use job queues to save users' requests in the order in which they are made. Another way such requests may be handled is according to how important the job request is. That is, the head of the company might get higher priority than the lowly junior programmer. Or an interactive program might get higher priority than a job to print out a report that isn't needed until the next day. To handle these requests efficiently, the operating system may use a structure called a *priority queue*. Because a heap gives us fast access to the largest (or highest-priority) element in the structure, it is a good way to implement a priority queue. We look at this structure in detail in the next section.

Heaps are also useful in sorting. It's easy to imagine how heaps relate to sorting an array if you consider a simple sorting technique that makes repeated searches through the array to locate the next-largest value and move it into its correct place. With heaps, we always know where to find the largest value. We look more at how heaps can be used in sorting in Chapter 10.

■|| *ADT Priority Queue*

Logical Level

A priority queue is an abstract data type with an interesting accessing protocol. Only the *highest-priority* element can be accessed. "Highest priority" can mean different things, depending on the application. Consider, for example, a small company with one secretary. When the other employees leave work on the secretary's desk, which jobs get done first? The jobs are processed in order of the employee's importance in the company; the secretary completes the president's work before starting the vice-president's, and does the marketing director's work before staff programmers'. The *priority* of each job relates to the level of the employee who initiated it.

In a telephone answering system, calls are answered in the order that they are received; that is, the highest-priority call is the one that has been waiting the longest. Thus a FIFO queue can be considered a priority queue whose highest-priority element is the one that has been queued the longest time.

The operations defined for the Priority Queue ADT include functions to enqueue items and dequeue items, as well as functions to test for an empty or full priority queue. These operations are very similar to those specified for the FIFO queue discussed in Chapter 4. The Enqueue operation adds a given element to the priority queue. The Dequeue operation removes the highest-priority element from the priority queue and returns it to the user.

■ Priority Queue ADT Specification

Structure: The Priority Queue is arranged to support access to the highest priority item.

Operations:

Assumption: Before any call is made to a priority queue operation, the queue has been declared and a constructor has been applied.

MakeEmpty
   Function: Initializes the queue to an empty state.
   Postcondition: Queue is empty.

Boolean IsEmpty
   Function: Tests whether the queue is empty.
   Postcondition: Function value = (queue is empty)

Boolean IsFull
   Function: Tests whether the queue is full.
   Postcondition: Function value = (queue is full)

Enqueue(ItemType newItem)
   Function: Adds newItem to the queue.
   Precondition: Queue is not full.
   Postcondition: newItem is in the queue.

Dequeue(ItemType& item)
   Function: Removes element with highest priority and returns it in item.
   Precondition: Queue is not empty.
   Postconditions: Highest priority element has been removed from queue. item is a copy of removed element.

Implementation Level

There are many ways to implement a priority queue. In any implementation, we want to be able to access the element with the highest priority quickly and easily. For instance, we can keep the elements in a linked list sorted from largest (highest-priority) element to smallest (lowest-priority) element, or in a binary search tree. We discuss these implementations more at the end of this section.

A heap is an excellent way to implement a priority queue. Here is how we declare our PQType class.

```
template<class ItemType>
class PQType
{
public:
    PQType(int);
    ~PQType();
    void MakeEmpty();
    bool IsEmpty() const;
    bool IsFull() const;
    void Enqueue(ItemType newItem);
    void Dequeue(ItemType& item);
private:
    int numItems;
    HeapType<ItemType> items;
    int maxItems;
};

template<class ItemType>
PQType<ItemType>::PQType(int max)
{
    maxItems = max;
    items.elements = new ItemType[max];
    numItems = 0;
}

template<class ItemType>
void PQType<ItemType::MakeEmpty()
{
    numItems = 0;
}

template<class ItemType>
PQType<ItemType>::~PQType()
{
    delete [] items.elements;
}
```

We keep the number of elements in a priority queue in data member numItems. Using the heap implementation described earlier, the elements are stored in the first numItems slots of array items.elements. Because of the order property, we know that the largest element is in the root—that is, in the first array slot (index 0).

Let's look first at the `Dequeue` operation. The root element is returned to the caller. After we remove the root, we are left with two subtrees, each of which satisfies the heap property. Of course, we cannot leave a hole in the root position, for that violates the shape property. Because we have removed an element, there are now `numItems - 1` elements left in the priority queue, stored in array slots 1 through `numItems - 1`. If we fill the hole in the root position with the bottom element, array slots 0 through `numItems - 2` contain the heap elements. The heap shape property is now intact, but the order property may be violated. The resulting structure is not a heap, but it is almost a heap—all of the nodes *except the root node* satisfy the order property. This is an easy problem to correct, for we have a heap operation to do exactly this task: `ReheapDown`. Here is our algorithm for `Dequeue`.

Dequeue

```
Set item to root element from queue
Move last leaf element into root position
Decrement numItems
items.ReheapDown(0, numItems-1)
```

The `Enqueue` operation involves adding an element in its "appropriate" place in the heap. Where is this place? If the new element's priority is larger than the current root element's priority, we know that the new element belongs in the root. But that's not the typical case; we want a more general solution. To start, we can put the new element at the bottom of the heap, in the next available leaf position (review Figure 9.14). Now the array contains elements in the first `numItems + 1` slots, preserving the heap shape property. The resulting structure is probably not a heap, but it's *almost* a heap—the order property is violated in the last leaf position. This problem is easy to solve using the `ReheapUp` operation. Here is our algorithm for `Enqueue`.

Enqueue

```
Increment numItems
Put newItem in next available position
items.ReheapUp(0, numItems-1)
```

```
template<class ItemType>
void PQType<ItemType>::Dequeue(ItemType& item)
// Post: element with highest priority has been removed
//       from the queue; a copy is returned in item.
{
    item = items.elements[0];
    items.elements[0] = items.elements[numItems-1];
    numItems--;
    items.ReheapDown(0, numItems-1);
}


template<class ItemType>
void PQType<ItemType>::Enqueue(ItemType newItem)
// Post: newItem is in the queue.
{
    numItems++;
    items.elements[numItems-1] = newItem;
    items.ReheapUp(0, numItems-1);
}



template<class ItemType>
bool PQType<ItemType>::IsFull() const
// Post: Function value = true if the queue is full;
//       false, otherwise
{
    return numItems == maxItems;
}

template<class ItemType>
bool PQType<ItemType>::IsEmpty() const
// Post: Function value = true if the queue is empty;
//       false, otherwise
{
    return numItems == 0;
}
```

Heaps vs. Other Representations of Priority Queues

How efficient is the heap implementation of a priority queue? The MakeEmpty, IsEmpty, and IsFull operations are trivial, so we only examine the operations to add and remove elements. Enqueue puts the new element into the next free leaf node in the heap. This array position can be accessed directly, so this part of the operation has O(1). ReheapUp is then invoked to correct the order. This operation moves the new element up the tree, level by level; because a complete tree is of minimum height, there are at most $\log_2 N$ levels above the new element (N = numItems). So Enqueue is an $O(\log_2 N)$ operation. Dequeue removes the element in the root node and replaces it with the bottom rightmost leaf node. Both of these elements in the array can be accessed directly, so this part of the operation has $O(1)$. Then ReheapDown is invoked to correct the order. This operation moves the root element down in the tree, level by level. There are at most $\log_2 N$ levels below the root; therefore Dequeue is also an $O(\log_2 N)$ operation.

How does this implementation compare to the others we mentioned earlier in this section? If we implement the priority queue with a linked list, sorted from largest to smallest priority, Dequeue merely removes the first node from the list—an $O(1)$ operation. Enqueue, however, must search up to all the elements in the list to find the appropriate insertion place; thus it is an $O(N)$ operation.

If the priority queue is implemented using a binary search tree, the efficiency of the operations depends on the shape of the tree. When the tree is bushy, both Dequeue and Enqueue are $O(\log_2 N)$ operations. In the worst case, if the tree degenerates to a linked list, sorted from smallest to largest priority, both Enqueue and Dequeue have $O(N)$. Table 9.1 summarizes the efficiency of the different implementations.

TABLE 9.1   Comparison of Priority Queue Implementations

	Enqueue	Dequeue
Heap	$O(\log_2 N)$	$O(\log_2 N)$
Linked List	$O(N)$	$O(1)$
Binary Search Tree		
Balanced	$O(\log_2 N)$	$O(\log_2 N)$
Skewed	$O(N)$	$O(N)$

Overall, the binary search tree looks good, if it is balanced. It can, however, become skewed, which reduces the efficiency of the operations. The heap, on the other hand, is always a tree of minimum height. The heap is not a good structure for accessing a randomly selected element, but that is not one of the operations defined for priority queues. The accessing protocol of a priority queue specifies that only the largest (or highest-priority) element can be accessed. The linked list is excellent for this operation (assuming the list is sorted from largest to smallest), but we may have to search the whole list to find the place to add a new element. For the operations specified for priority queues, therefore, the heap is an excellent choice.

▪▎ *Graphs*

Logical Level

Binary trees provide a very useful way of representing relationships in which a hierarchy exists. That is, a node is pointed to by at most one other node (its parent), and each node points to at most two other nodes (its children). If we remove the restriction that each node can have at most two children, we have a general tree, as pictured here.

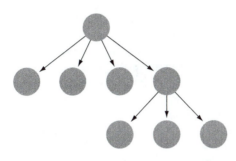

If we also remove the restriction that each node may have only one parent node, we have a data structure called a **graph**. A graph is made up of a set of nodes called **vertices** and a set of lines called **edges** (or **arcs**) that connect the nodes.

Graph   A data structure that consists of a set of nodes and a set of edges that relate the nodes to each other

Vertex   A node in a graph

Edge (Arc)   A pair of vertices representing a connection between two nodes in a graph

---

The set of edges describes relationships among the vertices. For instance, if the vertices are the names of cities, the edges that link the vertices could represent roads between pairs of cities. Because the road that runs between Houston and Austin also runs between Austin and Houston, the edges in this graph have no direction. This is called an **undirected graph**. However, if the edges that link the vertices represent flights from one city to another, the direction of each edge *is* important. The existence of a flight (edge) from Houston to Austin does not assure the existence of a flight from Austin to

Houston. A graph whose edges are directed from one vertex to another is called a **directed graph**, or **digraph**.

Undirected Graph   A graph in which the edges have no direction

Directed Graph (Digraph)   A graph in which each edge is directed from one vertex to another (or the same) vertex.

From a programmer's perspective, vertices represent whatever is the subject of our study: people, houses, cities, courses, and so on. However, mathematically, vertices are the undefined concept upon which graph theory rests. In fact, there is a great deal of formal mathematics associated with graphs. In other computing courses, you will probably analyze graphs and prove theorems about them. This textbook introduces the graph as an abstract data type, teaches some basic terminology, discusses how a graph might be implemented, and describes how algorithms that manipulate graphs make use of stacks, queues, and priority queues.

Formally, a graph G is defined as follows:

$$G = (V, E)$$

where

V(G) is a finite, nonempty set of vertices
E(G) is a set of edges (written as pairs of vertices)

The set of vertices is specified by listing them in set notation, within { } braces. The following set defines the four vertices of the graph pictured in Figure 9.18(a):

V(Graph1) = {A, B, C, D}

The set of edges is specified by listing a sequence of edges. Each edge is denoted by writing the names of the two vertices it connects in parentheses, with a comma between them. For instance, the vertices in Graph1 in Figure 9.18(a) are connected by the four edges described below:

E(Graph1) = {(A, B), (A, D), (B, C), (B, D)}

Because Graph1 is an undirected graph, the order of the vertices in each edge is unimportant. The set of edges in Graph1 can also be described as follows:

(a) Graph1 is an undirected graph.

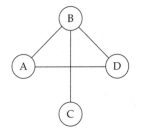

V(Graph1) = { A, B, C, D }
E(Graph1) = { (A, B), (A, D), (B, C), (B, D) }

(b) Graph2 is a directed graph.

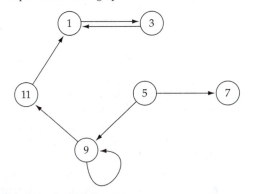

V(Graph2) = { 1, 3, 5, 7, 9, 11 }
E(Graph2) = { (1, 3), (3, 1), (5, 7), (5, 9), (9, 11), (9, 9), (11, 1) }

(c) Graph3 is a directed graph.

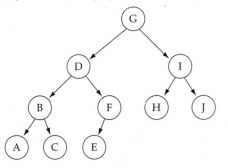

V(Graph3) = { A, B, C, D, E, F, G, H, I, J }
E(Graph3) = { (G, D), (G, J), (D, B), (D, F) (I, H), (I, J), (B, A), (B, C), (F, E) }

FIGURE 9.18 *Some examples of graphs.*

E(Graph1) = {(B, A), (D, A), (C, B), (D, B)}

If the graph is a digraph, the direction of the edge is indicated by which vertex is listed first. For instance, in Figure 9.18(b), the edge (5, 7) represents a link from vertex 5 to vertex 7. However, there is no corresponding edge (7, 5) in Graph2. Note that in pictures of digraphs, the arrows indicate the direction of the relationship.

If two vertices in a graph are connected by an edge, they are said to be **adjacent**. In Graph1 (Figure 9.18a), vertices A and B are adjacent, but vertices A and C are not. If the vertices are connected by a directed edge, then the first vertex is said to be *adjacent to* the second, and the second vertex is said to be *adjacent from* the first. For example, in Graph2 (in Figure 9.18b), vertex 5 is adjacent to vertices 7 and 9, while vertex 1 is adjacent from vertices 3 and 11.

Adjacent Nodes   Two nodes in a graph that are connected by an edge

---

The picture of Graph3 in Figure 9.18(c) may look familiar; it is the tree we looked at earlier in connection with the nonlinked representation of a binary tree. A tree is a special case of a directed graph, in which each vertex may only be adjacent from one other vertex (its parent node) and one vertex (the root) is not adjacent from any other vertex.

A **path** from one vertex to another consists of a sequence of vertices that connect them. For a path to exist, there must be an uninterrupted sequence of edges from the first vertex, through any number of vertices, to the second vertex. For example, in Graph2, there is a path from vertex 5 to vertex 3, but not from vertex 3 to vertex 5. Note that in a tree, such as Graph3 (Figure 9.18c), there is a unique path from the root to every other node in the tree.

Path   A sequence of vertices that connects two nodes in a graph

---

A **complete graph** is one in which every vertex is adjacent to every other vertex. Figure 9.19 shows two complete graphs. If there are N vertices, there are $N * (N - 1)$ edges in a complete directed graph and $N * (N - 1) / 2$ edges in a complete undirected graph.

Complete Graph   A graph in which every vertex is directly connected to every other vertex

---

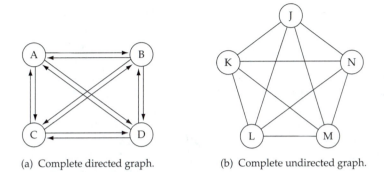

(a) Complete directed graph.　　(b) Complete undirected graph.

FIGURE 9.19 *Two complete graphs.*

A **weighted graph** is a graph in which each edge carries a value. Weighted graphs can be used to represent applications in which the *value* of the connection between the vertices is important, not just the *existence* of a connection. For instance, in the weighted graph pictured in Figure 9.20, the vertices represent cities and the edges indicate the Air Busters Airlines flights that connect the cities. The weights attached to the edges represent the air distances between pairs of cities.

Weighted Graph A graph in which each edge carries a value

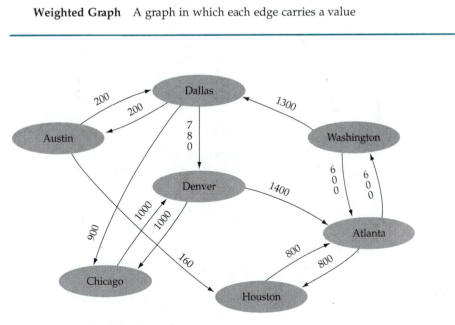

FIGURE 9.20 *A weighted graph.*

To see whether we can get from Denver to Washington, we look for a path between them. If the total travel distance is determined by the sum of the distances between each pair of cities along the way, we can calculate the travel distance by adding the weights attached to the edges that constitute the path between them. Note that there may be multiple paths between two vertices. Later in this chapter, we talk about a way to find the shortest path between two vertices.

We have described a graph at the abstract level as a set of vertices and a set of edges that connect some or all of the vertices one to another. What kind of operations are defined on a graph? In this chapter we specify and implement a small set of useful graph operations. Many other operations on graphs can be defined; we have chosen operations that are useful in the graph applications described later in the chapter. Here is the specification for the ADT Graph.

■ | **Graph ADT Specification**

Structure:	The graph consists of a set of vertices and a set of weighted edges that connect some or all of the vertices.

Operations:

Assumption:	Before any call is made to a graph operation, the graph has been declared and a constructor has been applied.

MakeEmpty
Function:	Initializes the graph to an empty state.
Postcondition:	Graph is empty.

Boolean IsEmpty
Function:	Tests whether the graph is empty.
Postcondition:	Function value = (graph is empty)

Boolean IsFull
Function:	Tests whether the graph is full.
Postcondition:	Function value = (graph is full)

AddVertex(VertexType vertex)
Function:	Adds vertex to the graph.
Precondition:	Graph is not full.
Postcondition:	vertex is in V(graph).

AddEdge(VertexType fromVertex, VertexType toVertex, EdgeValueType weight)
Function:	Adds an edge with the specified weight from fromVertex to toVertex.
Precondition:	fromVertex and toVertex are in V(graph).

Postcondition: (fromVertex, toVertex) is in E(graph) with the specified weight.

EdgeValueType WeightIs(VertexType fromVertex, VertexType toVertex)
Function: Determines the weight of the edge from fromVertex to toVertex.
Precondition: fromVertex and toVertex are in V(graph).
Postcondition: Function value = weight of edge from fromVertex to toVertex, if edge exists. If edge does not exist, function value = special "null-edge" value.

GetToVertices(VertexType vertex, QueType& vertexQ)
Function: Returns a queue of the vertices that are adjacent from vertex.
Precondition: vertex is in V(graph).
Postcondition: vertexQ contains the names of all the vertices that are adjacent from vertex.

Application Level

The Graph specification given in the last section included only the most basic operations. It did not include any traversal operations. As you might imagine, there are many different orders in which we can traverse a graph. As a result, we consider a traversal a graph application rather than an innate operation. The basic operations given in our specification allow us to implement different traversals *independent* of how the graph itself is actually implemented.

In Chapter 8, we discussed the postorder tree traversal, which goes to the deepest level of the tree and works up. This strategy of going down a branch to its deepest point and moving up is called a *depth-first* strategy. Another systematic way to visit each vertex in a tree is to visit each vertex on level 0 (the root), then each vertex on level 1, then each vertex on level 2, and so on. Visiting each vertex by level in this way is called a *breadth-first* strategy. With graphs, both depth-first and breadth-first strategies are useful. We outline both algorithms within the context of the airline example.

Depth-First Searching   One question we can answer with the graph in Figure 9.20 is "Can I get from city X to city Y on my favorite airline?" This is equivalent to asking "Does a path exist in the graph from vertex X to vertex Y?" Using a depth-first strategy, let's develop an algorithm that finds a path from startVertex to endVertex.

We need a systematic way to keep track of the cities as we investigate them. With a depth-first search, we examine the first vertex that is adjacent from startVertex; if this is endVertex, the search is over. Otherwise, we examine all the vertices that can be reached in one step (are adjacent from) this vertex. Meanwhile, we need to store the other vertices that are adjacent from `startVertex`. If a path does not exist from the first vertex, we come back and try the second, third, and so on. Because we want to travel as far as we can down one path, backtracking if the `endVertex` is not found, a stack is a good structure for storing the vertices. Here is the algorithm we use:

DepthFirstSearch

```
Set found to false
stack.Push(startVertex)
DO
      stack.Pop(vertex)
      IF vertex = endVertex
            Write final vertex
            Set found to true
      ELSE
            Write this vertex
            Push all adjacent vertices onto stack
WHILE !stack.IsEmpty() AND !found
IF (!found)
      Write "Path does not exist"
```

Let's apply this algorithm to the sample airline-route graph in Figure 9.20. We want to fly from Austin to Washington. We initialize our search by pushing our starting city onto the stack (Figure 9.21a). At the beginning of the loop we pop the current city, Austin, from the stack. The places we can reach directly from Austin are Dallas and Houston; we push both these vertices onto the stack (Figure 9.21b). At the beginning of the second iteration we pop the top vertex from the stack—Houston. Houston is not our destination, so we resume our search from there. There is only one flight out of Houston, to Atlanta; we push

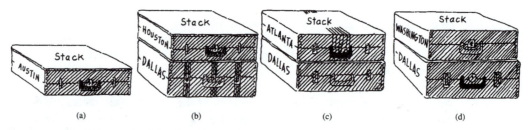

    (a)   (b)   (c)   (d)

FIGURE 9.21   *Using a stack to store the routes.*

Atlanta onto the stack (Figure 9.21c). Again we pop the top vertex from the stack. Atlanta is not our destination, so we continue searching from there. Atlanta has flights to two cities: Houston and Washington.

But we just came from Houston! We don't want to fly back to cities that we have already visited; this could cause an infinite loop. We have to take care of cycling in this algorithm. We must mark a city as having been visited so that it is not investigated a second time. Let's assume that we have marked the cities that have already been tried, and continue our example. Houston has already been visited, so we ignore it. The second adjacent vertex, Washington, has not been visited so we push it onto the stack (Figure 9.21d). Again we pop the top vertex from the stack. Washington is our destination, so the search is complete. The path from Austin to Washington, using a depth-first search, is illustrated in Figure 9.22.

This search is called a depth-first search because we go to the deepest branch, examining all the paths beginning at Houston before we come back to search from Dallas. When you have to backtrack, you take the branch closest to where you dead-ended. That is, you go as far as you can down one path before you take alternative choices at earlier branches.

Before we look at the source code of the depth-first search algorithm, let's talk a little more about "marking" vertices on the graph. Before we begin the search, any marks in the vertices must be cleared to indicate they are not yet visited. Let's call this function `ClearMarks`. As we visit each vertex during the search, we mark it. Let's call this function `MarkVertex`. Before we process each vertex we can ask, "Have we visited this vertex before?" The answer to this question is returned by function `IsMarked`. If we have already visited this vertex, we ignore it and go on. We must add these three functions to the specifications of the Graph ADT.

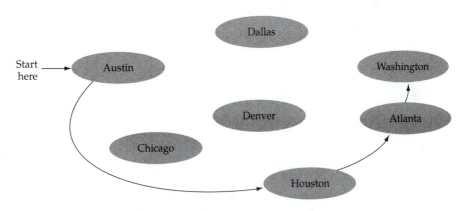

FIGURE 9.22   *The depth-first search.*

ClearMarks
Function:	Sets marks for all vertices to false.
Postcondition:	All marks have been set to false.

MarkVertex(VertexType vertex)
Function:	Sets mark for vertex to true.
Precondition:	vertex is in V(graph).
Postcondition:	IsMarked(vertex) is true.

Boolean IsMarked(VertexType vertex)
Function:	Determines if vertex has been marked.
Precondition:	vertex is in V(graph)
Postcondition:	Function value = (vertex is marked true)

Function `DepthFirstSearch` receives a graph object, a starting vertex, and a target vertex. It uses the depth-first strategy to determine if there is a path from the starting city to the ending city, displaying the names of all the cities visited in the search. Note that there is nothing in the function that depends on the implementation of the graph. The function is implemented as a graph application; it uses the Graph ADT operations (including the mark operations), without knowing how the graph is represented. In the following function, we assume that the header files for `StackType` and `QueType` have been included. We also assume that `VertexType` is a type for which the "==" and the "<<" operators are defined.

```
template<class VertexType>
void DepthFirstSearch(GraphType<VertexType> graph,
    VertexType startVertex, VertexType endVertex)
// Assumes VertexType is a type for which the ''=='' and ''<<''
// operators are defined.
{
    StackType<VertexType> stack;
    QueType<VertexType> vertexQ;

    bool found = false;
    VertexType vertex;
    VertexType item;

    graph.ClearMarks();
    stack.Push(startVertex);

    do
    {
        stack.Pop(vertex);
        if (vertex == endVertex)
```

```
        {
            cout << vertex;
            found = true;
        }
        else
        {
            if (!graph.IsMarked(vertex))
            {
                graph.MarkVertex(vertex);
                cout << vertex;
                graph.GetToVertices(vertex, vertexQ);

                while (!vertexQ.IsEmpty())
                {
                    vertexQ.Dequeue(item);
                    if (!graph.IsMarked(item))
                        stack.Push(item);
                }
            }
        }
    } while (!stack.IsEmpty() && !found);
    if (!found)
        cout << "Path not found." << endl;
}
```

Breadth-First Searching   A breadth-first search looks at all possible paths at the same depth before it goes to a deeper level. In our flight example, a breadth-first search checks all possible one-stop connections before checking two-stop connections. Most travelers prefer this approach for booking flights.

When we come to a dead end in a depth-first search, we back up as *little* as possible. We try another route from a recent vertex—the route on top of our stack. In a breadth-first search, we want to back up as *far* as possible to find a route originating from the earliest vertices. The stack is not the right structure for finding an early route. It keeps track of things in the order opposite of their occurrence—the latest route is on top. To keep track of things in the order in which they happened, we use a FIFO queue. The route at the front of the queue is a route from an earlier vertex; the route at the back of the queue is from a later vertex.

To modify the search to use a breadth-first strategy, we change all the calls to stack operations to the analogous FIFO queue operations. Searching for a path from Austin to Washington, we first enqueue all the cities that can be reached directly from Austin: Dallas and Houston (Figure 9.23a). Then we dequeue the front queue element. Dallas is not the destination we seek, so we enqueue all the adjacent cities that have not yet been visited: Chicago and Denver (Figure 9.23b). (Austin has been visited already, so it is not enqueued.) Again we dequeue the front element from the queue. This element is the other

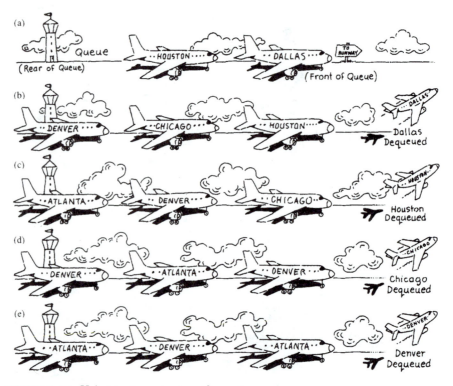

FIGURE 9.23   *Using a queue to store the routes.*

"one-stop" city, Houston. Houston is not the desired destination, so we continue the search. There is only one flight out of Houston, and it is to Atlanta. Because we haven't visited Atlanta before, it is enqueued (Figure 9.23c).

Now we know that we cannot reach Washington with one stop, so we start examining the two-stop connections. We dequeue Chicago; this is not our destination, so we put its adjacent city, Denver, into the queue (Figure 9.23d). Now this is an interesting situation: Denver is in the queue twice. Should we mark a city as having been visited when we put it in the queue or after it has been dequeued, when we are examining its outgoing flights? If we mark it only after it is dequeued, there may be multiple copies of the same vertex in the queue (so we need to check to see if a city is marked *after* it is dequeued).

An alternative approach is to mark the city as having been visited before it is put into the queue. Which is better? It depends on the processing. You may want to know whether there are alternative routes, in which case you would want to put a city into the queue more than once.

Back to our example. We have put Denver into the queue in one step and removed its previous entry at the next step. Denver is not our destination, so we put its adjacent cities that we haven't already marked (only Atlanta) into the

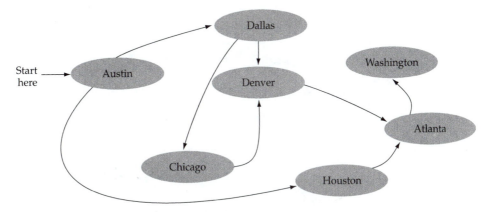

FIGURE 9.24 *The breadth-first search.*

queue (Figure 9.23e). This processing continues until Washington is put into the queue (from Atlanta), and is finally dequeued. We have found the desired city, and the search is complete. This search is illustrated in Figure 9.24.

The source code for the `BreadthFirstSearch` function is identical to the depth-first search, except for the replacement of the stack with a FIFO queue.

```
template<class VertexType>
void BreadthFirstSearch(GraphType<VertexType> graph,
    VertexType startVertex, VertexType endVertex)
// Assumes VertexType is a type for which the "==" and "<<"
// operators are defined.
{
    QueType<VertexType> queue;
    QueType<VertexType> vertexQ;

    bool found = false;
    VertexType vertex;
    VertexType item;

    graph.ClearMarks();
    queue.Enqueue(startVertex);

    do
    {
        queue.Dequeue(vertex);
        if (vertex == endVertex)
        {
            cout << vertex;
            found = true;
        }
        else
```

```
    {
        if (!graph.IsMarked(vertex))
        {
            graph.MarkVertex(vertex);
            cout << vertex;
            graph.GetToVertices(vertex, vertexQ);

            while (!vertexQ.IsEmpty())
            {
                vertexQ.Dequeue(item);
                if (!graph.IsMarked(item))
                    queue.Enqueue(item);
            }
        }
    }
} while (!queue.IsEmpty() && !found);
if (!found)
    cout << "Path not found." << endl;
}
```

The Single-Source Shortest-Paths Problem We know from the two search operations just discussed that there may be multiple paths from one vertex to another. Suppose that we want to find the *shortest path* from Austin to each of the other cities that Air Busters serves. By "shortest path" we mean the path whose edge values (weights), added together, have the smallest sum. Consider the following two paths from Austin to Washington:

Austin			Austin		
	160 miles			200 miles	
Houston			Dallas		
	800 miles			780 miles	
Atlanta			Denver		
	600 miles			1400 miles	
Washington			Atlanta		
				600 miles	
			Washington		
Total miles	1560 miles		Total miles	2980 miles	

Clearly the first path is preferable, unless you want to collect frequent-flyer miles.

Let's develop an algorithm that displays the shortest path from a designated starting city to *every other city* in the graph—this time we are not searching for a path between a starting city and an ending city. As in the two graph searches described earlier, we need an auxiliary structure for storing cities that we process later. By retrieving the city that was most recently put into the structure, the depth-first search tries to keep going "forward." It tries a one-flight solution, then a two-flight solution, then a three-flight solution, and so on. It backtracks to a fewer-flight solution only when it reaches a dead end. By retrieving the city that had been in the structure the longest time, the breadth-first search tries all one-flight solutions, then all two-flight solutions and so on. The breadth-first search finds a path with a minimum number of flights.

But a minimum *number* of flights does not necessarily mean the minimum total distance. Unlike the depth-first and breadth-first searches, this shortest-path traversal must use the number of miles (edge weights) between cities. We want to retrieve the vertex that is *closest* to the current vertex—that is, the vertex connected with the minimum edge weight. If we consider minimum distance to be the highest priority, then we know of a perfect structure—the priority queue. Our algorithm can use a priority queue whose elements are flights (edges) with the distance from the starting city as the priority. That is, the items on the priority queue are struct variables with three data members: `fromVertex`, `toVertex`, and `distance`.

ShortestPaths

```
graph.ClearMarks()
Set item.fromVertex to startVertex
Set item.toVertex to startVertex
Set item.distance to 0
pq.Enqueue(item)

DO
    pq.Dequeue(item)
    IF item.toVertex is not marked
        Mark item.toVertex
        Write item.fromVertex, item.toVertex, item.distance
        Set item.fromVertex to item.toVertex
        Set minDistance to item.distance
        Get queue vertexQ of vertices adjacent from item.fromVertex
        WHILE more vertices in vertexQ
            Get next vertex from vertexQ
            IF vertex not marked
                Set item.toVertex to vertex
                Set item.distance to minDistance +
                    graph.WeightIs( fromVertex, vertex)
                pq.Enqueue(item)
WHILE !pq.IsEmpty()
```

The algorithm for the shortest-path traversal is similar to those we used for the depth-first and breadth-first searches, but there are two major differences:

1. We use a priority queue rather than a FIFO queue or stack.
2. We stop only when there are no more cities to process; there is no destination.

Here is the source code for the shortest-path algorithm. This code assumes that the header files for `QueType` and `PQType` have been included. Notice that `ItemType` (the type of the items to be placed into the priority queue) must overload the relational operators such that a smaller distance indicates a *higher* priority. As a result, the priority queue is implemented with a *minimum heap*, as described earlier in this chapter. That is, for every item in the heap, `item.distance` is less than or equal to the `distance` member of each of its children.

```
template<class VertexType>
struct ItemType
{
    bool operator<(ItemType otherItem);
    // < means greater distance
    bool operator==(ItemType otherItem);
    bool operator<=(ItemType otherItem);
    VertexType fromVertex;
    VertexType toVertex;
    int distance;
};

template<class VertexType>
void ShortestPath(GraphType<VertexType> graph,
    VertexType startVertex)
{
    ItemType item;
    int minDistance;
    PQType<ItemType> pq(10);      // Assume at most 10 vertices
    QueType<VertexType> vertexQ;
    VertexType vertex;

    graph.ClearMarks();
    item.fromVertex = startVertex;
    item.toVertex = startVertex;
    item.distance = 0;
    pq.Enqueue(item);
    cout  << "Last Vertex    Destination   Distance" << endl;
    cout  << "-----------------------------------------" << endl;

    do
    {
```

```
    pq.Dequeue(item);
    if (!graph.IsMarked(item.toVertex))
    {
        graph.MarkVertex(item.toVertex);
        cout << item.fromVertex;
        cout << "   ";
        cout << item.toVertex;
        cout << "   " << item.distance << endl;
        item.fromVertex = item.toVertex;
        minDistance = item.distance;
        graph.GetToVertices(item.fromVertex, vertexQ);

        while (!vertexQ.IsEmpty())
        {
            vertexQ.Dequeue(vertex);
            if (!graph.IsMarked(vertex))
            {
                item.toVertex = vertex;
                item.distance = minDistance +
                    graph.WeightIs(item.fromVertex, vertex);
                pq.Enqueue(item);
            }
        }
    }
} while (!pq.IsEmpty());
}
```

The output from this function is a table of city pairs (edges), showing the total distance from startVertex to each of the other vertices in the graph, as well as the last vertex visited before the destination. If graph contains the information shown in Figure 9.20, the function call

```
ShortestPath(graph, startVertex);
```

where startVertex corresponds to Washington produces a table like the following:

Last Vertex	Destination	Distance
Washington	Washington	0
Washington	Atlanta	600
Washington	Dallas	1300
Atlanta	Houston	1400
Dallas	Austin	1500
Dallas	Denver	2080
Dallas	Chicago	2200

The shortest-path distance from Washington to each destination is shown in the two columns to the right. For example, our flights from Washington to Chicago total 2200 miles. The left-hand column shows which city immediately preceded the destination in the traversal. Let's figure out the shortest path from Washington to Chicago. We see from the left-hand column that the next-to-last vertex in the path is Dallas. Now we look up Dallas in the Destination (middle) column: the vertex before Dallas is Washington. The whole path is Washington-Dallas-Chicago. (We might want to consider another airline for a more direct route!)

Implementation Level

Array-Based Implementation   A simple way to represent V(graph), the vertices in the graph, is with an array where the elements are of the type of the vertices (`VertexType`). For example if the vertices represent cities, `VertexType` would be some representation of strings. A simple way to represent E(graph), the edges in a graph, is by using an **adjacency matrix**, a two-dimensional array of edge values (weights). Thus a graph consists of a data member `numVertices`, a one-dimensional array `vertices`, and a two-dimensional array `edges`. Figure 9.25 depicts the implementation of the graph of Air Busters flights between seven cities. For simplicity, we omit additional Boolean data needed to mark vertices as "visited" during a traversal. While the city names in Figure 9.25 are in alphabetical order, there is no requirement that the elements in this array be sorted.

Adjacency Matrix   For a graph with *N* nodes, an *N* by *N* table that shows the existence (and weights) of all edges in the graph

---

At any time, within this representation of a graph,

- `numVertices` is the number of vertices in the graph.
- V(graph) is contained in `vertices[0]..vertices[numVertices-1]`.
- E(graph) is contained in the square array
  `edges[0][0]..edges[numVertices-1][numVertices-1]`.

The names of the cities are contained in `graph.vertices`. The weight of each edge in `graph.edges` represents the air distance between two cities that are connected by a flight. For example, the value in `graph.edges[1][3]` tells us that there is a direct flight between Austin and Dallas, and that the air distance is 200 miles. A `NULL_EDGE` value (0) in `graph.edges[1][6]` tells us that the airline has no direct flights between Austin and Washington. Because this is a weighted graph with weights being air distances, we use `int` for

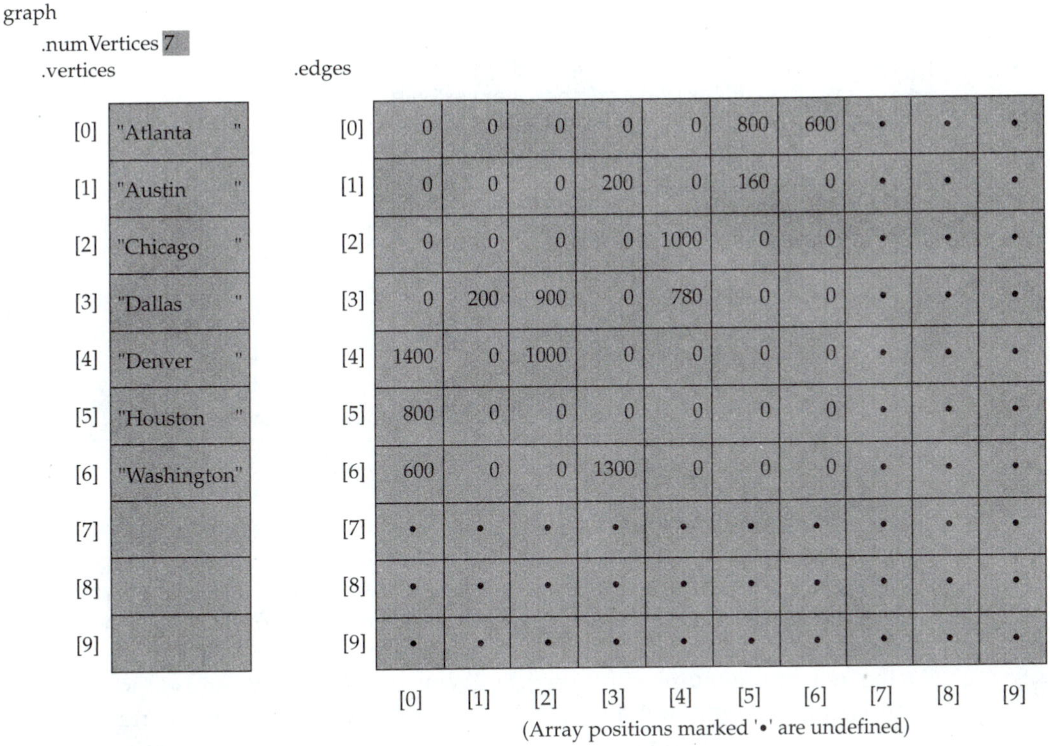

graph
.numVertices 7
.vertices   .edges

	.vertices			.edges									
				[0]	[1]	[2]	[3]	[4]	[5]	[6]	[7]	[8]	[9]
[0]	"Atlanta "	[0]		0	0	0	0	0	800	600	•	•	•
[1]	"Austin "	[1]		0	0	0	200	0	160	0	•	•	•
[2]	"Chicago "	[2]		0	0	0	0	1000	0	0	•	•	•
[3]	"Dallas "	[3]		0	200	900	0	780	0	0	•	•	•
[4]	"Denver "	[4]		1400	0	1000	0	0	0	0	•	•	•
[5]	"Houston "	[5]		800	0	0	0	0	0	0	•	•	•
[6]	"Washington"	[6]		600	0	0	1300	0	0	0	•	•	•
[7]		[7]		•	•	•	•	•	•	•	•	•	•
[8]		[8]		•	•	•	•	•	•	•	•	•	•
[9]		[9]		•	•	•	•	•	•	•	•	•	•

(Array positions marked '•' are undefined)

FIGURE 9.25 *Graph of flight connections between cities.*

EdgeValueType. If this were not a weighted graph, EdgeValueType would be Boolean, and each position in the adjacency matrix would be true if an edge exists between the pair of vertices, and false if no edge exists.

Here is the definition of class GraphType. For simplicity we assume that EdgeValueType is int.

```
template<class VertexType>
// Assumption: VertexType is a type for which the "=",
// "==", and "<<" operators are defined
class GraphType
{
public:
    GraphType();              // Default of 50 vertices.
    GraphType(int maxV);      // maxV <= 50.
    ~GraphType();
    void MakeEmpty();
```

```
       bool IsEmpty() const;
       bool IsFull() const;
       void AddVertex(VertexType);
       void AddEdge(VertexType, VertexType, int);
       int WeightIs(VertexType, VertexType);
       void GetToVertices(VertexType, QueType<VertexType>&);
       void ClearMarks();
       void MarkVertex(VertexType);
       bool IsMarked(VertexType) const;
private:
       int numVertices;
       int maxVertices;
       VertexType* vertices;
       int edges[50][50];
       bool* marks;     // marks[i] is mark for vertices[i].
};
```

The class constructors are usually the easiest operations to write. However, this is not true for class `GraphType`. We have to allocate the space for `vertices` and `marks` (the Boolean array indicating whether a vertex has been marked or not). The default constructor sets up space for 50 `vertices` and `marks`. The parameterized constructor lets the user specify the maximum number of vertices. Why don't we put `edges` in dynamic storage? We could; but allocating storage for a two-dimensional array is rather complex, and we do not wish to divert our attention from the main issue: the Graph ADT.

```
template<class VertexType>
GraphType<VertexType>::GraphType()
// Post: Arrays of size 50 are dynamically allocated for
//       marks and vertices. numVertices is set to 0;
//       maxVertices is set to 50.
{
    numVertices = 0;
    maxVertices = 50;
    vertices = new VertexType[50];
    marks = new bool[50];
}

template<class VertexType>
GraphType<VertexType>::GraphType(int maxV)
// Post: Arrays of size maxV are dynamically allocated for
//       marks and vertices.
//       numVertices is set to 0; maxVertices is set to maxV.
```

```
{
    numVertices = 0;
    maxVertices = maxV;
    vertices = new VertexType[maxV];
    marks = new bool[maxV];
}

template<class VertexType>
GraphType<VertexType>::~GraphType()
// Post: arrays for vertices and marks have been deallocated.
{
    delete [] vertices;
    delete [] marks;
}
```

The `AddVertex` operation puts `vertex` into the next free space in the array of vertices. Because the new vertex has no edges defined yet, we also initialize the appropriate row and column of `edges` to contain NULL_EDGE (0 in this case).

```
const int NULL_EDGE = 0;

template<class VertexType>
void GraphType<VertexType>::AddVertex(VertexType vertex)
// Post: vertex has been stored in vertices.
//       Corresponding row and column of edges have been set
//       to NULL_EDGE.
//       numVertices has been incremented.
{
    vertices[numVertices] = vertex;

    for (int index = 0; index < numVertices; index++)
    {
        edges[numVertices][index] = NULL_EDGE;
        edges[index][numVertices] = NULL_EDGE;
    }
    numVertices++;
}
```

To add an edge to the graph, we must first locate the `fromVertex` and `toVertex` that define the edge we want to add. These parameters to `AddEdge` are of type `VertexType`. To index the correct matrix slot, we need the *index* in the `vertices` array that corresponds to each vertex. Once we know the indexes, it is a simple matter to set the weight of the edge in the matrix. Here is the algorithm:

AddEdge

Set fromIndex to index of fromVertex in V(graph)
Set toIndex to index of toVertex in V(graph)
Set edges[fromIndex][toIndex] to weight

To find the index of each vertex, let's write a little search function that receives the name of a vertex and returns its location (index) in `vertices`. Because the precondition of `AddEdge` states that `fromVertex` and `toVertex` are in V(graph), the search function is very simple. We code it as helper function `IndexIs`.

```
template<class VertexType>
int IndexIs(VertexType* vertices, VertexType vertex)
// Post: Function value = index of vertex in vertices.
{
    int index = 0;

    while (!(vertex == vertices[index]))
        index++;
    return index;
}


template<class VertexType>
void GraphType<VertexType>::AddEdge(VertexType fromVertex,
    VertexType toVertex, int weight)
// Post: Edge (fromVertex, toVertex) is stored in edges.
{
    int row;
    int column;

    row = IndexIs(vertices, fromVertex);
    col = IndexIs(vertices, toVertex);
    edges[row][col] = weight;
}
```

The `WeightIs` operation is the mirror image of `AddEdge`.

```
template<class VertexType>
int GraphType<VertexType>::WeightIs(VertexType fromVertex,
    VertexType toVertex)
// Post: Function value = weight associated with the edge
//       (fromVertex, toVertex).
```

```
{
    int row;
    int column;

    row = IndexIs(vertices, fromVertex);
    col = IndexIs(vertices, toVertex);
    return edges[row][col];
}
```

The last graph operation that we specified is `GetToVertices`. This function receives a vertex, and returns a queue of vertices that are adjacent from the designated vertex. That is, it returns a queue of all the vertices that you can get to from this vertex in one step. Using an adjacency matrix to represent the edges, it is a simple matter to determine the nodes to which `vertex` is adjacent. We merely loop through the appropriate row in `edges`; whenever a value is found that is not `NULL_EDGE`, we add another vertex to the queue.

```
template<class VertexType>
void GraphType<VertexType>::GetToVertices(VertexType vertex,
    QueType<VertexType>& adjvertexQ)
{
    int fromIndex;
    int toIndex;

    fromIndex = IndexIs(vertices, vertex);
    for (toIndex = 0; toIndex < numVertices; toIndex++)
        if (edges[fromIndex][toIndex] != NULL_EDGE)
            adjvertexQ.Enqueue(vertices[toIndex]);
}
```

We leave `MakeEmpty`, `IsFull`, `IsEmpty`, and the marking operations (`ClearMarks`, `MarkVertex`, and `IsMarked`) as a programming assignment.

Linked Implementation   The advantages to representing the edges in a graph with an adjacency matrix are its speed and simplicity. Given the indexes of two vertices, determining the existence (or the weight) of an edge between them is an O(1) operation. The problem with adjacency matrices is that their use of *space* is $O(N^2)$, where N is the *maximum* number of vertices in the graph. If the maximum number of vertices is large, adjacency matrices may waste a lot of space. In the past, we have tried to save space by allocating memory as we need it at run time, using linked structures. We can use a similar approach to implementing graphs. **Adjacency lists** are linked lists, one list per vertex, that identify the vertices to which each vertex is connected. There are several ways to implement adjacency lists. Figure 9.26 shows two different adjacency list representations of the graph in Figure 9.20.

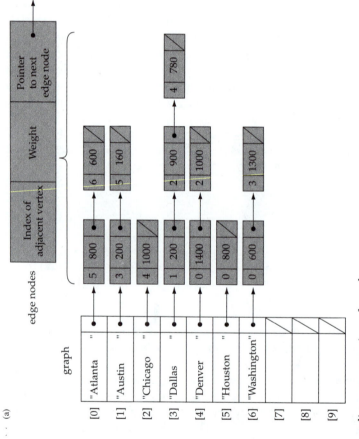

FIGURE 9.26 *Adjacency list representation of graphs.*

(b)

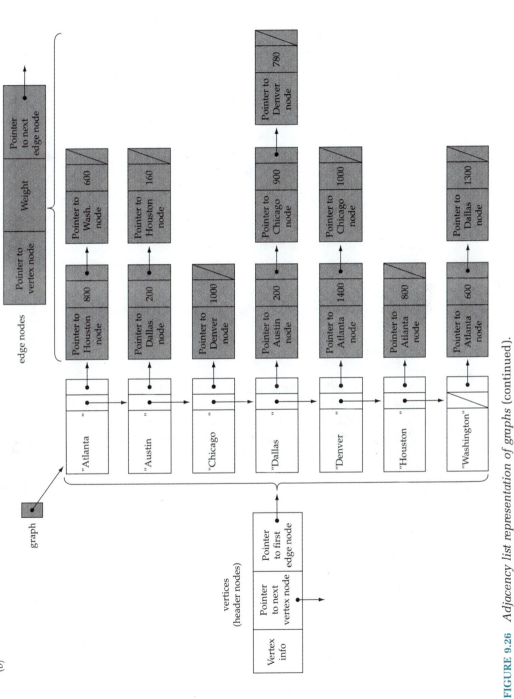

FIGURE 9.26 *Adjacency list representation of graphs* (continued).

Adjacency List A linked list that identifies all the vertices to which a
particular vertex is connected; each vertex has its own adjacency list

---

In Figure 9.26(a), the vertices are stored in an array. Each component of this
array contains a pointer to a linked list of edge nodes. Each node in these linked
lists contains an index number, a weight, and a pointer to the next node in the
adjacency list. Let's look at the adjacency list for Denver. The first node in the
list indicates that there is a 1400 mile flight from Denver to Atlanta (the vertex
whose index is 0) and a 1000 mile flight from Denver to Chicago (the vertex
whose index is 2).

No arrays are used in the implementation illustrated in Figure 9.26(b). The
list of vertices is implemented as a linked list. Now each node in the adjacency
lists contains a pointer to the vertex information rather than the index of the
vertex. Because there are so many of these pointers in Figure 9.26(b), we have
used text to describe the vertex that each pointer designates rather than draw
them as arrows.

We leave the implementation of the `GraphType` member functions using
these implementations as Chapter 9's Programming Assignment 2.

■|| *Summary*

In this chapter we have discussed several branching structures: trees, heaps, and
graphs. Branching structures are very versatile and are a good way to model
many real-world objects and situations. Because there are many different types
of applications for these data structures, there are all kinds of variations and
generalizations of trees and graphs. These topics are introduced here in order to
show the wide variety of applications for which programmers must create
appropriate data structures. They are generally covered in detail in more
advanced computer science courses.

■|| *Exercises*

1. Show the preorder, inorder, and postorder notation of the following binary expression trees. (Remember that you must supply parentheses for the inorder notation.)

(a)

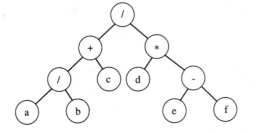

(b)

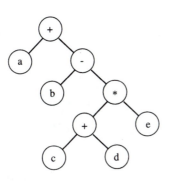

2. Evaluate the binary expression tree in Exercise 1(a) where
   a = 6   d = 2
   b = 2   e = 8
   c = 5   f = 7

3. Evaluate the binary expression tree in Exercise 1(b) where
   a = 5   d = 3
   b = 12   e = 2
   c = 2

4. Draw the binary expression tree that represents this preorder expression:

$$+ * a b / + c d e$$

5. Draw the binary expression tree that represents this inorder expression:

$$(((a - b) + c) * ((d + e) / f)) - g$$

6. Draw the binary expression tree that represents this postorder expression:

$$a \ b + c \ / \ d \ *$$

7. Write a recursive function to print the postorder representation of a binary expression tree. Use the variant record implementation of the nodes in the tree.

8. (a) Which of the following trees are complete?
   (b) Which of the following trees are full?
   (c) Which of the following trees are heaps?

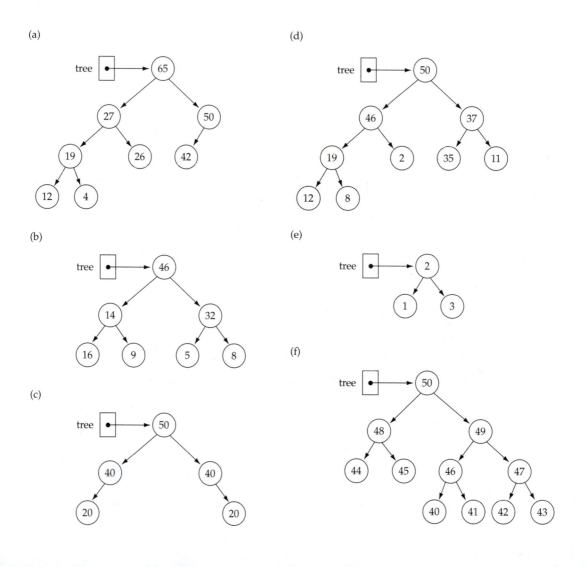

9. The elements in a binary tree are to be stored in an array, as described in the chapter. Each element is a nonnegative `int` value.
   (a) What value can you use as the dummy value, if the binary tree is not complete?
   (b) Show the contents of the array, given the tree illustrated below.

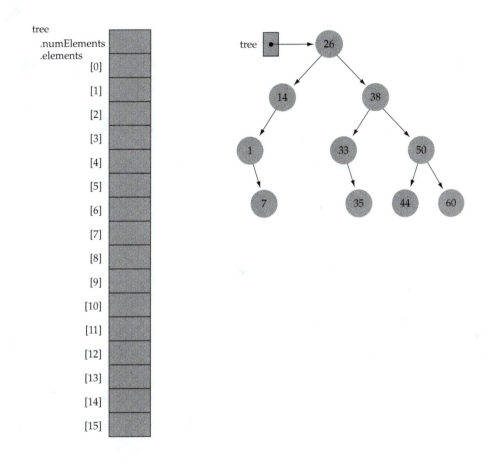

10. The elements in a complete binary tree are to be stored in an array, as described in the chapter. Each element is a nonnegative `int` value.
    (a) Show the contents of the array, given the tree illustrated on the next page.
    (b) Is this tree a heap?

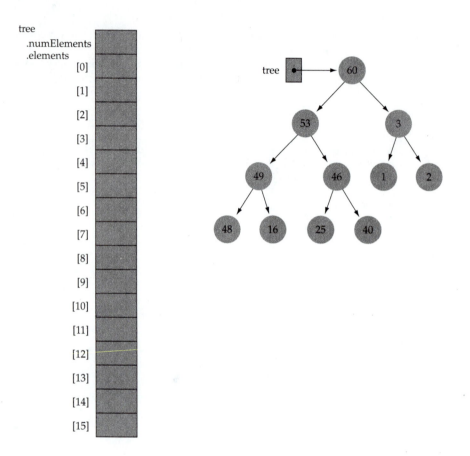

11. (a) Given the array pictured on the next page, draw the binary tree that can be created from its elements. (The elements are arranged in the array as discussed in the chapter.)

    (b) Is this tree a heap? If not, what function call(s) can be used to make the tree into a heap?

tree.numElements   9
tree.elements

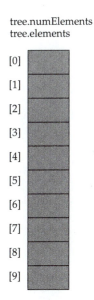

12. Draw a tree that satisfies both the binary search property and the order property of heaps.

13. A binary tree is stored in an array called `treeNodes`, which is indexed from 0 to 99, as described in the chapter. The tree contains 85 elements. Mark each of the following statements as True or False, and correct any false statements.
    (a) `treeNodes[42]` is a leaf node.
    (b) `treeNodes[41]` has only one child.
    (c) The right child of `treeNodes[12]` is `treeNodes[25]`.
    (d) The subtree rooted at `treeNodes[7]` is a full binary tree with four levels.
    (e) The tree has seven levels that are full, and one additional level that contains some elements.

14. A *minimum heap* has the following order property: the value of each element is less than or equal to the value of each of its children. What changes must be made in the heap operations given in this chapter?

15. (a) Write a nonrecursive version of `ReheapDown`.
    (b) Write a nonrecursive version of `ReheapUp`.
    (c) Describe the nonrecursive versions of these operations in terms of Big-O.

16. A priority queue containing characters is implemented as a heap stored in an array (see diagram on next page). The precondition states that this priority queue cannot contain duplicate elements. There are ten elements currently in the priority queue. What values might be stored in array positions 7–9 so that the properties of a heap are satisfied?

pq.items.elements

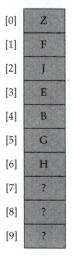

[0]	Z
[1]	F
[2]	J
[3]	E
[4]	B
[5]	G
[6]	H
[7]	?
[8]	?
[9]	?

17. A priority queue is implemented as a heap:

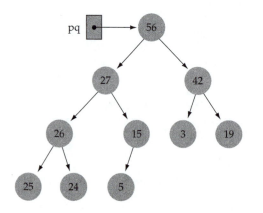

(a) Show how the heap above would look after this series of operations:
```
pq.Enqueue(28);
pq.Enqueue(2);
pq.Enqueue(40);
pq.Dequeue(x);
pq.Dequeue(y);
pq.Dequeue(z);
```
(b) What would the values of x, y, and z be after the series of operations in Part (a)?

18. A priority queue is implemented as a linked list, sorted from largest to smallest element.
    (a) How would the definition of PQType change?
    (b) Write the Enqueue operation, using this implementation.
    (c) Write the Dequeue operation, using this implementation.
    (d) Compare the Enqueue and Dequeue operations to those for the heap implementation, in terms of Big-O.

19. A priority queue is implemented as a binary search tree.
    (a) How would the definition of PQType change?
    (b) Write the Enqueue operation, using this implementation.
    (c) Write the Dequeue operation, using this implementation.
    (d) Compare the Enqueue and Dequeue operations to those for the heap implementation, in terms of Big-O. Under what conditions would this implementation be better or worse than the heap implementation?

20. A priority queue is implemented as a sequential array-based list. The highest-priority item is in the first array position, the second-highest priority item is in the second array position, and so on.
    (a) Write the declarations in the private part of the priority queue class definition needed for this implementation.
    (b) Write the Enqueue operation, using this implementation.
    (c) Write the Dequeue operation, using this implementation.
    (d) Compare the Enqueue and Dequeue operations to those for the heap implementation, in terms of Big-O. Under what conditions would this implementation be better or worse than the heap implementation?

21. A stack is implemented using a priority queue. Each element is time-stamped as it is put into the stack. (The time stamp is a number between 0 and INT_MAX. Each time an element is pushed onto the stack, it is assigned the next larger number.)
    (a) What is the highest-priority element?
    (b) Write the Push and Pop algorithms, using the specifications in Chapter 4.
    (c) Compare these Push and Pop operations to the ones implemented in Chapter 4, in terms of Big-O.

22. A FIFO queue is implemented using a priority queue. Each element is time-stamped as it is put into the queue. (The time stamp is a number between 0 and INT_MAX. Each time an element is enqueued, it is assigned the next larger number.)
    (a) What is the highest-priority element?
    (b) Write the Enqueue and Dequeue operations, using the specifications in Chapter 4.
    (c) Compare these Enqueue and Dequeue operations to the ones implemented in Chapter 4, in terms of Big-O.

23. A priority queue of strings is implemented using a heap. The heap contains the following elements:

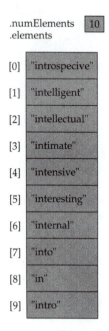

.numElements 10
.elements

[0] "introspecive"

[1] "intelligent"

[2] "intellectual"

[3] "intimate"

[4] "intensive"

[5] "interesting"

[6] "internal"

[7] "into"

[8] "in"

[9] "intro"

(a) What feature of these strings is used to determine their priority in the priority queue?

(b) Show how this priority queue is affected by adding the string "interviewing".

Use the following description of an *undirected graph* in Exercises 24–27.

EmployeeGraph   = (V, E)
V(EmployeeGraph) = {Susan, Darlene, Mike, Fred, John, Sander, Lance, Jean, Brent, Fran}
E(EmployeeGraph) = {(Susan, Darlene), (Fred, Brent), (Sander, Susan), (Lance, Fran), (Sander, Fran), (Fran, John), (Lance, Jean), (Jean, Susan), (Mike, Darlene), (Brent, Lance), (Susan, John)}

24. Draw a picture of EmployeeGraph.

25. Draw EmployeeGraph, implemented as an adjacency matrix. Store the vertex values in alphabetical order.

26. Using the adjacency matrix for EmployeeGraph from Exercise 25, describe the path from Susan to Lance
    (a) using a breadth-first strategy,
    (b) using a depth-first strategy.

27. Which one of the following phrases best describes the relationship represented by the edges between the vertices in EmployeeGraph?
    (a) "works for"
    (b) "is the supervisor of"
    (c) "is senior to"
    (d) "works with"

Use the following specification of a *directed graph* in Exercises 28–31.

ZooGraph   = (V, E)
V(ZooGraph) = {dog, cat, animal, vertebrate, oyster, shellfish, invertebrate, crab, poodle, monkey, banana, dalmatian, dachshund}
E(ZooGraph) = {(vertebrate, animal), (invertebrate, animal), (dog, vertebrate), (cat, vertebrate), (monkey, vertebrate), (shellfish, invertebrate), (crab, shellfish), (oyster, shellfish), (poodle, dog), (dalmatian, dog), (dachshund, dog)}

28. Draw a picture of ZooGraph.

29. Draw the adjacency matrix for ZooGraph. Store the vertices in alphabetical order.

30. To tell if one element in ZooGraph has relation X to another element, you look for a path between them. Show whether the following statements are true, using the picture or adjacency matrix.
    (a) dalmatian X dog
    (b) dalmatian X vertebrate
    (c) dalmatian X poodle
    (d) banana X invertebrate
    (e) oyster X invertebrate
    (f) monkey X invertebrate

31. Which of the following phrases best describes relation X in the previous question?
    (a) "has a"
    (b) "is an example of"
    (c) "is a generalization of"
    (d) "eats"

Use the following graph for Exercises 32–34.

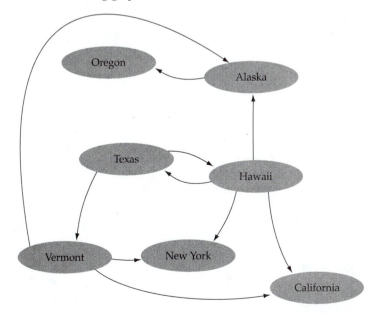

32. Describe the graph on page 583, using the formal graph notation.

    V(StateGraph) =
    E(StateGraph) =

33. (a) Is there a path from Oregon to any other state in the graph?
    (b) Is there a path from Hawaii to every other state in the graph?
    (c) From which state(s) in the graph is there a path to Hawaii?

34. (a) Show the adjacency matrix that would describe the edges in this graph. Store the vertices in alphabetical order.
    (b) Show the array-of-pointers adjacency lists that would describe the edges in this graph.

35. Class `GraphType` in this chapter is to be extended to include a Boolean `EdgeExists` operation, which determines whether two vertices are connected by an edge.
    (a) Write the declaration of this function. Include adequate comments.
    (b) Using the adjacency matrix implementation developed in the chapter and the declaration from Part (a), implement the body of the function.

36. Class `GraphType` in this chapter is to be extended to include a `DeleteEdge` operation, which deletes a given edge.
    (a) Write the declaration of this function. Include adequate comments.
    (b) Using the adjacency matrix implementation developed in the chapter and the declaration from Part (a), implement the body of the function.

37. Class `GraphType` in this chapter is to be extended to include a `DeleteVertex` operation, which deletes a vertex from the graph. Deleting a vertex is more complicated than deleting an edge from the graph. Discuss why.

38. The `DepthFirstSearch` operation can be implemented without a stack by using recursion.
    (a) Name the base case(s). Name the general case(s).
    (b) Write the algorithm for a recursive depth-first search.

Sorting and Searching Algorithms

GOALS

- To be able to design and implement the following sorting algorithms:

straight selection sort	insertion sort	heap sort
bubble sort (two versions)	merge sort	radix sort

- To be able to compare the efficiency of the sorting algorithms, in terms of Big-O and of space requirements
- To be able to discuss other efficiency considerations: sorting small numbers of elements, programmer time, sorting arrays of large data elements
- To be able to sort on several keys
- To be able to discuss the performances of the following search algorithms:

sequential search of an unsorted list	binary search
sequential search of a sorted list	searching a high-probability sorted list

- To be able to define the following terms:

hashing	collisions	clustering
rehashing	linear probing	

- To be able to design and implement an appropriate hashing function for an application
- To be able to design and implement a collision-resolution algorithm for a hash table
- To be able to discuss the efficiency considerations for the searching and hashing algorithms, in terms of Big-O

At many points in this book, we have gone to great trouble to keep lists of elements in sorted order: student records sorted by ID number, integers sorted from smallest to largest, words sorted alphabetically. The goal of keeping sorted lists, of course, is to facilitate searching: given an appropriate data structure, a particular list element can be found faster if the list is sorted.

In this chapter we examine strategies for both sorting and searching: two tasks that are fundamental to a variety of computing problems. In fact, we challenge you to look back at the programs you have written. Are there any that do *not* include a sort or a search?

■Ⅱ *Sorting*

Putting an unsorted list of data elements into order—*sorting*—is a very common and useful operation. Whole books have been written about various sorting algorithms, as well as algorithms for searching a sorted list to find a particular element. The goal is to come up with better, more efficient, sorts. Because sorting a large number of elements can be extremely time-consuming, a good sorting algorithm is very desirable. This is one area in which programmers are sometimes encouraged to sacrifice clarity in favor of speed of execution.

How do we describe efficiency? We pick an operation central to most sorting algorithms: the operation that compares two values to see which is smaller. In our study of sorting algorithms, we relate the number of comparisons to the number of elements in the list (N) as a rough measure of the efficiency of each algorithm. The number of swaps made is another measure of sorting efficiency. In the exercises we ask you to analyze the sorting algorithms developed in this chapter in terms of data movements.

Another efficiency consideration is the amount of memory space required. In general, memory space is not a very important factor in choosing a sorting algorithm. We look at only two sorts in which space would be a serious consideration. The usual time versus space trade-off applies to sorts—more space often means less time, and vice versa.

Because processing time is the factor that applies most often to sorting algorithms, we consider it in detail here. Of course, as in any application, the programmer must determine goals and requirements before selecting an algorithm and starting to code.

We review the straight selection sort, bubble sort, and insertion sort, three simple sorts that students often write in their first course. Then we review a more complex sorting algorithm that we looked at in Chapter 7 (quick sort) and introduce two additional complex sorts: merge sort and heap sort. We assume that the actual data type that replaces the template parameter `ItemType` in the rest of the chapter is either a simple built-in type or a class that overloads the relational operators. For simplicity, we assume that the keys are unique.

As we pointed out in Chapter 7, at the logical level, sorting algorithms take an unsorted list object and convert it into a sorted list object. At the implementation level, sorting algorithms take an array and reorganize the values in the array so that they are in order by key. The number of values to be sorted and the array in which they are stored are parameters to our sorting algorithms. Note that we are not sorting an object of type UnsortedType, but the values stored in an array. We call the array values, and its elements are of type ItemType.

Straight Selection Sort

If you were handed a list of names and asked to put them in alphabetical order, you might use this general approach:

1. Find the name that comes first in the alphabet, and write it on a second sheet of paper.
2. Cross the name out on the original list.
3. Continue this cycle until all the names on the original list have been crossed out and written onto the second list, at which point the second list is sorted.

This algorithm is simple to translate into a computer program, but it has one drawback: it requires space in memory to store two complete lists. Although we have not talked a great deal about memory space considerations, this duplication is clearly wasteful. A slight adjustment to this manual approach does away with the need to duplicate space, however. As you cross a name off the original list, a free space opens up. Instead of writing the minimum value on a second list, you can exchange it with the value currently in the position where the crossed-off item should go. Our "by-hand list" is represented in an array. Let's look at an example—sorting the five-element array shown in Figure 10.1(a). Because of this algorithm's simplicity, it is usually the first sorting method that students learn. Therefore, we go straight to the algorithm:

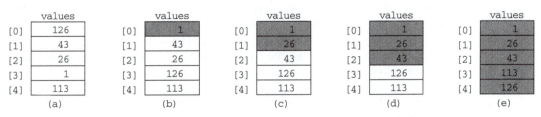

FIGURE 10.1 *Example of straight selection sort (Sorted elements are shaded.)*

Selection Sort

> Set current to the index of first item in the array
> WHILE more items in unsorted part of array
>   Find the index of the smallest unsorted item
>   Swap the current item with the smallest unsorted one
>   Shrink the unsorted part of the array by incrementing current

Although you could go immediately to writing the code, we use this algorithm to practice designing correct loops.

We use a variable, `current`, to mark the beginning of the unsorted part of the array. We start out by setting `current` to the index of the first position (index 0). This means that the unsorted part of the array goes from index `current` to `numValues-1`.

The main sort processing is in a loop. In each iteration of the loop body, the smallest value in the unsorted part of the array is swapped with the value in the `current` location. After the swap, `current` is in the sorted part of the array, so we shrink the size of the unsorted part by incrementing `current`. The loop body is now complete.

Back at the top of the loop body, the unsorted part of the array goes from the (now incremented) `current` index to position `numValues-1`. We know that every value in the unsorted part is greater than (or equal to, if duplicates are permitted) any value in the sorted part of the array.

How do we know when "there are more elements in the unsorted part"? As long as `current <= numValues-1`, the unsorted part of the array (`values[current]..values[numValues-1]`) contains values. In each iteration of the loop body, `current` is incremented, shrinking the unsorted part of the array. When `current = numValues-1`, the "unsorted" part contains only one element, and we know that this value is greater than (or equal to) any value in the sorted part. So the value in `values[numValues-1]` is in its correct place, and we are done. The condition for the While loop is `current < numValues-1`. A snapshot picture of the selection sort algorithm is illustrated in Figure 10.2.

Now all we have to do is to locate the smallest value in the unsorted part of the array. Let's write a function to do this task. Function `MinIndex` receives the array elements and the first and last indexes of the unsorted part, and returns the index of the smallest value in this part of the array.

Now that we know where the smallest unsorted element is, we swap it with the element at index `current`. Because swapping data values between two

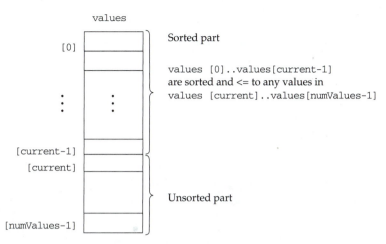

FIGURE 10.2 *A snapshot of the selection sort algorithm.*

int MinIndex(values, startIndex, endIndex)

```
Set indexOfMin to startIndex
FOR index going from startIndex + 1 to endIndex
  IF values[index] < values[indexOfMin]
    Set indexOfMin to index
Return indexOfMin
```

array locations is common in many sorting algorithms, let's write a little function, `Swap`, to accomplish this task.

```
template<class ItemType>
inline void Swap(ItemType& item1, ItemType& item2)
// Post: Contents of item1 and item2 have been swapped.
{
    ItemType tempItem;

    tempItem = item1;
    item1 = item2;
    item2 = tempItem;
}
```

The word `inline` before the function heading is called a *specifier*. `inline` suggests that the compiler insert the code for the function every time a call is issued rather than actually making a function call. We use "suggests that" rather than "tells," because compilers are not obligated to implement the `inline` specifier. Here are the rest of the function templates for this sorting algorithm.

```
template<class ItemType>
int MinIndex(ItemType values[], int startIndex, int endIndex)
// Post: Function value = index of the smallest value in
//       values[startIndex]..values[endIndex].
{
    int indexOfMin = startIndex;
    for (int index = startIndex + 1; index <= endIndex; index++)
        if (values[index] < values[indexOfMin])
            indexOfMin = index;
    return indexOfMin;
}

template<class ItemType>
void SelectionSort(ItemType values[], int numValues)
// Post: The elements in the array values are sorted by key.
{
    int endIndex = numValues-1;
    for (int current = 0; current < endIndex; current++)
        Swap(values[current],
            values[MinIndex(values, current, endIndex)]);
}
```

Analyzing Selection Sort   Now let's try measuring the amount of "work" required by this algorithm. We describe the number of comparisons as a function of the number of items in the array. To be concise, in this discussion we refer to `numValues` as N.

The comparison operation is in function `MinIndex`. We know from the loop condition in the `SelectionSort` function that `MinIndex` is called $N-1$ times. Within `MinIndex`, the number of comparisons varies, depending on the values of `startIndex` and `endIndex`:

```
for (int index = startIndex + 1; index <= endIndex; index++)
    if (values[index] < values[indexOfMin])
        indexOfMin = index;
```

In the first call to `MinIndex`, `startIndex` is 0 and `endIndex` is `numValues-1`, so there are $N-1$ comparisons; in the next call there are $N-2$ comparisons, and so on, until in the last call, there is only one comparison. The total number of comparisons is

$$(N - 1) + (N - 2) + (N - 3) + ... + 1 = N(N - 1)/2$$

To accomplish our goal of sorting an array of N elements, the straight selection sort requires $N(N - 1)/2$ comparisons. Note that the particular arrangement of values in the array does not affect the amount of work done at all. Even if the array is in sorted order *before* the call to SelectionSort, the function still makes $N(N - 1)/2$ comparisons. Table 10.1 shows the number of comparisons required for arrays of various sizes. Note that doubling the array size roughly quadruples the number of comparisons.

TABLE 10.1   Number of Comparisons Required to Sort Arrays of Different Sizes Using Selection Sort

Number of Items	*Number of Comparisons*
10	45
20	190
100	4,950
1,000	499,500
10,000	49,995,000

How do we describe this algorithm in terms of Big-O? If we express $N(N - \frac{1}{2})$ as $\frac{1}{2}N^2 - \frac{1}{2}N$, it is easy to see. In Big-O notation we only consider the term $\frac{1}{2}N^2$, because it increases fastest relative to N. (Remember the elephants and goldfish?) Further, we ignore the constant, $\frac{1}{2}$, making this algorithm $O(N^2)$. This means that, for large values of N, the computation time is *approximately proportional* to N^2. Looking back at the previous table, we see that multiplying the number of elements by 10 increases the number of comparisons by more than a factor of 100. That is, the number of comparisons is multiplied by approximately the square of the increase in the number of elements. Looking at this chart makes us appreciate why sorting algorithms are the subject of so much attention: using SelectionSort to sort an array of 1000 elements requires almost a half million comparisons!

The identifying feature of a selection sort is that, on each pass through the loop, one element is put into its proper place. In the straight selection sort, each iteration finds the smallest unsorted element and puts it into its correct place. If we had made the function find the largest value, instead of the smallest, the algorithm would have sorted in descending order. We could also have made the loop go down from numValues-1 to 1, putting the elements into the bottom of the array first. All these are variations on the straight selection sort. The variations do not change the basic way that the minimum (or maximum) element is found.

Bubble Sort

The bubble sort is a selection sort that uses a different scheme for finding the minimum (or maximum) value. Each iteration puts the smallest unsorted element into its correct place, but it also makes changes in the locations of the other elements in the array. The first iteration puts the smallest element in the array into the first array position. Starting with the last array element we compare successive pairs of elements, swapping whenever the bottom element of the pair is smaller than the one above it. In this way the smallest element "bubbles up" to the top of the array. The next iteration puts the smallest element in the unsorted part of the array into the second array position, using the same technique. As you look at the example in Figure 10.3, note that in addition to putting one element into its proper place, each iteration causes some intermediate changes in the array.

The basic algorithm for the bubble sort is

Bubble Sort

Set current to the index of first item in the array
WHILE more items in unsorted part of array
   "Bubble up" the smallest item in the unsorted part, causing
     intermediate swaps as needed
   Shrink the unsorted part of the array by incrementing current

---

The structure of the loop is much like that of the `SelectionSort`. The unsorted part of the array is the area from `values[current]` to `values[numValues-1]`. The value of `current` begins at 0, and we loop until `current` reaches `numValues-1`, with `current` incremented in each iteration. On entrance to each iteration of the loop body, the first `current` values are already sorted, and all the elements in the unsorted part of the array are greater than or equal to the sorted elements.

The inside of the loop body is different, however. Each iteration of the loop

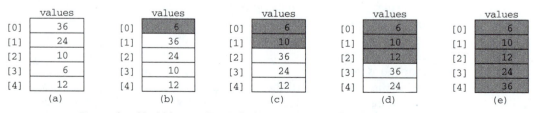

FIGURE 10.3   *Example of bubble sort (Sorted elements are shaded.)*

"bubbles up" the smallest value in the unsorted part of the array to the current position. The algorithm for the bubbling task is

BubbleUp(values, startIndex, endIndex)

FOR index going from endIndex DOWNTO startIndex +1
  IF values[index] < values[index-1]
    Swap(values[index], values[index-1])

A snapshot of this algorithm is shown in Figure 10.4. Using the Swap function coded earlier, the code for function BubbleSort follows.

```
template<class ItemType>
void BubbleUp(ItemType values[], int startIndex, int endIndex)
// Post: Adjacent pairs that are out of order have been switched
//       between values[startIndex]..values[endIndex] beginning at
//       values[endIndex].
{
```

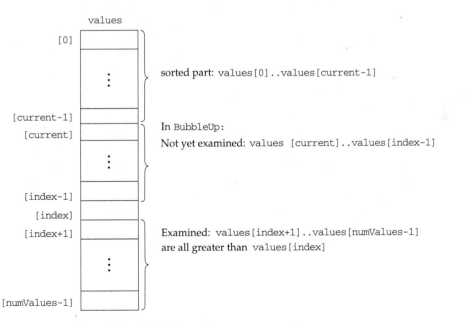

FIGURE 10.4 *Snapshot of bubble sort.*

```
        for (int index = endIndex; index > startIndex; index--)
            if (values[index] < values[index-1])
                Swap(values[index], values[index-1]);
}

template<class ItemType>
void BubbleSort(ItemType values[], int numValues)
// Post: The elements in the array values are sorted by key.
{
    int current = 0;

    while (current < numValues - 1)
    {
        BubbleUp(values, current, numValues-1);
        current++;
    }
}
```

Analyzing Bubble Sort   To analyze the work required by `BubbleSort` is easy. It is the same as for the straight selection sort algorithm. The comparisons are in `BubbleUp`, which is called *N* - 1 times. There are *N* - 1 comparisons the first time, *N* - 2 comparisons the second time, and so on. Therefore `BubbleSort` and `SelectionSort` require the same amount of work, in terms of the number of comparisons. `BubbleSort` does more than just make comparisons, though; while `SelectionSort` has only one data swap per iteration, `BubbleSort` may do many additional data swaps.

What is the purpose of these intermediate data swaps? By reversing out-of-order pairs of data as they are noticed, the function might get the array in order before *N* - 1 calls to `BubbleUp`. However, this version of the bubble sort makes no provision for stopping when the array is completely sorted. Even if the array is already in sorted order when `BubbleSort` is called, this function continues to call `BubbleUp` (which changes nothing) *N* - 1 times.

We could quit before the maximum number of iterations if `BubbleUp` returns a Boolean flag, `sorted`, to tell us when the array is sorted. Within `BubbleUp`, we initially set `sorted` to true; then in the loop, if any swaps are made, we reset `sorted` to false. If no elements have been swapped, we know that the array is already in order. Now the bubble sort only needs to make *one* extra call to `BubbleUp` when the array is in order. This version of the bubble sort is as follows:

```
template<class ItemType>
void BubbleUp2(ItemType values[], int startIndex, int endIndex,
        bool& sorted)
// Post: Adjacent pairs that are out of order have been switched
//          between values[startIndex]..values[endIndex] beginning at
```

```
//         values[endIndex].
//         sorted is false if a swap was made; otherwise, true.
{
    sorted = true;
    for (int index = endIndex; index > startIndex; index--)
        if (values[index] < (values[index-1])
        {
            Swap(values[index], values[index-1]);
            sorted = false;
        }
}


template<class ItemType>
void ShortBubble(ItemType values[], int numValues)
// Post: The elements in the array values are sorted by key.
//       The process stops as soon as values is sorted.
{
    int current = 0;
    bool sorted = false;

    while (current < numValues - 1 && !sorted)
    {
        BubbleUp2(values, current, numValues-1, sorted);
        current++;
    }
}
```

The analysis of ShortBubble is more difficult. Clearly, if the array is already sorted to begin with, one call to BubbleUp tells us so. In this best case scenario, ShortBubble is $O(N)$; only N - 1 comparisons are required for the sort. What if the original array was actually sorted in *descending* order before the call to ShortBubble? This is the worst possible case: ShortBubble requires as many comparisons as BubbleSort and SelectionSort, not to mention the "overhead"—all the extra swaps and setting and resetting the sorted flag. Can we calculate an average case? In the first call to BubbleUp, when current is 0, there are numValues - 1 comparisons; on the second call, when current is 1, there are numValues - 2 comparisons. The number of comparisons in any call to BubbleUp is numValues - current - 1. If we let N indicate numValues and K indicate the number of calls to BubbleUp executed before ShortBubble finishes its work, the total number of comparisons required is

$$(N - 1) \quad + (N - 2) \quad + \quad (N - 3) \quad + \ldots + \quad (N - K)$$

1st call   2nd call   3rd call   Kth call

A little algebra[1] changes this to

$$(2KN - K^2 - K) / 2$$

In Big-O notation, the term that is increasing the fastest relative to N is $2KN$. We know that K is between 1 and $N - 1$. On average, over all possible input orders, K is proportional to N. Therefore, $2KN$ is proportional to N^2; that is, the ShortBubble algorithm is also $O(N^2)$.

Why do we even bother to mention the bubble sort algorithm if it is $O(N^2)$ and requires extra data movements? Because, ShortBubble is the only sorting algorithm that recognizes when the array is already sorted and stops. If the original array is already sorted when ShortBubble is called, only one pass is made through the array. If you are going to sort a file that you know is almost in order, ShortBubble is a good choice.

Insertion Sort

In Chapter 3 we created a sorted list by inserting each new element into its appropriate place in an array. We can use a similar approach for sorting an array. The principle of the insertion sort is quite simple: each successive element in the array to be sorted is inserted into its proper place with respect to the other, already sorted elements. As with the previous sorts, we divide our array into a sorted part and an unsorted part. Initially, the sorted portion contains only one element: the first element in the array. Now we take the second element in the array, and put it into its correct place in the sorted part; that is, values[0] and values[1] are in order with respect to each other. Now the value in values[2] is put into its proper place, so values[0]..values[2] are in order with respect to each other. This process continues until all the elements have been sorted. Figure 10.5 illustrates this process, which we describe in the following algorithm, and Figure 10.6 shows a snapshot of the algorithm.

In Chapter 3, our strategy was to search for the insertion point from the beginning of the array and shift the elements from the insertion point down one slot to make room for the new element. We can combine the searching and shifting by beginning at the *end* of the sorted part of the array. We compare the item at values[current] to the one before it. If it is less, we swap the two items. We then compare the item at values[current-1] to the one before it, and swap if necessary. The process stops when the comparison shows that the values are in order or we have swapped into the first place in the array.

---

1. For those of you who want to see the algebra:

$(N - 1) + (N - 2) + \ldots (N - K)$

$= KN - (\text{sum of 1 through } K)$

$= KN - [\frac{1}{2}KK + 1)]$

$= KN - (\frac{1}{2}K^2 + \frac{1}{2}K)$

$= (2KN - K^2 - K) / 2$

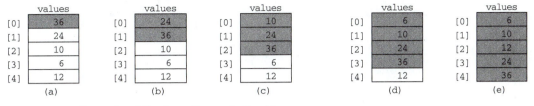

FIGURE 10.5 *Example of the insertion sort algorithm.*

Insertion Sort

> FOR count going from 0 through numValues-1
>   InsertItem(values, 0, count)

InsertItem(values, startIndex, endIndex)

> Set finished to false
> Set current to endIndex
> Set moreToSearch to (current does not equal startIndex)
> WHILE moreToSearch AND NOT finished
>   IF values[current] < values[current-1]
>   Swap(values[current], values[current-1])
>   Decrement current
>   Set moreToSearch to (current does not equal startIndex)
>   ELSE
>   Set finished to true

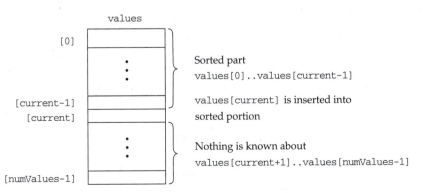

FIGURE 10.6 *A snapshot of the insertion sort algorithm.*

Here are the coded versions of `InsertItem` and `InsertionSort`.

```
template<class ItemType>
void InsertItem(ItemType values[], int startIndex, int endIndex)
// Post: values[startIndex]..values[endIndex] are now sorted.
{
    bool finished = false;
    int current = endIndex;
    bool moreToSearch = (current != startIndex);

    while (moreToSearch && !finished)
    {
        if (values[current] < values[current-1])
        {
            Swap(values[current], values[current-1]);
            current--;
            moreToSearch = (current != startIndex);
        }
        else
            finished = true;
    }
}


template<class ItemType>
void InsertionSort(ItemType values[], int numValues)
// Post: The elements in the array values are sorted by key.
{
    for (int count = 0; count < numValues; count++)
        InsertItem(values, 0, count);
}
```

Analysing Insertion Sort   The general case for this algorithm mirrors the `SelectionSort` and the `BubbleSort`, so the general case is $O(N^2)$. But like `ShortBubble`, `InsertionSort` has a best case: the data are already sorted in ascending order. When the data are in ascending order, `InsertItem` is called N times, but only one comparison is made each time and no swaps are necessary. The maximum number of comparisons are made only when the elements in the array are in reverse order.

If we know nothing about the original order in the data to be sorted, `SelectionSort`, `ShortBubble`, and `InsertionSort` are all $O(N^2)$ sorts and are too time-consuming for sorting large arrays. Thus we need sorting methods that work better when N is large.

O(N log$_2$ N) Sorts

Considering how rapidly N^2 grows as the size of the array gets larger, can't we do better? We note that N^2 is a lot larger than $(\frac{1}{2}N)^2 + (\frac{1}{2}N)^2$. If we could cut the array into two pieces, sort each segment, and then merge the two back together, we should end up sorting the entire array with a lot less work. An example of this approach is shown in Figure 10.7.

The idea of "divide and conquer" has been applied to the sorting problem in different ways, resulting in a number of algorithms that can do the job much more efficiently than O(N^2). In fact, there is a category of sorting algorithms that are O(Nlog$_2N$). We looked at one of these in Chapter 7: QuickSort. We examine two additional sorting algorithms here: MergeSort and HeapSort. As you might guess, the efficiency of these algorithms is achieved at the expense of the simplicity seen in the straight selection, bubble, and insertion sorts.

Merge Sort

The merge sort algorithm is taken directly from the idea in the previous section:

MergeSort

Cut the array in half
Sort the left half
Sort the right half
Merge the two sorted halves into one sorted array

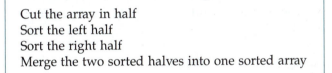
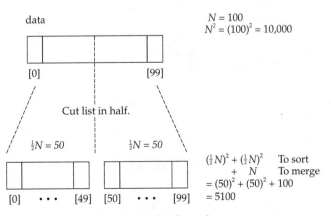

FIGURE 10.7 *Rationale for divide-and-conquer sorts.*

Merging the two halves together is an O(*N*) task: we merely go through the sorted halves, comparing successive pairs of values (one in each half) and putting the smaller value into the next slot in the final solution. Even if the sorting algorithm used for each half is O(*N*²), we should see some improvement over sorting the whole array at once.

Actually, because `MergeSort` is itself a sorting algorithm, we might as well use it to sort the two halves. That's right—we can make `MergeSort` a recursive function and let it call itself to sort each of the two subarrays:

MergeSort—Recursive

> Cut the array in half
> *MergeSort* the left half
> *MergeSort* the right half
> Merge the two sorted halves into one sorted array

This is the general case, of course. What is the base case, the case that does not involve any recursive calls to `MergeSort`? If the "half" to be sorted doesn't have more than one element, we can consider it already sorted and just return.

Let's summarize `MergeSort` in the format we used for other recursive algorithms. The initial function call would be `MergeSort(values, 0, numValues-1)`.

■■ **Function MergeSort(values, first, last)**

Definition:	Sorts the array items in ascending order.
Size:	values[first]..values[last]
Base Case:	If fewer than 2 items in values[first]..values[last], do nothing.
General Case:	Cut the array in half.
	MergeSort the left half.
	MergeSort the right half.
	Merge the sorted halves into one sorted array.

Cutting the array in half is simply a matter of finding the midpoint between the first and last indexes:

```
middle = (first + last) / 2;
```

Then, in the smaller-caller tradition, we can make the recursive calls to `MergeSort`:

```
MergeSort(values, first, middle);
MergeSort(values, middle+1, last);
```

So far this is pretty simple. Now we only have to merge the two halves and we're done.

Merging the Sorted Halves   Obviously all the serious work is in the merge step. Let's first look at the general algorithm for merging two sorted arrays, and then we can look at the specific problem of our subarrays.

To merge two sorted arrays, we compare successive pairs of elements, one from each array, moving the smaller of each pair to the "final" array. We can stop when the shorter array runs out of elements, and then move all the remaining elements (if any) from the other array to the final array. Figure 10.8 illustrates the general algorithm. We use a similar approach in our specific problem, in which the two "arrays" to be merged are actually subarrays of the original array (Figure 10.9). Just as in Figure 10.8 where we merged array1 and array2 into a third array, we need to merge our two subarrays into some auxiliary data structure. We only need this data structure, another array, temporarily. After the merge step, we can copy the now-sorted elements back into the original array. The whole process is shown in Figure 10.10.

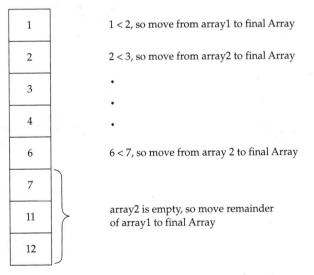

FIGURE 10.8   *Strategy for merging two sorted arrays.*

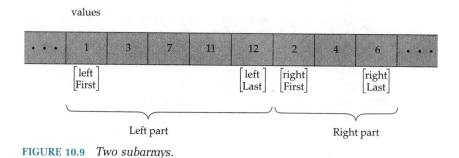

FIGURE 10.9   *Two subarrays.*

Let's specify a function, `Merge`, to do this task:

■▌ **Merge(ItemType values[ ], int leftFirst, int leftLast,**
  int rightFirst, int rightLast)

Function:	Merges two sorted subarrays into a single sorted piece of the array.
Preconditions:	values[leftFirst]..values[leftLast] are sorted;
	values[rightFirst]..values[rightLast] are sorted.
Postcondition:	values[leftFirst]..values[rightLast] are sorted.

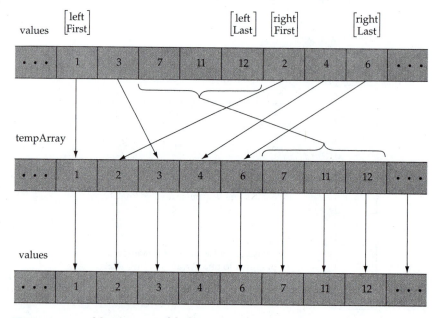

FIGURE 10.10   *Merging sorted halves.*

Here is the algorithm for `Merge`:

Merge (uses a local array, tempArray)

> Set saveFirst to leftFirst // to know where to copy back
> Set index to leftFirst
> WHILE more items in left half AND more items in right half
>   IF values[leftFirst] < values[rightFirst]
>   Set tempArray[index] to values[leftFirst]
>   Increment leftFirst
>   ELSE
>   Set tempArray[index] to values[rightFirst]
>   Increment rightFirst
>   Increment index
> Copy any remaining items from left half to tempArray
> Copy any remaining items from right half to tempArray
> Copy the sorted elements from tempArray back into values

In the coding of function `Merge`, we use `leftFirst` and `rightFirst` to indicate the "current" position in the left and right halves, respectively. Because these are not reference parameters, copies of these parameters are passed to function `Merge`. These copies are changed in the function, but the changed values are not passed out of `Merge`. Note that both of the "copy any remaining elements ..." loops are included. During the execution of this function, one of these loops never executes. Can you explain why?

```
template<class ItemType>
void Merge(ItemType values[], int leftFirst, int leftLast,
      int rightFirst, int rightLast)
// Post: values[leftFirst]..values[leftLast] and
//       values[rightFirst]..values[rightLast] have been merged.
//       values[leftFirst]..values[rightLast] are now sorted.
{
    ItemType tempArray[MAX_ITEMS];
    int index = leftFirst;
    int saveFirst = leftFirst;

    while ((leftFirst <= leftLast) && (rightFirst <= rightLast))
    {
        if (values[leftFirst] < values[rightFirst])
        {
            tempArray[index] = values[leftFirst];
            leftFirst++;
        }
```

```
        else
        {
            tempArray[index] = values[rightFirst];
            rightFirst++;
        }
        index++;
    }

    while (leftFirst <= leftLast)
    // Copy remaining items from left half.
    {
        tempArray[index] = values[leftFirst];
        leftFirst++;
        index++;
    }

    while (rightFirst <= rightLast)
    // Copy remaining items from right half.
    {
        tempArray[index] = values[rightFirst];
        rightFirst++;
        index++;
    }

    for (index = saveFirst; index <= rightLast; index++)
        values[index] = tempArray[index];
}
```

The MergeSort Function   As we said, most of the work is in the merge task. The actual `MergeSort` function is short and simple:

```
template<class ItemType>
void MergeSort(ItemType values[], int first, int last)
// Post: The elements in values are sorted by key.
{
    if (first < last)
    {
        int middle = (first + last) / 2;
        MergeSort(values, first, middle);
        MergeSort(values, middle + 1, last);
        Merge(values, first, middle, middle + 1, last);
    }
}
```

Analyzing MergeSort   We already pointed out that sorting two half-arrays is less work than sorting one whole array. How much less work is it? The bulk of the work occurs in the merge processing. In the `Merge` function we make comparisons on each element in the subarrays; this is an O(N) process. We also copy all the elements in the subarray back from `tempArray` into the original array, which is also O(N). This makes a total of 2N, but we drop constants. So the `Merge` function is O(N).

Now, how many times is the `Merge` function called? It is called in function `MergeSort` after the array has been divided in half and each of those halves has been sorted (using `MergeSort`, of course). In each of the recursive calls, one for the left half and one for the right, the array is divided in half again, making four pieces. Each of these pieces is similarly subdivided. At each level the number of pieces doubles (see Figure 10.11). We can keep dividing the array in half $\log_2 N$ times. (This is just like the analysis of the binary search algorithm.)

Each time the array is divided, we perform the O(N) `Merge` function to put it back together again. This gives us a product of $N \times \log_2 N$. Thus the whole algorithm is O($N\log_2 N$). Table 10.2 illustrates that, for large values of N, O($N\log_2 N$) is a big improvement over O(N^2).

The disadvantage of `MergeSort` is that it requires an auxiliary array that is as large as the original array to be sorted. If the array is large and space is a

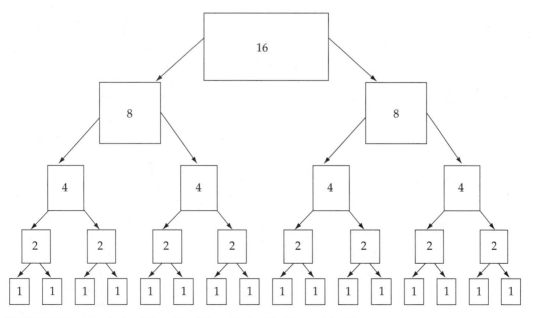

FIGURE 10.11   *Analysis of function MergeSort with N equal to 16.*

TABLE 10.2   Comparing N^2 and $N \log_2 N$

N	$\log_2 N$	N^2	$N\log_2 N$
32	5	1,024	160
64	6	4,096	384
128	7	16,384	896
256	8	65,536	2,048
512	9	262,144	4,608
1024	10	1,048,576	10,240
2048	11	4,194,304	22,528
4096	12	16,777,216	49,152

critical factor, this sort may not be an appropriate choice. Next we discuss two sorts that move elements around in the original array and do not need an auxiliary array.

QuickSort

We used QuickSort as the Case Study for Chapter 7. Like MergeSort, QuickSort is a "divide-and-conquer" algorithm that is inherently recursive. We postponed the analysis of QuickSort until this chapter.

The analysis of QuickSort is very similar to that of MergeSort. On the first call, every element in the array is compared to the dividing value (the "split value"), so the work done is O(N). The array is divided into two parts (not necessarily halves), which are then examined.

Each of these pieces is then divided in two, and so on. If each piece is split approximately in half, there are O($\log_2 N$) splits. At each split, we make O(N) comparisons. So QuickSort is also an O($N\log_2 N$) algorithm, which is quicker than the O(N^2) sorts we discussed at the beginning of this chapter.

But QuickSort isn't *always* quicker. Note that there are $\log_2 N$ splits *if* each split divides the segment of the array approximately in half. As we've seen, QuickSort is sensitive to the order of the data.

What happens if the array is already sorted when our first version of QuickSort is called? The splits are very lopsided, and the subsequent recursive calls to QuickSort break into a segment of one element and a segment containing all the rest of the array. This situation produces a sort that is not at all quick. In fact, there are $N - 1$ splits; in this case QuickSort is O(N^2).

Such a situation is very unlikely to occur by chance. By way of analogy, consider the odds of shuffling a deck of cards and coming up with a sorted deck. On the other hand, in some applications you may know that the original array is likely to be sorted or nearly sorted. In such cases you would want to

use either a different splitting algorithm or a different sort—maybe even
ShortBubble!

Heap Sort

In each iteration of the selection sort, we searched the array for the next-smallest
element and put it into its correct place in the array. Another way to write a
selection sort is to find the maximum value in the array and swap it with the
last array element, then find the next-to-largest element and put it into its place,
and so on. Most of the work in this sorting algorithm comes from searching
the remaining part of the array in each iteration, looking for the maximum
value.

In Chapter 9 we discussed the *heap*, a data structure with a very special
feature—we always know where to find its greatest element. Because of the
order property of heaps, the maximum value of a heap is in the root node. We
can take advantage of this situation by using a heap to help us sort. The general
approach of the heap sort is as follows:

1. Take the root (maximum) element off the heap, and put it into its place.
2. Reheap the remaining elements. (This puts the next-largest element into the
   root position.)
3. Repeat until there are no more elements.

The first part of this algorithm sounds a lot like the straight selection sort.
What makes the heap sort fast is the second step: finding the next-largest
element. Because the shape property of heaps guarantees a binary tree of
minimum height, we make only $O(\log_2 N)$ comparisons in each iteration, as
compared with $O(N)$ comparisons in each iteration of the selection sort.

Building a Heap   By now you are probably protesting that we are dealing
with an unsorted array of elements, not a heap. Where does the original heap
come from? Before we go on, we have to convert the unsorted array, values,
into a heap.

Let's take a look at how the heap relates to our array of unsorted elements.
In Chapter 9 we saw how heaps can be represented in an array with implicit
links. Because of the shape property, we know that the heap elements take up
consecutive positions in the array. In fact, the unsorted array of data elements
already satisfies the shape property of heaps. Figure 10.12 shows an unsorted
array and its equivalent tree.

We also need to make the unsorted array elements satisfy the order
property of heaps. First let's see if there's any part of the tree that already
satisfies the order property. All of the leaf nodes (subtrees with only a single
node) are heaps. In Figure 10.13(a) the subtrees whose roots contain the values
19, 7, 3, 100, and 1 are heaps because they are root nodes.

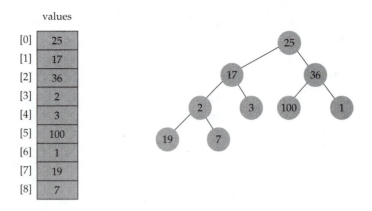

values

[0]	25
[1]	17
[2]	36
[3]	2
[4]	3
[5]	100
[6]	1
[7]	19
[8]	7

FIGURE 10.12 *An unsorted array and its tree.*

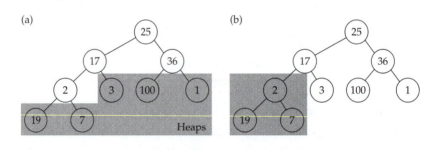

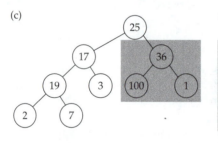

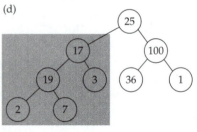

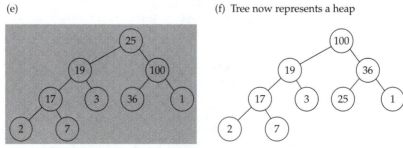

(f) Tree now represents a heap

FIGURE 10.13 *The heap-building process.*

Now let's look at the first *nonleaf* node, the one containing the value 2 [Figure 10.13(b)]. The subtree rooted at this node is not a heap, but it is *almost* a heap—all of the nodes *except the root node* of this subtree satisfy the order property. We know how to fix this problem. In Chapter 9 we developed a heap utility function, ReheapDown, that can be used to correct this exact situation. Given a tree whose elements satisfy the order property of heaps except (perhaps) at the root node, ReheapDown rearranges the nodes, leaving the (sub)tree as a heap.

We apply this function to all the subtrees on this level, then we move up a level in the tree and continue reheaping until we reach the root node. After ReheapDown has been called for the root node, the whole tree should satisfy the order property of heaps. This heap-building process is illustrated in Figure 10.13; the changing contents of the array are shown in Figure 10.14.

(In Chapter 9, we defined ReheapDown to be a member function of HeapType, a struct type. There, the function had two parameters, the indexes of the root node and the bottom node. Here, we assume a slight variation: ReheapDown is a global function that takes a third parameter—an array that is to be treated as a heap.)

The algorithm for building a heap is summarized below:

Build Heap

> FOR index going from first nonleaf node up to the root node
>   ReheapDown(values, index, numValues - 1)

We know where the root node is stored in our array representation of heaps—it's in values[0]. Where is the first nonleaf node? Because half the nodes of a complete binary tree are leaves (prove this yourself), the first nonleaf node may be found at position numValues/2 - 1.

	[0]	[1]	[2]	[3]	[4]	[5]	[6]	[7]	[8]
Original values	25	17	36	2	3	100	1	19	7
After ReheapDown index = 3	25	17	36	19	3	100	1	2	7
After index = 2	25	17	100	19	3	36	1	2	7
After index = 1	25	19	100	17	3	36	1	2	7
After index = 0	100	19	36	17	3	25	1	2	7

Tree is a heap.

FIGURE 10.14 *Changing contents of the array.*

Sorting Using the Heap   Now that we are satisfied that we can turn the unsorted array of elements into a heap, let's take another look at the sorting algorithm.

We can easily access the largest element from the original heap—it's in the root node. In our array representation of heaps, that is `values[0]`. This value belongs in the last-used array position `values[numValues-1]`, so we can just swap the values in these two positions. Because `values[numValues-1]` now contains the largest value in the array (its correct sorted value), we want to leave this position alone. Now we are dealing with a set of elements, from `values[0]` through `values[numValues-2]`, that is almost a heap. We know that all of these elements satisfy the order property of heaps, except (perhaps) the root node. To correct this condition, we call our heap utility, `ReheapDown`.

At this point we know that the next-largest element in the array is in the root node of the heap. To put this element in its correct position, we swap it with the element in `values[numValues-2]`. Now the two largest elements are in their final correct positions, and the elements in `values[0]` through `values[numValues-3]` are almost a heap. So we call `ReheapDown` again, and now the third-largest element is in the root of the heap.

This process is repeated until all of the elements are in their correct positions; that is, until the heap contains only a single element, which must be the smallest item in the array, in `values[0]`. This is its correct position, so the array is now completely sorted from the smallest to the largest element. Notice that at each iteration the size of the unsorted portion (represented as a heap) gets smaller and the size of the sorted portion gets larger. At the end of the algorithm, the size of the sorted portion is the size of the original array.

The heap sort algorithm, as we have described it, sounds like a recursive process. Each time we swap and reheap a smaller portion of the total array. Because it uses tail recursion, we can code the repetition just as clearly using a simple For loop. The node sorting algorithm is

Sort Nodes

FOR index going from last node up to next-to-root node
  Swap data in root node with values[index]
  ReheapDown(values, 0, index - 1)

Function `HeapSort` first builds the heap and then sorts the nodes, using the algorithms just discussed.

```
template<class ItemType>
void HeapSort(ItemType values[], int numValues)
// Post: The elements in the array values are sorted by key.
{
    int index;

    // Convert the array of values into a heap.
    for (index = numValues/2 - 1; index >= 0; index--)
        ReheapDown(values, index, numValues-1);

    // Sort the array.
    for (index = numValues-1; index >=1; index--)
    {
        Swap(values[0], values[index]);
        ReheapDown(values, 0, index-1);
    }
}
```

Figure 10.15 shows how each iteration of the sorting loop (the second For loop) would change the heap created in Figure 10.14. Each line represents the array after one operation. The sorted elements are shaded.

We entered the HeapSort routine with a simple array of unsorted values and returned to the caller with an array of the same values sorted in ascending order. Where did the heap go? The heap in HeapSort is just a temporary structure, internal to the sorting algorithm. It is created at the beginning of the function, to aid in the sorting process, and then is methodically diminished element by element as the sorted part of the array grows. At the end of the function, the sorted part fills the array and the heap has completely disappeared. When we used heaps to implement priority queues in Chapter 9, the heap structure stayed around for the duration of the use of the queue. The heap in HeapSort, in contrast, is not a retained data structure. It only exists for a while inside the HeapSort function.

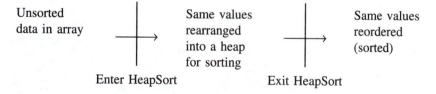

Analyzing Heap Sort   The code for function HeapSort is very short—only a few lines of new code plus the utility function ReheapDown that we developed in Chapter 9. These few lines of code, however, do quite a bit. All of the elements in the original array are rearranged to satisfy the order property of heaps, moving the largest element up to the top of the array, only to put it immediately into its place at the bottom. It's hard to believe from a small example such as the one in Figure 10.15 that HeapSort is really very efficient.

For small arrays, HeapSort is not very efficient because of all the "overhead." For large arrays, however, HeapSort is very efficient. Let's consider the sorting loop. We loop through N - 1 times, swapping elements and reheaping. The comparisons occur in ReheapDown. A complete binary tree with N nodes has $O(\log_2(N + 1))$ levels. In the worst cases, then, if the root element had to be bumped down to a leaf position, the ReheapDown function would make $O(\log_2 N)$ comparisons. So function ReheapDown is $O(\log_2 N)$. Multiplying this activity by the N - 1 iterations $[O(N)]$ shows that the sorting loop is $O(N\log_2 N)$.

Combining the original heap build, which is $O(N)$, and the sorting loop, we can see that HeapSort requires $O(N\log_2 N)$ comparisons. Note that, unlike QuickSort, HeapSort's efficiency is *not* affected by the initial order of the elements. HeapSort is just as efficient in terms of space; only one array is used to store the data.

	[0]	[1]	[2]	[3]	[4]	[5]	[6]	[7]	[8]
values	100	19	36	17	3	25	1	2	7
Swap	7	19	36	17	3	25	1	2	100
ReheapDown	36	19	25	17	3	7	1	2	100
Swap	2	19	25	17	3	7	1	36	100
ReheapDown	25	19	7	17	3	2	1	36	100
Swap	1	19	7	17	3	2	25	36	100
ReheapDown	19	17	7	1	3	2	25	36	100
Swap	2	17	7	1	3	19	25	36	100
ReheapDown	17	3	7	1	2	19	25	36	100
Swap	2	3	7	1	17	19	25	36	100
ReheapDown	7	3	2	1	17	19	25	36	100
Swap	1	3	2	7	17	19	25	36	100
ReheapDown	3	1	2	7	17	19	25	36	100
Swap	2	1	3	7	17	19	25	36	100
ReheapDown	2	1	3	7	17	19	25	36	100
Swap	1	2	3	7	17	19	25	36	100
ReheapDown	1	2	3	7	17	19	25	36	100
Exit from sorting loop	1	2	3	7	17	19	25	36	100

FIGURE 10.15   *Effect of HeapSort on the array.*

Other Efficiency Considerations

When N Is Small   As we have stressed throughout this chapter, we have based our analysis of efficiency on the number of comparisons made by a sorting algorithm. This number gives us a rough estimate of the computation time involved. The other activities that accompany the comparison (swapping, keeping track of Boolean flags, and so forth) contribute to the "constant of proportionality" of the algorithm.

In comparing Big-O evaluations, we ignored constants and smaller-order terms, for we wanted to know how the algorithm would perform for large values of N. In general, an $O(N^2)$ sort requires few extra activities in addition to the comparisons, so its constant of proportionality is fairly small. On the other hand, an $O(N\log_2 N)$ sort may be more complex, with more overhead and thus a larger constant of proportionality. This situation may cause anomalies in the relative performances of the algorithms when the value of N is small. In this case N^2 is not much greater than $N\log_2 N$, and the constants may dominate instead, causing an $O(N^2)$ sort to run faster than an $O(N\log_2 N)$ sort.

We have discussed sorting algorithms that have complexity either $O(N^2)$ or $O(N\log_2 N)$. The obvious question is: are there algorithms that are better than $O(N\log_2 N)$? No, it has been proven theoretically that we cannot do better than $O(N\log_2 N)$ for sorting algorithms that are based on comparing keys.

Eliminating Calls to Functions   We mentioned at the beginning of this chapter that it may be desirable, for efficiency considerations, to streamline the code as much as possible, even at the expense of readability. For instance, we have consistently written

```
Swap(item1, item2)
```

instead of the in-line expansion:

```
tempItem = item1;
item1 = item2;
item2 = temp;
```

Similarly, in `SelectionSort`, we coded the operation to find the minimum element as a function, `MinIndex`, and in `BubbleSort`, we coded a function `BubbleUp`. Coding such operations as functions made the code simpler to write and to understand, avoiding a more complicated nested loop structure.

Though the function calls are clearer, in the actual coding it may be better to use the in-line expansion (or at least to define the function using the `inline` specifier, which encourages the compiler to do so). Function calls require extra overhead that you may prefer to avoid in a sort, where these routines are called within a loop.

The recursive sorting functions, `MergeSort` and `QuickSort`, have a similar situation: they require the extra overhead involved in executing the recursive calls. You may want to avoid this overhead by coding nonrecursive versions of these functions.

Programmer Time   If the recursive calls are less efficient, why would anyone ever decide to use a recursive version of a sort? The decision involves a choice between types of efficiency. Up until now, we have only been concerned with minimizing computer time. While computers are becoming faster and cheaper, however, it is not at all clear that computer *programmer*s are following that trend. Therefore in some situations programmer time may be an important consideration in choosing a sort algorithm and its implementation. In this respect, the recursive version of `QuickSort` is more desirable than its nonrecursive counterpart, which requires the programmer to simulate the recursion explicitly.

Space Considerations   Another efficiency consideration is the amount of memory space required. In general, memory space is not a very important factor in choosing a sorting algorithm. We only looked at one sort, `MergeSort`, in which space would be a serious consideration. The usual time versus space trade-off applies to sorts—more space often means less time, and vice versa.

Because processing time is the factor that applies most often to sorting algorithms, we have considered it in detail here. Of course, as in any application, the programmer must determine goals and requirements before selecting an algorithm and starting to code.

More About Sorting in General

Keys   In our descriptions of the various sorts, we showed examples of sorting arrays using unique keys. In addition, a record may contain secondary keys, which may or may not be unique. For instance a student record may contain the following data members:

```
studentNumber   Primary unique key
name       ⎫
address    ⎬       Secondary keys
major      ⎭
```

If the data elements are only single integers, it doesn't matter whether the original order of duplicate values is kept. However, preserving the original order of records with identical key values may be desirable. If a sort preserves this order, it is said to be **stable**.

Stable Sort   A sorting algorithm that preserves the order of duplicates

---

Suppose the items on our array are student records with the following declarations:

```
struct AddressType
{
    .
    .
    .
    StrType city;
    long zip;
};

struct NameType
{
    StrType firstName;
    StrType lastName;
};

struct PersonType
{
    long studentNumber;
    NameType name;
    AddressType address;
};
```

The list may normally be sorted by the unique key `studentNumber`. For some purposes we might want to see a listing in order by name. In this case the sort key would be the `name` data member. To sort by zip code, we would sort on the `address.zip` data member.

If the sort is stable, we can get a listing by zip code, with the names in alphabetical order within each zip code, by sorting twice: the first time by name and the second time by zip code. A stable sort preserves the order of the records when there is a match on the key. The second sort, by zip code, produces many such matches, but the alphabetical order imposed by the first sort is preserved.

To get a listing by city, with the zip codes in order within each city and the names alphabetically sorted within each zip code, we would sort three times, on the following keys:

```
name
address.zip
address.city
```

The file would first be put into alphabetical order by name. The output from the first sort would be input to a sort on zip code. The output from this sort would be input to a sort on city name. If the sorting algorithms used were stable, the final sort would give us what we were looking for.

Of the sorts that we have discussed in this book, only HeapSort is inherently unstable. The stability of the other sorts depends on what the code does with duplicate values. In the exercises you are asked to examine the code for the other sorts as we have coded them and determine if they are stable.

Sorting with Pointers   Sorting large records using some kind of sort that swaps the contents of two places may require a lot of computer time just to move sections of memory from one place to another every time we make a swap. This move time can be reduced by setting up an array of *pointers* to the records and then rearranging the pointers instead of the actual records. This scheme is illustrated in Figure 10.16.

Note that after the sort the records are still in the same physical arrangement, but they may be accessed in order through the rearranged array of pointers.

This scheme may be extended to allow us to keep a large array of data sorted on more than one key. The data can be physically stored according to the primary key and auxiliary arrays can contain pointers to the same data but be sorted on secondary keys.

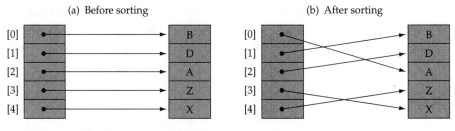

FIGURE 10.16   *Sorting arrays with pointers.*

▆❙ *Searching*

As we discussed in Chapter 2, for each particular structure used to hold data, the functions that allow access to elements in the structure must be defined. In some cases access is limited to the elements in specific positions in the structure, such as the top element in a stack or the front element in a queue. Often, when data is stored in a list or a table, we want to be able to access any element in the structure.

Sometimes the retrieval of a specified element can be performed directly. For instance, the fifth element of the list stored *sequentially* in an array-based list called `list` is found in `list.info[4]`. Often, however, you want to access an element according to some key value. For instance, if a list contains student records, you may want to find the record of the student named Suzy Brown or the record of the student whose ID number is 203557. In cases like these, some kind of *searching technique* is needed to allow retrieval of the desired record.

For each of the techniques we review or introduce, our algorithm must meet the following specifications. Note that we are talking about techniques within the class, not client code.

■❙ **FindItem(item, location)**

Function: Determines if an item in the list has a key that matches item's
Preconditions: List has been initialized.
              item's key has been initialized.
Postcondition: location = position of element whose key matches item's key, if it
■❙   exists; otherwise, location = NULL.

This specification has been written to apply to both array-based and linked lists, where `location` would be either an index in an array-based list or a pointer in a linked list, and NULL would be either -1 in an array-based list or the null pointer in a linked list.

Linear Searching

We cannot discuss efficient ways to find an element in a list without considering how the elements were inserted into the list. Therefore, our discussion of search algorithms is related to the issue of the list's `InsertItem` operation. Suppose that we want to insert elements as quickly as possible, and we are not as concerned about how long it does take to find them. We would put the element into the last slot in an array-based list and the first slot in a linked list. These are O(1) insertion algorithms. The resulting list is sorted according the time of insertion, not according to key value.

To search this list for the element with a given key, we must use a simple *linear* (or *sequential*) *search*. Beginning with the first element in the list, we search for the desired element by examining each subsequent item's key until either the search is successful or the list is exhausted:

Linear Search (unsorted data)

Initialize location to position of first item
Set found to false
Set moreToSearch to (have not examined Info(last))
WHILE moreToSearch AND NOT found
    IF item equals Info(location)
        Set found to true
    ELSE
        Set location to Next(location)
        Set moreToSearch to (have not examined Info(last))
IF NOT found
    Set location to NULL

Based on the number of comparisons, it should be obvious that this search is O(N), where N represents the number of elements. In the worst case, in which we are looking for the last element in the list or for a nonexistent element, we have to make N key comparisons. On the average, assuming that there is an equal probability of searching for any item in the list, we make N/2 comparisons for a successful search; that is, on the average we have to search half of the list.

High-Probability Ordering   The assumption of equal probability for every element in the list is not always valid. Sometimes certain list elements are in much greater demand than others. This observation suggests a way to improve the search: put the most-often-desired elements at the beginning of the list. Using this scheme, you are more likely to make a hit in the first few tries, and rarely do you have to search the whole list.

If the elements in the list are not static or if you cannot predict their relative demand, you need some scheme to keep the most frequently used elements at the front of the list. One way to accomplish this goal is to move each element accessed to the front of the list. Of course, there is no guarantee that this element is later frequently used. If the element is not retrieved again, however, it drifts toward the end of the list as other elements are moved to the front. This scheme is easy to implement for linked lists, requiring only a couple of pointer changes, but it is less desirable for lists kept sequentially in arrays, because of the need to move all the other elements down to make room at the front.

A second approach, which causes elements to move toward the front of the list gradually, is appropriate for either linked or sequential list representations. When an element is found, it is swapped with the element that precedes it. Over many list retrievals, the most frequently desired elements tend to be grouped at the front of the list. To implement this approach, we only need to modify the end of the algorithm to exchange the found element with the one before it in the list (unless it is the first element). If we had made `FindItem` a `const` member function and made this modification, we would have to remove the `const` declaration as the list is actually changed by the search operation. This change should be documented; it is an unexpected side effect of searching the list.

Keeping the most active elements at the front of the list does not affect the worst case; if the search value is the last element or is not in the list, the search still takes N comparisons. This is still an $O(N)$ search. The *average* performance on successful searches should be better, however. Both of these algorithms depend on the assumption that some elements in the list are used much more often than others. If this assumption is not applicable, a different ordering strategy is needed to improve the efficiency of the search technique.

Lists in which the relative positions of the elements are changed in an attempt to improve search efficiency are called *self-organizing* or *self-adjusting* lists.

Key Ordering   If a list is sorted according to the key value, we can write more efficient search routines. To support a sorted list, we must either insert the elements in order, or we must sort the list before searching it. (Note that inserting the elements in order is an $O(N^2)$ process, as each insertion is $O(N)$. If we insert each element into the next free slot, and then sort the list with a "good" sort, the process is $O(N\log_2 N)$.)

If the list is sorted, a sequential search no longer needs to search the whole list to discover that a element does *not* exist. It only needs to search until it has passed the element's logical place in the list—that is, until an element with a larger key value is encountered. Versions of the Sorted List ADT in Chapters 3 and 5 implement this search technique.

The advantage of linear searching of a sorted list is the ability to stop searching before the list is exhausted if the element does not exist. Again, the search is $O(N)$—the worst case, searching for the largest element, still requires N comparisons. The average number of comparisons for an unsuccessful search is now $N/2$, however, instead of a guaranteed N.

The advantage of linear searching is its simplicity. The disadvantage is its performance: in the worst case you have to make N comparisons. If the list is sorted and stored in an array, however, you can improve the search time to a worst case of $O(\log_2 N)$ by using a binary search. However, efficiency is improved at the expense of simplicity.

Binary Searching

We know of a way to improve searching from $O(N)$ to $O(\log_2 N)$. If the data elements are sorted and stored sequentially in an array, we can use a *binary search*. The binary search algorithm improves the search efficiency by limiting the search to the area where the element might be. The binary search algorithm takes a divide-and-conquer approach. It continually pares down the area to be searched until either the element is found or the search area is gone (the element is not in the list). We developed the `BinarySearch` function in Chapter 3, and converted it to a recursive function in Chapter 7.

The binary search, however, is not guaranteed to be faster for searching very small lists. Notice that even though the binary search generally requires fewer comparisons, each comparison involves more computation. When N is very small, this extra work (the constants and smaller terms that we ignore in determining the Big-O approximation) may dominate. Although fewer comparisons are required, each involves more processing. For instance, in one assembly-language program, the linear search required 5 time units per comparison, whereas the binary search took 35. For a list size of 16 elements, therefore, the worst-case linear search would require 5 * 16 = 80 time units. The worst-case binary search only requires 4 comparisons, but at 35 time units each, the comparisons take 140 time units. In cases where the number of elements in the list is small, a linear search is certainly adequate and sometimes faster than a binary search.

As the number of elements increases, however, the disparity between the linear search and the binary search grows very quickly. Look back at Table 1 in Chapter 3 to compare the rates of growth for the two algorithms.

Note that the binary search discussed here is appropriate only for list elements stored in a sequential array-based representation. After all, how can you efficiently find the midpoint of a linked list? However, you already know of a structure that allows you to perform a binary search on a linked data representation, the binary search tree. The operations used to search a binary tree are discussed in Chapter 8.

Hashing

So far, we have succeeded in paring down our $O(N)$ search to $O(\log_2 N)$ by keeping the list sorted sequentially with respect to the key value—that is, the key in the first element is less than (or equal to) the key in the second element, which is less than the key in the third, and so on. Can we do better than that? Is it possible to design a search of $O(1)$—that is, one that has a constant search time, no matter where the element is in the list?

In theory, that is not an impossible dream. Let's look at an example, a list of employees of a fairly small company. Each of the 100 employees has an ID number in the range 0 to 99, and we want to access the employee records by the key idNum. If we store the elements in an array that is indexed from 0 to 99, we can directly access any employee's record through the array index. There is a one-to-one correspondence between the element keys and the array index; in effect the array index functions as the key of each element.

In practice, however, this perfect relationship between the key value and the location of an element is not easy to establish or maintain. Consider a similar small company that uses its employees' five-digit ID number as the primary key. Now the range of key values is from 00000 to 99999. Obviously it is impractical to set up an array of 100,000 elements, of which only 100 are needed, just to make sure that each employee's element is in a perfectly unique and predictable location.

What if we keep the array size down to the size that we actually need (an array of 100 elements) and just use the last two digits of the key to identify each employee? For instance, the element of employee 53374 is in employeeList.info[74], and the element of employee 81235 is in employeeList.info[35]. Note that the elements are not sorted according to the *value* of the key as they were in our earlier discussion; the position of employee 81235's record precedes that of employee 53374 in the array, even though the value of its key is larger. Instead, the elements are sorted with respect to some *function* of the key value.

This function is called a **hash function**, and the search technique we are using is called **hashing**. In the case of the employee list above, the hash function is (Key % 100). The key (idNum) is divided by 100, and the remainder is used as an index into the array of employee elements, as illustrated in Figure 10.17. This function assumes that the array is indexed from 0 to 99 (MAX_ITEMS

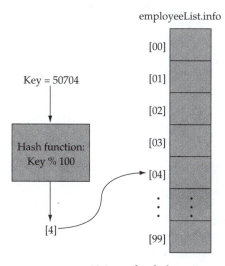

FIGURE 10.17 *Using a hash function to determine the location of the element in an array.*

= 100). The function to perform the conversion of key values to indexes is very simple:

```
int ItemType::Hash() const
// Post: Function value = an integer between 0 and MAX_ITEMS-1.
{
    return (idNum % 100);
}
```

Here we assume that Hash is a member function of ItemType, the type of the items in the list, and that idNum is a data member of ItemType.

Hash Function   A function used to manipulate the key of an element in a list to identify its location in the list

Hashing   The technique used for ordering and accessing elements in a list in a relatively constant amount of time by manipulating the key to identify its location in the list

---

This hash function has two uses. As we have seen, it is used as a method of accessing the list element. The result of the hash function tells us where to *look* for a particular element—information we need to retrieve, modify, or delete the element. Here, for example, is a simple version of function RetrieveItem, which assumes that the element is in the list.

```
template<class ItemType>
void ListType<ItemType>::RetrieveItem(ItemType& item)
// Post: item is a copy of the element in the array
//       at position item.Hash().
{
    int location;

    location = item.Hash();
    item = info[location];
}
```

There is a second use of the hash function. It determines where in the array to *store* the element. If the employee list elements were inserted into the list using an insert operation from Chapter 3—into sequential array slots or into slots with their relative order determined by the key value—we could not use the hash function to retrieve them. We have to create a version of an insert operation that puts each new element into the correct slot *according to the hash function*. Here is a simple version of `InsertItem`, which assumes that the array slot at the index returned from the hash function is not in use:

```
template<class ItemType>
void ListType<ItemType>::InsertItem(ItemType item)
// Post: item is stored in the array at position item.Hash().
{
    int location;

    location = item.Hash();
    info[location] = item;
    length++;
}
```

Figure 10.18(a) shows an array whose elements—records for the employees with the key values (unique ID numbers) 12704, 31300, 49001, 52202, and 65606—were added using `InsertItem`. Note that this function does not fill the array positions sequentially. Because we have not yet inserted any elements whose keys produce the hash values 3 and 5, the array slots [3] and [5] are logically "empty." This is different from the approach we used in Chapter 3 to create a sorted list. In Figure 10.18(b), the same employee records have been inserted into a sorted list using the `InsertItem` operation from Chapter 3. Note that, unless the hash function was used to determine where to insert an element, the hash function is *useless* for finding the element.

Collisions   By now you are probably objecting to this scheme on the grounds that it does not guarantee unique hash locations. ID number 01234 and ID

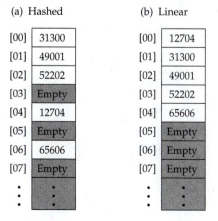

(a) Hashed

[00]	31300
[01]	49001
[02]	52202
[03]	Empty
[04]	12704
[05]	Empty
[06]	65606
[07]	Empty

(b) Linear

[00]	12704
[01]	31300
[02]	49001
[03]	52202
[04]	65606
[05]	Empty
[06]	Empty
[07]	Empty

FIGURE 10.18   *Comparing hashed and sequential lists of identical elements.*

number 91234 both "hash" to the same location: `list.info[34]` The problem of avoiding these **collisions** is the biggest challenge in designing a good hash function. A good hash function *minimizes collisions* by spreading the elements uniformly throughout the array. We say "minimizes collisions," for it is extremely difficult to avoid them completely.

Collision   The condition resulting when two or more keys produce the same hash location

---

Assuming that there are some collisions, where do you store the elements that cause them? We briefly describe several popular collision-handling algorithms in the next sections. Note that the scheme that is used to find the place to store an element determines the method that is subsequently used to retrieve it.

Linear Probing   A simple approach to resolving collisions is to store the colliding element into the next available space. This technique is known as **linear probing**. In the situation in Figure 10.19, we want to add the employee element with the key ID number 77003. The hash function returns 3. But there already is an element stored in this array slot, the record for Employee 50003. We increment `location` to 4 and examine the next array slot. `list.info[4]`

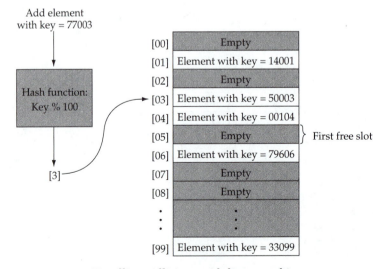

FIGURE 10.19 *Handling collisions with linear probing.*

is also in use, so we increment `location` again. This time we find a slot that is empty, so we store the new element into `list.info[5]`.

Linear Probing Resolving a hash collision by sequentially searching a hash table beginning at the location returned by the hash function

---

What happens if the key hashes to the last index in the array and that space is in use? We can consider the array as a circular structure and continue looking for an empty slot at the beginning of the array. This situation is similar to our circular array-based queue in Chapter 4. There we used the % operator when we incremented our index. We can use similar logic here.

How do we know whether an array slot is "empty"? We can initialize the array slot to contain a special `emptyItem` value. This value (a parameter to the class constructor) must be syntactically legal, but semantically illegal. For instance, if all employees have nonnegative integer `idNum` keys, we can use -1 as the key value for an "empty" slot. Now it is easy to tell if the slot is free. We compare the value in the position to `emptyItem`.

Here is a version of `InsertItem` that uses linear probing to find a place to store a new element. It assumes that there is room in the array for another element; that is, a check has been made for `IsFull` before the function is called. (We have retained the `length` member. Even though it no longer tells us where the end of the list is, it is still useful in determining if the list is full.)

```
template<class ItemType>
void ListType<ItemType>::InsertItem(ItemType item)
// Post: item is stored in the array at position item.Hash()
//       or the next free spot.
{
    int location;

    location = item.Hash();
    while (info[location] != emptyItem)
        location = (location + 1) % MAX_ITEMS;
    info[location] = item;
    length++;
}
```

To search for an element using this collision-handling technique, we perform the hash function on the key, then compare the desired key to the actual key in the element at the designated location. If the keys do not match, we use linear probing, beginning at the next slot in the array. Following is a version of function `RetrieveItem` that uses this approach. If the element is not found in the list, the outgoing parameter `found` is false, and `item` is undefined.

```cpp
template<class ItemType>
void ListType<ItemType>::RetrieveItem(ItemType& item, bool& found)
{
    int location;
    int startLoc;
    bool moreToSearch = true;

    startLoc = item.Hash();
    location = startLoc;
    do
    {
        if (info[location] == item || info[location] == emptyItem)
            moreToSearch = false;
        else
            location = (location + 1) % MAX_ITEMS;
    } while (location != startLoc && moreToSearch);
    found = (info[location] == item);
    if ( found)
        item = info[location];
}
```

We have discussed the insertion and retrieval of elements in a hash table, but we have not yet mentioned how to delete an element from the table. If we did not need to concern ourselves with collisions, the deletion algorithm would be simple:

Delete

> Set location to item.Hash()
> Set info[location] to emptyItem

Collisions, however, complicate the matter. We can find the element using the same search approach as we used for `RetrieveItem`. But when we locate the element in the hash table, we cannot merely replace the item with `emptyItem`. A review of `RetrieveItem` above shows the problem. In the loop, the detection of an empty slot ends the search. If `DeleteItem` "empties" the slot occupied by a deleted element, we may terminate a subsequent search prematurely.

Let's look at an example. In Figure 10.20, suppose we delete the element with the key 77003 by setting the array slot [5] to emptyItem. A subsequent search for the element with the key 42504 would begin at the hash location [4]. The record in this slot is not the one we are looking for, so we increment the hash location to [5]. This slot, which formerly was occupied by the record that we deleted, is now empty (contains emptyItem), so we terminate the search. We haven't really finished searching, however—the record that we are looking for is in the next slot.

One solution to this problem is to create a third constant value, deletedItem, to use in slots that were occupied by deleted records. If a slot contains deletedItem, it means that this slot is currently free, but the slot was previously occupied.

With this change, we must modify both the insertion and retrieval operations to process slots correctly. The insertion algorithm treats a slot with deletedItem and emptyItem the same; the search for an available slot for the new element ends. emptyItem halts the search in function RetrieveItem, but deletedItem does not.

This solution corrects the search problem, but generates another: after many deletions, the search "path" to a record may travel through many array slots with deletedItem. This may cause the efficiency of retrieving an element to deteriorate. These problems illustrate that hash tables, in the forms that we have studied thus far, are not the most effective data structure for implementing lists whose elements may be deleted.

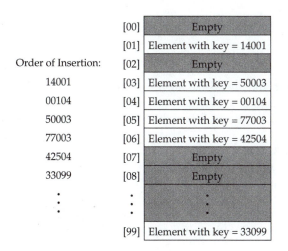

FIGURE 10.20 *A hash table with linear probing.*

Clustering One problem with linear probing is that it results in a situation called **clustering**. A good hash function results in a uniform distribution of indexes throughout the array's index range. Initially, therefore, records are inserted throughout the array, each slot equally likely to be filled. Over time, however, after a number of collisions have been resolved, the distribution of records in the array becomes less and less uniform. The records tend to cluster together, as multiple keys begin to compete for a single hash location.

Clustering The tendency of elements to become unevenly distributed in the hash table, with many elements clustering around a single hash location

---

Consider the hash table in Figure 10.20. Only a record whose key produces the hash value 8 would be inserted into array slot [8]. However, any records with keys that produce the hash values 3, 4, 5, 6, or 7 would be inserted into array slot [7]. That is, array slot [7] is five times as likely as array slot [8] to be filled. Clustering results in inconsistent efficiency of insertion and retrieval operations.

Rehashing The technique of linear probing discussed here is an example of collision resolution by **rehashing**. If the hash function produces a collision, the hash value is used as the input to a *rehash function* to compute a new hash value. In the previous section, we added 1 to the hash value to create a new hash value; that is, we used the rehash function:

(HashValue + 1) % 100

For rehashing with linear probing, you can use any function

(HashValue + *constant*) % *array-size*

as long as *constant* and *array-size* are relatively prime—that is, if the largest number that divides both of them evenly is 1. For instance, given the 100-slot array in Figure 10.21, we might use the constant 3 in the rehash function:

(HashValue + 3) % 100.

(Though 100 is not a prime number, 3 and 100 are relatively prime; they have no common factor larger than 1.)

Suppose that we want to add a record with the key 14001 to the hash table in Figure 10.21. The original hash function (Key % 100) returns the hash value

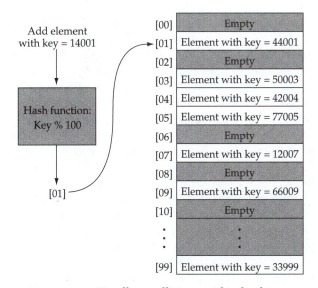

FIGURE 10.21 *Handling collisions with rehashing.*

Rehashing Resolving a collision by computing a new hash location from a hash function that manipulates the original location rather than the element's key

1, but this array slot is in use; it contains the record with the key 44001. To determine the next array slot to try, we apply the rehash function using the results of the first hash function as input: $(1 + 3) \% 100 = 4$. The array slot at index [4] is also in use, so we reapply the rehash function until we get an available slot. Each time, we use the value computed from the previous rehash as input to the rehash function. The second rehash gives us $(4 + 3) \% 100 = 7$; this slot is in use. The third rehash gives us $(7 + 3) \% 100 = 10$; the array slot at index [10] is empty, so the new element is inserted there.

To understand why the constant and the number of array slots must be relatively prime, consider the rehash function

$$(\text{HashValue} + 2) \% 100.$$

We want to add the record with the key 14001 to the hash table pictured in Figure 10.21. The original hash function, Key % 100, returns the hash value 1. This array slot is already occupied. We resolve the collision by applying the rehash function above, examining successive odd-numbered indexes until a free slot is found. What happens if *all* of the slots with odd-numbered indexes are already in use? The search would fail—even though there are free slots with even-numbered indexes. This rehash function does not cover the full index range of the array. However, if the constant and the number of array slots are relatively prime (like 3 and 100), the function produces successive rehashes that eventually cover *every* index in the array.

Rehash functions that use linear probing do not eliminate clustering (although the clusters are not always visually apparent in a figure). For example, in Figure 10.21, any record with a key that produces the hash value 1, 4, 7, or 10 would be inserted into the slot at index [10].

In linear probing, we add a constant (usually 1) in each successive application of the rehash function. Another approach, called **quadratic probing**, makes the result of rehashing dependent on how many times the rehash function has been applied. In the *I*'th rehash, the function is

(HashValue + I^2) % *array-size*.

The first rehash adds 1 to HashValue, the second rehash adds 4, the third rehash adds 9, and so on. Quadratic probing reduces clustering, but it does not necessarily examine every slot in the array. For example, if *array-size* is a power of 2 (512 or 1024, for example), relatively few array slots are examined. However, if *array-size* is a prime number of the form (4 * *some-integer* + 3), quadratic probing does examine every slot in the array.

Quadratic Probing   Resolving a hash collision by using the rehashing formula (HashValue + I^2) % array-size, where *I* is the number of times that the rehash function has been applied

---

A third approach uses a pseudorandom number generator to determine the increment to HashValue in each application of the rehash function. **Random probing** is excellent for eliminating clustering, but it tends to be slower than the other techniques we have discussed.

Random Probing   Resolving a hash collision by generating pseudorandom hash values in successive applications of the rehash function

---

Buckets and Chaining   Another alternative for handling collisions is to *allow* multiple element keys to hash to the same location. One solution is to let each computed hash location contain slots for multiple elements, rather than just a single element. Each of these multi-element locations is called a **bucket**. Figure 10.22 shows a hash table with buckets that can contain three elements each. Using this approach, we can allow collisions to produce duplicate entries at the same hash location, up to a point. When the bucket becomes full, we must again deal with handling collisions.

Bucket   A collection of elements associated with a particular hash location

Another solution, which avoids this problem, is to use the hash value not as the actual location of the element, but as the index into an array of pointers. Each pointer accesses a **chain** of elements that share the same hash location. Figure 10.23 illustrates this solution to the problem of collisions. Rather than rehashing, we simply allow both elements to share hash location [3]. The entry in the array at this location contains a pointer to a linked list that includes both elements.

Chain   A linked list of elements that share the same hash location

To search for a given element, you first apply the hash function to the key and then search the chain for the element. Searching is not eliminated, but it is limited to elements that actually share a hash location. In contrast, with linear probing you may have to search through many additional elements if the slots following the hash location are filled with elements from collisions on other hash locations.

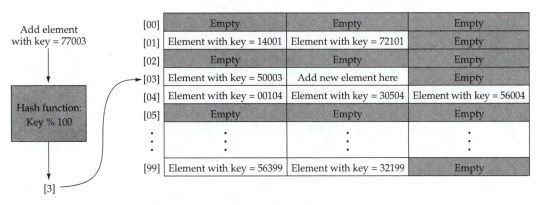

FIGURE 10.22 *Handling collisions by hashing with buckets.*

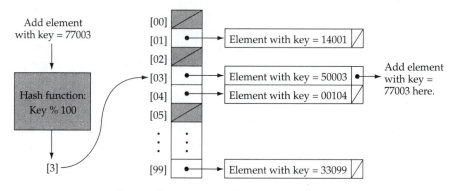

FIGURE 10.23   *Handling collisions by hashing with chaining.*

Figure 10.24 illustrates a comparison of the chaining and hash-and-search schemes. The elements were added in the following order:

45300
20006
50002
40000
25001
13000
65905
30001
95000

Figure 10.24(a) represents the linear probing approach to collision handling; Figure 10.24(b) shows the result of chaining the colliding elements. Let's search for the element with the key 30001.

Using linear probing, we apply the hash function to get the index [1]. Because list.info[1] does not contain the element with the key 30001, we search sequentially until we find the element in list.info[7].

Using the chaining approach, we apply the hash function to get the index [1]. list.info[1] directs us to a chain of elements whose keys hash to 1. We search this linked list until we find the element with the desired key.

Another advantage of chaining is that it simplifies the deletion of records from the hash table. We apply the hash function to obtain the index of the array slot that contains the pointer to the appropriate chain. The node can then be deleted from this chain using the linked-list algorithm from Chapter 5.

Choosing a Good Hash Function   One way to minimize collisions is to use a data structure that has more space than is actually needed for the number of elements, in order to increase the range of the hash function. In practice it is

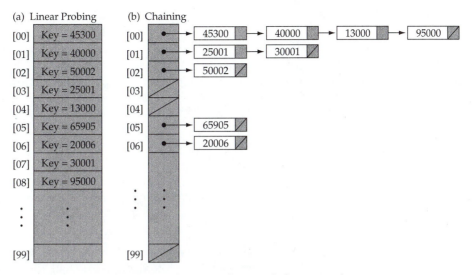

FIGURE 10.24 *Comparison of linear probing and chaining schemes.*

desirable to have the array size somewhat larger than the number of elements required, in order to reduce the number of collisions.

Selecting the table size involves a space vs. time trade-off. The larger the range of hash locations, the less likely it is that two keys hash to the same location. However, allocating an array that contains a large number of empty slots wastes space.

More important, you can design your hash function to minimize collisions. The goal is to distribute the elements as uniformly as possible throughout the array. Therefore you want your hash function to produce unique values as often as possible. Once you admit collisions, you must introduce some sort of searching, either through array or chain searching or through rehashing. The access to each element is no longer direct, and the search is no longer O(1). In fact, if the collisions cause very disproportionate chains, the worst case may be almost O(N)![2]

To avoid such a situation, you need to know something about the statistical distribution of keys. Imagine a company whose employee records are sorted according to a company ID six digits long. There are 500 employees, and we decide to use a chained approach to handling collisions. We set up 100 chains (expecting an average of five elements per chain) and use the hash function

---

2. This is O(N) "exclamation point," not O(N) factorial, as one long ago student complained when he got the answer wrong on a quiz.

```
idNum % 100
```

That is, we use the last two digits of the six-digit ID number as our index. The planned hash scheme is shown in Figure 10.25(a). Figure 10.25(b) shows what happened when the hash scheme was implemented. How could the distribution of the elements have come out so skewed? It turns out that the company's ID number is a concatenation of three fields:

X X X	X	X X
⌣	⌣	⌣
3 digits,	1 digit,	2 digits,
unique number	dept. number	year hired
(000–999)	(0–9)	(e.g., 89)

The hash scheme depended solely on the year hired to produce hash values. Because the company was founded in 1987, all the elements were crowded very disproportionately into a small subset of the hash locations. A search for an employee element, in this case, is $O(N)$. Although this is an exaggerated example, it illustrates the need to understand as completely as possible the domain and predicted values of keys in a hash scheme.

Division Method   The most common hash functions use the division method (%) to compute hash values. This is the type of function used in the preceding examples. The general function is

    Key % TableSize

We have already mentioned the idea of making the table somewhat larger than the number of elements required, in order to increase the range of hash values. In addition, it has been found that better results are produced with the division method when the table size is a prime number.

    The advantage of the division hash function is simplicity. Sometimes, however, it is necessary to use a more complicated (or even exotic) hash function to get a good distribution of hash values.

Other Hash Methods   How can we use hashing if the element key is a string instead of an integer? One approach is to use the internal representations of the string's characters to create a number that can be used as an index. (Recall that each ASCII character is represented in memory as an integer in the range 0 through 127.) For instance, here is a simple hash function that takes a five-element `char` array and produces a hash value in the range 0 through `MAX_ITEMS-1`:

(a) The plan

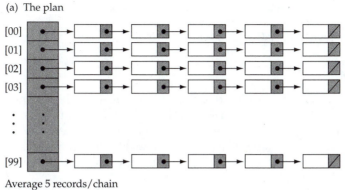

Average 5 records/chain
5 records x 100 chains = 500 emploees
Expected search — 0(5)

(b) The reality

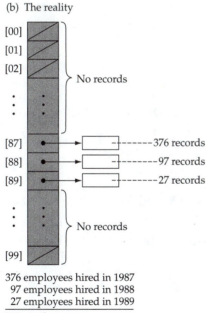

376 employees hired in 1987
 97 employees hired in 1988
 27 employees hired in 1989
_____
500 employees
Actual search 0(N)

FIGURE 10.25 *Hash scheme to handle employee records.*

```
int Hash(char letters[])
// Post: Function value = an integer between 0 and MAX_ITEMS-1.
{
    int sum = 0;
```

```
for (int index = 0; index < 5; index++)
    sum = sum + int(letters[index]);
return sum % MAX_ITEMS;
}
```

A hash method called **folding** involves breaking the key into several pieces and concatenating or exclusive-OR'ing some of them to form the hash value. Another method is to square the key and then use some of the digits (or bits) of the key as a hash value. There are a number of other techniques, all of which are intended to make the hash location as unique and random (within the allowed range) as possible.

Folding   A hash method that breaks the key into several pieces and concatenates or exclusive-ORs some of them to form the hash value

---

Let's look at an example of folding. Suppose we want to devise a hash function that results in an index between 0 and 255, and the internal representation of the int key is a bit string of 32 bits. We know that it takes 8 bits to represent the 256 index values ($2^8 = 256$). A folding algorithm to create a hash function might

1. break the key into four bit strings of 8 bits each,
2. exclusive-OR the first and last bit strings,
3. exclusive-OR the two middle bit strings, and
4. exclusive-OR the results of steps 2 and 3 to produce the 8-bit index into the array.

We illustrate this scheme using the key 618403. The binary representation of this key is

00000000000001001011011111010011.

We break this bit string into four 8-bit strings:

00000000   (leftmost 8 bits)
00001001   (next 8 bits)
01101111   (next 8 bits)
10100011   (rightmost 8 bits)

The next step is to exclusive-OR the first and last bit strings. (The exclusive OR of two bits is 0 if the two bits are the same, and 1 if they are different. To exclusive-OR (denoted as XOR) bit strings, we apply this rule to successive pairs of bits.)

```
        00000000
(XOR) 10100011
        10100011
```

Then we exclusive-OR the middle two bit strings:

```
        00001001
(XOR) 01101111
        01100110
```

Finally we exclusive-OR the results of the preceding two steps:

```
        10100011
(XOR) 01100110
        11000101
```

This binary number is equivalent to the decimal number 197. So the key 618403 hashes into the index 197.

The relationship between the key and the index is not intuitively obvious, but the indexes produced are likely to be uniformly distributed through the range of possible values.

When using an exotic hash function, you should keep two considerations in mind. First, you should consider the efficiency of calculating the function. Even if a hash function always produces unique values, it is not a good hash function if it takes longer to calculate the hash value than to search half the list. Second, you should consider programmer time. An extremely exotic function that somehow produces unique hash values for all of the known key values may fail if the domain of possible key values changes in a later modification.

Finally, we should mention that if you know all of the possible keys ahead of time, it is possible to determine a *perfect* hash function. For example, if you needed a list of elements whose keys were the reserved words in a computer language, it is possible to find a hash function that hashes each word to a unique location. In general, it takes a great deal of effort to discover a perfect hash function. And usually, we find that its computational complexity is very high, perhaps comparable to the effort required to do a binary search.

Analyzing Hashing   We began the discussion of hashing by trying to find a list implementation in which the insertion and deletion operations were O(1). If our hash function never produces duplicates or if the array size is very large compared to the expected number of items in the list, then we have reached our goal. In general, this is not the case. Clearly, as the number of elements approaches the array size, the efficiency of the algorithms deteriorates. A precise analysis of the complexity of hashing is beyond the scope of this book.

Informally we can say that the larger the array is relative to the expected number of elements, the more efficient the algorithms are.

■❙❙ *Radix Sort*

We have placed radix sort in a section by itself after sorting and searching for two reasons. First, radix sort is not a *comparison* sort; that is, the algorithm does not compare two items in the list. Therefore, we cannot analyze the amount of work done in terms of comparisons. In fact, the only thing that radix sort has in common with the other sorts is that it takes an unsorted list as input and returns a sorted list as output. The second reason for including radix sort here is that radix sort is to sorting as hashing is to searching. Radix sort makes use of the *values* in the individual keys to order the items just as hashing makes use of the values in the individual keys to determine where to place items. As in the other sorting algorithms, the number of values to be sorted and the array in which they are stored are parameters.

The idea behind radix sort is to divide the values to be sorted into as many subgroups as there are possible alternatives for each position in the key. For example, if the key is an integer number, each position is a digit and has ten possibilities: 0..9. If the key is a string of letters and case is not important, then each position has 26 possibilities: 'a'..'z'. The number of possibilities is called the **radix**. After subdividing the values into radix subgroups, we combine them back into one array and repeat the process. If we begin with the *least-significant* position in the key, regroup the values in order, repeat the process as many times as there are positions in the key, moving one position to the left each time, the array is sorted when we finish.

Radix   The number of possibilities for each position; the digits in a number
system

Let's illustrate the algorithm by sorting three-digit positive integers. Within a three-digit number, let's refer to the units, tens, and hundreds positions as positions 1, 2, and 3 respectively. We divide the values into ten subgroups based on the digit in the units position (position 1). Let's create an array of queues, `queues[0]..queues[9]`, to hold the groups. All items with 0 in the units position are enqueued into `queues[0]`; all items with a 1 in the units position are enqueued into `queues[1]`; etc. After the first pass through the array, we collect the subgroups (queues) with the one in `queues[0]` on top and the one in `queues[9]` on the bottom. We repeat the process using the tens position and the hundreds position. When we collect the queues the last time, the values in the array are in order. This algorithm is illustrated in Figures 10.26 and 10.27.

Look at the array after each pass; the digits in the position that corresponds to the pass number are sorted (Figure 10.26). Likewise, the digits in the pass number position are the same as the index of the queue that it is in (Figure 10.27).

Original Array	Array After 1st Pass	Array After 2nd Pass	Array After 3rd Pass
762	800	800	001
124	100	100	100
432	761	001	124
761	001	402	402
800	762	124	432
402	432	432	761
976	402	761	762
100	124	762	800
001	976	976	976
999	999	999	999

FIGURE 10.26 *Array after each pass.*

[0]	[1]	[2]	[3]	[4]	[5]	[6]	[7]	[8]	[9]
800	761	762		124		976			999
100	001	432							
		402							

(a) Queues after 1st pass

[0]	[1]	[2]	[3]	[4]	[5]	[6]	[7]	[8]	[9]
800		124	432			761	976		999
100						762			
001									
402									

(b) Queues after 2nd pass

[0]	[1]	[2]	[3]	[4]	[5]	[6]	[7]	[8]	[9]
001	100			402			761	800	976
	124			432			762		999

(c) Queues after 3rd pass

FIGURE 10.27 *Queues after each pass.*

Let's first write the algorithm for radix sort that matches our example and then examine ways to make it more general.

RadixSort(values, numValues)

FOR position going from 1 to 3
  FOR counter going from 0 to numValues-1
    Set whichQueue to digit at position "position" of values[counter]
    queues[whichQueue].Enqueue(values[counter])
  Collect queues

In this algorithm, each iteration of the outer loop corresponds to one pass in Figures 10.26 and 10.27. In the first pass we use the units digit of an integer item to determine the appropriate queue for the item. In the second pass we use the tens digit, and in the third we use the hundreds digit. Next we need to write the Collect Queues step of the algorithm. Here we collect the items from all of the queues and put them back into the `values` array.

CollectQueues

Set index to 0
FOR counter going from 0 to 9
  WHILE !queues[counter].IsEmpty()
    queues[counter].Dequeue(item)
    Set values[index] to item
    Increment index

Now that we understand the algorithm for three-digit integer keys, let's look at how we can make it more general before we code it. When we examined inserting an item into a sorted list in Chapter 3, we required the comparison of two items to be a member function of `ItemType`. The corresponding idea here is to make accessing the correct position in the key a function. For example, with an integer key, the digits must be extracted using / and %. If the key is a string, then access into an array of characters is needed. The point is that *only the user knows*, so the user should provide a member function for `ItemType` to access successive positions in the key. This function (`SubKey`) requires the position number as a parameter.

The radix sort function itself, however, must know the number of positions in the key (`numPositions`) and the number of possible values for each position in the key (radix). We make numPositions and radix parameters to the function.

```cpp
template<class ItemType>
void RadixSort(ItemType values[], int numValues,
    int numPositions, int radix)
// Post: Elements in values are in order by key.
{
    QueType<ItemType> queues[radix];
    // With default constructor, each queue size is 500
    int whichQueue;

    for (int position = 1; position <= numPositions; position++)
    {
        for (int counter = 0; counter < length; counter++)
        {
            whichQueue = values[counter].SubKey(position);
            queues[whichQueue].Enqueue(values[counter]);
        }
        CollectQueues(values, queues, radix);
    }
}

template<class ItemType>
void CollectQueues(ItemType values[], QueType<ItemType> queues[],
    int radix)
// Post: queues are concatenated with queues[0]'s on top and
//       queues[9]'s on the bottom and copied into values.
{
    int index = 0;
    ItemType item;

    for (int counter = 0; counter < radix; counter++)
    {
        while (!queues[counter].IsEmpty())
        {
            queues[counter].Dequeue(item);
            values[index] = item;
            index++;
        }
    }
}
```

If the keys are integer values, function SubKey must take the position number and extract the digit in that position. Let's calculate a few positions and look for a pattern. Assume itemKey is the four-digit integer 8749.

Position is 1: `itemKey % 10` = 9
Position is 2: `(itemKey / 10) % 10` = 4
Position is 3: `(itemKey / 100) % 10` = 7
Position is 4: `(itemKey / 1000) % 10` = 8

Notice that as the position number gets larger, the second operand of the `/` operation increases. If we rewrite the first calculation as

Position is 1: `(itemKey / 1) % 10`

the pattern is clearer:

Result = `(itemKey / 10`$^{\text{position-1}}$`) % 10`

If the key is alphabetic, function `SubKey` must take each character and convert it to a number between 0 and 25 (if case does not count) or between 0 and 51 (if case does matter). The algorithm that you use depends on the character set of the machine you are using.

Analyzing RadixSort   The amount of work done by radix sort is more complicated than any we have examined so far. Each item in the array is processed `numPositions` times, making the Big-O analysis a function of two variables: N (the number of items to be sorted) and P (the number of positions in the key). The processing includes extracting a value from the key, inserting the item into a queue, dequeueing each item, and copying each item back into the array. We know that each operation has O(1). So an approximation is O($N*P$). However, when N is large, it dominates P. (N is the elephant and P is the goldfish.)

In each iteration of the radix sort, the queues were collected, meaning that each item to be sorted is processed twice on each iteration: once to put it into a queue and once when the queues are collected. The processing in the radix sort could be shortened somewhat if we use the linked queue implementation and access the queues directly to recreate the intermediate list in linked form. However, this would require copying the final linked version back into the array-based form.

What about space requirements? Our `RadixSort` requires space for at least two copies of each element: one place in the array and one place in the queue. If the queues are array based, the amount of space is prohibitive because there must be room in each queue for every element. If the queues are linked, additional space for N pointers is required. We can cut the space requirements if we realize that this algorithm works just as well if the values to be sorted are in linked form. Nodes can be removed from the linked structure and moved to the appropriate queue; then the linked structure can be recreated by concatenating the queues. In this way, only one copy of an item (plus a pointer) exists: either in the linked structure or in a subgroup (queue).

Hence, both time and space requirements can be improved in the radix sort, if the linked versions of the queue and list are used.

■ ‖ *Summary*

We have not attempted in this chapter to describe every known sorting algorithm. We have presented a few of the popular sorts, of which many variations exist. It should be clear from this discussion that no single sort is best for all applications. The simpler, generally $O(N^2)$ sorts work as well, and sometimes better, for fairly small values of N. Because they are simple, these sorts require relatively little time to write and maintain. As you add features to improve sorts, you add to the complexity of the algorithms, increasing both the work required by the routines and the programmer time needed to maintain them.

Another consideration in choosing a sort algorithm is the order of the original data. If the data are already sorted (or almost sorted), ShortBubble is $O(N)$, whereas some versions of a QuickSort are $O(N^2)$.

As always, the first step in choosing an algorithm is to determine the goals of the particular application. This step usually narrows down the options considerably. After that, knowledge of the strong and weak points of the various algorithms assists you in making a choice.

The following table summarizes the comparison among the sorts discussed in this chapter, in terms of Big-O.

TABLE 3.3   Comparison of Sorting Algorithms

	Order of Magnitude		
Sort	Best Case	Average Case	Worst Case
SelectionSort	$O(N^2)$	$O(N^2)$	$O(N^2)$
BubbleSort	$O(N^2)$	$O(N^2)$	$O(N^2)$
ShortBubble	$O(N)$ (*)	$O(N^2)$	$O(N^2)$
InsertionSort	$O(N)$ (*)	$O(N^2)$	$O(N^2)$
MergeSort	$O(N\log_2 N)$	$O(N\log_2 N)$	$O(N\log_2 N)$
QuickSort	$O(N\log_2 N)$	$O(N\log_2 N)$	$O(N^2)$ (depends on split)
HeapSort	$O(N\log_2 N)$	$O(N\log_2 N)$	$O(N\log_2 N)$

* Data almost sorted.

Radix sort is not shown in this table because it is not based on key comparisons. Radix sort uses the values in different key positions to successively divide the list into sublists and collects the sublists back together again. After this process is repeated as many times as there are positions in the key, the list is sorted.

Searching, like sorting, is a topic that is closely tied to the goal of efficiency. We speak of a sequential search as an $O(N)$ search, because it may require up to N comparisons to locate an element. (N refers to the number of elements in the list.) Binary searches are considered to be $O(\log_2 N)$ and are appropriate for arrays only if they are sorted. A binary search tree may be used to allow binary searches on a linked structure. The goal of hashing is to produce a search that approaches $O(1)$. Because of collisions of hash locations, some searching or rehashing is usually necessary. A good hash function minimizes collisions and distributes the elements randomly throughout the table.

To solve a problem, programmers usually would rather create a new algorithm than review someone else's solution. Why then have we devoted the past chapter to a discussion of well-known sorting and searching algorithms? First, it is important to be familiar with several of the basic sorting and searching techniques. These are tools that you will use over and over again in a programming environment, and you need to know which ones are appropriate solutions to different problems. Second, a review of sorting and searching techniques has given us another opportunity to examine a measuring tool—the Big-O approximation—that helps us determine how much work is required by a particular algorithm. Both building and measuring tools are needed to construct sound program solutions.

■‖ *Exercises*

1. Show the contents of the array

43	7	10	23	18	4	19	5	66	14
[0]	[1]	[2]	[3]	[4]	[5]	[6]	[7]	[8]	[9]

   after the fourth iteration of
   (a) `BubbleSort`
   (b) `SelectionSort`
   (c) `InsertionSort`

2. (a) Show how the values in the array in Exercise 1 would have to be rearranged to satisfy the heap property.
   (b) Show how the array would look with four values in the sorted portion after reheaping.

3. Show how the values in the array in Exercise 1 would be arranged immediately before the execution of function `Merge` in the original (nonrecursive) call to `MergeSort`.

4. Given the array

26	24	3	17	25	24	13	60	47	1
[0]	[1]	[2]	[3]	[4]	[5]	[6]	[7]	[8]	[9]

tell which sorting algorithm would produce the following results after four iterations:

(a)

1	3	13	17	26	24	24	25	47	60
[0]	[1]	[2]	[3]	[4]	[5]	[6]	[7]	[8]	[9]

(b)

1	3	13	17	25	24	24	60	47	26
[0]	[1]	[2]	[3]	[4]	[5]	[6]	[7]	[8]	[9]

(c)

3	17	24	26	25	24	13	60	47	1
[0]	[1]	[2]	[3]	[4]	[5]	[6]	[7]	[8]	[9]

5. How many comparisons would be needed to sort an array containing 100 elements using `ShortBubble`?
   (a) in the worst case?
   (b) in the best case?

6. A sorting function is called to sort a list of 100 integers that have been read from a file. If all 100 values are zero, what would the execution requirements (in terms of Big-O) be if the sort used was
   (a) `QuickSort`, with the first element used as the split value?
   (b) `ShortBubble`?
   (c) `SelectionSort`?
   (d) `HeapSort`?
   (e) `InsertionSort`?
   (f) `MergeSort`?

7. How many comparisons would be needed to sort an array containing 100 elements using `SelectionSort` if the original array values were already sorted?
   (a) 10,000
   (b) 9,900
   (c) 4,950
   (d) 99
   (e) None of the above

8. A merge sort is used to sort an array of 1000 test scores in descending order. Which of the following statements is true?
   (a) The sort is fastest if the original test scores are in order from smallest to largest.
   (b) The sort is fastest if the original test scores are in completely random order.

(c) The sort is fastest if the original test scores are in order from largest to smallest.

(d) The sort is the same, no matter what the order of the original elements.

9. A list is in order from smallest to largest when a sort is called. Which of the following sorts would take the longest time to execute and which would take the shortest time?

(a) `QuickSort`, with the first element used as the split value

(b) `ShortBubble`

(c) `SelectionSort`

(d) `HeapSort`

(e) `InsertionSort`

(f) `MergeSort`

10. (a) In what case(s), if any, is the bubble sort $O(N)$?

(b) In what case(s), if any, is the selection sort $O(\log_2 N)$?

(c) In what case(s), if any, is quick sort $O(N^2)$?

11. A very large array of elements is to be sorted. The program is to be run on a personal computer with limited memory. Which sort would be a better choice: heap sort or merge sort? Why?

12. Use the Three-Question Method to verify `MergeSort`.

13. True or False? Correct the false statements.

(a) `MergeSort` requires more space to execute than `HeapSort`.

(b) `QuickSort` (using the first element as the split value) is better for nearly sorted data than `HeapSort`.

(c) The efficiency of `HeapSort` is not affected by the order of the elements on entrance to the function.

14. Which is true about `QuickSort`?

(a) A recursive version executes faster than a nonrecursive version.

(b) A recursive version has fewer lines of code than a nonrecursive version.

(c) A nonrecursive version takes more space on the run-time stack than a recursive version.

(d) It can only be programmed as a recursive function.

15. What is meant by the statement that programmer time is an efficiency consideration? Give an example of a situation in which programmer time is used to justify the choice of an algorithm, possibly at the expense of other efficiency considerations.

16. Identify one or more correct answers: reordering an array of pointers to list elements, rather than sorting the elements themselves, is a good idea when

(a) the number of elements is very large.

(b) the individual elements are large in size.

(c) the sort is recursive.

(d) there are multiple keys on which to sort the elements.

17. Go through the sorting algorithms coded in this chapter and determine which ones are stable as coded. If there are unstable algorithms (other than `HeapSort`), make them stable.

18. Give arguments for and against using functions (such as Swap) to encapsulate frequently used code in a sorting routine.

19. Write a version of the bubble sort algorithm that sorts a list of integers in descending order.

20. We said that HeapSort is inherently unstable. Explain why.

21. Sooey County is about to have its annual Big Pig Contest. Because the sheriff's son, Wilbur, is majoring in computer science, the county hires him to computerize the Big Pig judging. Each pig's name (string) and weight (integer) are to be read in from the keyboard. The county expects 500 entries this year.

    The output needed is a listing of the ten heaviest pigs, sorted from biggest to smallest. Because Wilbur has just learned some sorting methods in school, he feels up to the task of writing this "pork-gram." He writes a program to read in all the entries into an array of records, then uses a selection sort to put the whole array in order according to the pigWeight member. He then prints the 10 largest values from the array.

    Can you think of a more efficient way to write this program? If so, write the algorithm.

22. State University needs a listing of the overall SAT percentiles of the 14,226 students it has accepted in the past year. The data are in a text file, with one line per student. That line contains the student's ID number, SAT overall percentile, math score, English score, and high school grade point average. (There is at least one blank between each two fields.) The output needed is a listing of all the percentile scores, one per line, sorted from highest to lowest. Duplicates should be printed. Outline an $O(N)$ algorithm to produce the listing.

23. Which sorting algorithm would you *not* use under the following conditions?
    (a) The sort must be stable.
    (b) Data is in descending order by key.
    (c) Data is in ascending order by key.
    (d) Space is very limited.

24. Determine the Big-O measure for SelectionSort based on the number of elements moved rather than on the number of comparisons,
    (a) for the best case.
    (b) for the worst case.

25. Determine the Big-O measure for BubbleSort based on the number of elements moved rather than on the number of comparisons,
    (a) for the best case.
    (b) for the worst case.

26. Determine the Big-O measure for QuickSort based on the number of elements moved rather than on the number of comparisons,
    (a) for the best case.
    (b) for the worst case.

27. Determine the Big-O measure for `MergeSort` based on the number of elements moved rather than on the number of comparisons,
    (a) for the best case.
    (b) for the worst case.

28. Fill in the following table, showing the number of comparisons needed either to find the value or to determine that the value is not in the array, given the following values:

    26, 15 27, 12, 33, 95, 9, 5, 99, 14

Value	Unsorted	Sorted, Sequential Search	Sorted, Binary Search	Binary Search Tree (entered as shown)
15				
17				
14				
5				
99				
100				
0				

For Exercises 29–32 use the following values:

66 47 87 90 126 140 145 153 177 285 393 395 467 566 620 35

29. Store the values into a hash table with 20 positions, using the division method of hashing and the linear probing method of resolving collisions.

30. Store the values into a hash table with 20 positions, using rehashing as the method of collision resolution. Use key % tableSize as the hash function, and (key + 3) % tableSize as the rehash function.

31. Store the values into a hash table with 10 buckets, each containing three slots. If a bucket is full, use the next (sequential) bucket that contains a free slot.

32. Store the values into a hash table that uses the hash function key % 10 to determine which of 10 chains to put the value into.

33. Fill in the following table, showing the number of comparisons needed to find each value using the hashing representations given in Exercises 29–32.

Number of Comparisons

Value	Exercise 29	Exercise 30	Exercise 31	Exercise 32
66				
467				
566				
735				
285				
87				

34. If you know the index of an element stored in an array of N unsorted elements, which of the following best describes the order of the algorithm to retrieve the element?
    (a) $O(1)$
    (b) $O(N)$
    (c) $O(\log_2 N)$
    (d) $O(N^2)$
    (e) $O(0.5\ N)$

35. The element being searched for is *not* in an array of 100 elements. What is the *average* number of comparisons needed in a sequential search to determine that the element is not there
    (a) if the elements are completely unsorted?
    (b) if the elements are sorted from smallest to largest?
    (c) if the elements are sorted from largest to smallest?

36. The element being searched for is *not* in an array of 100 elements. What is the *maximum* number of comparisons needed in a sequential search to determine that the element is not there
    (a) if the elements are completely unsorted?
    (b) if the elements are sorted from smallest to largest?
    (c) if the elements are sorted from largest to smallest?

37. The element being searched for *is* in an array of 100 elements. What is the *average* number of comparisons needed in a sequential search to determine the position of the element
    (a) if the elements are completely unsorted?
    (b) if the elements are sorted from smallest to largest?
    (c) if the elements are sorted from largest to smallest?

38. Choose the answer that correctly completes the following sentence: the elements in an array may be reordered by highest probability of being requested in order to reduce
    (a) the average number of comparisons needed to find an element in the list.
    (b) the maximum number of comparisons needed to detect that an element is not in the list.
    (c) the average number of comparisons needed to detect that an element is not in the list.
    (d) the maximum number of comparisons needed to find an element that is in the list.

39. Identify the following statements as True or False. Correct any false statements.
    (a) A binary search of a sorted set of elements in an array is always faster than a sequential search of the elements.
    (b) A binary search is an $O(N\log_2 N)$ algorithm.
    (c) A binary search of elements in an array requires that the elements be sorted from smallest to largest.
    (d) A high-probability ordering scheme would be a poor choice for arranging an array of elements that are equally likely to be requested.
    (e) When a hash function is used to determine the placement of elements in an array, the order in which the elements are added does not affect the resulting array.
    (f) When hashing is used, increasing the size of the array always reduces the number of collisions.
    (g) If we use buckets in a hashing scheme, we do not have to worry about collision resolution.
    (h) If we use chaining in a hashing scheme, we do not have to worry about collision resolution.
    (i) The functions in this chapter are used only for external searching (i.e., for disk searching).
    (j) The goal of a successful hashing scheme is an $O(1)$ search.

40. Choose the answer that correctly completes the following sentence: the number of comparisons required to find an element in a hash table with N buckets, of which M are full,
    (a) is always 1.
    (b) is usually only slightly less than N.
    (c) may be large if M is only slightly less than N.
    (d) is approximately $\log_2 M$.
    (e) is approximately $\log_2 N$.

41. How might you order the elements in a list of C++'s reserved words to use the idea of high-probability ordering?

42. How would you modify the radix sort algorithm to sort the list in descending order?

43. The radix sort algorithm uses an array of queues. Would an array of stacks work just as well?

Appendixes

APPENDIX A Reserved Words

The following identifiers are *reserved words*—identifiers with predefined meanings in the C++ language. The programmer cannot declare them for other uses in a C++ program.

asm	double	new	template
auto	else	operator	this
bool	enum	private	throw
break	extern	protected	true
case	false	public	try
catch	float	register	typedef
char	for	return	union
class	friend	short	unsigned
const	goto	signed	virtual
continue	if	sizeof	void
default	inline	static	volatile
delete	int	struct	while
do	long	switch	

APPENDIX B Operator Precedence

The following is a complete list of the C++ operators. Operators are binary unless marked unary.

Operators	*Associativity*
::	Left to right
() [] -> .	Left to right
++ -- ~ ! + - & * new (all unary)	Right to left
delete (cast) sizeof (all unary)	Right to left
->* .*	Left to right
* / %	Left to right
+ -	Left to right
<< >>	Left to right
< <= > >=	Left to right
== !=	Left to right
&	Left to right

^	Left to right
|	Left to right
&&	Left to right
||	Left to right
? :	Right to left
= += -+ etc.	Right to left
, (the operator, not the separator)	Left to right

APPENDIX C   Description of Selected Operators

Type of Operator	Operator	Meaning
arithmetic	*	Unary plus
	-	Unary minus
	+	Addition
	-	Subtraction
	*	Multiplication
	/	Floating point operands: floating point result Integer operands: integer quotient Mixed operands: floating point result
	%	Modulus (remainder from integer division; operands must be integral)
	++	Increment by one; can be prefix or postfix
	--	Decrement by one; can be prefix or postfix
	sizeof	Returns the size in bytes of its operand
assignment	=	Assignment; evaluate expression on the right and store in variable named on the left
I/O	<<	Insertion; insert the characters (if a string) or the value (if a variable or constant) in the output stream named on the left of the first insertion operator
	>>	Extraction; extract the value from the input stream named on the left of the first extraction operator and store in the place named on the right
relational	==	Equal to
	!=	Not equal to
	>	Greater than
	<	Less than
	>=	Greater than or equal to
	<=	Less than or equal to
logical	&&	AND is a binary Boolean operator. If both operands are true, the result is true. Otherwise, the result is false.
	||	OR is a binary Boolean operator. If at least one of the operands is true, the result is true. Otherwise, the result is false.

	!	NOT is a unary Boolean operator. NOT returns the opposite of the value of its operand: if the operand is true, the result is false; if the operand is false, the result it true.
pointer related	*	(postfix on a type or prefix on a variable in a pointer variable declaration) Declare a variable that is a *pointer to* a place that can contain a variable of the type; must be dereferenced to access the place pointed to
	*	(prefix on a pointer variable in an expression) Dereferencing operator; accesses *place pointed to*
	&	(postfix on a type or prefix on a variable in a reference variable declaration) Declare a variable that holds the address of a place that can contain a variable of the type; dereferenced automatically by the compiler
	&	(prefix on a variable) *Address of* a variable
	->	(infix between a pointer to `struct` or `class` variable and member name) Dereferences a pointer variable and accesses a member
	new	Returns the address of new space allocated for a dynamic variable of the type named on the right
	delete	Returns the space allocated for the dynamic variable whose pointer is on the right to the heap to be allocated again
selection	.	(infix: `struct` variable.member) Accesses the member of the `struct` variable
	.	(infix: `class` variable.member) Accesses the member data or function of the `class` variable
	[]	(postfix: encloses an integral expression) Accesses a position within the array variable named on the left
scope resolution	::	(infix: `class` type::function) Associates a function with the `class` in which it is declared

APPENDIX D   C++ Library Routines and Constants

Header File `ctype.h`

`isalnum(ch)`	Returns true if `ch` is a letter or a digit; false otherwise.
`isalpha(ch)`	Returns true if `ch` is a letter; false otherwise.
`iscntrl(ch)`	Returns true if `ch` is a control character; false otherwise.
`isdigit(ch)`	Returns true if `ch` is a digit; false otherwise.
`isgraph(ch)`	Returns true if `ch` is a nonblank printable character; false otherwise.
`islower(ch)`	Returns true if `ch` is lowercase; false otherwise.

`isprint(ch)`	Returns true if `ch` is a printable character; false otherwise.
`ispunct(ch)`	Returns true if `ch` is a nonblank printable character and is not a letter or a digit; false otherwise.
`isspace(ch)`	Returns true if `ch` is a whitespace character; false otherwise.
`isupper(ch)`	Returns true if `ch` is an uppercase letter; false otherwise.
`toupper(ch)`	Returns `ch` in uppercase regardless of original case.
`tolower(ch)`	Returns `ch` in lowercase regardless of original case.

HEADER FILE `string.h`

`strcat(s1, s2)`	Returns the base address of `s1` with `s2` concatenated on the end.
`strcmp(s1, s2)`	Returns a negative integer if `s1` comes before `s2`; returns zero if `s1` is equal to `s2`; and returns a positive integer if `s2` comes before `s1`.
`strcpy(s1, s2)`	Returns the base address of `s1` with `s2` copied in it.
`strlen(s)`	Returns the number of characters in `s`.

HEADER FILE `stddef.h`

`NULL`	The system-dependent null pointer constant (usually 0).

HEADER FILE `float.h`

`FLT_DIG`	Approximate number of significant digits in a `float` value on your machine.
`FLT_MAX`	Maximum positive `float` value on your machine.
`FLT_MIN`	Minimum positive `float` value on your machine.
`DBL_DIG`	Approximate number of significant digits in a `double` value on your machine.
`DBL_MAX`	Maximum positive `double` value on your machine.
`DBL_MIN`	Minimum positive `double` value on your machine.
`LDBL_DIG`	Approximate number of significant digits in a `long double` value on your machine.
`LDBL_MAX`	Maximum positive `long double` value on your machine.
`LDBL_MIN`	Minimum positive `long double` value on your machine.

HEADER FILE `limits.h`

`CHAR_BITS`	Number of bits in a byte on your machine.
`CHAR_MAX`	Maximum `char` value on your machine.
`CHAR_MIN`	Minimum `char` value on your machine.
`SHRT_MAX`	Maximum `short` value on your machine.
`SHRT_MIN`	Minimum `short` value on your machine.

INT_MAX	Maximum int value on your machine.
INT_MIN	Minimum int value on your machine.
LONG_MAX	Maximum long value on your machine.
LONG_MIN	Minimum long value on your machine.
UCHAR_MAX	Maximum unsigned char value on your machine.
USHRT_MAX	Maximum unsigned short value on your machine.
UINT_MAX	Maximum unsigned int value on your machine.
ULONG_MAX	Maximum unsigned long value on your machine.

APPENDIX E   The Character Sets

The following charts show the ordering of the two most common character sets: ASCII (American Standard Code for Information Interchange) and EBCDIC (Extended Binary Coded Decimal Interchange Code). The internal representation for each character is shown in decimal. For example, the letter A is represented internally as the integer 65 in ASCII and as 193 in EBCDIC. The blank character is denoted by a "□".

ASCII

Left Digit(s)	Right digit 0	1	2	3	4	5	6	7	8	9
0	NUL	SOH	STX	ETX	EOT	ENQ	ACK	BEL	BS	HT
1	LF	VT	FF	CR	SO	SI	DLE	DC1	DC2	DC3
2	DC4	NAK	SYN	ETB	CAN	EM	SUB	ESC	FS	GS
3	RS	US	□	!	"	#	$	%	&	'
4	(	)	*	+	,	-	.	/	0	1
5	2	3	4	5	6	7	8	9	:	;
6	<	=	>	?	@	A	B	C	D	E
7	F	G	H	I	J	K	L	M	N	O
8	P	Q	R	S	T	U	V	W	X	Y
9	Z	[	\	]	^	_	`	a	b	c
10	d	e	f	g	h	i	j	k	l	m
11	n	o	p	q	r	s	t	u	v	w
12	x	y	z	{	|	}	~	DEL		

Codes 00–31 and 127 are the following nonprintable control characters:

NUL	Null character	ENQ	Enquiry
SOH	Start of header	ACK	Acknowledge
STX	Start of text	BEL	Bell character (beep)
ETX	End of text	BS	Back space
EOT	End of transmission	HT	Horizontal tab

(ASCII control characters cont.)

LF	Line feed
VT	Vertical tab
FF	Form feed
CR	Carriage return
SO	Shift out
SI	Shift in
DLE	Data link escape
DC1	Device control one
DC2	Device control two
DC3	Device control three
DC4	Device control four

NAK	Negative acknowledge
SYN	Synchronous idle
ETB	End of transmitted block
CAN	Cancel
EM	End of medium
SUB	Substitute
ESC	Escape
FS	File separator
GS	Group separator
RS	Record separator
US	Unit separator
DEL	Delete

EBCDIC

Left Digit(s)	0	1	2	3	4	5	6	7	8	9
6					□					
7					¢	.	<	(	+	|
8	&									
9	!	$	*	)	;	¬	-	/		
10							^	,	%	_
11	>	?								
12		`	:	#	@	'	=	"		a
13	b	c	d	e	f	g	h	i		
14						j	k	l	m	n
15	o	p	q	r						
16		~	s	t	u	v	w	x	y	z
17								\	{	}
18	[	]								
19				A	B	C	D	E	F	G
20	H	I								J
21	K	L	M	N	O	P	Q	R		
22							S	T	U	V
23	W	X	Y	Z						
24	0	1	2	3	4	5	6	7	8	9

Nonprintable control characters—codes 00–63, 250–255, and those for which empty spaces appear in the chart—are not shown.

Answers to Selected Exercises

CHAPTER 1

Many of the questions in this chapter's exercises are "thought questions." The answers given here are typical or suggested responses, but they are not the only possible answers.

1. Software engineering is a disciplined approach to the creation and maintenance of computer programs throughout their whole life cycle.
2. (d) is correct. Although there is a general order to the activities, and in some cases it is desirable to finish one phase completely before beginning another, often the software phases overlap one another.
6. (a) When the program's requirements change; when a better solution is discovered in the middle of the design phase; when an error is discovered in the requirements due to the design effort.

    (b) When the program is being debugged, because of compilation errors or errors in the design; when a better solution is found for a part of the program that was already implemented; or when any of the situations in Part (a) occur.

    (c) When there are errors that cause the program to crash or to produce wrong answers; or when any of the situations in Parts (a) or (b) occur.

    (d) When an error is discovered during the use of the program; when additional functions are added to an existing software system; when a program is being modified to use on another computer system; or when any of the situations in Parts (a), (b), or (c) occur.
11. Customer, bank card, ATM, PIN, account, account number, balance, display
12. This is a thought question; answers vary by student.
13. The correction of errors early in the program's life cycle involves less rework. The correction can be incorporated into the program design. Detected late in the life cycle, errors may necessitate redesign, recoding, and/or retesting. The later the error is detected, the more rework one is likely to have to do to correct it.
17. The body of the While loop is not in braces.

    The comments include the call to Increment.

    The parameter to Increment is not a reference parameter.
18. A single programmer could use the inspection process as a way to do a structured "deskcheck" of his or her program and would especially benefit from inspection checklists of errors to look for.

19. (a) It is appropriate to start planning a program's testing during the earliest phases of program development.

20. *Unit testing* is the testing of a single unit of the program (for instance, a function). *Integration testing* is the testing of groups of already tested units to make sure that they interact correctly and that the whole program works according to its specification.

25. Top-down integration testing, using stubs, is performed to test the program in pieces, beginning with the top levels and continuing through the lower levels. Bottom-up integration testing, using test drivers, is used to test the lower level program pieces independently of the higher levels of the program.

26. Life-cycle verification refers to the idea that program verification activities can be performed throughout the program's life cycle, not just by testing the program after it is coded.

CHAPTER 2

1. *Data abstraction* refers to the logical picture of the data—what the data represent rather than how they are represented.

2. *Data encapsulation* is the separation of the physical representation of data from the applications that use the data at a logical (abstract) level. When data abstraction is protected through encapsulation, the data user can deal with the data abstraction but cannot access its implementation, which is encapsulated. The data user accesses data that are encapsulated through a set of operations specified to create, access, and change the data. Data encapsulation is accomplished through a programming language feature.

3. (a) Application level (e.g., College of Engineering's enrollment information for 1988)

   (b) Abstract level (e.g., list of student academic records)

   (c) Implementation level (e.g., array of records that contain the members studentID (an integer), lastName (a string of characters), firstName (a string of characters), etc.)

4. (a) Applications of type GroceryStore include shopping at the Safeway on Main Street, the Piggly Wiggly on Broadway, and the Kroger's on First Street.

   (b) User operations include SelectItem, CheckOut, PayBill, and so on.

(c)

▪️ Specification of CheckOut operation:

CheckOut (basket, bill)

Function:	Presents basket of groceries to cashier to check out; receives bill.
Precondition:	basket is not empty.
Postconditions:	bill = total charge for all the groceries in basket.
	basket contains all groceries arranged in paper sacks.

(d)

CheckOut

```
InitRegister
Set bill to 0
DO
    OpenSack
    WHILE More objects in basket AND NOT sackFull
        Take object from basket
        Set bill to bill + cost of this object
        Put object in sack
    Put full sack aside
WHILE more objects in basket
Put full sacks into basket
```

(e)

The customer does not need to know the procedure that is used by the grocery store to check out a basket of groceries and to create a bill. The logical level (c) above provides the correct interface, allowing the customer to check out without knowing the implementation of the process.

9. Each array has a base address. The index and the base address are used to access the items in the structure.

10. (a) `char name[20];`
    (b) 1009

15. `student.gpa=3.87;`
    Base + offset of gpa field = 100 + 21 = 121.

16. Number of slots * cells/slot = 100 * 25 = 2500.

19. In a struct, members are public by default and private only when marked. In a class, members are private by default and public only when marked.

20. The members of a class are private unless specified as public. Client code cannot access private members.

23. (a)

■ | **SquareMatrix ADT Specification**

Structure: An $N \times N$ square integer matrix.

Operations:

MakeEmpty(int n)
  Function: Initializes the size of the matrix to $n \times n$ and sets the values to zero.
  Precondition: n is less than or equal to 50.
  Postcondition: Matrix contains all zero values.

StoreValue(int i, int j, int value)
  Function: Stores value into the i, jth position in the matrix.
  Preconditions: Matrix has been initialized; i and j are between 0 and the size minus 1.
  Postcondition: value has been stored into the i, jth position of the matrix.

Add(SquareMatrixType one, Square MatrixType result)
  Function: Adds self and matrix one and stores the result in result.
  Preconditions: one and two have been initialized and are the same size.
  Postcondition: result = self + two.

Subtract(SquareMatrixType one, SquareMatrixType result)
  Function: Subtracts two from one and stores the result in result.
  Preconditions: self and one have been initialized and are the same size.
  Postcondition: result = self - two.

Print
  Function: Prints the matrix on the screen.
  Precondition: Matrix has been initialized.
  Postcondition: The values in the matrix have been printed by row on the screen.

Copy(SquareMatrixType one, SquareMatrixType two)
  Function: Copies two into one.
  Precondition: two has been initialized.
  Postcondition: one = two.

24. (a)

```
RelationType StrType::ComparedTo(StrType otherString) const
{
    int result;

    result = strcmp(letters, otherString.letters);
    if (result < 0)
        return LESS;
    else if (result > 0)
        return GREATER;
    else return EQUAL;
}
```

(b)

```
RelationType StrType::ComparedTo(StrType otherString) const
{
    int count = 0;
    bool equal = true;

    while (equal && letters[count] != '\0')
        if (letters[count] != otherString.letters[count])
            equal = false;
        else
            count++;
    if (otherString.letters[count] == '\0' && equal)
        return EQUAL;
    else if (equal) // more characters in otherString
        return LESS;
    else if (letters[count] < otherString.letters[count])
        return LESS;
    else return GREATER;
}
```

25.

```
void StrType::CopyString(StrType& newString)
{
    int count = 0;

    do
    {
        newString.letters[count] = letters[count];
        count++;
    }
    while (letters[count-1] != '\0');
}
```

CHAPTER 3

1. (a)

> ◼️ **Boolean IsThere(ItemType item)**
>
> *Function:*   Determines if item is in the list.
> *Precondition:*   List has been initialized.
> *Postcondition:* Function value = there exists an item in the list whose
>   key is the same as item's.
> ◼️

(b) `bool IsThere(ItemType item) const;`

(c)
```
bool UnsortedType::IsThere(ItemType item)
{
    bool moreToSearch;
    int location = 0;
    bool found = false;

    moreToSearch = (location < length);
    while (moreToSearch && !found)
    {
        switch (item.ComparedTo(info[location]))
        {
            case LESS    :
            case GREATER : location++;
                           moreToSearch = (location < length);
                           break;
            case EQUAL   : found = true;
                           break;
        }
    }
    return found;
}
```

(d) O(N) where N is the number of items in the list.

3. The specification and prototype are identical for the unsorted and sorted versions. Only the algorithm used to implement the search differs. Because the values in the list are sorted by key in Exercise 2, the binary search can be used to look for `item`. The binary search has O($\log_2 N$) in contrast to the O(N) linear search that must be used in an unsorted list.

4. (a)

■| **Boolean IsThere(ItemType item, UnsortedType list)**
Function: Determines if item is in the list.
Precondition: List has been initialized.
Postcondition: Function value = there exists an item in the list whose key
■ is the same as item's.

(b)
```
bool IsThere(ItemType item, UnsortedType list)
{
    ItemType item2;
    int counter = 1;
    bool found = false;

    list.ResetList();
    int length = list.LengthIs();
    while (counter <= length && !found)
    {
        list.GetNextItem(item2);
        if (item.ComparedTo(item2) == EQUAL)
            found = true;
        counter++;
    }

    return found;
}
```
or
```
bool IsThere(ItemType item, UnsortedType list)
{
    bool found;
    list.RetrieveItem(item, found);
    return found;
}
```

(c) Both of these functions are O(N) The first is obviously O(N); the second lets `RetrieveItem`, which is O(N), do the search.

(d) The member function has direct access to the array where the items are stored; the client has to use the class access functions to retrieve each item in turn or call the member function `RetrieveItem`. The order of `IsThere` is the same in both cases, but the overhead included in the constant is greater in the client version because of the extra function calls.

6. (a)
```
void MergeLists(SortedType list1, SortedType list2,
    SortedType& result);
```
(b)
```
void MergeLists(SortedType list1, SortedType list2,
    SortedType& result)
```

```
{
    int length1;
    int length2;
    int counter1 = 1;
    int counter2 = 1;
    ItemType item1;
    ItemType item2;

    length1 = list1.LengthIs();
    length2 = list2.LengthIs();
    list1.ResetList();
    list2.ResetList();
    list1.GetNextItem(item1);
    list2.GetNextItem(item2);
    result.MakeEmpty();

    while (counter1 <= length1 && counter2 <= length2)
        switch (item1.ComparedTo(item2))
        {
            case LESS    : result.InsertItem(item1);
                           if (counter1 < length1)
                               list1.GetNextItem(item1);
                           counter1++;
                           break;
            case GREATER: result.InsertItem(item2);
                           if (counter2 < length2)
                               list2.GetNextItem(item2);
                           counter2++;
                           break;
        }
    for (; counter1 <= length1; counter1++)
    {
        result.InsertItem(item1);
        if (counter1 < length1)
            list1.GetNextItem(item1);
    }
    for (; counter2 <= length2; counter2++)
    {
        result.InsertItem(item2);
        if (counter2 < length2)
            list2.GetNextItem(item2);
    }
}
```

9. (a)

> ■| **DeleteItem (ItemType item)**
>
> *Function*:   Deletes the element whose key matches item's key.
> *Preconditions*: List has been initialized.
>   Key member of item is initialized.
>   At most one element in list has a key matching item's key.
> *Postcondition*: If an element in list had a key matching item's key, the item has been removed; otherwise, the list is unchanged.

(b)

```
void UnsortedType::DeleteItem(ItemType item)
{
    int location = 0;
    bool found = false;

    while (!found && location < length)
    {
        if (item.ComparedTo(info[location]) == EQUAL)
            found = true;
        else
            location++;
    }
    if ( found)
    {
        info[location] = info[length - 1];
        length--;
    }
}
```

(c)

> ■| **DeleteItem (ItemType item)**
>
> *Function*:   Deletes the element whose key matches item's key.
> *Preconditions*: List has been initialized.
>   Key member of item is initialized.
> *Postcondition*: No element in list has a key matching item's key.

(d)

```
void UnsortedType::DeleteItem(ItemType item)
{
    int location = 0;

    while (location < length)
    {
```

```
                    if (item.ComparedTo(info[location]) == EQUAL)
                    {
                        info[location] = info[length - 1];
                        length--;
                    }
                    else
                        location++;
            }
        }
```

10. (a) Same as Exercise 9 (a).
    (b)
```
        void SortedType::DeleteItem(ItemType item)
        {
            int location = 0;
            bool found = false;

            while (!found && location < length)
            {
                if (item.ComparedTo(info[location]) == EQUAL)
                    found = true;
                else
                    location++;
            }
            for (int index = location + 1; index < length; index++)
                info[index - 1] =  info[index];
            length--;
        }
```

    (c) Same as Exercise 9 (c).
    (d)
```
        void SortedType::DeleteItem(ItemType item)
        {
            int location = 0;

            while (location < length)
            {
                if (item.ComparedTo(info[location]) == EQUAL)
                {
                    for (int index = location + 1; index < length;
                       index++)
                        info[index - 1] =  info[index];
                    length--;
                }
                else
                    location++;
            }
        }
```

CHAPTER 4

1. (a) Yes   (e) Yes
    (b) No   (f) No
    (c) Yes   (g) No
    (d) No   (h) Yes

2. The accessing protocol of a stack is summarized as follows: both to retrieve elements and to store new elements, access only the top of the stack. Access is through the Pop and Push member functions.

3. (a)

    3 5 4 (each on a separate line)

    5 16 1 0 (each on a separate line)

    (b)

    0 5 6 5 (each on a separate line)

    5 4 5 (each on a separate line)

8. (a) Set secondElement to the second element in the stack, leaving the stack without its original top two elements.

```
{
    stack.Pop(secondElement);
    stack.Pop(secondElement);
}
```

    (b) Set bottom equal to the bottom element in the stack, leaving the stack empty.

```
{
    while (!stack.IsEmpty())
        stack.Pop(bottom);
}
```

    (c) Set bottom equal to the bottom element in the stack, leaving the stack unchanged.

```
{
    StackType tempStack;
    ItemType tempItem;

    while (!stack.IsEmpty())
    {
        stack.Pop(tempItem);
        tempStack.Push(tempItem);
    }
    bottom = tempItem;
    // restore stack
    while (!tempStack.IsEmpty())
    {
        tempStack.Pop(tempItem);
        stack.Push(tempItem);
    }
}
```

12. (a) Draw a diagram of how the stack might look.

smallTop: top for the stack of small values, initialized to -1 and incremented.

largeTop: top for the stack of large values, initialized to 200 and decremented.

[0]	[1]	[2]	[3]	....	[197]	[198]	[199]

(b)
```
class DStack
{
public:
    DStack();
    void Push(int item);
    void PopLarge(int& item);
    void PopSmall(int& item);
private:
    int smallTop;
    int largeTop;
    int item[200];
};
```
(c)
```
void DStack::Push(int item)
{
    if (item <= 1000)
    {
        smallTop++;
        items[smallTop] = item;
    }
    else
    {
        largeTop--;
        items[largeTop] = item;
    }
}
```

13. (a) Although the items are technically homogeneous (all integers), they are not semantically homogeneous. The value in the [0] slot has a different meaning from the values in all the other slots.

(b) The specifications would not change; all of the implementations would change.

15.

```
void ReplaceItem(StackType& stack, ItemType oldItem, ItemType
newItem)
{
    StackType tempStack;
    ItemType tempItem;
    while (!stack.IsEmpty())
    {
        stack.Pop(tempItem);
        if (tempItem.ComparedTo(oldItem) == EQUAL)
            tempStack.Push(newItem);
        else
            tempStack.Push(tempItem);
    }
    // restore stack
    while (!tempStack.IsEmpty())
    {
        tempStack.Pop(tempItem);
        stack.Push(tempItem);
    }
}
```

16.

```
// Represent candy container as a stack pezJar.
// Eat yellow candies
WHILE pezJar is not empty
    pezJar.Pop(candy)
    IF candy != yellow candy
        tempJar.Push(candy)
// Restore candy container
WHILE tempJar is not empty
    tempJar.Pop(candy)
    pezJar.Push(candy)
```

17.

Stack ADT Specification

Structure: Elements are added to and removed from the top of
                      the stack.

Definitions   (provided by user):

MAX_ITEMS: Maximum number of items that might be on the stack.

ItemType: Data type of the items on the stack.

Operations   (provided by the ADT):

MakeEmpty

Function: Sets stack to an empty state.

Precondition: None

Postcondition: Stack is empty.

Boolean IsEmpty

Function: Determines whether the stack is empty.

Precondition: Stack has been initialized.

Postcondition: Function value = (stack is empty)

Boolean IsFull

Function: Determines whether the stack is full.

Precondition: Stack has been initialized.

Postcondition: Function value = (stack is full)

Push(ItemType newItem, Boolean& error)

Function: Adds newItem to the top of the stack.

Precondition: Stack has been initialized.

Postcondition: If stack on entry is not full, newItem is at the top of the stack and error is false; otherwise, error is true and the stack is unchanged.

Pop(ItemType& item, Boolean& error)

Function: Removes top item from stack and returns it in item.

Preconditions: Stack has been initialized.

Postcondition: If the stack on entry is not empty, the top element has been removed from stack, item is a copy of removed element, and error is false; otherwise, error is true and the stack is unchanged.

(b) None

(c) None

An alternative implementation would add an error data member to the class. This error flag would be set if underflow or overflow occurred and the operation would not be performed. A member function would have to be added to the class to allow the user to check the error flag.

20. Yes, this sequence is possible.

23. The accessing protocol is summarized as follows: items are inserted at the rear and removed from the front. Accessing is done through the `Enqueue` and `Dequeue` member functions.

24. (a)

　　1　0　4 (on separate lines)
　　5　16　0　3 (on separate lines)

(b)

　　6　4　6　0 (on separate lines)
　　6　5　0 (on separate lines)

25.

(a)

■| **Queue ADT Specification**

Structure:	Elements are added to rear and removed from the front of the queue.
Definitions	(provided by user):
MAX_ITEMS:	Maximum number of items that might be on the queue.
ItemType:	Data type of the items on the queue.
Operations	(provided by ADT):

MakeEmpty

Function:	Initializes the queue to an empty state.
Precondition:	None
Postcondition:	Queue is empty.

Boolean IsEmpty

Function:	Determines whether the queue is empty.
Precondition:	Queue has been initialized.
Postcondition:	Function value = (queue is empty)

Boolean IsFull

Function:	Determines whether the queue is full.
Precondition:	Queue has been initialized.
Postcondition:	Function value = (queue is full)

Enqueue(ItemType newItem, Boolean& error)

Function:	Adds newItem to the rear of the queue.
Precondition:	Queue has been initialized.

Postcondition: If the queue on entry is not full, newItem is at rear of queue and error is false; otherwise the queue is unchanged and error is true.

Dequeue(ItemType& item, Boolean& error)

Function: Removes front item from queue and returns it in item.

Precondition: Queue has been initialized.

Postcondition: If the queue on entry is not empty, the front element has been removed from the queue, item is a copy of removed element, and error is false; otherwise the queue is unchanged and error is true.

(b) What new data members must be added to the class? None.

(c) What new member functions must be added to the class? None.

26. `queue.Enqueue(letter);`

27. `queue.Enqueue (letter);`

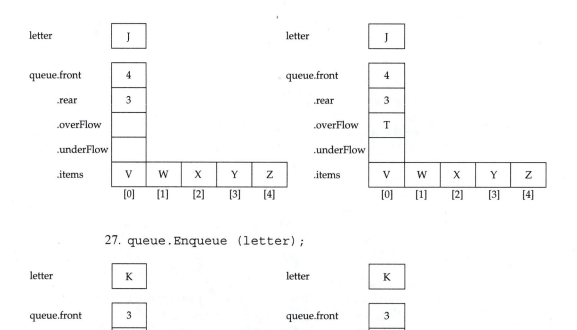

28. `queue.Dequeue (letter);`

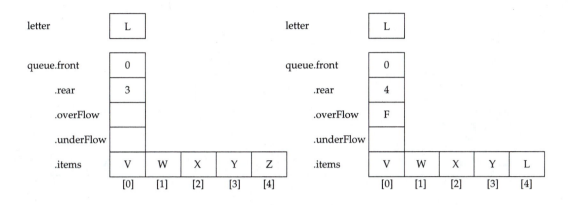

29. `queue.Dequeue (letter);`

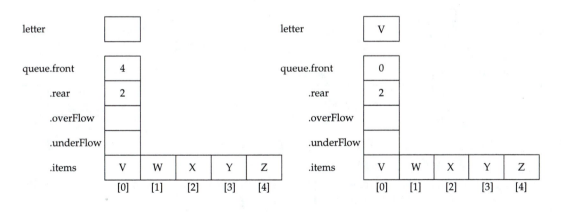

30. `queue.Dequeue (letter);`

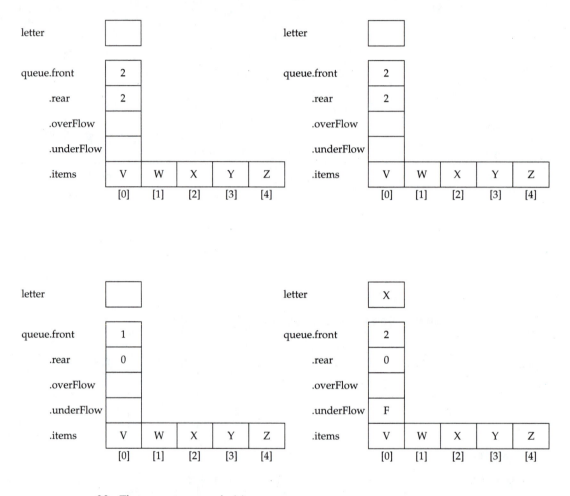

33. The correct answer is (a).

34. The correct answer for the first statement is (d); the correct answer for the second statement is (a).

36.

```
{
        QueType<int> tempQ;
        int item;

        while (!queue.IsEmpty())
        {
            queue.Dequeue(item);
            if (item == oldItem)
```

```
                    tempQ.Enqueue(newItem);
            else
                    tempQ.Enqueue(item);
        }
        while (!tempQ.IsEmpty())
        {
            tempQ.Dequeue(item);
            queue.Enqueue(item);
        }
    }
```

37. (a) No
(b) Yes
(c) No
(d) No
(e) Yes
(f) Yes
(g) No
(h) Yes
(i) No

38.
```
bool Identical(QueType<float> queue1, QueType<float> queue2)
    {
        QueType<float> tempQ1;
        QueType<float> tempQ2;
        float item1, item2;
        bool same = true;

        while (!queue1.IsEmpty() && !queue2.IsEmpty())
        {
            queue1.Dequeue(item1);
            queue2.Dequeue(item2);
            tempQ1.Enqueue(item1);
            tempQ2.Enqueue(item2);
        }
        // Check for same size.
        same = queue1.IsEmpty() && queue2.IsEmpty();
        if (same) // Check for matching items while copying.
            while (!tempQ1.IsEmpty())
            {
                tempQ1.Dequeue(item1);
                tempQ2.Dequeue(item2);
                queue1.Enqueue(item1);
                queue2.Enqueue(item2);
                if (item1 != item2)
                    same = false;
            }
        else
```

```
{    // Process rest of queue1 and copy back.
    while (!queue1.IsEmpty())
    {
        queue1.Dequeue(item1);
        tempQ1.Enqueue(item1);
    }
    while (!tempQ1.IsEmpty())
    {
        tempQ1.Dequeue(item1);
        queue1.Enqueue(item1);
    }
    // Process rest of queue2 and copy back.
    while (!queue2.IsEmpty())
    {
        queue2.Dequeue(item2);
        tempQ2.Enqueue(item2);
    }
    while (!tempQ2.IsEmpty())
    {
        tempQ2.Dequeue(item2);
        queue2.Enqueue(item2);
    }
    return same;
}
```

42. The `MakeEmpty` operation is a logical operation that sets the structure to empty. A class constructor is a C++ construct that is implicitly called when an object of the type is defined. `MakeEmpty` is under the control of the client program and can be applied any number of times.

44. No, this sequence is not possible.

CHAPTER 5

1. (a) The client code does not change when the implementation of the class changes. The solution to Chapter 4, Exercise 11(a) works for this problem also.

    (b)

```
ItemType Top(); const;                              // prototype
template<class ItemType>
ItemType StackType<ItemType>::Top() const
{
    return topPtr->info;
}
```

3.

```
bool Identical(StackType<Item Type> stack1) const    // prototype
template<class ItemType>
bool StackType<ItemType>::
```

```
        Identical(StackType<ItemType> stack1) const
{
    NodeType<ItemType>* selfPtr;
    NodeType<ItemType>* otherPtr;
    bool same = true;
    selfPtr = topPtr;
    otherPtr = stack1.topPtr;
    while (same)
    {
        same = (selfPtr != NULL && otherPtr != NULL
                && selfPtr->info == otherPtr->info);
        if (same)
        {
            selfPtr = selfPtr->next;
            otherPtr = otherPtr->next;
        }
    }
    if (selfPtr == NULL && otherPtr == NULL)
        return true;
    else
        return false;
}
```

6.
```
int Length() const;        // prototype
template<class ItemType>
int QueType<ItemType>::Length() const
{
    NodeType<ItemType>* location = qFront;
    int length = 0;

    while (location != NULL)
    {
        length++;
        location = location->next;
    }
    return length;
}
```

7.
```
template<class ItemType>
bool UnsortedType<ItemType>::IsThere(ItemType item) const
{
    NodeType<ItemType>* location = listData;
    bool found = false;

    while (!found && location != NULL)
    {
        found = location->info == item;
        location = location->next;
```

```
        }
        return found;
}
```
10. (b)
```
void SplitLists(SortedType<ItemType>& list1,
     SortedType<ItemType>& list2, ItemType item);// prototype
template<class ItemType>
void SortedType<ItemType>::SplitLists(SortedType<ItemType>& list1,
     SortedType<ItemType>& list2,  ItemType item)
{
    NodeType<ItemType>* listPtr = listData;

    List1.MakeEmpty();
    List2.MakeEmpty();
    while (listPtr!= NULL && listPtr->info <= item)
    {
        list1.InsertItem(listPtr->info);
        listPtr = listPtr->next;
    }
    while (listPtr != NULL)
    {
        list2.InsertItem(listPtr->info);
        listPtr = listPtr->next;
    }
}
```
   (c) See Chapter 3, Exercise 8.
14. (a) True
   (b) True
   (c) False. A linked list is not a random-access structure.
   (d) False. A sequential list may be stored in a statically allocated or a dynamically allocated structure.
   (e) True
   (f) False. A queue is not a random-access structure; access is always to the first one stored.
15. (a) 30
   (b) 90
   (c) 45
16. (a) `true`
   (b) `false`
   (c) `false`
   (d) `true`
17. (a) `ok`
   (b) You cannot assign a struct to a pointer.
   (c) You cannot assign a pointer to a struct.
   (d) You cannot assign an `info` member to a pointer.
   (e) `ok`

(f) ok

18. (a) `listData = ptr1->next;`

(b) `ptr2 = ptr2->next;`

(c) `listData = NULL;`

(d) `ptr1->next->info = 60;`

CHAPTER 6

1. (a) The special case of changing the external list pointer when a node is added at or deleted from the beginning of the list.

(b) The check for the end of the list is eliminated from the search function.

(c) No. Popping and pushing always change the external pointer.

(d) Yes. The special cases of adding a new node to an empty queue and removing the last node from a queue can be eliminated with dummy nodes.

(e) The special case of changing the external list pointer when a node is added to an empty list or when the last node is deleted from the list, leaving it empty.

3. Member functions `Enqueue` and `Dequeue` would have to be changed.

4.
```
template<class ItemType>
void SortedType<ItemType>::PrintReverse() const
    // Pre:  List is not empty.
    // Post: List is printed in reverse order.
    {
        NodeType<ItemType>* location = listData;
        StackType<ItemType> stack;
        ItemType item;

        do
        {
            stack.Push(location->info);
            location = location->next;
        } while (location != listData);
        while (!stack.IsEmpty())
        {
            stack.Pop(item);
            cout << item << endl;
        }
    }
```

5. Class `List2Type` provides no way to directly access the items in the list, so a derived class couldn't insert into the list. The only accessing mechanisms provided are insertion at the beginning and insertion at the end.

6. No, the class definition would not have to be changed. Only the definition of `NodeType` would have to be changed.

9. Write a member function `Copy` of the Stack ADT, assuming that self is copied into the stack named in the parameter list.

```
template <class ItemType>
void StackType<ItemType>::Copy(StackType<ItemType>& anotherStack)
{
    NodeType<ItemType>* ptr1;
    NodeType<ItemType>* ptr2;

    if (topPtr == NULL)
        anotherStack.topPtr = NULL;
    else
    {
        anotherStack.topPtr = new NodeType<ItemType>;
        anotherStack.topPtr->info = topPtr->info;
        ptr1 = topPtr->next;
        ptr2 = anotherStack.topPtr;
        while (ptr1 != NULL)
        {
            ptr2->next = new NodeType<ItemType>;
            ptr2 = ptr2->next;
            ptr2->info = ptr1->info;
            ptr1 = ptr1->next;
        }
        ptr2->next = NULL;
    }
}
```

12. (a) Doubly linked
    (b) Circular
    (c) List with header and trailer

13. Initialization has $O(N)$ complexity where N is the size of the array of records; `GetNode` and `FreeNode` have $O(1)$.

15. (a)

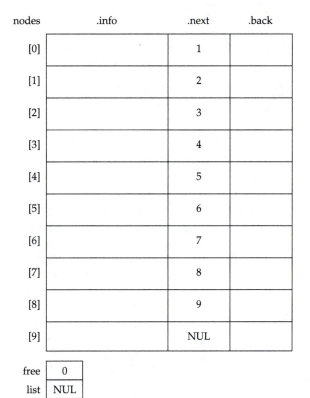

nodes	.info	.next	.back
[0]		1	
[1]		2	
[2]		3	
[3]		4	
[4]		5	
[5]		6	
[6]		7	
[7]		8	
[8]		9	
[9]		NUL	

free	0
list	NUL

16. Classes can relate to each other by inheritance, by composition, or not at all.

17. Two classes are related by composition when one class has a data member of the type of the other class. Two classes are related by inheritance when one is derived from the other.

18. A base class is the class being inherited from; the derived class is the class that inherits.

21. Define and implement a `CountedStack` class that inherits from `StackType`.

```
template<class ItemType>
class CountedStack : public StackType<ItemType>
{
public:
    CountedStack();
    void Push(ItemType newItem);
    void Pop(ItemType& item);
    int LengthIs() const;
        // Returns the number of items on the stack.
```

```
private:
    int length;
};

template<class ItemType>
void CountedStack<ItemType>::Push(ItemType newItem)
{
    length++;
    StackType<ItemType>::Push(newItem);
}

template<class ItemType>
void CountedStack<ItemType>::Pop(ItemType& item)
{
    length--;
    StackType<ItemType>::Pop(item);
}

template<class ItemType>
int CountedStack<ItemType>::LengthIs() const
{
    return length;
}

template<class ItemType>
CountedStack<ItemType>::CountedStack() : StackType<ItemType>()
{
    length = 0;
}
```

CHAPTER 7

1. (a) The base case is a nonrecursive exit from the recursive routine.
    (b) The general (or recursive) case is a path that includes a recursive call to
        the routine, to solve a smaller version of the original problem.
    (c) The run-time stack is a structure that keeps track of the activation records
        at run time, in order to preserve the values of parameters, return
        addresses, registers, and so on.
    (d) Binding time refers to the point in the compile/execution cycle when
        variable names are associated with addresses in memory.
    (e) Tail recursion occurs when the recursive call is the last statement
        executed in a recursive function.

2. True or False? If false, correct the statement. *Recursive functions* ...
    (a) True
    (b) False

(c) False

(d) False

(e) False. Recursive routines are often shorter and clearer but not always.

(f) True

(g) False. Recursive routines are often the same as the nonrecursive solution, in terms of Big-O.

3. (1) *Base Case:* One base case occurs when the value is found on this call and the function is exited without any further calls to itself. A second base case occurs when the end of the list is reached without the value's having been found and the function is exited without any further recursive calls. The answer is yes.

   (2) *Smaller Caller:* The recursive call in the general case increments the value of `startIndex`, making the part of the list left to be searched smaller. The answer is yes.

   (3) *General Case:* Let's assume that the recursive call in the general case correctly tells us whether the value is found in the second through last elements in the list. Then Base Case 1 gives us the correct answer of true if the value is found in the first element in the list, and Base Case 2 gives us the correct answer of false if the value is not in the first element and the first element is the *only* element in the list. The only other possible case is that the value exists somewhere in the rest of the list. Assuming that the general case works correctly, the whole function works, so the answer to this question is also yes.

8. (a) -1

   (b) 120

   (c) 1

9. (a) Yes, `num` must be zero or a negative number.

   (b) No

   (c) Yes. 0 is returned.

   (d) Yes. -15 is returned.

12. (a) This answer is incorrect. The value 0 is returned; the recursive case is never reached. This solution gets half credit, because it correctly calculates the base case (even if it doesn't reach it).

    (b) This solution correctly calculates the sum of squares but gets no credit because it is not a *recursive* solution.

    (c) This answer is correct and gets full credit.

    (d) This answer is functionally equivalent to (c); it just avoids the last recursive call (to an empty list) by returning the sum of the last squares as the base case. This answer runs into problems if the list is empty, but the specification states that the list is not empty. This answer gets full credit.

    (e) This solution is incorrect. The general case does not correctly calculate the sum of the squares. Quarter credit is given for using the correct control structure and for getting the base case correct.

13. (a)
```
int Fibonacci(int number)
{
    if (number <= 1)
        return number;
    else
        return Fibonacci(number - 2) + Fibonacci(number - 1);
}
```
(b)
```
int Fibonacci(int number)
{
    int current;
    int previous;
    int temp;

    if (number <= 1)
        return 1;
    else
    {
        previous = 0;
        current = 1;
        for (int count = 2; count <= number; count++)
        {
            temp = previous;
            previous = current;
            current = temp + previous;
        }
        return current;
    }
}
```
(c)
```
#include <iostream.h>
int Fibonacci(int number);
int main()
{
    int number;
    cout << "Input the fibonacci number you wish." << endl
         << "Input a negative number to quit."  << endl;
    cin  >> number;
    while (number >= 0)
    {
        cout << "number: "  << number  << endl;
             << "Fibonacci number: "  << Fibonacci(number)
             << endl;
```

```
        cout << "Input the fibonacci number you wish." << endl
            << "Input a negative number to quit." << endl;
        cin >> number;
    }
    return 0;
}
// Put the function version you are testing here.
```

(d) The recursive solution is inefficient because some of the intermediate values are calculated more than once.

(e) The following version, which uses an auxiliary recursive function, is more efficient. Note that the recursive parameters are used to keep track of the current and previous numbers, rather than recalculating them.

```
int Fibonacci(int number)
{
    return Fib(number, 1, 1);
}
int Fib(int number, int previous, int current)
{
    if (number == 0)
        return previous;
    else
        return Fib(number - 1, current, current + previous)
}
```

17. (a) It is difficult to establish that the recursive calls satisfy Question 2, that they are moving toward the base case.

(b)
```
cout << Ulam(7) << endl;   16 recursive calls
cout << Ulam(8) << endl;    3 recursive calls
cout << Ulam(15) << endl;  17 recursive calls
```

21. (a)
```
NodeType* MinLoc(NodeType* list, NodeType* minPtr)
{
    if (list != NULL)
    {
        if (list->info < minPtr->info)
            minPtr = list;
        return MinLoc(list->next, minPtr);
    }
    else
        return minPtr;
}
```

(b)
```
void Sort(NodeType* list)
{
    NodeType* minPtr;
    int temp;
```

```
            if (list != NULL)
            {
                minPtr = MinLoc(list, list);
                temp = minPtr->info;   // swap
                minPtr->info = list->info;
                list->info = temp;
                Sort(list->next); // sort rest of list
            }
        }
```

22. (a) False. Recursive solutions are often less efficient in terms of computing time.

(b) True

(c) False. Recursive solutions generally require more space in the run-time stack.

(d) True. (Don't you want a good grade in this course?)

CHAPTER 8

1. (a) The level of a binary search tree determines the maximum number of comparisons that are required to find an element in the tree.

(b) 100

(c) 7

2. (c) is the correct answer

6.

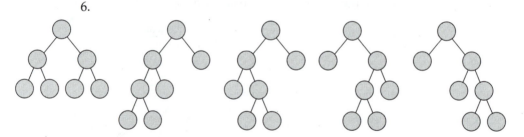

7. The queue is used to hold the values in the tree so that the user can access them one at a time. A linked structure would require an extra pointer for each value in the tree. If an array-based queue of just the right size could be dynamically allocated, it would be much more efficient. However, the implementation presented here makes the queue a part of the private data of the tree object, and the number of nodes (data values) is not known at the time of instantiation.

8. (a) Q, K, and M

(b) B, D, J, M, P, and N

(c) 8

(d) 16

(e) 63

9.

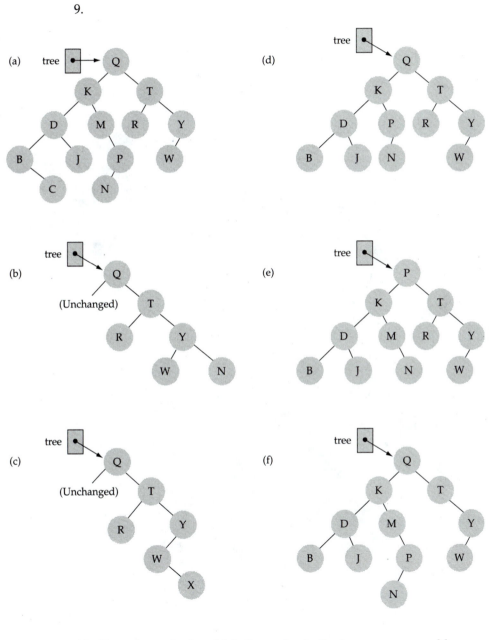

10. Show the order in which the nodes in the tree are processed by
    (a) BDJKMNPQRTWY
    (b) BJDNPMKRWYTQ
    (c) QKDBJMPNTRYW

11.

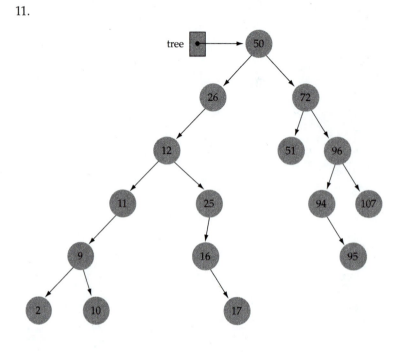

15.

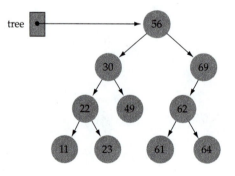

16.

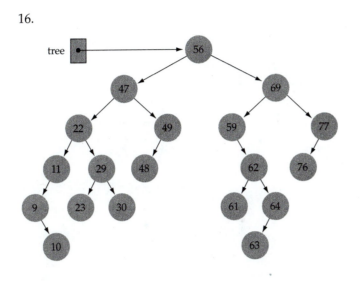

17. (a) False
    (b) False
    (c) True
    (d) False
18. No; an inorder traversal would leave the elements in a sorted order, so that when you went to rebuild the tree, you would have a stalk instead of a tree.
19. (a) Elements inserted in random order:
    Linked list: O(N)
    Binary search tree: O($\log_2 N$)
    (b) Elements inserted in order:
    Linked list: O(N)
    Binary search tree: O(N)

20.

(a) Insert order: monkey, canary, donkey, deer, zebra, yak, walrus, vulture, penguin, quail.

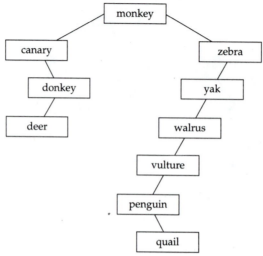

(b) Insert order: quail, walrus, donkey, deer, monkey, vulture, yak, penguin, zebra, canary.

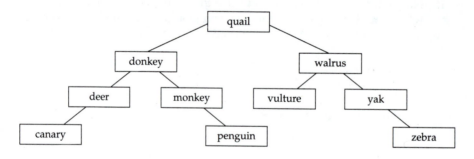

(c) Insert order: zebra, yak, walrus, vulture, quail, penguin, monkey, donkey, deer, canary.

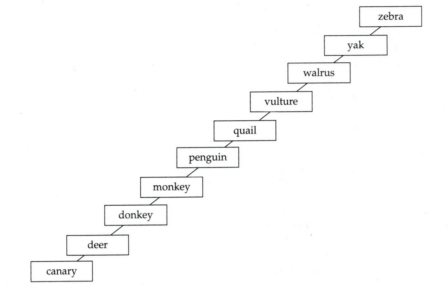

26. (a)
```
void Ancestors(ItemType value) const;          // prototype
// Pre:  A node whose info member is value is in the tree.
// Post: The ancestors of the node whose info member is value
//       have been printed.
```
(b)
```
template<class ItemType>
void TreeType<ItemType>::Ancestors(ItemType value) const
{
    TreeNode<NodeType>* location;

    while (location->info != value)
    {
        cout << location->info << endl;
        if (location->info < value)
            location = location->right;
        else
            location = location->left;
    }
}
```

27.

```
template<class ItemType>
void PrintAncestors(TreeNode<ItemType>* tree,
    ItemType value) const;
// prototype
template<class ItemType>
void TreeType<ItemType>::Ancestors(ItemType value) const
// Calls recursive function PrintAncestors to print the
// ancestors.
{
    PrintAncestors(root, value);
}


template<class ItemType>
void PrintAncestors(TreeNode<ItemType>* tree, ItemType value)
const
{
    if (tree->info != value)
    {
        cout << tree->info << endl;
        if (tree->info < value)
            PrintAncestors(tree->right, value);
        else
            PrintAncestors(tree->left, value);
    }
}
```

30.

```
int LeafCount()const;             // prototype
// Post: Function value = number of leaf nodes in the tree.

template<class ItemType>
int Count(TreeNode<ItemType>* tree) const;      // prototype

template<class ItemType>
int TreeType<ItemType>::LeafCount() const
// Calls recursive function Count to count the number
// of leaf nodes.
{
    return Count(root);
}

template<class ItemType>
int Count(TreeNode<ItemType>* tree) const
{
    if (tree == NULL)
        return 0;
    else if (tree->left == NULL) && (tree->right == NULL)
        return 1;
```

```
        else
            return Count(tree->left) + Count(tree->right);
    }
```

31.

```
    int SingleParentCount() const;        // prototype
    // Post: Number of nodes with only one child is returned.
    template<class ItemType>
    int SingleCount(TreeNode<ItemType>* tree) const;
    // prototype

    template<class ItemType>
    int TreeType<ItemType>::SingleParentCount() const
    // Calls recursive function SingleCount to count the number of
    // nodes with only one child.
    {
        return SingleCount(root);
    }

    template<class ItemType>
    int SingleCount(TreeNode<ItemType>* tree) const
    {
        if (tree == NULL)
            return 0;
        else if (tree->left == NULL && tree->right != NULL)
            return 1 + Count(tree->right);
        else if (tree->right == NULL && tree->left != NULL)
            return 1 + Count(tree->left);
        else
            return Count(tree->left) + Count(tree->right);
    }
```

32.

```
    template<class ItemType>
    int Count(TreeType<ItemType> tree, ItemType value) const
    // Pre:  tree has been initialized.
    // Post: Function value = the number of nodes in tree that
    //       contain values that are greater than value.
    {
        ItemType item;
        bool finished = false;
        int number = 0;      // sum of number of items < value

        if (tree.IsEmpty())
            return 0;
        else
        {
```

```
                    tree.ResetTree(IN_ORDER);
                    // By using an inorder traversal, the process can stop
                    // when a larger value is returned.
                    while (!finished)
                    {
                        tree.GetNextItem(item, finished, IN_ORDER);
                        if (value < item)
                            number++;
                        else
                            finished = true;
                    }
                    return number;
                }
            }
```

35.

```
        template<class ItemType>
        void MakeTree(TreeType<ItemType>& tree, ItemType info[],
            int length)
        // Creates a binary tree from a sorted array.
        {
            tree.MakeEmpty();
            AddElements(tree, info, 0, length-1);
        }


        template<class ItemType>
        void AddElements(TreeType<ItemType>& tree, ItemType info[],
            int fromIndex, int toIndex)
        {
            int midIndex;

            if ( fromIndex <= toIndex)
            {
                midIndex = ( fromIndex + toIndex) / 2;
                tree.InsertItem(info[midIndex]);
                AddElements(tree, info, fromIndex, midIndex - 1);
                // Complete the left subtree.
                AddElements(tree, info, midIndex+1, toIndex);
                // Complete the right subtree.
            }
        }
```

38. Either the value in node 5 or the value in node 6.
39. Inorder
40. Preorder

CHAPTER 9

4.

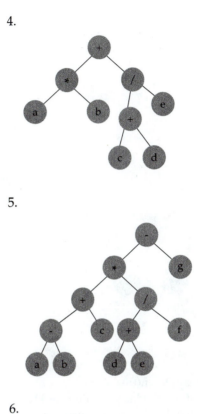

5.

6.

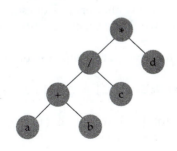

7.

```
void Print(TreeNode* tree)
// Post: Expression tree has been printed in postorder.
{
    if (tree->info.whichType == OPERAND)
        cout << tree->info.operand;
```

```
        else
        {
                Print(tree->left);
                Print(tree->right);
                cout << tree->info.operation;
        }
    }
```
8. (a) b, d, and e
   (b) b and e
   (c) d
11. (a)

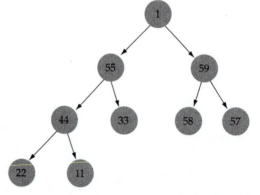

    (b) No, it is not a heap. ReheapDown(tree, 0, 8)
12. Any tree whose root node contains the largest value, and whose other nodes
    are linearly linked through the `left` pointer member, each containing a
    smaller value than its parent, correctly answers this question.
13. (a) True. Its smallest child index would be 85, but the tree only contains 85
    elements.
    (b) False. `treeNodes[41]` has two children: `treeNodes[83]` and
    `treeNodes[84]`.
    (c) False. The left child of `treeNodes[12]` is `treeNodes[25]`.
    (d) True.
    (e) False. The tree contains six full levels (containing 63 elements), with 22
    additional elements on the seventh level.

17. (a)

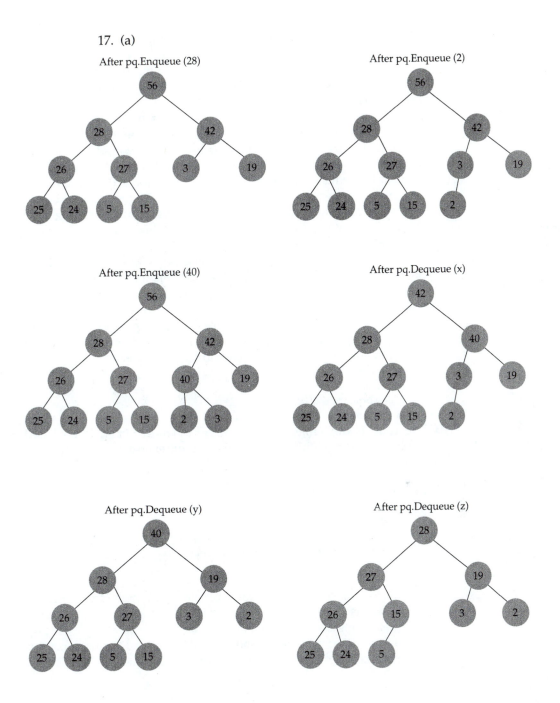

(b) **x** = 56, y = 42, z = 40

18. (a) The member functions would not change, but the private data members would change. The only data member would be a pointer to a linked list.
    (b) The code for `SortedType::InsertItem` (linked implementation) can be used directly with the relational operator reversed.
    (c) The code is identical to `StackType::Pop`.
    (d) `Dequeue` for a priority queue implemented as a linked list (sorted from highest to lowest priority) is very simple and efficient; we have direct access to the largest element. There is less work involved in fixing the structure after the largest element is removed, because the next-largest element immediately follows it. Thus the operation is O(1). In the heap implementation we have immediate access to the largest element, but we have to perform a reheap operation to fix the structure, resulting in an $O(\log_2 N)$ operation. The linked-list implementation is more efficient, in terms of Big-O.

    When the priority queue is implemented as a linked list, the efficiency of `Enqueue` varies according to the position that the new element occupies in the list. If the new element belongs in the last position, the whole list is searched before the insertion place is found. Thus the operation is O(N). Using heaps, the insertion operation is $O(\log_2 N)$. The linked-list implementation might be better if the elements were inserted in largely sorted order from smallest to largest value.

20. (a)
```
private:
    ItemType items[MAX_PQ];
    int length;
```
    (b) The code is the same as `SortedList::InsertItem` (array-based implementation) with the relational operator reversed.
    (c)
```
template<class ItemType>
void PQType<ItemType>::Dequeue(ItemType& item)
{
    item = items[0];
    for (int count = 1; count < length; count++)
        items[count - 1] = items[count];
    length--;
}
```
    (d) `Enqueue` has O(N), the order of `SortedList::InsertItem`. `Dequeue` has O(N): O(1) to find the item to remove, and O(N) to shift all the elements down one to remove it.

21. (a) The highest-priority element is the one with the largest time stamp. (This assumes that the time stamp never reaches `INT_MAX`.)

(b)

Push

> Assign the next largest time stamp to the new element
> Put new element in the stack (position is unimportant)

Pop

> Find the element with the largest time stamp
> Assign this element to item (to be
> returned)
> Remove the element

(c) The Push operation has O(1) because it doesn't matter where the item is stored in the structure. The Pop operation has O(N), because the item with the largest time stamp must be searched for. Therefore, Push is the same in both implementations, but Pop is not. If the priority queue is implemented using a heap with largest value the highest priority, Pop and Push have $O(\log_2 N)$.

24.

EmployeeGraph

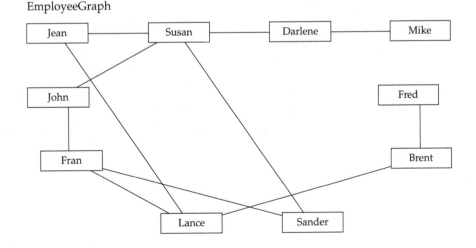

25.

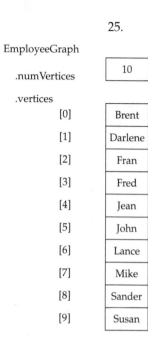

EmployeeGraph

.numVertices   10

.vertices

[0]	Brent
[1]	Darlene
[2]	Fran
[3]	Fred
[4]	Jean
[5]	John
[6]	Lance
[7]	Mike
[8]	Sander
[9]	Susan

.edges

	[0]	[1]	[2]	[3]	[4]	[5]	[6]	[7]	[8]	[9]
[0]	F	F	F	T	F	F	T	F	F	F
[1]	F	F	F	F	F	F	F	T	F	T
[2]	F	F	F	F	F	T	T	F	T	F
[3]	T	F	F	F	F	F	F	F	F	F
[4]	F	F	F	F	F	F	T	F	F	T
[5]	F	F	T	F	F	F	F	F	F	T
[6]	T	F	T	F	T	F	F	F	F	F
[7]	F	T	F	F	F	F	F	F	F	F
[8]	F	F	T	F	F	F	F	F	F	T
[9]	F	T	F	F	T	T	F	F	T	F

26.

(a) Susan, Jean, Lance

(b) Susan, Sander, Fran, Lance

27. "works with" is the best description of the relationship represented by the edges between vertices in EmployeeGraph, because it is an undirected graph. The other relationships listed have an order implicit in them.

28.

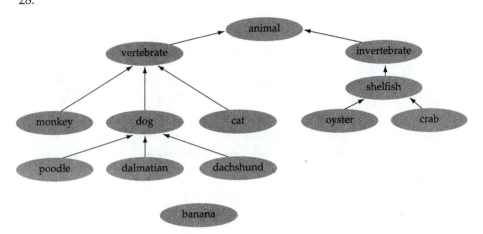

31. The correct answer is (b). For example, a dalmatian *is an example of* a dog.

32. V(StateGraph) = {Oregon, Alaska, Texas, Hawaii, Vermont, New York, California}

E(StateGraph) = {(Alaska, Oregon), (Hawaii, Alaska), (Hawaii, Texas), (Texas, Hawaii), (Hawaii, California), (Hawaii, New York), (Texas, Vermont), (Vermont, California), (Vermont, Alaska)}

Note: The order of the elements in the sets is not important.

33. (a)

no

(b) yes

(c) Texas

35. (a)

```
template<class VertexType>
bool EdgeExists(VertexType vertex1, VertexType vertex2);
// prototype
// Pre:  vertex1 and vertex2 are in the set of vertices.
// Post: Function value = (vertex1, vertex2) is in the set of
// edges.
```

(b)

```
template<class VertexType>
bool GraphType<VertexType>::EdgeExists(VertexType vertex1,
    VertexType vertex2)
{
    return edges[indexIs(vertices, vertex1),
             // indexIs(vertices, vertex2)] != NULL_EDGE;
}
```

38. (a) *Base cases*: (1) If `endVertex` has been previously found, stop. (2) If `startVertex` equals `endVertex`, found is true, stop. (3) If no more untried vertices adjacent to `startVertex`, found is false, stop.
General case: If `endVertex` is not yet found, DepthFirstSearch all the untried adjacent vertices.

(b)

DepthFirstSearch

IF !found
   IF startVertex = endVertex
      Write startVertex
      Set found to true
ELSE
   IF startVertex is not yet tried
      Mark startVertex as tried
      Write startVertex
      Get list of adjacent vertices
      DepthFirstSearch all untried adjacent vertices

CHAPTER 10

4. (a) bubble sort
   (b) selection sort
   (c) insertion sort
5. (a) 4950
   (b) 99
6. (a) $O(N^2)$
   (b) $O(N)$
   (c) $O(N^2)$
   (d) $O(N\log_2 N)$
   (e) $O(N)$
   (f) $O(N\log_2 N)$
7. The correct answer is (c).

8. The correct answer is (d).
9. QuickSort and SelectionSort would take the longest; InsertionSort and ShortBubble would take the shortest.
10. (a) Bubble sort is O(N) if the values are already sorted, and if the algorithm stops processing when the sorting is complete (like ShortBubble).
    (b) None.
    (c) QuickSort is O(N^2) if the values are already sorted and the split algorithm causes the array to be split into one element and the rest of the array.
13. (a) True
    (b) False. HeapSort is better for nearly sorted data than QuickSort.
    (c) True
14. Only (b) is true.
15. Programmer time refers to the amount of time it takes a programmer to generate a piece of software, including the time to design, code, and test it. If a programmer needs to finish a software project quickly, sometimes the programmer's time is a more critical efficiency consideration than how fast the resulting program runs on a computer. In this chapter, recursive sorting algorithms are cited as time-savers for the programmer, possibly at the expense of computing time.
16. The correct answer is (b).
17. All of the algorithms are stable except HeapSort.
22. Declare an array indexed from 0 through 99. Use the slots in the array as counters for that percentile score; that is, the slot indexed by 0 is the counter for percentile scores of 0; the slot indexed by 2 is the counter for percentile scores of 2; and so on. To produce the required output, go through the array from 99 down to 0, printing the loop counter as many times as there are values in that slot.
23. Which sorting algorithm would you *not* use under the following conditions?
    (a) HeapSort
    (b) QuickSort or InsertionSort
    (c) QuickSort
    (d) MergeSort
24. (a) for the best case. O(N)
    (b) for the worst case. O(N)
25. (a) for the best case. O(1)
    (b) for the worst case. O(N^2)

29.

[0]	140
[1]	620
[2]	
[3]	
[4]	
[5]	145
[6]	66
[7]	47
[8]	87
[9]	126
[10]	90
[11]	285
[12]	467
[13]	153
[14]	393
[15]	395
[16]	566
[17]	177
[18]	735
[19]	

30.

[0]	140
[1]	
[2]	467
[3]	620
[4]	
[5]	145
[6]	66
[7]	47
[8]	285
[9]	126
[10]	87
[11]	
[12]	566
[13]	90
[14]	
[15]	395
[16]	153
[17]	177
[18]	735
[19]	393

31.

HashTable

[0]	90	140	620
[1]			
[2]			
[3]	153	393	
[4]			
[5]	145	285	395
[6]	66	126	566
[7]	47	87	177
[8]	467	735	
[9]			

32.

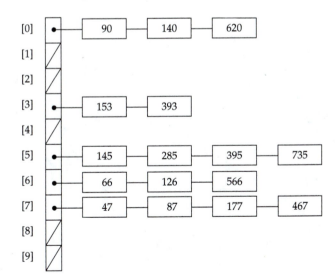

37. (a) 50
    (b) 50
    (c) 50
38. The correct answer is (a)

42. To sort the file in descending order, collect the queues from `queues[9]` down to `queues[0]`.
43. No. Simply substituting the Stack ADT for the Queue ADT would not work. The elements would be gathered in the wrong order.

Programming Assignments

In this section, we have included a number of programming assignments, keyed by chapter. Some of the programs are to be written "from scratch," to give students the opportunity to design, code, and test a whole program from written specifications. Other programming assignments are designed to give students experience in modifying an existing program. For instance, for each chapter that contains an application section, there are suggested modifications to the original program. We hope that, by having the opportunity to modify an existing program, students will gain important experience in program reading and "maintenance."

There are many additional programming assignments included in the *Instructor's Guide*.

A collection of programming assignments, each much altered over time, is part of the folklore of every department. In the assignments that follow we have tried to attribute ones we didn't write ourselves to their original authors. If you recognize one of your own and we didn't credit you, forgive us: the oversight was unintentional.

CHAPTER 1

1. Write a program to grade a set of true/false tests. There are 15 true/false questions. True is represented by T, and false is represented by F. The key to the quiz is on file "Quiz.dat" followed by the student responses. Each student's name (maximum of 15 characters) immediately follows the student's last answer. For each student write out the name followed by the number answered correctly and the number missed. Use stream failure to terminate processing.

INPUT

The data as described in the Problem Statement. Here are the first three lines of input.

```
TFTFTFTFTTTFFFT
TFTFTFTFTTTFFFTJoe Jones
TFTFTFTFTTTFFFFJanet Jerome
```

OUTPUT

Each student's name followed by the number answered correctly and the number missed.

PROCESSING NOTES

Your solution must use an integer function to calculate the number of answers correct (or missed).

DELIVERABLES

- A listing of your program
- A listing of your output file
- An implemented test plan

2. Write a program that processes the lines of source code in a C++ program, producing a listing of the program, with line numbers preceding each executable line of source code, followed by a report of the counts of executable and comment lines of source code.

DEFINITIONS

Lines of source code: A line of a C++ program file (all characters up to the end of line), which may contain statements or parts of statements, comments, and/or blanks.

Blank line: A line of source code that does not contain any nonblank characters.

Executable line: A line of source code that contains C++ statements, declarations, definitions, reserved words, etc. (*Note*: It may contain comments in addition to functional code.)

Comment line: A line of source code that contains only C++ comments. A comment must terminate on the same line as it begins; it cannot span more than one line.

INPUT

The C++ program to be processed is contained in a single text file. The user should be prompted to supply the file name.

OUTPUT

The lines are echo printed to the screen as they are read from the source file.

The formatted report output is written to file "count.out." The output contains two sections:

1. The *Program Listing* consisting of all the lines of the C++ program. Three types of lines are treated as follows:
   (a) Blank line: Print a blank line.
   (b) Executable line: The line is printed, preceded by the current line count printed in eight character spaces.
   (c) Comment line: The line is printed, preceded by eight blank spaces (to maintain program formatting and indention).
2. The *Count Report* consisting of the following elements, printed with appropriate labels:
   (a) Number of executable lines of code
   (b) Number of comment lines.

Assumptions

1. The C++ program in the input file is syntactically correct. (For example, you can assume that all comments terminate.)
2. The program contains only printable characters.
3. Only // comment delimiters are supported. /**/ comments are not.
4. Nested comments are not supported.
5. An executable line cannot begin with a comment.

Deliverables

- The Program Listing
- The Count Report
- An implemented test plan

3. You are the manager of a team of ten programmers who have just completed a seminar on software design and implementation. To prove to your boss that these techniques pay off, you decide to run the following contest. You number the programmers 1 through 10, based on their performance in the seminar (1 is poorest, 10 is best), and monitor their work. As each does his or her part of your project, you keep track of the number of lines of debugged code turned in by each programmer. (You get this information from the program written in Assignment 2.) You record this number as a programmer turns in a debugged module. The winner of the contest is the first person to reach 1000 lines of debugged code. (You hope this is programmer #9 or #10.) As further proof of the value of these new techniques, you want to determine how many poor programmers it takes to surpass the winner's figure; that is, find the smallest k such that programmers 1 through k have turned in more lines than the winner.

INPUT

The input consists of a sequence of pairs of integers. The first integer in each pair is the programmer's number (an integer from 1 to 10), and the second is the number of lines of code turned in. The pairs occur in the same order as that in which the modules were turned in.

PROCESSING/OUTPUT

Read in pairs of integers until someone's total goes over 1000. Print out (echo print) each pair as you read it. Ignore any input after someone's total exceeds 1000. Then print out a table listing the ten programmers and their totals, with the winner flagged as shown in the example that follows. Finally, find the smallest k such that the sum of the totals for programmers 1–k exceeds the winner's total. Print k in an explanatory sentence.

Sample Input:

```
10 230
 8 206
 7 111
 3 159
 9 336
 1 51
10 250
 4 101
 9 341
 2 105
 8 256
10 320
 3 150
 5 215
 7 222
 9 400  #9 goes over 1000.
```

Sample Output:
```
    PROGRAMMER PROGRESS
Programmer  Lines of Code
10             230  ⎫
  .                 ⎬ Echo print the first 16 pairs.
  .                 ⎭
 9             400
    FINAL TOTALS
Programmer  Lines of Code
 1              51
 2             105
 3             309
 4             101
 5             215
 6               0
 7             333
 8             462
 9            1077  *** THE WINNER ***
10             800
```

It took programmers 1 through 7 to produce more than the winner.

DELIVERABLES

- A program listing produced by running your program through ListAndCount (Assignment 2)
- Run your program twice with different input data. Turn in a listing of the program output for each test.

4. Finish the coding and testing of the `FractionCalc` program described in Chapter 1.

CHAPTER 2

1. Many mathematical problems require the addition, subtraction, and multiplication of two matrices. Write an ADT Matrix. You may use the following class definition.

```
const int MAX_ROWS = 10;
const int MAX_COLS = 10;
class MatrixType
{
public:
  MatrixType();
  void MakeEmpty();
```

```
    void SetSize(int rowSize, int colSize);
    void StoreItem(int item, int row, int col);
    void Add(MatrixType otherOperand, MatrixType& result);
    void Sub(MatrixType otherOperand, MatrixType& result);
    void Mult(MatrixType otherOperand, MatrixType& result);
    void Print(ofstream& outfile);
    bool AddSubCompatible(MatrixType otherOperand) const;
    bool MultCompatible(MatrixType otherOperand) const;
private:
    int values[MAX_ROWS][MAX_COLS];
    int numRows;
    int numCols;
};
```

Before you start looking at how to implement this class, you must determine the appropriate preconditions and postconditions for each operation. Note that the class provides the member functions to allow the client to determine if the binary matrix operations are possible. Before this class can become a permanent part of your program library, it must be thoroughly tested. Write a menu-driven testing program to test your MatrixType.

MENU-DRIVEN TESTING INTERFACE

The menu should contain the following options.
GetNewMatrix <matrix>

> Number of rows and number of columns are on the next line.

> Number of column values on each of the next number of rows lines

AddMatrices <matrix> <matrix> <matrix>

> Add first and second, leaving the result in the third

SubMatrices <matrix> <matrix> <matrix>

> Subtract second from first, leaving the result in the third

MultiplyMatrices <matrix> <matrix> <matrix>

> Multiply first and second, leaving the result in the third

PrintMatrix <matrix>

> Print the matrix one row per line on DataOut

Quit

PROCESSING NOTES

1. <matrix> is a number between 0 and 9. This value is used as an index into a one-dimensional array of MatrixType objects.
2. The main function must include a Switch statement where the switch expression is of a user-defined enumeration type. This means that the command is recognized and its enumeration equivalent is sent back to be used in the switch statement.

3. The driver must ensure the preconditions of the member functions of `MatrixType`. Print an error message if a precondition is violated.
4. Echo print each command on file DataOut.

DELIVERABLES

- A listing of the specification file for class `MatrixType` with the preconditions and postconditions specified
- A listing of the implementation file for class `MatrixType`
- A listing of the test driver
- An implemented test plan

2. Your assignment is to extend and test the String ADT that was developed in the Case Study of this chapter. Add the following four operations to the String ADT:

void Concat(StrType& otherString, Boolean& error)

Function:	Concatenates self to the back of otherString.
Precondition:	Self and otherString have been initialized.
Postcondition:	If original Length(otherString) + Length(self) <= MAX_CHARS, otherString has self appended to the rear of original otherString and error is false; otherwise otherString is unchanged and error is true.

void Delete(int startPos, int numChars, Boolean& error)

Function:	Deletes numChars characters from self, beginning with the character in startPos position.
Preconditions:	Self has been initialized.
	0 <= startPos < Length(self)
	numChars <= MAX_CHARS
Postcondition:	If startPos + numChars > original Length(self), error is true and self is unchanged; otherwise, error is false and self = original self with numChars characters deleted, beginning at position startPos.

void Insert(StrType inString, int pos, Boolean& error)

Function:	Inserts inString into self at the position specified by pos, moving the following characters to make room for the new characters.
Preconditions:	Self has been initialized.
	0 <= pos <= Length(String)
Postconditions:	If original Length(self) + Length(inString) > MAX_CHARS, error is true and self is unchanged; otherwise, error is false and self = original self with

inString inserted beginning at position pos. Any characters in self that follow the inserted characters are moved to make room for inString.

void Search(StrType pattern, int& pos, Boolean& found)

Function: Searches for the first occurrence of pattern in self. If it is found, pos indicates its starting position in self.
Precondition: Self and pattern have been initialized.
Postconditions: found = (pattern was found in self).
                  If found, pos = position of first pattern character within self; otherwise, pos is undefined.

PROCESSING REQUIREMENTS

As part of the String ADT, the operations specified above should be implemented to manipulate the strings directly, without the use of functions in <string.h>.

DELIVERABLES

- A listing of the specification file for StrType
- A listing of the implementation file for StrType
- A listing of your implemented test plan

CHAPTER 3

1. An organization that your little cousin belongs to is selling low-fat cookies. If your cousin's class sells more cookies than any other class, the teacher has promised to take the whole class on a picnic. Of course, your cousin volunteered you to keep track of all the sales and determine the winner. Each class has an identification number. Each sales slip has the class identification number and the number of boxes sold.

INPUT

Here is a sample of the data. (The classes are numbered from 1 through 10.)

Id. Number	Boxes Sold
3	23
4	1
2	13
2	7
4	5
1	6
10	16

OUTPUT

The following information written on file "boxes.out", all properly labeled.
The total number of boxes sold by each class.
The identification number of the winning class. If there is a tie, list all winners.

DELIVERABLES

- The listing of your source program
- A listing of your implemented test plan

2. Your assignment is to track the corporate careers of some up-and-coming executives who are busily changing jobs, being promoted and demoted, and, of course, getting paid.

In this (admittedly unrealistic) version of the corporate world, people either belong to a company or are unemployed. The list of people the program must deal with is not fixed: initially there are none, and new people may be introduced by the JOIN command (see below).

Executives within a company are ordered according to a seniority system and are numbered from 1 to N (the number of people in the company) to indicate their rank: 1 is the lowest rank and N is the highest. A new employee always enters at the bottom of the ladder and hence always starts with a rank of 1. When a new person joins a company, the rank of everyone in the company is increased by one, and when an employee quits, the rank of employees above him or her in that company is decreased by one. Promotions can also occur and affect the ranks in the obvious way.

Naturally, salaries are based on rank. An employee's salary is Rank*$1000. Unemployed people draw $50 in unemployment compensation.

INPUT

1. From file "company": The company names are listed one per line. There are at most 20 companies. Company names are at most 10 characters and do not contain embedded blanks.
2. From the keyboard: Commands, as listed below. <Person> and <Company> names are at most 10 characters and do not contain embedded blanks.

JOIN <person> <company>

<Person> joins the specified <company>. This may be the first reference to this person, or he or she may be unemployed. The person does not currently belong to another company. Remember that when a person joins a company, he or she always starts at the bottom.

QUIT <person>

<Person> quits his or her job and becomes unemployed. You may assume that the person is currently employed.

CHANGE <person> <company>

<Person> quits his or her job and joins the specified new <company>. You may assume that the person is currently employed.

PROMOTE <person>

<Person> is moved up one step in the current company, ahead of his or her immediate superior. If the person has highest rank within the company, no change occurs.

DEMOTE <person>

<Person> is moved one step down in the current company, below his or her immediate subordinate. If the person has lowest rank within the company, no change occurs.

PAYDAY

Each person is paid his or her salary as specified in the Problem Statement. (You must keep track of the amount each person has earned from the start of the program.)

EMPLOYEES <company>

The current list of employees should be printed for the specified <company>. The employees must be printed in order of rank; either top to bottom or bottom to top is appropriate.

UNEMPLOYED

The list of unemployed people should be printed.

DUMP

Print the employees in each company, as specified under the EMPLOYEES command above, then print the unemployed people. Label the output appropriately.

END

Stop accepting commands.

Note that the CHANGE, PROMOTE, and DEMOTE commands do not tell you the person's current employer; you have to search the data structure to find the person.

OUTPUT (to screen and file "employee.out")

1. Echo print all commands, and print out a message that indicates what action has been taken. (For the EMPLOYEES and UNEMPLOYED commands, print out the information specified in the Input section.)
2. After all the commands have been processed, print out one list consisting of all the people who have been mentioned in any command and the total amount of money they have accumulated.

DATA STRUCTURES

The list of employees for each company should be implemented using the appropriate List ADT.

TESTING

You must write and implement a test plan. The following are some sample data:

File COMPANY:
```
Borland
Microsoft
IBM
Digital
Compaq
NEC
XEROX
```

Commands from the Keyboard:
```
JOIN David XEROX
JOIN Mario XEROX
JOIN John Digital
JOIN Fred Digital
JOIN Phil IBM
CHANGE Fred NEC
JOIN Miriam Digital
JOIN Sharon Microsoft
JOIN Harvey Digital
CHANGE Miriam Borland
PAYDAY
EMPLOYEES Digital
JOIN Marge Borland
JOIN Lesley Microsoft
JOIN Sam Digital
JOIN George NEC
JOIN Bob Borland
JOIN Susan IBM
JOIN Joshua Digital
JOIN Max NEC
PAYDAY
EMPLOYEES IBM
EMPLOYEES Digital
EMPLOYEES NEC
JOIN Tim IBM
DEMOTE Harvey
PROMOTE Max
DEMOTE Marge
```

```
CHANGE Marge IBM
QUIT John
PAYDAY
QUIT Mario
QUIT David
PROMOTE Marge
PROMOTE Marge
PAYDAY
EMPLOY
EMPLOYEES IBM
EMPLOYEES XEROX
JOIN John Compaq
JOIN Ralph Compaq
QUIT Phil
JOIN Phil Compaq
DUMP
CHANGE Marge Compaq
CHANGE Miriam Compaq
CHANGE Fred Compaq
CHANGE Susan Compaq
QUIT Tim
PAYDAY
EMPLOYEES Compaq
JOIN Mario XEROX
JOIN David XEROX
EMPLOYEES XEROX
JOIN Tim Compaq
PROMOTE Tim
PROMOTE Fred
DEMOTE Miriam
JOIN Laszlo Digital
PROMOTE Laszlo
CHANGE Joshua Compaq
PAYDAY
PROMOTE Sharon
DEMOTE Lesley
PROMOTE Bob
DEMOTE Bob
DEMOTE John
UNEMPLOYED
PAYDAY
DUMP
END
```

DELIVERABLES

- A listing of your source program including a listing of any classes used

- A listing of file "employee.out"
- A listing of your implemented test plan

(This programming assignment was developed from an idea by Jim Bitner).

3. Design a black box test plan for the Case Study in Chapter 3. Implement your test plan.

DELIVERABLES

- A listing of your implemented test plan
- A listing of your test driver

CHAPTER 4

1. Complete the coding and testing of the Postfix Evaluation Program as specified in Figure 4.6.

DELIVERABLES

- The output specified in Figure 4.6
- A listing of your source file
- A listing of your implemented test plan

2. This problem requires you to write a program to convert an infix expression to postfix format. The evaluation of an infix expression such as A + B * C requires knowledge of which of the two operations, + or *, should be performed first. In general, A + B * C is to be interpreted as A + (B * C) unless otherwise specified. We say that multiplication takes *precedence* over addition. Suppose that we would now like to convert A + B *C to postfix. Applying the rules of precedence, we begin by converting the first portion of the expression that is evaluated, namely the multiplication operation. Doing this conversion in stages, we obtain

A + B * C	*Given infix form*
A + <u>B C *</u>	*Convert the multiplication*
<u>A B C * +</u>	*Convert the addition*

(The part of the expression that has been converted is underlined.)

The major rules to remember during the conversion process are that the operations with highest precedence are converted first and that after a portion of an expression has been converted to postfix it is to be treated as a single operand. Let us now consider the same example with the precedence of operators reversed by the deliberate insertion of parentheses:

(A + B) * C *Given infix form*
<u>A B +</u> * C   *Convert the addition*
<u>A B + C</u> *   *Convert the multiplication*

Note that in the conversion from "A B + * C" to "A B + C *", "A B +" was treated as a single operand. The rules for converting from infix to postfix are simple, provided that you know the order of precedence.

We consider four binary operations: addition, subtraction, multiplication, and division. These operations are denoted by the usual operators, +, -, *, and /, respectively. There are two levels of operator precedence. Both *and / have higher precedence than + and −. Furthermore, when unparenthesized operators of the same precedence are scanned, the order is assumed to be left to right. Parentheses may be used in infix expressions to override the default precedence.

As we discussed in this chapter, the postfix form requires no parentheses. The order of the operators in the postfix expressions determines the actual order of operations in evaluating the expression, making the use of parentheses unnecessary.

INPUT

The input file contains a collection of *error-free* infix arithmetic expressions, one expression per line. Expressions are terminated by semicolons, and the final expression is followed by a period. An arbitrary number of blanks and end-of-lines may occur between any two symbols in an expression. A symbol may be an operand (a single upper-case letter), an operator (+, -, *, or /), a left parenthesis, or a right parenthesis.

Sample Input

```
A + B - C ;
A + B * C ;
( A + B ) / ( C - D ) ;
(/ * /( A + B ) * ( C - D ) + E ) / ( F + G) .
```

OUTPUT

Your output should consist of each input expression, followed by its corresponding postfix expression. All output (including the original infix expressions) must be clearly formatted (or reformatted) and also clearly labeled.

Sample Output:
```
    Infix:    A + B - C ;
    Postfix:  A B + C -
```

```
Infix:     A + B * C ;
Postfix:   A B C * +

Infix:     ( A + B ) / ( C - D ) ;
Postfix:   A B + C D - /

Infix:     ( ( A + B ) * ( C - D ) + E ) / ( F + G ) .
Postfix:   A B + C D - * E + F G + /
```

DISCUSSION

In converting infix expressions to postfix notation, the following fact should be taken into consideration: in infix form the order of applying operators is governed by the possible appearance of parentheses and the operator precedence relations; however, in postfix form the order is simply the "natural" order—i.e., the order of appearance from left to right.

Accordingly, subexpressions within innermost parentheses must first be converted to postfix, so that they can then be treated as single operands. In this fashion, parentheses can be successively eliminated until the entire expression has been converted. The *last* pair of parentheses to be opened within a group of nested parentheses encloses the *first* subexpression within that group to be transformed. This last-in, first-out behavior should immediately suggest the use of a stack. Your program may utilize any of the operations in the Stack ADT.

In addition, you must devise a Boolean function that takes two operators and tells you which has higher precedence. This is helpful because in Rule 3 below you need to compare the next input symbol to the top stack element. Question: What precedence do you assign to '('? You need to answer this question because '(' may be the value of the top element in the stack.

You should formulate the conversion algorithm using the following six rules:

Rule 1: Scan the input string (infix notation) from left to right. One pass is sufficient.

Rule 2: If the next symbol scanned is an operand, it may be immediately appended to the postfix string.

Rule 3: If the next symbol is an operator,

    (a) Pop and append to the postfix string every operator on the stack that
        (i) is above the most recently scanned left parenthesis, and
        (ii) has precedence higher than or equal to that of the new operator symbol.

    (b) Then push the new operator symbol onto the stack.

Rule 4: When an opening (left) parenthesis is seen, it must be pushed onto the stack.

Rule 5: When a closing (right) parenthesis is seen, all operators down to the most recently scanned left parenthesis must be popped and appended to the postfix string. Furthermore, this pair of parentheses must be discarded.

Rule 6: When the infix string is completely scanned, the stack may still contain some operators. (No parentheses at this point. Why?) All these remaining operators should be popped and appended to the postfix string.

DATA STRUCTURE

You may use either stack implementation from the chapter. Outside of the Stack ADT operations, your program may not assume knowledge of the stack implementation. If you need additional stack operations, you should specify and implement them using the operations for the Stack ADT.

EXAMPLES

Here are two examples to help you understand how the algorithm works. Each line in the following tables demonstrates the state of the postfix string and the stack when the corresponding next infix symbol is scanned. The rightmost symbol of the stack is the top symbol. The rule number corresponding to each line demonstrates which of the six rules was used to reach the current state from that of the previous line.

Example 1: Input expression is A + B * C / D − E.

Next Symbol	Postfix String	Stack	Rule
A	A		2
+	A	+	3
B	A B	+	2
*	A B	+ *	3
C	A B C	+ *	2
/	A B C *	+ /	3
D	A B C * D	+ /	2
−	A B C * D / +	−	3
E	A B C * D / + E	−	2
	A B C * D / + E		6

Example 2: Input expression is (A + B * (C − D)) / E.

Next Symbol	Postfix String	Stack	Rule
(		(	4
A	A	(	2
+	A	(+	3
B	A B	(+	2
*	A B	(+ *	3
(	A B	(+ * (	4
C	A B C	(+ * (	2
-	A B C	(+ * (-	3
D	A B C D	(+ * (-	2
)	A B C D -	(+ *	5
)	A B C D - * +		5
/	A B C D - * +	/	3
E	A B C D - * + E	/	2
	A B C D - * + E /		6

DELIVERABLES

- A listing of your source program
- A listing of your implemented test plan

3. Complete the queueing system simulation specified in Figure 4.15.

DELIVERABLES

- The output specified in Figure 4.15
- A listing of your source program
- A listing of your implemented test plan

4. The local medical clinic has decided to automate its scheduling services. You have been assigned to design the initial version of the schedules. The basic functions that the clinic has in mind are doctor check-in and check-out and patient check-in and check-out.

A doctor checks in by telling the scheduler his or her name, an examination room number, and a medical specialty code. Each doctor has a favorite room. The scheduler checks to see whether the room is free. If so, it assigns this doctor to the room; if not, it rejects the request with a message, and the doctor can try again to check in. When a doctor checks out, the examination room is freed.

A patient checking in gives a name, age, and specialist code indication. The scheduler tries to match up the patient with a doctor according to a set of rules that are described here. If there is a match, the patient is seen by the assigned doctor. If this doctor is currently seeing a patient, the new patient is queued to see the doctor.

The rules for assigning doctors to patients are as follows:

1. Any patient under age 16 is assigned to see a pediatrician.
2. Patients age 16 and older are assigned a doctor according to the specialty requested. If there is no doctor in the clinic with the requested specialty, the patient is assigned to a general practitioner (GP). If there is no GP, the patient can be assigned to any doctor.
3. If there is more than one doctor of the requested specialty, the patient is assigned to the doctor with the shortest waiting list.

   When a patient checks out, the doctor he or she was assigned to is available to see the next patient if there is anyone in the waiting list.

INPUT

Because this is an interactive system, your program should prompt the users to input the correct information. The initial prompt is

`Type D for Doctor or P for Patient:`

The next prompt is

`Type I for check-in or O for check-out:`

According to the request, your program should prompt the user for any other needed information, as indicated in the following table:

Action	Additional Information
Doctor check-in	Doctor's name
	Room number
	Specialty code
Doctor check-out	Doctor's name
Patient check-in	Patient's name
	Age
	Specialty (code requested)
Patient check-out	Patient's name
	Room number

You may define the format for the input processed by your program.

OUTPUT

The output for each request is in the form of messages to the user, according to the request, as indicated in the following table.

Action	Message
Doctor check-in	Confirmation that room is available or Error message if room is in use
Doctor check-out	Good-bye message
Patient check-in	Message telling patient which room to go to and which doctor has been assigned. If no doctor is available, apologetic message.
Patient check-out	Good-bye message. At a later time we may add billing information at this point.

In addition to printing the messages on the screen, you should also write the requests and messages to a transaction file ("trans.out"), to be turned in with your program listing.

DETAILS AND ASSUMPTIONS

1. There are 100 examination rooms at the clinic, each with a waiting room attached.
2. Specialty codes are as follows:

Pediatrics	PED
General practice	GEN
Internal medicine	INT
Cardiology	CAR
Surgeon	SUR
Obstetrics	OBS
Psychiatry	PSY
Neurology	NEU
Orthopedics	ORT
Dermatology	DER
Ophthalmology	OPT
Ear, Nose, and Throat	ENT

3. You may assume that no patient leaves without checking out. (That is, every doctor becomes free eventually.)
4. No one leaves before he or she sees the assigned doctor. (That is, no one has to be taken out of the waiting queue.) The clinic is open 24 hours a day, 7 days a week.
5. If a doctor checks out while there is still a waiting list of patients assigned to him or her, the patients must be reassigned to other doctors.

DATA STRUCTURES

The basic data structure is a list of examination rooms with waiting lists attached to each. Because the number of rooms is fixed, you may use an array of records to represent it. It is the waiting list attached to each examination room that is of interest to us. We have seen that patients are seen in the order in which they are added to the list (a simple queue).

DELIVERABLES

- A listing of your source program including all included files
- A listing of your implemented test plan
- A listing of your output file "trans.out"

CHAPTER 5

1. Many mathematical problems require the addition, subtraction, and multiplication of two matrices. Chapter 2, Programming Assignment 1, was to write and test a class that implemented the ADT Matrix using the built-in two-dimensional array data structure. This assignment requires you to implement the same operations using another underlying data structure. This new structure is appropriate for *sparse matrices*: matrices with many zero elements. You are to use the same class specification as your interface, changing only the private data members. `values` should be of type `SortedType` in this implementation.

As always, before this class can become a permanent part of your program library, it must be thoroughly tested. To test this implementation, use the command-driven testing program you wrote to test your first matrix class.

SPARSE MATRIXES

A sparse matrix is one in which there are many zero elements. For example, Matrix A:

```
3 0 4 0 5
0 0 2 0 1
1 0 0 0 2
0 0 0 0 0
```

Matrix A has 4 rows and 5 columns. Of the 20 places in the matrix, 13 of them are zero. We represent this matrix as a sorted list of <row, column, value> triples as shown below. The matrix operations become operations on lists.

Row	Column	Value
1	1	3
1	3	4
1	5	5
2	3	2
2	5	1
3	1	1
3	5	2

PROCESSING NOTES

1. The list of values should be kept ordered by column within rows. (Is this necessary or just preferable?)
2. The test plan for an array-based implementation should have been based on the shape of the matrices. A test plan for a list implementation should include cases dealing with the length of the list (empty, only one item, etc.). In addition, because this is a sparse array implementation, cases must be tried with missing rows and missing columns. Write a test plan appropriate for a list implementation of a sparse array and execute it.

DELIVERABLES

- A listing of your source program including any included files
- A listing of your implemented test plan

2. Rewrite Programming Assignment 2, Chapter 3, using a linked implementation of the List ADT. The specifications, input, output, and deliverables remain the same.
3. Rewrite StrType specified in Chapter 2 using a linked implementation. Use a class template, and include the overloaded relational operators. Use the test plan outlined in Chapter 2 to test your implementation.

DELIVERABLES

- A listing of your class StrType
- A listing of your implemented test plan

4. Implement the Queue ADT using a circular linked list. Test your implementation using the test plan developed in Chapter 4.

DELIVERABLES

- A listing of your class QueType
- A listing of the driver program used to implement the test plan
- A listing of your implemented test plan

CHAPTER 6

1. Enhance classes `UnsortedType` and `SortedType` with overloaded assignment operators and copy constructors.

    ### DELIVERABLES
    - A listing of specification and implementation files for `UnsortedType` and `SortedType`
    - A listing of the implemented test plan for testing the new member functions of `UnsortedType` and `SortedType`

2. Implement the following specification of `UnsortedType` using a circular linked list as the implementation structure.

```
template <class ItemType>
struct NodeType;

/* Assumption: ItemType is a type for which the operators
"<" and "==" are defined—either an appropriate built-in type or a
class that overloads these operators. */

template <class ItemType>
class UnsortedType
{
public:
    // Class constructor, destructor, and copy constructor
    UnsortedType();
    ~UnsortedType();
    UnsortedType(const UnsortedType<ItemType>&);

    void operator=(UnsortedType<ItemType>);

    bool IsFull() const;
    // Determines whether list is full.
    // Post: Function value = (list is full)

    int LengthIs() const;
    // Determines the number of elements in list.
    // Post: Function value = number of elements in list.

    void MakeEmpty();
    // Initializes list to empty state.
    // Post: List is empty.

    void RetrieveItem(ItemType& item, bool& found);
    // Retrieves list element whose key matches item's key
    // (if present).
```

```
// Pre:  Key member of item is initialized.
// Post: If there is an element someItem whose key matches
//       item's key, then found = true and item is a copy of
//       someItem; otherwise found = false and item is
//       unchanged.
//       List is unchanged.
void InsertItem(ItemType item);
// Adds item to list.
// Pre: List is not full.
//      item is not in list.
// Post: item is in list.

void DeleteItem(ItemType item);
// Deletes the element whose key matches item's key.
// Pre: Key member of item is initialized.
//      One and only one element in list has a key matching
//      item's key.
// Post: No element in list has a key matching item's key.

void ResetList();
// Initializes current position for an iteration through the
// list.
// Post: Current position is prior to first element in list.

void GetNextItem(ItemType& item);
// Gets the next element in list.
// Pre: Current position is defined.
//      Element at current position is not last in list.
// Post: Current position is updated to next position.
//       item is a copy of element at current position.

private:
    NodeType<ItemType>* listData;
    int length;
    NodeType<ItemType>* currentPos;
};
```

DELIVERABLES

- A listing of the specification and implementation files for
  UnsortedType
- A listing of the driver program for your test plan
- A listing of the implemented test plan for this class

3. Implement class UnsortedType as specified in Assignment 2 using a doubly linked list.

DELIVERABLES

- A listing of the specification and implementation files for
  `UnsortedType`
- A listing of the driver program for your test plan
- A listing of the implemented test plan for this class

4. Implement class `UnsortedType` as specified in Assignment 2 using a singly linked list implemented in an array of records in dynamically allocated storage as described in this chapter.

DELIVERABLES

- A listing of the specification and implementation files for
  `UnsortedType`
- A listing of the driver program for your test plan
- A listing of the implemented test plan for this class

5. Implement class `SortedType` as specified in the following class definition using a circular linked list.

```
template <class ItemType>
struct NodeType;

/* Assumption: ItemType is a type for which the operators
"<" and "==" are defined—either an appropriate built-in type
or a class that overloads these operators. */

template <class ItemType>
class SortedType
{
public:
    // Class constructor, destructor, and copy constructor.
    SortedType();
    ~SortedType();
    SortedType(const SortedType<ItemType>&);

    void operator=(SortedType<ItemType>);

    bool IsFull() const;
    // Determines whether list is full.
    // Post: Function value = (list is full)

    int LengthIs() const;
    // Determines the number of elements in list.
    // Post: Function value = number of elements in list.

    void MakeEmpty();
```

```
// Initializes list to empty state.
// Post: List is empty.

// All of the following operations have the pre/post
// condition that the list items are sorted.

void RetrieveItem(ItemType& item, bool& found);
// Retrieves list element whose key matches item's key
// (if present).
// Pre:  Key member of item is initialized.
// Post: If there is an element someItem whose key matches
//       item's key, then found = true and item is a copy of
//       someItem; otherwise found = false and item is
//       unchanged.
//       List is unchanged.

void InsertItem(ItemType item);
// Adds item to list.
// Pre: List is not full.
//      item is not in list.
// Post: item is in list.

void DeleteItem(ItemType item);
// Deletes the element whose key matches item's key.
// Pre: Key member of item is initialized.
//      One and only one element in list has a key
//      matching item's key.
// Post: No element in list has a key matching item's key.

void ResetList();
// Initializes current position for an iteration through the
// list.
// Post: Current position is prior to first element in list.

void GetNextItem(ItemType& item);
// Gets the next element in list.
// Pre: Current position is defined.
//      Element at current position is not last in list.
// Post: Current position is updated to next position.
//       item is a copy of element at current position.

private:
 NodeType<ItemType>* listData;
 int length;
 NodeType<ItemType>* currentPos;
};
```

DELIVERABLES

- A listing of the specification and implementation files for `SortedType`
- A listing of the driver program for your test plan
- A listing of the implemented test plan for this class

6. Implement class `SortedType` as specified in Assignment 5 using a doubly linked list.

DELIVERABLES

- A listing of the specification and implementation files for `SortedType`
- A listing of the driver program for your test plan
- A listing of the implemented test plan for this class

7. Implement class `SortedType` as specified in Assignment 5 using a singly linked list implemented in an array of records in dynamically allocated storage as described in this chapter.

DELIVERABLES

- A listing of the specification and implementation files for `SortedType`
- A listing of the driver program for your test plan
- A listing of the implemented test plan for this class

8. Implement the following specification.

■ Set ADT Specification

Structure:	Elements are inserted into and deleted from a set.
Operations	(provided by the ADT):

MakeEmpty
Function:	Sets set to an empty state.
Preconditions:	None
Postcondition:	Set is empty.

Store(ItemType item)
Function:	Stores item into the set.
Precondition:	Set has been initialized.
Postconditions:	item is in the set.
	Set does not contain duplicates.

Delete(ItemType item)

Function:	Removes an item from a set.
Precondition:	Set has been initialized.
Postcondition:	item is not in the set.

int Card

Function:	Determines the number of items in the set.
Precondition:	Set has been initialized.
Postcondition:	Function value = number of items in the set.

Boolean IsIn(ItemType item)

Function:	Determines if item is in the set.
Precondition:	Set has been initialized.
Postcondition:	Function value = (item is in the set).

Difference(SetType operand2, SetType& result)

Function:	Calculates set difference: all the elements in self that are not in operand2.
Preconditions:	Self and operand2 have been initialized.
Postconditions:	result = self - operand2 result does not contain duplicates.

Intersection(SetType operand2, SetType& result)

Function:	Calculates set intersection: all the elements that are in both self and operand2.
Preconditions:	Self and operand2 have been initialized.
Postconditions:	result = intersection of self and operand2. result does not contain duplicates.

Union(SetType operand2, SetType& result)

Function:	Calculates set union: all the elements in self and all the elements in operand2.
Preconditions:	Self and operand2 have been initialized.
Postconditions:	result = union of self and operand2. result does not contain duplicates.

Boolean IsSubset(SetType operand2)

Function:	Determines if operand2 is a subset of self.
Preconditions:	Self and operand2 have been initialized.
Postcondition:	Function value = (operand2 is a subset of self).

INPUT/OUTPUT

Because you are implementing an abstract data type, there are no specific inputs or outputs. Your test plan, however, dictates both inputs and outputs.

PROCESSING NOTES

There are two basic ways to implement sets. The first explicitly records the presence or absence of each item in the base type (ItemType) in the representation of the set variable. The second only records those items that are in a set variable at a particular time. If an item is not listed as being in the set, it is not in the set. That is, the presence of each item in the set is explicitly recorded; the absence of an item is implicit. You are to use the second method.

Although sets are themselves unordered structures, the algorithms for the binary set operations are more efficient if the list of set items is kept ordered.

DATA STRUCTURES

You must use either `SortedType` or `UnsortedType`. You are not to rewrite the list operations.

DELIVERABLES

- A listing of the file containing the specification and implementation of the Set ADT
- A listing of the driver program used to implement your test plan
- A listing of your implemented test plan including any output generated

9. Complete the implementation and testing of the following class

```
enum SignType {PLUS, MINUS};

class LargeInt
{
public:
    LargeInt();
    bool operator<(LargeInt second);
    bool operator ==(LargeInt second);
    LargeInt operator+(LargeInt second);
    LargeInt operator-(LargeInt second);
    void InsertDigit(int);
    void Write(ofstream&);
private:
    List2Type<int> number;
    SignType sign;
    int numDigits;
};
```

This assignment also requires the completion of the implementation of class `List2Type`.

DELIVERABLES

- A listing of your source program including any included files
- A listing of your driver program used to implement the test plan
- A listing of the implemented test plan

10. Enhance class `LargeInt` with the following member functions.

```
LargeInt operator*(LargeInt second);
// Returns the result of multiplying self by second.
LargeInt operator/(LargeInt second);
// Returns the result of dividing self by second.
```

PROCESSING NOTES

There are two ways to implement multiplication and division. One is to use repeated addition (or subtraction); the other is to simulate how we do multiplication (and division) by hand. You may use either method.

DELIVERABLES

- A listing of your source program including any included files
- A listing of your driver program used to implement the test plan
- A listing of the implemented test plan

CHAPTER 7

1. As a child, did you ever dream of playing in a maze? How fun and scary it would have been to get lost and then, just at sundown, find your way out. If you had thought about it, you might have come up with the idea of marking your path as you went along. If you were trapped, you could then go back to the last crossing and take the other path. This technique of going back to the last decision point and trying another way is called *backtracking*. You are to use backtracking to simulate escaping from a maze.

INPUT

The input comes from a text file, "mazeFile." It contains the original maze, represented as a square table of symbols, with one row of the table per line. Each symbol is a character that indicates whether the corresponding maze position is an open path ('O'), a trap ('+'), or the exit ('E'). The size of the maze is 10 × 10 positions.

Following the original maze in the file, there are a series of starting position coordinates. Each line contains a pair of values, representing the row and column of the starting position in the maze. You are to process each of these starting points until you reach the end of the file.

Output

For each starting position, print the following:

1. The maze, with the starting point represented by an '*' symbol.
2. A message that indicates the result of the escape attempt:
   "Hooray! I am free!" or "Help! I am trapped."
3. The number of positions tried before a solution was found.

Processing Requirements

Begin processing each starting position at the specified coordinates, and continue moving until you find the way out or have no more moves to try. You may move horizontally or vertically into any position that is an open path ('O'), but not into a position that is blocked ('+'). If you move into the exit position ('E'), you have exited the maze. (Don't worry if the number of positions tried is greater than the number of positions in the maze; there may be positions that were duplicated during backtracking.)

Deliverables

- A listing of your program and any included files
- A listing of your test driver
- A listing of your implemented test plan

2. Your assignment is to (1) write a function that computes an approximation to a definite integral that is within a given tolerance of the exact answer, (2) write a sorting function that helps monitor the behavior of the integration function, and (3) test your function on several prescribed integrals.

Method

The integration function implements an adaptive algorithm based on the trapezoid rule of integration and its associated error estimate. The trapezoid rule for integration is

$$\int_a^b f(x)dx = (f(a) + f(b)) * (b - a)/2$$

If the interval [a, b] is divided into two equal subintervals, another estimate of the integral can be obtained by applying the trapezoid rule to each half interval and adding the two results. This new result is normally more accurate, and an estimate of the error in the better result is given by

Error = (T(a, b) - (T(a, c) + T(c, b))) / 3.0

where $c = (a + b)/2$ and $T(x, y)$ is the result of applying the trapezoid rule to function f on the interval $[x, y]$.

The integral is to be computed to within a given degree of accuracy by a divide-and-conquer strategy. With the given formulas, the integral can be approximated and the error in the approximation can be estimated. If the absolute value of the error is small enough, the calculation terminates. Otherwise, the integral is computed on each half interval separately with an error tolerance that is half the original one.

All the real numbers at which the function is evaluated should be inserted into a Sorted List ADT. This helps monitor the behavior of the integration algorithm by showing where the function f was evaluated. The evaluations should be concentrated where the function is badly behaved (that is, poorly approximated by straight-line pieces).

SPECIFICATION

The integration function should be

Q (f, a, b, eps, $maxFun$, err)

f	is the name of the function to be integrated.[1]
a	is the left endpoint of the interval.
b	is the right endpoint of the interval.
eps	is the maximum allowed absolute value of the error.
$maxFun$	is the maximum number of function evaluations to be used.
err	is a Boolean error flag: err is true if more than $maxFun$ function values would be needed to satisfy the error test.
q	returns the estimate of the integral.

IMPLEMENTATION DETAILS

1. The name of the function f, which is to be integrated, should be passed by the main function as a parameter to the integration function Q. One execution of the main function should call the integration function for each of the functions whose integrals are to be estimated. It is not acceptable to include the code of a function to be integrated inside the integration function Q.
2. To prevent the possibility of infinite recursion, the integration function should terminate if the function f is called $maxFun$ times. In this case, the best available approximation to the integral should be returned and an error flag should be set.

---

1. We have not covered the syntax for passing a functon as a parameter. You must consult a C++ reference book

3. The primary cost of using an integration routine is in the cost of evaluating the function f. Write your code so that it never evaluates the function twice at the same point.
4. The divide-and-conquer approach should be implemented by a recursive function. This recursive function is not called directly, but is called by the nonrecursive driver function Q, described above.
5. The straightforward way to compute the midpoint of an interval is not the best. To ensure that the computed midpoint in an interval $[a, b]$ is not outside the interval, the formula $a + (b - a)/2$ should be used.
6. The main function should do the following, once for each function in the test data.
    (a) Call Q with the appropriate arguments
    (b) Print the estimate of the interval
    (c) Print an error message if *err* is true
    (d) Print the list of real numbers at which the function f was evaluated

TESTING THE FUNCTION

Test your integration function by computing the following integrals:

f	a	b	eps	$maxFun$
1	0.0	1.0	10^{-3}	5
x	-1.0	3.0	10^{-5}	3
x	-1.0	3.0	10^{-5}	2
e^{-x*x}	0.0	5.0	10^{-3}	1000
$(\frac{1}{3} - x)^{1/3}$	0.0	1.0	10^{-2}	10
$(\frac{1}{3} - x)^{1/3}$	0.0	1.0	10^{-3}	1000
$\frac{4}{(1+x^2)}$	0.0	1.0	10^{-3}	1000

DELIVERABLES

- A listing of your program
- A listing of your output from the test data

(*This programming assignment was written by Alan Cline and David Scott.*)

CHAPTER 8

1. There is a real program developed by a computer company that reads a report (running text), issues warnings on style, and partially corrects bad style. You are to write a simplified version of this program with the following features.

STATISTICS

A statistical summary is prepared for each report processed with the following information:

- total number of words in the report;
- number of unique words;
- number of unique words of more than three letters;
- average word length, average sentence length; and
- a listing of special words (as specified by the user), with the number of times each was used in the report.

STYLE WARNINGS

Issue a warning in the following cases:

- Word used too often: List each unique word of more than three letters if its usage is more than 5% of the total number of words of more than three letters.
- Sentence length too long: Write a warning message if the average sentence length is greater than 10.
- Words too big: Write a warning message if the average word length is greater than 5.

RUN SUMMARY

At the end of the run the special words are written to a file with the number of times each was used during the run of the program.

INPUT

From the keyboard:
1. The name of the file containing the text to be analyzed
2. List of special words

From the input file:
The report to be analyzed. Allow the user to continue with another file name or quit.

OUTPUT

1. For each report being analyzed, write the following information to a file.

- The name of the input file
- A listing of the file
- The statistical summary of the report (See Statistics above.)
- The style warnings given (See Style Warnings above.)

2. An alphabetical listing of the special words, one per line with the number of times each was used throughout the run of the program.

DATA STRUCTURES

1. A list to contain the special words
2. A list of unique words in the report, created as the file is read. If a word is not in the list, put it there. If it is in the list, increment a counter showing how many times the word has been used.

DEFINITIONS

Word: A sequence of letters ending in a blank, a period, an exclamation point, a question mark, a colon, a comma, a single quote, a double quote, or a semicolon. You may assume that numbers do not appear in words.

Unique words: Words that are spelled the same, ignoring uppercase and lowercase distinctions.

Sentence: Words between end-of-sentence markers (., !, ?) or between the beginning of the report and the first end-of-sentence marker.

DELIVERABLES

- A listing of your source program including any included files
- A listing of your executed test plan

(This programming assignment was developed from an idea by Gael Buckley.)

2. The Case Study in Chapter 8 was to create an index. We divided the task into two parts: producing a list of unique words in the text and producing the index. The first part was designed and coded in the text. You should take the list of unique words and determine which ones should be included in the index and complete the index.

INPUT

- From the keyboard: a "yes" or "no" indicating whether or not a word should be included in the index.
- The output from the program written to generate the unique words, file "words.out".
- The text for which the index is to be constructed.

Output

- To the screen: each word in file "words.out" with a question as to whether or not the word should be in the index.
- An index that shows each word and the pages on which the word occurs.

Data Structure

A list to hold the words to be in the index. Associated with each word is a list of pages on which the word occurs.

Processing

1. Read the file of words one at a time. Print each word to the screen and ask the user if the word should be included in the index. Words that should go in the index are put into the list of words.
2. Read the text word-by-word, looking to see if each word is in the index. If it is, add the current page number to the list associated with that word.
3. Print each word in the index with its associated page numbers.

Deliverables

- A listing of your source program including any included files
- A listing of your test data file
- A listing of your implemented test plan

3. Implement the following class using a binary search tree as the implementation structure.

```
template <class ItemType>
struct NodeType;

/* Assumption: ItemType is a type for which the operators
"<" and "==" are defined—either an appropriate built-in type
or a class that overloads these operators. */

template <class ItemType>
class SortedType
{
public:
    // Class constructor, destructor, and copy constructor
    SortedType();
    ~SortedType();
    SortedType(const SortedType<ItemType>&);

    void operator=(SortedType<ItemType>);
```

```
bool IsFull() const;
// Determines whether list is full.
// Post: Function value = (list is full)

int LengthIs() const;
// Determines the number of elements in list.
// Post: Function value = number of elements in list.

void MakeEmpty();
// Initializes list to empty state.
// Post: List is empty.

// All of the following operations have the pre/postcondition
// that the list items are sorted.

void RetrieveItem(ItemType& item, bool& found);
// Retrieves list element whose key matches item's key
// (if present).
// Pre: Key member of item is initialized.
// Post: If there is an element someItem whose key matches
//       item's key, then found = true and item is a copy of
//       someItem; otherwise found = false and item is
//       unchanged.
//       List is unchanged.

void InsertItem(ItemType item);
// Adds item to list.
// Pre: List is not full.
//      item is not in list.
// Post: item is in list.

void DeleteItem(ItemType item);
// Deletes the element whose key matches item's key.
// Pre: Key member of item is initialized.
//      One and only one element in list has a key matching
//      item's key.
// Post: No element in list has a key matching item's key.

void PrintList(ofstream& outFile);
// Prints the items in the list in ascending order on outFile.
// Pre: outFile has been opened.
// Post: List items have been written in ascending order on
//       file outFile.
private:
 // To be filled in.
};
```

DELIVERABLES

- A listing of the specification and implementation files
- A listing of the driver program used to implement the test plan
- A listing of the implemented test plan

CHAPTER 9

1. Your assignment is to write and compare two implementations of a priority queue whose highest priority element is the one with the *smallest key* value.

PRIORITY QUEUE IMPLEMENTATIONS

1. The first implementation uses a minimum heap. You need to modify the heap operations to keep the minimum, rather than maximum, element in the root. The comparison function should compare key fields.
2. The second implementation uses a linear linked list, whose elements are ordered by key value.

TEST DATA

Create a data set that contains 50 items with priorities generated by a random-number generator.

COMPARING THE IMPLEMENTATIONS

To compare the operations, you must modify the Enqueue and Dequeue operations to count how many elements are accessed (compared or swapped, in the case of reheaping) during its execution.

Write a driver to enqueue and dequeue the 50 test items and print out the number of elements accessed for the Enqueue and Dequeue operations. Run your driver once with each implementation.

DELIVERABLES

- A listing of specification and implementation files for both priority queue implementations
- A listing of your driver
- A listing of your test data
- A listing of the output from both runs
- A report comparing the number of elements accessed in executing each operation.

2. Reimplement the Graph ADT using an *adjacency list* representation. Figure 9.26 suggests two ways that the graph could be implemented. The class definition is repeated here.

```
template<class VertexType>
// Assumption: VertexType is a type for which the "=",
// "==", and "<<" operators are defined
class GraphType
{
public:
    GraphType();           // Default of 50 vertices.
    GraphType(int maxV); // maxV <= 50.
    ~GraphType();
    void MakeEmpty();
    bool IsEmpty() const;
    bool IsFull() const;
    void AddVertex(VertexType);
    void AddEdge(VertexType, VertexType, int);
    int WeightIs(VertexType, VertexType) const;
    void GetToVertices(VertexType, QueType<VertexType>&);
    void ClearMarks();
    void MarkVertex(VertexType);
    bool IsMarked(VertexType) const;
private:
    int numVertices;
    int maxVertices;
    VertexType* vertices;
    int edges[50][50];
    bool* marks;    // marks[i] is mark for vertices[i].
};
```

INPUT

Input the graph depicted in Figure 9.20, and perform the following depth-first *and* breadth-first searches:

Houston to Denver
Washington to Chicago
Austin to Washington

All output should be directed to both the screen and file "graph.out".

DELIVERABLES

- A listing of the specification and implementation files for the class
- A listing of the driver program used to implement the test plan
- A listing of the implemented test plan for the class
- A listing of the output from "graph.out"

CHAPTER 10

1. The object of this programming assignment is twofold. First, you are to compare the relative performance of different sorting algorithms on the same data set. Second, you are to compare the relative performance of the same algorithm on two different data sets.

   Seven sorting algorithms are to be tested:
   1. SelectionSort
   2. BubbleSort
   3. ShortBubble
   4. InsertionSort
   5. MergeSort
   6. Quicksort
   7. HeapSort

PROCESSING REQUIREMENTS

You must modify each sort to include a counter to keep track of the number of comparisons made.

INPUT

Two files of integers to be sorted. There are a maximum of 100 integers in the first data set and a maximum of 1000 integers in the second data set. Generate these data sets using a random-number generator.

OUTPUT

The following output should be repeated for each sort for each file:
   1. The name of the sort
   2. An echo print of the input file
   3. The sorted file
   4. The number of comparisons required

DELIVERABLES

   - A listing of each sort function
   - A listing of the driver
   - A listing of the output specified in the Output section

2. The object of this assignment is twofold. First, you are to compare the relative performance of different searching algorithms on the same data set. Second, you are to compare the performance of the same algorithm on data sets of different sizes.

Your program should compare the following three search strategies:
1. Linear search in an unsorted list
2. Linear search in a sorted list
3. Binary search

You need to write each search function with a counter that keeps track of how many comparisons are made.

INPUT

Create a data set of 100 integers. Do 10 searches with each algorithm. Be sure the searches include values not in the list as well as those in the list.

Create a second data set made up of three different sets of data to be searched. The first set of data should have 6 values, the second 50, and the third 150. Run each routine with five searches within each of the three data sets.

OUTPUT

The following should be supplied for each data set:
1. An echo print of the input data
2. A print-out of the following, for each search value:
   (a) the value being searched for
   (b) the algorithm name, the success of the search, and the number of comparisons made

DELIVERABLES

- A listing of the driver program
- A listing of the output specified in the Output section

3. Create a data set with 100 integer values. Use the division method of hashing to store the data values into hash tables with table sizes of 7, 51, and 151. Use the linear probing method of collision resolution. Print out the tables after the data values have been stored. Search for 10 different values in each of the three hash tables, counting the number of comparisons necessary. Print out the number of comparisons necessary in each case, in tabular form.

DELIVERABLES

- A listing of the program
- A listing of the output

Glossary

abstract data type   a data type whose properties (domain and operations) are specified independently of any particular implementation; a class of data objects with a defined set of properties and a set of operations that process the data objects while maintaining the properties

abstract step   an algorithmic step for which some implementation details remain unspecified

abstraction   a model of a complex system that includes only the details essential to the perspective of the viewer of the system; the separation of the logical properties of data or actions from their implementation details

abstraction (in OOD)   the essential characteristics of an object from the viewpoint of the user

acceptance tests   the process of testing the system in its real environment with real data

activation record (stack frame)   a record used at run time to store information about a function call, including the parameters, local variables, register values, and return address

actual parameter   a variable, constant, or expression listed in the call to a function

adjacency list   a linked list that identifies all the vertices to which a particular vertex is connected; each vertex has its own adjacency list

adjacency matrix   for a graph with N nodes, an $N \times N$ table that shows the existence (and weights) of all edges in the graph

adjacent nodes   two nodes in a graph that are connected by an edge

aggregate operation   an operation on a data structure as a whole, as opposed to an operation on an individual component of the data structure

algorithm   a logical sequence of discrete steps that describes a complete solution to a given problem computable in a finite amount of time; a step-by-step procedure for solving a problem in a finite amount of time; a verbal or written description of a logical sequence of actions

ALU   see *arithmetic/logic unit*

anonymous type   a user-defined type that does not have an identifier (a name) associated with it

arithmetic/logic unit (ALU)   the component of the central processing unit that performs arithmetic and logical operations

array data type   a collection of components, all of the same type, ordered on N dimensions ($N >= 1$); each component is accessed by N indices, each of which represents the component's position within that dimension

assembler   a program that translates an assembly language program into machine code

assembly language   a low-level programming language in which a mnemonic represents each of the machine language instructions for a particular computer

assertion   a logical proposition that is either true or false

assignment expression   a C++ expression

with a value and the side effect of storing the expression value into a memory location

assignment statement   a statement that stores the value of an expression into a variable

atomic data type   a data type that allows only a single value to be associated with an identifier of that type

automatic variable   a variable for which memory is allocated and deallocated when control enters and exits the block in which it is declared

auxiliary storage device   a device that stores data in encoded form outside the computer's memory

base address   the memory address of the first element in an array

base case   the case for which the solution can be stated nonrecursively

base class   the class being inherited from

batch processing   a technique for entering data and executing programs without intermediate user interaction with the computer

big-O notation   a notation that expresses computing time (complexity) as the term in a function that increases most rapidly relative to the size of a problem

binary   expressed in terms of combinations of the numbers 1 and 0 only

binary search   a search algorithm for sorted lists that involves dividing the list in half and determining, by value comparison, whether the item would be in the upper or lower half; the process is performed repeatedly until either the item is found or it is determined that the item is not on the list

binary search tree   a binary tree in which the key value in any node is greater than the key value in its left child and any of its children (the nodes in the left subtree)

and less than the key value in its right child and any of its children (the nodes in the right subtree)

binary tree   a structure with a unique starting node (the root), in which each node is capable of having two child nodes, and in which a unique path exists from the root to every other node

binding time   the time at which a name or symbol is bound to the appropriate code

bit   short for binary digit; a single 1 or 0

black box testing   testing a program or function based on the possible input values, treating the code as a "black box"

block   in C++, a group of zero or more statements enclosed in braces

body   the statement(s) to be repeated within the loop; the executable statement(s) within a function

Boolean   a data type consisting of only two values: true and false

Boolean expression   an assertion that is evaluated as either true or false, the only values of the Boolean data type

Boolean operators   operators applied to values of the type Boolean; in C++ these are the special symbols &&, ||, and !

booting the system   the process of starting up a computer by loading the operating system into its main memory

branch   a code segment that is not always executed; for example, a Switch statement has as many branches as there are case labels

branching control structure   see *selection control structure*

bucket   a collection of elements associated with a particular hash location

byte   eight bits

call   the point at which the computer begins following the instructions in a subprogram is referred to as the subprogram call

cancellation error a form of representational error that occurs when numbers of widely differing magnitudes are added or subtracted

central processing unit (CPU) the part of the computer that executes the instructions (program) stored in memory; consists of the arithmetic/logic unit and the control unit

chain a linked list of elements that share the same hash location

char a data type whose values consist of one alphanumeric character (letter, digit, or special symbol)

character set a standard set of alphanumeric characters with a given collating sequence and binary representation

circular linked list a list in which every node has a successor; the "last" element is succeeded by the "first" element

class an unstructured type that encapsulates a fixed number of data components with the functions that manipulate them; the predefined operations on an instance of a class are whole assignment and component access

class constructor a special member function of a class that is implicitly invoked when a class object is defined

class destructor a special member function of a class that is implicitly invoked when a class object goes out of scope

class member a component of a class; class members may be either data or functions

class object (class instance) a variable of a class type

clear (white) box testing testing a program or function based on covering all of the branches or paths of the code

client software that declares and manipulates objects (instances) of a particular class

clustering the tendency of elements to become unevenly distributed in the hash table, with many elements clustering around a single hash location

code coverage see *clear (white) box testing*

code walk-through a verification process for a program in which each statement is examined to check that it faithfully implements the corresponding algorithmic step, and that the preconditions and postconditions of each module are preserved

coding translating an algorithm into a programming language; the process of assigning bit patterns to pieces of information

collating sequence the ordering of the elements of a set or series, such as the characters (values) in a character set

collision the condition resulting when two or more keys produce the same hash location

communication complexity a measure of the quantity of data passing through a module's interface

compiler a program that translates a high-level language (such as C++, Pascal, or FORTRAN) into machine code

compiler listing a copy of a program into which have been inserted messages from the compiler (indicating errors in the program that prevent its translation into machine language if appropriate)

complete binary tree a binary tree that is either full or full through the next-to-last level, with the leaves on the last level as far to the left as possible

complete graph a graph in which every vertex is directly connected to every other vertex

complexity a measure of the effort expended by the computer in performing a computation, relative to the size of the computation

composite type a data type that allows a collection of values to be associated with an object of that type

composition (containment) a mechanism by which an internal data member of one class is defined to be an object of another class type

computer a programmable device that can store, retrieve, and process data

computer program a list of instructions to be performed by a computer

computer programming the process of planning a sequence of steps for a computer to follow

concrete step a step for which the implementation details are fully specified

conditional test the point at which the Boolean expression is evaluated and the decision is made to either begin a new iteration or skip to the first statement following the loop

constant an item in a program whose value is fixed at compile time and cannot be changed during execution

constant time an algorithm whose Big-O work expression is a constant

constructor an operation that builds new instances of an abstract data type (such as a list)

control abstraction the separation of the logical properties of a control structure from its implementation

control structure a statement used to alter the normally sequential flow of control

control unit the component of the central processing unit that controls the action of other components so that instructions (the program) are executed in sequence

conversion function a function that converts a value of one type to another type so that it can be assigned to a variable of the second type; also called *transfer function* or *type cast*

copy constructor a special member function of a class that is implicitly invoked when passing parameters by value, initializing a variable in a declaration, and returning an object as the value of a function

count-controlled loop a loop that executes a predetermined number of times

counter a variable whose value is incremented to keep track of the number of times a process or event occurs

CPU see *central processing unit*

crash the cessation of a computer's operations as a result of the failure of one of its components; cessation of program execution due to an error

cursor control keys a special set of keys on a computer keyboard that allow the user to move the cursor up, down, right, and left to any point on the screen

data information that has been put into a form a computer can use

data abstraction the separation of a data type's logical properties from its implementation

data coverage see *black box testing*

data encapsulation the separation of the representation of data from the applications that use the data at a logical level; a programming language feature that enforces information hiding

data flow the flow of information from the calling code to a function and from the function back to the calling code

data representation the concrete form of data used to represent the abstract values of an abstract data type

data structure a collection of data elements whose organization is characterized by accessing operations that are used to store and retrieve the individual data elements; the implementation of the composite data members in an abstract data type

data type the general form of a class of data items; a formal description of the set of values (called the domain) and the basic set of operations that can be applied to it

data validation a test added to a program or a function that checks for errors in the data

debugging the process by which errors are removed from a program so that it does exactly what it is supposed to do

decision see *selection control structure*

declaration a statement that associates an identifier with a process or object so that the user can refer to that process or object by name

deep copy an operation that not only copies one class object to another but also makes copies of any pointed-to data

`delete` a C++ operator that returns the space allocated for a dynamic variable back to the heap to be used again

delimiter a symbol or keyword that marks the beginning or end of a construct (e.g., statement, comment, declaration, and parameter list)

demotion (narrowing) the conversion of a value from a "higher" type to a "lower" type according to a programming language's precedence of data types; may cause loss of information

dereference operator an operator that when applied to a pointer variable denotes the variable to which the pointer points

derived class the class that inherits

deskchecking tracing an execution of a design or program on paper

development environment a single package containing all of the software required for developing a program

directed graph (digraph) a graph in which each edge is directed from one vertex to another (or the same) vertex

documentation the written text and comments that make a program easier for others to understand, use, and modify

doubly linked list a linked list in which each node is linked to both its successor and its predecessor

down a descriptive term applied to a computer when it is not in a usable condition

driver a simple dummy main program that is used to call a function being tested; a main function in an object-oriented program

dynamic allocation allocation of memory space for a variable at run time (as opposed to static allocation at compile time)

dynamic binding the run-time determination of which implementation of an operation is appropriate

dynamic data structure a data structure that can expand and contract during program execution

dynamic variable a variable created during execution of a program and hence not declared in the declaration section of a program

echo printing printing the data values input to a program to verify that they are correct

edge (arc) a pair of vertices representing a connection between two nodes in a graph

editor an interactive program used to create and modify source programs or data

encapsulation (in OOD) the bundling of data and actions in such a way that the logical properties of the data and actions are separated from the implementation details; the practice of hiding a module implementation in a separate block with a formally specified interface

enumeration data type   a data type in which the formal description of the set of values is an ordered list of literal values

enumerator   one of the values in the domain of an enumeration type

event counter   a variable that is incremented each time a particular event occurs

event-controlled loop   a loop that terminates when something happens inside the loop body to signal that the loop should be exited

exception report   a set of messages in a program that explains the actions taken when an invalid data item is encountered during execution

executing   the action of a computer performing as instructed by a given program

execution summary   a computer-generated list of all commands processed and any system messages generated during batch processing

execution trace   a testing procedure that involves simulating by hand the computer executing a program

expression   an arrangement of identifiers, literals, and operators that can be evaluated to compute a value of a given type

expression statement   a statement formed by appending a semicolon to an expression

external file   a file that is used to communicate with people or programs and is stored externally to the program

external pointer   a named pointer variable that references the first node in a linked list

external representation   the printable (character) form of a data value

fetch-execute cycle   the sequence of steps performed by the central processing unit for each machine language instruction

field   a group of character positions in a line of output

field identifier (member identifier in C++)   the name of a component in a record (struct)

field of a record   a component of a record data type

field member selector   the expression used to access components of a record variable; formed by using the record variable name and the field identifier, separated by a period

file   a named area in secondary storage that is used to hold a collection of data; the collection of data itself

finite state machine   an idealized model of a simple computer consisting of a set of states, the rules that specify when states are changed, and a set of actions that are performed when changing states

flag   a Boolean variable that is set in one part of the program and tested in another to control the logical flow of a program

flat implementation   the hierarchical structure of a solution written as one long sequence of steps; also called *inline implementation*

floating point number   the value stored in a type `float` variable, so called because part of the memory location holds the exponent and the balance of the location the mantissa, with the decimal point floating as necessary among the significant digits

flow of control   the order of execution of the statements in a program

folding   a hash method that breaks the key into several pieces and concatenates or exclusive-ORs some of them to form the hash value

formal parameter   a variable declared in a function heading

formal parameter declaration   the code that associates a formal parameter identifier with a data type and a passing mechanism

formatting the planned positioning of statements or declarations and blanks on a line of a program; the arranging of program output so that it is neatly spaced and aligned

free store (heap) a pool of memory locations reserved for dynamic allocation of data

full binary tree a binary tree in which all of the leaves are on the same level and every nonleaf node has two children

function a subprogram in C++

function call an expression or statement requiring the computer to execute a function subprogram

function definition a function declaration that includes the body of the function

function prototype a function declaration without the body of the function

function result the value computed by the function and then returned to the main program; often just called the *result*

function result type the data type of the result value returned by a function; often referred to simply as *function type*

function type see *function result type*

functional cohesion a property of a module in which all concrete steps are directed toward solving just one problem, and any significant subproblems are written as abstract steps

functional domain the set of valid input data for a program or function

functional equivalence a property of a module that performs exactly the same operation as the abstract step it defines, or when one module performs exactly the same operation as another module

functional modules in top-down design, the structured tasks and subtasks that are solved individually to create an effective program

functional problem description a description that clearly states what a program is to do

garbage memory locations that can no longer be accessed

general (recursive) case the case for which the solution is expressed in terms of a smaller version of itself

generic data type a type for which the operations are defined but the types of the items being manipulated are not

global a descriptive term applied to an identifier declared outside any function, so called because it is accessible to everything that follows it

graph a data structure that consists of a set of nodes and a set of edges that relate the nodes to each other

hardware the physical components of a computer

hash function a function used to manipulate the key of an element in a list to identify its location in the list

hashing the technique used for ordering and accessing elements in a list in a relatively constant amount of time by manipulating the key to identify its location in the list

header node a placeholder node at the beginning of a list; used to simplify list processing

heap a complete binary tree, each of whose elements contains a value that is greater than or equal to the value of each of its children; see also *free store*

heuristics assorted problem-solving strategies

hierarchical implementation a process in which a modular solution is implemented by subprograms that duplicate the hierarchical structure of the solution

hierarchical records records in which at least one of the fields is itself a record

hierarchy (in OOD)   the structuring of abstractions in which a descendant object inherits the characteristics of its ancestors

high-level programming language   any programming language in which a single statement translates into one or more machine language instructions

homogeneous   a descriptive term applied to structures in which all components are of the same data type (such as an array)

identifier   a name associated with a process or object and used to refer to that process or object

implementation phase   the second set of steps in programming a computer: translating (coding) the algorithm into a programming language; testing the resulting program by running it on a computer, checking for accuracy, and making any necessary corrections; using the program

implementing   coding and testing an algorithm

implementing a test plan   running the program with the test cases listed in the test plan

implicit matching   see *positional matching*

in place   describes a kind of sorting algorithm in which the components in an array are sorted without the use of a second array

index   a value that selects a component of an array

infinite loop   a loop whose termination condition is never reached and that therefore is never exited without intervention from outside of the program

infinite recursion   the situation in which a subprogram calls itself over and over continuously

information   any knowledge that can be communicated

information hiding   the practice of hiding the details of a function or data structure with the goal of controlling access to the details of a module or structure; the programming technique of hiding the details of data or actions from other parts of the program

inheritance   a design technique used with a hierarchy of classes by which each descendant class inherits the properties (data and operations) of its ancestor class; the language mechanism by which one class acquires the properties—data and operations—of another class; a mechanism for automatically sharing data and methods among members of a class and its subclasses

inline implementation   see *flat implementation*

inorder traversal   a systematic way of visiting all the nodes in a binary tree that visits the nodes in the left subtree of a node, then visits the node, and then visits the nodes in the right subtree of the node

input   the process of placing values from an outside data set into variables in a program; the data may come from either an input device (keyboard) or an auxiliary storage device (disk or tape)

input prompts   messages printed by an interactive program, explaining what data are to be entered

input transformation   an operation that takes input values and converts them to the abstract data type representation

input/output (I/O) devices   the parts of a computer that accept data to be processed (input) and present the results of that processing (output)

insertion sort   a sorting algorithm in which values are placed one at a time into their proper position within a list that was originally empty

inspection   a verification method in which one member of a team reads the program or design line by line and the others point out errors

integer number a positive or negative whole number made up of a sign and digits (when the sign is omitted, a positive sign is assumed)

integration testing testing performed to integrate program modules that have already been independently unit tested

interactive system a system that allows direct communication between the user and the computer

interface a connecting link (such as a computer terminal) at a shared boundary that allows independent systems (such as the user and the computer) to meet and act on or communicate with each other; the formal definition of the behavior of a subprogram and the mechanism for communicating with it

internal file a file that is created but not saved; also called a *scratch file*

interpreter a program that inputs a program in a high-level language and directs the computer to perform the actions specified in each statement; unlike a compiler, an interpreter does not produce a machine language version of the entire program

invoke to call on a subprogram, causing the subprogram to execute before control is returned to the statement following the call

iteration an individual pass through, or repetition of, the body of a loop

iteration counter a counter variable that is incremented with each iteration of a loop

iterator an operation that allows us to process all the components in an abstract data type sequentially

leaf node a tree node that has no children

length the actual number of values stored in a list or string

lifetime the period of time during program execution when an identifier has memory allocated to it

linear probing resolving a hash collision by sequentially searching a hash table beginning at the location returned by the hash function

linear time for an algorithm, when the Big-O work expression can be expressed in terms of a constant times N, where N is the number of values in a data set

linked list a list in which the order of the components is determined by an explicit link field in each node, rather than by the sequential order of the components in memory

listing a copy of a source program, output by a compiler, containing messages to the programmer

literal value any constant value written in a program

local variable a variable declared within a block; it is not accessible outside of that block

logarithmic order for an algorithm, when the Big-O work expression can be expressed in terms of the logarithm of N, where N is the number of values in a data set

logging off informing a computer— usually through a simple command— that no further commands will follow

logging on taking the preliminary steps necessary to identify yourself to a computer so that it will accept your commands

logical order the order in which the programmer wants the statements in the program to be executed, which may differ from the physical order in which they appear

loop a method of structuring statements so that they are repeated while certain conditions are met

loop control variable (LCV)   a variable whose value is used to determine whether the loop executes another iteration or exits

loop entry   the point at which the flow of control first passes to a statement inside a loop

loop exit   that point when the repetition of the loop body ends and control passes to the first statement following the loop

loop invariant   assertions about the characteristics of a loop that must always be true for a loop to execute properly; the assertions are true on loop entry, at the start of each loop iteration, and on exit from the loop, but are not necessarily true at each point in the body of the loop

loop test   the point at which the loop expression is evaluated and the decision is made either to begin a new iteration or skip to the statement immediately following the loop

machine language   the language, made up of binary-coded instructions, that is used directly by the computer

mainframe   a large computing system designed for high-volume processing or for use by many people at once

maintenance   the modification of a program, after it has been completed, in order to meet changing requirements or to take care of any errors that show up.

maintenance phase   the period during which maintenance occurs

mantissa   with respect to floating point representation of real numbers, the digits representing a number itself and not its exponent

member selector   the expression used to access components of a `struct` or `class` variable. It is formed by using the variable name and the member name, separated by a dot (period)

memory leak   the loss of available memory space that occurs when memory is allocated dynamically but never deallocated

memory unit   internal data storage in a computer

metalanguage   a language that is used to write the syntax rules for another language

method   a function declared as a member of a class object

metric based testing   testing based on measurable factors

microcomputer   see *personal computer*

minicomputer   a computer system larger than a personal computer but smaller than a mainframe; sometimes called an entry-level mainframe

mixed mode expression   an expression that contains operands of different data types

modular programming   see *top-down design*

modularity (in OOD)   the meaningful packaging of objects

module   a self-contained collection of steps that solves a problem or subproblem; can contain both concrete and abstract steps

module nesting chart   a chart that depicts the nesting structure of modules and shows calls among them

name precedence   the priority treatment accorded a local identifier in a block over a global identifier with the same spelling in any references that the block makes to that identifier

named constant   a location in memory, referenced by an identifier, where a data value that cannot be changed is stored

named type   a type that has an identifier (a name) associated with it

nested control structure   a program structure consisting of one control statement (selection, iteration, or subprogram) embedded within another control statement

nested If   an If statement that is nested within another If statement

nested loop   a loop that is within another loop

new   a C++ operator that returns the address of new space allocated for a dynamic variable

nodes   the building blocks of dynamic structures, each made up of a component (the data) and a pointer (the link) to the next node

nonlocal   a descriptive term applied to any identifier declared outside of a given block

nonlocal access   access to any identifier declared outside of its own block

null statement   an empty statement

nybble   four bits; half of a byte

object class (class)   the description of a group of objects with similar properties and behaviors; a pattern for creating individual objects

object program   the machine language version of a source program

object-based programming language   a programming language that supports abstraction, and encapsulation but not inheritance

object-oriented design   a building-block design technique that incorporates abstraction, encapsulation, modularity, and hierarchy

object-oriented programming   a method of implementation in which programs are organized as cooperative collections of objects, each of which represents an instance of some class, and whose classes are all members of a hierarchy of classes united via inheritance relationships

observer   an operation that allows us to observe the state of an instance of an abstract data type without changing it

one-dimensional array   a structured collection of components of the same type given a single name; each component is accessed by an index that indicates its position within the collection

operating system   a set of programs that manages all of the computer's resources

out-of-bounds array index   an index value that, in C++, is either less than zero or greater than the array size minus one

output transformation   an operation that takes an instance of an abstract data type and converts it to a representation that can be output

overflow   the condition that arises when the value of a calculation is too large to be represented

overloading   giving the same name to more than one function or using the same operator symbol for more than one operation; usually associated with static binding

overriding   reimplementing a member function inherited from a parent class

parameter   a literal, constant, variable, or expression used for communicating values to or from a subprogram

parameter list   a mechanism by which functions communicate with each other

pass by address   a parameter-passing mechanism in which the memory address of the actual parameter is passed to the formal parameter; also called *pass by reference*

pass by name   a parameter-passing mechanism in which the actual parameter is passed to a subprogram as a literal character string and interpreted by a thunk

pass by reference   see *pass by address*

pass by value   a parameter-passing

mechanism in which a copy of an actual parameter's value is passed to the formal parameter

password a unique series of letters assigned to a user (and known only by that user) by which that user identifies himself or herself to a computer during the logging-on procedure; a password system protects information stored in a computer from being tampered with or destroyed

path a combination of branches that might be traversed when a program or function is executed; a sequence of vertices that connects two nodes in a graph

path testing a testing technique whereby the tester tries to execute all possible paths in a program or function

PC see *personal computer*

peripheral device an input, output, or auxiliary storage device attached to a computer

personal computer (PC) a small computer system (usually intended to fit on a desktop) that is designed to be used primarily by a single person

pointer a simple data type consisting of an unbounded set of values, each of which addresses or otherwise indicates the location of a variable of a given type; operations defined on pointer variables are assignment and test for equality

polymorphic operation an operation that has multiple meanings depending on the type of the object to which it is bound at run time

polymorphism The ability to determine which of several operations with the same name is appropriate; a combination of static and dynamic binding

positional matching a method of matching actual and formal parameters by their relative positions in the two parameter lists; also called *relative* or

implicit matching

postconditions assertions that must be true after a module is executed

postfix operator an operator that follows its operand(s)

postorder traversal a systematic way of visiting all the nodes in a binary tree that visits the nodes in the left subtree of a node, then visits the nodes in the right subtree of the node, and then visits the node

precision a maximum number of significant digits

preconditions assertions that must be true before a module begins execution

prefix operator an operator that precedes its operand(s)

preorder traversal a systematic way of visiting all the nodes in a binary tree that visits a node, then visits all the nodes in the left subtree of the node, and then visits the nodes in the right subtree of the node

priming read an initial reading of a set of data values before entry into an event-controlled loop in order to establish values for the variables

problem-solving phase the first set of steps in programming a computer: analyzing the problem; developing an algorithm; testing the algorithm for accuracy

procedural abstraction the separation of the logical properties of an action from its implementation

program validation the process of determining the degree to which software fulfills its intended purpose

program verification the process of determining the degree to which a software product fulfills its specifications

programming planning, scheduling, or performing a task or an event; see also *computer programming*

programming language a set of rules, symbols, and special words used to construct a program

pseudocode a mixture of English statements and C++-like control structures that can easily be translated into a programming language

quadratic probing resolving a hash collision by using the rehashing formula (HashValue + I^2) % *array-size*, where *I* is the number of times that the rehash function has been applied

queue a data structure in which elements are added to the rear and removed from the front; a "first in, first out" (FIFO) structure

radix the number of possibilities for each position; the digits in a number system

random probing resolving a hash collision by generating pseudorandom hash values in successive applications of the rehash function

range of values the interval within which values must fall, specified in terms of the largest and smallest allowable values

real number a number that has a whole and a fractional part and no imaginary part

record (struct) data type a composite data type with a fixed number of components called fields (members); the operations are whole record assignment and selection of individual fields by name

recursion the situation in which a function calls itself

recursive algorithm a solution that is expressed in terms of (a) smaller instances of itself and (b) a base case

recursive call a function call in which the function being called is the same as the one making the call.

recursive case see *general case*

recursive definition a definition in which something is defined in terms of smaller versions of itself

reference parameter a formal parameter that receives the location (memory address) of the caller's actual parameter

reference type a simple data type consisting of an unbounded set of values, each of which is the address of a variable of a given type. The only operation defined on a reference variable is initialization, after which every appearance of the variable is implicitly dereferenced

refinement in top-down design, the expansion of a module specification to form a new module that solves a major step in the computer solution of a problem

regression testing re-execution of program tests after modifications have been made in order to ensure that the program still works correctly

rehashing resolving a collision by computing a new hash location from a hash function that manipulates the original location rather than the element's key

relational operators operators that state that a relationship exists between two values; in C++, symbols that cause the computer to perform operations to verify whether the indicated relationship exists

relative matching see *positional matching*

representational error arithmetic error caused when the precision of the true result of arithmetic operations is greater than the precision of the machine

requirements a statement of what is to be provided by a computer system or software product

reserved word a word that has special meaning in a programming language; it cannot be used as an identifier

result see *function result*

return   the point at which the computer comes back from executing a function

right-justified   placed as far to the right as possible within a fixed number of character positions

robust   a descriptive term for a program that can recover from erroneous inputs and keep running

robustness   the ability of a program to recover following an error; the ability of a program to continue to operate within its environment

root   the top node of a tree structure; a node with no parent

run-time stack   a data structure that keeps track of activation records during the execution of a program

scope   the region of program code where it is legal to reference (use) an identifier

scope rules   the rules that determine where in a program a given identifier may be accessed, given the point at which the identifier is declared

scratch file   see *internal file*

secondary storage device   see *auxiliary storage device*

selection control structure   a form of program structure allowing the computer to select one of possibly several actions to perform based on given circumstances; also called a *branching control structure*

self   the object to which a member function is being applied

self-documenting code   a program containing meaningful identifiers as well as judiciously used clarifying comments

semantics   the set of rules that gives the meaning of instructions written in a programming language

semihierarchical implementation   a modular solution implemented by functions in a manner that preserves the hierarchical design, except that a function

used by multiple modules is implemented once, outside of the hierarchy, and called in each place it is needed

sentinel   a special data value used in certain event-controlled loops as a signal that the loop should be exited

sequence   a structure in which statements are executed one after another

shallow copy   an operation that copies one class object to another without copying any pointed-to data

side effect   any effect of one function on another that is not part of the explicitly defined interface between them

significant digits   those digits from the first nonzero digit on the left to the last nonzero digit on the right (plus any zero digits that are exact)

simulation   a problem solution that has been arrived at through the application of an algorithm designed to model the behavior of physical systems, materials, or processes

size (of an array)   the physical space reserved for an array

software   computer programs; the set of all programs available on a computer

software engineering   a disciplined approach to the design, production, and maintenance of computer programs that are developed on time and within cost estimates, using tools that help to manage the size and complexity of the resulting software products; the application of traditional engineering methodologies and techniques to the development of software

software life cycle   the phases in the life of a large software project including requirements analysis, specification, design, implementation, testing, and maintenance

software piracy   the unauthorized copying

of software for either personal use or use by others

software specification a detailed description of the function, inputs, processing, outputs, and special requirements of a software product. It provides the information needed to design and implement the program

sorting arranging the components of a list in order (for instance, words in alphabetical order, numbers in ascending or descending order)

source program a program written in a high-level programming language

stable sort a sorting algorithm that preserves the order of duplicates

stack an abstract data type in which elements are added and removed from only one end; a "last in, first out" (LIFO) structure

stack frame See *activation record*

stack overflow the condition resulting from trying to push an element onto a full stack

stack underflow the condition resulting from trying to pop an empty stack

standardized made uniform; most high-level languages are standardized, as official descriptions of them exist

static binding The compile-time determination of which implementation of an operation is appropriate

static variable a variable for which memory remains allocated throughout the execution of the entire program

stepwise design see *top-down design*

stepwise refinement see *top-down design*

string a collection of characters that is interpreted as a single data item; in C++, a null-terminated sequence of characters stored in a `char` array

stub a special function that can be used in top-down testing to stand in for a lower level function

style the individual manner in which computer programmers translate algorithms into a programming language

subprogram see *function*

supercomputer the most powerful class of computers

switch expression the expression in a Switch statement whose value determines which case label is selected; it cannot be a floating point expression

syntax the formal rules governing how valid instructions (constructs) are written in a programming language

system software a set of programs—including the compiler, the operating system, and the editor—that improves the efficiency and convenience of the computer's processing

tail recursion the case in which a function contains only a single recursive invocation and it is the last statement to be executed in the function

team programming the use of two or more programmers to design a program that would take one programmer too long to complete

template A C++ language construct that allows the compiler to generate multiple versions of a class type or a function by allowing parameterized types

temporary file a file that exists only during the execution of a program

termination condition the condition that causes a loop to be exited

test driver see *driver*

test plan a document showing the test cases planned for a program or module, their purposes, inputs, expected outputs, and criteria for success

test plan implementation see *implementing a test plan*

testing checking a program's output by

comparing it to hand-calculated results; running a program with data sets designed to discover any errors

testing the state of a stream the act of using a C++ stream variable in a logical expression as if it were a Boolean variable; the result is true if the last I/O operation on that stream succeeded, and false otherwise

text file a file in which each component is a character; each numeric digit is represented by its code in the collating sequence

top-down design a technique for developing a program in which the problem is divided into more easily handled subproblems, the solutions of which create a solution to the overall problem; also called stepwise refinement and modular programming

trailer node a placeholder node at the end of a list; used to simplify list processing

transfer function see *conversion function*

transformer an operation that builds a new value of an ADT, given one or more previous values of the type

traverse a list to access the components of a list one at a time from the beginning of the list to the end

two-dimensional array a collection of components, all of the same type, structured in two dimensions; each component is accessed by a pair of indices that represent the component's position within each dimension

type cast see *conversion function*

type coercion an automatic conversion of a value of one type to a value of another type

type definition the association of a type identifier with the definition of a new data type

unary operator an operator that has just one operand

underflow the condition that arises when the value of a calculation is too small to be represented

undirected graph a graph in which the edges have no direction

unit testing testing a module or function by itself

unstructured data type a collection consisting of components that are not organized with respect to one another

user name the name by which a computer recognizes the user, and which must be entered to log on to a machine

value parameter a formal parameter that receives a copy of the contents of the corresponding actual parameter

value-returning function a function that returns a single value to its caller and is invoked from within an expression

variable a location in memory, referenced by an identifier, in which a data value that can be changed is stored

vertex a node in a graph

virtual function a function in which each invocation cannot be matched with the proper code until run time

virus a computer program that replicates itself, often with the goal of spreading to other computers without authorization, possibly with the intent of doing harm

visible accessible; a term used in describing a scope of access

void function (procedure) a function that does not return a function value to its caller and is invoked as a separate statement

walk-through a verification method in which a *team* performs a manual simulation of the program or design

weighted graph a graph in which each edge carries a value

word a group of 16, 32, or 64 bits; a group of bits processed by the arithmetic-logic unit in a single instruction

work a measure of the effort expended by the computer in performing a computation

workstation a minicomputer or powerful microcomputer designed to be used primarily by one person at a time

Index